Zope™ Bible

Zope™ Bible

Michael R. Bernstein, Scott Robertson,
and the Codeit Development Team

Hungry Minds™

Best-Selling Books • Digital Downloads • e-Books • Answer Networks • e-Newsletters • Branded Web Sites • e-Learning

New York, NY ✦ Cleveland, OH ✦ Indianapolis, IN

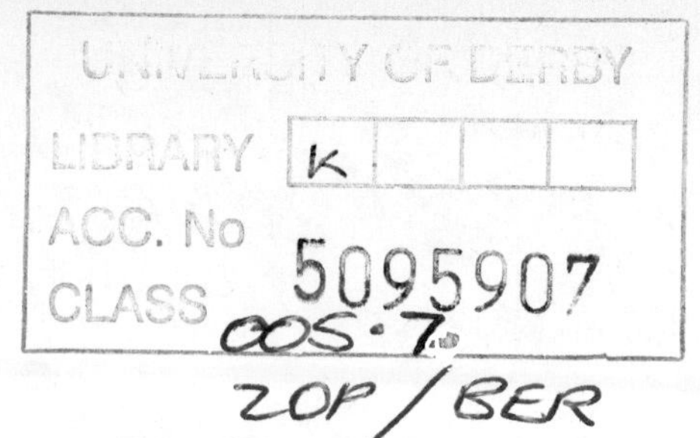

Zope™ Bible

Published by
Hungry Minds, Inc.
909 Third Avenue
New York, NY 10022
www.hungryminds.com

Library of Congress Control Number: 2001118285

ISBN: 0-7645-4857-3

Printed in the United States of America

10 9 8 7 6 5 4 3 2 1

1B/SQ/QT/QS/IN

Distributed in the United States by Hungry Minds, Inc.

Distributed by CDG Books Canada Inc. for Canada; by Transworld Publishers Limited in the United Kingdom; by IDG Norge Books for Norway; by IDG Sweden Books for Sweden; by IDG Books Australia Publishing Corporation Pty. Ltd. for Australia and New Zealand; by TransQuest Publishers Pte Ltd. for Singapore, Malaysia, Thailand, Indonesia, and Hong Kong; by Gotop Information Inc. for Taiwan; by ICG Muse, Inc. for Japan; by Intersoft for South Africa; by Eyrolles for France; by International Thomson Publishing for Germany, Austria, and Switzerland; by Distribuidora Cuspide for Argentina; by LR International for Brazil; by Galileo Libros for Chile; by Ediciones ZETA S.C.R. Ltda. for Peru; by WS Computer Publishing Corporation, Inc., for the Philippines; by Contemporanea de Ediciones for Venezuela; by Express Computer Distributors for the Caribbean and West Indies; by Micronesia Media Distributor, Inc. for Micronesia; by Chips Computadoras S.A. de C.V. for Mexico; by Editorial Norma de Panama S.A. for Panama; by American Bookshops for Finland.

For general information on Hungry Minds' products and services please contact our Customer Care department within the U.S. at 800-762-2974, outside the U.S. at 317-572-3993 or fax 317-572-4002.

For sales inquiries and reseller information, including discounts, premium and bulk quantity sales, and foreign-language translations, please contact our Customer Care department at 800-434-3422, fax 317-572-4002 or write to Hungry Minds, Inc., Attn: Customer Care Department, 10475 Crosspoint Boulevard, Indianapolis, IN 46256.

For information on licensing foreign or domestic rights, please contact our Sub-Rights Customer Care department at 212-884-5000.

For information on using Hungry Minds' products and services in the classroom or for ordering examination copies, please contact our Educational Sales department at 800-434-2086 or fax 317-572-4005.

For press review copies, author interviews, or other publicity information, please contact our Public Relations department at 317-572-3168 or fax 317-572-4168.

For authorization to photocopy items for corporate, personal, or educational use, please contact Copyright Clearance Center, 222 Rosewood Drive, Danvers, MA 01923, or fax 978-750-4470.

About the Authors

Michael Bernstein is an information architect for Codeit. He has been a member of the Zope development community since it was released as Open Source in late 1998, and wrote the first community-contributed "How-To" for Zope in February of 1999. Michael was one of the technical reviewers for *The Zope Book* published by New Riders in 2001, and created the Zope category in the Open Directory Project (dmoz.org). Currently residing in Las Vegas, he has worked for two start-ups before joining Codeit and has built and managed various Content Management Systems and intranets using Zope. His interests include Science Fiction Fandom, Open Source, and other self-organizing emergent phenomena. His personal Web site is at `http://www.michaelbernstein.com`.

Scott Robertson co-founded Codeit in 1997, a company dedicated to building custom applications that help businesses increase productivity and lower expenses. In 1998, he discovered a technology named Bobo that was so compelling that he learned Python and swore off Perl forever. When Principia (an application built on Bobo) was renamed Zope and released as Open Source, he selected it as Codeit's preferred Web platform. An ardent believer in Open Source, he has contributed several products to the community and encourages his employees to do the same. When he's not working he can usually be found creating strategies for achieving world domination, or at the very least devising ones that will annoy his partners.

The Codeit Development Team has over 15 years of combined Zope experience. Besides the primary authors, other Codeit developers and staff contributed material to this book, including Nick Garcia, Erik Burrows, Forest Zachman, Brent Rogan, and Sam Stimson.

The entire Codeit team is dedicated to using Open Source technologies on behalf of our customers, so that at the conclusion of a project they have the skills, code, and documentation on how to change and scale each application we build, enabling them to be as self-reliant as they wish to be. Beyond development, Codeit also offers Zope hosting as one of its services.

Credits

Acquisitions Editor
Terri Varveris

Project Editor
Barbra Guerra

Technical Editor
Tom Deprez

Copy Editors
Katherine Dvorak
Ryan Rader

Permissions Editor
Carmen Krikorian

Editorial Manager
Kyle Looper

Project Coordinator
Ryan Steffen

Graphics and Production Specialists
Sean Decker
Joyce Haughey
Gabriele McCann
Heather Pope
Betty Schulte

Quality Control Technicians
Laura Albert
John Greenough
Andy Hollandbeck
Carl Pierce
Linda Quigley
Charles Spencer

Media Development Specialist
Travis Silvers

Proofreading and Indexing
TECHBOOKS Production Services

Cover Illustration
Kate Shaw

To Ruth, for doing such a good job raising me; to Roxanne, for making my life complete; and to Talia, for the future.

—Michael

To Kyle Reid, welcome to the party. Glad you could make it.

—Scott

Preface

Hi! You're holding the *Zope Bible,* a book we suspect will change how you look at building Web sites and Web applications. If you're like most Web developers and designers, you're probably always looking for ways to improve your process, both for building and for maintaining Web sites. Whether the sites you're building are consumer-oriented Web applications, content-centric publishing sites, intranets, or even vanity sites, you want to build them faster, maintain them easier, and integrate other people into your workflow with a minimum of hassle and fuss.

Zope is a tool that is hard to describe, as in many ways it's in a category all its own. So, rather than describe what it *is*, it's better to describe what Zope can *do* for you:

- ✦ Zope contains a templating language for creating dynamic pages, making it easier to create and maintain a common look and feel for your site.
- ✦ Zope uses a powerful scripting language (Python) for creating business logic, making it easy to create powerful Web applications.
- ✦ Zope has a built-in Web management interface so you can create and maintain entire sites with nothing more than a standard browser and an Internet connection.
- ✦ Zope has a built-in object database, making it easy to store content, logic, and presentation in a single place.
- ✦ Zope has a built-in security framework, making it easy and safe to delegate maintenance of sections or subsections of the site to other people.
- ✦ Zope sites are also accessible via FTP and WebDAV, making it easier to leverage the desktop site creation tools you already use.
- ✦ Zope is written in Python, making it easy to extend and enhance with your own customizations.
- ✦ Zope has built-in content management tools such as Version objects and Undo, which make it easier to safely modify and update a site while it's "live."

In other words, if you build Web sites, Zope is the tool for you.

Why We Wrote This Book

In the two years since Zope was open-sourced, the user and developer communities have grown tremendously. However, while Zope itself has grown and become both more powerful and easier to use, the documentation has not kept pace.

The most glaring omission, the lack of a user manual, was remedied last year with the release of *The Zope Book* by Amos Latteier and Michel Pelletier (New Riders, 2001). This was a very important milestone, as *The Zope Book* was a complete reference for using Zope to build Web sites and simple applications. However, by focusing on thoroughly covering the basics, it left those who wanted to take advantage of Zope's more advanced features out in the cold.

At Codeit Computing, we've long wanted a book that could serve as a textbook for educating our own employees, not only teaching them the basics, but more advanced topics as well, such as extending Zope with Python products and building advanced user interfaces. We've also wanted a book that we could hand to our clients and their IT staff to make it easier for them to assume the maintenance of the projects that we complete.

When we were approached to write this book, we determined that this would be our opportunity to write the book that we wished we had all along.

What You Need

To follow along with the steps in this book you need to know how to use your browser. Don't laugh! Zope is very browser-centric. Knowing what the "Back" button does, or that right-clicking a link lets you launch the link target in another window is kind of important when you're actually using your browser to develop a Web site.

This book assumes that you already know how to build Web sites "the old fashioned way." A basic familiarity and ability to write HTML, including tables and forms and using a text editor, will be very handy. In fact, we assume that you're sick and tired of maintaining your sites by hand.

A familiarity with some other application server or middleware technology is helpful, but not really required. Examples of these are Macromedia ColdFusion, Microsoft Active Server Pages, Java Servlets, Java Server Pages, or PHP.

Regardless of your operating system, you'll need to have the appropriate privileges to install software on your computer. Zope is very lightweight, and can be installed on most desktops with a minimum of fuss, but many corporate environments don't give users the ability to install software.

DTML, Python, and ZPT Code Conventions

This book contains many small snippets of code, as well as complete code listings. Each listing appears in a `monospace font`.

If a line of code doesn't fit on a single line in this book, We use the arrow (⮐) symbol. For example, the following two lines comprise a single line of code:

```
<dtml-in "listEntriesByGroup(_['SelectedGroup'])" size=20 ⮐
start=start sort_expr="sort_by">
```

What the Icons Mean

Throughout the book, we've used *icons* in the left margin to call your attention to points that are particularly important.

We use Note icons to tell you that something is important—perhaps a concept that may help you master the task at hand or something fundamental for understanding subsequent material.

Tip icons indicate a more efficient way of doing something, or a technique that may not be obvious.

These icons indicate that an example file is on the companion CD-ROM.

We use Caution icons when the operation that we are describing can cause problems if you're not careful.

We use this icon to indicate that the material discussed is new to the latest Zope version.

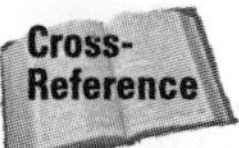

We use the Cross-Reference icon to refer you to other chapters that have more to say on a subject.

How This Book Is Organized

This book is organized into four parts that are meant to be read in order if you're a complete newcomer to Zope.

Part I: Getting Started with Zope

In this section Zope is introduced, as are the fundamentals of coding in DTML and Python. If you are already an experienced Zope user, and want to jump to Part II and start developing Python Zope Products, we suggest reading Chapter 5, "Object-Oriented Programming and Python," in this section first, even if you're already familiar with Python.

Part II: Building Zope Products

In this section, we build upon the material from Part I, and show you how to extend Zope with new object types. At the end of this section, you will have built a powerful and useful Web application.

Part III: Zope Management

Zope provides powerful tools for building and maintaining Web sites. In this section, several aspects of Zope are explored in-depth. Chapter 11 covers content management strategies using Zope, Chapter 12 explains data management including integrating external RDBMSs, and Chapter 13 deals with security and user management.

Part IV: Advanced Zope Concepts

In this section, we've put the advanced topics that are relatively independent of each other and the rest of the book. Chapter 14 describes in detail the various parts and pieces that Zope is built out of and how they fit together; Chapter 15 covers writing scripts for Zope using Python and/or Perl Script Objects; Chapter 16 covers ZClasses for those who wish to develop products entirely within the browser; Chapter 17 explains Zope's Searching and indexing framework, and how to create automatically indexed content objects; Chapter 18 introduces Zope Page Templates, a new presentation scripting technology introduced in Zope 2.5; Chapter 19 covers Debugging; and Chapter 20 addresses creating and running clusters of Zope servers.

Appendixes

Appendix A describes the material included on the CD-ROM, and Appendix B covers installing Zope from source code or RPM files.

Web Site

We, the authors of the *Zope Bible,* have set up a Web site specifically for the readers of this book at `http://www.zopebible.com`. The Web site contains additional information, sample code from the book, links to Zope-related Web sites, and other items and information we think you'll find useful.

Acknowledgments

This book represents a great deal of very hard work (if only we had known what we were getting into), and the authors couldn't have succeeded without the following list of extremely pushy people who insisted they get some credit:

The other employees at Codeit Computing, who pitched in to help with individual chapters when we realized we needed their expertise, particularly: Erik Burrows, who wrote a phenomenal chapter on RDBMS integration (Chapter 12); Nick Garcia, who has debugged enough of our code that he was able to write a chapter on how to debug yours (Chapter 19); and Forest Zachman, Zope scripting dude number one (Chapter 15).

The incredible Zope Development Community, including the following folks from the #zope IRC channel who helped answer both newbie and advanced questions: Kapil Thangavelu (hazmat); Ron Bickers (rbickers); George A. Runyan Jr. (runyaga); Andrew Milton (TheJester); Chris McDonough (chrism); Andreas Jung (YET); R. David Murray (rdmurray); Alex Verstraeten (zxc); M. Adam Kendall (DaJoker); and Morten W. Petersen (Morphex). A special thanks goes to Chris Withers for pitching in on the final review at the last minute. Far too many others in the Zope community, on the mailing lists and in the IRC channel, helped with suggestions, code snippets, HowTos, tutorials, and detailed explanations on every aspect of Zope over the years than could be listed here. We couldn't have learned as much as we did without the rest of you. The community is a big part of what makes Zope a success.

Any remaining bugs in the book's example code are definitely their fault.

Many thanks go to the great folks at Hungry Minds: Terri Varveris, our acquisitions editor, for understanding that we have day jobs and whose efforts went above and beyond the call of duty; Barb Guerra, our project editor, whose gentle guidance forced us into submitting our chapters; Tom Deprez, our technical editor, for helping to make the book both clearer and more complete; and Katharine Dvorak and Ryan Rader, our copy editors, who fixed punctuation gaffes, rephrased subjunctive sentences, and cut out unnecessary prepositions with reckless abandon.

And of course, all the great folks at Zope Corporation, for creating an open-source Web application platform that lets us solve our customer's problems without creating new ones.

Michael adds:

Besides the folks mentioned above, I'd also like to extend my personal thanks to the following people:

My co-author Scott Robertson and Codeit CEO Jason Reid deserve my thanks for giving me the opportunity to write this book and accepting my tendency to perfectionism.

Roxanne, for encouraging me when I was down, and keeping my eye on the ball when things just seemed too hard, even though she really deserved my attention more.

The members of the Southern Nevada Area Fantasy and Fiction Union (snaffu.org), who deserve my thanks for not complaining even though they didn't really get the club Vice President they voted for (no, guys, I am *not* taking you all to Disneyland).

Scott adds:

Thanks to my partners, Chris Klein and Jason Reid, who told me to not write a book because I didn't have time and I'd hate the process (they know me too well) and then helped out in every possible way when I ran into trouble because I never listen.

Contents at a Glance

Contents

Part IV: Advanced Zope Concepts 387

Getting Started with Zope

P A R T

I

✦ ✦ ✦ ✦

In This Part

✦ ✦ ✦ ✦

Overview of Zope

In This Chapter

History of Zope

Zope features

Zope architecture

The advantages of Zope

If you are picking up this book, you probably fall into one of three categories: the tech book browser who wants to know what the application with the funny name is, the Web developer who is looking into application platforms to develop on top of, or your company's HTML resource, looking for something that will help you build the intranet your boss wants online yesterday. No matter which of these categories you fall under, this book is for you. Not only do we explain what Zope is and how it can help you, but we also get into the nitty-gritty of building Web applications in Zope from back to front.

What Is Zope?

Put quite simply, Zope is an open source Web application server. Published by Zope Corporation (formerly Digital Creations) and supported by a large, active community of users, it was designed with the idea in mind that a successful Web application requires the collaboration of many people in an organization. Zope runs on almost all UNIX systems, as well as on Windows, plus it can be run with most Web servers or its own built-in Web server. The few platforms that are not officially supported (such as Apple MacOS) nevertheless have their own community supporters who can almost certainly provide a version of Zope pre-compiled for your platform. Since Zope is open source, you also always have the option (as a last resort) of compiling Zope for your platform yourself with some assistance from the community. In practice, this is rarely necessary.

One of Zope's biggest attractions is that it contains everything you need to build secure, speedy, and reliable Web-based applications. You can create community Web sites, sell products online, streamline your business with an intranet/extranet, or invent the next Internet fad. Instead of having to buy several components separately and getting them to work together, Zope provides many (if not most) of the features you need, including content management features, adapters to common databases (such as Oracle, PostGreSQL,Sybase, MySQL, MS SQL Server, Interbase, or any other ODBC (Open Database Connectivity)-compliant database), and a rich security model.

As an open source technology, especially with its rapidly growing user base and the ease with which it can be extended, it is unlikely Zope will end up as a "dead technology." There is a wide selection of third-party products and plug-ins created by other Zope users that you can use to customize your site. And, because of Zope's non-proprietary license, you have access to the source code in case you would like to add or tweak anything on your own. In fact, in the second part of this book, we'll show you exactly how to do just that.

History of Zope

The World Wide Web originally consisted of a series of documents used by scientists and researchers to share ideas and information. As more and more people used the Internet and for different purposes, there developed a need to interact with these documents. Thus, CGI (Common Gateway Interface) was created to enable such interaction between people and Web sites, and significantly increased the practical functionality of the Internet. This transformed the Web from a collection of static documents to a place where things could be done. Suddenly documents could change depending on parameters that were provided to them, incorporating data from other sources, or modifying and storing data.

CGI is used to collect user input from the Web through the use of forms. Because CGI only defines how Web servers communicate with programs designed to process input from the Web, programmers found themselves constantly recreating all of the other necessary components of a Web application every time they wanted to write something new.

To resolve this limitation, programmers created reusable libraries of common functions and routines, saving themselves some of the time and trouble involved in creating Web applications. Enterprising individuals collected these libraries into programs capable of performing multiple tasks, such as communicating with databases and managing content. This made the process of building applications more convenient by concealing many of the low-level functions programmers found themselves rewriting.

Up until this point most of the application servers were procedural based. This may be due to the fact that the first thing most programmers wanted to do was to connect a Web site with organizations' databases, which are procedural in nature. (Java wasn't nearly as prevalent on the Web as it is today.)

In 1996, Jim Fulton needed to learn about CGI scripting to give a tutorial on the subject and, while traveling, came up with a way to publish objects on the Web as a better alternative to CGI scripts. Jim had been working for Zope Corporation (then Digital Creations) for about a week at that point and coded most of an ORB on the flight back.

There was much rejoicing in the OOP (object-oriented programming) community. They released several components: *Bobo*, *BoboPOS*, and *Document Template* as open source, but built a proprietary product called *Principia* with those components that they attempted to sell. In 1998 an investor by the name of Hadar Pedahazur convinced Digital Creations that its product would be more successful if it, too, was released as open source. Thus, Principia became *Zope*, and a movement began.

Zope exploded onto the scene and immediately the user base increased significantly, proving that Pedahazur's decision was a good one. The user base became an integral part of the development of Zope, becoming a full-blown community centered on this product. Currently Zope applications are developed all over the world to suit all sorts of Web-application needs, and recently Zope Corporation has opened up the development process for more community participation in Zope's development, with promising results.

More businesses now are adopting Zope as their Web-development toolkit every day, increasing the pool of available developers and third-party products for each new user. Organizations such as Red Hat, NASA, Bell Atlantic Mobile, CBS, and the U.S. Navy all have chosen to use Zope for various Web applications, and the list keeps growing.

Features of Zope

Zope has a lot of moving parts that are put together in a very integrated way. This gives Zope many features that are not present in other application servers. In many ways, calling Zope an application server ignores additional features such as the integrated object database that other application servers simply don't have.

Platforms

Because Zope is written in Python (you'll meet the computer language *Python* in Chapter 5), Zope can run on any platform Python can run on (which is virtually every platform in use today). Currently, Zope is officially supported on the following platforms:

- Windows 95/98/NT/2000
- Linux
- Solaris

Zope has also been run successfully on the following platforms:

- NetBSD/OpenBSD/FreeBSD
- HP-UX
- MacOS X
- BeOS

Database adapters

Name a database and a Zope adapter probably already exists for it. Adapters exist to talk to various traditional databases such as Oracle, Sybase, MSSQL, Access, MySQL, PostgresSQL, and many others. There is even a wide variety of adapters for non-traditional databases such as LDAP and IMAP.

Web-based user interface

Everything in Zope can be managed through a Web browser. Maintenance and support are simplified due to the independence from any required client-side utilities. In addition, building and editing your site can be accomplished from anywhere you have access to the Internet.

Integration with existing tools

Zope has built-in support for FTP and WebDAV, which enables existing client-side tools to access Zope easily. When combined with Zope Page Templates (discussed in Chapter 18), you'll find that developers and designers can work together more smoothly than ever before.

Open source

Zope is an open source technology, which means not only that is it free but also that there exists a large community that has adopted the product and is constantly contributing to its growth and well-being. In addition, there is the added advantage of not being locked in to a single vendor for extensions and upgrades. Of course, for those organizations desiring it, support contracts are available from a variety of vendors.

Extendibility

Zope has an easy, consistent architecture built with the powerful Python language, so in the rare event that you cannot find a product to do your bidding, you can write your own. Chapter 5 is an introduction to Python, and chapters 6 through 10 provide a detailed tutorial on extending Zope with your own Python products. Chapter 16 deals with extending Zope through the Web by using ZClasses.

Built-in Web server

Zope includes its own built-in multi-threaded Web server, which you can use to quickly get Zope up and running. In many (if not most) cases you won't need anything else.

Plays nice with third-party Web servers

Zope can be run on any of the leading Web servers. It can interface with Apache, Microsoft IIS, Netscape Enterprise Server, and many others.

Multiple protocol support

Zope supports many existing Internet standards such as HTTP, FTP, SQL, and ODBC, as well as many emerging standards such as DOM, XML, SOAP, XML-RPC, and WebDAV.

Indexing and searching

Powerful search functions put every object in your Zope installation at your fingertips. You can search your entire architecture for a particular object, or search for all of the objects that match an extensive list of criteria. You can also incorporate this functionality into your Zope Web applications (discussed in Chapter 17).

Built-in object database

Every object you create—including documents, files, images, folders, and more—is stored in Zope's integrated, easy-to-manage object database.

Built-in security model

Zope's dynamic security model offers a powerful range of options and capabilities. It enables you to protect entire sections of your Web site by simply editing one list of permissions, and protect individual objects by setting permissions on an object-by-object basis. (Chapter 9 shows you how to incorporate security into your Zope Products, and Chapter 13 explains how to leverage Zope security in your site.)

Clustering and load balancing

ZEO (Zope Enterprise Options) is an open source add-on that is included with the Zope package. Using ZEO and a variety of load-balancing options, you can scale a site up from running on a single server to one that spans the globe. Chapter 20 explains these alternatives in detail.

Transactions

Zope works off of transactions. What this means is that a series of changes made to the database is stored in a transaction. If that transaction causes an error or is somehow invalid, all of the changes are rolled back and the database remains unaltered. In addition, Zope plays well with other systems that support transactions, such as Oracle.

Versions

All development in Zope can be done in Versions. This means many changes (transactions) can be made and reviewed on the live site without affecting what a visitor sees until the changes are approved and the version committed.

Undo support

Just about everything you do in Zope can be *un*done with Zope's transactional undo support. If you don't like a change you just made or you accidentally broke a part of your Web site, fixing the problem takes just a few clicks.

Zope Architecture

You are probably wondering how Zope accomplishes all of the features we have been preaching about. At the heart of Zope is a series of components that provides services for handling tasks such as Internet requests, object persistence, transaction management, content indexing/searching, undo support, RDBMS (Relational DataBase Management System) access, and plug-in support. Most of these components can be embedded into other Python applications without Zope. Figure 1-1 shows an overview of the various Zope components and their relations to each other.

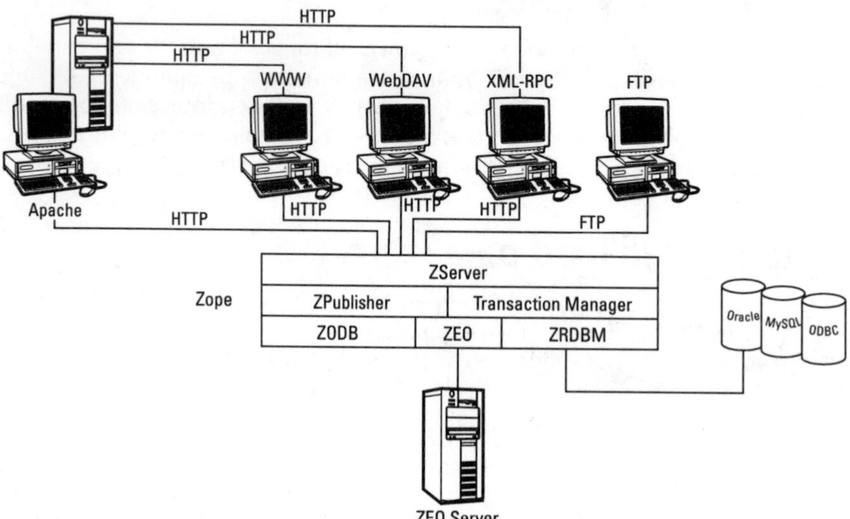

Figure 1-1: The server bone is connected to the backbone . . .

ZServer

To understand what ZServer is and how it works, imagine that you are a translator for the United Nations. Every culture has different customs, expressions, and other idioms that to the uninitiated are not understood or might even be considered offensive. Your job then is to not only translate the words of one diplomat into the language of another, but you also must help each diplomat understand the other's point of view. To do this you might have to rephrase what a diplomat asked so as to not upset the other, which requires that you be well-versed in both cultures in order to know the right way to phrase something.

ZServer performs a similar job. Except in this case instead of diplomats speaking foreign languages, you have client programs speaking a specific Internet protocol. ZServer translates a specific protocol into a request that Zope understands and then translates Zope's response into a format the client understands.

However, this is a gross understatement of the work ZServer does. ZServer also performs many other complex server operations as well. This way a developer can extend Zope to speak another protocol without having to get bogged down in the details of writing a server application from scratch.

ZServer is based on Sam Rushing's Medusa server (`http://www.nightmare.com/medusa/`) and could, if your needs were different enough from other Zope users, be replaced with some other integrated server architecture. In practice, it's often easier to run Zope behind Apache or another Web server instead.

ZPublisher

Zope is an object-publishing environment. That means that when Zope is asked for an object, it is searched for and published back to the requester. This is done by what some developers call an *ORB* (Object Request Broker). ZPublisher is Zope's ORB component. You can think of ZPublisher as a helpful librarian. Instead of asking the librarian to help you search through all of the bookshelves to find a specific book, you ask ZPublisher to search through the ZODB (Z Object Database) to find an object, typically by specifying a URL in an HTTP request.

Once ZPublisher finds an object, and you have the appropriate permissions, ZPublisher checks to see if the object is callable (in other words, it checks to see whether the object is a function), or to see whether the object has a callable attribute named `index_html`. In which case ZPublisher runs the function and returns the results back to ZServer.

Just as a librarian keeps the library tidy and efficient by returning books back to the shelves when inconsiderate people come along and leave them out on the tables, ZPublisher also performs house keeping functions, such as starting/ending transactions and rolling failed transactions back in case there was an error.

Transaction Manager

Zope supports *atomic transactions*, which means that all operations in a transaction must be successful or the whole database must be restored to the state it was before the beginning of the transaction. The Transaction Manager is responsible for keeping track of all objects that have changed during the publishing process. At the end of the request, after ZServer has returned Zope's response back to the client, the Transaction Manager either commits the changes (permanently accepts them) or if there was an error, it loops through each changed object and tells the database to abort the changes (and hence revert back to the database's original state).

Persistent objects (objects that are stored in the ZODB) and RDBMS adapters that support transactions are integrated with the Transaction Manager, which means that you never have to worry about managing your own transactions (unless you want to).

A good example of the necessity for atomic transactions is an account balance transfer. Suppose two users — Margaret and Todd — each have an account on your system, and that you have enabled your users to initiate balance transfers from their accounts to any other account on the system. One day, as Margaret is transferring about $1,000 from her account to Todd's account, a rat chews through the power cord of your server. The *good* news is that the rat was electrocuted, and won't be taking down any of your *other* servers. The *bad* news is that while Margaret's account balance was reduced by the transferred amount, Todd's account was never increased by the equivalent amount. The money disappeared. In a Zope implementation of this system, both accounts would be updated with their new balances, or neither would be, as the balance transfer operation would be contained in a single transaction, rats be damned.

ZODB

The ZODB (Z Object Database) provides transparent persistent object support. What this means is that developers can create instances of objects and manipulate them, and they will automatically be saved with little or no intervention from the developer.

Refer to Chapters 5 for more information on objects and Chapter 6 to see persistent objects in action.

Engineered from the ground up to be robust, ZODB uses a simple journaling schema for saving changes to the object. When an object is changed, a new version of the object is saved at the end of the database and the database is then saved to disk. This way you never run the risk of having corrupt data due to Zope unexpectedly quitting (maybe you had a loss of power or someone randomly killing your Zope process). The worst that could happen is that you will lose the transaction that Zope was in the middle of committing to disk. One side effect of this approach of saving versions of objects is that you have the ability to undo changes that you previously made.

ZEO

ZEO (Zope Enterprise Option) allows one ZODB to be shared with multiple Zope instances running on different machines. This option enables you to quickly scale a site to handle more traffic with use of additional hardware.

ZRDBM

ZRDBM (Zope Relational Database management) provides an abstracted interface layer to relational databases. This enables you to swap different database adapters without having to rewrite major portions of your site, and to access multiple databases at the same time. If your database supports transactions, the ZRDBM will manage them for you.

Zope Advantages

"That's nice and all," you may be thinking. "But why should I stick my neck out and tell my project manager that this is the way to go when there are so many other well-known Web-development platforms out there?" A good question. Besides having a cool name (which lends itself to such phrases and terms as "Zope-It!" and "Zope-ification"), there are several aspects to it that make Zope an attractive option for your development needs.

Low cost of ownership

Probably Zope's most enticing aspect is its price tag. At the low, low price of *free*, it's a deal that's hard to beat. Other Web development toolkits can cost upwards of six figures when you factor in associated software and licenses for multiple systems, not including the price for the training that is often required, and customization that is frequently available only from a single vendor, if it's available at all. With Zope, you get a complete package for absolutely nothing. Also, with Zope's public license, you are free to do whatever you wish with the software, including creating your own tweaks and add-ons. Even if you do decide to go with another product, it's worth the time to download Zope and see what it's capable of.

Fast development/deployment time

Zope was designed with your entire development team in mind. With Zope's Versions and flexible security model, you can minimize the possibility that one change may override another. Zope Page Templates, introduced in Zope 2.5 (Chapter 18) separate presentation from logic in a way that let your designers use their favorite WYSIWYG HTML editors while collaborating with the coders on your team. As well, Zope's acquisition helps make for *less* coding. For example, if a section of the Web site is supposed to have a universal look, you can set up a template with universal headers and footers and have the pages dynamically rendered from stored information, whether from within Zope itself or from external databases.

Reliability

Because of Zope's transactional method of changing the database, it's virtually impossible to have invalid entries in the database that might break your site. Coupled with the easy undo system, even if a change is made that does break some portion of your site, you can quickly recover with minimum hassle.

Scalability

Zope runs smoothly on single machines, but the nifty thing about Zope is that it can easily be scaled to a much larger operation with hardly any fuss at all using the ZEO package. If your Web site grows from 100 hits a day to 100,000, you will be able to spread across as many machines as you will need to handle the load.

Summary

It all sounds pretty interesting, doesn't it? The great thing about Zope is that you can download it, install it, and have it up and running to play with in less time than it would take to wash your car. And because it's free, you have no major commitment if it's not what you're looking for. We suspect that you will be pleased with the surprising power Zope offers. So let's go get it installed!

✦ ✦ ✦

Installation

In the last chapter we discussed Zope's many features. Now it is time to install the application so that we can get you started working with it.

This chapter is served to you in two parts. The first part is designed to give you everything you need to get Zope installed and running on your computer. The second part deals mostly with modifying the behavior of Zope's built-in Web server, ZServer. (You may want to skip this part until later.)

✦ ✦ ✦ ✦

In This Chapter

What you need to run Zope

Finding Zope

Installing Zope under Windows

Installing Zope under Linux

Firing Zope up for the first time

Starting up Zope's Web server application, ZServer

Installing additional products

Troubleshooting tips

✦ ✦ ✦ ✦

What You Need to Run Zope

Zope is remarkably easy on your system. In the past, we have set Zope up on everything from Sun SPARC stations to laptops running Microsoft's Windows 95. In this chapter, we discuss how to install Zope on a Windows or Linux machine.

To install Zope under Linux or Windows, you only need the following:

- ✦ An Intel x86 or compatible chipset *or* a SPARC machine
- ✦ At least 128 MB of RAM
- ✦ At least 16 MB of hard drive space

Zope consumes 16 MB of hard drive space once it is installed. The space that it takes will grow significantly once you start adding content, so you will want to have plenty of room available.

This is also all you need to get going with the software we provide on the CD-ROM that accompanies this book.

Where to Find Zope

The easiest place to find the Zope installation files is on the CD-ROM supplied with this book. In the /Zope directory, you will find all of the files necessary to get started with Zope, which are listed as follows:

Zope-2.5.0-win32-x86.exe	This is the file to install under Microsoft Windows 9*x*/NT/2000.
Zope-2.5.0-linux2-x86.tgz	This is the binary used to install under the various Linux operating systems.
Zope-2.5.0-solaris-2.6-sparc.tgz	This is the file to install on a SPARC station.
Zope-2.5.0-src.tgz	This file contains the source code, in case you wish to compile straight from the source.

You can also find the most recent version of Zope at http://www.zope.org. You will find the naming convention of the files identical.

If you want Zope in Red Hat's *RPM* or Debian's *deb* formats, then you will have to look elsewhere. Zope RPMs can be found at http://starship.python.net/crew/jrush/Zope/, while the deb packages can be found on Debian's Web site, http://www.debian.org.

Check out Appendix B for instructions on how to compile Zope from the source code or install it using the Red Hat RPMs.

Installing Zope Under Windows

Installing Zope on Windows 9*x*/NT/2000 is a quick and easy process. To start, run the .exe file that is on the CD-ROM that accompanies this book or in whatever directory you downloaded it by double-clicking it or using "Run" in the Windows Start menu. This will start a simple installation wizard that will ask you for a few things and then install Zope.

While you can run Zope on Windows 95, 98, or ME for exploring and experimenting, you will definitely want to choose a more stable operating system if you plan to produce a site that will be receiving any sort of traffic.

After the usual licensing agreement, you will be asked to name your Web site, as you can see in Figure 2-1. The default is imaginatively named "WebSite." One effect the name of your Web site has is that it determines the default directory to which Zope will be installed. For example, if you kept "Website," Zope will be installed to C:\Program Files\WebSite. You can still change the default installation directory in the next step of the wizard, but the name of your site is also listed in the Add/Remove Programs dialog of your control panel.

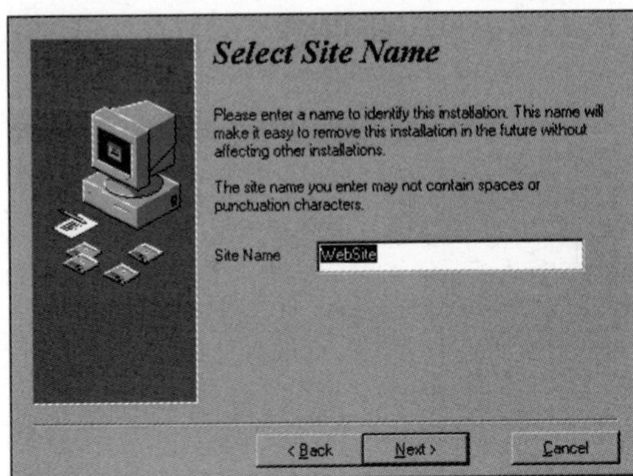

Figure 2-1: Naming your Web site

The final step in the installation process is setting the username and password of the *initial user*. This first user that is created will have the manager *role*. Roles will be explained in Chapter 3; however, for now, just know that this initial user will have the ability to add and remove any Zope object, such as documents, methods, or even other users.

After these three steps are completed, Zope will auto install itself onto your computer. To start Zope after it is installed, go to the directory that was defined above and run the `start.bat` that you find there. You may notice that Zope starts in a command prompt. Once the batch file runs, you will be ready to log on to Zope using your Web browser and start building your application. Logging on will be explained in the next section. There are various command line options that you can use to alter Zope's behavior and configuration, and we'll cover them later in the chapter in "Modifying ZServer's behavior with switches."

When you are installing Zope on Windows NT/2000, you may choose to set Zope as a service. Refer to the appropriate Microsoft documentation for more information on services.

Following are the quick steps to get Zope running on Windows 9*x*/NT/2000:

1. Run the installation .exe file by either clicking it in Windows Explorer, by typing **Zope-2.5.0-win32-x86** in the command prompt, or by typing the full path to the .exe file in Run.
2. Accept the License Agreement.
3. Name your Web site. (This will affect the next step, and the name used in the Add/Remove programs dialog.)

4. Select the directory to which you wish to install. The default is `C:\Program Files\WebSite`.
5. Choose the username and password for the initial user.
6. Choose whether or not you wish to have Zope run as a service if installing under Windows NT/2000. (See Figure 2-2.)

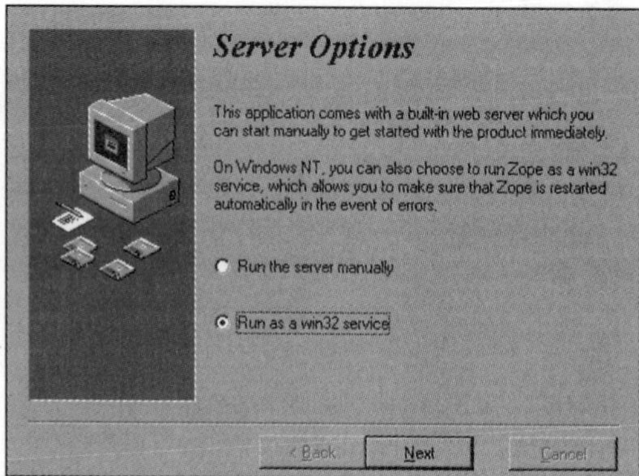

Figure 2-2: Setting Zope up as a service on Windows NT/2000

7. Start Zope by running the start.exe in Zope's installation directory.
8. Log onto Zope by pointing your Web browser to `http://localhost:8080/`. (This is explained in the next section.)

Installing Zope Under Linux

Installing Zope with the UNIX binaries isn't much more of a hassle than installing under Windows, especially if you are familiar with the use of the *tar* and *chown* commands. Go to the directory off of which you would like to have your Zope directory (we recommend `/usr/local`; you will also need to be logged in as the root user as well) and extract the tarball that you downloaded from the Internet or copied off of the CD-ROM that accompanies this book with tar. The following tar command should work: **tar xvfz Zope-2.5.0-linux2-x86.tgz**.

Another task that you may wish to do, though isn't necessary, is to rename the directory to which Zope is installed. By default the directory will be named something such as `/usr/local/Zope-2.5.0`. Type **mv Zope-2.5.0 Zope** from the `/local` directory. (This will make it easier to change directories.)

You will then want to use the `cd` command to change to the directory that will be created. Once in this directory, run the installer script with `./install`. The output from the script should look something like the following:

```
# ./install

------------------------------------------------------------
Compiling python modules
------------------------------------------------------------
------------------------------------------------------------
creating default access file
Note:
        The admin name and password are 'admin'
        and 'VjLk2UV8'.

        You can change the superuser name and password with the
        zpasswd script.  To find out more, type:

        /usr/local/zope/2-5-0/bin/python zpasswd.py

chmod 0600 /usr/local/zope/2-5-0/access
chmod 0711 /usr/local/zope/2-5-0/var
------------------------------------------------------------
setting dir permissions
------------------------------------------------------------
creating default database
chmod 0600 /usr/local/zope/2-5-0/var/Data.fs
------------------------------------------------------------
Writing the pcgi resource file (ie cgi script),
/usr/local/zope/2-3-0/Zope.cgi
chmod 0755 /usr/local/zope/2-5-0/Zope.cgi
------------------------------------------------------------
Creating start script, start
chmod 0711 /usr/local/zope/2-5-0/start
------------------------------------------------------------
Creating stop script, stop
chmod 0711 /usr/local/zope/2-5-0/stop
------------------------------------------------------------

Done!
```

Make note of the initial username and password that are printed in the installer script, as these are what you will use to access Zope for the first time. If you would like to install Zope with a specific name for the initial user, try running the installer script like: **./install -u name -g users**, where “name” is the name you would like and “users” is group to which “name” belongs.

You may also create the initial user yourself using the `zpasswd.py` script. You can do this by typing **python zpasswd.py inituser** (assuming that you have Python in your path). The script will prompt you for a username, a password, and allowed domains. *Allowed domains* are explained in Chapter 3, so for the time being do not enter anything. Note that this can be done at any time, and is especially handy if you lost your Zope password.

One thing you will need to do before starting up Zope for the first time is change the ownership of the contents of Zope's `/var` directory to the "nobody" user by using the chown command. We do this by typing **chown –R nobody var** from the directory of your Zope installation. This is because Zope switches user contexts to "nobody" if you start it as the root user, so you will need to allow "nobody" access to Zope's database files. Under the nobody user, the likelihood of an external user gaining access to your file system through Zope is minimized, as the nobody user has no power other than what is explicitly assigned by an administrator (you). You can also make Zope run as a different user with the –u switch. (The –u switch is explained later in this chapter when we discuss ZServer options.)

To start up the Zope processes, simply run the `./start` script in the directory to which Zope is installed. You will see information printed on your screen, including what ports on which Zope is running. This means you can now log onto Zope with your Web browser by going to `http://localhost:8080/`.

As we mentioned before, Zope's startup scripts have many optional arguments. We'll cover those options a little later in the chapter.

Following is a summary of the steps for installing under Linux:

1. Uncompress the Zope tarball with **tar xvfz Zope-2.5.0-linux2-x86.tgz**.
2. Change to the newly created directory with **cd Zope-2.5.0-linux2-x86**.
3. Run the installation script by typing **./install**. Make note of the name and password of the initial user that will be printed while the script runs.
4. Change the ownership of the `/var` directory with **chown –R nobody var**.
5. To start Zope, run the startup script with **./start**.
6. Log onto Zope by pointing your Web browser to `http://localhost:8080/`.

Finding Your Way around Zope's Directory Tree

There are several points in this book where we direct you to copy files to or from some directory of your Zope installation. We'll explain some of the directories you may need to be familiar with later. Figure 2-3 is of a Zope installation's directory tree.

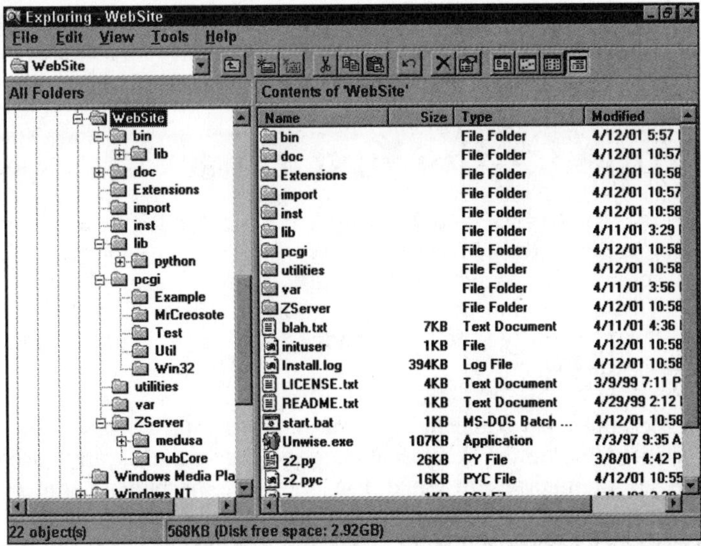

Figure 2-3: Zope's Directory Tree

The *bin* directory contains the Python application that Zope uses. As well, in the *lib* directory below it are all of the Python modules. You probably will not need to mess with this directory unless you are a Python programmer and wish to tweak Zope itself.

You may notice that the *Extensions* directory is empty but for a .txt file when you first install Zope. This is not a mistake. As you can read in the .txt, this will be the place where you will place any External Methods.

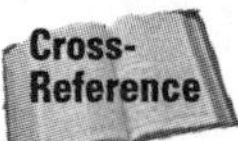

External Methods are explained in Chapter 14.

Likewise, the *import* directory is empty. If you are importing Zope files from another Zope installation, this is where you will want to place them. Likewise, this location is where you will find files that you export to the server (rather than automatically downloaded to your desktop).

Importing and exporting are discussed in Chapter 3.

The *var* directory will start off with a small `Data.fs` file. This is one of the most important files in your Zope installation as it is the ZODB, or Z\ Object Database, and contains the contents of your Zope Web site. If you need to copy in a new `Data.fs` or restore an old one, this is where you'll want to take care of that.

If you ever start Zope with no `Data.fs` in the `var` directory, Zope will create a new, empty `Data.fs` file to work from.

Starting up Zope for the First Time

Once you have the Zope processes up and running, it is time to log in and start playing. Zope's interface is entirely browser-based, which means you can log into it with any Web browser such as Mozilla, Internet Explorer, or Netscape Navigator. Point your browser (from the same computer that Zope is installed on) to `http://localhost:8080/`. If you see the "Zope Quick Start" page (Figure 2-4), then you will know Zope is running.

"localhost" is the equivalent of saying "this machine" to your browser. So when you give "localhost:8080" to the browser, it goes and checks the current machine, port 8080. As an alternative, you could also enter the machine's name or IP address and achieve the same result. There is also a 'special' IP address (127.0.0.1) that is equivalent to 'localhost' in that it means 'this machine'. To change the port number, use the -w switch when starting ZServer (see "Modifying ZServer's behavior with switches").

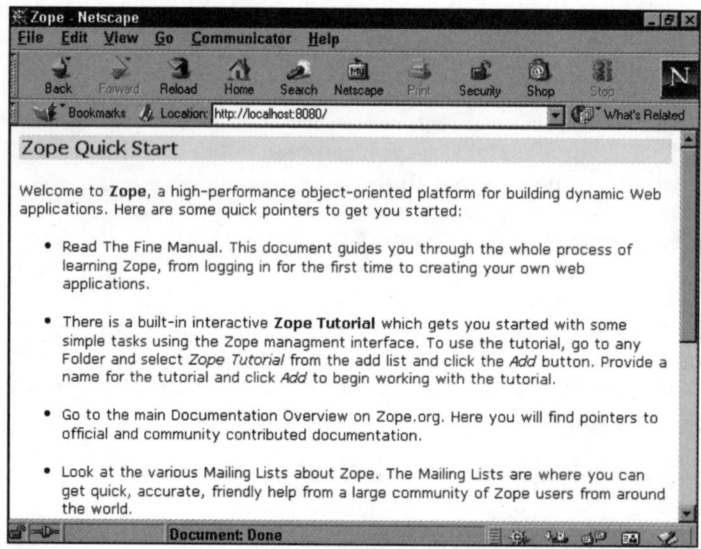

Figure 2-4: Starting Zope quickly with the Zope Quick Start

If you have trouble getting Zope to start up, check to make sure that no other application is running on the same port on which that Zope is trying to start. To change the port number that Zope will use, use the -w switch when starting ZServer (see "Modifying ZServer's behavior with switches"').

Logging in

Most of the true work in Zope is done via the management interface, which you can see in Figure 2-5. You will find several links to the management interface throughout the Zope Quick Start page. If you follow any of these links (or go directly to `http://localhost:8080/manage/`, which is much easier), the first thing you will see is a login prompt. This is where you enter the username and password that were defined when you installed Zope. Once you login, your authentication information is cached, so you won't need to re-enter it unless you exit all instances of your browser.

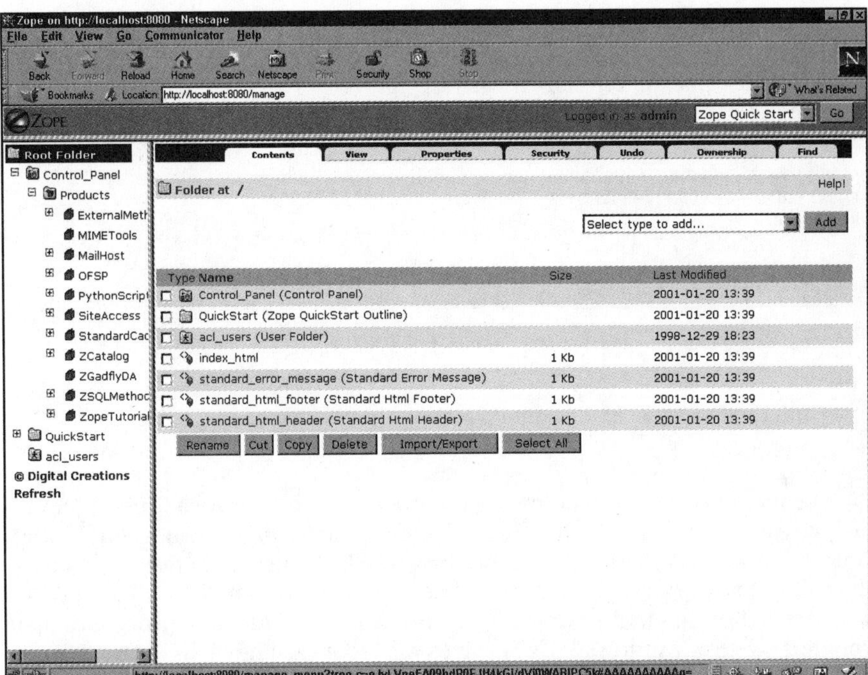

Figure 2-5: The Zope Management Interface should look familiar if you use Windows.

Shutting down

In most cases there are three "proper" ways to shut down Zope. The first can be accomplished from Zope's management interface by going into the Control Panel folder (which is in the root folder of the Zope management interface) and clicking the Shutdown button (see Figure 2-6). A message will appear that the Zope processes have been stopped (more information about the Management Interface can be found in Chapter 3). The second way to shut down Zope is by pressing Ctrl-C in the Command Prompt window while Zope is in Debug mode. You will get a message that there has been a keyboard interrupt and Zope will stop running. The third way to shut down Zope can only be accomplished under Linux, and that is using the stop batch file. Simply go to the Zope directory and type **./stop**, and the Zope processes will be shut down.

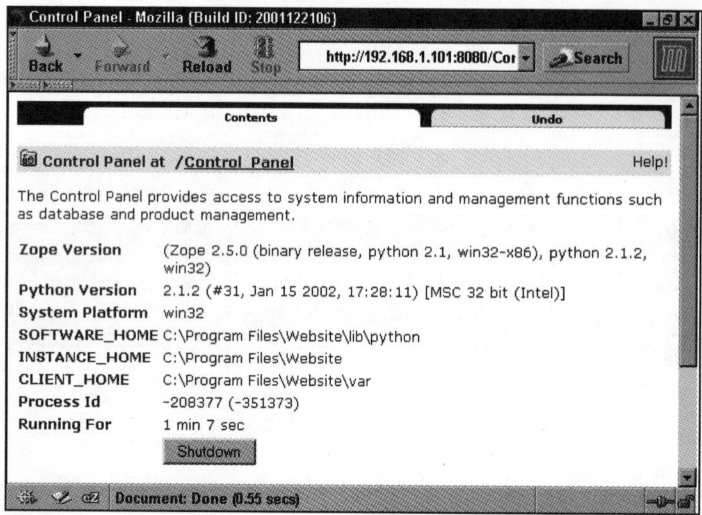

Figure 2-6: Shut it down!

The Control Panel and its other functions are discussed in Chapter 3.

When running Zope as a Windows NT service, things operate a little differently. For one, it will start automatically when Windows starts, shut down when Windows is shut down, and it will not have to be restarted if the user logs out. This saves you the trouble of starting up the Zope processes with the start batch file that you would usually need to do. However, to start and stop the Zope processes manually, you must access Windows NT's Services Manager (as shown in Figure 2-7).

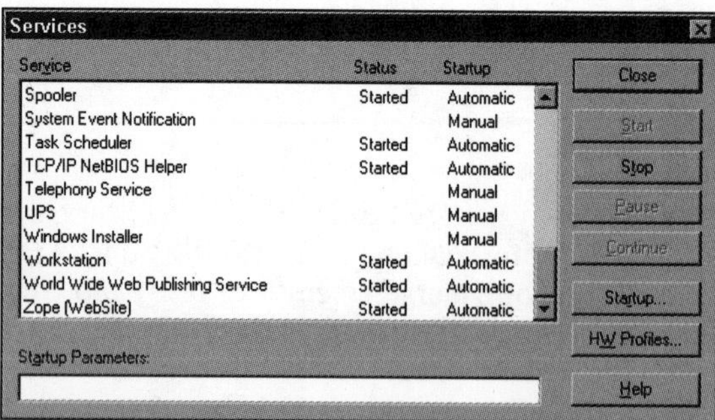

Figure 2-7: Windows NT's Services manager

If you double-click Services under Window NT's Control Panel, you will bring up the Services manager. Zope will be listed as "Zope (SiteName)" along with its status ("Started" or blank) and whether it starts up automatically or not. Click Zope's name to highlight it, then choose the function you wish to do.

You cannot Pause the Zope service, only turn it on or off.

Copying your Web site to a different machine

Everything in your Web site is saved in the ZODB. The representation of this in your file structure is the `Data.fs` file found in the `/usr/local/Zope/var` directory (on UNIX-like systems). This file contains basically everything in your application, from the objects you have added to any Undo information. Under Windows this file is located in the `C:/Program Files/WebSite/var` directory.

Sometimes it is necessary to add a new `Data.fs` file to your application whether you are reverting to a previously saved backup or copying in a `Data.fs` to a brand new installation. Most likely you will be moving your Web site to a more powerful machine or copying it to other Zope instances.

To copy your Web site to a different machine, first shut down any running copies of Zope using one of the methods discussed earlier in this chapter.

Now go to the `./Zope/var` directory. Before you copy anything, you may want to name the existing `Data.fs` to a name such as **Data.fs.old**, just in case you might need it later. Then all you need to do is copy in the new `Data.fs` file. Restart Zope, and you should see the change immediately when you log into the management screen.

If you have packed your database at some point, you might already find a file named `Data.fs.old`. It is safe to delete this file.

Running Zope with ZServer

ZServer is the Web server that comes packaged with Zope. Essentially, this is what enables you to publish anything you create in Zope on the World Wide Web. Besides coming with Zope and allowing you to get going without the use of a third-party Web server, ZServer allows you to access Zope through protocols other than HTTP, such as FTP, WebDAV, or LDAP. As well, ZServer is multi-threaded, allowing for multiple Web requests at the same time.

See Chapter 17 to find out how to run Zope behind other third-party Web servers, such as Apache, IIS, and Netscape.

If you are playing around with Zope for the first time, you can skip this section and come back to it later. Here we explain how to modify how ZServer runs and behaves, and most likely it should be operating properly to suit our needs right out of the box.

When you run the startup script for Zope, you will see an output similar to what is listed here:

```
------
2001-04-04T21:53:38 INFO(0) ZServer HTTP server started at Wed
Apr 04 14:53:38 2001
        Hostname: localhost
        Port: 8080
------
2001-04-04T21:53:38 INFO(0) ZServer FTP server started at Wed
Apr 04 14:53:38 2001
        Hostname: sam.moosestore.com
        Port: 8021
------
2001-04-04T21:53:38 INFO(0) ZServer PCGI Server started at Wed
Apr 04 14:53:38 2001
        Inet socket port: 8090
```

This is Zope's ZServer getting up and running. When this is started, three main processes are begun: the HTTP server, the FTP server, and a secure monitor service that allows interactive Python-style access to a running ZServer. Once ZServer is running, you can publish Zope content or python modules via HTTP and/or FTP.

The output to the console basically just informs you what machine name Zope recognizes, and what port numbers different protocols are running on. In this case, it's informing you that HTTP access is at `localhost:8080`, that FTP access is at `sam.moosestore.com:8021`, and that the Persistent CGI service is at port `8090` on that machine.

Modifying ZServer's behavior with switches

As you can see from the previous section, the basic command to get ZServer started under Linux is `/usr/local/Zope/bin/python.exe /usr/local/Zope/z2.py -D`. Under Windows, it might look like `C:/Program Files/Zope/python z2.py -D`. If you wish, you can modify the script to incorporate several different startup command line options. Table 2-1 contains the most common ZServer command line options. (You can also see this table by running **./python z2.py -h**.)

Table 2-1
ZServer Command Line Switches

Command line option	***What it does***
-h	Displays this list of commands.
-z path	The location of the Zope installation. The default is the location of this script.
-Z path	UNIX only! This option is ignored on Windows. If this option is specified, a separate management process will be created that restarts Zope after a shutdown (or crash). The path must point to a `pid` file that the process will record its process id in. The path may be relative, in which case it will be relative to the Zope location. To prevent use of a separate management process, provide an empty string: -Z ' '
-t n	The number of threads to use, if ZODB3 is used. The default is 4. The older ZODB2 file format was deprecated as of Zope 2.0. If you're unsure which format you're using, check the filename in the /var subdirectory of your Zope installation. ZODB3 files are named `Data.fs`, and ZODB2 files are named `Data.bbb`.
-i n	Set the interpreter check interval. This integer value determines how often the interpreter checks for periodic things such as thread switches and signal handlers. The Zope default is 120, but you may want to experiment with other values that may increase performance in your particular environment.
-D	Run in Zope debug mode. This causes the Zope process not to detach from the controlling terminal, and is equivalent to supplying the environment variable setting Z_DEBUG_MODE=1
-a ipaddress	The IP address to listen on. If this is an empty string (-a ' '), then all addresses on the machine are used.
-d ipaddress	IP address of your DNS server. If this is an empty string (-d ' '), then IP addresses will not be logged. If you have DNS service on your local machine then you can set this to 127.0.0.1.

Continued

Table 2-1 (continued)

Command line option	*What it does*
-u username or uid number	The username to run ZServer as. You may want to run ZServer as "nobody" or some other user with limited resources. This only works under UNIX-like operating systems, and if ZServer is started by root.
-P [ipaddress:] number	Set the Web, FTP, and monitor port numbers simultaneously as offsets from the number. The Web port number will be number+80. The FTP port number will be number+21. The monitor port number will be number+99. The number can be preceded by an IP address followed by a colon to specify an address to listen on. This allows different servers to listen on different addresses. Multiple -P options can be provided to run multiple sets of servers.
-w [ipaddress:] port	The Web server (HTTP) port. This defaults to 8080. The standard port for HTTP services is 80. If this is an empty string (-w ' '), then HTTP is disabled. The number can be preceded by an IP address followed by a colon to specify an address to listen on. This allows different servers to listen on different addresses. Multiple –w options can be provided to run multiple servers.
-f [ipaddress:] port	The FTP port. If this is an empty string (-f ' '), then FTP is disabled. The standard port for FTP services is 21. The default is 8021. The port can be preceded by an IP address followed by a colon to specify an address to listen on. This allows different servers to listen on different addresses. Multiple -f options can be provided to run multiple servers.
-p path	Path to the PCGI resource file. The default value is Zope.cgi, relative to the Zope location. If this is an empty string (-p ' ') or the file does not exist, then PCGI is disabled.
-F path or port	Either a port number (for inet sockets) or a path name (for UNIX domain sockets) for the FastCGI Server. If the flag and value are not specified then the FastCGI Server is disabled.

Command line option	What it does
-m [ipaddress:] port	The secure monitor server port. If this is a dash (-m -), then the monitor server is disabled. The monitor server allows interactive Python style access to a running ZServer. To access the server see `medusa/monitor_client.py` or `medusa/monitor_client_win32.py`. The monitor server password is the same as the Zope emergency user password set in the `access` file. The default is to not start up a monitor server. The port can be preceded by an IP address followed by a colon to specify an address to listen on. This allows different servers to listen on different addresses. Multiple –m options can be provided to run multiple servers.
-l path	Path to the ZServer log file. If this is a relative path then the log file will be written to the `var` directory. The default is `Z2.log`.
-r	Run ZServer is read-only mode. ZServer won't write anything to disk. No log files, no pid files, nothing. This means that you cannot do a lot of things such as use PCGI and zdaemon. ZServer will log hits to STDOUT and zLOG will log to STDERR.
-L	Enable locale (internationalization) support. The value passed for this option should be the name of the locale to be used (see your operating system documentation for locale information specific to your system). If an empty string is passed for this option (-L ''), Zope will set the locale to the user's default setting (typically specified in the $LANG environment variable). If your Python installation does not support the locale module, the requested locale is not supported by your system or an empty string was passed but no default locale can be found, an error will be raised and Zope will not start.
-X	Disable servers. This might be used to effectively disable all default server settings or previous server settings in the option list before providing new settings. For example, to provide just a Web server use: `z2.py -X -w80`
-M file	Save detailed logging information to the given file. This log includes separate entries for the start of a request; the start of processing the request in an application thread; the start of response output; and the end of the request.

Generally speaking, if an option is omitted, the default value is used, so you only have to specify those options which you want set to some non-default value.

Using the command line switches when running Zope as a service

To modify the command line switches when running Zope as a service under Windows NT, you cannot just edit the batch file that Zope uses to start up. What you will need to do is actually edit the registry key directly in the Windows registry.

To edit the registry key, select Run from the Start menu, type **regedit32**, and click OK. This will enter the Registry Editor. Once in the registry, the path is `HKEY_LOCAL_MACHINE\SYSTEM\CurrentControlSet\Services\SiteName\Parameters\Start`, where *SiteName* is the name you gave your Web site when installing Zope (see Figure 2-8). Add the switches that you would like and click OK. The changes will take effect when you restart the Zope service.

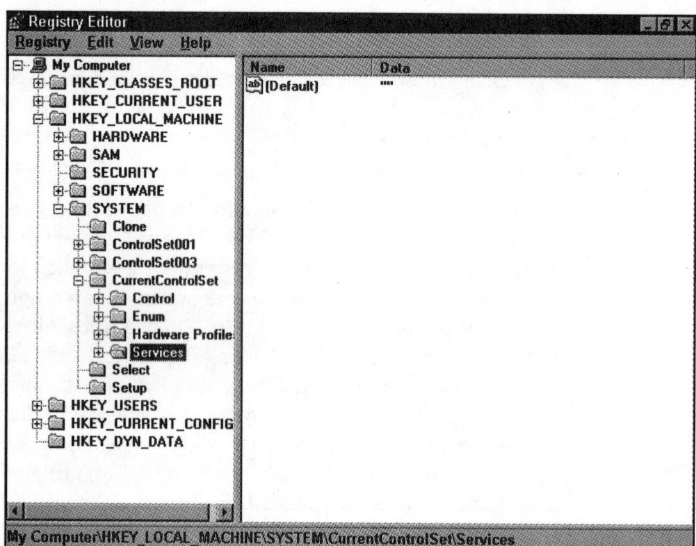

Figure 2-8: Editing the Registry Key

Editing the Windows registry makes it really easy to truly mess up your system if you are not careful. We advise not touching anything besides the `HKEY_LOCAL_MACHINE\SYSTEM\CurrentControlSet\Services\SiteName\Parameters\Start` key unless you really know what you are doing.

Expanding Zope with Products

Products are essentially "plug-ins" for Zope usually created by other Zope users like you. There are products for many uses, from simple database adapters to full e-commerce suites. If you go to `http://www.zope.org/Products`, you will see a wide range of products available for download.

Installing new products

The procedure for installing new products should be exactly the same on both UNIX and Windows, with a few syntactic differences.

First, download the product you want to install. Typically, you will receive a compressed archive with the name and version number of the product. Let's say for example that we have just downloaded `ZLDAPConnection.tgz`, the Zope LDAP Connection Product, and placed it in `/tmp/` for UNIX or in `C:\Downloads\forWindows`.

If they have been constructed correctly, most products will need to be uncompressed into your Zope installation directory. Under UNIX, you will have to change to the Zope directory: **cd /usr/local/Zope-2.5.0** (or whatever you named your Zope installation directory). From there, you will do **tar xvfz /usr/downloads/ZLDAPConnection.tgz**, which will extract the product and place it in the directory, `/lib/python/Products/ZLDAPConnection/`.

Under Windows, you must use a program that understands the tar and gzip compression schemes, such as WinZip. Instruct your program to extract the files, using full path information, to your Zope installation directory.

Check the directory where the product was installed for any `README` or `INSTALL` files. If any exist, you should read them thoroughly and follow any other installation instructions that they may have.

After this, your product should be ready to go. Restart your Zope server by going into the Zope Control Panel and clicking the Shutdown button. Start your Zope server back up the way you normally would.

Once you are back in Zope's management interface, you want to verify that you can use the product. All you have to do in this case is click the list of items to add and verify that the product, in this case, "ZLDAPConnection," is listed in there.

Check out Chapter 3 for more on products and the Product Management screen.

Product troubleshooting

If the product does not show up in the add list, you can get more information as to what the problem might be. In the Control Panel is a special folder called *Product Management*. This folder has a list of all the products currently installed on your system. If a product is broken, it will say so next to the name of the product, as well as display an icon of a broken box. Clicking the product will take you to a page that has a link to a Traceback (a listing of the sequence of object and method calls that lead to the error) that will tell you what error the product is giving. More information on this can be found in Chapter 19.

Getting Support

If you can't figure out a problem, help is always only an e-mail message away. Zope currently has two mailing lists for getting help or discussing Zope-related issues. The `zope@zope.org` list provides help for people using Zope to develop Web sites and Web applications, while the `zope-dev@zope.org` list provides a place for people developing Zope itself to discuss problems. You can subscribe to either list or search their archives by going to `http://www.zope.org/Resources/MailingLists`. If you do have a question, it is generally considered polite to search the archives first to make sure your question has not been asked (and answered) before.

Summary

In this chapter we installed and ran Zope for the first time. We also explained the Zope directory structure before moving on to help you get Zope running with its built-in Web server, ZServer. Finally, we explained how to add new products that you may have downloaded from the CD-ROM that accompanies this book or off of the Web.

In the next chapter we start working in Zope, helping you become familiar with the work interface and how to use Zope objects.

✦ ✦ ✦

Zope Objects and the Management Interface

In this chapter, we introduce you to Zope's unique browser-based management interface. The management interface is the default tool you use to create and manipulate your Web application (other tools can also be used, since Zope provides FTP and WebDAV access as well). As we mentioned earlier in this book, Zope uses objects to store and manage information over the Web. Some of the more commonly used objects, which are also described in this chapter, include *Folders*, *DTML Documents*, *DTML Methods*, *Images*, *Files*, and *Users*. Following a detailed look at the management interface itself, the functions and features of each of these objects are thoroughly described.

It is our goal that by the end of this chapter, you will be familiar enough with Zope objects and the management interface to begin building your own Web site. If after reading this chapter some subjects still seem confusing, don't worry; most of the concepts introduced here are described throughout the book in greater detail. In an effort to minimize any confusion you may experience, this chapter is infested with examples. While some of the examples we present are more extensive than others, they are all designed to get you more comfortable with the objects and ideas as they are introduced over the course of the chapter.

✦ ✦ ✦ ✦

In This Chapter

✦ ✦ ✦ ✦

Object Basics

The word *object* is used extensively in modern computer literature. You might be unsure of what an object really is because you've heard it used just about everywhere. The reason for this confusion and seemingly over usage of the word is that "object" means "a thing." It is hard to precisely explain what an "object" or even "a thing" is because it's a generic word that is used to reference . . . well, other *things*. Now that we have done our best to thoroughly confuse you we'll attempt to explain what objects are to Zope.

Throughout this book we will constantly be referring to *things* in Zope as *objects*, so we should probably begin by telling you what an object *is*. To put it simply, everything you use to build a Web site or an application in Zope is an object, from the document that stores data, to the template that presents that data, to the script that adds to or manipulates that data. As far as Zope is concerned, even the users of your application are objects. For the purposes of this chapter, you only need to realize that with Zope you are working with these things called *objects*.

Objects in Zope have a number of characteristics that are, if not unique to Zope, are at least uncommon in other systems, and are unique in combination:

✦ Objects can be identified and accessed via a unique, human readable URL, and can be accessed via HTTP, FTP, XML-RPC, or WebDAV like this: `http://myzopesite.com/book/cover/large`

✦ Changes to objects are persistent, and are stored in the ZODB

✦ Objects can acquire attributes from their containers, even if they don't have those attributes themselves, so that in the above book cover example, a book that has no cover image can acquire a default one from the containing folder

Objects are discussed in more detail in Chapter 5.

The Zope Management Interface

Almost everything you do in Zope is through the management interface. The management interface is accessed by starting up your Web browser and going to `http://localhost:8080/manage`. After successfully logging in, you are presented with the management screen like the one shown in Figure 3-1. Note the similarity between the management screen and your system's File Manager (on Microsoft Windows this is the Windows Explorer). This is the default way of accessing Zope, and is one of the things that makes Zope very convenient for website development.

Using the management interface you can build and maintain a Zope site from any Internet connected computer, without having to install any software. Other methods of accessing Zope, such as FTP, may require downloading and installing special software on your system (such as an FTP client) but make it easier to access Zope from within any special development tools that you may be used to using, however, even experienced developers who use their own favorite tools with Zope find themselves using the management interface occasionally, especially when working from someone else's computer.

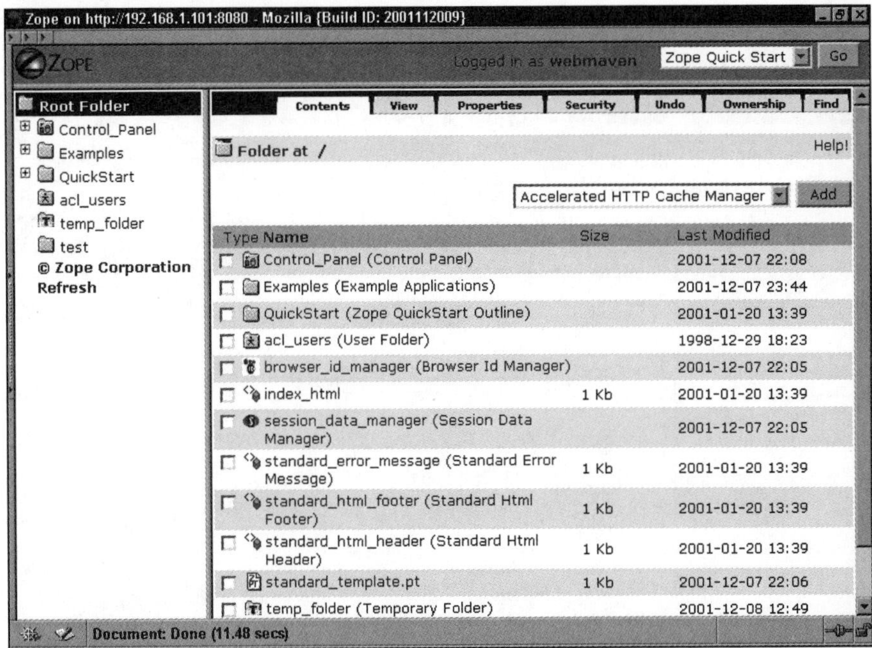

Figure 3-1: The Zope management interface

As you can see, the management screen is broken up into three frames. The top frame that extends the width of the screen contains the Zope logo; the username you are currently logged in as; and a drop-down list containing Zope Quick Start, Set Preferences, and Logout. The left frame, called the *Navigator* frame, shows all of the current folders off of the Root Folder, a link to the Zope Corporation copyright, and a Refresh link. The right frame, called the *Workspace* frame, contains the path of the current folder, all of its contents, and several tabs and buttons, which are discussed in the following section.

Using the top frame

The topmost frame has only a few functions in the current release, though that may change in future versions of Zope. Currently the top frame houses the Zope logo, which if clicked, opens a new browser window pointed toward `http://www.zope.org`; the username that you are currently logged on as; and a short drop-down list of options. The topmost option, Zope Quick Start, is a simple page that contains some useful links, including those to Zope's online documentation at `http://www.zope.org`, Zope mailing lists, and the built-in help system.

Customizing the interface

A new feature in Zope 2.3 was the ability to loosely customize the default settings of Zope's management interface. From the drop-down list in the top frame, select Set Preferences and click the Go button. You are taken to the screen shown in Figure 3-2.

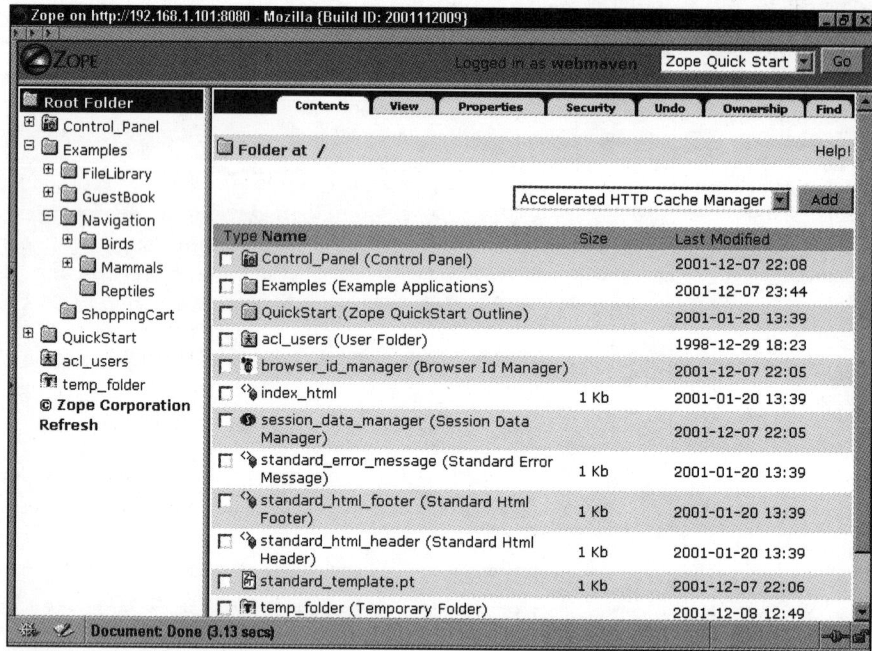

Figure 3-2: Setting your preferences for the management interface

Show Top Frame determines whether the top navigation bar is shown with a simple Yes/No radio button. *Yes* is the default setting. If set to *No*, the top frame is removed and the name of the current user and the drop-down list is relocated to the bottom of the Navigator frame. Any changes you make will not 'take' until after you click the *Change* button, and you must refresh your browser to see this change take effect.

Use Style Sheets is another Yes/No radio button, which is defaulted to *Yes*. This setting determines whether the management interface uses style sheets to determine its look. When set to *No*, none of the text in the interface is formatted in any way and will appear in your browser's default formatting.

The next two options, Text Area Width and Text Area Height, determine the size of the text area seen when working in objects such as DTML Documents or Methods. The defaults are set at 100 columns for width and 20 rows for height. A sample text box is provided at the bottom of the Browser Preferences page so you can fiddle with the settings until they are comfortable for you.

To enact any changes you make, simply click the *Change* button. With the exception of the Show Top Frame option, any changes you make should become immediately visible. The Show Top Frame option also requires that you refresh your browser after clicking the *Change* button.

Logging out

This simple-seeming function is a feature that was added to Zope 2.3. Its operation is as straightforward as it looks. Click the Logout option in the drop-down list in the top frame and a login dialog box appears. Simply enter a valid username and password and you should be working under that username from then on.

If you have multiple browser windows open, they probably will still show that you are logged in under the old username in the top frame. If you reload the top frame, it should update to the current username that you are logged in as.

The function of switching authentication is often browser-dependent. If you have any trouble logging in as a new identity, simply close all of your browser windows and restart Zope with a fresh login.

Exploring folders with the Navigator frame

The Navigator frame shows all of the folders off of the Root Folder in a tree layout, including the Control_Panel, acl_users, and temp_folder folders. If a folder has subfolders, a plus sign in a box will appear beside its icon, indicating that it can be expanded. Clicking the plus sign changes it into a minus sign and expands the folder one more level. You can see the expanded tree in Figure 3-3. Clicking the minus sign collapses the folders back down.

Sometimes when adding new subfolders, the Navigator frame doesn't properly update to reflect the change. If this happens, click the Refresh link at the bottom of the Navigator frame and Zope will update the frame so that it is accurate.

Manipulating objects in the Workspace frame

The Workspace frame is where you will do the majority of your work in Zope. Within the Workspace frame, you view, manipulate, and edit the various objects that make up your Zope Web site and applications.

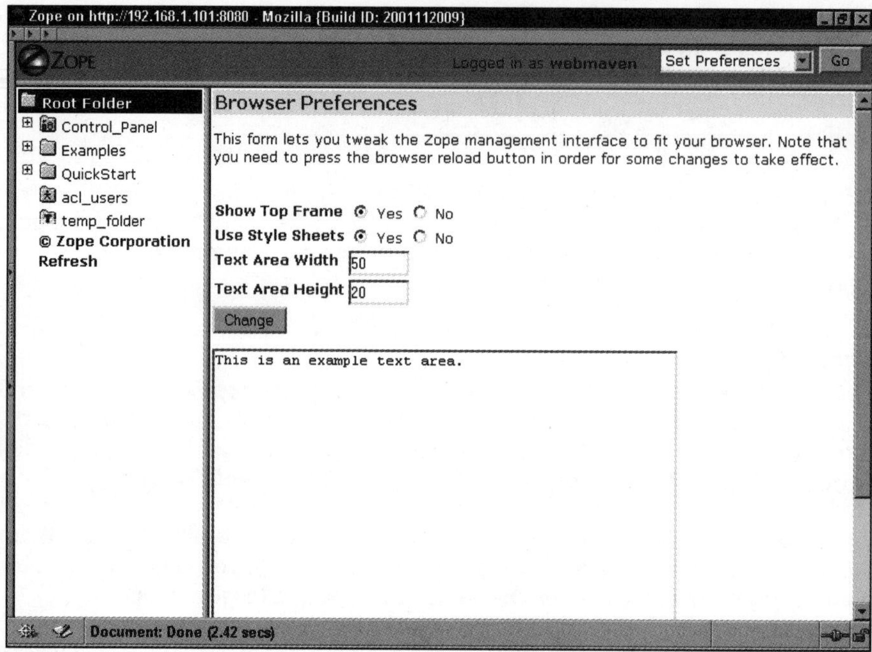

Figure 3-3: An expanded folder tree in the Root Folder

Along the top of the Workspace are several tabs that let you switch between the different views of an object. The number and labels of these tabs depend on the type of the object that you are currently working with. Below these tabs is listed the type of object you are working in, as well as its path. For example, if you were working in a document called "meeting" that was in an "Events" folder off of the Root Folder, you would see `DTML Document at / Events/meeting` (notice that the current object you are in is also underlined).You would also see that the first slash and the containing folder were links: the slash link would take you to the Root Folder, while the other would take you to the Events folder.

Let's use an existing example to make sure that this is clear. Click on the plus sign next to the Examples folder in the Navigator Frame. You should see several new folders there, including FileLibrary. Click on the FileLibrary in the Naviagtor frame, and the contents of the Workspace Frame will change to display the FileLibrary folder. Just below the tabs, you should see a folder icon, and the text Folder at /Examples/FileLibrary.

To the far right of the location, there is also a Help! link, which will pop up a help window that will display help for the object you are currently examining.

What is displayed below this depends not only on the type of object you are currently in, but also on which tab you have selected. For example, in Figure 3-1 you are looking at the Content view of the Root Folder. You can tell this because the Content tab is in front of the others (the other tabs are slightly grayed out, and have a line dividing them from the rest of the workspace frame).

Common Views

The tabs along the top of the Workspace frame represent different views of the current object. *Views* show you different aspects of the information about an objects attributes and/or enable you to edit its attributes, from defining their security settings to undoing any changes made. To access a view, simply click its title.

What follows is a brief tour through the views found on most objects, to get you acquainted with their look and feel. Although explaining each one fully is far more complex than we can get into at this point, each are explained in much more detail in the coming chapters. Keep in mind, that custom objects that are added to Zope have their own specialized views, and it's up to the Product developer to decide how those are displayed. We'll be discussing building custom Products in Section II of the book.

Viewing objects through the Default view

All Zope objects have URLs that can be accessed through a Web browser. Whenever you click the View tab, it merely replaces the Workspace frame with a view of the object as if you had gone to its absolute URL through the Web. You might use this to check your work in a DTML (Document Template Markup Language) method, or see how an image would appear when rendered by a browser. This basic functionality is important to Zope's design, so it bears repeating: All Zope objects can be uniquely accessed through a human readable URL. Calling an object through its URL will give you that object's default rendering: Image objects display themselves, Folder objects display a contained index_html object if they have one (if they don't, then they acquire one), and method and document objects render themselves and display the rendered result to the browser.

Examining an object and its Properties

Many objects in Zope can have properties attached to them. *Properties* are bits of data associated with an object, such as the object's title or content type. The Properties view displays all of the properties associated with an object, showing the property names, values, and types. In this view you may also define new properties and edit or delete old properties. You display this view by clicking on the View tab of an object. Clicking on a folder's Properties view will result in a display something like Figure 3-4.

In Chapter 4, you will see how you can use object properties when building your application.

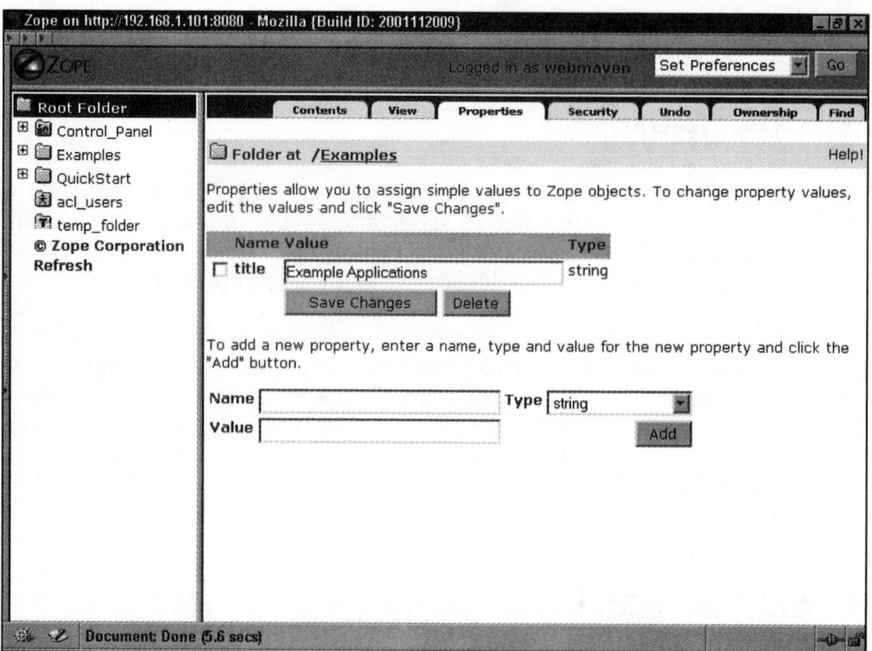

Figure 3-4: The Properties view

You can see that the properties view first lists the existing properties, along with their values and types in a list. Below the list, there are two buttons: Save Changes and Delete. Below that, there is another form for adding new Properties to an object with a Name field, a Value field, and a Type drop-down box.

Adding a new property

To add a new property, enter a name for the property into the Name field at the bottom of the Properties view, select the property's type from the drop-down menu, and enter a value for that property into the Value field. Click the Add button, and the property will be added to the property list above the Add Property form.

Suppose you want to add a new property to the `index_html` Document in the Root Folder of your site that reflects the last time it was updated. Click `index_html` to get into the document object, then click the Properties tab at the top of the page to enter the Properties view. In the Name field, enter **last_updated**, then click the Type drop-down list and select `date`. Finally, enter the current date in the format: YYYY/MM/DD into the Value field. For example, January 1, 2001 would be entered as **2001/01/01**. Now click the Add button and voila! A new property has been added to your `index_html` document.

Most property types correspond to their equivalent Python types, with the exceptions of the lines, text, tokens, selection and multiple selection' types. For a discussion of these special types, see Chapter 16. The python equivalents of the 'normal' property types (Boolean, date, float, int, long, string) are discussed in Chapter 5.

Editing or deleting an existing property

To edit the value of an existing property, simply change whatever is in the Value field to what you desire and then click the Save Changes button. To delete properties, place checkmarks in the boxes beside the properties you wish to remove, then click the Delete button. Changes or deletions will become immediately visible.

Changing permissions in the Security view

The Security view shows you all of the security settings of the current object. By manipulating these settings, you can allow some users to view certain parts of your site, while denying access to others. It lists all of the permissions available for the object in rows, and all of the roles in columns. The roles that have permissions assigned to them have checkmarks. Figure 3-5 shows this View.

The Security view is covered in greater detail in Chapter 13.

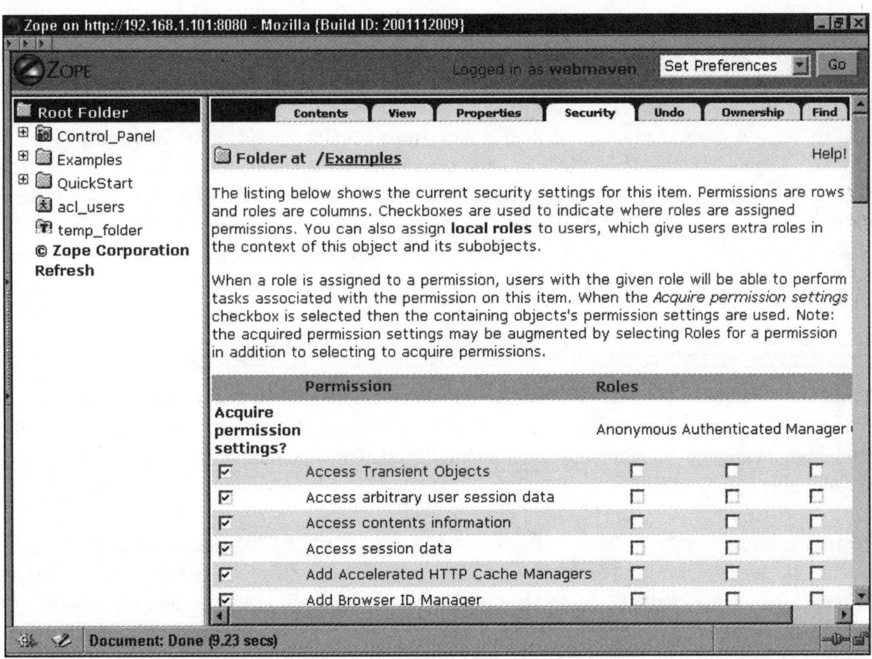

Figure 3-5: The Security view

Simulating roles with the Proxy view

Usually when objects are invoked, they have the same privileges as the user that invokes them. Using proxy roles, you can allow DTML documents or methods to run using a different role than that of the user who invokes it. The Proxy view shows what proxy roles the DTML document or method has, if any. Proxy roles replace the roles of the user who is viewing the document or method, enabling you to give greater or lesser control over what the document or method may access. For example, you could give a method being viewed by an anonymous user the ability to create other objects, which an anonymous user is normally not allowed to do.

As is the Security view discussed earlier in this chapter, the Proxy view is explained in more detail in Chapter 13. User roles and their privileges are discussed in Chapter 11 (Content Management).

Viewing ownership information

Any object, except those found in the Control Panel, can be owned. The Ownership view displays the name of the user that currently owns the object and enables you to change that status.

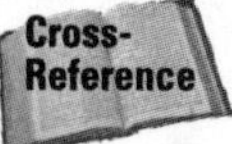

Ownership is discussed in more detail in Chapter 13.

Fixing mistakes in the Undo view

Any change you make to an object constitutes a *transaction*. Zope automatically tracks which object was modified and which method was used to make that modification. These transactions are listed in the object's Undo tab, along with the username of the person who made the change and the date the change was made. For example, if you were logged in as Bob and modified the index_html object in the Root Folder, the record of the transaction in the Undo tab would look something like the following:

```
/index_html/manage_edit by Bob      2001-02-05 04:36:00 PM
```

The Undo tab in a folder shows all of the transactions of the objects contained within that folder, including those in any subfolders. This means that if you are in the Root Folder you can see all of the transactions performed in Zope. Figure 3-6 shows the Undo view.

To undo any change, place a checkmark in the box beside the listing of the transactions you would like to remove, then click the Undo button at the bottom of the screen. It is important to note that you cannot undo a transaction for an object if any later transactions modify the same object. The way around this is to simply select all of the later transactions as well as the one you wish to remove. Also, you cannot undo an Undo—once a transaction is removed, it is permanently gone.

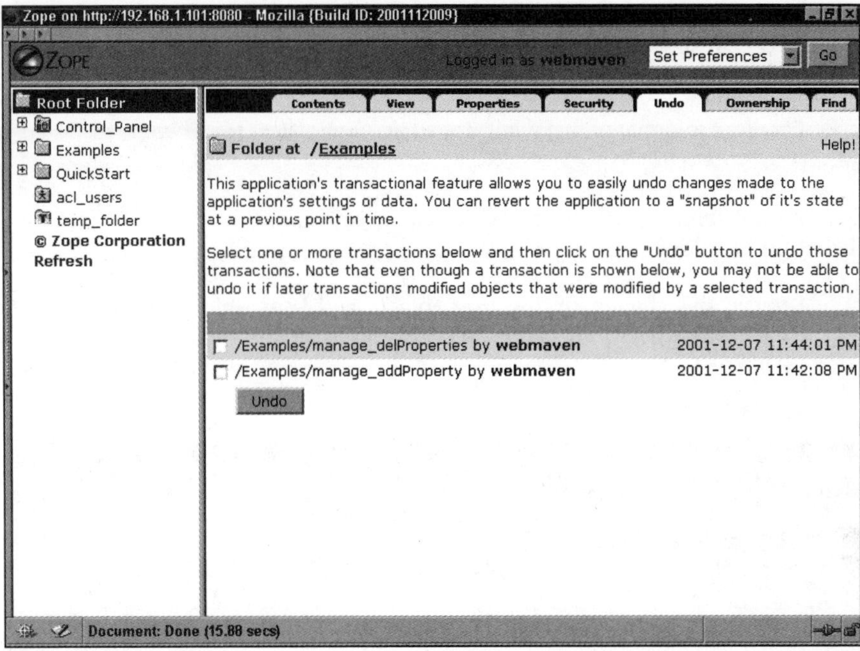

Figure 3-6: The Undo view

Folder Objects

Folders provide the framework around which you build your application. Essentially, Folders are similar to directories on your computer, containing the other objects that make up your Web site, including other folders. More important, the security and behavior of your Web site can be affected by how you organize your folder structure. Here we show you the basic functions of the Folder object, but you will see as we go on how it affects the rest of your site.

Adding folders

If you are not already looking at the Root Folder object, click the Root Folder in the Navigation Frame. From the Root Folder of your Zope site (your browser should look like Figure 3-1) click the drop-down list of available objects (this drop down is between the location bar and the contents list). Select the item labeled Folder from the list. The form shown in Figure 3-7 will appear.

The Add Folder form prompts you for an id, title, and whether you want to create a public interface and/or user folder. Zope creates a default Zope Page Template called index_html if you select "Create public interface." This is the default document that is displayed by Zope when you access the URL for the folder. For example, if your folder is named "products," you could then type `http://localhost:8080/products/` into your browser and you will see the contents of the `index_html` Method in the products folder.

For more information regarding Zope Page Templates, see Chapter 18.

Zope creates an `acl_users` folder for you in your new folder if you select the "Create user folder" option.

Later in this chapter (in the User Folders and User Objects section) we briefly explain what User Folders are and how they work, but for in-depth coverage, see Chapter 13.

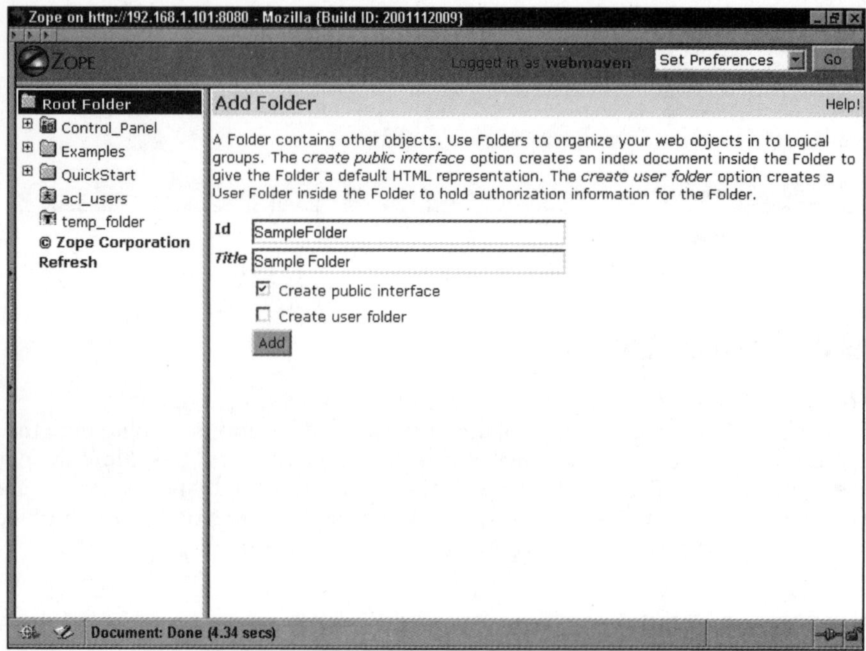

Figure 3-7: The Add Folder form

To become familiar with how this works, let's add a Folder object to our example site. Enter "SampleFolder" for the Folder's id and "Sample Folder" for the title. Check "Create public interface" but leave the "Create user folder" unchecked. Then click add. Now you should have a brand-new folder with a public interface.

Now, open another browser window, and type in the URL `http://localhost:8080/SampleFolder`. Congratulations! You've just created your first Zope object, and displayed it in a browser.

The folder object you just added to your site is similar, in most respects to the Root Folder itself. There are only a few differences in the Root Folder from a regular Folder object. You cannot delete the Control_Panel for example.

The contents View

When you click a folder in the Zope management screen, you are presented with the folder's Contents view as can be seen in Figure 3-8. The Contents view displays an id for each of the objects in a folder, as well as the size of the object and the date the object was last modified. If any of those objects has a title property, the title is displayed in parentheses beside the id.

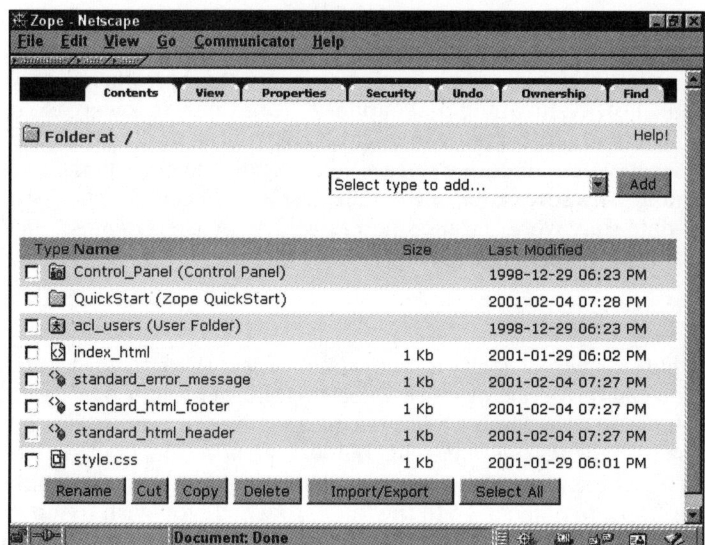

Figure 3-8: The folder content list

Adding objects

Just as you added a Folder to the Root Folder, you add new objects to a Folder by clicking the drop-down list titled "Select type to add . . . ." This list contains all of the available objects that you can add to a Folder. Select the type of object you wish to add. If you have JavaScript enabled in your browser, Zope will automatically load the add form (if you do not have JavaScript enabled, you'll need to click the Add button). Each object type has its own add form.

Removing objects

Removing objects you no longer need is simple. Click the checkbox next to the object(s) you want to remove and click the Delete button. The object(s) will be deleted and you will be returned to the folder's contents. Deleting objects from a folder is considered a transaction, and will appear in the Folder's Undo tab as a transaction that can be undone. There are certain objects in the Root Folder like the Control Panel and the standard_error_message that Zope will not allow you to delete, as they are necessary for Zope to function.

Renaming objects

Renaming an object involves a similar process as removing objects. Place a checkmark in the box beside the object you wish to rename and click the Rename button. A page will appear with a text box, an OK button, and a Cancel button. Simply erase the old name and enter the new one, then click the OK button. If the new name has invalid characters or is blank, Zope displays an error and the old name will remain unchanged. Renaming objects is also an undo-able transaction that will be listed in the object's Undo tab.

Sorting objects

By default Zope sorts all of the objects in folder according to their ids in case-sensitive, alphabetical order, meaning that capital *Z* comes before lowercase *a*. If you have a lot of objects in one folder, you might have trouble finding the object with which you want to work. Since the release of 2.3 Zope lets you click on the column headers to change the sort order of the objects. Objects can now be sorted by type, size, and the date they were last modified as well as by their names. Clicking a column header again will reverse the sorting order.

Cutting and pasting objects

The Cut and Copy buttons work exactly as you would expect them to work in traditional programs. You can move one or more objects to another folder by selecting the checkbox to the left of the object name and then clicking the Cut button. The browser will redisplay the same page you were viewing but with an additional button labeled Paste. The presence of this button indicates that there are objects on your clipboard that you can paste. To paste objects, go to the folder to which you wish to move your object(s), then click the Paste button. The object(s) that you have previously cut will be moved from their current folder and placed into the new folder.

Copying works in the same way. The only difference is that the original objects remain where they were. If there is already an object in the destination folder with the same name as the one you are moving or copying, your new object will be prefixed with the name `copy_of_`. If you copied an `index_html` into a folder that already contains an `index_html`, your new object will be named `copy_of_index_html`. (You can then use the rename function to fix this problem.) As with other changes, cutting and pasting, and copying and pasting are undoable transactions that will show up in the Undo tab.

The prefix *copy_of_* can be something of a misnomer as the object may not really be a copy of the object of the same name in that folder. For example, if you copied an `index_html` from one folder to another folder that already had an `index_html`, the copy will show up in the second folder as `copy_of_index_html` but will actually be identical to the `index_html` in the original folder.

Importing and exporting objects

If you work with multiple Zope sites, you may want to export an object to a different installation of Zope instead of recreating it there from scratch. Using Zope's Import/Export facilities you can copy objects between two different Zope installations.

To export an object to a different Zope installation, place a checkmark beside the object you wish to export and then click the Import/Export button. Zope will display the Import/Export page, like you see in Figure 3-9. The top part of the page is for exporting objects from the current folder, while the bottom part is for importing objects into the current folder. If you clicked on the button without first checking an object to export, the Export Object id field will be blank, and you can enter the id of the object in the current folder that you wish to export. If you leave the id blank, Zope will let you export the current folder and all of its contents. This is the only way to export an entire Zope site (since the Root Folder isn't contained in anything else, and doesn't have an Id).

Below the object's id, you will be presented with two choices on how to export the file: you may either save it to your local machine or you may save it to the server. If you save it to your local machine, your browser will bring up the save box and you can pick where you want it to be saved. Notice that the name of the file is the id of the object plus the extension, `.zexp` (if you export the Root Folder, the file will be named `.zexp`). If you save the object to the server, Zope will save the export file to the `var` directory of the current Zope installation (refer to Chapter 2 if you do not know where this directory is). After exporting a file to the server, you will be presented with a message notifying you that the export was successful. You can only export one object at a time.

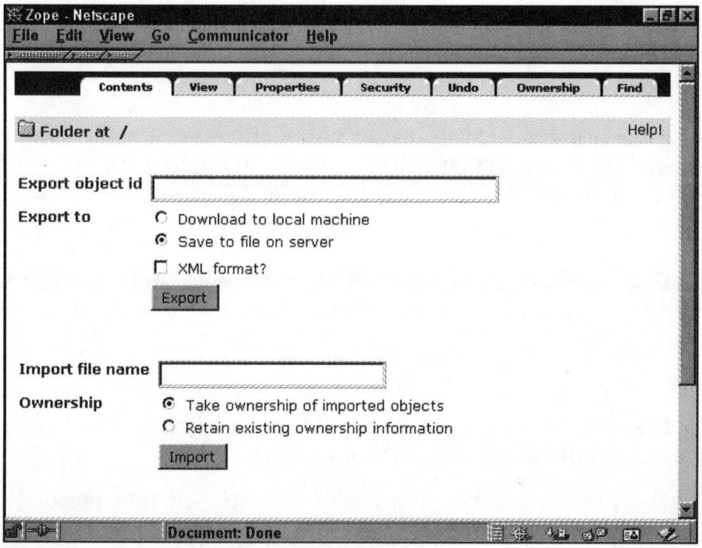

Figure 3-9: The Zope Import & Export screen

The export file is usually saved as a binary file, but you have the option to instead save it in XML (eXtensible Markup Language) format by placing a checkmark in the "XML format" checkbox. The XML file is significantly larger than its binary counterpart, but it enables you to actually look at the exported object in a somewhat intelligible light. You may also do some limited editing if you need to, though messing with the data is inadvisable unless you know what you are doing. Importing an object saved as an XML file is no different than importing one saved as a binary.

To import objects, place the `.zexp` file into the import directory of the Zope installation to which you wish to import (refer to Chapter 2 if you do not know where this is). Then, in Zope, go to the folder where you want to import the object and click the Import/Export button. Type the name of the file into the "import filename" field in the bottom portion of the screen and select Import. By default, the username you are logged in as will become the object's owner, but you may have the object keep its original ownership information by selecting "Retain existing ownership information" before you import it. More information on Ownership can be found in Chapter 13.

Viewing a folder

The View tab operates just as we discussed earlier in this chapter, showing you the default view of the folder, as if you went to the folder's URL in your Web-browser. For example, if you had a folder named "Widgets" that was under the "Products" folder, which happened to be in the Root Folder, the View tab will show you what it would look like if you went to the URL, `http://localhost:8080/Products/Widgets`, in your browser. One thing to note, though, is that the View tab only works if the current folder either has or inherits an `index_html` object. This is assuming that you are running Zope using ZServer as we discussed in Chapter 2. Essentially, you would see the exact same thing if you were to go to `http://localhost:8080/Products/Widgets/index_html`.

The Find view

Zope provides a method for you to search your entire site for a specific object based on custom search criteria. When you click the Find tab you are presented with the basic searching functions. The basic functions will perform a search using the following fields:

- ✦ **Find objects of type.** The type of objects to find, such as Folders, Images, DTML Documents, and so on. You may also search by all object types.
- ✦ **With ids.** The ids of objects to find. You may specify one or more ids, separated by spaces.
- ✦ **Containing.** The text that must be contained in the body of found items. Text in the title or other attribute fields will not be searched.
- ✦ **Modified.** Enables you to restrict your search to a specific time period. You can choose objects before or after a specified date/time.

The date should be a DateTime string such as YYYY/MM/DD hh:mm:ss, YYYY-MM-DD, or hh:mm.

You can also limit or expand the scope of the search by telling Zope to only search the current folder or to search all of the current folder's sub-folders.

You can specify additional criteria by clicking on the "Advanced" link. An advanced search adds the following fields to the search form:

✦ **expr.** A DTML expression to restrict found items. If the expression equals false in the context of the found object, the object is rejected. For example, try searching with the expression `id is not "Control_Panel"`. It will bring up every object in the site except the Control Panel, for which the expression evaluates as false.

✦ **Where the roles.** Use in combination with the "have permission" option. Restricts found objects to those that provide the indicated permissions for the indicated roles.

✦ **Have permission.** Use in combination with "Where the roles" option. Restricts found objects to those that provide the indicated permissions for the indicated roles.

DTML Documents

DTML Documents are the building blocks of any Web site created with Zope. Documents are used to display Web content to users over the Internet. As they are most commonly used, a DTML Document is basically the equivalent of a Web page. Among other formats, Documents can contain textual information in the form of plain text, HTML (Hypertext Markup Language), XML, or structured-text. DTML scripting commands (or tags) can be added to create dynamic Web pages capable of performing calculations, connecting to databases, sending mail, and even conditional or iterative insertion.

For a complete description of the scripting capabilities of DTML, refer to Chapter 4.

Adding a DTML document

In the Root Folder, select DTML Document from the drop-down list of available objects at the top of the Workspace, and click the Add button next to the list. The form shown in Figure 3-10 should appear on your screen.

You will see form inputs for Id, Title, and File. Of these, only Id is required. For example, enter **sampleDoc** for Id and **Sample Document** for Title. The file input is only used if you already have an HTML file in another location that you want to insert into a document when it is created. If so, click the Browse button and locate the file on your local drive. To just create this document and return to the list of contents, click Add. If you want to begin working on it right away, click the Add and Edit button and you will be taken to the Edit view of the newly created document.

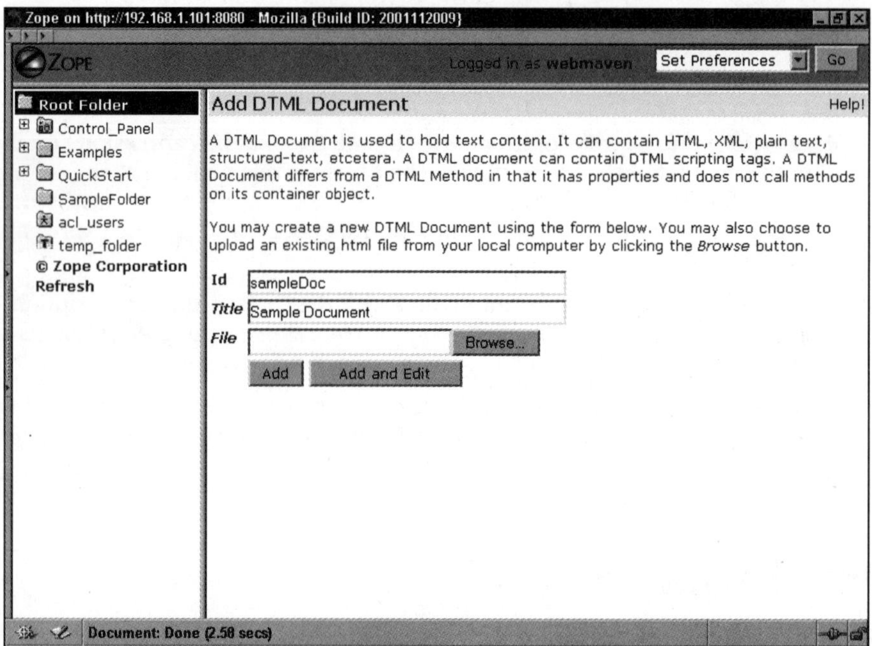

Figure 3-10: The Add DTML Document form

Editing a DTML document

To edit a DTML Document, find the object in the list of contents and click its name or the document icon that appears just to the left. This opens the Edit view for the document you selected. To continue with the previous example, find the document, `Sample Document` that you just created and click it. (See Figure 3-11.)

The Edit view includes an input for changing the title of the document and a text area for changing its content. The text area can be resized to fit your preference by clicking the Taller, Shorter, Wider, and Narrower buttons (don't forget you can also set a preference for the field size by choosing the Set Preferences option from the drop-down box in the Top Frame). To save any changes to your document, click the Save Changes button. Before your changes are actually saved, Zope parses the content of the text area for proper DTML syntax. If no syntax errors are found, the page is reloaded with a confirmation that your changes were saved and when. To overwrite the current contents of the document, you can upload the contents of another file by browsing your local drive for the location of the file and clicking Upload File.

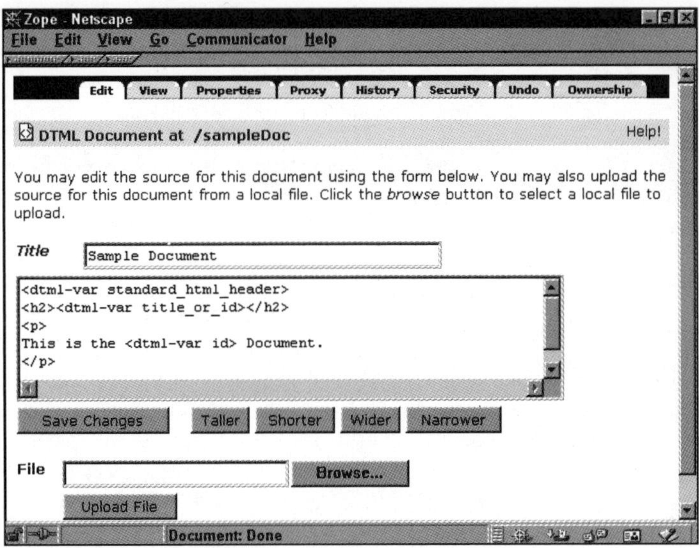

Figure 3-11: The Edit DTML Document view

Viewing a DTML Document

Viewing a DTML Document is a fairly simple process and can be achieved a couple of different ways. To view the document without leaving the management interface, click the View tab. This replaces the Workspace frame with a view of the document as it will be rendered on the Web.

Another way to view a DTML Document is by entering the URL of the object directly into your browser. As stated earlier in this chapter, a Zope object's URL is based on its id. So if we had a DTML Document in the Root Folder called "sampleDoc," its URL would be `http://localhost:8080/sampleDoc`. If the same document were in a folder called "sampleFolder," the URL would be `http://localhost:8080/sampleFolder/sampleDoc`.

Reviewing changes with the History view

The History view is used to track changes made to a DTML Document. It displays a list of every revision made to the document in descending order starting with the most recent. Each item on the list shows you when the revision was made, what type of action was taken, and by whom. See Figure 3-12 for an example of the History view of a DTML Document.

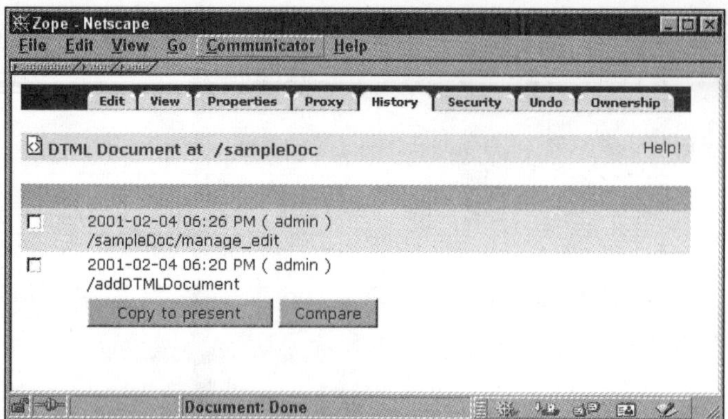

Figure 3-12: The History view

The History view enables you to undo changes to the text content stored in a DTML Document without affecting any changes you may have made to other properties (such as the id or the location of the document). To revert back to a particular revision in the history of the document, check the box next to that item in the list and click "Copy to present." You can view the document as it existed at the time of that revision by clicking the time date stamp.

You can also selectively compare revisions by checking the box next to any two items on the list and clicking "Compare." Selecting only one item will compare that revision to the current state of the document. The comparison is shown in *diff* format. Lines added to the new document appear with a plus sign next to them, while lines that have been removed from the old document appear with a minus sign. Lines that have been replaced or changed are signified with an exclamation point.

DTML Methods

DTML Methods are almost identical to DTML Documents, except for a few fundamental differences. On the surface, both documents and methods have the same user interface, are added, edited, viewed, and uploaded in the same way, and act the same when called through the Web. Then why have two different object types?

The most important distinction between DTML Methods and DTML Documents is how they are intended to be used. Simply put, documents are meant to contain and display information, while methods are meant to control dynamic behavior. In other words, methods are used when you need to display a smaller section of dynamic content that is designed to perform some action or manipulate another object. The practical upshot is that when a method looks for an attribute — for example, title — it starts its search in its container, not itself. Adding a title to a Method accomplishes nothing, as it would never be acquired. A Document on the other hand, looks at itself first when looking for attributes, so a title attribute attached to a document will be found and used.

When you edit a DTML Method you may notice that it does not have a Properties tab. Methods do not need their own set of properties; they share the properties of the folder they are in. This is because Folders were originally intended to behave like objects themselves with DTML Methods performing the duties of traditional methods in OOP (Object Oriented Programming).

OOP is covered in more detail in Chapter 4.

Following are a few examples of how DTML Methods are commonly used in Zope. These examples have code in them that we do not expect you to understand just yet, since we haven't really gotten to DTML yet. In the next chapter (Chapter 4), we'll discuss DTML syntax.

Introducing the standard header

The concept of the `standard_html_header` is great example of how DTML Methods are often used. When you log into Zope for the first time, you will see a method labeled `standard_html_header` among the list of contents in the Root Folder. This method is designed to contain a section of HTML content shared by a series of pages. This not only reduces the size and redundancy of your Web site in terms of the amount of text needed to render all of your Web pages, but it also makes maintaining your Web site much easier. Look at the simple example of the default `standard_html_header` that Zope comes installed with by clicking on the DTML method:

```
<HTML>
<HEAD>
 <TITLE><dtml-var title_or_id></TITLE>
</HEAD>
<BODY BGCOLOR="#FFFFFF">
```

Chances are, with the exception of a few pages, your entire Web site will have the same few lines of HTML at the beginning of every page. By putting these shared lines into one DTML Method, you eliminate the task of finding and modifying that same HTML several times when a change is needed. To illustrate this concept using the previous example, open the `standard_html_header` method and change the last line to:

```
<BODY BGCOLOR="#0000CC">
```

Viola! Whenever any document using this Method is rendered by a Web browser, it will use the updated background color. Return to the Root Folder in the Workspace frame and view the `index_html` document. Notice that the background color has changed from white to blue even though you never touched the `index_html`. This works because the index_html document has at its beginning a line that says:

```
<dtml-var standard_html_header>
```

Overriding the standard header

This concept can be taken one step further by using a special feature called acquisition in Zope. Say, for example, you have a subfolder named "NotBlue." We want every document in this folder to have the original white background, but the rest of the site will still use (acquire) the new blue background. This can be easily accomplished by copying the `standard_html_header` from the Root Folder into the NotBlue folder and changing the last line back to its original color:

```
<BODY BGCOLOR="#FFFFFF">
```

Because Zope looks inside the current folder for the `standard_html_header` before looking elsewhere, all of the documents that use this method in the NotBlue folder will now have a white background.Check it out by viewing `http://localhost:8080/NotBlue/`.

For more information about acquisitions, see Chapter 11.

File Objects

Files provide a way to contain raw data as objects in Zope. You can put just about any type of binary information in a file. Microsoft Word documents, PDF (portable document format) files, Lotus spreadsheets, and even movies and sound files can be made available on your Web site by uploading them as Zope File objects.

Adding a file

Adding a file is similar to creating a DTML Document or Method. The forms to add files and document are almost identical. Upon selecting "File" from the Add List, you will see a form with inputs for Id, Title, and File. As with all Zope objects, the id is required and the title is optional. For file objects, if an id is not specified, the name of the file you upload will be used. Click the Browse button to find the file you want on your local drive. To save the new file object, click Add. Although technically you can create a file object without specifying a file on your local drive to upload, it will create an empty object.

If you did not specify an id and the name of the file you are uploading contains illegal characters, Zope will return an exception once the file is finished uploading and you will be forced to re-upload the file.

Editing a file

To edit a file, find the file you want to edit in the list of contents and click the id or the icon of that file. The Edit view for the file object is shown in Figure 3-13.

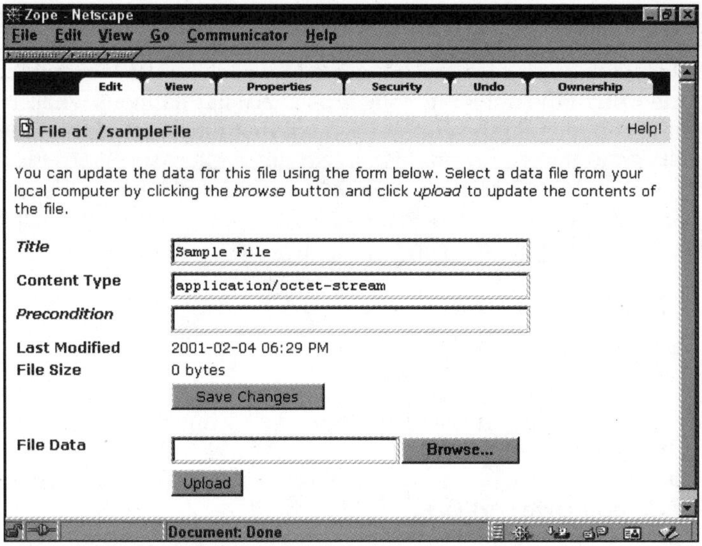

Figure 3-13: The Edit File view

From this form, you can change the title of the file or replace the binary content of the file by uploading a new file from your local drive. Although the layout of this form should be fairly familiar to you by now, there are a couple of fields here that are unique to file objects. These are Content Type and Precondition.

Content type

When you upload a file, Zope attempts to determine what type of file you are adding by the extension in the filename. If you upload a file with a `.pdf` extension, Zope assumes the file is an Adobe Acrobat PDF file, and sets its content type to `application/pdf`. The content type field is used to tell your computer what program to use when you try to open this file over the Web. So technically, if you wanted to, you can change this field on the Edit view without changing the file type and fool your computer into opening the file with a different program. If Zope does not recognize the file extension or an extension is not included in the path of the file when you upload, Zope will classify the object as a generic file. Zope uses `application/octet-stream` to describe the content type of generic files.

Precondition

When editing a file, you can set a method or document located elsewhere on the site as a *Precondition.* Zope will run the precondition method before it allows the object to be viewed. If any exceptions are raised by the precondition, then the file cannot be viewed. You might use this to verify an authenticated user or to update a database that tracks the number of downloads of the file, by having the precondition set to trigger a Python Script object that incremented an int property

Viewing a file

Like most other objects in Zope, files can be viewed by clicking the View tab or by going directly to the URL of the object in your browser. What happens when you attempt to view a file depends on the content type of that file. Most of the time, your computer will know what to use to open a text file, a Microsoft Word file, and so forth. If the file doesn't have a content type or is considered generic (see the section, "Content type," earlier in this chapter), Zope tells your computer to just save the file to your local drive so that you can figure out what to do with it.

Image Objects

Image objects are used to display graphics over the Web. Zope recognizes many of the more popular image formats including

- GIF (Graphics Interchange Format)
- JPEG (Joint Photographic Experts Group)
- BMP (Bitmaps)
- PNG (Portable Network Graphics)

Images in Zope are a specialized kind of file object. They have the same interface and share all of the same features common to files with the exception of a precondition. Zope also automatically determines the height and width of the image when it is added or uploaded and sets each as an object property of the image, though they may remain undefined for image types that Zope does not understand. If necessary, the height and width can be altered via the image's Properties view.

Adding an image

The process for adding an image is identical to that of adding a file. Upon selecting "Image" from the Add list, you will see a form with inputs for Id, Title, and File. As with all Zope objects, the id is required and the title is optional. For image objects, if an id is not specified, the name of the image you upload will be used. Click Browse to find the image you want on your local drive. To save the new image object, click Add. Again, while technically you can create an image object without specifying a file on your local drive to upload, when the image is viewed over the Web it will appear broken.

Editing an image

Editing an image is like editing any other type of file object. The Edit view enables you to change the title of the image, alter the content type if necessary, and replace the image with a different image by clicking Browse and selecting a new file from your local drive. The Edit view also displays a thumbnail of the image that it currently contains. As mentioned previously, Zope creates a height and a width property when an image is added. These properties change automatically if a new image with different dimensions is uploaded into the object.

Viewing an image

Images can be viewed like other objects in Zope by either going directly to the absolute URL of the image with your browser or by clicking the View tab while managing the object. For the sake of the following example, let's say you created an image you want to display on the Web. You gave this image an id of **sampleImage**.

This image can be displayed with or without the use of DTML. If you want to, you can write out the `<img>` tag by hand to look something like this:

```
<img src="sampleImage" height="50" width="50" alt="Sample">
```

Alternatively, this image object can be displayed with the use of DTML scripting tags that will do most of this writing for you. See Chapter 4 for more on using DTML to display images over the Web.

User Folders and User Objects

Although Chapter 13 is devoted entirely to security, the following section serves as an introduction to adding, editing, and managing User Folders and Users. Almost every object in Zope has a Security view, meaning security can be controlled on an object-by-object basis. For the purpose of this introduction (and everyday use), this level of control can be time consuming and is probably excessive. The most common way to limit viewing and management access to parts of a Zope Web site is at the folder level.

A *User Folder* is a specialized Zope object that acts as a user database in the folder in which it is created. User Folders are used to ensure security and manage the delegation of content development. For example, someone with the responsibility of managing the content of a website might want to give a developer access to work on only a certain part of a Web site. This can be achieved relatively easily by creating a user for that developer in a subfolder and giving that user access to content only in that subfolder. For the subjects covered in the next few chapters, it is only important that you understand that a User Folder is used to control which users are allowed to perform certain functions on the Web site, and that this access is only granted for the contents of the folder the user folder is in (as well as the containing Folder's remaining subfolders).

User objects on the other hand represent an individual user. They are created within User Folders, and generally have a username and a password. When someone accesses a website and authenticates themselves using a username and password, they then can operate within the site with the privileges associated with that User Object.

Adding a User Folder

View the contents of the Root Folder on your Zope site. You will see that a User Folder already exists. Each folder can only contain one User Folder, so we will need to create a subfolder for this example. If you have not done so already, create a new folder with an id of "sampleFolder." Open the contents of sampleFolder by clicking its name or icon.

User Folders are about the easiest objects in Zope to create. Select "User Folder" from the Add list. There, you're done. The folder contents will be refreshed with a new User Folder object. All User Folders are given an id of `acl_users` and a title of `User Folder`. These properties cannot be changed.

Editing a User Folder

User Folders don't support most of the common editing functions associated with other types of objects. Without a Properties view, User Folder properties such as title cannot be changed and new ones cannot be added. Although User Folders do have an absolute URL, they cannot be viewed directly through the Web, and therefore do not have a View manage tab. The functions under the Security and Undo views pertain only to managing the users within that User Folder.

Adding a user

To view a list of users already in a User Folder or to add a new user, view the list of contents for that User Folder by clicking its name or icon. Find the `acl_users` folder in the Root Folder and view its list of contents. When you installed Zope, you were asked for a username and password for the initial manager, which is the user you are probably logged in as right now. You should see this user in the list of contents of this User Folder.

To add a new user, click the Add button at the bottom of the user list. Figure 3-14 shows the Add User form.

Enter a name and password for the new user. To be sure that you typed it correctly, you will be asked to confirm the password. For additional security, you have the option of limiting the Internet domains that this user can log in from. Enter these in the input for *Domains* and be sure to separate them by spaces (for example, "zope.org MooseStore.com"). *Roles* are used to control which users are allowed to perform certain actions in Zope. For example, the initial user you create has the "Manager" role. This is required to access the Zope management interface you are currently using. Although you are not required to specify any roles for a new user, logging in for a user without any roles would be a pointless endeavor, as he or she is essentially an unauthenticated user. (Authentication is fully explained in Chapter 13.) For our purposes here, consider an unauthenticated user as a user who has not been given any roles by the Web site.

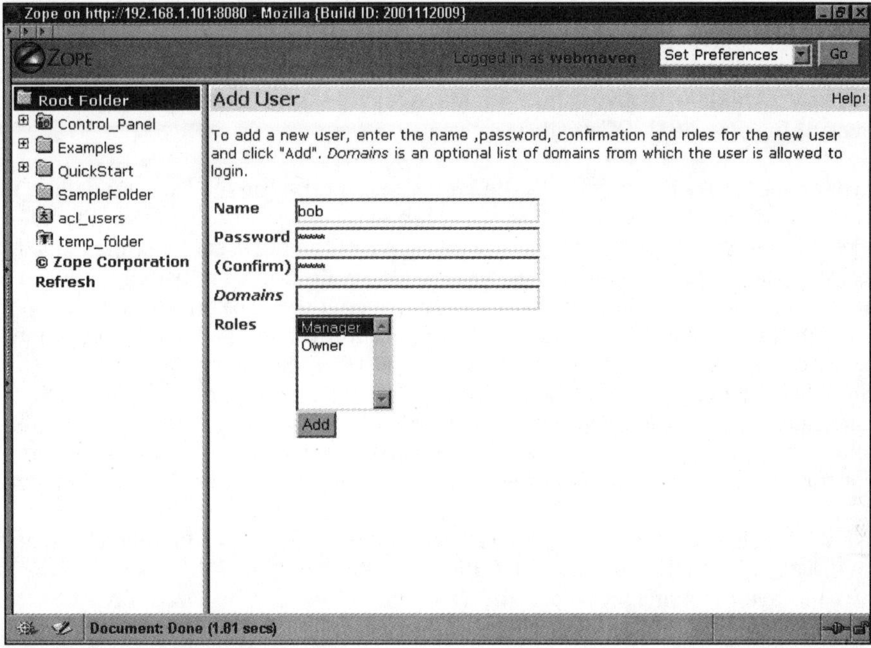

Figure 3-14: The Add User form

Editing a user

The form used to edit an existing user is the same form used to add a new one. Click the name or icon of one of the users in the list of contents. All of the roles this user has been given will be highlighted on the drop-down list of available roles. Notice hat both the password field and the confirm field have eight hidden characters (these appear as *). If, when the form is saved, these two fields are unchanged, the user's actual password is not changed. This allows someone with access to the user folder to make changes to a user's other properties (such as roles or domains) without knowing or changing his or her password. The name of a user object cannot be changed. If a someone wants a different name, a new user object will have to made.

Managing users

Now that we have discussed the nuts and bolts of users and User Folders, let's look at a simple example of how they are commonly implemented. Create a new folder in the Root Folder called `MooseStore`. Put a subfolder called `Products` and a User Folder in MooseStore. Finally, add a new user, Bob, to the User Folder.

View the list of contents for the User Folder in the MooseStore folder. You should see a user called "Bob." For the sake of this example, let's say you decide to put Bob in charge to maintaining all of the content in the MooseStore folder, but you are not comfortable with giving him the Manager role (and therefore top-level access to everything else on the Web site).

Every time a user interacts with the Web site (whether he or she is managing the Web site or simply viewing it over the Internet), Zope verifies whether the user attempting to perform the action in question has the necessary permissions. Many permissions, such as View and Access Database Methods, are usually granted to the anonymous user. In other words, everyone, even if they are not logged in, can perform these actions. Other more sensitive operations such as View management screens are limited to authenticated users with the Manager role. Zope looks first in the folder in which the operation is requested. If a user object with properties matching those of the person logged in (username, password, and roles) is not found in the User Folder at the level at which the operation is being performed, Zope continues up the folder tree in search of a user that does have the necessary roles.

What this means for Bob is that he will be granted access to the management interface, but only for the MooseStore folder and all its contents. This also means that he will have the manager role in the Products folder, as it is a subfolder of MooseStore. But, Bob would be denied if he attempted to perform a privileged operation in the Root Folder. This example can be extended into infinite subfolders, granting any level of access to any user in any subfolder anywhere on your site, without allowing them access up the folder tree in the opposite direction.

Control Panel

The Control Panel is a special object in Zope. This object is created for you during installation. You cannot create a new one or remove the existing one.

The Control Panel provides the interfaces for administrating and maintaining Zope. Clicking `Control_Panel` (located in the Root Folder) will show the view displayed in Figure 3-15.

In this screen you are presented with information about the current Zope process; what version of Zope and Python you are using, what platform the system is running on, the current process id, and how long the process has been running.

Two controls are provided as well as one for restarting the server and another for shutting the server down. In addition, there are links to Database Management, Version Management, Product Management, and Debugging Information.

Note The Restart button only appears when Zope is being run on a platform that is capable of supporting restarts. That is, under Windows 9*x*, Zope will not display the button, but if you install Zope as a service on Windows NT, it will. UNIX-like operating systems generally support the restart functionality.

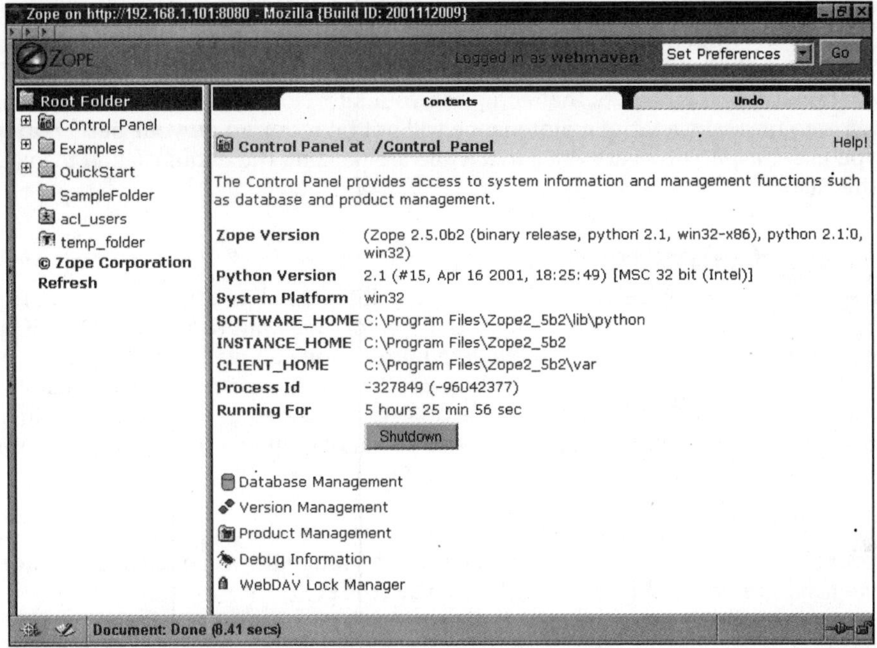

Figure 3-15: The Control Panel

Stopping and restarting Zope

Even though the two buttons we mentioned labeled Restart and Shutdown are probably self-explanatory, let's review how they work.

Clicking the Restart button restarts the server, as the name implies. This is useful when you are installing new Products. The server will shutdown for a moment and then go through the startup process.

The only difference between Shutdown and Restart is that the server will not automatically be brought back online after you click the Shutdown button. You will have to bring the server back online by following the instructions in Chapter 2 for your particular installation.

In Version 2.5, Zope incorporated new functionality that made it possible to update Products that had been installed by refreshing them. Previously, upgrading a product required restarting Zope.

Managing the database

This link will take you to the pages that enable you to manage the ZODB. The ZODB contains all of the objects that comprise your site. Not very much can go wrong here, so normally a lot of maintenance will not be required on your part. Two things you may have to do every once in a while are packing the database and managing the cache.

Packing the database

Zope provides a sophisticated Undo system. It tracks all of the changes you make. So, if you accidentally make changes that you do not want to keep, or maybe you got a little trigger happy with the delete button, you can revert. This feature comes with the slight penalty of using up diskspace. Zope keeps track of each change on the hard disk, so the file that all of the objects are stored in will grow over time. To reclaim this space, periodically you need to remove the old object versions from the database. This is called *packing the database*.

The Database view is shown in Figure 3-16. This view shows you the location of your Zope database and its current size. Even though it can be in various places on your hard drive, the file is always named `Data.fs`.

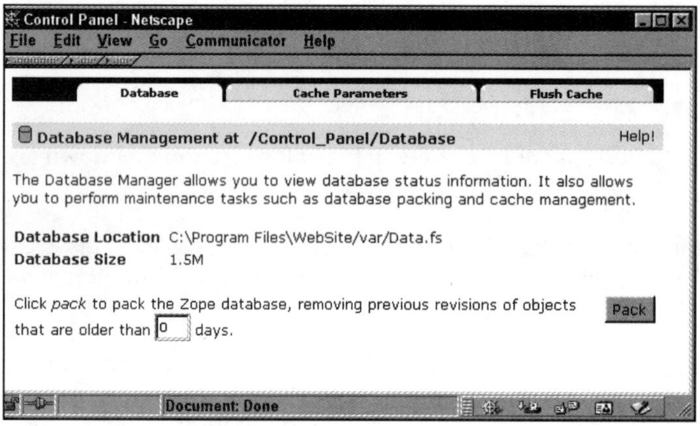

Figure 3-16: The Database view

Using this view you can remove revisions based on the date you entered. For example, if you entered 1 in the box and click the Pack button, Zope will discard all of the previous changes you made more than 24 hours ago. This means that you will only be able to undo changes that you made more recently than 24 hours ago. The default number of days is set to 0, which would mean that when you pack all the previous changes that you have made to the objects in your site will be discarded, leaving only the current version. If you do this, keep in mind that you cannot undo any changes made before the moment you packed the database, and that you cannot undo the pack operation itself.

When you pack the database, Zope will first copy your existing database to a file named `Data.fs.old` in the same location as your current directory. If you forget where your current directory is, take a look at the "Database Location" section in the Database view (shown in Figure 3-16). Zope will then remove the previous versions of your objects out of the database and you should see a significantly reduced database after pressing the Pack button. You can delete the `Data.fs.old` file at anytime to free up more diskspace.

Because Zope makes a copy of the `Data.fs` before performing the packing operation, you might run into a situation in which you do not have enough diskspace. Make sure you have at least two times the size of your current `Data.fs` in diskspace available before performing the pack operation. If not, Zope will return an IO error in the middle of the operation.

Managing the Object Cache

Zope caches each object in memory as it retrieves them from the computer's hard disk. This increases performance because Zope does not need to constantly perform time-consuming disk operations on every request. Keeping large objects (or large numbers of objects) around in the cache can quickly fill your computer's memory. To conserve space in memory, Zope keeps track of how long since each object has been used. If an object has not been used for period of time (which you can set), the objects will be removed from the cache to free up memory for other objects.

You can adjust how many objects Zope will attempt to keep in memory before grooming the cache, and how long an object can sit unused before it should be removed. Take a look at Figure 3-17.

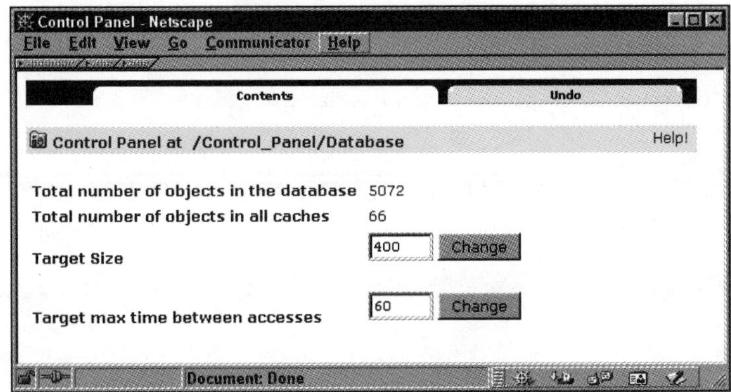

Figure 3-17: Adjusting the cache parameters

The Cache Parameters view tells you how many objects are in the database and how many are cashed in memory. From here, you can change the target size for the number of objects to be kept in cache. The default value for this parameter is 400 objects. You can also alter the maximum number of seconds that an object can remain idle before it can be removed from the cache.

If you find that Zope is using too much memory on your system, you can try reducing either of these parameters, but that will lead to a greater reliance on disk access for retrieving objects, and may result on slower performance.

Managing versions

This screen (found by clicking on version Management in the Control Panel) contains a list of each version that has changes in it. It is here as a convenience so that you do not have to search the entire site to find a particular version.

Versions allow you to make changes to the site that are temporarily hidden from other people. This lets you redesign or rebuild parts or aspects of your site, without having to show the world your work in progress. When you are satisfied with your changes, you can commit them, and as far as anyone else is concerned, the entire site is changed at once. Conversely, if you are unhappy with your changes, you can undo them within the version, or just discard all the version's changes wholesale (Refer to Chapter 11 for more information on versions).

Managing products

The Manage Product view gives you a list of all the products that you have installed. Take a look at Figure 3-18. This view shows all of the products that were successfully installed (closed box icon), those that you have created through the Web (open boxed icon), and those that are broken (shattered icon).

We discuss through-the-Web products in more detail in Chapter 16.

If you have the base Zope 2.5 package installed without any additional Products, your Product list should contain the following:

- ExternalMethod
- MIMETools
- MailHost
- OFSP
- Page Templates
- PluginIndexes
- PythonScripts

- ✦ Sessions
- ✦ SiteAccess
- ✦ StandardCacheManagers
- ✦ TemporaryFolder
- ✦ Transience
- ✦ ZCatalog
- ✦ ZGadflyDA
- ✦ ZSQLMethods
- ✦ ZopeTutorial

If you click any one of these Products you will be presented with the content list screen that you should be familiar with by now. The only thing you will see is an object labeled help.

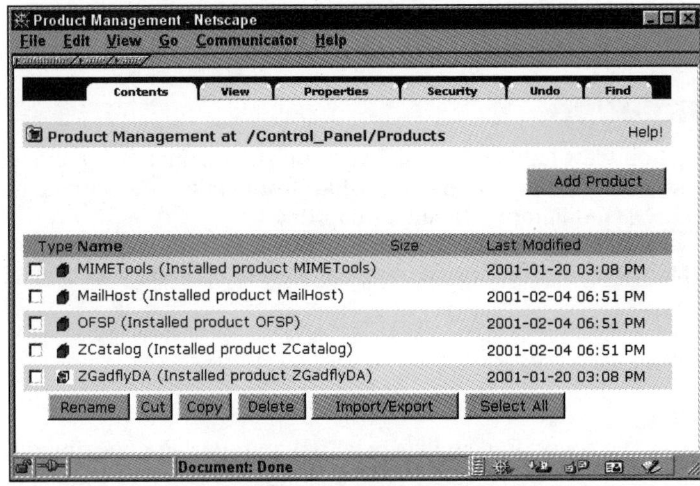

Figure 3-18: Products, products everywhere

If you are developing (or installing someone else's Product) and for some reason Zope had a problem initializing the Product, it will mark the Product as broken in the Product list. Broken Products are displayed as a box that has been shattered into many pieces. Clicking a broken Product displays some interesting information. This information is only of interest to you if you are developing or installing Products. Zope provides you with the *traceback* that Python produced when it encountered the error. (See Figure 3-19.)

For information on reading tracebacks see Chapter 19.

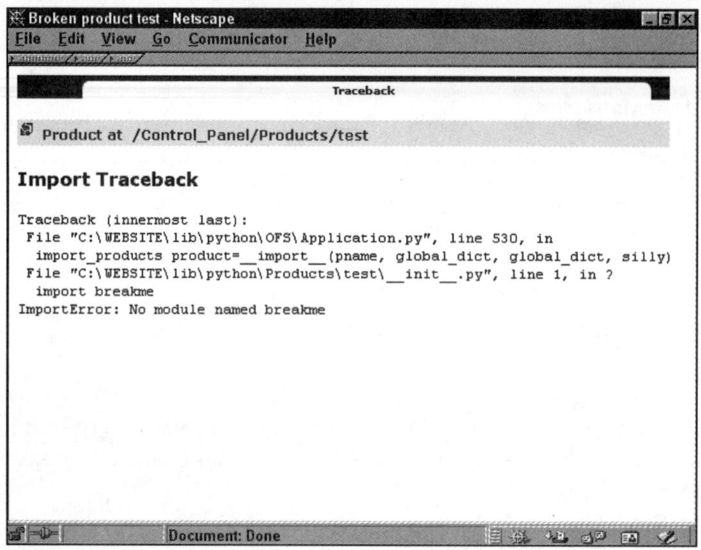

Figure 3-19: Traceback from a broken product

Debug information

The Debug Information view helps you optimize Zope's performance by showing you what Zope is spending its time doing and what products are consuming memory. This topic is discussed in more detail in Chapter 19.

Refer to Chapter 19 for instructions on using this view to optimize your site.

Summary

By now, you should have a working familiarity with manipulating Zope objects in the management interface, as well as have seen a glimpse of some of what is to come. With what you have learned in this chapter, you can put together a traditional Web site of static documents, and maybe even augment it with some of Zope's features, such as user folders and object properties.

In the next chapter, you will learn about Zope's special Document Template Markup Language, or DTML, in more detail. With DTML, you can turn that static Web site into one that is capable of becoming a true Web application by taking information from users, databases, and even other programs, and displaying it in a dynamically created page.

✦ ✦ ✦

Document Template Markup Language

In This Chapter

DTML concepts

DTML tags

By now you have had a chance to play with some of the basic features of Zope and you've probably already used some of the concepts in this chapter, even if you didn't know it. Now it's time to roll up our sleeves and really dig into one of the reasons why you bought this book: to build powerful, dynamic Web sites that will revolutionize the Internet! Okay, maybe we'll hold off on the revolution for now, but we will take a hard look at the concepts and components of Document Template Markup Language (DTML).

In this chapter we start with a discussion of how to write DTML and discuss some of the magic that goes on behind the scenes when Zope renders your documents for the rest of the world to see. Most of the chapter is then devoted to examining each DTML tag (or command) individually, picking apart its uses and limitations and suggesting how each might best be used to achieve whatever effect you have in mind for you Web site.

This chapter is intended to be both an introduction to DTML for those new to Zope and a reference for more experienced users in search of specific information on individual tags.

DTML Concepts

In technical terms, DTML (Document Template Markup Language) is a tag-based template language that lets you insert dynamically generated text into HTML documents. Zope combines DTML tags and static HTML (Hypertext Markup Language) text to create document templates. These templates are used to display dynamic content over the Web. When a document is requested by a Web browser, Zope evaluates the DTML tags in the document template and converts them into source text that can be rendered by the browser and shown over the Web.

A simple HTML document might look like this:

```
<html>
<body>
Hello World!
</body>
</html>
```

A DTML document template looks likes a HTML document but it contains DTML tags that Zope reads and replaces with HTML text. For example, the following DTML would dynamically change the text on your Web page to greet whomever happened to be logged into your Web site by inserting the value of one of the many default variables that Zope makes available to DTML authors.

```
<html>
<body>
Hello <dtml-var name="AUTHENTICATED_USER">!
</body>
</html>
```

When this is rendered into HTML source text, it would look like:

```
<html>
<body>
Hello Bob!
</body>
</html>
```

Basically, DTML enables you to present and manipulate data dynamically on your Web site. It is most often used to substitute data in your Web pages in the form of object properties or other types of variables that we discuss a little later in this chapter. DTML can also be used to evaluate Python expressions and conditionally insert or modify content in your documents. You can iterate through a list of results from a database query or even check for errors and provide custom instructions for handling any problems that might come up when your pages are rendered or a form is submitted. Before we tell you more than you ever wanted to know about what DTML can do for you, let's take a look at how to write DTML tags and some of the features that most tags have in common.

For a basic description of object properties and for instructions on how to create and edit DTML Documents, please refer to Chapter 3. Detailed descriptions of the different property types can be found in Chapter 16.

Where data comes from

As the chapter deals with generating HTML documents using dynamic data, it's helpful to understand where this data comes from and how to use it. Data can come from the following three sources:

1. **Zope objects.** These include all of the objects you add under the root folder. Every object has a set of properties and methods that can be used from within DTML and scripts. For instance, all of the objects that come with the standard installation of Zope have a `title` property and a `getId` method.

   All of the objects, their methods, and their properties are collectively known as the *Zope API* (application program interface). We introduce you to some of these methods and properties from the API for demonstrative purposes in this chapter. For the API complete reference, click the help link from the Zope Management page.

2. **External sources.** These sources can include just about anything, such as RDBMS databases (Oracle, MSSQL, PostgreSQL, MySQl); LDAP servers; IMAP; and many more. Technically this data is accessed through other Zope objects that you create such as ZSQLMethods.

3. **The user's browser.** Information can include user input from HTML forms and other information that is part of normal HTTP request such as cookies and header information. All of these values are placed in a special variable called "REQUEST."

Understanding variables, properties, and methods

In this book we assume that you have at least some programming experience and understand concepts such as *variables* and *functions*. This is because DTML is a type of programming language (one that is designed for formatting data not necessarily manipulating it) and as such you need this type of background to be effective using it.

DTML tag syntax

In this section we introduce the basic syntax and structure for using tags. In order to demonstrate the tag structure we need to use variable names (dynamic data) and other tag elements that we haven't had a chance to explain. For now, concentrate on the syntax. In the sections that follow we explain where your dynamic data comes from and how you can use it.

All tags in DTML have the same basic structure. Each tag starts with a tag name that determines the type of tag being used. Most tags also have attributes that tell Zope how find the data the tag is accessing and what to do with that data. The format of a DTML tag is identical to the format used to write HTML tags. The standard syntax for a DTML tag is shown here:

```
<dtml-name attribute1="argument1" attribute2="argument2">
```

Although many tag attributes require some kind of argument to function properly, there are a number of attributes that are essentially a predefined instruction on how to handle the data the tag is accessing. The `dtml-var` tag is used to substitute data in a document. In the example that follows, the `name` attribute indicates the name of the object to be inserted by the `dtml-var` tag and always requires an argument. The `upper` attribute converts all lowercase letters in the inserted string to uppercase and does not require any kind of argument.

```
<dtml-var name="title" upper>
```

Just as in HTML, DTML uses both *block* and *singleton* tags. Block tags are actually two-part tags that consist of an open and a close tag. Any attributes needed to perform the desired actions are placed in the open tag. The close tag is written in the same way as the open tag except that the tag name is preceded by a /. Close tags never contain attributes and are only used to tell Zope that the tag is done doing its job. The real work of the tag is done by the enclosed text between the open and close tags. These tags can also contain other DTML tags. The `dtml-if` tag is a good example of a block tag:

```
<dtml-if expr="age > 5">
  I am <dtml-var name="age"> years old!
</dtml-if>
```

Singleton tags are able to perform their functions using only the attributes contained in one tag and therefore do not need to be closed. The `dtml-call` tag is a commonly used singleton tag in DTML.

```
<dtml-call name="documentAdd">
```

The name attribute

Because of the frequency with which the `name` attribute is used, there is a special shorthand notation for writing this variable in DTML tags. In this notation the `name` attribute is written before any other attributes in the tag and is not enclosed in quotation marks. Until now, all of our examples have used the more formal notation of the name attribute, as shown here:

```
<dtml-var name="title" upper>
```

In all future examples we use the following shorthand notation:

```
<dtml-var title upper>
```

The `name` attribute is used during data substitution and evaluation to look up objects by name. The rules for this process are explained in more detail in the section, "Name Lookup," later in this chapter. For now, we focus on what happens when the value of a name attribute is requested.

If the value of the `name` attribute is an object property or REQUEST variable, the value is returned directly to the current document. In the previous example, the value of the *title* property of the current document or folder would replace the `dtml-var` tag when the document is rendered.

When the `name` attribute requests a method, Zope attempts to evaluate the method by mapping any properties from the object hierarchy and/or the REQUEST object to the arguments the method needs. For instance, imagine you want to insert the results of a method that expects two arguments, `foo` and `bar`, using the `var` tag. It doesn't matter where `foo` or `bar` are located; if Zope can locate them, it will pass them to the method for you.

If the `name` attribute requests a Zope Document or Python document template, the contents of the document or template are rendered into source text before they are returned to the object making the request. To illustrate a common application of this process, create a DTML Method like we did in Chapter 3 and examine its default content.

```
<dtml-var standard_html_header>
<h2><dtml-var title_or_id></h2>
<p>
This is the <dtml-var id> Document.
</p>
<dtml-var standard_html_footer>
```

Most of your DTML Documents and Methods will start with a `standard_html_header` and end with a `standard_html_footer`. These are DTML Methods that are created in the Root Folder by Zope during installation and cannot be moved, deleted, or renamed. Each contains a section of HTML and DTML that is inserted into the beginning and end, respectively, of all of the pages on your Web site. The contents of the default `standard_html_header` created by Zope appear as follows:

```
<HTML>
<HEAD><TITLE><dtml-var title_or_id></TITLE></HEAD>
<BODY BGCOLOR="#FFFFFF">
```

When this method is requested by a document, the three lines shown previously are rendered as HTML source text and inserted into the document.

If the `name` attribute is used in block tags such as in the `dtml-if`, `dtml-elif`, `dtml-unless`, `dtml-in`, or `dtml-with` the value associated with the name is cached until the tag is closed. This allows references to the name to be made faster inside the block tag. This is one way of reducing the burden placed on your system by having to request a large or complicated function more than once. The example that follows shows the value of `reallyBigMethod` being cached by a `dtml-if` tag and then referenced again by a `dtml-var` tag:

```
<dtml-if reallyBigMethod>
  <dtml-var reallyBigMethod>
</dtml-if>
```

The expr attribute

The `expr` attribute is a powerful tool that enables you to evaluate Python expressions in your DTML tags. This can solve a multitude of problems and issues that simply cannot be handled using DTML alone. If, for example, you want to perform a function with a variable in one of your documents but you need to make sure that the data has a certain value first. You can use an expression to evaluate the value of the data and see if it fits your requirements. Following is an example of the expr attribute syntax:

```
<dtml-if expr="tickets_sold < 1000">
  There are still tickets available for this event!
</dtml-if>
```

Everything between the quotation marks in the `expr` attribute will be evaluated as if it were Python code.

For more on Python syntax, please see Chapter 5.

The `expr` attribute can also be used to explicitly pass arguments into a method as you are calling it:

```
<dtml-var expr="getClients('New')">
```

You can also use an expression to access the objects that Zope cannot find using the normal rules of acquisition. Usually, Zope only looks *up* through the folder hierarchy of your Web site to find objects. If you needed to access a method in a subfolder below the folder you are currently working in, you could use the following syntax:

```
<dtml-var expr="Subfolder.methodObject()">
```

See Chapter 14 for more information on the rules of acquisition in Zope.

The `expr` attribute can also be used to look *sideways*, in effect, and access the contents of another folder that is neither above nor below the folder you are in. Take a look at Figure 4-1.

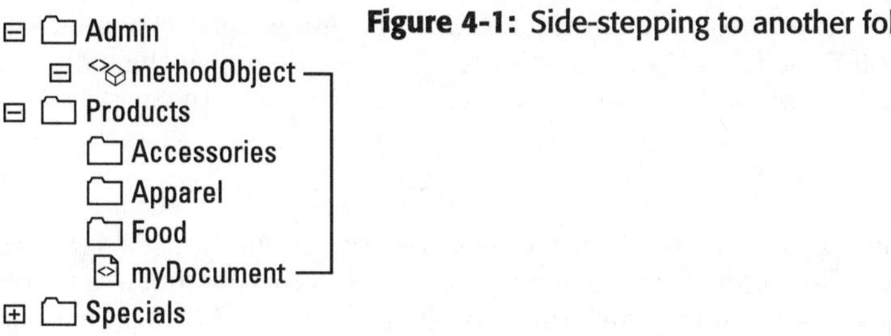

Figure 4-1: Side-stepping to another folder

Say, for example, we are displaying a document in the Products folder, but we need access to a method in the Admin folder. To do this, you could use:

```
<dtml-var expr="Admin.methodObject()">
```

As with the `name` attribute syntax, there is a shorthand notation used to write the `expr` attribute syntax in DTML tags. In this notation, the `"expr="` is omitted and the expression is simply enclosed in double quotes. For this reason, double quotes are not allowed inside the expression. Following is the previous example rewritten to use the shorthand notation of the expr attribute:

```
<dtml-var "getClients('New')">
```

The creators of Zope recommend *against* using this shortcut because it can be the source of some confusion. They believe that the two lines below are too easily confused:

```
<dtml-var getClients>
<dtml-var "getClients">
```

These two lines will return completely different results. In the first line, `getClients` is the value of the *name* attribute written in the shorthand `name` attribute notation. Zope looks for `getClients` by name and render whatever it finds into the document that requested it. In the second line, `getClients` is evaluated as a Python *expression*. Instead of figuring out what `getClients` is and what it should do with it, Zope simply tries to insert the results of the expression. In this case, Zope returns something like the following as source text to your browser:

```
<ExternalMethod instance at 869f6e0>
```

This isn't always true. In Python, object designers can override how objects are formatted when they are converted to a string. For instance, Python scripts return a blank string when the objects are referenced using the expression syntax but don't have the suffix "(" and ")".

Namespaces

When you look past all of the fancy features and terminology, one of the most basic and essential functions of DTML is to generate dynamic Web pages using your objects and your instructions in the form of tags. In order to work its magic, Zope must first find the objects to which you refer. Unfortunately, it's pretty much up to you to figure out if Zope finds the *right* objects or not. Let's look at the simple example of inserting the value of a variable into your document with the `dtml-var` tag:

```
<dtml-var my_name>
```

When Zope comes across this tag as it renders your document, it uses a process called *Name Lookup* to search for the `my_name` variable in the document's namespace. We will talk more about Name Lookup in just minute, but first let's focus on namespaces.

The concept of namespaces can be a bit tricky to explain, especially in Zope. Simply put, a *namespace* is a collection of names arranged in a predefined order. A *name* is a reference or a link to an object that exists in your ZODB (Zope Object Database). Zope uses names to find a specific object when it is executing the DTML tags in your documents. Although this is a bit of a simplification, it is easier to think of namespaces as stacked one on top of the other. A stack of namespaces is initially made up of two layers, the DTML Client Object and the DTML Request Object. Although we will explain the process that Zope goes through when it looks up an object later in this chapter, for now it is important that you understand that a namespace is where Zope looks for references to the objects that are used to create your Web site.

For more on Zope objects, refer to Chapter 3.

Name Lookup

Understanding the process of how Zope looks up a variable is the key to understanding how your objects will behave when they are rendered. By knowing exactly where your variables are coming from (from which namespace, that is), you can avoid much of the confusion that can occur with Zope's somewhat complicated process of Name Lookup.

When a DTML tag tries to perform some action with an object, Zope must first find that object before it can use it. Zope looks for an object by searching for object names in the namespace stack of the document it is rendering. When Zope starts to render a document, it creates a namespace stack to resolve all of the name lookups it needs to evaluate the various DTML tags in that document.

Initially, there are two layers in the namespace stack: the DTML Client Object and the DTML Request Object. There are a few DTML tags that can be used to modify an existing namespace stack by changing the objects in one of the layers or adding a new layer, but we'll get to those a little later in this chapter. Unless the namespace stack has been modified by one of these tags, the Client Object is at the top of the stack and is the first place Zope looks for the name of an object. If a reference to the name of your object cannot be found in the namespace of the Client Object, Zope then looks in the Request Object. The Request Object namespace is usually the last place Zope looks for an object reference because it is at the bottom of the stack.

For more on modifying existing namespaces see the sections, "The dtml-with Tag," "The dtml-let Tag," and "The dtml-in Tag," later in this chapter.

The DTML Client Object

The DTML Client Object layer of the namespace stack is actually made up of a series of objects. Which object Zope looks at first depends on whether you are using a DTML Document or a DTML Method.

If you are using a DTML Document, the first object in the Client Object namespace is the document itself. That means when Zope searches the Client Object for a name, it first searches the object properties and methods of the document in which you are working. If the document does not contain the variable you need, Zope then uses acquisition to search all of the document's parents. If, after searching all the way up to the Root Folder a reference to the name of the object you are looking for still cannot be found, Zope then searches the DTML Request Object.

For a more information on the rules of Zope Acquisition, please refer to Chapter 14.

If, however, you are using a DTML Method, the Client Object becomes the folder that contains that DTML Method. This is because DTML Methods are not designed to have their own object properties; they inherit the properties of their parent folder. If a reference to the object for which you are looking cannot be found in the properties of the method's parent folder or in the properties of the other objects in the same folder, Zope continues the same process of searching up through the folder hierarchy that it performs when searching the Client Object of a DTML Document.

In a sense, this layer of the namespace can be thought of as a stack of objects, with the document (or the parent folder in the case of a method) at the top of the stack. Below that is each successive parent folder.

The DTML REQUEST Object

Usually, the DTML REQUEST Object is the last namespace that Zope searches for a reference to the name of your object. You could also think of this layer of the namespace as always at the bottom of the namespace stack. The Request Object contains all of the information about the current Web request, including form data, cookies, and a number of useful variables defined by the CGI (Common Gateway Interface) and Zope. The intimate workings of the Request Object are out of the scope of this chapter. For now, it is important that you understand that the Request Object, like any other layer of the namespace, can be thought of as a stack of objects in a predetermined order.

For a complete explanation of the Request Object and the variables that it provides see Chapter 14.

The _ variable

The _ variable (also referred to as the *special namespace variable*) is a special object in Zope that enables you to access the namespace object directly when using the `expr` attribute of a tag. The _ is used because some of the special variables that certain block tags provide within their block have hyphens in them. While it's perfectly legal for hyphens to be included in DTML, it's not legal to include hyphens within Python expressions. This is because Python treats the hyphen as the subtraction operator.

This DTML quirk is a historical problem that developed when DTML variables with hyphens in them were introduced before tags could use Python expressions. In order to maintain backwards' compatibility, this cumbersome work around was created.

To understand the use of the _ to get around this problem, it's best to refer to the `in` tag, which is explained later in this chapter.

The second use of the _ variable is for accessing certain Python modules such as `string` and `math` within your expressions. Here's an example of using the `lower` method, which converts a string of characters to all lower case, within an expression:

```
<dtml-var "_.string.lower('I\'M NOT SHOUTING!')">
```

which produces this result:

```
i'm not shouting
```

For security reasons Zope doesn't allow you to use all of the standard Python modules. Table 4-1 includes a list of all Python modules and their methods that can be used with DTML. For further information on how to use these methods refer to the Python Library reference at `http://www.python.org/doc/current/lib/lib.html`.

Table 4-1
Modules and Methods Available from DTML

Module	*Methods*
math	abs(number): Returns the absolute value of a number. number may be a plain or long integer or a floating point number. If number is a complex number, its magnitude is returned.
	divmod(number1, number2): Takes two numbers as arguments and returns a pair of numbers consisting of their quotient and remainder when using long division. With mixed operand types, the rules for binary arithmetic operators apply. For plain and long integers, the result is the same as (a / b, a % b). For floating point numbers the result is (q, a % b), where q is usually math.floor(a / b) but may be 1 less than that. q * b + a % b is very close to *a*. If a % b is non-zero, it has the same sign as *b*, and 0 <= abs(a % b) < abs(b).
	float(number): Converts a string or a number to floating point. If the argument is a string, it must contain an optionally signed decimal or floating-point number, possibly embedded in whitespace. This behaves identical to string.atof(number). Otherwise, the argument may be a plain or long integer or a floating-point number, and a floating-point number with the same value (within Python's floating-point precision) is returned.
	hash(object): Returns the hash value of the object if the object has one. Hash values are integers. Hashes are used to quickly compare dictionary keys during a dictionary lookup. Numeric values that test true for equality (even if not for identity) have the same hash value (even if they are of different types, such as 1 and 1.0).
	hex(integer): Converts an integer number (of any size) to a hexadecimal string. The result is a valid Python expression. Note: this always yields an unsigned literal. (For example, on a 32-bit machine, hex(-1) yields 0xffffffff.) When evaluated on a machine with the same word size, this literal is evaluated as -1; at a different word size, it may turn up as a large positive number or raise an OverflowError exception.
	int(number): Converts a string or number to a plain integer. If the number is a string, it must contain an (optionally signed) decimal number that can be represented as a Python integer, possibly embedded in whitespace. This has identical behavior to string.atoi(number[, radix]). The radix parameter gives the base for the conversion and may be any integer in the range 2 to 36. If radix is specified and number is not a string, TypeError is raised. Otherwise, the argument may be a plain or long integer or a floating-point number. Conversion of floating-point numbers to integers is defined by the C semantics. (Usually the conversion truncates toward zero.)

Continued

Table 4-1 (continued)	
Module	***Methods***
	`oct(integer)`: Converts an integer number (of any size) to an octal string. The result is a valid Python expression. Note: this always yields an unsigned literal. (For example, on a 32-bit machine, `oct (-1)` yields `037777777777`.) When evaluated on a machine with the same word size, this literal is evaluated as -1; at a different word size, it may turn up as a large positive number or raise an `OverflowError` exception.
	`pow(x, y [,z])`: Returns `x` to the power `y`; if `z` is present, returns `x` to the power `y`, modulo `z` (computed more efficiently than `pow(x, y) % z`). The arguments must have numeric types. With mixed operand types, the rules for binary arithmetic operators apply. The effective operand type is also the type of the result; if the result is not expressible in this type, the function raises an exception. (For example, `pow(2, -1)` or `pow(2, 35000)` is not allowed.)
	`round(x [,n])`: Returns the floating-point value `x` rounded to `n` digits after the decimal point. If `n` is omitted, it defaults to zero. The result is a floating-point number. Values are rounded to the closest multiple of 10 to the power minus `n`; if two multiples are equally close, rounding is done away from 0. (`round(0.5)` is 1.0 and `round(-0.5)` is -1.0.)
`sequence`	`len(sequence)`: Returns the length (the number of items) of an object. The argument may be a sequence (for example, a string, tuple, or list) or a mapping (dictionary).
	`max(s)`: With a single argument `s`, returns the largest item of a non-empty sequence (for example, a string, tuple, or list). With more than one argument, it returns the largest of the arguments.
	`min(s)`: With a single argument `s`, returns the smallest item of a non-empty sequence (for example, a string, tuple, or list). With more than one argument, returns the smallest of the arguments.
	`reorder(s [,with] [,without])`: Reorders the items in `s` according to the order given in `with` and without the items mentioned in `without`. Items from `s` not mentioned in `with` are removed. `s`, `with`, and `without` are all either sequences of strings or sequences of key-value tuples, with ordering done on the keys. This function is useful for constructing ordered select lists.
`string`	`chr(integer)`: Returns a string of one character whose ASCII code is the integer. (For example, `chr(97)` returns the string `a`.) This is the inverse of `ord()`. The argument must be in the range 0 to 255, inclusive. A `ValueError` exception is raised if the integer is outside that range.

Module	Methods
	ord(character): Returns the ASCII value of a string of one character. (For example, ord("a") returns the integer 97.) This is the inverse of chr().
	Zope specific functions, and Zope versions of Python core functions DateTime(): Returns a Zope DateTime object given constructor arguments.
	getattr(object, name[,default]): Returns the value of the named attribute of object. name must be a string. If the string is the name of one of the object's attributes, the result is the value of that attribute. (For example, getattr(x, "foobar") is equivalent to x.foobar.) If the named attribute does not exist, default is returned if provided. Otherwise AttributeError is raised.
	getitem(variable, render=0): Returns the value of a DTML variable. If render is true, the variable is rendered. (See the render() function.)
	has_key(variable): Returns true if the DTML namespace contains the named variable.
	hasattr(object, string): The arguments are an object and a string. The result is 1 if the string is the name of one of the object's attributes; 0 if not. (This is implemented by calling getattr(object, name) and seeing whether it raises an exception.)
	namespace([name=value]...): Returns a new DTML namespace object. Keyword arguments of name=value pairs are pushed into the new namespace.
	range([start,] stop [,step]): This function creates lists containing arithmetic progressions. The arguments must be plain integers. If the step argument is omitted, it defaults to 1. If the start argument is omitted, it defaults to 0. The full form returns a list of plain integers [start, start + step, start + 2 * step, ...]. If step is positive, the last element is the largest start + i step that is still smaller than stop. If step is negative, the last element is the largest start + i step that is larger than stop. step must not be zero (or else ValueError is raised).
	render(object): Renders the object. For DTML objects this evaluates the DTML code with the current namespace. For other objects, this is equivalent to str(object).
	SecurityCalledByExecutable(): Returns true if the current object (DTML document or method) is being called by an executable (another DTML document or method, a script or a SQL method).

Continued

Table 4-1 *(continued)*

Module	*Methods*
	`SecurityCheckPermission(permission, object)`: Checks whether the security context allows the given permission on the given object. For example, `SecurityCheckPermission("Add Documents, Images, and Files", this())` would return true if the current user was authorized to create documents, images, and files in the current location.
	`SecurityGetUser()`: Returns the current user object. This is normally the same as the `REQUEST.AUTHENTICATED_USER` object. However, the `AUTHENTICATED_USER` object is insecure since it can be replaced.
	`SecurityValidate([object] [,parent] [,name] [,value])`: Returns true if the value is accessible to the current user. `object` is the object the value was accessed in, `parent` is the container of the value, and `name` is the name used to access the value. (For example, if it was obtained via 'getattr'.) You may omit some of the arguments; however, it is best to provide all available arguments.
	`SecurityValidateValue(object)`: Returns true if the object is accessible to the current user. This function is the same as calling `SecurityValidate(None, None, None, object)`.
	`str(object)`: Returns a string containing a nicely printable representation of an object. For strings, this returns the string itself.
	`test(condition, result [,condition, result]... [,default])`: Takes one or more `condition, result` pairs and returns the `result` of the first true `condition`. Only one `result` is returned, even if more than one `condition` is true. If no `condition` is true and `default` is given, the default is returned. If no condition is true and there is no default, `None` is returned.
`unicode`	`unichr(number)`: Returns a unicode string representing the value of `number` as a unicode character. This is the inverse of `ord()` for unicode characters.
	`unicode(string[, encoding[, errors ] ])`: Decodes `string` using the codec specified for `encoding`. Error handling is done according to errors. The default behavior is to decode UTF-8 in strict mode, meaning that encoding errors raise `ValueError`.

The dtml-var Tag

One of the most basic yet powerful functions of DTML is *variable substitution*. The dtml-var tag is used to insert objects into DTML Documents and Methods. You may find yourself using this tag more often than any other when creating dynamic Web pages.

Although you have already seen this tag in action in some of the previous examples, the dtml-var tag can be used to substitute all kinds of data. It can be used to dynamically display object properties such as id or title:

```
<dtml-var expr="myDocument.title">
```

You can also use the dtml-var tag to generate dynamic hyperlinks to your documents and other objects:

```
<a href="<dtml-var absolute_url>"><dtml-var title></a>
```

Entity syntax

Zope provides an alternate syntax for writing simple dtml-var tags. To make your HTML a little easier to read, dtml-var tags that do not require attributes or expressions can be written using the *HTML entity* syntax. Following is an example of a variable called title written in this syntax:

```
&dtml-title;
```

This is the same as writing:

```
<dtml-var title>
```

The reason this style of DTML is called *entity syntax* is because HTML uses a similar format for inserting special characters that you can't type into your document from the keyboard. To insert an HTML entity (such as the copyright symbol) into an html document, you must enter a & (ampersand) symbol followed by the entity's special code followed by ; (semicolon). For example, to insert a copyright symbol, embed © into your HTML.

The entity is primarily used to avoid writing normal DTML tag syntax inside HTML tags. For example, instead of writing:

```
<input type="hidden" name="title" value="<dtml-var title>">
```

You can use the entity syntax to make your DTML and HTML text easier to read:

```
<input type="hidden" name="title" value="&dtml-title;">
```

This syntax is also often used to generate dynamic URLs in HTML hyperlinks:

```
<a href="&dtml-Web_address;">Click Here</a>
```

As you will see in this section and throughout the rest of this chapter, there is virtually no limit to the number of uses for the `dtml-var` tag. Let's take a look at some of the attributes that make this tag tick.

Attributes of the dtml-var tag

The `dtml-var` tag has a multitude of attributes that enable you to control how the data you are inserting is presented. These attributes are described in Table 4-2.

Table 4-2
The dtml-var Tag Attributes

Attribute	Requires an Argument	Description
`name`	Yes	Used to look up the object you are trying to insert; the argument is the name of the object you are looking up
`expr`	Yes	Evaluate a Python expression and return a value
`fmt`	Yes	Specifies a format for the data you are inserting; format can be custom, special, or C-style
`null`	Yes	Specifies a string to be inserted if value of object is null
`lower`	No	Converts all uppercase letters to lowercase
`upper`	No	Converts all lowercase letters to uppercase
`capitalize`	No	Converts the first character in the object to uppercase
`spacify`	No	Converts all underscores to spaces

Attribute	Requires an Argument	Description
thousands_commas	No	If object is a number, inserts a comma every three digits left of the decimal point
html_quote	No	Converts all characters that have a special meaning in HTML into HTML entities
url_quote	No	Converts all characters that have a special meaning in URLs into HTML entities using decimal values
url_quote_plus	No	Same as url_quote except spaces are converted to into plus signs (+)
sql_quote	No	Converts a single quotation mark into a pair of single quotation marks; required to include values that contain single quotes in a SQL string
newline_to_br	No	Converts new lines (including carriage returns) to HTML break tags
size	Yes	Truncates an object to a specified number of characters
etc	Yes	Used to change the text that is added to the end of a string that as been truncated with the size attribute; default text is "..."
missing	No	Specifies a value to be inserted if object is missing and prevents a KeyError if object cannot be found

Some of these attributes require a little more explanation. Those dtml-var tag attributes that are not relatively self-explanatory in their use are described in more detail here.

Null and missing values

The null attribute enables you to specify a default string of text if the value of the object you are trying to insert is a null value. A *null value* is a value that cannot be formatted with the specified format, a special Python value None, or is false and yields an empty string. Following is an example of a dtml-var tag the null attribute:

```
<dtml-var phone_number null="No Number Listed">
```

The missing attribute enables you to specify a default value if the object you are trying to insert cannot be found. Usually, when Zope cannot find an object it is looking for by name, it returns a KeyError. If you specify a value for the missing attribute, Zope inserts that value if the object cannot be found instead of returning an error. Note that the missing attribute can only be used to prevent a KeyError returned by unsuccessful name lookup. It cannot be used to prevent a NameError that is returned by an invalid expression in a `dtml-var` tag.

For more on Zope errors and debugging, please refer to Chapter 19

Variable truncation

Sometimes the design of your Web pages limits the amount of space you have to work with when inserting variables. This can be especially true when you are using a carefully constructed HTML table layout with predetermined pixel widths for each cell. It then becomes necessary to truncate long strings to prevent them from stretching out your table and visually disrupting your Web page. The `size` attribute truncates a variable to a number of characters specified by the value of the attribute. In the following example, the value of the variable `too_long` is "This sentence is way too long to fit on my page."

```
<dtml-var too_long size=24>
```

This would render the following string when displayed on your Web page:

```
This sentence is way too...
```

The `etc` attribute is used to change the text that is added to the end of a string that as been truncated with the `size` attribute. As you can see from the results of the previous example, when the `size` attribute truncates an object and no value is specified for the `etc` attribute, the default value of "..." is used. Any text string can be substituted for the default value, but the `etc` attribute is often used to prevent any text from being added to the end of a truncated object by setting the value to an empty string. For example:

```
<dtml-var too_long size=24 etc="">
```

URL and HTML quotes

Sometimes, in order for your variables to be included in URLs and other kinds of query strings, certain reserved or illegal characters must be converted. The `dtml-var` tag offers a few useful attributes for just this purpose.

The `url_quote` attribute is used to convert all characters in your variable that have special meaning in URLs into HTML entities using decimal values. Here's a quick example:

```
<a href="<dtml-var salesReport url_quote>">Click Here</a>
```

If the value of `salesReport` was "Weekly Sales Report.txt," for example, the spaces in this string will cause a problem when you try to click this hyperlink. The `url_quote` attribute can be used to solve this sort of problem by converting the spaces (and any other illegal characters) into HTML entities. Therefore, the previous example is rendered as the following HTML source text:

```
<a href="Weekly%20Sales%20Report.txt">Click Here</a>
```

The `url_quote_plus` attribute works the same way as the `url_quote` attribute except that it replaces each empty space character with a plus sign (+). Sometimes this is required when passing a query string through an URL.

The `html_quote` converts all characters in your variable that have a special meaning in HTML into HTML entities. That means that `<`, `>`, and `&` are converted respectively into `<`, `>`, and `&`.

Formatting your data with the fmt attribute

The `fmt` attribute gives you more specific control over the format of the data being inserted by the `dtml-var` tag. There are three basic formats used by the `fmt` attribute: Special, Custom, and C-style.

Special formats

There are a few special formats that have been predefined as part of the `dtml-var` tag because of their common use in data presentation. These formats are described in Table 4-3.

Table 4-3
Special Formats for the dtml-var Tag fmt Attribute

Format	*Description*
Whole-dollars	Converts a number value into a whole dollar amount preceded by a dollar sign ($)
Dollars-and-cents	Converts a number value into a dollar amount out to two decimal places, preceded by a dollar sign ($); numbers more specific than two decimal places are rounded
Collection-length	If the variable is a sequence, this format returns its length
Structured-text	Converts the variable to structured text

Following is a quick example of one of these special formats in action. An object for sale in our online store has a float property price that we want to display as a dollar amount. In this example, the value of price is 10.5.

```
<dtml-var price fmt="dollars-and-cents">
```

This format displays the price property of our object as:

```
$10.50
```

Custom format methods

Zope supports the use of custom formats for greater control over the presentation of objects in your Web pages. Although the most often used custom formats are related to the formatting of date-time strings, any method evaluated on an object that returns a string can be used as a custom format.

Date-time strings can be formatted in just about any way you can imagine with the various date-time methods available in Python. Chances you are working with a date-time string retrieved from a form or a database, but if you need to display (and format) the current date and time, you can use the `ZopeTime` object:

```
<dtml-var ZopeTime>
```

The date-time string that follows shows how the ZopeTime method is displayed without any custom formatting:

```
2001/01/01 12:00:00.00 US/Pacific
```

That's great and all but you may want to display your date-time strings in a format that is a little easier to read:

```
<dtml-var ZopeTime fmt="aCommon">
```

The `aCommon` format is a fairly common way of displaying a date and time. When rendered, the line above will look like this:

```
Jan 1, 2001 12:00 pm
```

For your convenience, the custom date-time formats from the Python DateTime Library are show in Table 4-4.

Table 4-4
Custom date-time Formats for the dtml-var Tag fmt Attribute

Method	*Description*
AMPM	Returns the time to the nearest second
AMPMMinutes	Returns the time to the nearest minute
aCommon	Returns a string with the format: Jan 1, 1980 12:00 pm
aCommonZ	Returns a string with the format: Jan 1, 1980 12:00 pm US/Eastern

Method	Description
aDay	Returns the abbreviated name of the day of the week
aMonth	Returns the abbreviated month name
ampm	Returns the appropriate time modifier (am or pm)
Date	Returns the date string for the object
Day	Returns the full name of the day of the week
DayOfWeek	Returns the full name of the day of the week
day	Returns the day of the object as an integer
dayOfYear	Returns the day of the year in context of the time-zone representation of the object
dd	Returns day as a 2-digit string
fCommon	Returns a string with the format: January 1, 1980 12:00 pm
fCommonZ	Returns a string with the format: January 1, 1980 12:00 pm US/Eastern
H_12	Returns the 12-hour clock representation of the hour
h_24	Returns the 24-hour clock representation of the hour
hour	Returns the 24-hour clock representation of the hour
isCurrentHour	Returns true if this object represents a date/time that falls within the current hour in the context of this object's time-zone representation
isCurrentMonth	Returns true if this object represents a date/time that falls within the current month in the context of this object's time-zone representation
isFuture	Returns true if this object represents a date/time later than the time of the call
isLeapYear	Returns true if the current year (in the context of the object's time zone) is a leap year
isPast	Returns true if this object represents a date/time earlier than the time of the call
Month	Returns the full month name
minute	Returns the minute
mm	Returns month as a 2-digit string
month	Returns the month of the object as an integer
PreciseAMPM	Returns a precise time string for the object on a 12-hour clock
PreciseTime	Returns a precise time string for the object on a 24-hour clock
pCommon	Returns a string with the format: Jan. 1, 1980 12:00 pm

Continued

Table 4-4 *(continued)*

Method	***Description***
pCommonZ	Returns a string with the format: Jan. 1, 1980 12:00 pm US/Eastern
pDay	Returns the abbreviated (with a period) name of the day of the week
pMonth	Returns the abbreviated (with a period) month name
Rfc822	Returns the date in RFC 822 format
second	Returns the second
timezone	Returns the time zone in which the object is represented
year	Returns the calendar year of the object
yy	Returns calendar year as a 2-digit string

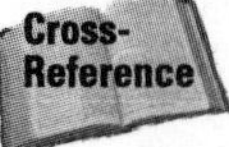

For more information about DateTime objects see the Zope API reference in Zope's Online Help System.

You might be thinking, "Great! I can combine a few of these formats to display my dates and times in whatever way I want." You can, but not in the same `dtml-var` tag. Cramming a few of these methods into the same `fmt` attribute won't display what you had in mind. Let's say you want to show a date string in the following format: mm/dd/yy. To do this using the methods in Table 4-3, you would have to write something like this:

```
<dtml-var ZopeTime fmt="mm">/<dtml-var ZopeTime fmt="dd">/ _
<dtml-var ZopeTime fmt="yy">
```

This isn't very pretty, but that's the way the tag is designed. However, you can use string formats for the Python strftime module to achieve a similar result with only one `dtml-var` tag:

```
<dtml-var ZopeTime fmt="%d/%m/%y">
```

See Chapter 5 for more information on Python strings.

C-style format strings

The `fmt` attribute supports the use of C-style format strings to control the format of your data. Although you will find a more complete discussion of string formatting in Chapter 5, here we show you a quick example of how these formats are used.

Basically, C-style formats are used to convert an object or variable of one type to another. In the following example we convert a floating point value into an integer:

```
<dtml-var expr="12345.6789" fmt="%d">
```

When rendered, this tag will insert the following integer:

```
12345
```

For more about string formatting, please refer to Chapter 5.

The dtml-if Tag

Variable substitution with the `dtml-var` tag is one of the most powerful and most often used functions of DTML. As in any kind of scripting or even programming, it is often necessary to evaluate a number of conditions before your script or program can know what variables are to be substituted and how to present them. This process is referred to *conditional insertion.*

DTML primarily uses the `dtml-if` tag to perform conditional insertion. The `dtml-else` and `dtml-elif` tags are also used to evaluate alternate conditions in your Web pages and enable you to create different sets of instructions for how and what data is to be inserted based on the conditions that exist when your Web page is loaded.

The basics of conditional insertion

As far as DTML is concerned, conditions are either true or false. Generally, all objects are considered true unless they are 0, None, or an empty string or sequence. Whether a condition is true or not can be evaluated using both the `name` attribute syntax and the `expr` attribute syntax.

For more on the `name` attribute syntax and the `expr` attribute syntax, see "DTML Concepts" earlier in this chapter.

Sometimes in order to prevent an error, the existence of a variable must be verified before your Web page tries to use that variable. The `name` attribute syntax can be used to evaluate both the existence and the value of an object. Following is a simple example using this syntax in a `dtml-if` tag to see whether the title variable exists before inserting it. In this example, Zope renders the contents of the `dtml-if` tag block if the value of `title` is not 0, None, or an empty string or sequence.

```
<dtml-if title>
  <dtml-var title>
</dtml-if>
```

You may find that it is often necessary to evaluate the value of your variables with an expression before performing some function with that object. Following is an example of conditionally inserting content based on the value of a variable using the expression attribute syntax. In this example, the text is displayed if the value of `tickets_sold` is less than 1000.

```
<dtml-if expr="tickets_sold < 1000">
  There are still tickets available for this event!
</dtml-if>
```

Note that the `expr` attribute syntax does not check for the existence of the variable and returns an error if the variable cannot be found. For this reason, you must be sure to use a valid Python expression.

The dtml-else and dtml-elif tags

By itself, the `dtml-if` tag will only evaluate the truth of a single condition. Often, you may want to provide an alternate set of instructions for presenting your content if the condition you are evaluating is false. This can be achieved with the `dtml-else` tag. Following is an example of how to use the `dtml-else` tag to insert content if the condition in the `dtml-if` tag is false:

```
<dtml-if "color == 'blue'">
  Good guess!
<dtml-else>
  Sorry, guess again.
</dtml-if>
```

There are no valid attributes for the `dtml-else` tag. Each `dtml-if` tag block can only contain one `dtml-else` tag. However, you can nest `dtml-if` tags within other `dtml-if` tags. In the next example, we first verify that a color variable exists with the name attribute syntax, and then we use the `expr` attribute syntax to see if it matches a certain value.

```
<dtml-if color>
 <dtml-if "color == 'blue'">
   Good guess!
 <dtml-else>
   Sorry, guess again.
 </dtml-if>
<dtml-else>
  No color provided.
</dtml-if>
```

Sometimes it can be helpful to evaluate several conditions in the same `dtml-if` tag block. You can evaluate multiple conditions by adding a `dtml-elif` tag for each additional condition you need to evaluate. The `dtml-elif` tag uses the same syntax and attributes as the dtml-if tag. If the condition specified in the initial dtml-if tag is false, each dtml-elif tag is evaluated in the order in which they are presented until one is evaluated as true. If none of the conditions specified are found to be true, Zope renders the contents of the dtml-else tag if one is present.

A dtml-if tag block can contain any number of dtml-elif tags but only one dtml-else tag. The dtml-else tag must always come after the dtml-elif tags. An additional condition is added to one of the previous examples in the code that follows:

```
<dtml-if "color == 'blue'">
  Good guess!
<dtml-elif "color == 'green'">
  Green is not a valid choice, guess again.
<dtml-else>
  Sorry, guess again.
</dtml-if>
```

The dtml-unless Tag

The dtml-unless tag offers another way to perform conditional insertion. It has the same basic functions as the dtml-if tag, except that the contents of the dtml-unless tag are only rendered if the condition being evaluated is false. The same effect could be created by specifically testing for a false condition with a dtml-if tag, but sometimes it is more convenient (and easier to read) if a dtml-unless tag is used. The following two examples return the same result, but the first is written with a dtml-if tag and the second uses a dtml-unless:

```
<dtml-if expr="sum != 10">
  Sorry, that answer is incorrect. Please try again.
</dtml-if>

<dtml-unless expr="sum == 10">
  Sorry, that answer is incorrect. Please try again.
</dtml-unless>
```

Although this example doesn't illustrate much of a convenience by choosing the dtml-unless tag over the dtml-if tag when a false condition must be tested for, it does show that the two tags work pretty much the same way. One simply looks for a true condition and the other looks for a false condition.

The dtml-unless tag is more limited than the dtml-if tag in that it cannot be used with the dtml-else or dtml-elif tags. However, the dtml-unless tag is great for when you only want to insert dynamic content if an object does not exist in the current namespace. Take a look at the following example:

```
<dtml-unless daily_sales>
  No sales today!</dtml-unless>
```

This tag checks to see whether the object `daily_sales` exists. If it cannot be found in the current namespace, then the phrase "No sales today!" is inserted into the document. This is just one of many ways of achieving the same result with DTML, but you might find this method more convenient or easier to read than if a `dtml-if` or some other tag were used.

The dtml-in Tag

So far, we have looked at variable substitution with the `dtml-var` tag and setting conditions for when and how to insert those variables with the `dtml-if` tag. As your Web pages become more complex, especially if they interact with some kind of database, it may become necessary to loop through and manipulate a list of some kind of objects. Often this list will be a set of results from a database query. The `dtml-in` tag is used to iterate (or loop) through these results and perform a specified set of actions for each item in the sequence. This process is referred to as *iterative insertion.*

The basics of iterative insertion

Like the `dtml-if` tag, `dtml-in` is a block tag. The object or sequence to be iterated over is specified either by name or by an expression in the open tag and there are a significant number of specialized variables for use with the `dtml-in` tag. We will take a look at these attributes in much closer detail later in this section, but for now let's look at a simple example of how the `dtml-in` tag works. In the example that follows, we use a `dtml-in` tag to generate a list of employees from an imaginary database:

```
<dtml-in listEmployees>
  <dtml-var employee_name></br>
</dtml-in>
```

Depending on your database, this might look something like:

```
Tom
Dick
Harry
```

The method `listEmployees` is used to generate a result set containing a list of all of the employees stored in our database. A result set is an object that acts like a list. In this result set, we have a sequence of values associated with a variable called `employee_name`. The `dtml-in` tag in this example iterates through this result set and render the `<dtml-var employee_name>` tag and a line break for each item in the sequence.

We can perform a similar function using an expression instead of calling a method by name. The next example uses the Zope API method objectValues to query the ZODB for a list of all of the DTML Document objects in the current folder.

```
<dtml-in expr="objectValues('DTML Document')">
  <dtml-var title_or_id><br>
</dtml-in>
```

The objectValues method in this example is the same method the Zope management interface uses to generate a list of all the objects in a folder. This is done by using the same DTML shown the previous example without specifying an object type as an argument in the expression that calls the objectValues method. (An object type is the same names that you see in the drop-down box for adding objects.)

Also be aware that the dtml-in tag does change the namespace stack by pushing the contents of the tag (all of the objects in the result set) to the top of the stack. In other words, if the results of your dtml-in tag contain a variable name that also appears elsewhere in your page, Zope finds the value associated with the name that appears in the dtml-in tag for the duration of the block. Once the dtml-in tag block is closed, the order of the namespace stack returns to its usual state.

The dtml-else tag and empty sequences

As we have seen, the dtml-in tag is used to iterate through a sequence of objects and insert the same dynamic content for each item in the list. But what happens if the list is empty? If there were no DTML Documents in the current folder of our previous example, the objectValues returns an empty sequence. In this case, Zope doesn't do anything. No content is inserted and Zope continues rendering the rest of the document as though the dtml-in tag wasn't even there. You can account for this possibility by using a dtml-else tag. Using the previous example, we could display a string of text to the user instead of nothing at all if the method returns an empty sequence:

```
<dtml-in expr="objectValues('DTML Document')">
  <dtml-var title_or_id><br>
<dtml-else>
  No documents were found.
</dtml-in>
```

The previous example assumes that the code is within a DTML Method and not within a DTML Document.

Attributes of the dtml-in tag

The `dtml-in` tag has specialized attributes that enable you to manipulate the iteration of the data in your sequence. These attributes are described in Table 4-5.

Table 4-5
The dtml-in Tag Attributes

Attribute	*Requires an Argument*	*Description*
`Name`	Yes	Name of the object that returns the sequence you want to iterate over
`Expr`	Yes	Evaluates a Python expression to return the sequence you want to iterate over
`Mapping`	No	Iterates over mapping objects rather than instances; this allows values of the mapping objects to be accessed as DTML variables. Mapping objects are explained within Chapter 5.
`Sort`	Yes	Sorts the sequence based on the specified attribute of the result set
`Reverse`	No	Causes the order of the sequence to be reversed
`Start`	Yes	Specifies the index of the row on which to start a batch
`Size`	Yes	Specifies the maximum size of the batch; value of the argument is the maximum number of rows to be processed
`skip_unauthorized`	No	Causes an item to be skipped if access to the item is unauthorized; this attribute prevents an error from being raised if unauthorized items are encountered
`Orphan`	Yes	Specifies the minimum desired size of the batch; value of argument is the minimum number of rows to be processed
`Overlap`	Yes	Specifies the number of rows to overlap between batches

Attribute	Requires an Argument	Description
`Previous`	No	Prevents iterative insertion; provides processing variables associated with the previous batch in the sequence (if one exists)
`Next`	No	Prevents iterative insertion; provides processing variables associated with the next batch in the sequence (if one exists)

Many of the attributes of the `dtml-in` tag are used to perform *batch processing*. Batch processing can add powerful dynamic capabilities to your Web pages by breaking up a long sequence of objects into manageable bits, but it can also be somewhat complicated. Before we get in to that, let's take a look at some of the more basic attributes of the `dtml-in` tag.

Sorting the contents of your sequence

The `sort` attribute enables you to control the order in which the contents of your sequence are processed. The `dtml-in` tag uses the value of the `sort` attribute to sort the sequence before the results are iterated into your document. In the example that follows, a ZSQLMethod `listClients` returns a result set that contains several rows of data with the following attributes: `first_name`, `last_name`, `phone`, and `address`. The list of clients displayed in the HTML table is sorted in ascending order by the `last_name` attribute of the result set.

```
<table>
  <dtml-in listClients sort="last_name">
    <tr>
      <td><dtml-var last_name>, <dtml-var first_name></td>
      <td><dtml-var phone></td>
      <td><dtml-var address></td>
    </tr>
  </dtml-in>
</table>
```

The `reverse` attribute is fairly straightforward. Including the `reverse` attribute in a `dtml-in` tag reverses whatever order the sequence already has and can be used with the `sort` attribute, but does not require it.

Changing the size of your sequence

Sometimes you may only be interested in displaying part of a sequence. In the code that follows, only the first ten rows of the result set will be displayed, the rest will be ignored. (Please note that this will only work inside of a DTML method.)

```
<dtml-in "objectValues()" size=10>
  <dtml-var title_or_id><br>
</dtml-in>
```

The previous example assumes that the code is within a DTML Method and not within a DTML Document.

Current item variables

Zope provides several variables with the `dtml-in` tag that are used to access information about the current item in the sequence of objects you are iterating through. These current item variables are described in Table 4-6.

Table 4-6
The dtml-in Tag Current Item Variables

Variable	*Description*
sequence-item	The current item in the iteration
sequence-key	The current key in the iteration, only useful when iterating over a mapping object
sequence-index	The current number of iterations completed so far starting from 0
sequence-number	The current number of iterations completed so far starting from 1
sequence-roman	The current number of iterations completed so far; displayed in lowercase Roman numerals starting from *i*
sequence-Roman	The current number of iterations completed so far; displayed in uppercase Roman numerals starting from *I*
sequence-letter	The current number of iterations completed so far; displayed incrementally in lowercase letters
sequence-Letter	The current number of iterations completed so far; displayed incrementally in uppercase letters
sequence-start	True if the current item is the first item in the iteration
sequence-end	True if the current item is the last item in the iteration

Variable	*Description*
sequence-even	True if the index of the current item is 0 or even
sequence-odd	True if the index of the current item is odd
sequence-var-*variable*	Used to access a variable of the current item
sequence-index-*variable*	The index of a variable of the current item

To get a better idea of how some of these variables are used, let's take a look at a few examples. First, we use the `dtml-in` tag and the `sequence-item` variable to dynamically generate a list of options in a HTML select form input. In the example that follows, the method `listMonths` generates a list of the months of the year as a sequence of strings.

```
<select name="month">
<dtml-in _
expr="['Jan','Feb','Mar','Apr','May','Jun','Jul','Aug','Sep','Oct','Nov','Dec']"
>
  <option value="&dtml-sequence-item;"><dtml-var sequence-item></option>
</dtml-in>
</select>
```

This `dtml-in` tag generates a select form input with an option for each month of the year that was listed in our sequence. In the next example, let's say a value for *month* already exists in our namespace and we want this select input to default to the that value automatically when the page is loaded. A `dtml-if` tag is used to see whether the value of the month variable matches each item in the list of months, assuming it's in the namespace.

```
<select name="month">
  <dtml-in _
expr="['Jan','Feb','Mar','Apr','May','Jun','Jul','Aug','Sep','Oct','Nov','Dec']"
>
    <option<dtml-if expr="month == _.['sequence-item']"> SELECTED</dtml-if> _
value="&dtml-sequence-item;"><dtml-var sequence-item></option>
   </dtml-in>
</select>
```

For information on simplifying this DTML and eliminating the `_.['sequence-item']` portions of the expression, read the "Using the <dtml-in> Prefix Attribute" sidebar.

Using the <dtml-in> Prefix Attribute

The dtml-in tag has several attributes that are hyphenated, such as sequence-item and XX. These attributes are difficult to use within Python expressions, as they require cryptic notations such as:

```
<dtml-if expr="month == _.['sequence-item']">
```

This notation is necessary because Python would otherwise interpret sequence-item as sequence minus item. The prefix attribute (added in Zope 2.4) enables you to circumvent this limitation and increase the clarity of your code. When you specify a prefix for a dtml-in tag, all hyphenated attributes have the sequence portion of their names replaced with the value of prefix, and the hyphens are replaced with underscores. This lets you write DTML code as follows:

```
<dtml-in expr="objectValues('Folder','DTML Document')"
prefix="objects">
 <dtml-if "objects_item.meta_type = 'Folder'">
  <b><dtml-var "objects_item.id"></b>
 <dtml-else>
  <dtml-var "objects_item.id">
 </dtml-if>
```

The prefix notation also has another use. It allows access to the outer iteration's attributes from nested inner iterations. Without the prefix notation, the attribute names of nested iterations mask the outer iteration's attributes, as the attribute names are identical. With the prefix attribute set, you can get around this limitation without having to use dtml-let, like so:

```
<dtml-in expr="[1,2,3]" prefix="outer">
 <dtml-in expr="[4,5,6]" prefix="inner">
 <dtml-var expr="outer_item * inner_item"><br>
 </dtml-in>
</dtml-in>
```

As you can see, the prefix attribute of dtml-in is a powerful tool for simplifying your code.

The *sequence-even* variable can be used to create the alternating gray and white table cells seen in the list of contents for each folder in the Zope management interface. The following example generates a list of links to all of the objects contained in the current folder and highlights every other row with a light gray background:

```
<table>
  <dtml-in expr="objectValues()">
    <tr<dtml-if sequence-even> bgcolor="#EFEFEF"</dtml-if>>
      <td><a href="&dtml-absolute_url;"><dtml-var title_or_id></a></td>
    </tr>
  </dtml-in>
</table>
```

The previous example assumes that the code is within a DTML Method and not within a DTML Document.

Summary statistic variables

The `dtml-in` tag can calculate statistical information about a sequence with the use of a number of summary statistic variables. See Table 4-7 for a complete list of these variables.

Table 4-7
The dtml-in Tag Summary Statistic Variables

Variable	*Description*
total-nnn*	Returns the sum of a sequence of numeric values
count-nnn	Returns the total number of non-missing values in a sequence
min-nnn	Returns the smallest number in a sequence of non-missing values
max-nnn	Returns the largest number in a sequence of non-missing values
median-nnn	Returns the median of a sequence of non-missing values
mean-nnn	Returns the mean of a sequence of numeric values
variance-nnn	Returns the variance of a sequence of numeric values computed with a degrees of freedom equal to the (count - 1)
variance-n-nnn	Returns the variance of a sequence of numeric values computed with a degrees of freedom equal to the count
standard-deviation-nnn	Returns the standard deviation of a sequence of numeric values computed with a degrees of freedom equal to the (count - 1)
standard-deviation-n-nnn	Returns the standard deviation of a sequence of numeric values computed with a degrees of freedom equal to the count

* nnn is the name of an attribute or key. For example, to get the mean price in a list of products each with the attribute price, type *mean-price*.

If you are using another database besides the ZODB, you may already be able to perform many of these functions. Nevertheless, these variables do offer a quick and easy way of accessing certain statistics about your sequence without having to write other database queries to calculate them. The following example is only concerned with displaying some statistical data about our sequence, not with actually displaying the sequence itself. The method showSalesReport returns a list of objects with two attributes: product_name and price.

```
<table>
  <dtml-in showSalesReport size="1">
    <tr>
      <td>Total Products Sold:</td>
      <td><dtml-var count-product_name></td>
    </tr><tr>
      <td>Total Sales:</td>
      <td><dtml-var total-price fmt="dollar-and-cents"></td>
    </tr><tr>
      <td>Average Price:</td>
      <td><dtml-var mean-price fmt="dollar-and-cents"></td>
    </tr>
  </dtml-in>
</table>
```

This example displays the following text (assuming some imaginary values for the summary statistic variables):

```
Total Products Sold: 24
Total Sales:         $3620.00
Average Price:       $150.83
```

Because the dtml-in tag is designed to iterate through a sequence of objects and perform a predefined set of actions for each object, it is necessary to set the size of the batch in the preceding example to "1". Otherwise, the contents of the dtml-in tag block would be displayed once for every item in the sequence.

Grouping variables

The dtml-in tag also supports two variables that are used to test when a grouping of data within your sequence starts or ends. You can group your data by sorting the sequence by a particular attribute and then testing to see when that variable changes with the grouping variables described in Table 4-8.

Table 4-8
The dtml-in Tag Grouping Variables

Variable	*Description*
First-nnn	true if the current item is the first item in the sequence that has the current value for the variable *nnn*; otherwise false
Last-nnn	true if the current item is the last item in the sequence that has the current value for the variable *nnn*; otherwise false

The following example groups the sequence we are displaying by the `type` attribute. The product type is printed in `<H1>` text at the beginning of each new group and a `<hr>` is inserted at the end of every group.

```
<dtml-in listProducts sort="type">

  <dtml-if first-type>
    <H1><dtml-var type></H1>
  </dtml-if>

  <P><dtml-var name></P>

  <dtml-if last-type>
    <hr size="1" noshade>
  </dtml-if>

</dtml-in>
```

Batch processing

When you are working a large sequence of items, it is not practical to display the entire sequence all at once. To make your Web interface easier to use and to decrease size of your Web pages (and therefore the amount time they take to load), you may want to display your sequence in little chunks. Breaking up your sequence into digestible bits is called *batching*. The `dtml-in` tag is equipped with several variables that enable you to perform some powerful batch processing. These variables are described in Table 4-9.

Table 4-9
The dtml-in Tag Batch Processing Variables

Variable	*Description*
sequence-query	Returns the HTTP query string with the start variable removed; this variable can be used to construct links to next and previous batches
sequence-step-size	Returns the batch size
previous-sequence	True when the first item in the current batch is displayed *and* when that item is not the first item in the entire sequence
previous-sequence-start-index	Returns the index (starting from 0) of the first item in the previous batch

Continued

Table 4-9 (continued)

Variable	*Description*
previous-sequence-start-number	Returns the number (starting from 1) of the first item in the previous batch
previous-sequence-end-index	Returns the index (starting from 0) of the last item in the previous batch
previous-sequence-end-number	Returns the number (starting from 1) of the last item in the previous batch
previous-sequence-size	Returns the size of the previous batch
previous-batches	A sequence of mapping objects with information about all previous batches; each mapping object has these keys: batch-start-index, batch-end-index, and batch-size
next-sequence	True when the last item in the current batch is displayed *and* when that item is not the last item in the entire sequence
next-sequence-start-index	Returns the index (starting from 0) of the first item in the next batch
next-sequence-start-number	Returns the number (starting from 1) of the first item in the next batch
next-sequence-end-index	Returns the index (starting from 0) of the last item in the next batch
next-sequence-end-number	Returns the number (starting from 1) of the last item in the next batch
next-sequence-size	Returns the size of the next batch
next-batches	A sequence of mapping objects with information about all following batches; each mapping object has these keys: batch-start-index, batch-end-index, and batch-size

Instead of looking at these variables one or two at a time, we are going to go ahead and hit you with whole thing at once. Take a look at the example that follows, but don't get too upset; we will every part of it in just a minute.

```
<dtml-var standard_html_header>

<dtml-in listCustomers size=10 sort=name start=query_start>

<dtml-if sequence-start>
  <H1>Customer List</H1>
  <dtml-if previous-sequence>
    <P><a href="&dtml-URL;&dtml-sequence-query;query_start=&dtml-previous-
sequence-start-number;">Previous <dtml-var previous-sequence-size></a></P>
```

```
  </dtml-if>
  <table>
    <tr>
      <th>Customer</th>
      <th>Phone</th>
      <th>Address</th>
    </tr>
</dtml-if>

    <tr<dtml-if sequence-even> bgcolor="#EFEFEF"</dtml-if>>
      <td><dtml-var name></td>
      <td><dtml-var phone></td>
      <td><dtml-var address></td>
    </tr>

<dtml-if sequence-end>
  </table>
  <dtml-if next-sequence>
    <P><a href="&dtml-URL;&dtml-sequence-query;query_start=&dtml-next-sequence-
start-number;">Next <dtml-var next-sequence-size></a></P>
  </dtml-if>
</dtml-if>

</dtml-in>

<dtml-var standard_html_footer>
```

This isn't really as bad as it looks. Let's start from the beginning. The method `listCustomers` creates a list of customers with attributes for `name`, `phone`, and `address`. The `size` attribute limits our batches to a maximum of 10 results, and the `sort` attribute sorts the entire sequence by the name attribute. The `start` attribute tells the `dtml-in` tag which index (of the entire sequence) it should use to start the current batch.

Next we have two nested `dtml-if` tags. The first checks to see whether `sequence-start` is true, meaning it checks to see whether the current item is the first item in this batch. If it is, it prints the `<H1>` text, evaluates a second `dtml-if` tag, and then inserts some column headers for the table we will use to display our results. This second `dtml-if` tag checks to see whether `previous-sequence` is true, meaning it checks for any items in the sequence before the first one of the current batch. If the first item in the current batch is not the first item in the entire sequence, a link to the previous batch of 10 results is inserted.

Below this, we create the table row that will be inserted for each item in the current batch. There isn't much going on here that hasn't already been discussed under previous sections.

Toward the end of the example you will see two more nested `dtml-if` tags. This section performs basically the same function as the first set of nested `dtml-if` tags except that here we are testing to see if the current item is the last item in this batch. If it is, the table is closed and another if check is evaluated to see whether this is the last batch in the sequence. Unless the current batch is the last batch of 10 results (or part-thereof), a link to the next batch is inserted.

A few of the batch processing variables can be used to display statistics about the next and previous batches. In the previous example, the `previous-sequence-size` and *n*ext-sequence-size variables are used to show the number of results in the previous and next batches, respectively. There are also variables to display the starting and ending index of the next and previous batches.

The dtml-with Tag

The `dtml-with` tag is used to push a particular object to the top of the namespace. This enables you to either add new attributes to the namespace by including an object outside of the normal chain of acquisition (like a subfolder), or look for variables in a particular object before searching the rest of the namespace.

In the example that follows, we must access several objects in another folder. This can be accomplished without the `dtml-with` tag by using an expression to access the objects of another container:

```
<dtml-in expr="Clients.getClientInfo(client_id=client_id)">
  <H1><dtml-var name></H1>
  <dtml-if "employees > 50">
    <dtml-var expr="Clients.addInsuranceForm">
  <dtml-else>
    <dtml-var expr="Clients.smallBusinessMethod()">
  </dtml-if>
</dtml-in>
```

As you can see, this can make for a lot of extra work if you need to access another folder like this more than once or twice. By using a `dtml-with` tag to push the Clients folder (and its contents) to the top of the namespace, this example becomes a little easier to read and a lot easier to write. Everything inside the `dtml-with` tag block will look for objects in the Clients folder before following the normal pattern of acquisition.

```
<dtml-with Clients>
  <dtml-in expr="getClientInfo(client_id=client_id)">
    <H1><dtml-var name></H1>
    <dtml-if "employees > 50">
      <dtml-var addInsuranceForm>
    <dtml-else>
      <dtml-var smallBusinessMethod>
    </dtml-if>
  </dtml-in>
</dtml-with>
```

Usually, the Request is at the bottom the namespace stack. In other words, it's the last place Zope looks when searching for a variable. The `dtml-with` tag is often used to push the Request to the top of the namespace. This can be useful if you need to access a variable in the Request that also exists somewhere else in the namespace.

Let's say you need to access a variable in the Request called *title*. Finding the right title variable can be a problem as Zope looks for the name title in the client object before it looks in the Request. If you are working in a DTML Document, the client object is likely to have a title attribute and Zope will think this must be what you were looking for. By enclosing your `dtml-var` tag in a `dtml-with` tag block, you can force Zope to look in the Request before it looks anywhere else.

```
<dtml-with REQUEST>
  <dtml-var title>
</dtml-with>
```

In the previous example, if the Request does not contain a title variable, it is still possible that a title variable from somewhere else in the namespace stack could be returned. Chances are, this is the wrong title. The `only` attribute prevents Zope from looking up objects outside the namespace specified in the `dtml-with` tag. This enables you to be sure about which variables are being inserted into your documents.

```
<dtml-with REQUEST only>
  <dtml-var title>
</dtml-with>
```

The dtml-let Tag

The `dtml-let` tag is used to create a new layer at the top of the namespace stack and assign multiple variables to that namespace. Although both the `dtml-with` and `dtml-let` tags are used to modify namespaces, the `dtml-let` tag is better suited for setting one or more new variables in the namespace instead of accessing the attributes or contents of an existing object. As with the `dtml-with` tag, any changes to the namespace stack are undone when the `dtml-let` tag is closed. In other words, the namespace stack is only changed for the contents of the `dtml-let` tag block.

In the next example, the method `getShoppingCart` returns a list of objects with the following properties: sku, cost, and inventory. For each object in the sequence, the `dtml-let` assigns a value to the `date` and `subtotal` variables.

```
<dtml-in getShoppingCart sort="sku">
  <dtml-let date="ZopeTime()" subtotal="cost*inventory">
    <dtml-call
"addToReceipt(sku=sku,date=date,subtotal=subtotal)">
  </dtml-let>
</dtml-in>
```

This shows how multiple assignment with the `dtml-let` tag can help make simple scripting a little easier.

The dtml-call Tag

Sometimes you may find it necessary to call a method without displaying the results on your Web page. You may need to define a new a variable in the Request or insert some form elements into a database. The dtml-call tag is intended for just this purpose. Unlike the dtml-var tag, the dtml-call tag enables you to run a method without inserting any results into your document.

For example, let's say you want to insert the contents of an online questionnaire (an HTML form) into a MySQL database. One efficient way to achieve this is to have the form post to a DTML Method that contains only two dtml-call tags. The first tag calls a method insertQuestionnaire that inserts the form elements from the Request into a MySQL database, and the second tag redirects the user to another document, possibly a thank you page.

```
<dtml-call insertQuestionnaire>
<dtml-call "RESPONSE.redirect('thank_you.html')">
```

This DTML Method is completely transparent to the user. Without any dtml-var tags or other forms of output, the user will not see the contents of this DTML method. For the user, it is a simple process of submitting the form and being taken to the thank_you.html page.

The dtml-call tag is also commonly used to define a new variable in the current namespace by calling the set method of the Request object. For example, if a document always requires a certain variable but for some reason that variable is not always passed in when the document is loaded, you can set a default value for that variable in the Request.

```
<dtml-unless new_variable>
  <dtml-call "REQUEST.set('new_variable', 1)">
</dtml-unless>
```

As with many things in Zope, there are other ways of achieving the same result, but sometimes how you perform a certain action with DTML is a function of personal preference and sometimes it is determined by the overall design of your Web site.

The dtml-return Tag

In earlier versions of Zope (before 2.3.0), the dtml-return tag was used to perform script-like computations with DTML Documents or Methods. If Zope encounters a dtml-return tag while rendering a document, only the results of the expression or name lookup in the tag itself will be displayed. All other content in the page is ignored. In other words, when a valid dtml-return tag is parsed, Zope stops evaluating the rest of page and returns only the value of the tag.

```
<H1>Ignore me!</H1>
<dtml-return expr="ZopeTime()">
```

When rendered, the previous example would return only:

```
2001/01/01 12:00:00.0 US/Pacific
```

All content in the document or method other than the value of the `dtml-return` tag is ignored when the template is parsed. The `dtml-return` tag even stops block tags like the `dtml-if` and `dtml-in` tags from being completely evaluated.

```
<dtml-in shortLivedMethod>
  <dtml-return sequence-item>
</dtml-in>
```

In this example, only the first item in the sequence is returned. The rest of the sequence is not processed or displayed.

With the development of script objects, this tag is now basically useless. Anything that is possible with the `dtml-return` tag is probably easier to achieve with a script object. In fact, in a way, this tag now contradicts the purpose of DTML as it was intended to be used: for presentation only. This tag is left over from a time when there was no other way to achieve these kind of computations in DTML. With the addition of Python Scripts and other features, there is no reason to use DTML to perform any kind of serious logic or computation.

Please see Chapter 15 for more information on Python Script objects.

The dtml-comment Tag

The `dtml-comment` tag is primarily used to remove a piece of text from a DTML Document or Method. When a document is requested by the client, any content in the `dtml-comment` tag block is not rendered, even in the HTML source of the document. This is different from the behavior of HTML comments that hide their contents when the page is displayed, but still show up when the source for the Web page is viewed. The following document would appear blank when viewed regularly with a browser:

```
<dtml-var standard_html_header>

<!-- You must be viewing the source if you can see this. -->

<dtml-comment>
  <P>You shouldn't see any of this, even when viewing the
source</P>
  <P>The current time is <dtml-var ZopeTime fmt="AMPM">.</P>
</dtml-comment>

<dtml-var standard_html_footer>
```

If you were to view the HTML source for this page, you would see the following:

```
<html>
<head>
 <title>Test Page</title>
</head>

<body bgcolor="#FFFFFF">

<!-- You must be viewing the source if you can see this. -->


</body>

</html>
```

As far your browser is concerned, the `dtml-comment` tag block and all of its contents aren't even there. For this reason, the `dtml-comment` tag can be used to document your DTML by making notes to yourself (or to others) that no one on the client server side will ever see.

The dtml-raise Tag

The `dtml-raise` tag is used to raise an exception, usually in the event of an error. An *exception* is an unexpected error encountered while Zope is rendering a DTML Document or Method. Once an exception is raised by you or by Zope, the execution of the Document or Method being accessed is stopped and a Zope Error explaining what went wrong is displayed.

There are a couple of advantages to using a `dtml-raise` tag to report errors. First, the `dtml-raise` tag enables you to raise specific HTTP errors or even generate custom exceptions based on certain conditions in your documents. You can even insert a special error message in the `dtml-raise` tag block that will displayed when the exception is raised. If your error message contains any HTML formatting, the standard Zope Error will be replaced with the contents of the `dtml-raise` tag block. In the next example, a Moose Error exception is raised if the object `moose_info` is not true:

```
<dtml-if moose_info>
  <dtml-call expr="createMooseProfile()">
  <dtml-call "RESPONSE.redirect('thank_you.html')">
<dtml-else>
  <dtml-raise type="Moose Error">
    <H1>Moose Error</H1>
    <I>Profile information missing, cannot generate Moose Profile.</I>
  </dtml-raise>
</dtml-if>
```

The other advantage to using a `dtml-raise` tag to report errors is that the current transaction is rolled back if an exception is detected. This means that all changes to other objects that are part of the current request are undone. If, for example, you were making a series of changes to an object and one or more of your methods encountered some kind of error, you wouldn't have to worry about keeping track of which changes were successful and which ones weren't. To preserve the integrity of the object or the data you are trying to change, the entire transaction is rolled back.

The dtml-try Tag

When Zope encounters an exception while rendering a document or method, either because an error prevented your document from being displayed correctly or because an exception was generated with a `dtml-raise` tag, Zope stops whatever it was doing and displays an error message. Sometimes you may need to know whether an exception will be raised by running a method or performing some other action, but you don't want to show a cryptic error message to everyone in the event that an error does occur. The `dtml-try` tag enables you to detect and handle exceptions by specifying alternate sets of instructions based on the outcome of whatever action you are trying. By providing Zope with another set of instructions in the event of an exception, the rest of the document or method can be rendered even if an error is encountered. Another way to think about this is to say that the `dtml-try` tag works sort of like the `dtml-if` tag, except that instead of evaluating objects or expressions as true or false, the `dtml-try` tag evaluates whether or not an object or an expression raises an exception.

Checking for errors

Let's take a look at how we can perform some simple error checking with the `dtml-try` tag. In the next example, we receive a variable, `hourlyWage`, from a form input and we need to make sure that the value is a floating point number. If `hourlyWage` cannot be converted into a float, a ValueError exception will be raised and Zope renders the contents of the `dtml-except` tag. Instead of displaying a ZopeError, the string `hourlyWage` is added to a list of problem fields that will be dealt with later and Zope can continue about its business of rendering the rest of the document.

```
<dtml-try>
  <dtml-call "_.float(hourlyWage)">
<dtml-except ValueError>
  <dtml-call "error_list.append('hourlyWage')">
</dtml-try>
```

In the `dtml-except` tag in the previous code, we are only looking for a ValueError exception. If any other type of exception is raised by our `dtml-try` tag, a ZopeError is displayed. It is possible to have more than one `dtml-except` tag if you expect to be raising different types of exceptions. If you do not specify an exception type in the `dtml-except` tag, it catches any kind of exception.

See Chapter 19 for more information on exceptions and ZopeErrors.

Handling multiple exceptions

The following example shows a dtml-try tag with multiple dtml-except tags. The first dtml-except tag is only concerned with a ZeroDivisionError that would be raised if the value of managers is equal to zero. The second dtml-except does not specify a type of exception to look for, so it will handle any exception. If you want to include a catch-all dtml-except tag like this, it must be the last one in the list.

```
<dtml-try>
  <dtml-var expr="_.float(sales_week/managers)" fmt="dollars-and-cents">
<dtml-except ZeroDivisionError>
  $0.00
<dtml-except>
  N/A
</dtml-try>
```

Some exceptions in Python (and therefore Zope) are grouped together in what are called *base classes*. For example, the LookupError base class includes both the IndexError and KeyError exceptions. A base class is never raised as an exception, but they can be used to catch multiple types of exceptions with one dtml-except tag.

```
<dtml-try>
  <dtml-var Hoffa>
<dtml-except LookupError>
  Sorry, your variable could not be found.
</dtml-try>
```

The dtml-except tag in the previous example uses the LookupError base class and would handle either an IndexError or KeyError exception.

Optional dtml-else and dtml-finally tags

The dtml-try tag supports two optional tags that can be used to handle almost any other conditions that aren't covered by the dtml-except tag. The dtml-else tag is used to provide content to be rendered if no exceptions are raised, and the dtml-finally tag inserts content whether an exception is raised or not.

The dtml-else tag works basically the same way here as it does with the dtml-if tag. If the contents of the dtml-try tag do not raise any exceptions, all of the dtml-except tags are ignored and the contents of the dtml-else tag (if one exists) are rendered. This is really more useful when the dtml-try tag itself isn't returning any input. In the next example, the dtml-else tag is used to confirm that the method updateWage was run successfully:

```
<dtml-try>
  <dtml-call "_.float(hourlyWage)">
  <dtml-call expr="updateWage(hourlyWage)">
<dtml-except ValueError>
  <dtml-call "error_list.append('hourlyWage')">
<dtml-else>
  <H1>Thank you!</H1>
  <P>Your hourly wage has been updated.</P>
</dtml-try>
```

You can use the `dtml-finally` tag to insert content regardless of whether your objects or methods raised any exceptions. Instead of preventing exceptions, the `dtml-finally` tag is designed to allow the exceptions to be raised and then cleanup after them. Usually, a failed transaction is rolled back, but there are some tasks, such as unlocking a locked table in a database, that the Transaction Manager might not (depending on the Database you are using) take care of. In the following example, a method locks a table in a database from being accessed by anyone else and then runs a method. In this case, it is important to always unlock the table, even if an error occurred so that the table can be accessed again.

```
<dtml-try>
  <dtml-call expr="lockTable(table_name)">
  <dtml-call expr="updateTable(table_name)">
<dtml-finally>
  <dtml-call expr="unlockTable(table_name)">
</dtml-try>
```

The creators of Zope contend that whatever results you might achieve with this use of the `dtml-finally` tag are probably outside the intended realm of the capabilities of DTML and would be better if done in Python or Perl.

Writing your own error messages

Zope gives you access to the same variables it uses to display ZopeErrors. These exception variables are described in Table 4-10.

Table 4-10
The dtml-try tag Exception Variables

Variable	*Description*
error_type	Returns the type of the handled exception
error_value	Returns the value of the handled exception, usually the name of the object or method that caused the error
error_tb	Returns the traceback of the handled exception; this is displayed on all ZopeErrors when Zope is in debug mode

The following DTML is an excerpt from the `standard_error_message` method. It can be found in the root folder. Zope uses it to report most types of ZopeErrors. This is included to show how these variables can be used to create your own custom error messages or to change the default message Zope uses.

```
<dtml-try>
  <dtml-call brokenMethod>
<dtml-except>
  <H2>Zope Error</H2>
  <P>Zope has encountered an error while publishing this resource.</P>

  <P>
    <STRONG>Error Type: <!--#var error_type--></STRONG><BR>
    <STRONG>Error Value: <!--#var error_value--></STRONG><BR>
  </P>
</dtml-try>
```

The dtml-tree Tag

The `dtml-tree` tag is a specialized tag that is used to display object hierarchies in an expandable tree format. The Navigator frame on the left side of the Zope management interface is generated using a `dtml-tree` tag. Each folder object in the Root Folder is displayed in this frame and those with subfolders have a plus (+) sign to the left of the folder name. Clicking this plus sign expands a branch to show a list of all the folder objects that are contained in the folder you selected. To collapse that branch of the tree again, click the minus (-) sign that now appears to the left of the folder name. Figure 4-2 is an example of a partially expanded Navigator frame in the Zope management interface.

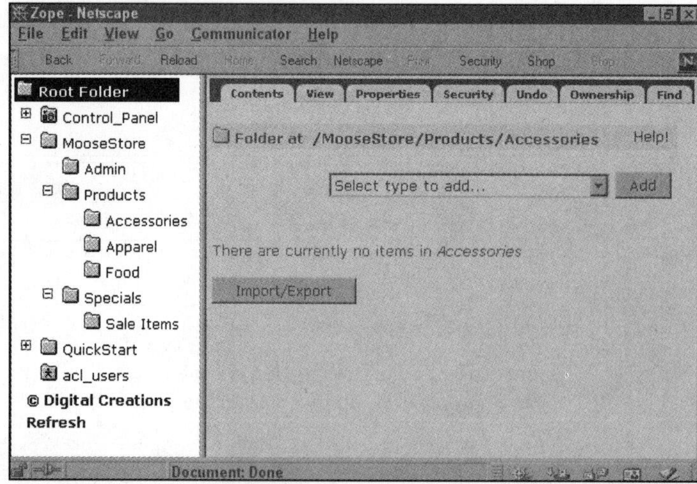

Figure 4-2: The Navigator Frame is made with a `dtml-tree` tag

The `tree` tag is usually used in conjunction with folders. As such, make sure that you use DTML Methods, because DTML Documents use their own namespaces, preventing you from working with most of the folders methods without explicitly referencing the folder in your code. Most of the examples in this section assume that the code is in a DTML Method.

Displaying objects in a tree

Creating a tree to display the contents of your folders is pretty easy with the `dtml-tree` because it does most of the work for you. To generate a basic tree, you only really need to specify what objects you want the `dtml-tree` tag to show.

```
<dtml-var standard_html_header>

<dtml-tree>
  <dtml-var getId>
</dtml-tree>

<dtml-var standard_html_footer>
```

This is about as simple as a `dtml-tree` tag gets. In this tree, we are only displaying the id of any object that can contain other objects (all folder-ish objects). This might be useful for using a tree to display a sitemap, but it doesn't enables you to do much else besides show the contents of all of your folders. The Navigator frame takes this a step further by adding some functionality to this list. Each object in the tree generated by the DTML that follows is now also a hyperlink to the contents of that object:

```
<dtml-var standard_html_header>

<dtml-tree>
  <a href="&dtml-tree-item-url;/manage_workspace"><dtml-var getId></a>
</dtml-tree>

<dtml-var standard_html_footer>
```

The tree that is generated here is basically the same tree that Zope uses in the Navigator frame of the management interface. Let's take a look now at some of the other features of the `dtml-tree` tag.

Attributes of the dtml-tree tag

The `dtml-tree` tag has several attributes that provide you with greater control over how the tree is displayed. These attributes are described in Table 4-11.

Table 4-11
The dtml-tree Tag Attributes

Attribute	*Requires an Argument*	*Description*
`Name`	Yes	Used to specify the root object (usually a folder) of the tree: defaults to the current folder
`Expr`	Yes	Inserts an expression that evaluates to the value to be inserted
`Branches`	Yes	The name of the method used to find the objects to be included on the tree: defaults to tpValues (a method defined by container objects)
`Branches_expr`	Yes	Performs the same function as the branches attribute but uses an expression rather than the name of a method.
`Id`	Yes	The name of a method or attribute used to determine the id of an object for the purposes of calculating tree state: defaults to tpId
`url`	Yes	The name of a method or attribute used to determine the url of an object: defaults to tpURL
`leaves`	Yes	The name of a DTML Document or Method rendered when a node without a child is expanded
`header`	Yes	The name of a DTML Document or Method rendered at the beginning of every expanded branch
`footer`	Yes	The name of a DTML Document or Method rendered at the end of every expanded branch
`nowrap`	No	If branch text exceeds available space, this attribute is used to truncate text instead of wrapping it
`sort`	Yes	Sorts branches based on the name of the specified attribute
`reverse`	No	Causes the order of the branches to be reversed

Attribute	Requires an Argument	Description
assume_children	No	Assumes that all nodes have children: useful for large trees because sub-objects will only be looked up when the node is actually expanded
single	No	Allows only one branch to be expanded at a time; all other branches are closed when a new one is opened
skip_unauthorized	No	Skips nodes that the user is not authorized to see; this attribute prevents an unauthorized error
urlparam	Yes	Specifies a query string to be included as branches are expanded and collapsed

Now that you have seen a couple of simple trees, lets take a look at some of the more advanced attributes of the dtml-tree tag.

Changing the type of objects in your tree

By default, the dtml-tree tag uses a method called *tpValues* to determine which objects are used to build your tree. This method is defined by most container objects such as folders, user folders, and even the Control Panel object. (This method can also be defined by objects you build, but that topic is covered later in this book.)

The branches attribute enables you to specify the name of the method used to generate a list of objects instead of tpValues. The method objectValues is often used with the branches attribute. The following example generates a tree using all of the objects it finds, not just container-like objects:

```
<dtml-tree branches="objectValues">
  <dtml-var getId>
</dtml-tree>
```

Alternately, the branches_expr attribute enables you to use an expression to the determine which objects are used to build your tree. This is useful if you only want to specify a list of certain objectValues to be used instead of all objectValues.

```
<dtml-tree branches_expr="objectValues(['Folder','File'])">
  <dtml-var getId>
</dtml-tree>
```

This dtml-tree tag will build a tree of folders and file objects. All other object types are ignored when the tree is built.

Inserting leaves, headers, and footers

The `leaves`, `header`, and `footer` attributes of the `dtml-tree` tag enable you to insert the contents of other DTML Documents and Methods into the branches of your tree. The `leaves` attribute enables you to specify a document or method to be rendered when a node without a child is expanded. In other words, the contents of the document or method are displayed when an object that does not contain other objects is expanded. This can be useful for displaying the contents of a database. The branches of the tree are used to organize the content of the database and the leaves are used to display actual data.

The `header` and `footer` attributes can also be used to insert the content of other documents into your tree, but they are only displayed in branches that contain other sub-branches. The header document is displayed before the list of objects is any expanded branch of your tree that contains other sub-branches. The `footer` attribute performs the same function, except that its document is displayed after the list of contents.

Changing how your tree is displayed

The `sort` attribute of the `dtml-tree` tag works the same way as the `sort` attribute of the `dtml-in` tag. The value of the `sort` attribute is used to sort the list of objects in each branch before the objects are displayed in the tree. If a list of objects is used to generate your tree (as opposed to a result set from a database), the objects are sorted according to their id by default. The objects can be sorted by any property they all have in common, but generally you want to sort the objects in your tree according to the same property you are using to display them.

The `reverse` attribute is fairly straightforward. Including the `reverse` attribute in a `dtml-tree` tag reverses whatever order the sequence already has and can be used with the `sort` attribute, but does not require it.

The `assume_children` attribute is unique to the `dtml-tree` tag. If this attribute is true, Zope assumes that all of the objects in your tree have children, meaning that initially every object in the tree will have a plus (+) sign next to it. Usually, when Zope displays a tree, it looks in the current container (usually a folder object) and returns whatever you told it look for. It then has to look at each object individually to see if that object contains any other objects This is how Zope knows to put the plus (+) sign next to each object that can be expanded. Another way to think of this is to say that Zope always looks one level deeper into the tree than it is actually showing you. If you are building a large tree, the `assume_children` attribute can be used to save some system resources by not looking at each item being displayed to see if it contains any other objects. Zope simply assumes that everything is expandable and won't look to see whether a particular branch actually contains anything until you try to expand it.

Passing variables within your tree

The `urlparam` attribute is used to pass along any variables that exist when your tree is first generated. The value of the `urlparam` attribute is whatever query string you want to pass along every time your tree is redrawn when a branch is expanded or collapsed. The use of this attribute is somewhat limited because Zope simply passes along whatever string you specify as the value for the `urlparam` attribute. Expressions, and therefore the dynamic insertion of variables, are not possible with this attribute under the current version of Zope.

Current item variables

Zope provides several variables with the `dtml-tree` tag that are used to access information about the current item in the sequence of objects displayed in your tree. These current item variables are described in Table 4-12.

Table 4-12
The dtml-tree Tag Current Item Variables

Variable	*Description*
tree-item-expanded	True if the current item is expanded
tree-item-url	The URL of the current item relative to the URL of the DTML Document or Method in which the dtml-tree tag appears
tree-root-url	The URL of the DTML Document or Method in which the dtml-tree tag appears
tree-level	The depth (in expanded nodes) of the current item, items at the top of the tree have a level of 0
tree-colspan	The total number of columns that the table is currently using to display the tree (equal to one greater than the current number of expanded nodes)
tree-state	The tree state expressed as a list of ids and sub-lists of ids

These variables are similar in function to the current item variables of the `dtml-in` tag. They are used to determine or display information about each object displayed in your tree. The tree-item-expanded variable is used when the tree is created to see whether the object being displayed is expanded or not. This, among other possibilities, enables you to visually differentiate expanded items form collapsed ones. Take a look at the following example:

```
<dtml-tree branches="objectValues">
  <dtml-if tree-item-expanded>
    <font size="+2"><dtml-var getId></font>
  <dtml-else>
    <dtml-var getId>
  </dtml-if>
</dtml-tree>
```

This example illustrates a simple use of the tree-item-expanded variable to test whether each item is expanded as it is being generated and to render it in a slightly larger font if it is.

At some point, you may want to turn the objects in your tree into hyperlinks to other documents. The `tree-item-url` and `tree-root-url` are useful for generating dynamic relative and absolute URLs to the objects displayed in your tree. The following example is similar to the Navigator frame in the Zope management interface in that each item in the tree is a hyperlink to either its Contents or Edit tab, depending on the type of object:

```
<dtml-tree branches="objectValues">
  <a href="&dtml-tree-root-url;/manage_workspace"><dtml-var getId></a>
</dtml-tree>
```

Control variables

The `dtml-tree` tag offers a couple of variables that are used to control the state of the entire tree. The expand_all and collapse_all variables are described in Table 4-13.

Table 4-13
The dtml-tree Tag Control Variables

Variable	*Description*
expand_all	If set to a true value, this variable causes the entire tree to be expanded
collapse_all	If set to a true value, this variable causes the entire tree to be collapsed

There isn't much mystery to the use of these variables, but the following example shows how they can be used to expand or collapse your entire tree with the click of a hyperlink:

```
<dtml-var standard_html_header>

<P>
  <a href="&dtml-URL0;?expand_all=1">Expand</a>
   | 
  <a href="&dtml-URL0;?collapse_all=1">Collapse</a>
</P>

<dtml-tree>
  <dtml-var getId>
</dtml-tree>

<dtml-var standard_html_footer>
```

The dtml-sendmail and dtml-mime Tags

The `dtml-sendmail` tag is used to generate and send dynamic e-mail messages in DTML or Python scripts. The `dtml-mime` tag encodes data using MIME (Multipurpose Internet Mail Extensions) so that it can be sent as an attachment with a message generated by the `dtml-sendmail` tag.

To send an e-mail with the `dtml-sendmail` tag, you must specify either the `MailHost` object or the address of the SMTP server that you want to use to send the message.

Creating dynamic e-mail messages

Although it can be used in many different ways, the `dtml-sendmail` tag is often used to dynamically generate and send an e-mail using data from a HTML form. In the following example, we assume a customer has already filled out a request form asking to receive an online newsletter. The form posts to the following method, which generates the e-mail and assures the customer that his or her message has been sent:

```
<dtml-var standard_html_header>

<dtml-sendmail mailhost="MailHost">
To: editor@moosenews.com
From: <dtml-var e-mail>
Subject: Moose News Magazine

I would like to subscribe to Moose News Magazine!
Name:    <dtml-var first_name> <dtml-var last_name>
Address: <dtml-var address>
Phone:   <dtml-var phone>
E-mail:   <dtml-var e-mail>
</dtml-sendmail>

<H1>Thank you <dtml-var first_name>!</H1>
<p>Your request has been sent to the editor.</p>

<dtml-var standard_html_footer>
```

There are a few things to notice about how the `dtml-sendmail` tag is written. First, the content of the tag is broken into two parts: the mail headers and the body of the message. Although the `dtml-sendmail` tag supports all of the standard mail headers (To, From, Subject, Cc, Bcc, and Reply To), you must specify a value for at least the To, From, and Subject mail headers. Also note that the mail headers and the rest of the contents of the tag are separated by a line break. This is used to identify where the body of the message begins. Although the contents of the `dtml-sendmail` tag can contain additional line breaks, Zope uses the first one it finds to start the body of the e-mail message. Also, the body of the message is formatted as though it were in a HTML `<pre>` tag. In other words, the body of the message will be displayed exactly as it is typed, including all additional spaces and line breaks between words. Lastly, the `dtml-sendmail` tag itself does not generate any output the current document. When the method in this example is displayed to the customer, the customer will only see the text that thanks him or her for filling out the form.

Notice also that the body of the message in this example contains a `dtml-var` tag. Any DTML tag can be used inside a `dtml-sendmail` tag to dynamically generate the body of the message.

All valid attributes of the `dtml-sendmail` tag are described in Table 4-14. If used, each attribute does require some kind of argument to be specified.

Table 4-14
The dtml-sendmail Tag Attributes

Attribute	*Description*
`Mailhost`	This attribute specifies the id of the mailhost object that will deliver the message; not to be used with the `smtphost` attribute
`Smtphost`	This attribute specifies the address of the SMTP server that will deliver the message; not to be used with the `mailhost` attribute
`Port`	If the `smtphost` attribute is used this attribute specifies the port number to connect to; the default value of 25 will be used if the port attribute is not specified.
`Mailto`	The e-mail address of the recipient of the message or list of address separated by commas
`Mailfrom`	The e-mail address of the sender of the message
`Subject`	The subject of the message

Sending attachments

The `dtml-mime` tag is used to send attachments with the `dtml-sendmail` tag. In the next example, a `dtml-in` tag is used to iterate through a result set of subscriber information generated by the ZSQLMethod `listSubscribers`. An individualized e-mail message is generated with a newsletter attachment and sent to each subscriber in the sequence.

```
<dtml-in listSubscribers>

<dtml-sendmail mailhost="MailHost">
To: <dtml-var e-mail>
From: editor@moosenews.com
Subject: Moose News Magazine
<dtml-mime type=text/plain encode=7bit>
```

```
Hi <dtml-var first_name>,
Here is this month's copy of Moose News Magazine. Enjoy!

<dtml-boundary type=text/plain disposition=attachment
encode=base64><dtml-var newsletter></dtml-mime>

</dtml-sendmail>

</dtml-in>
```

If you compare the text in this example to the previous `dtml-sendmail` example, you may notice that using the `dtml-mime` tag changes a few things. First, there is no line break between the mail headers and the open `dtml-mime` tag. The first line break is inside the `dtml-mime` tag, and therefore, so is the body of the message. For most e-mail messages, you may need to set the `encode` attribute of the `dtml-mime` tag to "7bit." This means that the body of the e-mail messagse will not be encrypted. After the body of the message, there is a `dtml-boundary` tag that indicates the next part of the e-mail message is an attachment. A `dtml-var` tag is then used to insert the file you want to attach to the e-mail. Notice also that there are no line breaks between the `dtml-boundary` tag, `dtml-var` tag and the close `dtml-mime` tag. Any line breaks between these tags will be encoded and sent along with the MIME part of the e-mail.

The `dtml-mime` tag has three attributes, which are listed in Table 4-15. The `dtml-boundary` tag uses the same attributes as the `dtml-mime` tag.

Table 4-15
The dtml-mime and dtml-boundary Tag Attributes

Attribute	*Description*
`Type`	Sets the MIME header, Content-Type, of the subsequent data
`Disposition`	Sets the MIME header, Content-Disposition, of the subsequent data (If disposition is not specified in a mime or boundary tag Content-Disposition MIME header is not included.)
`Encode`	Sets the MIME header, Content-Transfer-Encoding, of the subsequent data (f encode is not specified, base64 is used as default. The options for encode are: base64, uuencode, x-uuencode, quoted-printable, uue, x-uue, and 7bit. No encoding is done if set to 7bit.)

Summary

Chances are, the reason you bought this book in the first place has something to do with a desire to build a powerful and dynamic Web site that will meet and exceed all of your business or personal Internet needs. If you've gotten this far into the book, we shouldn't have to spend any more time shouting from our soapbox about why Zope is great platform for building such a Web site. Although DTML is by no means the answer to every problem, most of Zope and the current add-on products rely on it.

DTML provides you with a powerful way to separate the presentation of your Web site from the logic that makes it work. It also enables two different groups of people (content managers and developers) to manage either task. This capability, combined with a large variety powerful options and special variables, makes DTML one of the most powerful tools in your Zope toolbox.

✦ ✦ ✦

Object-Oriented Programming and Python

✦ ✦ ✦ ✦

In This Chapter

Using the interactive interpreter

Running Python commands from a file

Variables

Types and operators

Control statements

Understanding namespaces

Modules and packages

Classes and objects

Exception handling

✦ ✦ ✦ ✦

This chapter is intended as a brief introduction to the Python programming language. As Zope is written in Python, some of the obscure syntax that you encounter in DTML pages will become obvious. Additionally a good working knowledge of Python will help you conquer certain tasks more easily or accomplish ones that are just plain impossible to do with a template language.

Python is an interpreted scripting language. This means that it is not necessary to compile Python files in order to get them to run on the computer. In this respect it is similar to the Perl programming language.

Python is object-oriented. This means that besides the procedural (step-by-step) features of most programming languages, it has features that enable you to define the problem you want your program to solve in terms of objects, which can have their own traits and data attached to them. If you're not already familiar with object-oriented programming, Python is one of the easiest ways to learn about it. In this respect it is often compared to both the C++ and Java programming languages. Python is as or more object-oriented than any other language, and makes it easier to apply an object-oriented methodology to your programming efforts.

Python is portable. The examples in this chapter should work on any platform for which Python is available with little or no changes to the examples. This means that the programs that you write using Python are write-once-run-anywhere (WORA), and are even more portable than Java programs in that regard. One practical upshot of this is that any enhancements you make to Zope will almost certainly work regardless of what platform on which you're running Zope, whether it's a Windows variant (95/98/NT/2000), Linux, Sun Solaris, or one of the BSD variants.

Using the Interactive Interpreter

Python comes bundled with the pre-compiled versions of Zope. Assuming that you have followed the instructions for installing Zope in Chapter 2, you already have a copy of Python installed on your computer and you are ready to begin working. If you have not yet installed Zope, please read Chapter 2.

Alternatively, you can visit the Python Web site at `http://www.python.org` and follow the instructions there for downloading and installing Python on your computer. Be advised that directories and paths we refer to in this chapter assume that you are working with a copy of Python that was installed with a pre-built version of Zope. If you have installed a separate version of Python or placed Zope in a directory other than the default, you will have to take that into account while reading our examples.

How you start the Python interpreter depends on what operating system you are running.

If you are using Windows (Win95/98/NT/2000), open the MS-DOS prompt and follow these steps:

```
C:\>cd "c:\program files\website\bin"
C:\Program Files\WebSite\bin>python
```

If you are running Linux (or other UNIX variant) follow these steps from the console or a terminal window:

```
$ cd /usr/local/Zope/bin
$ ./python
```

Python will start up and will print a short copyright notice. It then displays the Python command prompt similar to the one shown here:

```
Python 1.5.2 (#0, Jul 30 1999, 09:52:18) [MSC 32 bit (Intel)]
on win32
Copyright 1991-1995 Stichting Mathematisch Centrum, Amsterdam
>>>
```

The interpreter lets you evaluate the results of Python statements directly from your terminal. This is a great method for learning and/or experimenting with new Python commands. To get a feel for how the interpreter works, type **1001 + 1** and press Enter. Python will evaluate the expression you entered and will return back a result of `1002`:

```
C:\Program Files\WebSite\bin>python
Python 1.5.2 (#0, Jul 30 1999, 09:52:18) [MSC 32 bit (Intel)]
on win32
Copyright 1991-1995 Stichting Mathematisch Centrum, Amsterdam
>>> 1001 + 1
1002
>>>
```

The interactive interpreter has two prompts to indicate the "mode" the interpreter is in. The first is the one you've seen in the previous example: >>>. The second prompt type is the "continuation" prompt, which looks like this: .... Python uses the two types of prompt to indicate whether it is expecting further input before a statement can be evaluated. The `1001 + 1` statement did not require any further input in order to be evaluated, so it was evaluated and the result displayed.

Let's take a look at a statement that requires a continuation before it can be evaluated:

```
>>> x = "eggs and spam"
>>> for y in x:
...     print y, " ",
...
e g g s   a n d   s p a m
>>>
```

Caution

When entering this statement into the interpreter, make sure that you precede the `print y, " ",` with at least one space (or more). It doesn't matter how many spaces, so long as the `print` line is indented more than the `for` statement. We'll explain later in this chapter how and why indentation is important to Python.

The assignment of `"eggs and spam"` to `x` did not require a continuation in order to be evaluated, but also did not produce a result.

The second statement, `for y in x:` is a multi-line statement (in this case, a loop), as indicated by the colon at the end of the line. Accordingly, on the subsequent line, the prompt changed to `...` and you were required to indent the statement before you entered it (in fact you would have received an error I you didn't). `print y, " "`. The statement, `print y, " ",` will be evaluated once for every step through the loop, printing the current offset into the string `x` and a space.

Finally, pressing Enter key at the second continuation prompt without any further input indicates that the `for` statement is now complete and can be evaluated. The indentation of the second line of the `for` statement is very significant. Python uses indentation to identify blocks of code that belong to the same statement. A statement sequence is identified by its indentation level, so that when the indentation returns to its previous level, the interpreter assumes that the current sequence has ended. Because statements of various sorts can be nested within each other, indentation is very significant in determining to which statement a particular line of code belongs.

The interpreter is more than a glorified calculator; it can be used to perform just about any command that you would write in a Python program. Before we get into the various different commands you can use, we will show you how to write and run your first Python program. For now you need to exit the interpreter. If you are using Windows, press ^Z and hit the Enter key. If you are using Linux, press ^D. Python will return you to your operating system's respective command prompt.

Running Python Commands from a File

The program we are going to write, if you have not guessed it by now, is the venerable "Hello, world!" program that is used to introduce most computer languages. This program when invoked will simply print out the words "Hello, world!" on the screen and then quit. Creating this program quickly introduces you to the process of writing and running a program in Python.

To create this program, open your favorite text editor and type this line of code exactly as shown:

```
print "Hello, world!"
```

Save this as a plain text file named `hello.py`, and exit your editor.

That's it, you have written your first Python program! Now you need to run it to see what it does. You will invoke your program in a similar fashion to starting the interpreter. Go back to your Command Prompt or Terminal Window and change the current directory to the directory where you saved `hello.py`. Type in the complete path to the Python interpreter and pass `hello.py` as an argument.

Saving Time Running Python

Having to type the full path to the Python interpreter to invoke a program every time gets tedious. Fortunately there are several methods, operating system-dependent of course, that can minimize the amount of typing you need to do in order to run a program.

The first thing you should do is to make sure that the Python executable is in your path. This way you can just type `python` at the prompt instead of the full path to the program. If you are using windows the path to Python should be `"c:\program files\website\bin"`. So, add the following line to your `autoexec.bat` file, located in the root directory of your C:\ drive:

PATH=%PATH%;"C:\Program Files\WebSite\bin"Making this change will let you run Python programs like so:

```
C:\>Python hello.py
```

On Windows NT, you can go a step further and eliminate the necessity of specifying the .py extension. You do this by utilizing the PATHTEXT environment variable. Check to see what extensions are currently executable:

```
C:>\echo %PATHTEXT%
.exe;.bat;.cmd

C:\>
```

You can add Python .py files to this list like so:

```
C:\>set PATHTEXT=%PATHTEXT%;.py
```

And then test your change:

```
C:\>echo %PATHTEXT%
.exe;.bat;.cmd;.py
```

Voilà! You can now run Python scripts from the command line, just by using the following command under Windows NT:

```
C:\>python hello
```

Most versions of Linux already have Python installed. Testing this is fairly simple, just type **python** at the command prompt:

```
$ python

>>>Python 1.5.2 (#1 Aug 25 2000, 09:33:37) [GCC 2.96 20000731
(experimental)] on Linux-i386
>>>
```

Making your Python scripts executable is a fairly simple procedure. First, you need to tell the UNIX shell to use the Python interpreter when running the script. This is done by making the following modification at the beginning of your script:

```
#! /usr/bin/python

print "Hello, world!"
```

The string `#!` at the beginning of your script will tell the UNIX shell where to find the interpreter for the rest of the script. In this case, the shell will look for the Python interpreter at `/usr/bin/python`, which is the standard location for Red Hat Linux–based distributions. Your distribution may place the Python in another location.

Next, you need to change the permissions on the `hello.py` file itself in order for the shell to recognize it as an executable file.

In the same directory as the `hello.py` file, execute the following command:

```
$ chmod 755 hello.py
```

This will set the permissions on the file as follows: The file owner can read, write, or execute the file; other users in the owners group can read or execute the file, and users not in the owners group can also read or execute the file.

Once this is done you can type the script name directly at the prompt.

```
$ ./hello.py
Hello, World!
$
```

For example, in Windows, if you saved `hello.py` to `c:\temp` you would run your program like this:

```
C:\>cd temp
C:\temp>"c:\program files\website\bin\python" hello.py
Hello, world!

C:\temp>
```

If you are using Linux and you saved `hello.py` to `/tmp` you would run the program like this:

```
$ cd /tmp
$ /usr/local/Zope/bin/python hello.py
Hello, world!
$
```

You can also run your script directly in the interactive interpreter. To do this, start the interpreter as we did in the previous section. Make sure the current directory is the same place where your hello.py file is, first. Once you are at the Python prompt type `import hello`. Python will print out the words, "Hello, world!" as in the previous examples, and will then redisplay the Python prompt >>> and wait for you to enter another command.

Notice that you did not need to type the file extension .py. In fact, if you did, Python would print out `ImportError: No module named py`. The reason for this is that the period, also known as the "dot," has a special meaning to Python. It is used for attribute look up on an object. We explain what this means in the section regarding objects.

That is all there is to writing and running Python scripts. Of course printing out a bunch of words on a screen is pretty pointless by itself. In the next sections we discuss the other fundamental building blocks of any programming language; variables, control statements, functions, and so on.

Variables

One could make the generalization that all programs do the same thing. They take data in the form of input (usually from a human via a keyboard and mouse, but not always) and perform a series of calculations or transformation on it and then output the results (normally to a monitor but not always). The program you created in the previous section was useless because every time you ran the program it would do the exact same thing. In order for a program to have any merit it needs to interact with data. Data can come from a variety of sources; a user could type a key on the keyboard, click a mouse button or the data could come from a file or across the network. Programs do not always interact with one source of data either, actually most programs work with several sources of data to get the job done.

So you as the programmer need a way to tell the computer where to get its data. You need the ability to take information and ferret it away for later reference. This is what variables are for.

Consider the `Hello, world!` program that you created earlier. Pretend that you need to change this program so that it will say hello to your friend Sally. You could change your program to print `"Hello, Sally!"`, which would get the job done. But would you want to rewrite your program every time that you got a new friend. What you ideally would like is to have your program say hello to that person. This way you only have to write your program once. The following code contains all the change necessary to make your program ask for a name and then say hello.

```
name = raw_input("What is your name? ")
print "Hello, " + name + "!"
```

Create a new file with the above listing in it. If you run this code it will look something like this.

```
$ python hello2.py
What is your name? Bob
Hello, Bob!
```

Here is an explanation of what each line of code is doing. `raw_input` is a built-in Python function that will prompt a user with a specified string, in this case, "What is your name?" It then waits for the user to type a few keys and press Enter. Whatever the user has entered will be stored in the variable, `name`. The next line contains the print statement that is similar to our "hello world" example. The difference here is that we are constructing a new string by adding the string `Hello` to whatever is in the name variable. You have also tacked on an exclamation point to the end, so that the user knows that your program is really excited to great them.

In the previous example you used the `name` variable to hold the users input until your program had the chance to print it. One thing to note is that you could have called the variable anything you wanted. You could have just as easily written your program like this:

```
user = raw_input("What is your name? ")
print "Hello " + user + "!"
```

All you need to do is store that results of `raw_input` into a legally named Python variable and then update your print statement to use the same variable. A Python variable must be a single word (no spaces) start with a letter or the underscore ("_") and can have any number of alpha or numeric characters.

So, for example, the following are legal variable names:

```
user
your_name
name1
```

While the following are not

```
2name
your name
*!#%user
```

If you try to use a variable name with illegal characters Python will stop the program at the line in your code where you first tried to use the illegal variable and will complain that you have a SyntaxError.

Types and Operators

Everything in Python is implemented as an object. Numbers, characters, arrays, and even functions are objects. The rich set of built in object types is one of the things that make Python such a pleasure to program in. Unlike lower-level languages, with Python you do not have to manage your own memory and strings and arrays do not have to be initialized to a specific size prior to their use (they grow and shrink as needed without intervention from you). Nor do you need to worry about crashing your computer because you improperly initialized a variable or inadvertently wrote to the wrong location in memory. If you are a user of a higher-level language such as Perl or Visual Basic you probably take some of these features for granted, but you will find that some of the features that are uniquely Python are so convenient you will wonder how you lived without them.

Numbers

Python supports the usual number types that you find in other programming languages such as integers, long integers, and floating points. The different numeric types refer to the largest value that a number can hold and how precise (the number of digits to the right of the decimal point) the number is.

Table 5-1 lists the different number types and how they can be expressed in Python.

Table 5-1
Numeric Types

Type	*Literal*
Integer	0, -1, 10
Long integer	10923809128309019832L
Float	2.1, 1.0, 3.14e-10, 4E210, 4.0e+210
Octal Notation	012
Hex	0xff, 0x1A
Complex	23+10j, 8j, 4+1.1j

Understanding the number syntax

Integers are written as either positive or negative numbers without a decimal point. They are limited in size based on your hardware. Refer to the sidebar "Determining How Large an Integer Can Be" to find out what the limits are for your machine. Examples of using integers:

```
>>> x = 1
>>> x + 2
3
```

Integers can also be expressed in either octal or hexadecimal notation. To express a number in hex format you would prefix your number with a `0x`. Similarly, you can express an integer in octal format by prefix the number with a `0`. You cannot write a normal base 10 number starting with a `0`, because Python interprets it as an octal. For example:

```
>>>  x  =  010
```

is equivalent to writing

```
>>> x = 8
```

Normally Python will raise an OverflowError exception when you try to create an integer bigger than what is allowed for your particular architecture. If you have the need for numbers that are bigger than the limit you can use a long integer. The difference between long integers and normal ones is that the only size limit is based upon the amount of available memory, and are slightly less efficient. To create a long integer you add either a lower or uppercase L to the end of the number. (It is usually recommended that you use the capital L because the lowercase L sometimes looks like the number one.)

Floats, on the other hand, are numbers that contain decimal points and exponents. Exponents are denoted with either an uppercase or lowercase E. The compiler that was used to compile your version of Python determines the precision of a float; generally you do not need to worry about precision unless you are doing calculations that are used in scientific applications and the like.

Complex numbers are composed of a real and an imaginary part. To create a complex number you add either a lowercase or uppercase J to your number. The plus symbol is used to denote where the real number ended and the imaginary one begins. Once you have assigned a complex number to a variable you can access the real and imaginary parts like so:

```
>>> x = 2+1j
>>> x.real
2.0
>>> x.imag
1.0
```

Determining How Large an Integer Can Be

The largest number that an integer can contain depends on your system architecture. For instance, on a 32-bit Intel machine (running either Windows or Linux) the largest positive integer you can have is 2,147,483,647 and the largest negative number is –2,147,483,648. If you try to create a number larger or smaller than these limits Python will raise an OverflowError.

If you are not running an Intel-based machine you can determine the maximum positive size for yourself by running this command from the Python interpreter.

```
>>> import sys
>>> sys.maxint
2147483647
```

To determine the largest negative number (assuming that you ran the example above and already imported the `sys` module) you would type.

```
>>> -sys.maxint-1
```

Add one to `sys.maxint` to see how Python handles a number larger than the maximum.

Evaluating numbers

You perform calculations on numbers by using the operators in Table 5-2. If you perform a calculation using two different types of numbers Python will automatically convert the number to the larger type. If you have an integer and a long Python will convert both numbers to a long before performing your calculations.

Table 5-2
Numeric Operations

Operation	*Result*
x + y	sum of x and y
x – y	difference of x and y
x * y	product of x and y
x / y	quotient of x and y
x % y	remainder of x / y
-x	x negated
+x	x unchanged
x<y	1 (true) if x is less than y, 0 if x is greater or equal to y

Operation	Result
x<=y	1 if x is less than or equal to y, 0 if x is greater than y
x>y	1 if x is greater than y, 0 if x is less than or equal to y
x>=y	1 if x is greater than or equal to y, 0 if x is less than y
x==y	1 if x equals y, 0 if x does not equal y
x!=y	1 if x does not equal y, 0 if x equals y
x<>y	1 if x does not equal y, 0 if x equals y
x and y	if x is false, then x, else y
x or y	if x is false, then y, else x

These operations are straightforward and work like you would expect them to work in other languages. Here are some examples and their result. You can try these out for yourself by typing them directly into the Python interpreter.

Adding to integers:

```
>>> 1 + 1
2
```

Adding an integer to a float:

```
>>> 1 + 13.2
14.2
```

Python will evaluate your expressions according to the order of precedence. This means that if your expression contains addition and multiplication, the multiplication is evaluated first before the numbers are added. You can use parentheses `()` to control the order in which numbers are evaluated. Consider the following examples.

Addition and multiplication without grouping:

```
>>> 1 + 2 * 3
7
```

Here is the same example but this time we control the order in which the expression is evaluated using parentheses. (Notice that you get a completely different result.)

```
>>> (1 + 2) * 3
9
```

When dividing integers the result is an integer. Python does not do any rounding it ignores the remainder. So for example:

```
>>> 1 / 2
0
>>> 3/2
1
>>> 4/1
4
```

To discover what the remainder is you can you can use the modulus operator `%`. For example, 20 divided by 7 is 2 with a remainder of 6. To find both these numbers you would first divide then perform the modulus operation.

```
>>> 20 / 7
2
>>> 20 % 7
6
```

Alternatively, you can include a float in your expression and Python will return the results as a decimal:

```
>>> 20 / 7.0
2.85714285714
```

Manipulating numbers using Python's built-in functions

The following list contains Python's built-in functions for manipulating numbers:

abs(x)	Returns the absolute vale of x
complex(real [, imag])	Creates a complex number, using real and imaginary components
divmod(x, y)	Returns the quotient and remainder of long division as a tuple. For integers, the tuple (x / y, x % y) is returned. Floating point numbers return (math.floor(x / y), x % y)
float(x)	Returns a floating point number
hex(x)	Returns a hexadecimal string
long(x)	Returns a long integer, if given a number or a string
max(seq [, arg1, ...])	For a single sequence argument seq, returns the largest item in the sequence. If supplied with multiple arguments, returns the largest argument.

min(seq [,arg1, ...])	For a single sequence argument seq, returns the smallest item in the sequence. If supplied with multiple arguments, returns the smallest argument.
oct(x)	Returns an octal string
pow(x, y [, z])	Returns x ** y. if z is supplied, returns (x ** y) % z
round(x [,y])	Returns the result of rounding a floating-point number x to the closest multiple of 10^y. If y is not supplied, y defaults to a value of 0.

Sequences

Python has a "family" of types called sequences. There are three sequence types:

- Strings
- Lists
- Tuples

All sequences are ordered collections of objects. Strings are immutable ordered collections of characters; lists are mutable ordered collections of arbitrary objects; and tuples are immutable ordered collections of arbitrary objects.

All sequences have some common methods and operations:

- Elements of the sequence can be accessed by index: s[i]
- A subset of the elements can be returned using slice notation: s[i:j]
- The number of elements in the sequence can be returned: len(s)
- The value of the element with the largest value can be returned: max(s)
- The value of the element with the smallest value can be returned: min(s)

If you have programmed with other languages, you are probably familiar with all the previous notations except for slicing. Have no fear. We'll explain this powerful feature under the section dealing with lists.

Strings

Strings are used for manipulating text and binary data. They are a sequence of character elements surrounded by either double or single quotations. Python does not have a built-in type specifically designed for the handling of single characters as some other programming languages do. The letter "a" is a sequence 1 item long.

Accessing a particular character from within a string is fairly simple:

```
>>> x = "spam and eggs"
>>> x[6]
'n'
>>>
```

You indicate which element you want out of the sequence by specifying its index within square brackets. Notice how the x[6] operation returns the seventh element in the string. This is because sequence element indexes begin with 0 not 1. So a ten-element sequence's last element would be accessed using s[9].

Strings can be created in one of four ways in Python.

You can enclose a string in double quotes as in the previous example:

```
>>> text = "I'm a string!"
>>> print text
I'm a string
```

Also notice that a string is created by using double quotes in the assignment. Certain characters in a string have special meanings to Python. For example, the double quote character tells Python that you are either starting or ending a string. If your string contains double quotes as one of its characters you must prefix the \ character to it so that Python knows that the double quote is part of your string. For example:

```
>>> quote = "\"A penny saved is a penny earned.\" - Ben Franklin"
>>> print quote
"A penny saved is a penny earned." - Ben Franklin
```

Having to escape all of your double quotes can be tedious if you are creating a string that contains a lot of them. This is why Python also lets you create a string using single quotes. When you use single quotes you do not need to escape the double quotes. You will, however, need to escape all of your single quotes.

```
>>> text = 'I\'m a string!'
>>> print text
I'm a string!
```

There is no difference between strings created with either single or double quotes. Python provides this feature purely for your convenience and because it is easier to read strings that are not cluttered with a bunch of back slash characters. If you spend any time reading other peoples Python code you will notice that an author will use both methods indiscriminately.

Your string cannot span multiple lines when using the double or single quote method of creating strings. For example, if you try starting a string with the first double quote but press enter instead of closing the string with the second quote Python will raise a `SyntaxError` because it is expecting another quote before it reads the next line

```
>>> "This string is missing the closing quote.
  File "<stdin>", line 1
    "This string is missing the closing quote.
                                              ^
SyntaxError: invalid token
>>>
```

You have a couple options available to you if you want your string to span multiple lines. Normally you do this to keep your code pretty—other programmers will appreciate your thoughtfulness when they do not have to repeatedly scroll left and right to read what you have written.

First you can use the backslash character to escape the end of the line. This tells Python to continue your statement on the following line.

```
>>> x = "This string \
... spans two lines!"
>>> print x
This string spans two lines!
```

Once again Python has a more convenient method for inputting strings that span multiple lines called *triple quoting*. As the name implies instead of opening and closing your code with one quote you enclose your quotes with three quotes (either `"""` or `'''`) in a row. Your strings can then span an unlimited amount of lines as in the following example:

```
>>> x = """This is a triple quoted
... string. Not only can it span
... multiple lines. It can contain
... double quotes that do not need
... to be "escaped".
... """
>>> print x
This is a triple quoted
string. Not only can it span
multiple lines. It can contain
double quotes that do not need
to be "escaped".

>>>
```

Escape sequences

When you use the backslash (\) to escape a character you are telling Python to change the meaning of the character following the backslash. From the previous sections you have already seen two different uses of the backslash one to escape a quote so that Python does not think that you want the string closed and the other to tell Python to ignore the end of the line. Table 5-3 contains all of Python's escape codes.

Table 5-3
Character Escape Codes

Code	*Description*
\\	Backslash
\'	Single quote
\"	Double quote
\a	Bell
\b	Backspace
\e	Escape
\000	Null
\n	Newline
\v	Vertical tab
\t	Horizontal tab
\r	Carriage return
\f	Form feed
\0XX	Octal value XX
\xXX	Hex value XX

To get a feel for how these work, create a few strings in the interpreter. For instance, to include a backslash in your string you need to escape it as well.

```
>>> s1 = "This string has a backslash (\\) in it."
>>> print s1
This string has a backslash (\) in it.
```

To include a newline in your string you would use `\n`. This makes the text wrap to the next line when you print it.

```
>>> s2 = "This is the first line.\nThis is the second!"
>>> print s2
This is the first line.
This is the second!
```

The newline can be different depending on what platform it runs on. Under UNIX, the newline is represented as the line feed character `\n` or the ASCII character number 12. In Windows the newline is actually represented by two characters, the carriage return `\r` or ASCII character 15 and then the line feed `\n` ASCII character number 12. While on the Macintosh the newline is represented as just the carriage return.

Formatting strings

There are several ways to format strings in Python. Perhaps the simplest to understand is string concatenation. This is when you take two or more strings and add them together to make a new string. For instance:

```
>>> s1 =  "This is the first part of the string,"
>>> s2 = " and this is the second."
>>> s3 = s1 + s2
>>> print s3
This is the first part of the string, and this is the second.
```

If you wanted to add a number to your string you would first need to convert the number to a string using Python's built in `str()` function and then add the string together.

```
>>> s1 = "I saw " + str(10) + " dead birds."
>>> print s1
I saw 10 dead birds.
```

Python provides another method that you can use to format strings using the `%` operator. Table 5-4 contains a list of all the string formatting codes. With the `%` operator you can create new strings by first creating a format string (a string that holds special markers that tells Python where you will be inserting objects) and then use the `%` operator like you used the + operator to format a list of objects into the string.

```
>>> s1 = "Format string %d" % 10
>>> print s1
Format string 10
>>> s1 = "A %s, %d, %f oh my!" % ('string', 5, 3.14)
>>> print s1
A string, 5, 3.14 oh my!
```

Table 5-4
String Formatting Codes

Code	*Description*
%s	String conversion of any object
%c	Character conversion of an int
%d	Decimal integer
%l	Integer
%u	Unsigned integer
%o	Octal integer without a leading "0"
%x	Hexadecimal integer without leading "0x"
%X	Uppercase Hexadecimal integer
%e	Floating point with exponent
%E	Floating point
%f	Floating point
%g	Floating point with or without exponent
%G	Floating point
%%	Literal %

When Python sees the `%` in the format string it looks at the next character to determine how to format the next object in the list. There must be exactly the same number of format directives in the string as there are objects to format. If not, Python will raise TypeError.

Not all objects can be converted to all types. Just about every object type in Python can be converted to a string representation, but not all strings can be converted to, say, a floating-point number.

```
>>> x = '2'
>>> x
'2'
>>> x * 2
'22'
>>> y = int(x)
>>> y
2
>>> y * 2
4
```

```
>>> x = 'a 2'
>>> x * 2
'a 2a 2'
>>> y = int(x)
Traceback (innermost last):
  File "<stdin>", line 1, in ?
ValueError: invalid literal for int(): a 2
>>>
```

Similarly, %f will not work correctly for `s1 = "%f" % (x)` if x is a string object, even one that could be converted to a float:

```
>>> x = 2
>>> s1 = "%f" % (x)
>>> s1
'2.000000'
>>> x = '2'
>>> s1 = "%f" % (x)
Traceback (innermost last):
  File "<stdin>", line 1, in ?
TypeError: illegal argument type for built-in operation
>>>
```

Lists

Lists are one of the real workhorses in Python. They are analogous to arrays in other languages. There are some key differences. First, they are dynamic—they automatically grow or shrink as needed and you do not have to specify its size when you initialize it. Second, they can contain any combination of Python objects even other lists (some languages only allow arrays to be all of one type).

Creating and filling lists

Lists are created either empty or containing objects. You create an empty list by typing the open and close brackets with nothing in between them (for example, `[]`). Once this is done you can use the list's `append()` method to dynamically add items. The following code creates an empty list and then adds one of each object type that you have learned so far (a number, a string, and an empty list):

```
>>> mylist = []
>>> mylist.append(1)
>>> mylist.append("string")
>>> mylist.append([])
>>> mylist
[1, "string", []]
```

Although most programs you write will probably create empty lists in the beginning and dynamically fill them in as your program runs, sometimes you need to pre-populate lists with objects. To create a list containing elements you type in the open bracket and then a comma-separated list of each variable name (or expression that evaluates to an object) followed by the closing bracket. Here is a condensed version of the code you just wrote:

```
>>> mylist = [1, "string", []]
>>> mylist
[1, 'string', []]
```

Working with elements in a list

As in other sequence types, list elements can be accessed individually by using the sequence index notation. For example, `mylist[1]`, will return the second element in the list. The index of the first element is 0. So, if your list were 10 elements large, the last element's index would be 9. The difference between lists and strings in this regard is that string sequence elements are single characters, and list sequence elements can be any type of object that exists in Python.

```
>>> mylist = ['a','b','c']
>>> print mylist[1]
'b'
```

You can use an entry from a list just like you would use a normal variable. For example, you can change the value of an element in place, using the same method you use to set a variable to an object.

```
>>> mylist[1] = 'd'
>>> print mylist[1]
d
```

To access the last element of a list under most programming languages requires that you know the size of your list first. You then subtract one from the size to access the last element, subtract two to access the second to last element and so on. To determine the size of your list you use the built-in `len()` method, as in the next example:

```
>>> mylist = ['a','b','c','d']
>>> size = len(mylist)
>>> print size
4
>>> print mylist[size -1]
d
```

Accessing the element at the end of a list is done so often Python provides a shortcut. Normal indexing (using the elements position in the list to access it) is preformed from the beginning to the end. Using a negative index you can access the elements from end to beginning. To access the last element you would use an index of `-1`, as in `mylist[-1]`. To access the second to last element use `-2` and `-3` to access the third from last. You get the idea.

```
>>> mylist = [1,2,3,4]
>>> print mylist[-1]
4
```

A two-dimensional list is a list that has elements that are lists (say that three times fast). To work with the second lists third element, you would type `mylist[1][2]`. A list of any dimension (three, four, and so on) is accessed in the same manner. If this seems confusing, the following example should clear things up:

```
>>> list2d = [['a', 'b', 'c'],
...         ['d', 'e', 'f'],
...         ['g', 'h', 'i']]
>>> print list2d
[['a', 'b', 'c'], ['d', 'e', 'f'], ['g', 'h', 'i']]
>>> list2d[0]
['a', 'b', 'c']
>>> list2d[2][0]
'g'
```

Inserting elements into a list

We have already introduced you to list's `append()` method. This adds an element to the end of a list. You can also insert new items into any place in the list your heart desires. Using the aptly named `insert()` method, you can specify where in the list to insert your new item. When you insert an item, the size of the list is increased by one. All the items in the list, starting at the position you specified, are shifted to the right to make room for the new item.

To insert the value three into the third position in a list you would type `mylist.insert(2, 3)`. Remember that the third position is index referenced with index number 2.

```
>>> mylist = [1,2,4]
>>> print mylist
[1, 2, 4]
>>> mylist.insert(2,3)
>>> print mylist
[1, 2, 3, 4]
```

Similarly, to insert the number 100 to the beginning of the list you would type `mylist.insert(0, 100)`.

Slicing and dicing lists

Python sequences also provide another unique access method called slicing. Slicing allows you to work with a series of consecutive elements at once. Slices are written using a pair of indexes in between the brackets. For example `mylist[2:4]`, tells Python to return a new sub-list (or slice) from the list starting at index two and up to but not including index four. In other words `mylist[2:4]` returns a list containing the third and fourth elements in the list.

```
>>> mylist = [1,2,3,4,5,6,7,8,9,10]
>>> sublist = mylist[2:4]
>>> print sublist
[3,4]
```

Accessing elements using slice notation is something that all types in the sequence group share, including strings and tuples. So you can easily grab the first two characters in a string by using s[0:2].

Slices can sometimes be confusing if you forget that the first element in the sequence starts at position 0. This is why `mylist[2:4]` returns the third and fourth entries not the second and third.

There are a few other slice notations that are handy for you to know. Omitting the first index as in `mylist[:10]` is equivalent to `mylist[0:10]`. Omitting the second index in your slice is equivalent to saying slice from this index to the end. Finally, you can omit both the first and the second index, to make a copy of your list. Try playing with these examples in the interpreter:

```
>>> mylist = [1, 2, 3, 4]
>>> print mylist[:2]
[1, 2]
>>> print mylist[1:]
[2, 3, 4]
>>> print mylist[:]
[1, 2, 3, 4]
```

You can assign multiple entries in a list in one pass using a slice. In the next example we change the second and third entries in a list:

```
>>> mylist = ['a','b','c','d']
>>> mylist[1:3] = ['x', 'x']
>>> print mylist
['a', 'x', 'x', 'd']
```

Removing items from a list

What goes in might need to come out. Hence you can use the `del` statement to remove items from a list. You can either specify one item to remove or you can remove a whole selection at a time using a slice.

```
>>> mylist = ['a','b','c','d']
>>> del mylist[1]
>>> print mylist
['a', 'c', 'd']
>>> del mylist[1:]
>>> print mylist
['a']
```

Lists are mutable sequences. This means that they can be changed after they have been created. Strings, on the other hand, are immutable and so cannot be changed. For this reason, strings do not implement slice assignment or deletion, inserting, or appending. Immutable objects can always be replaced, though:

```
>>> x = "qwerty"
>>> x[2:4] = ['x', 'x']
Traceback (innermost last):
```

```
  File "<stdin>", line 1, in ?
TypeError: object doesn't support slice assignment
>>> x = x[0:2] + "xx" + x[4:6]
>>> x
'qwxxty'
>>>
```

Similarly, you can achieve the same result a bit more cleanly by converting the string into a list, manipulating it, and converting it back:

```
>>> import string
>>> x = "qwerty"
>>> xlist = list(x)
>>> xlist[2:4] = ['x', 'x']
>>> x = string.join(xlist, "")
>>> x
'qwxxty'
>>>
```

Tuples

Tuples share some of the characteristics of both strings and lists. Like lists, tuples are an ordered collection of arbitrary objects. Like strings, tuples are immutable, and so cannot be changed, only replaced.

Tuples use ordinary parentheses (for example, `'x(y, z)'`) to define its member sequence, unlike lists, which use square brackets.

Because tuples (like strings) are immutable, they do not support item or slice assignment, but they can be replaced:

```
>>> x = ('q', 'w', 'e', 'r', 't', 'y')
>>> x
('q', 'w', 'e', 'r', 't', 'y')
>>> x[2] = 'x'
TypeError: object doesn't support item assignment
>>> x = (x[0], x[1], 'x', x[3], x[4], x[5])
>>> x
('q', 'w', 'x', 'r', 't', 'y')
>>>
```

You can see from this example that tuples support element access by index, even though they don't allow slice or index assignment.

Because tuples use ordinary parentheses to surround their sequence definition, and parentheses are also used in Python to enclose expressions, an additional syntactical device must be used to distinguish single element tuples from expressions:

```
>>> x = 2
>>> y = 3
>>> z = (x + y)
```

```
>>> z
5
>>> z = (x + y, )
>>> z
(5,)
>>>
```

As you can see, you must use a trailing comma to create a single element tuple from the result of `x + y`, rather than simply assigning the result to the variable `z`.

Tuples, like lists, can hold any type of object, including lists and other tuples. This means that even though a tuple cannot itself be modified, its member elements can be modified, if they're of an appropriate type:

```
>>> x = (['1', '2', '3'], '123')
>>> x[0][1] = 'x'
>>> x
(['1', 'x', '3'], '123')
>>>
```

Dictionaries

Dictionaries are unordered collections of data. They use keys that you specify to store and retrieve items. This is different from lists where an items index is based upon its position in the list.

Lists excel at managing data that needs to be kept in order. A draw back to working with lists is that you need to know where the item is within the list. This isn't a problem if you are using a list as a queue or stack, where you either start at the beginning or end of the list and process one entry after the next. However, if you need to find a specific item (maybe you want to remove it from the list) you need to implement searching algorithms that are sometimes very complex.

Creating dictionaries

To create an empty dictionary you assign a variable to an empty set of braces. Dictionaries can also be pre initialized when they are created by using one or more `key:value` pairs separated by commas in between braces. Use these examples in the interpreter to get the feel for creating and using dictionaries.

```
>>> product = {'color': 'green', 'quantity': 10}
>>> print product
{'quantity': 10, 'color': 'green'}
>>> print product['quantity']
10
```

Adding and changing items

Instead of accessing an item in a dictionary based on its index, you access it by its key. A *key* is usually a string that you pick to uniquely identify the item in a dictionary. Unlike lists, dictionaries do not have an append method. To add an item to a dictionary you assign the value to a key. If there is an item already in the dictionary with the same key, it will be replaced. If the key does not exist, the key and the item will be added to the dictionary. Consider theses examples.

```
>>> d = {}
>>> d['John Doe'] = 40
>>> print d['John Doe']
40
>>> d['John Doe'] = 41
>>> print d['John Doe']
41
```

You can use numbers or any other immutable object as the keys instead of strings or a mix. In addition, instances of classes (we explain classes later in this chapter) that have a `__hash__()` method can be used as keys as well.

Removing items from a dictionary

Python's `del` statement is used to remove an item from a dictionary. Unlike lists, you can only remove one item at a time because dictionaries are unordered and do not support slicing, which depends on elements being in a particular order. However, dictionaries do support a `clear()` method to remove all items from a list at once.

```
>>> d = {'a' : 1, 'b' : 2, 'c' : 3}
>>> print d
{'b': 2, 'c': 3, 'a': 1}
>>> del d['b']
>>> print d
{'c': 3, 'a': 1}
>>> d.clear()
>>> print d
{}
```

Useful operations

Dictionaries provide a whole slew of operations that make finding out what's in them and manipulating their contents a snap. The examples in this section assume that you have created the following dictionary by typing this into the interpreter.

```
>>> d = {'color': 'red', 'size' : 'large', 'quantity' : 100}
```

✦ `has_key()`. This method is used to test if a particular item exists in a dictionary. It returns the value of 1 (true) if the item exists or 0 (false) if it doesn't.

```
>>> d.has_key('color')
1
>>> d.has_key('moose')
0
```

✦ `len`. This built-in function returns the number of items that are in a dictionary. Just like it does for lists.

```
>>> print len(d)
3
```

✦ `keys()`. This method returns a list of all the keys in the dictionary as in `dict.keys()`. This is useful for looping through the items of a dictionary. One caveat is that the order the keys are returned is not guaranteed. In the next example we give you a sneak preview of the `for` statement which lets you loop over a list of items.

```
>>> for x in d.keys():
...   print x
...
size
quantity
color
```

✦ `values()`. This method returns a list of all the values in a dictionary.

```
>>> for x in d.values():
...   print x
...
large
100
red
```

✦ `items()`. This method returns a list of list representing every key and value in the dictionary.

```
>>> for key, value in d.items():
...   print "Key: %s\tValue: %s" % (key, value)
...
Key: size       Value: large
Key: quantity   Value: 100
Key: color      Value: red
```

Control Statements

Now that you have learned the basic types, the last thing that you need to learn before you can write real programs are the statements that control the flow of your program. Python provides the `if` statement for performing evaluation, the `for` and `while` statements for looping, and the `def` statement for defining reusable functions.

An important note to keep in mind while reading this section is that how you indent your code determines how Python groups statements. Languages such as C, Perl, and Java use braces to group statements together. If you write a program in C that tests whether the "q" key was pressed, runs clean up code, and then quits, your code might look something like this:

```
if(key == "q"){
  do_cleanup();
  exit();
}
```

In C, all statements in between the opening and closing braces are part of one group (also known as block). C's `if` statement evaluates the expression and executes the statements within the group if it is true. In the previous example the functions `do_cleanup()` and `exit()` are ran only if the variable `key` is equal to the letter `"q"`. If `key` does not equal `"q"` the whole block of code is skipped.

Python, however, uses indentation to determine what statements are grouped together. Indenting can be done either with spaces or with the Tab key (one tab is equivalent to eight spaces). The snippet of code you wrote above would look like this in Python:

```
if key == "q":
  do_cleanup()
  exit()
```

Python knows that the `do_cleanup()` function and the `exit()` are to be run if key equals `"q"` because they are both indented two spaces under the `if` statement. Any code after the `if` statement that is not part of the `if` block will have the same indentation as the `if` statement.

In the next example, if the key does not equal the letter, `"q"` is printed to the screen.

```
if key == "q":
  do_cleanup()
  exit()

print key
```

It is important that you are consistent with your indentation. Each line in the same block must have the same indentation. If you have one line in an `if` statement that is indented with two spaces and one line that is indented four spaces a SyntaxError will be raised. Also pay attention when cutting and pasting. Sometimes when you paste text it is inserted in the wrong place and then you have to re-indent all of your code. The easiest way to avoid problems like this is to use a text editor that has Python support. We like XEmacs (available at `http://www.xemacs.org`) because it is available for both Windows and UNIX.

When editing Python code that was written on a different platform you might have a trouble with indentation. We have run into a problem sometimes with Python raising SyntaxErrors with code that looks correct. We only noticed this problem when we edit code on a UNIX-based system that was originally created on a Windows machine. The problem we discovered was due to the extra carriage return that ends every line in a Windows text file. When we tried to add new lines of code from a UNIX editor that only terminates lines with a single newline, our indentation was wrong. Python was counting on the carriage return to be there like the rest of the lines in the file. The solution was to strip the carriage returns from the file.

Most new users absolutely abhor this requirement because they are used to the conventional approach of grouping code in between braces or other delimiters. Trust us, if you give Python a shot you will grow to appreciate the benefits of indentation. Your code is easier to read because you are forced to indent your code. And you don't have to type as much.

Conditional testing with the If statement

Once you have stored data away into variables you can test their values and take different actions based on the test using the if clause.

Continuing our ridiculous "hello" example, modify your program to match the following code. In this listing we prompt the user to enter his or her name as before but this time we have included a test to determine whether the username is your best friend Bob, and if so, a special greeting is printed. If it is not Bob, the normal greeting prints.

```
best_friend = "Bob"
name = raw_input("What is your name? ")
if name == best_friend:
    print "Hello, " + name + ", I think you are swell!"
else:
    print "Hello, " + name + "!"
```

If you run the above example and enter `Bob` when it asks your name, your program will look something like this:

```
c:\temp\>python hello3.py
What is your name? Bob
Hello Bob, I think you are swell!
```

Now run the program again, but this time, enter a name other than Bob.

There are several new things we have introduced in this program. For starters, the first thing we do is create a variable and set it to the string containing the word, "Bob." You could have just as easily skipped this step and changed the line in your program from `if name == best_friend:` to `if name == "Bob":` and you would have seen the same results. The reason we do not do it this way is that it makes your program easier to maintain. Imagine that you have written a complicated program that makes several checks to see whether the user name matches "Bob". Now imagine that you had a falling out with Bob, maybe he told you that your program is silly, and you want to change your program so that it works for Sally (who happens to be a real program connoisseur). This would require that you run through the program and change every reference of "Bob" to "Sally", but if you had used a variable like we did (hurray for us) in the beginning of this program you would only have to change your program in one spot. You would set best_friend = "Sally" and be done.

The next new thing that you wrote in this program is line three, which reads, if name == best_friend: This statement tests to see whether the value of name equals whatever is stored in the best_friend variable. == is a value comparison. == will test to see whether two expressions have identical values.

If the test evaluates to true (for example, the input is equal to the content of the 'best_friend' variable), then the block of code indented under the if statement will execute. Some languages (such as BASIC) require an explicit then statement to specify what code to execute when the test evaluates to true. Because Python uses indentation to indicate block structure, this sort of device is unnecessary, along with other block delimiters.

In our case here, the code that executes when the if statement evaluates to true, is a print statement that outputs a greeting that indicates that you think the person is swell.

The else: statement

Continuing on down the program, we come to an else: statement, which contains code that executes when the if statement evaluates to false, or in other words, when the person's name does not match the name of your best friend.

The else: statement is optional. If the conditional does not evaluate to true, but no else: statement is present, the program does nothing.

The elif: statement

The elif: statement, like else:, is also optional. It is used when, upon evaluating an if: as false, you want to perform one or more other tests before executing some code. Continuing our "hello" example, modify the program to match the following code:

```
best_friend = "Bob"
worst_enemy = "Jimmy"
name = raw_input("What is your name? ")
if name == best_friend:
    print "Hello, " + name + ", I think you are swell!"
elif name == worst_enemy:
    print "I think you suck, " + name + "!"
else:
    print "Hello, " + name + "!"
```

Here you can see that if the name typed in by the user is not that of your best friend, the program then checks to see whether it matches that of your worst enemy. Only when the `elif:` statement also evaluates as false will the body of the `else:` statement be executed. In other words, the `else:` statement will be executed only if the name does not match your best friend's *or* your worst enemy's name.

While there can be only one `else:` statement following an `if` statement, you can have as many `elif:` statements as you need. The first condition that evaluates to true (whether it's the `if:` or an `elif:`) results in all the other conditions being ignored.

`elif` statements *must* be placed between the `if` and `else:` statements.

Nesting conditional statements

if/elif/else conditionals execute a single code block at most. More complex applications may require nesting conditionals. Consider the following program:

```
print "I can count to ten!"
number = raw_input("Give me a number:")
number = int(number)
if number >= 10:
    print "Wow, that's a big number!"
    if number == "10":
        print "That's a ten!"
    else:
        print "I can't count that high."
else:
    print "I know what that is!"
    if number == "1":
        print "That's a one!"
    elif number == "2":
        print "That's a two!"
    elif number == "3":
        print "That's a three!"
    elif number == "4":
        print "That's a four!"
    elif number == "5":
        print "That's a... umm... a six?"
    else:
        print "That's a... uhh... I'm not sure."
```

As you can see, this program doesn't count very well. Notice that the `if:` statements for dealing with single digits are never evaluated if the number input by the user is two or more digits long because they're nested within the first `else:` statement.

Similarly, the `if:` statement that tests whether the number is equal to "10" is never evaluated if the number is *shorter* than two digits.

By using nested conditionals in this way we avoided repeating some code, such as the printed statement that is impressed with "big" numbers of over 12 digits, and the one expressing a misplaced confidence with single digit numbers.

Looping

Python provides two loop constructs, `while` and `for`:

Looping with the While statement

The `while` statement is similar in syntax to the `if` statement. It starts with the keyword `while` and is followed by an expression and then a block of code. If the expression evaluates to true, the block of code following the while statement is executed. Unlike the `if` statement, after each statement in the while block has been evaluated, the whole process is started over again and continues until the expression evaluates to false. For example, the following statements print out the numbers one through ten and then quits:

```
>>> x = 0
>>> while x < 5:
...   x = x + 1
...   print x
...
1
2
3
4
5
>>>
```

It's very important to make sure that you do not set up a loop that will never have a valid exit condition. A loop without a valid exit condition, called an *infinite loop*, will continue indefinitely. Here is an example:

```
>>> x = 1
>>> while x > 0
...     x = x + 1
...     print x
...
```

This example, when run, will continue to increment `x` forever (or at least until the size limit for an integer is reached). You'll need to break the interpreter out of the loop manually by typing **^C** (in Windows) or **^Z** (in UNIX-based systems such as Linux).

The `while` statement also supports an optional `else` clause, which if present, is executed before the loop quits.

```
>>> l = ["dog", "cat", "frog", "horse"]
>>> while l:
...    print l[0]
...    del l[0]
... else:
...    print "List is empty!"
...
dog
cat
frog
horse
List is empty!
```

Looping with the For statement

We gave you a sneak peek of the `for` statement when we discussed lists. The `for` statement is used to loop through each item of a sequence (string, tuple, or list). The syntax is `for` *`variable`* `in` *`expression`*`:`. Just as with the `while` statement, you can optionally define an `else` clause. The following example loops through and prints out each animal from the list animals:

```
>>> animals = ["dog", "cat", "frog", "horse"]
>>> for animal in animals:
...    print animal
... else:
...    print "List is empty!"
...
dog
cat
frog
horse
List is empty!
```

As the `for` statement loops through the list, it assigns the variable `animal` to the next item and then prints out the value of `animal`. The first time through the list the `animal` variable is created.

The expression in a `for` loop needs to evaluate to a sequence. If it does not, a `TypeError` will be raised. Unlike the `while` loop, the expression in a `for` loop is only evaluated once at the beginning of the statement not every time.

It is unwise to modify the sequence you are looping over inside the `for` loop. If you need to modify your list, iterate over a sliced copy instead. For example:

```
>>> animals = ["dog", "cat", "frog", "horse"]
>>> for animal in animals[:]:
...    if animal == "cat":
...      animals.remove("cat")
```

```
...
>>> print animals
['dog', 'frog', 'horse']
```

Nesting loops

You can nest loops in order to repeat one sequence of actions within another sequence of actions:

```
>>> x = ["two", "three", "four"]
>>> animals = ["dog", "cat", "frog"]
>>> for animal in animals:
...     for y in x:
...         s = y + " " + animal + "s"
...         print s
...
two dogs
three dogs
four dogs
two cats
three cats
four cats
two frogs
three frogs
four frogs
>>>
```

You can see here that the outer loop iterates over the list of animals, and within each animal, loops through the list of numbers. For each number, the current number and current animal are printed.

Breaking and continuing in a loop

Python provides two methods to stop the execution of statements in the middle of a `for` or `while` statement. These are the `break` and the `continue` statement. The `break` statement immediately exits the innermost `for` or `while` statement and run the next statement outside of the loop. The `else` clause of the loop is ignored. The `continue` clause, on the other hand, ignores the rest of the statements in the block and will return to the top of the loop.

Take a look at `break` in action. In this example each animal is printed until the animal equals "frog."

```
>>> animals = ['dog', 'cat', 'frog', 'horse']
>>> for animal in animals:
...   if animal == 'frog':
...     break
...   else:
...     print animal
...
dog
cat
```

Use the same code but this time, substitute `continue` for the `break` statement. Notice that instead of quitting and not printing "frog" or "horse," the code skips over the "frog" entry and prints "horse."

```
>>> animals = ['dog', 'cat', 'frog', 'horse']
>>> for animal in animals:
...   if animal == 'frog':
...     continue
...   else:
...     print animal
...
dog
cat
horse
```

Functions

Functions are the foundation of any programming language. Functions let you define reusable sets of routines that can turn complex tasks into simple, one-line statements. Without them programmers would constantly be recreating code that is hard to read and even harder to maintain.

Python provides a whole slew of built-in functions for your convenience. We have introduced you to some of them, such as `int()`, `len()`, and `raw_input()`. Even more functions are available to you, which are part of the normal Python distribution. We explain how to use some of these functions in the section, "Modules and Packages" later in this chapter. But first we show you how to create and use your own function.

Defining functions

To create a function in Python you use the `def` statement. The syntax for a function is `def` *`function`*`([arg1], [arg2], ... [argX]):` followed by a block of code to be executed when a function is called. When Python encounters a `def` statement it creates a function object assigned to the function name you specified. For example, to create a function that prints your favorite saying, "Hello, world!" you would type the following:

```
>>> def hello():
...   print "Hello, world!"
...
>>>
```

Now, whenever you wan to print out "Hello, world!" you can just call the `hello()` function you created:

```
>>> hello()
Hello, world!
```

Passing variables to functions

You can specify that a function takes one or more arguments. This way you can pass the function variables to work with. For example, you can change the `hello()` function that you defined earlier to take an argument called `name`. Now your function can greet a specific person.

```
>>> def hello(name):
...     print "Hello, %s!" % name
...
>>> hello("Bob")
Hello, Bob!
```

To define a function that takes more than one argument, create a list of arguments separated by commas in between the parentheses. Try modifying the `hello()` function to take multiple arguments. The first argument will be the name of the person to whom you are saying hello. The second argument will be how many times to say hello.

```
>>> def hello(name, count):
...     for x in range(count):
...       print "Hello, %s!" % name
...
>>> hello("Bob", 2)
Hello, Bob!
Hello, Bob!
```

The previous bit of code uses a function called range. It's one of the built-in functions we mentioned. The `range` function produces a list of sequential numbers. To get a feel for how it works, enter `range(10)` in the interpreter.

The order that you pass arguments into a function must be the same order in which they were defined. If you tried to call the `hello()` function like this, `hello(2, "Bob")`, Python would assign the argument called `name` to the value of 2 and `count` would be assigned the string `"Bob"`.

Naming arguments

We were fibbing when we said that the order you pass arguments to a function must be the same order in which they were defined. Python provides a way to specify arguments out of order, called *keyword arguments*. Keyword arguments lets you specify which value is associated with which argument by using the form *`argument = value`*. For example, to switch up the order of the arguments you use to call the `hello()` function you would type:

```
>>> hello(count=2, name="Bob")
Hello, Bob!
Hello, Bob!
```

It is easy to accidentally mix-up the order of parameters when calling a function, especially if the function takes a lot of arguments. Python can sometimes detect that you passed the arguments in the wrong order, such as if you passed a number where a list was expected, but Python has no way to tell whether two strings (or two numbers) are flip-flopped. In theory, using keyword arguments would help you to avoid these kinds of errors because you can look at the function and know which value is being used for what in a function. In practice, passing arguments in the right position is less verbose, so keyword arguments don't always get used.

There are a couple of rules to follow in order to use keyword arguments and to keep Python happy. The first rule is that once you use a keyword argument when calling a function every other argument must be passed as a keyword. Python will raise a SyntaxError if you called the `hello()` function like `hello(count=1, "Bob")`. However, it is not an error to call the function like this, `hello("Bob", count=2)` because the non-keyword argument was passed first.

The second rule is that it is an error to use the same keyword twice. For instance, you can't call the function like `hello("Bob", name="Bob", count=3)`.

Assigning arguments default values

It is possible to specify a default value for a functions argument. You do not need to pass an argument to a function if it has default value. For instance, you can modify the `hello()` function so that name and count both have reasonable defaults.

```
>>> def hello(name="World", count=1):
...   for x in range(count):
...     print "Hello, %s!" % name
...
>>> hello()
Hello, world!
>>> hello("Frank")
Hello, Frank!
>>> hello("Frank", 3)
Hello, Frank!
Hello, Frank!
Hello, Frank!
```

Once you specify a default value for one argument all of the following arguments must have defaults.

The default value is only evaluated once. The drawback is that any changes made to a mutable object (such as list or dictionary) will be remembered. For instance, if you defined a function whose argument is defaulted to an empty list, every time you make changes to that list they are remembered the next time the function is called.

```
>>> def myFunction(x, mylist=[]):
...   mylist.append(x)
...   print mylist
...
```

```
>>> myFunction(1)
[1]
>>> myFunction(2)
[1, 2]
>>> myFunction(3)
[1, 2, 3]
```

This may cause problems if you expect `mylist` to be empty every time. The way around this is default `mylist` to `None` and then in your function set `mylist` to an empty list if it is the default.

```
>>> def myFunction(x, mylist=None):
...   if mylist is None:
...     mylist = []
...   mylist.append(x)
...   print mylist
...
>>> myFunction(1)
[1]
>>> myFunction(2)
[2]
>>> myFunction(3)
[3]
```

Returning values from a function

To return a value from a function use the `return` *`expression`* statement. Python exits the function and passes the object that expression evaluates to back to the caller. To get an idea how this works, create a function that computes the sum of two numbers and returns the results.

```
>>> def sum(x,y):
...   return x + y
...
>>> x = sum(10, 2)
>>> print x
12
```

Like the `break` statements in loops, any statements made after the `return` is ignored. Functions that do not return any values but need to quit before processing remaining statements can call return with no expression, in which case the value `None` is returned.

None is always returned when a function ends without using the `return` statement.

Assigning functions to names

Functions, like almost everything else in Python, are objects. By creating a function with the `def` statement you are actually creating a name that points to an object in the current namespace. If you defined the `sum()` function from the previous example you can manipulate it like other objects. For example, you can print it out or assign it to another name. You can use a variable that has been assigned a function like a normal function.

```
>>> def sum(x, y):
...     return x + y
...
>>> print sum
<function sum at 823ca8>
>>> print sum(2, 1)
3
>>> foo = sum
>>> foo(2, 5)
7
```

This demonstrates the difference between calling a function and using its reference. When you call a function you add the open and close parentheses to the end of a function. For example, `myfunction()`. Where as myfunction (without parentheses) tells Python that you are manipulating the function instead of its results.

This ability can lead to some interesting possibilities, such as appending several functions that transform data into a list. In the next example we create three functions. The first two functions perform minor calculations on whatever argument is passed to the function. The third function sticks these two functions into a list. When the third function is called and passed a number, it loops through the list and calls each function to transform the data.

```
>>> def subtracttwo(x):
...     return x - 2
...
>>> def multiplybyitself(x):
...     return x * x
...
>>> def transform(x, transformations=[subtracttwo,
multiplybyitself]):
...     for trans in transformations:
...       x = trans(x)
...     return x
...
>>> transform(10)
64
```

Arbitrary arguments

The last things we need to introduce in order to wrap up our discussion on Python functions are two ways to pass arbitrary arguments to a function. The first method lets you pass more arguments to a function than you have defined by prefixing an argument with an asterisk.

```
>>> def foo(*args):
...     for arg in args:
...      print arg
...
>>> foo(1,2,3)
1
2
3
```

The second method collects all keyword arguments that don't have a corresponding argument in the function definition into a dictionary. To specify what dictionary to store these arguments in you include an argument that is prefixed with two asterisks, as in the following example:

```
>>> def foo(**kw):
...   print kw
...
>>> foo(bar=10, blah="test")
{'blah': 'test', 'bar': 10}
```

You can specify normal arguments but they must be created at the beginning of the definition and there can be only one of each type of special argument in a function definition.

Understanding Namespaces

Before we progress from writing functions to higher-level constructs, some discussion is warranted on exactly what names mean in Python.

Whenever Python first comes across a name, the interpreter first looks in the local namespace for it, then in the global namespace, and finally in the built-in namespace, stopping at the first successful lookup.

Namespaces, then, are where names "live." Because names can be assigned and created without first being declared, the namespace a name lives in is determined by where it is assigned.

Namespaces within functions

Functions define a local namespace that will be looked in first when a variable is used. This is why you can define an *x* variable in two different functions where one function defines it as a list, and the other as a string, without a name conflict arising.

Because local namespaces are examined first, it's important not to define local names that are identical to those defined in other namespaces, such as the built-in namespace. So, for example, you shouldn't define a variable named `int` as that will override the built-in Python `int` function and make it unavailable within your function.

Global namespaces are defined at the module level. While we have not yet discussed writing modules, the top level of the interactive prompt is also considered a module, so we can demonstrate fairly easily:

```
>>> x = 5
>>> def func():
...     y = 6
...     x = 2
...     z = x + y
...     return z
...
>>> func()
8
>>> x
5
>>>
```

Here you first defined a global variable named x and assigned the value 5 to it. Next you defined a function, `func()`, that established its own local namespace, and created three local variables *y*, *x*, and *z*, assigning them values of 6, 2, and *x* + *y*, respectively. The `func()` function returns the value of `z`, so when we call it, we get 8 (6 +2).

Notice that while the local namespace overrides the global namespace, it does not replace it. When we call `x` again outside of the function, it still returns the value assigned to it at the beginning of the session.

Let's try something a little different:

```
>>> def func():
...     y = 6
...     z = x + y
...     return z
...
>>> func()
11
>>>
```

In this case, we did not create a local variable named x, so the interpreter, after looking in the local namespace, looked in the global namespace, where it found the *x* variable we defined earlier, and used its value when calculating *z*.

Creating and manipulating global variables

Interestingly, y and z don't even exist except while the `func()` function is executed.

```
>>> y
Traceback (innermost last):
  File "<interactive input>", line 1, in ?
NameError: There is no variable named 'y'
>>> z
Traceback (innermost last):
  File "<interactive input>", line 1, in ?
NameError: There is no variable named 'z'
>>>
```

There is also a way for a function to modify the value of a global variable, which can be used as an alternative to returning a result:

```
>>> x = 5
>>> z = None
>>> def func():
...      y = 6
...      global z
...      z = x+y
...
>>> z
>>> func()
>>> z
11
>>>
```

Here, we've shown you the use of the `global` statement. This statement caused the `z` variable assignment within the function to modify the value of the `z` variable in the global namespace, rather than creating a local variable. Note that the global statement will create a new variable in the global namespace if the name in question does not already exist within the global namespace.

Modules and Packages

We've hinted before that Python provides a way of reusing code. The way that Python provides this is through the use of *modules*.

Modules have several roles in Python. They enable you to do several important tasks, such as:

- ✦ Reuse your code within a project
- ✦ Isolate names within namespaces to avoid conflicts
- ✦ Reuse code across different projects

So, what are modules good for?

- ✦ **Reusing code within a project.** Modules enable you to define data structures and logic that are reused within several places within your project. This can be something simple, such as a list of U.S. state codes and state names, or something more complex, such as a custom sorting algorithm, or a special string processing function.
- ✦ **Isolating names within namespaces.** Python doesn't have a higher level of program organization than the module. Executed code and class instances are enclosed (wrapped) by their module. As a result, functions that are defined at the module level can be used by all of the code within that module, and will not conflict with functions defined in other modules that have the same name.
- ✦ **Reusing code across different projects.** Python modules can use the code and data in other modules be explicitly importing them.

Using modules

A module must be imported first in order to use any of its routines, classes, or variables in your script. You do this using the cleverly named `import` statement. When Python encounters this statement in your code it first checks to see whether the module has already been loaded in memory. If it hasn't, Python searches the module path for the first occurrence of a file with the same name as the module that you want to import. The file must either end in .py or .pyc. Python then attempts to parse the script. If it doesn't encounter any errors, it will create a name in the local namespace that matches the name of the file.

Loading the `hello` script in the previous interpreter is an example of using the `import` statement. To refresh your memory, import the string module. The string module provides a collection of useful (and optimized) methods for manipulating strings.

```
>>> import string
```

Once you have imported a module into the current namespace you can access the names in that module using the "." or dot operator. For instance, use the `split()` method from the `string` module we just imported:

```
>>> string.split("All good men")
['All', 'good', 'men']
```

As you can see, the split string is returned as a list of strings.

Playing with the module path

When you attempt to `import` a module, the interpreter searches for the module by name within the module path. You can see what module path Python is searching by examining the `path` attribute of the `sys` module:

```
>>> import sys
>>> sys.path
['', '/usr/lib/python1.5', '/usr/lib/python1.5/plat-linux-
i386', '/usr/lib/python1.5/site-packages',
'/usr/lib/python1.5/site-packages/PIL']
```

The result of `sys.path` will depend on how your system is set up.

By appending a directory of your choosing to the `path`, you can make your modules available for importing:

```
>>> import sys
>>> sys.path.append('/usr/local/me/python-modules')
>>> sys.path
['', '/usr/lib/python1.5', '/usr/lib/python1.5/plat-linux-
i386', '/usr/lib/python1.5/site-packages',
'/usr/lib/python1.5/site-packages/PIL', ('/usr/local/me/python-
modules']
```

Python searches the directories in the order in which they are defined in the path list. If you have two modules in different directories, the module in the directory that is at the head of the list will be found first.

Importing specific names from modules

Besides importing modules wholesale, you can import individual names with great specificity by using the `from module import name` syntax. This has the advantage of not having to qualify the specified names when they're used:

```
>>>from string import split
>>>split("more good men")
['more', 'good', 'men']
```

If you need to import all of a module's exported attributes but don't want to specify them all individually, Python has a special syntax: `from module import *`.

```
>>>from string import *
>>>join(['aren\'t', 'there', 'good', 'women', 'too?'])
'aren't there good women too?'
```

There is an exception to the `from module import *` syntax: names in modules that begin with an underscore (_) will not be imported into your module.

Creating and using packages

So, what do you do if you want to create and distribute several modules together? It may not make sense to stuff the modules into a single file, because even though they import from each other, you nevertheless may want to import form them separately. The answer is to use a *package*.

A package is a directory containing one or more modules and possibly further subdirectories. Just as a module derives its name from the .py file that contains its code, Packages derive their name from the directory name. Packages also help resolve namespace conflicts between imported modules.

Packages have one other requirement: they must contain a file named `__init__.py`, which fulfills two functions:

- ✦ Python requires a package directory to contain an `__init__.py` file for it to be recognized as a package, even if the `__init__.py` file is empty. This prevents just any directory containing some Python files from accidentally being recognized as a package and loaded.
- ✦ The `__init__.py` file can contain code that runs the first time the package is loaded, making it possible to do initialization of whatever code the programmer wants.

Create a `/helloproject` package directory in one of the directories from your Python installation's PYTHONPATH environment variable (for example, in the `/site-packages` directory), if you have one.

Then create an empty `__init__.py` file in the `/site-packages/helloproject` directory.

Now, create a `hellocode.py` file containing the following code:

```
def hello(name="World", count=1):
    for x in range(count):
        print "Hello, %s!" % name
```

One problem new programmers often run into is creating a package, module, and class that all have the same name. For example, imagine that you have a package, module, and class all named "Klass." If you want to use the class you would need to type from klass.klass import klass. A common coding mistake would be to type from klass import klass instead, and then try to instansiate Klass objects. But because you imported the module from the package, and did not import the class explicitly, this will not work and you would have to instantiate Klass.Klass instances. It's much better to name your packages, modules, and classes with distinct names instead to avoid this confusion.

Now, import the package, using the same syntax that you used to import a module:

```
>>>from helloproject import *
>>>from hellocode import *
Traceback (innermost last)
  File "<interactive input>", line 0, in ?
NameError: hellocode
>>>
```

Oops.

As this demonstrates, packages do not automatically import their contained files even when you use the `from package import *` syntax. Because some file systems are case-sensitive and others are not, you need to tell Python what names to expose to a request to get all importable objects. This is done by adding an `__all__` list into the `__init__.py` file, like so:

```
__all__ = [hellocode, goodbyecode]
```

Note that this is not entirely necessary. If you want to import objects more explicitly, you can still do so without using `__all__`:

```
>>>from helloproject import hellocode
>>>hellocode.hello()
Hello, World!
>>>
```

And you can drill down with even more accuracy like this:

```
>>>from helloproject.hellocode import hello
>>>hello()
Hello, World!
>>>
```

You should use the `__all__` attribute in your `__init__.py` files when you intend the entire package to be imported using `from package import *`.

While it may seem reasonable to "hide" names form being imported by failing to include them in the `__all__` list, this is actually a bad idea. Instead, names that need to remain private should begin with an underscore (_), as was discussed earlier in this chapter.

Examining the contents of a namespace with dir()

Let's say you want to find out what names are defined in an imported module, regardless of whether that module was in a package. You could examine the module's code directly, but that can be tedious and repetitive. Aren't computers good at automating repetitive tasks? Yes they are.

```
>>> from helloproject import hellocode
>>> dir(hellocode)
['__builtins__', '__doc__', '__file__', '__name__', 'hello']
```

The `dir()` function returns a list of all the names in the module. It's not limited to just modules either. For example, you can get a list of everything in the current namespace by calling `dir()` with no arguments, or you can use it on the objects that you create later in this chapter.

Understanding .pyc files

One of the side effects you may have noticed while working through the previous sections is that when you import a module (whether it's in a package or not), another file is created on the file system with the same name as the module, but ending in .pyc instead of .py.

.pyc files are Python bytecode files. *Bytecodes* are the instructions the Python interpreter runs on directly, and are created whenever a module is imported by another module. If a .pyc file is present for the module that the interpreter is trying to import, and the .pyc file is not older than the .py file, the .pyc file is loaded directly, saving the bytecode compilation time.

.pyc files can be used as a form of pre-compiled binary library. They can be imported into other modules and used in a portable fashion, as the interpreter will import a .pyc file if no .py file can be found.

Classes and Objects

You can create your own objects in Python. These objects can mimic the objects described in the section, "Types and Operators" earlier in this chapter, or you can define completely new behavior. Usually most programs create objects that describe things in real life. For example, imagine creating a program to keep track of the names and numbers of your friends. You might create an address book object that contains several person objects. Each person object would contain the name of the person and his or her phone number.

All user-defined objects in Python are instances of a class. Classes define how objects are created and what attributes and methods they have. In our imaginary application the address book and person are each examples of classes. For instance, the person class would define that all person objects will have a name and a phone number. The Address book would define methods, which are special types of functions that you, the programmer, would use to add and remove people from your address book.

You can visualize the relationship of classes and objects by imagining that classes are like cookie cutters. Once you have created a cookie cutter you can use it to stamp out multiple cookies.

Defining a new class

Classes are defined using the `class` statement as follows:

```
>>> class person:
...    firstName='Bob'
```

This statement creates a class in the current namespace called "person." Like functions and modules, each class gets its own private namespace. In this particular class we created the name called `firstName` and assigned it to the string, `Bob`. You can access and manipulate the namespace of a class just like you can with modules. For instance, you can print out the value of `firstName` from the person class:

```
>>> print person.firstName
Bob
```

Once you have defined a class you can create a new instance of the class by using the open and close parentheses. This is identical to how you would call a function.

```
>>> x = person()
>>> print x.firstName
Bob
```

Class scope versus object scope

Instances of classes get their own private namespaces. In addition, they share the namespace of their class. This means that when you are looking at attribute `x` on object `person` (in other words, `person.x`) Python first searches the object's private namespace for the attribute and if it doesn't find it there, looks for the attribute in the class.

If you assign the instance's attribute to a different value, the value is only changed in the instance's namespace and not in the classes. For example:

```
>>> x.firstName = 'Frank'
>>> print x.firstName
Frank
>>> print person.firstName
Bob
```

Assigning a new value to an instance attribute only changes that attribute. But if you modify the value of an attribute of a class, all instances that haven't overridden the attribute (as you did in the previous example) will be changed as well. In the next example you will create a couple of instances of the person class and reassign the `firstName` attribute at instance level and at the object level.

```
>>> p1 = person()
>>> p2 = person()
>>> print person.firstName, p1.firstName, p2.firstName
Bob Bob Bob
>>> p1.firstName = 'Frank'
>>> person.firstName = 'Sally'
>>> print person.firstName, p1.firstName, p2.firstName
Sally Frank Sally
>>>
```

Methods

Methods are functions that are bound to an object. In other words, methods know which specific object invoked the method. Methods are created by defining functions in the block part of a class definition. Unlike normal functions, every method must define at least one argument. This first argument is always assigned to the value of the object for which the method was invoked. You do not need to pass this argument. Python does it for you. Traditionally this argument is named "self."

The next couple of examples will be easier to work with if you create your classes in a file instead of directly in the interpreter. That way you do not have to completely rewrite the class definition every time you make a change. In the next couple of examples we assume that you will create your classes in file named `person.py`. To begin with, modify `person.py` as follows:

```
class person:
  firstName = 'Bob'
  lastName  = 'Flanders'

  def fullName(self):
    return self.firstName + ' ' + self.lastName
```

Now import the module into the interpreter, create a person object, and try out your first method.

```
>>> from person import person
>>> a = person()
>>> print a.fullName()
Bob Flanders
>>> a.firstName = 'Sally'
>>> print a.fullName()
Sally Flanders
```

As you can see, `self` is bound to the new instance you created. When you change that instance's attributes, the value returned by `fullName()` is changed as well.

Controlling how classes are initialized with __init__

Sometimes it is not always practical to initialize attributes of an object as you did with the `firstName` and `lastName` attributes. For instance, you may want to make it a requirement that when a person object is created, the first name and last name must be set. Python lets you define a method named `__init__` that is called whenever a new instance is created. In OOP (object-oriented programming) speak this is known as a *constructor method.* Rewrite your class to use `__init__` method:

```
class person:
  def __init__(self, firstName, lastName):
    self.firstName = firstName
    self.lastName = lastName
  def fullName(self):
    return self.firstName + ' ' + self.lastName
```

Now, whenever you create a new instance of the person class you must pass in a first name and a last name.

```
>>> a = person('Bob', 'Dylan')
>>> a.fullName()
'Bob Dylan'
```

One thing to note is that we removed the `firstName` and `lastName` from the classes namespace so that you can no longer access `person.firstName`. Although there are legitimate uses for using attributes at the class level, using the constructor function is the preferred method for initializing attributes.

Inheritance

Creating classes and class instances is only one aspect of object-orientation. Another important aspect is *inheritance*. Inheritance saves time because you can create common functionality in a base class and have another class inherit from it; you will not need to rewrite or copy any of the code. (Just like when you try to access an attribute in an object instance's namespace and if it's not there Python checks to see if it is in class's namespace.) Python also checks to see whether the name is in any of the base classes.

In Python, inheritance is accomplished fairly simply in the class definition. Consider the following rewritten `person.py` file:

```
from string import join

class person:
    def __init__(self, firstName='Bill', lastName='Bob'):
        self.firstName = firstName
        self.lastName = lastName
    def fullName(self):
        return join([self.firstName, self.lastName])
```

```
class employee(person):
    def __init__(self, firstName='Bill', lastName='Bob',
phoneExtension='000'):
        person.__init__(self, firstName, lastName)
        self.phoneExtension = phoneExtension
```

As you can see, the class definition of `employee` states that it is a kind of `person`. The employee class now has three parameters that it expects, along with default values for missing parameters. What the `employee` class does not have is the initialization code for the `firstName` and `lastName` attributes, and the `fullName` method definition. It is inheriting these from the person class. Also notice that the `__init__` method of the person class is explicitly called from within the `__init__` method of the employee class.

Let's test the new employee class:

```
>>> from person import employee
>>> a = employee('Jimbo', 'Jones', '002')
>>> a.fullName()
'Jimbo Jones'
>>>
```

Great! Our `employee` class has demonstrably inherited both the initialization code and the methods of its parent class, `person`.

It might seem that you've only saved a few lines of code in the employee class by having it inherit from the person class. This is true, but this example is a trivial one. The more complex the person class is, the greater the benefit of inheriting from it, rather than reimplementing the same functionality in the employee class. In particular, you can inherit from other people's classes that you install as third-party packages on your system. Some classes in third-party modules and packages run to thousands of lines of code. Using inheritance in such circumstances can lead to enormous savings in time.

Exception Handling

Whenever Python encounters an error it raises an exception (you can create custom exceptions as well). Your program will quit if your program does not explicitly handle it. The benefit from using an exception is that it forces you not to ignore errors. Compare this to the more traditional approach of error handling where you call a function and you must check the return value of the function. If the return value is not checked, it's possible that the error condition will cause other errors in the program.

Using the try statement

Various tasks you've been doing with Python so far can fail for various reasons. For example, you could attempt to import a module from code that does not exist in your Python installation.

Let's suppose, for example, that you've written a Python module that depends on a third-party module called `superstring`:

```
from superstring import *
```

When this fails, the interpreter will give you a not-very-helpful warning:

```
Traceback (most recent call last):
  File "C:\Python20\helloproject\person.py", line 2, in ?
    from superstring import *
ImportError: No module named superstring
```

Here's how to make this error message a bit more helpful:

```
try:
    from superstring import *
except:
    print 'you need the superstring third party module, from
www.super-string.org'
```

Now, when you try running the program, the raised exception is caught by the `try` statement, and the more helpful message is printed out at the console.

The except object

The previous example also introduced the except: clause. We'll deal with the details of this clause shortly, but meanwhile it's worthwhile to explain just what is happening here.

When Python encounters an error such as the one we've demonstrated, it "raises" an exception object. This exception object actually has a bit of data associated with it, which can be used for various purposes. Most important is the exception name. The code above could just as easily been written `except ImportError:` and achieved the same result, but what if there is more than one exception possible? Similarly, the exception object can have other data associated with it that can be helpful in analyzing failures, or put to other uses.

It's important to note that exception objects that are raised that do not get caught by try/except clauses continue to propagate upward until they manifest themselves at the top level, which runs the default action of producing a traceback.

Catching exceptions

The except clause can have several forms:

- ✦ except:
- ✦ except name:
- ✦ except name, variable:
- ✦ except (name1, name2):

The first, second, and fourth forms are fairly self-explanatory. The first catches all exceptions, the second catches an exception with a particular name, and the fourth catches exceptions whose names appear in the list of arguments.

The third form catches a named exception, but also catches optional data in a variable. The `raise` statement, which we will introduce in a moment, must pass this optional data, or it isn't available.

Using else: with try

The `else` clause of a try statement pretty much works the way it does in conditional statements and iterators. That is, they contain code that runs if no exceptions are raised by the code in the try block. While there may be several except blocks, there should only be a single else in a try. Modify the code as follows:

```
try:
    from string import join
except ImportError:
    print 'you need the string'
else:
    print 'you\'ve got string!'
```

Running this code produces the expected result of `'you've got string!'` at the command line, as an `ImportError` was not raised.

The finally clause

The finally clause is one that runs whether an exception is raised or not, on the way out of the try clause. It cannot be used with except: or else: clauses, but is a good way of adding additional commentary that will be displayed before the top level runs a traceback on the raised exception:

```
try:
    from superstring import *
finally:
    print 'get superstring at www.super-string.org\n'
```

This will produce the following result:

```
get superstring at www.super-string.org

Traceback (most recent call last):
  File "C:\Python20\helloproject\person.py", line 3, in ?
    from superstring import *
ImportError: No module named superstring
```

Raising exceptions

So far, we've shown you how to catch built-in exceptions that the Python interpreter can raise, but for more sophisticated flow control, you need to be able to raise your own custom exceptions, as well. This is done with the raise statement.

The following code demonstrates the use of the raise statement, along with handling optional data:

```
customException = 'Error'

def failedFunc():
    raise customException, "failure"

try:
    failedFunc()
except customException, report:
    print 'failedFunc reported: ', report
```

This produces the following output when run:

```
failedFunc reported:  failure
```

In this way, you can use custom exceptions to handle special cases within your code (such as input validation) by raising the appropriate exceptions and catching them, rather than having to pepper your code with special case handling code everywhere.

Where Do I Go From Here?

You can find some good libraries online at the following Web sites:

✦ **http://www.vex.net/parnassus/.** This is an extensive resource of third-party programs modules and packages for Python.

✦ **http://www.pythonware.com/products/pil/.** A popular image-processing library.

✦ **http://www.python.org/sigs/.** Python Special Interest Groups (SIGs). Python is useful for a great many different problem domains, and SIGs exists for such diverse topics as XML, databases, and internationalization.

A few other books that we would recommend include:

✦ *Python Bible* (Hungry Minds, Inc., 2001) by Dave Brueck and Stephen Tanner

✦ *Learning Python* (O'Reilly & Associates, Inc., 1999) by Mark Lutz and David Ascher

✦ *Core Python Programming* (Prentice Hall, PTR, 2000) by Wesley J. Chun

How will this help you using Zope?

As Zope is written in Python, knowledge of Python is necessary in order to extend Zope significantly.

For example, Python expressions in DTML can be used to join several variables into a single string using join. It is clear that PARENTS[-1] refers to the last item in the PARENTS sequence.

We discuss the PARENTS list in Chapter 14.

Most significantly complex programming needs to happen either inside a Python Script object, or in an external method. DTML is really not suited to complex programming tasks. Third-party modules must also be imported into an external method to be used from within Zope.

Furthermore, when you want to develop Python Products for Zope, you will find that they are basically packages that define classes, which inherit from existing Zope base classes.

Summary

This chapter has only been a very brief introduction to Python and object-oriented programming, intended in helping you get more out of Zope than you could otherwise. You have learned the Python syntax, basic Python data-types, operators, functions, and flow control. You learned about creating and importing modules, packages, and how Python allows object-oriented design with Classes and inheritance. You also learned about exceptions, which allow more sophisticated flow control and error handling.

✦ ✦ ✦

Building Zope Products

PART

✦ ✦ ✦ ✦

In This Part

✦ ✦ ✦ ✦

From Packages to Products

In This Chapter

Creating a Hello World package

Publishing objects

Changing a package into a product

Instantiating your object

Adding DTML methods

Processing form submissions and returning

In chapters 6 through 10 we are going to roll up our sleeves and get into the nitty-gritty details of writing a Zope application, but we are going to build this application in a nontraditional manner. Usually when building a Web site you would create the site using Zope through the Web interface (or through FTP), and you would use the components that are supplied with Zope (those discussed in Chapter 3), or other third-party components. So, for example, a perfectly functional address book application can be built using nothing more than DTML Documents, Folders, and DTML Methods, or with a combination of Page Templates and Python Scripts, but the resulting application would be extremely hard to reuse and upgrade to new versions. An improvement would be to use ZClasses (as described in Chapter 16) to define any new object types you might want, and this would certainly improve the reusability of your application, but it would still be extremely difficult to upgrade to a newer version.

If you are already familiar with Zope, you might be wondering why we decided to stick the chapters for building custom products in the middle of the book when it is customary to have these chapters at the end or even in another book. The reason we are taking you down the path less traveled first is because we feel that if we introduce you to the fundamental principles of Zope that are exposed at the component level, these principles will be easier for you to understand when we introduce some of Zope's other nuances — nuances that are typically described as "black magic" by first-time users of Zope, but are easily understood if you are already familiar with the concepts of Python programming.

If you are not a programmer or are only interested in building a simple site, feel free to skip over these chapters.

In Chapter 5, we introduced you to the basics of Python programming and object-oriented features. Specifically, you learned how to create and use Modules and Packages, and how to define and use Classes. While general Python programming skills are useful for working with Zope (such as in creating Python Script objects or external methods), understanding Packages is a necessary first step toward creating your own Python Zope products, and new Zope Object types are defined in products using Classes. If you've jumped directly to this section of the book without reading Chapter 5 and aren't already familiar with Python programming, we suggest you go back and read Chapter 5 now, before continuing. Don't worry, we'll wait for you right here.

Back so soon? See, Python wasn't difficult to learn, was it? Let's move on.

What's a Product?

Products are pre-packaged add-ons to Zope. They are most often custom objects that have some useful combination of functionality and presentation. Once the product is installed, you can add these objects to your Zope site through the management interface just like any of the built-in objects by using the Add Objects drop-down menu.

An example of a popular Zope Product is the Photo product (`http://www.zope.org/Members/rbickers/Photo`), which is used for organizing Photos into an online photo album. The Photo product has presentation methods for displaying thumbnails of photos, forms for uploading photos, and management interfaces for configuring the default sizes for photo objects, as well as other features that make creating and maintaining an online photo album easier.

Because the developer included so much functionality in the Photo Product, Zope site administrators can simply install the Photo Product without having to redevelop the same functionality.

You'll notice that the argument for creating and using Zope Products is very similar to the one for creating and using Modules and Packages (namely, reusability. This is not surprising, as Zope Products are just Packages with some additional features. In this chapter, we walk you through the process of creating a simple Product from a Package.

A few products don't define new object types at all, but instead modify or enhance Zope's core functionality in some way. This second type of product is usually more trouble than it's worth, at least until its functionality is added to the standard Zope distribution.

An example of the second type of product is the Refresh product, whose functionality allows modifying other installed products and refreshing them so Zope doesn't need to be restarted in order for the product changes to take. This functionality was incorporated into Zope as of version 2.4 (making the product unnecessary), and you'll be using it a lot throughout this section of the book.

Creating a Hello World Package

So let's get started. First, locate a directory that is included in your PYTHONPATH environment variable (for example, `/site-packages`), and create a `/helloPackage` subdirectory. Refer to "Playing with the Module Path" in Chapter 5 to help identify the appropriate directories.

If you are using a binary installation of Zope, then you can find the Python directory under the `/bin` directory of your Zope installation.

In your new Package subdirectory, create an empty `__init__.py` file and a `helloModule.py` file. You'll recall from Chapter 5 that the presence of an `__init__.py` file (even an empty one) signals to Python that the directory is a Package.

Edit the `helloModule.py` file as follows:

```
class helloClass:
    def __init__(self, Name = 'World'):
        self.Name = Name

    def saySomething(self):
        return "Hello, " + self.Name

    def edit(self, Name):
        self.Name = Name
```

This class has three methods:

- An `__init__` method that takes a `Name` argument that defaults to 'World'
- A `saySomething` method that returns a greeting
- An `edit` method that takes a `Name` argument and changes the value of `self.Name`

As you can see, each of the methods in the class makes use of the `self` object to refer to the actual object instance. Thus `self.Name` refers to the name attribute of the object, both for assignment (via the `edit` method) and display (through the `saySomething` method). For more information on Class methods, refer back to Chapter 5.

After saving the files in the `/helloPackage` subdirectory, import and instantiate the Class:

```
>>> from helloPackage import helloModule
>>> from helloModule import helloClass
>>> a = helloClass()
>>> a.saySomething()
'Hello, World'
>>>
```

Next, use the class's `edit` method to change the value of `Name`:

```
>>> a.edit('Bob')
>>> a.saySomething()
'Hello, Bob'
>>>
```

Okay, so we've demonstrated creating a rudimentary Package. Next you're going to turn it into a rudimentary Zope Product, but before we do that you should understand the concept of publishing objects.

Publishing Objects

In Chapter 1, we briefly introduced you to ZServer and ZPublisher, which are two of Zope's core components. Their job is to handle a request from the network, find the objects that the request refers to, run its method, and return the results. (We explain the process in more detail in this section, which will be helpful when you read the next couple of chapters.)

For the real nitty-gritty details of the publishing process and how you can exert more control over it refer to Chapter 14.

To better explain how this works we'll show you how to publish your hello object's `saySomething()` method on the Web. What this means is when somebody enters the URL, `http://www.yourdomain.com/hello/saySomething`, into his or her browser, he or she will get a page that says, "Hello, World!"

Here's an over view of the publishing process:

1. When ZPublisher receives the URL from ZServer, ZPublisher creates an object named REQUEST (a mapping, really) that contains everything that ZPublisher knows about the HTTP request that called the object, and the context within which the request was made. It starts at the root folder and looks for the object named `hello`.
2. If ZPublisher finds that object, it looks to see if the object has a sub-object named `saySomething`.
3. ZPublisher expects that the last name in a URL is the name of an object that is callable. In other words, it expects that the last object is a method or that the object has a default method named `index_html`.
4. Once ZPublisher finds the final method, it examines what arguments the method expects and tries to pass them from the REQUEST object to the method in the proper order. Any URL parameters or form fields submitted through the HTTP request are also found in the REQUEST object, and passed to the method.
5. ZPublisher returns the results of the method back to ZServer, which in turn returns the results back to the client packaged in the appropriate protocol.

In order to publish your hello object you will need to create an instance of the hello class somewhere in the Zope object hierarchy. In this example you create the object in the root folder object. This is accomplished by modifying your `helloClass` to inherit from a few Zope-specific base classes (in Chapter 5 you learned about creating classes that inherit from other classes) and creating two constructor methods (in Zope, you need special methods to create instances of your class within the ZODB). Once you've done this you will be able to enter the Zope management screen and add a hello object to the root folder by selecting it from the Add Object drop-down menu.

Changing a Package into a Product

Creating a Product from a Package is not difficult. The first step is copying the `/helloPackage` directory into your Zope installation's `./lib/python/Products` directory and renaming it `/helloProduct`.

When Zope starts up it looks in the `./lib/python/Products` directory for any Packages (such as directories that have a `__init__.py` module). For each Package it finds it attempts to call a method named `initialize`, which should be defined in your `__init__.py` file.

In order to define the initialize method, edit the `__init__.py` file as follows:

```
import helloModule

def initialize(context):
    context.registerClass(
        helloModule.helloClass,
        permission="Add Hello Object",
        constructors=(helloModule.manage_addHelloForm,
                      helloModule.manage_addHello)
        )
```

These changes to `__init__.py` call Zope's Product registration machinery and pass in the following:

- ✦ The `helloClass`
- ✦ A name for the Permission that will allow adding an instance of the Class
- ✦ The form to display when you want to add an instance of the Class
- ✦ The method that will actually add the Class

Permissions, by the way, are what Zope uses to protect certain objects and actions from being available to all users who access your site. This is dealt with more in depth in Chapters 9 and 13. For now, you just need to know that the permission added here will only allow manager users to add hello Objects to the site.

The last thing that you need to do is add an empty `refresh.txt` file to the `helloProduct` directory. This enables Zope's refresh functionality, which is very useful when developing products, as it makes it unnecessary to constantly shut down and restart Zope between making changes to Products.

The Product registration machinery is run when Zope starts up. Don't start Zope just yet, as there are a few small changes still to be made to the Module before the registration can succeed.

Edit the `helloModule.py` file as follows:

```
def manage_addHelloForm(self):
    " "
    return ""

def manage_addHello(self):
    " "
    return ""

class helloClass:
    def __init__(self, Name = 'World'):
        self.Name = Name

    meta_type = "Hello Object"

    def hello(self):
        return "Hello, " + self.Name

    def edit(self, Name):
        self.Name = Name
```

Note the following changes we made:

- ✦ We added two dummy methods to the Module that match the names given in the `initialize` method we added to the `__init__.py` file.
- ✦ We added a `meta_type` declaration to the class.

The meta_type declaration sets the object's meta type, which is useful when you are trying to filter a list of objects to only those that you want. An example is when you want to return all the subfolders from the current folder using (from DTML) `<dtml-in objectValues('Folder')>`.

Notice that both of the placeholder methods that we added to the Module have as their first line a one-space string. The contents of this string are unimportant at this stage, but the string must be present. This is the method's docstring, and Zope will not expose to the Internet any method that does not have a docstring.

Now that we've made the minimum necessary changes to the Package, Zope can correctly register it as a Product when it finds the `__init__.py` file and calls the `initialize` method (which calls `registerClass`), when you start (or restart) the Zope server.

As you can see in Figure 6-1, the helloProduct Product registered correctly. (You can tell this from the fact that the icon shown for the product is not broken.) If the icon shown for the Product is broken, then you need to verify that the code is correct. The Product also appears in the Add list drop-down menu as shown in Figure 6-2.

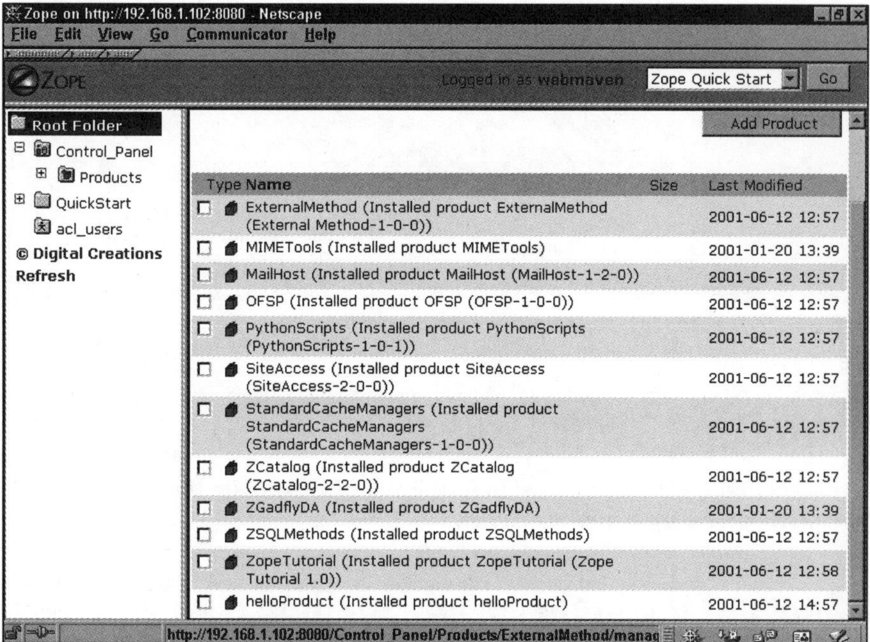

Figure 6-1: The Registered Product listing

However, the Product as it is will not yet add itself to a folder. If you try, nothing will happen. This is because the `manage_addHelloForm` and `manage_addHello` methods are dummies, and because the `helloClass` doesn't know enough about Zope's persistence machinery to interact with it correctly. The persistence machinery is the code that Zope uses to save (or persist) objects and their attributes even between Zope restarts. In other words it's the mechanism by which data is stored in the ZODB. We'll show you how to fix both of these situations in the next section.

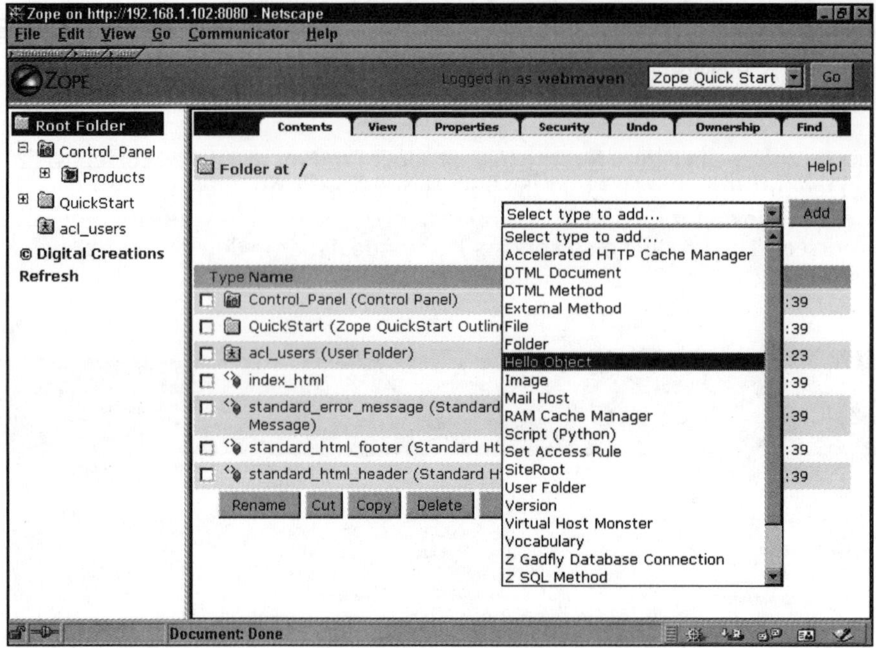

Figure 6-2: The Add list drop-down menu

Instantiating Your Object

In this section we show you how to further modify the hello Product so that it can instantiate correctly inside of a folder.

Filling out the manage_add methods

First, you need to fill out the two placeholder methods that you already added to the `helloModule.py` file:

```
def manage_addHelloForm(self, REQUEST):
    "Form for adding a Hello Object"
    return """
    <html>
    <head></head>
    <body>
    <form method="post" action="./manage_addHello">
    <input type="text" name="id">
    <input type="submit" value="Add Hello">
    </form>
    </body>
    </html>
    """
```

```
def manage_addHello(self, id, REQUEST):
    "Method for adding a Hello object"
    newHello = helloClass(id)
    self._setObject(id, newHello)
    return self.manage_main(self, REQUEST)
```

Another change is required in the `helloClass` itself, so that the object "knows" its own id:

```
class helloClass:
    def __init__(self, id, Name = 'World'):
        self.id = id
        self.Name = Name

    meta_type = "Hello Object"

    def hello(self):
        return "Hello, " + self.Name

    def edit(self, Name):
        self.Name = Name
```

As you can see, the class's `__init__` method is altered so that it takes `id` as its second parameter, and then sets the id attribute, in addition to the Name attribute. Without this change, various things will break, in some subtle ways. For example, the object will not report its id correctly to the containing object, resulting in a blank id field in the folder contents view. This would also prevent the object from being renamed (via the management interface) to a different id.

After you've made and saved these changes, you can refresh the Zope product by going into the Products Refresh tab, and clicking the Refresh This Product button. This will cause Zope to re-initialize the product code from the file system, and enable the changes that you just made without having to restart Zope. This is a feature that was introduced into Zope in version 2.4.

When you try to select Hello Object from the list of objects in the drop-down menu, a simple form consisting of a single Add Hello button appears, as shown in Figure 6-3.

Zope's registration machinery automatically builds the drop-down menu so that selecting the `meta_type` listed will cause the `manage_addHelloForm` method to be called. In this case, the `manage_addHelloForm` method returns the contents of a string, which consists of some HTML defining a simple form. The form defined by the `manage_addHelloForm` method has as its target the `manage_addHello` method.

The code you added to the `manage_addHello` method is a little more complex, but if you remember that the method is a Module level method (and not a class method), it becomes clearer.

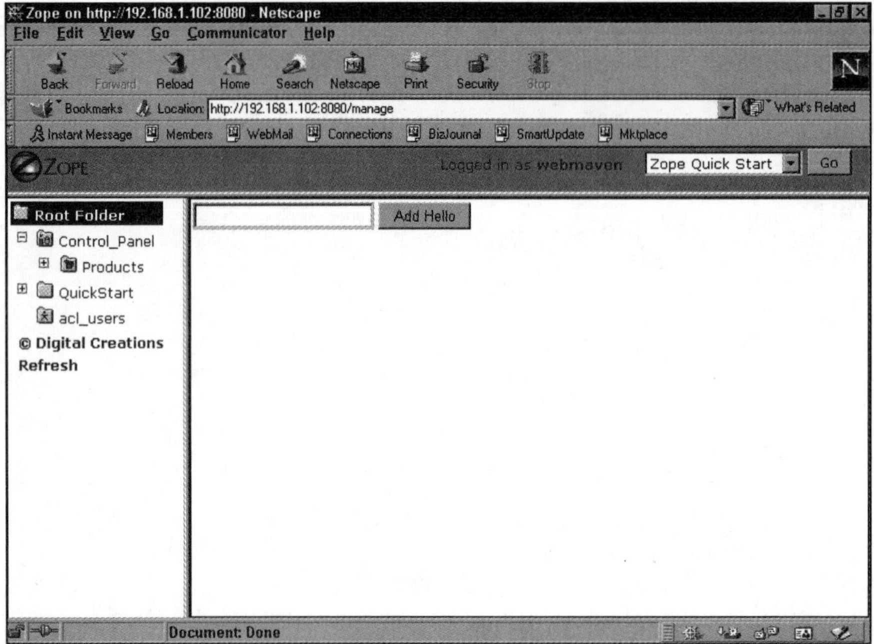

Figure 6-3: The Hello Product's Add form

The first line is again a docstring, necessary for exposing the method to the Internet. The second line simply assigns a new instance of the class to `newHello`. The third is where things start getting interesting. The `_setObject` method is not one you may have seen before, as it is a standard method of the Folder class. It is through this method that the instance of the `helloClass` is placed inside the folder with the appropriate `id`.

The last line we added to `manage_addHello` tells Zope what to display after adding an instance of your class to the folder. Here we tell Zope to display the current object's (the folder we're in) `manage_main` method. This is standard behavior for the Zope management interface, in that after you add an object to a folder, you are brought back to the folder where you can see the object you just added.

Subclassing from Zope base classes

The helloProduct Product seems ready to work. However, if you were to refresh the product at this point and try to add a Hello object to a folder, Zope will report a strange error and not add the object to the folder. The problem is that the `helloClass` doesn't have any notion of how to represent itself in the Zope management interface, or the persistence machinery that allows objects to be stored in the Zope Object Database (ZODB). As far as Zope is concerned, Python objects or attributes that aren't stored persistently largely don't exist, in the sense that if Zope is shut down or restarted, whatever changes were made to the object or attribute will be lost.

The remedy for this is fairly painless. The `helloClass` must inherit from one or more of the base classes the Zope developers have thoughtfully provided.

Therefore, in order for the `helloClass` instances to interact correctly with the management interface, they need to inherit from `OFS.SimpleItem.Item`:

```
from OFS.SimpleItem import Item
```

In order for the class instances to store themselves in the ZODB, they must inherit from `Globals.Persistent`:

```
from Globals import Persistent
```

And in order for the class instances to acquire attributes and methods from their containers, they need to inherit from `Acquisition.Implicit`:

```
from Acquisition import Implicit
```

Add the previous three lines to the top of the `helloModule.py` file, and then change the `helloClass` class definition as follows so the helloClass inherits from these three base classes:

```
class helloClass(Item, Persistent, Implicit):
```

After making these changes and refreshing the Product, try adding the Hello object again. Select the Hello Object option from the drop-down menu. The Add form should appear as shown in Figure 6-3. Type **TestHello** into the form and click the Add Hello button. You should be brought back to the folder's main view, and you should see a TestHello object listed, as shown in Figure 6-4.

Congratulations! You've successfully created a Product that you can add through the Zope management interface. In the next section, we show you how to improve the Product further, so that it actually does something.

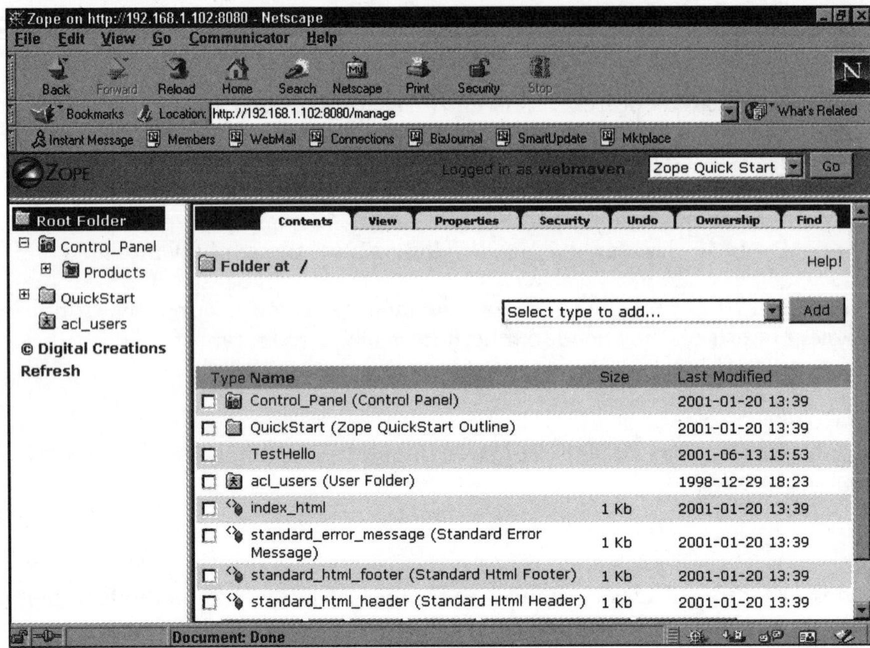

Figure 6-4: An Instance of helloClass added to the folder

Adding DTML Methods

In the previous section, we added the `manage_addHelloForm` method to the `helloModule` Module:

```
def manage_addHelloForm(self, REQUEST):
    "Form for adding a Hello Object"
    return """
    <html>
    <head></head>
    <body>
    <form method="post" action="./manage_addHello">
    <input type="text" name="id">
    <input type="submit" value="Add Hello">
    </form>
    </body>
    </html>
    """
```

The problem with embedding HTML code directly into your Module files like this is that it can make your Module difficult to read and debug, as you are actually mixing logic and presentation into the same source file. You wouldn't want to hand your Module file over to an HTML designer to improve the look and feel, would you?

There are a couple of other disadvantages, too: The Product needs to be refreshed every time you make a change to the Module, and the embedded HTML can't contain DTML for Zope to interpret, since it's just text returned directly to the browser, thereby throwing away most of the advantages of working with Zope in the first place, such as using standard headers and footers for look and feel.

The preferred alternative is to use external *.dtml files that you can bring into the Module as HTMLFile objects.

First add a `/DTML` subdirectory to your `/helloProduct` directory. Then add a `manage_addHelloForm.dtml` file in the `/helloProduct/DTML` subdirectory with the following contents:

```
<dtml-var manage_page_header>
 <form method="post" action="./manage_addHello">
  <input type="text" name="id">
  <input type="submit" value="Add Hello">
 </form>
<dtml-var manage_page_footer>
```

Notice that Zope has special headers and footers for the management interface.

Next, change the beginning of the `helloModule.py` file to match the following code:

```
from OFS.SimpleItem import Item
from Globals import Persistent, HTMLFile
from Acquisition import Implicit

manage_addHelloForm = HTMLFile('DTML/manage_addHelloForm',
globals())
```

You can see that two changes were made here. First, we are now importing `HTMLFile` from `Globals`, in addition to `Persistent`. Second, `manage_addHelloForm` is now an instance of HTMLFile. HTMLFiles, despite their name, are intended to contain DTML as well as HTML, so that Zope can interpret the DTML and display the result. As HTMLFiles are intended to be presented through the Web, they don't require a docstring as a Python method does.

If you now refresh the product and try adding a new Hello object, you'll see that the functionality is unchanged, even though we have moved the code for the form to an external file. As a result, our Module file is now shorter and easier to understand, and we can leverage the flexibility of DTML in our template.

If after refreshing the product it breaks, check to make sure you haven't made any typos. Remember that file names and directory names are case-sensitive!

Our Hello objects currently do not have any way of presenting themselves on the Internet because they lack an `index_html` method. This means that if you try to access them directly, they will acquire an `index_html` method from their container, which won't show you anything particularly interesting. This is easily remedied by adding an `index_html.dtml` file to your `Products /DTML` subdirectory with the following contents:

```
<dtml-var standard_html_header>
<h1>Hello, <dtml-var Name>!</h1>
<dtml-var standard_html_footer>
```

Then add the following to the end of the `helloModule.py` file inside the class:

```
    # Web Methods

    index_html = HTMLFile('DTML/index_html', globals())
```

Unlike the `manage_add*` Module methods at the top of the file, `index_html` is a method of the class, and must be indented accordingly. Your `helloModule.py` file should now look like this:

```
from OFS.SimpleItem import Item
from Globals import Persistent, HTMLFile
from Acquisition import Implicit

manage_addHelloForm = HTMLFile('DTML/manage_addHelloForm', ⮐
globals())

def manage_addHello(self, id, REQUEST):
    "Method for adding a Hello object"
    newHello = helloClass(id)
    self._setObject(id, newHello)
    return self.manage_main(self, REQUEST)

class helloClass(Item, Persistent, Implicit):
    def __init__(self, id, Name = 'World'):
        self.id = id
        self.Name = Name

    meta_type = "Hello Object"

    def hello(self):
        return "Hello, " + self.Name

    def edit(self, Name):
        self.Name = Name

    # Web Methods

    index_html = HTMLFile('DTML/index_html', globals())
```

Save the file and refresh the Product. Now you should be able to go to a URL such as `http://128.0.0.1:8080/TestHello` (or whatever your development machine's URL is), and see results similar to the results shown in Figure 6-5.

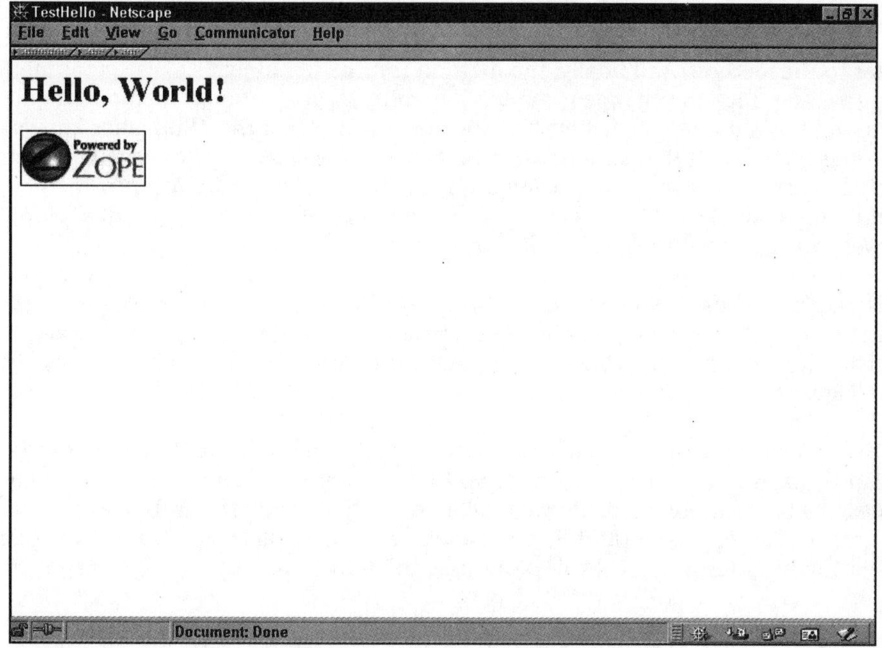

Figure 6-5: The Hello Products `index_html` method

From this we can also see that the Name property that we are initializing in the class's `__init__` method is working correctly, and that we can access the Name property of the class instance from DTML by using `<dtml-var Name>`.

Processing Form Submissions and Returning

Next, you'll learn how to process form submissions, and return the browser to a management screen. We'll use this to allow through the web editing of your objects.

Web-enabling the edit method

Our Hello Product now instantiates correctly, and even has a public viewing interface, but it doesn't let us change the attributes of its instances. The Hello Class has an edit method, which with a little work we can Web enable:

```
def edit(self, Name, REQUEST):
    "method to edit Hello instances"
    self.Name = Name
    return self.index_html(self, REQUEST)
```

What are the changes we've made here? First, we added a docstring so that the edit method could be called through the Web. Second, `REQUEST` was added as a parameter to the method. And finally, the method returns the object's `index_html` method as a result once the change is made. Generally, all presentation methods require `REQUEST` as a parameter (which contains everything that the ZPublisher knows about the request that caused a method to be called), so any Web-enabled methods that return a presentation method are going to need it, too, in order to correctly pass the context that the method was called from. (We refine this to deal with non-Web situations a little later in this chapter.)

Now, after refreshing the product, if you type into your browser a URL such as, `http://128.0.0.1:8080/TestHello/edit?Name=Bob`, you should get a browser page that demonstrates that the value of the `Name` attribute has been changed, as shown in Figure 6-6.

You can see that although the edit method itself is not a presentation method, by modifying it to return another method that *is* a presentation method after its processing is complete, it can now be called directly through the Web. Without that last line, calling the method through a browser will actually change the attribute, but the browser will not display anything to indicate that the change has taken.

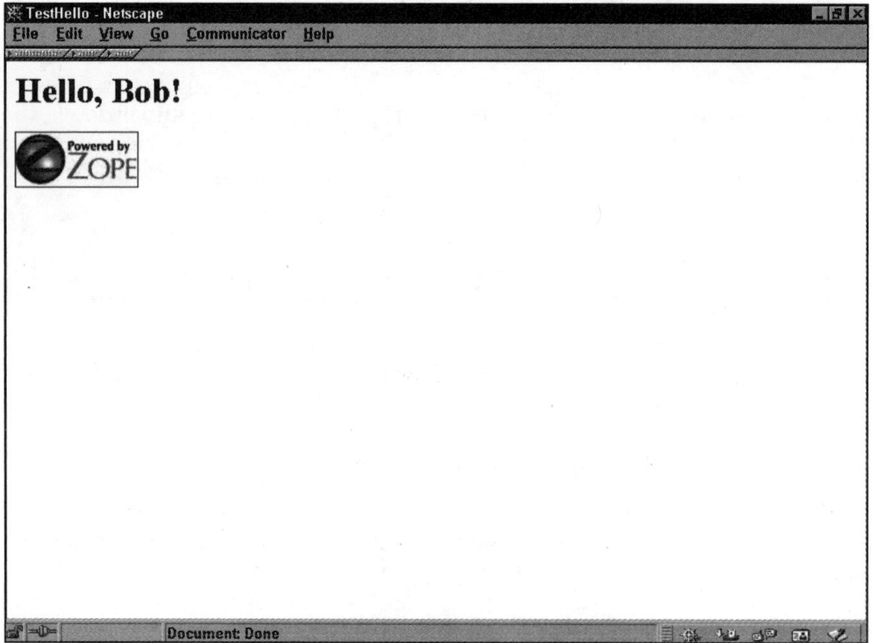

Figure 6-6: The Web-enabled `edit` method

Dealing with non-Web situations

The edit method as currently constructed now requires a REQUEST parameter that can only be had when then the method is accessed over the Web and returns the class index_html method, which also can only be accessed over the Web. In order to make sure that your Product is still accessible for non-Web uses, you need to make the following change:

```
def edit(self, Name, REQUEST=None):
    "method to edit Hello instances"
    self.Name = Name
    if REQUEST is not None:
        return self.index_html(self, REQUEST)
```

These two changes make sure that your class' edit method is still usable from the interactive interpreter or other non-Web situations. First, you made the REQUEST parameter optional, with a default value of None. Second, you added a conditional to test whether the REQUEST object was *not* None, and if so, only then return the object's index_html method.

Adding manage_editHelloForm

Obviously, calling an edit method directly through your browser is not very convenient. So we need to add a manage_editHelloForm method that will make it easier to work with. Add the following line to the helloClass, under the # Web Methods line:

```
manage_editHelloForm = HTMLFile('DTML/manage_editHelloForm', globals())
```

Of course this means that we also need a manage_editHelloForm.dtml file in the DTML subdirectory of our Product:

```
<dtml-var manage_page_header>
<dtml-var manage_tabs>
<p>Current Name is: <dtml-var Name></p><br>
<form method="post" action="./edit">
 <input type="text" name="Name">
 <input type="submit" value="Change Name">
</form>
<dtml-var manage_page_footer>
```

Refresh the product, and test the URL, http://128.0.0.1:8080/TestHello/manage_editHelloForm. You should be presented with a screen that resembles Figure 6-7.

Notice that Zope provides a manage_tabs method for Web management interface views. Right now, you haven't yet defined any tabs for your class, so Zope displays a default set of two tabs: Undo and Ownership.

If you type in some other name into the form and hit the Change Name button, the form will submit to the edit method, be processed, and redirect you back to the `index_html` method, where you will see a greeting for the new name you typed in.

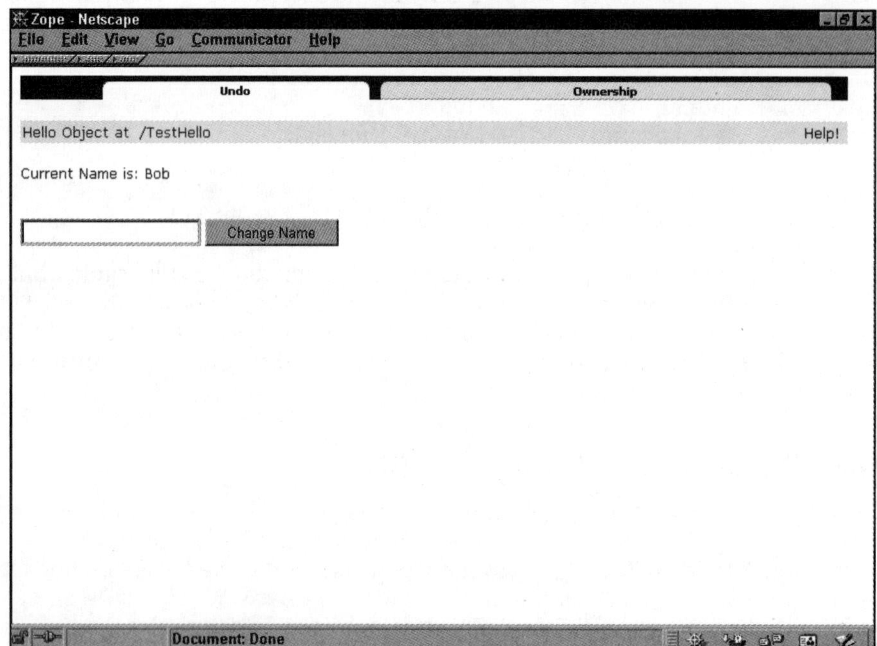

Figure 6-7: The `manage_editHelloForm` screen

Defining your own management tabs

The `manage_editHelloForm` method as it currently stands has a serious drawback in that you still have to type the URL directly into the browser in order to see it. What we really want is for the form to have its own tab that comes up automatically when we click the object in the management interface. As you might suspect, Zope provides a fairly simple way of adding this functionality into your Product.

Add the following line to `helloModule.py` inside the class, just after the `meta_type` declaration:

```
manage_options = ({'label':'Edit',
                   'action':'manage_editHelloForm'},
                 )
```

This might seem a little obscure, but the explanation is straightforward. `manage_options` is a tuple of two-item dictionaries. *Tuples* are sequences, so the order of the items in the tuple is significant. In this case, the order of items in the tuple represents the order of the tabs in the management interface. Each dictionary in the `manage_options` tuple represents a single tab and has two key/value pairs; the first pair is the text that will appear on the tab, with a key of label, and a value of Edit, and a second key/value pair with a key of action, and a value of manage editHelloForm that is used as the target for the tab hyperlink. So you can see that we've just defined a tab with a label of Edit that will send you to the `manage_editHelloForm` method.

Because tuples use regular parentheses to enclose their members, a single item tuple requires a trailing comma after the item to distinguish itself from a pair of parentheses grouping some items in an expression. If we had defined two tabs (each with its own dictionary) in the `manage_options` tuple, they would be separated by a comma, and we wouldn't need a trailing comma.

When you define more than one tab for a class in Zope, it's helpful to remember that the first tab defined in the `manage_options` tuple will be the default tab, and is the tab you will get when you click an object in the management interface.

Now, refresh the product, and click the TestHello Hello object instance in the management interface. You should see results similar to those shown in Figure 6-8.

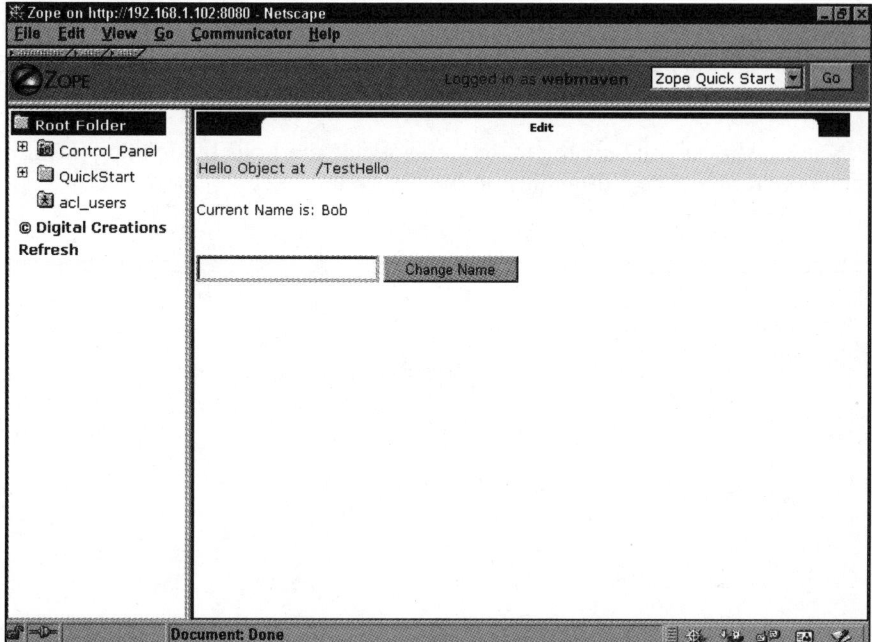

Figure 6-8: The Edit tab

The functionality of the manage_editHelloForm method is unaffected by the changes you've made, but you should nevertheless see that the method no longer displays the Undo and Ownership tabs. As long as you didn't define manage_options within your class, your class was acquiring a default manage_options attribute from the Zope environment via the Item base Class that helloClass inherits from. Now that you've defined manage_options for your class (overriding the inherited value), only the tabs you define are displayed.

Another common tab is a View tab, usually defined to point toward an object's index_html method. You can make that change by changing the definition of manage_options as follows:

```
manage_options = ({'label':'Edit',
                    'action':'manage_editHelloForm'},
                   {'label':'View', 'action':'index_html'}
                   )
```

This will add a View tab to the management interface.

Summary

As you've seen in this chapter, changing a Package into a Product is not very difficult. Mostly it involves changes to make your Package register with Zope automatically when Zope is started up, changes that enable your classes to interact with the management interface and be instantiated; changes that enable instances of your class to be stored persistently and interact with the acquisition machinery; and changes that enable your classes' methods to be called over the Web.

We've also shown you how to create Web-specific methods by defining HTMLFile objects that reference *.dtml files on the file system.

✦ ✦ ✦

Creating an AddressBook Application

✦ ✦ ✦ ✦

In This Chapter

The Addressit Product and the AddressBook class

Creating add, edit, and index_html methods

Creating an entry module in the Addressit Product

Adding, listing, and deleting entries from the AddressBook

Traversing the AddressBook into the entries

Editing an entry

✦ ✦ ✦ ✦

In Chapter 6, you learned about the similarities and differences between Python Packages and Zope Products, and how to take an existing Package and enhance it with the features that would make it into a Zope Product.

In this chapter and the following chapters in Part II, we build upon that knowledge to show you how to design and build more sophisticated Zope Products that you can use to enhance your Zope-based sites and intranets.

We chose an address book application to demonstrate how to design and build a Web application as a Zope Product. We feel that it is an appropriate example of an application that a developer wanting to enhance a Zope Web site or intranet with some additional functionality would consider developing. In addition, it possesses the appropriate levels of straightforwardness (to support ease of understanding) and complexity (to be a sufficiently challenging task) to make it a good first application.

At the end of this chapter, you will have a functional and useful Zope Product, which you will continue to enhance in subsequent chapters in the second part of this book.

The Addressit Product and the AddressBook Class

So, what are you actually going to build here? Typically, an address book can be thought of as containing entries (corresponding to people) that can be listed and navigated in various ways, and that have a number of attributes that can be used to contact those people. An AddressBook then is a containing class, and Entry instances are contained within it.

Creating the Addressit Product

We'll call this product the Addressit product, if you don't mind a little self-promotion for the authors' employer (Codeit Computing).

To begin, create an `Addressit` directory inside your Zope installation's `Products` directory, as you did for the `helloProduct` in the previous chapter. Then create an `__init__.py` file in your `Addressit` directory with the following code:

```
import AddressBook

def initialize(context):

    context.registerClass(
        AddressBook.AddressBook,
        permission="Add AddressBook",
        constructors=(AddressBook.manage_addAddressBookForm,
                      AddressBook.manage_addAddressBook)
        )
```

The structure of this file should be recognizable; it's essentially the same as the file you created for the `helloProduct` in the previous chapter, with a few name substitutions. You can see that the `__init__.py` file refers to an `AddressBook` class inside an `AddressBook` module, so you'll need to create that next. Place an `AddressBook.py` file with the code shown in Listing 7-1 into the same directory.

Listing 7-1: AddressBook.py

```
from OFS.SimpleItem import SimpleItem
from Globals import DTMLFile


# Module level declarations and methods

manage_addAddressBookForm = DTMLFile("dtml/addAddressBookForm", ⮐
globals())


def manage_addAddressBook(self, id, title, REQUEST):
    "Adds an AddressBook object to a folder"

    newAddressBook=AddressBook(id, title)
    self._setObject(id, newAddressBook)

    return self.manage_main(self, REQUEST)


# The Addressbook Class

class AddressBook(SimpleItem):
```

```
    "An AddressBook object"

    meta_type = "AddressBook"

    def __init__(self, id, title):
        self.id          = id
        self.title       = title
```

Here you can start to see some differences between helloProduct and the Addressit Product. Specifically, the base classes that the two Products inherit from are not the same. The helloProduct inherited from OFS.SimpleItem.Item, Globals.Persistent, and Acquisition.Implicit, whereas the AddressBook class inherits from a single class OFS.SimpleItem.SimpleItem. OFS.SimpleItem.SimpleItem is a base class provided to make creating Zope Products easier, as it is simply a class that inherits from the three base classes that we are already familiar with, plus one more: AccessControl.Role.RoleManager, which enables you to set local roles on instances of the class. This last base class isn't really important at the moment, as we don't discuss application security until Chapter 9, but meanwhile we can take advantage of the increased legibility that comes from using one base class (SimpleItem) instead of several base classes.

Another difference is the use of DTMLFile instances instead of HTMLFile instances. HTMLFile is actually a deprecated class that is a little simpler in some regards than its newer replacement, DTMLFile. The examples in Chapter 6 were straightforward enough that it didn't really make any difference which was used, but in this and subsequent chapters we're building a real product, so to speak, so we're using the more recent DTMLFile for the rest of this chapter and the subsequent chapters in this section.

The only thing that's missing to get this Product to register and instantiate correctly at this point is a manage_addAddressBookForm.dtml file, so that's what you're going to add next. Create the file in a /dtml subdirectory of the Product directory, with the code shown in Listing 7-2.

Listing 7-2: **manage_addAddressBook.dtml**

```
<dtml-var standard_html_header>

<form method=post action=manage_addAddressBook>
<table border=0 cellspacing=0 cellpadding=5>
 <tr>
  <td>Address book ID:</td>
  <td><input type=text name="id"></td>
 </tr>
```

Continued

Listing 7-2 *(continued)*

```
  <tr>
   <td>Title:</td>
   <td><input type=text name="title"></td>
  </tr>
  <tr>
   <td colspan=2><input type=submit value="Add
AddressBook"></td>
  </tr>
</table>
</form>

<dtml-var standard_html_header>
```

Start (or restart) your Zope installation and you should now see the Addressit Product show up in the `Control Panel/Products` folder, and the AddressBook should show up correctly in the Add drop-down menu. Adding an AddressBook should also work correctly. At this point, the Addressit Product can be described with the UML (Unified Modeling Language) diagram shown in Figure 7-1.

Address Book
title: id:
+ init (id: , title:)

Figure 7-1: The Addressit UML diagram

If you're not familiar with UML diagrams, we recommend that you take a look at *UML Distilled* by Martin Fowler and Kendall Scott (Addison-Wesley, 1999), which is an excellent introductory book.

The diagram in Figure 7-1 shows a single class (named AddressBook) that has two attributes, `title` and `id` (listed directly below the name of the class), and one method `__init__` listed below the attributes. We'll include explanations for other features of UML as we encounter them.

Of course, the Product doesn't actually do anything yet.

The code for the product at this point can be found in the `/chapter_07/Addressit_1` directory on the accompanying CD-ROM.

Creating edit and index_html Methods

Okay, so the AddressBook class needs a way of displaying itself in the management interface, and of editing its properties. Add the following code to the end of the AddressBook.py file, extending the AddressBook class definition:

```
manage_options=(
{'label':'Edit', 'action':'manage_main' },
)

manage_main = DTMLFile("dtml/mainAddressBook", globals())

def editAddressBook(self, title, REQUEST):
    "A method to edit Address Book Properties"

    self.title = title

    return self.manage_main(self, REQUEST)
```

You've done three things here:

- ✦ You've added a manage_options property to generate custom tabs for your Product, overriding the manage_options attribute inherited from SimpleItem.
- ✦ You've defined an external DTMLFile object to act as your main management view.
- ✦ You've defined an edit method to change the object's properties.

You may notice that manage_options refers to manage_main, and manage_main refers to an external DTMLFile that doesn't yet exist, so you need to create a mainAddressBook.dtml file in your Product's /dtml subdirectory with the code shown in Listing 7-3.

Listing 7-3: mainAddressBook.dtml

```
<dtml-var manage_page_header>
<dtml-var manage_tabs>

<form method=post action=editAddressBook>
<table border=0 cellspacing=0 cellpadding=5>
 <tr>
  <td>Title:</td>
  <td><input type=text name="title" value="&dtml-title;"></td>
 </tr>
 <tr>
```

Continued

Listing 7-3 (continued)

```
  <td colspan=2><input type=submit value="Edit
AddressBook"></td>
 </tr>
</table>
</form>
</body>
</html>

<dtml-var manage_page_footer>
```

As we explained in Chapter 6, Zope provides special header and footer methods for management screens, including a method for generating the tabs at the top of those screens. The rest of this DTML method is a simple form that has as its action the `editAddressBook` class method that we've already defined. An interesting enhancement to this form is the fact that it renders the current value of a property in the form field, which makes it easy to edit it rather than having to retype it from scratch. It does this by setting the value of the `title` input form element to `&dtml-title;` this HTML-entity syntax is equivalent to `<dtml-var title>`, and Zope would render both the same. The only difference is that the syntax that we chose to use here won't cause an HTML editor to choke on the invalid HTML syntax. In any case, rendering the current value of a property into the form element that is supposed to change it is good practice.

Add a refresh.txt file to the `/Addressit` product folder and refresh the Addressit product. The result is a main view for the AddressBook object that consists of a form to edit the title property of the instance. Add an AddressBook to your Root Folder with an id of *Test* and a title of *My AddressBook*. By clicking it in the management interface, you should see a screen resembling the one shown in Figure 7-2.

Changing the value in the field and clicking the Edit AddressBook button submits the form to the `editAddressBook` method of the class. The method will apply the changed values to the instance, and return the form again. You'll probably notice a brief flicker as the form is re-rendered, but it will appear otherwise unchanged, as the form re-renders with the changed values that you had already typed into the form. Check to see if it worked correctly by looking at the main view of the folder where you placed the AddressBook instance. You should see that the changed title is now listed in parentheses after the AddressBook id.

To round out this basic AddressBook Product, it needs an `index_html` method, so first change the class `manage_options` property as follows:

```
     manage_options=(
{'label':'Edit', 'action':'manage_main' },
                    {'label':'View', 'action':'index_html' }
                    )
```

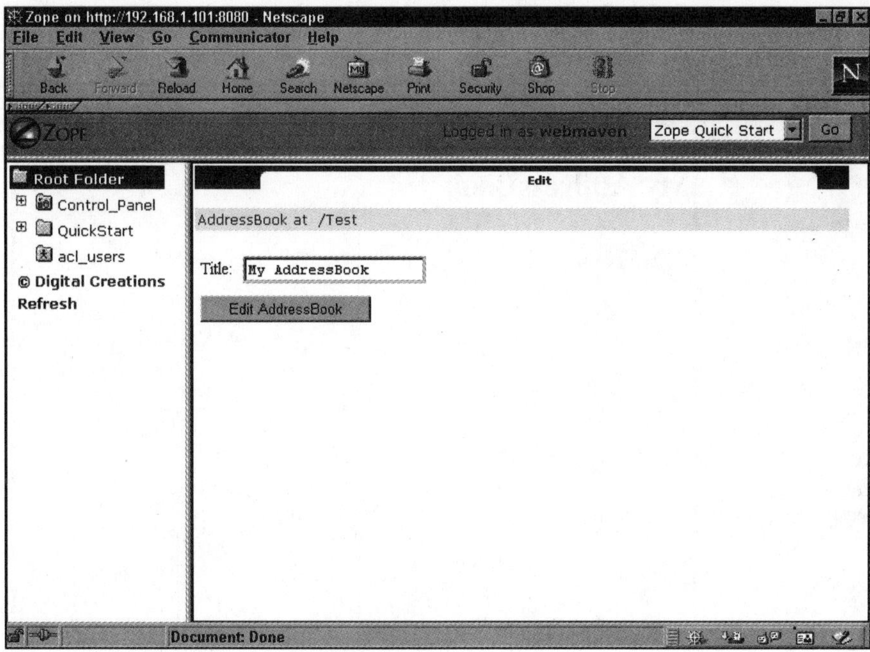

Figure 7-2: The AddressBook main view

This creates a *View* tab in the management interface linked to an `index_html` method. If you were to refresh the product at this point and click the View tab of an AddressBook instance (or type in its URL directly), the instance would display an acquired `index_html` method (from its parent folder). Add the following code to the end of the `AddressBook.py` file, indented so that it's within the class definition:

```
# Web Presentation Methods

index_html = DTMLFile("dtml/indexAddressBook", globals())
```

Next, create an `indexAddressBook.dtml` file in the `/Addressit/dtml` directory with the following code:

```
<dtml-var standard_html_header>
<h1><dtml-var title><h1>
<dtml-var standard_html_footer>
```

Now, if you refresh the product and click the View tab, you'll see the `AddressBook` class' `index_html` method, which should look something like Figure 7-3.

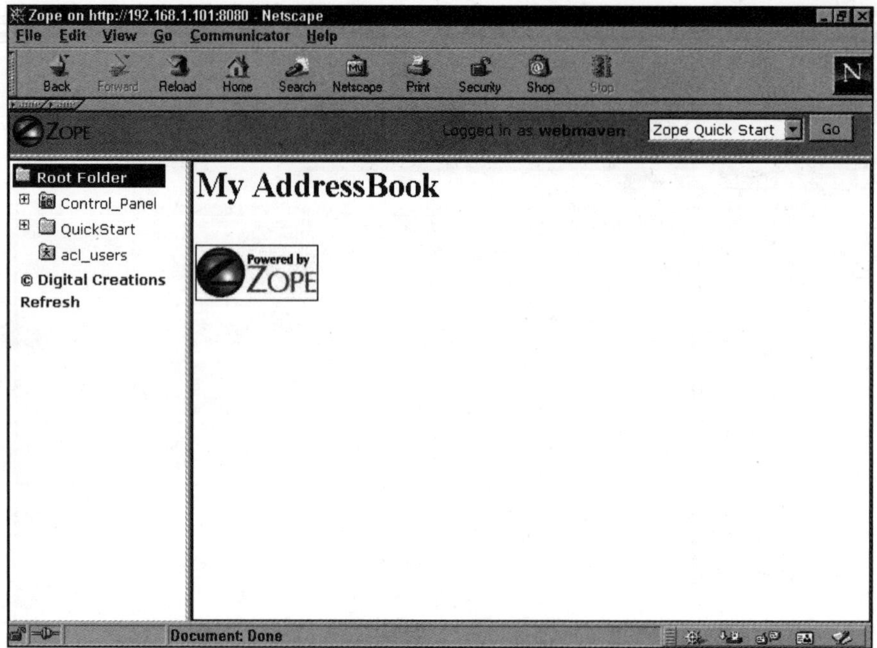

Figure 7-3: The Addressbook's `index_html` method

The methods we've added alter the UML diagram a little, so it should now look like Figure 7-4.

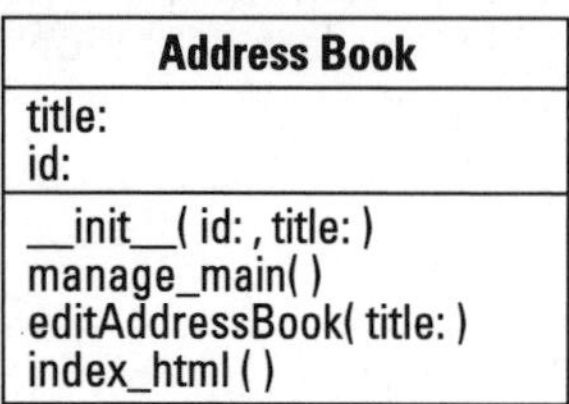

Figure 7-4: AddressBook UML diagram

The code for the Product at this point can be found in the `/chapter_07/Addressit_2` directory on the CD that accompanies this book.

Creating an Entry Module in the Addressit Product

Our Addressit Product now has a sort of generic object that will act as a container for our entries. However, there is as yet nothing for an AddressBook to contain. So we need to create an `Entry` class. While it is perfectly possible to define the `Entry` class within the `AddressBook` module, this is not something we recommend. Monolithic modules are generally harder to understand and maintain. Splitting a Product (or a Package) into several modules (one for each type of object) is usually a good idea. Because we have a container/contained-object pattern here, a module for each makes sense. Therefore, the `Entry` class will get its own Module, `Entry.py`.

What should an entry do? An entry should obviously have a number of attributes that store information about the person in question and information about how to contact the person. So our `Entry` class will have the following attributes:

- FirstName
- MiddleInitial
- LastName
- Address1
- Address2
- City
- State
- ZipCode
- Country
- Company
- Title

This should give us enough information about the person in question. But we also need to store contact information as well. Each entry will have up to six contacts associated with it, and each contact will have an associated contact type, like so:

Contact_1, Contact_Type_1

Contact_2, Contact_Type_2

...

Contact_6, Contact_Type_6

The class also needs (at a minimum) a constructor, a method for editing instances, a form for entering changed values, and an `index_html` presentation method. The UML diagram in Figure 7-5 shows this information, and the relationship between the `AddressBook` and `Entry` classes.

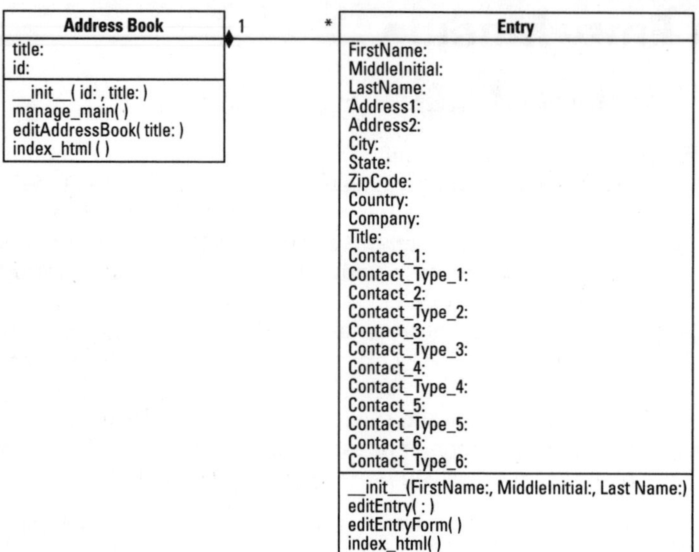

Figure 7-5: UML diagram of the `AddressBook` and `Entry` classes

Figure 7-5 shows a line connecting the two classes in the diagram, a black diamond and the number 1on one end, and an asterisk on the other.

The black diamond on the AddressBook end of the line denotes that the relationship between an AddressBook and an Entry is one of *Composition,* which means that if the AddressBook is deleted, its contained entries are to be deleted as well. The number 1 and the asterisk denote that the relationship is between a single AddressBook instance, and zero or more Entry instances.

Now, create an `Entry.py` file in your `Product` directory, with the code shown in Listing 7-4.

Listing 7-4: Entry.py

```
from Globals import Persistent, DTMLFile
from Acquisition import Implicit
from OFS.SimpleItem import Item

class Entry(Item, Persistent, Implicit):
    "Address Book Entry"

    meta_type = "AddressBook Entry"
```

```
def __init__ (self, id, FirstName, MiddleInitial,
              LastName):
    self.id = id
    self.editEntry(FirstName, MiddleInitial, LastName)



def editEntry (self, FirstName, MiddleInitial, LastName,
               Address1 = "",
               Address2 = "",
               City = "",
               State = "",
               ZipCode = "",
               Country = "",
               Company = "",
               Title = "",
               Contact_1 = "", ContactType_1 = "",
               Contact_2 = "", ContactType_2 = "",
               Contact_3 = "", ContactType_3 = "",
               Contact_4 = "", ContactType_4 = "",
               Contact_5 = "", ContactType_5 = "",
               Contact_6 = "", ContactType_6 = "",
               REQUEST = None
               ):
    "Method for updating Entries"
    self.FirstName = FirstName
    self.LastName = LastName
    self.MiddleInitial = MiddleInitial
    self.Address1 = Address1
    self.Address2 = Address2
    self.City = City
    self.State = State
    self.ZipCode = ZipCode
    self.Country = Country
    self.Company = Company
    self.Title = Title
    self.Contact_1 = Contact_1
    self.ContactType_1 = ContactType_1
    self.Contact_2 = Contact_2
    self.ContactType_2 = ContactType_2
    self.Contact_3 = Contact_3
    self.ContactType_3 = ContactType_3
    self.Contact_4 = Contact_4
    self.ContactType_4 = ContactType_4
    self.Contact_5 = Contact_5
    self.ContactType_5 = ContactType_5
    self.Contact_6 = Contact_6
    self.ContactType_6 = ContactType_6
    if REQUEST is not None:
        return self.editEntryForm(self, REQUEST)
```

Continued

Listing 7-4 *(continued)*

```
# Web Presentation Methods

    editEntryForm = DTMLFile("dtml/editEntryForm", globals())

    index_html = DTMLFile("dtml/entryDetails", globals())
```

Other than the greater number of attributes that this class has, there should be nothing intimidating about the code for this module and class. There are a few finer points that deserve some attention, though.

First, notice that other than the id attribute, the `__init__` method does not set any other attributes directly. Instead, it calls the `editEntry` method, passing in the three required parameters of `FirstName`, `MiddleInitial`, and `LastName`. `editEntry`, on the other hand, only requires those same three parameters — all others are optional and have default values consisting of empty strings.

The only optional parameter that does not default to an empty string is `REQUEST`, which defaults to the `None` object. In this way, when `editEntry` is called from `__init__` (and `REQUEST` is not passed in), the `editEntry` method only sets the values of the passed in parameters, and does nothing else. However, when `editEntry` is called from a Web form directly (and therefore `REQUEST` is passed in), `REQUEST` will not be `None`, and the method will return the `editEntryForm` after setting all of the class's attributes.

The second aspect of this class that is worth noting is that it does not have any add methods. This is because add methods actually operate on the container, not on the added object. One can legitimately ask then why the AddressBook's add methods and forms are contained within the `AddressBook` Module, and the Entry objects' add methods aren't contained in the Entry Module. The answer to that question is one of pragmatics: It would be impractical to have to add code to the Zope Folder implementation directly to deal with every Product added to a Zope installation, so Zope uses a bit of indirection, and registers the add methods of added products when they are set in the Package's `__init__.py` file's initialize method. The `Entry` class doesn't have to go through any such contortions since it is only addable in AddressBook instances, so we can safely place the methods to add entries into the `AddressBook` class.

Before we do that though, we still need to add two DTMLFiles to the `Entry`, `index_html`, and `editEntryForm`. Add an `editEntryForm.dtml` file to the `/Addressit/DTML` directory with the code in Listing 7-5.

Listing 7-5: editEntryForm.dtml

```
<dtml-var standard_html_header>

<form action="&dtml-absolute_url;/editEntry" method=POST>
<table>
<tr>
 <th>First Name:</th>
 <td><input type=text name=FirstName value="&dtml-
FirstName;"></td>
</tr>
<tr>
 <th>Last Name:</th>
 <td><input type=text name=LastName value="&dtml-
LastName;"></td>
</tr>
<tr>
 <th>Middle Initial:</th>
 <td><input type=text name=MiddleInitial size=1 ⮐
value="&dtml-MiddleInitial;"></td>
</tr>
<tr>
  <th>Title:</th>
  <td>
    <input type=text name=Title value="&dtml-Title;">
  </td>
</tr>

<tr>
  <th>Company Name:</th>
  <td>
    <input type=text name=Company value="&dtml-Company;">
  </td>
</tr>

<tr>
  <th>Contact 1:</th>
  <td>
   <select size=1 name="ContactType_1">
    <option  value="">Contact Type:
<dtml-in listContactTypes>
    <option value="&dtml-sequence-item;"<dtml-if ⮐
"_['sequence-item']==ContactType_1">selected</dtml-if>> ⮐
<dtml-var sequence-item>
</dtml-in>
   </select>
   <input type=text name=Contact_1 value="&dtml-Contact_1;">
  </td>
</tr>
```

Continued

Listing 7-5 *(continued)*

```
<tr>
  <th>Contact 2:</th>
  <td>
   <select size=1 name="ContactType_2">
    <option  value="">Contact Type:
<dtml-in listContactTypes>
    <option value="&dtml-sequence-item;"<dtml-if ⮐
"_['sequence-item']==ContactType_2">selected</dtml-if>> ⮐
<dtml-var sequence-item>
</dtml-in>
   </select>
   <input type=text name=Contact_2 value="&dtml-Contact_2;">
  </td>
</tr>


<tr>
  <th>Contact 3:</th>
  <td>
   <select size=1 name="ContactType_3">
    <option  value="">Contact Type:
<dtml-in listContactTypes>
    <option value="&dtml-sequence-item;"<dtml-if ⮐
"_['sequence-item']==ContactType_3">selected</dtml-if>> ⮐
<dtml-var sequence-item>
</dtml-in>
   </select>
   <input type=text name=Contact_3 value="&dtml-Contact_3;">
  </td>
</tr>


<tr>
  <th>Contact 4:</th>
  <td>
   <select size=1 name="ContactType_4">
    <option  value="">Contact Type:
<dtml-in listContactTypes>
    <option value="&dtml-sequence-item;"<dtml-if ⮐
"_['sequence-item']==ContactType_4">selected</dtml-if>> ⮐
<dtml-var sequence-item>
</dtml-in>
   </select>
   <input type=text name=Contact_4 value="&dtml-Contact_4;">
  </td>
</tr>
```

```
<tr>
  <th>Contact 5:</th>
  <td>
   <select size=1 name="ContactType_5">
    <option  value="">Contact Type:
<dtml-in listContactTypes>
    <option value="&dtml-sequence-item;"<dtml-if ⮐
"_['sequence-item']==ContactType_5">selected</dtml-if>> ⮐
<dtml-var sequence-item>
</dtml-in>
   </select>
   <input type=text name=Contact_5 value="&dtml-Contact_5;">
  </td>
</tr>


<tr>
  <th>Contact 6:</th>
  <td>
   <select size=1 name="ContactType_6">
    <option  value="">Contact Type:
<dtml-in listContactTypes>
    <option value="&dtml-sequence-item;"<dtml-if ⮐
"_['sequence-item']==ContactType_6">selected</dtml-if>> ⮐
<dtml-var sequence-item>
</dtml-in>
   </select>
   <input type=text name=Contact_6 value="&dtml-Contact_6;">
  </td>
</tr>

<tr>
  <th>Street Address 1:</th>
  <td>
    <input type=text name=Address1 value="&dtml-Address1;">
  </td>
</tr>

<tr>
  <th>Street Address 2:</th>
  <td>
    <input type=text name=Address2 value="&dtml-Address2;">
  </td>
</tr>

<tr>
  <th>City:</th>
  <td>
    <input type=text name=City value="&dtml-City;">
  </td>
</tr>
```

Continued

Listing 7-5 *(continued)*

```
<tr>
  <th>State:</th>
  <td>
    <input type=text name=State value="&dtml-State;">
  </td>
</tr>

<tr>
  <th>Zipcode:</th>
  <td>
    <input type=text name=ZipCode value="&dtml-ZipCode;"
size="5">
  </td>
</tr>

<tr>
  <th>Country:</th>
  <td>
    <input type=text name=Country value="&dtml-Country;">
  </td>
</tr>

<tr>
  <td> </td>
  <td><input type=submit value="Edit Entry"></td>
</tr>
</table>

</form>

<dtml-var standard_html_footer>
```

This form is much larger that the forms you've been creating so far, but a quick examination reveals that most of it is fairly straightforward. Most of the form elements are simple text fields that have as their value the current value of the associated attribute, for example:

```
<tr>
 <th>First Name:</th>
 <td><input type=text name=FirstName value="&dtml-
FirstName;"></td>
</tr>
```

The various Contact_Type fields, however, aren't simple text fields, but <select> elements:

```
    <select size=1 name="ContactType_1">
     <option  value="">Contact Type:
<dtml-in listContactTypes>
     <option value="&dtml-sequence-item;"<dtml-if ⮐
"_['sequence-item']==ContactType_1">selected</dtml-if>> ⮐
<dtml-var sequence-item>
</dtml-in>
    </select>
```

You can see that the form element is actually built by iterating over a listContactTypes method, and an <option> element is created for each item in the sequence. In each iteration, however, the value of sequence-item is compared to the current value of the ContactType attribute, and if they match, the <option> form element is marked as selected on the form.

Obviously, the listContactTypes method needs to come from somewhere. We could define it in the Entry module to have it be shared by all entries, but it actually makes more sense to define it as a method of the AddressBook class and have it return the contents of an AddressBook list property. This would enable us later to create a management interface for customizing the list of allowed ContactTypes on an AddressBook instance, and still have all entries contained in an AddressBook share the list, via acquisition. We won't be actually creating such a management interface for ContactTypes, but we demonstrate the use of this design pattern for another feature in Chapter 8.

Meanwhile, you still need to make the requisite changes to your AddressBook class. Change the __init__ method of the AddressBook class as follows and add the listContactTypes method immediately after it:

```
    def __init__(self, id, title):
        self.id             = id
        self.title          = title
        self.ContactTypeList = ['Email', 'Home', 'Mobile',
                                'Work', 'Pager', 'ICQ/IM',
                                'URL', 'Extension']

    def listContactTypes(self):
        "Returns a list of Contact Types"
        return self.ContactTypeList
```

The list of contact types given here should suffice for most corporate intranet applications.

Before we move on to the more extensive changes that are going to need to be made to the `AddressBook` class, there is still another DTMLFile that needs to be added to the Product: the `index_html DTMLFile`. At the end of Listing 7-4, you can see that the `Entry` class `index_html` method is pointing toward an `entryDetails.dtml` file. Create the `entryDetails.dtml` file in the `/Addressit/dtml/` directory, and place the contents of Listing 7-6 in it.

Listing 7-6: **entryDetails.dtml**

```
<dtml-var standard_html_header>
<h1><dtml-var FirstName> <dtml-var LastName></h1>
<table cellspacing="0" cellpadding="3" border="0">

<dtml-if Title>
 <tr>
  <th>Title:</th>
  <td><dtml-var Title>
 </tr>
</dtml-if>

<dtml-if Company>
 <tr>
  <th>Company Name:</th>
  <td><dtml-var Company>
 </tr>
</dtml-if>

<dtml-if "ContactType_1 or Contact_1">
 <tr>
  <th><dtml-var ContactType_1>:</th><td><dtml-var Contact_1>
 </tr>
</dtml-if>
<dtml-if "ContactType_2 or Contact_2">
 <tr>
  <th><dtml-var ContactType_2>:</th><td><dtml-var Contact_2>
 </tr>
</dtml-if>
<dtml-if "ContactType_3 or Contact_3">
 <tr>
  <th><dtml-var ContactType_3>:</th><td><dtml-var Contact_3>
 </tr>
</dtml-if>
<dtml-if "ContactType_4 or Contact_4">
 <tr>
  <th><dtml-var ContactType_4>:</th><td><dtml-var Contact_4>
 </tr>
</dtml-if>
<dtml-if "ContactType_5 or Contact_5">
 <tr>
  <th><dtml-var ContactType_5>:</th><td><dtml-var Contact_5>
 </tr>
```

```
</dtml-if>
<dtml-if "ContactType_6 or Contact_6">
 <tr>
  <th><dtml-var ContactType_6>:</th><td><dtml-var Contact_6>
 </tr>
</dtml-if>

<tr>
 <th valign="top">Address:</th>
 <td>
  <dtml-var Address1><br>
  <dtml-if Address2><dtml-var Address2><br></dtml-if>
  <dtml-if City><dtml-var City>, </dtml-if><dtml-var State> ⮐
<dtml-var ZipCode><br>
  <dtml-var Country><br>
 </td>

</table>
<dtml-var standard_html_footer>
```

In `entryDetails.dtml`, we can see a fairly simple presentation method. Other than the `FirstName` and `LastName` attributes and the various mailing address attributes, the rest of the object's attributes are only rendered if they are non-blank. This reduces clutter on the page by hiding fields that aren't used for a particular Entry.

Unfortunately, because we don't have a way of instantiating entries, we can't yet test the functionality of the `Entry` class, so that's what we show you next.

Adding, Listing, and Deleting Entries from the AddressBook

In the previous section, you added the necessary code to edit and render instances of the `Entry` class, but none of that will do your application any good if you don't have any instances to edit or render.

Adding entries to the AddressBook

The `AddressBook` class instances, as we told you earlier in this chapter, must be responsible for managing their own contents. While Zope has a base class (ObjectManager) specifically for creating container-type objects, the `AddressBook` class doesn't inherit from it. `ObjectManager`-derived classes are useful when you need an object that can contain a wide variety of object types, and that requires some functionality that you can't get with a regular folder (Folders subclass ObjectManager). If you need to manage the contained objects through the ZMI (Zope Management Interface), deriving from Folder may be more appropriate.

For this project, AddressBooks only need to contain `Entry` objects, and the `Entry` objects need to be managed from a custom interface, not through the ZMI, so we're not subclassing `ObjectManager` or `Folder`.

The next thing you need to do to the `AddressBook` class is to give it somewhere to store the Entry objects. Because we'll want to retrieve Entry objects later by their id, it makes most sense to store them in a dictionary, where the key is the id. So edit the `AddressBook` class `__init__` method (in `AddressBook.py`) as follows:

```
def __init__(self, id, title):
    self.id              = id
    self.title           = title
    self.ContactTypeList = ['Email', 'Home', 'Mobile',
                            'Work', 'Pager', 'ICQ/IM',
                            'URL', 'Extension']
    self.Entries         = {}
    self.LastEntryID     = 0
```

Notice the last line also defines a `LastEntryID` integer attribute. This will be incremented each time an Entry is added to the AddressBook, and will be used to ensure that each Entry has a unique id.

Next you need to add an `addEntry` method. Add the following code to the `AddressBook` class before the Web presentation methods section at the end of the `AddressBook.py` file:

```
# Methods to add, edit, delete and retrieve Entries


def addEntry(self, FirstName = "", MiddleInitial = "",
             LastName = "", REQUEST = None
             ):
    "Method to add an entry to an AddressBook"
    id = self.LastEntryID = self.LastEntryID + 1
    id = str(id)
    entry = Entry(id, FirstName, MiddleInitial, LastName)
    self.Entries[id] = entry
    self.__changed__(1)

    if REQUEST is not None:
        return self.index_html(self, REQUEST)
```

Let's explain how this `addEntry` method works. The method has four optional parameters: `FirstName`, `MiddleInitial`, and `LastName` default to an empty string, while `REQUEST` defaults to `None`. After the docstring, the first statement increments the `LastEntryID` (an integer) attribute of the AddressBook and assigns its value to id, which is then converted to a string. This conversion is necessary, because when we later try to access the entry in the Entries dictionary, the key we supply and the key that was used to assign the entry to the dictionary in the first place must be of the same type, or the lookup will fail. Converting the key to a string before the assignment helps ensure that, since the data from the HTML forms will default to strings. An alternative would be to leave the id as an integer and convert the incoming form values to integers as well, but that way requires slightly more code.

Next, the method creates an Entry object using the parameters passed into the method and the id attribute, and assigns it to `entry`.

The object assigned to `entry` is then assigned to the AddressBook's Entries dictionary, using id as the key.

Here is something that you may not have seen yet: `self.__changed__(1)`. Previously, whenever we've changed a property on a class, we haven't had to do anything special to get the changes to "stick," so to speak. The Persistence machinery took care of the rest. Up till now though, the attributes we've been changing have all been strings. Strings are one of the immutable types and the Zope persistence machinery treats mutable and immutable attributes differently. When you change a mutable attribute of a class you're storing persistently, you need to notify the persistence machinery that the class has changed by using `self.__changed__(1)`. Dictionaries have this requirement along with Lists as they are both mutable types. Because `Entries` is a dictionary, we need to give the AddressBook the proper notification after we've assigned `entry` to `Entries[id]`.

Finally, if the method was called through the Web (determined by checking whether `REQUEST` is `None`), it then returns the AddressBook's `index_html` method.

Because the `addEntry` method tries to instantiate an Entry object, the `AddressBook` module needs to know about the `Entry` class. In other words, the `Entry` class needs to be imported from the `Entry` module. Change the beginning of the `AddressBook.py` file as follows:

```
from OFS.SimpleItem import SimpleItem
from Globals import DTMLFile
from Entry import Entry
```

Finally, the AddressBook needs a presentation method to display an entry-adding form. Add the following to the Web presentation methods section at the end of the file:

```
    addEntryForm = DTMLFile("dtml/addEntryForm", globals())
```

Your AddressBook module should now look like Listing 7-7.

Listing 7-7: AddressBook.py

```
from OFS.SimpleItem import SimpleItem
from Globals import DTMLFile
from Entry import Entry


# Module level declarations and methods

manage_addAddressBookForm = DTMLFile ⮐
("dtml/addAddressBookForm", globals())


def manage_addAddressBook(self, id, title, REQUEST):
    "Adds an AddressBook object to a folder"

    newAddressBook=AddressBook(id, title)
    self._setObject(id, newAddressBook)

    return self.manage_main(self, REQUEST)


# The Addressbook Class

class AddressBook(SimpleItem):
    "An AddressBook object"

    meta_type = "AddressBook"

    def __init__(self, id, title):
        self.id             = id
        self.title          = title
        self.ContactTypeList = ['Email', 'Home', 'Mobile',
                                'Work', 'Pager', 'ICQ/IM',
                                'URL', 'Extension']
        self.Entries        = {}
        self.LastEntryID    = 0

    def listContactTypes(self):
        "Returns a list of Contact Types"
        return self.ContactTypeList

    manage_options=(
    {'label':'Edit', 'action':'manage_main' },
    {'label':'View', 'action':'index_html'}
    )

    manage_main = DTMLFile("dtml/mainAddressBook", globals())

    def editAddressBook(self, title, REQUEST):
        "A method to edit Address Book Properties"
```

```
        self.title = title

        return self.manage_main(self, REQUEST)

    # Methods to add, edit, delete and retrieve Entries


    def addEntry(self, FirstName = "", MiddleInitial = "",
                 LastName = "", REQUEST = None
                 ):
        "Method to add an entry to an AddressBook"
        id = self.LastEntryID = self.LastEntryID + 1
        id = str(id)
        entry = Entry(id, FirstName, MiddleInitial, LastName)
        self.Entries[id] = entry
        self.__changed__(1)

        if REQUEST is not None:
            return self.index_html(self, REQUEST)


    # Web Presentation Methods

    index_html = DTMLFile("dtml/indexAddressBook", globals())

    addEntryForm = DTMLFile("dtml/addEntryForm", globals())
```

Now add an `addEntryForm.dtml` file to the `/Addressit/DTML/` directory with the content from Listing 7-8:

Listing 7-8: addEntryForm.dtml

```
<dtml-var standard_html_header>

<form action=addEntry>

<table>
<tr>
 <th>First Name:</th>
 <td><input type=text name=FirstName></td>
</tr>
<tr>
 <th>Last Name:</th>
 <td><input type=text name=LastName></td>
</tr>
<tr>
```

Continued

Listing 7-8 *(continued)*

```
 <th>Middle Initial:</th>
 <td><input type=text name=MiddleInitial size=1></td>
</tr>

<tr>
<td colspan=2>
<input type=submit value="Add Entry">
</table>

</form>

<dtml-var standard_html_footer>
```

Testing the addEntryForm

After making all the modifications described in the previous section, refresh the Addressit product and add a new AddressBook called *Test.* Then click the Test object to see its management interface, and right-click the View tab. Open the link in a new window, and you should see a screen like the one shown in Figure 7-6.

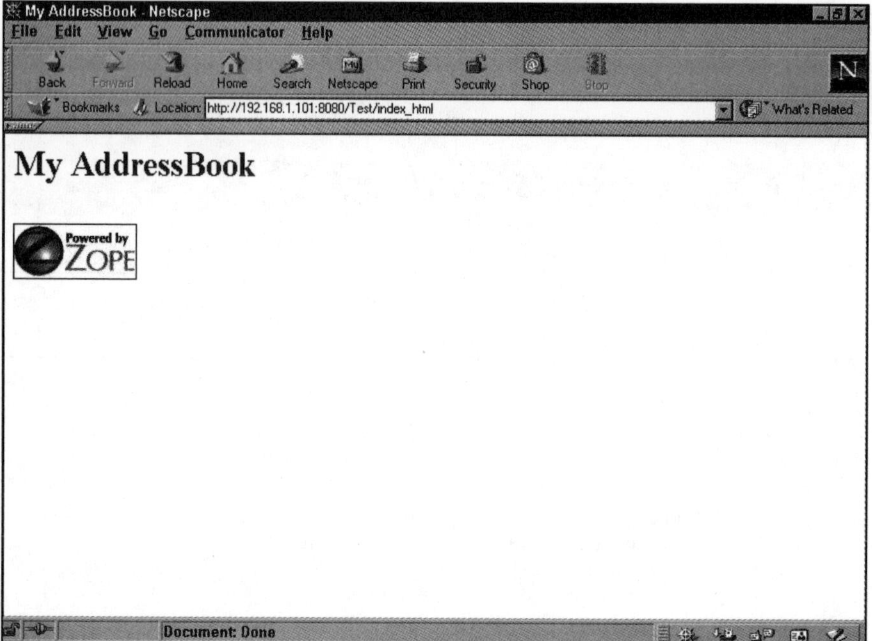

Figure 7-6: The AddressBook `index_html` **view**

In Figure 7-6, the URL in the browser is `http://192.168.1.101:8080/Test/index_html`. Your browser probably shows something else for the server portion of the URL, perhaps something like `128.0.0.1`, or perhaps something else. Rewrite the end portion of the URL from `/Test/index_html` to `/Test/addEntryForm`, and press Return.

You should now see a screen resembling the one shown in Figure 7-7.

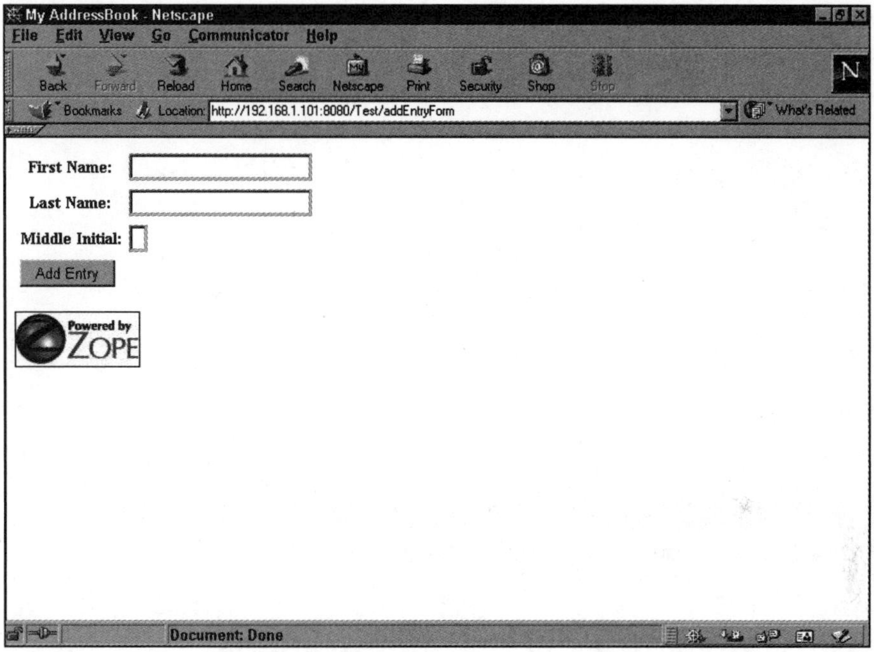

Figure 7-7: The AddressBook `addEntryForm`

Enter a first name, last name, and a middle initial, and then press the Add Entry button. You should now see a page resembling Figure 7-6 again. In order to verify that an entry object was actually added to the AddressBook's Entries dictionary, you need to add a `listEntries` method to the `AddressBook` class. Add the following method just below the `addEntry` method:

```
def listEntries(self):
    "Method to list Entries"
    return self.Entries.values()
```

Now restart Zope, and rewrite the URL to something like `http://192.168.1.101:8080/Test/listEntries`, and you should see a screen similar to the screen shown in Figure 7-8.

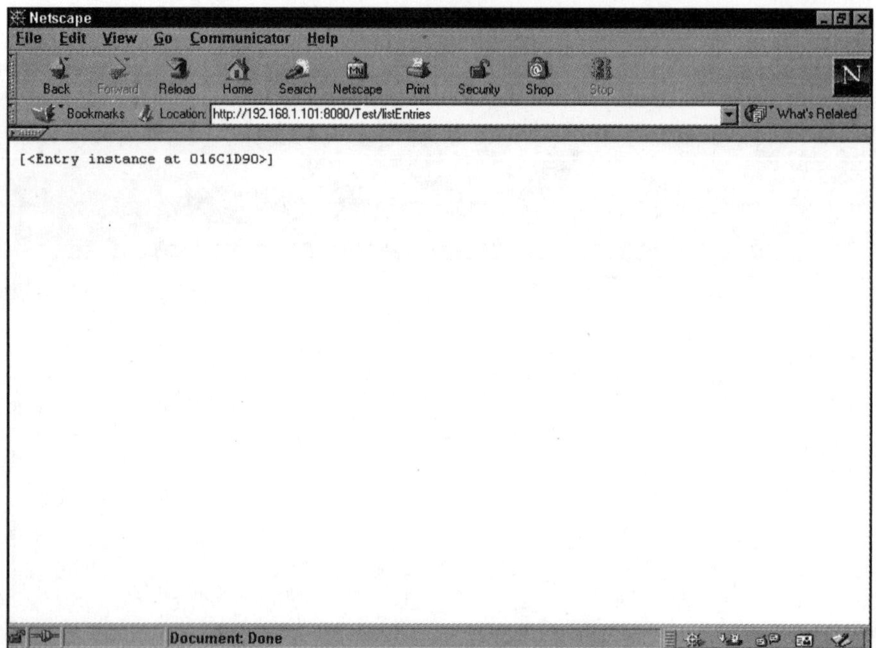

Figure 7-8: Demonstrating the successful adding of an Entry

Listing the entries in the AddressBook

Okay, now you need to be able to list the entries in the AddressBook's `index_html` method. Edit the `indexAddressBook.dtml` file as follows:

```
<dtml-var standard_html_header>
<h1><dtml-var title></h1>
<dtml-in listEntries>
<dtml-var FirstName> <dtml-var LastName><br>
</dtml-in>
<dtml-var standard_html_footer>
```

As when you developed the `helloProduct`, changes to DTMLFile DTML methods do not require restarting Zope or refreshing the product. Reload the `/Test/index_html` URL, and see the changes made to the page as shown in Figure 7-9

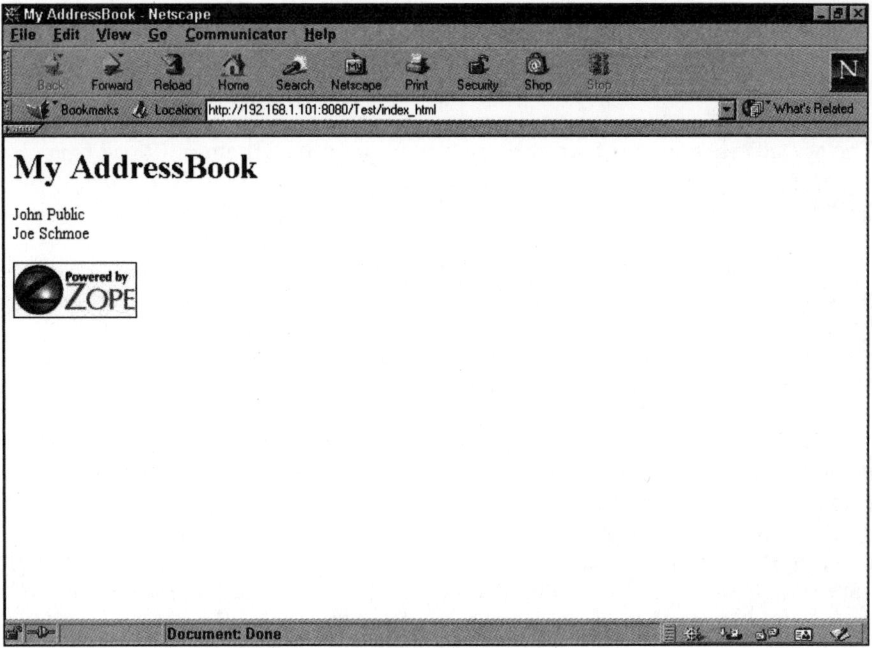

Figure 7-9: Listing the entries in the AddressBook

Deleting entries from the AddressBook

So far, we've shown you how to add entries to the AddressBook, and list them. Deleting entries is much the same as adding them, only in reverse. First add the following line at the top of the `AddressBook.py` file, just after the import statements:

```
ListType = type([])
```

Then add the following `delEntries` method to the `AddressBook` class in `AddressBook.py` immediately after the `addEntry` method:

```
    def delEntries(self, EntryIDs = [], REQUEST = None):
        "Method to delete Entries"

        if type(EntryIDs) != ListType:
            EntryIDs = [EntryIDs]

        for id in EntryIDs:
            try:
                del self.Entries[id]
            except KeyError:
                pass
```

```
        self.__changed__(1)

        if REQUEST is not None:
            return self.index_html(self, REQUEST)
```

The `delEntries` method takes two parameters, both of them optional: `EntryIDs` and `REQUEST`. EntryIDs is set by default to an empty list, and REQUEST is set by default to the None object.

The first thing that the `delEntries` method does is to check whether the `EntryIDs` parameter is actually a list by comparing its type with the ListType that is set at the top of the module. If it isn't, then it takes the `EntryIDs` string and turns it into a one-element list. We're assuming that EntryIDs is a String if it isn't a List because form submitted values default to a string representation.

Next, the method iterates over the members of the list, and for each one tries to delete the dictionary member whose key matches the id. Because more than one user could be deleting entries at more—or less the same time, the `delEntries` method could conceivably attempt to delete a dictionary member that has already been deleted and no longer exists. When you try to delete a member from a dictionary that doesn't have a matching key, Python raises a KeyError exception. The try/except block will pass on to the next member of `EntryIDs` if a keyError exception is raised, avoiding crashing the application with an error.

After completing the removal of the appropriate entries from the AddressBook, the `delEntries` method notifies the AddressBook instance that a mutable attribute has changed, and then returns the `index_html` method of the class.

So, where does this list of `EntryIDs` come from? You might think that you would need to create a separate `delEntriesForm.dtml` file, but that's actually unnecessary. We are already listing all of the entries in the `index_html` method, so a few tweaks will make it work for this purpose as well, as shown in Listing 7-9.

Listing 7-9: **IndexAddressBook.dtml**

```
<dtml-var standard_html_header>
<h1><dtml-var title></h1>
<form action="." method="post">
<input type="submit" name="delEntries:method" value="Delete">
<input type="submit" name="addEntryForm:method"
value="Add"><br>
<dtml-in listEntries>
<input type="checkbox" name="EntryIDs:list" value="&dtml-id;">
<dtml-var FirstName> <dtml-var LastName><br>
</dtml-in>
<dtml-var standard_html_footer>
```

There are several interesting tricks being used in this revised `index_html` method. First, Zope is resolving the form action from the names of the two submit buttons. The action of the form is ".", which is an alias for the current directory, and Zope resolves the method to call on the object from the name of the submit button, which is designated using a special `:method` convention.

Second, the checkboxes are collated into a list of values whether there is one or several checkboxes marked. Ordinarily, a single marked checkbox would be interpreted by Zope as a string, and only if more than one checkbox was marked would Zope interpret it as a list of strings. But by appending the checkbox form element's name with *:list*, Zope will always coerce the results to a list, even if only one checkbox is marked. This might be seen as overkill, as the `delEntries` method already takes the precaution of making sure to change any single strings it gets into lists, but we feel that this "suspenders-and-belt" approach is a good one.

Refresh the product, and take a look at `/Test/index_html`. You should see something like Figure 7-10:

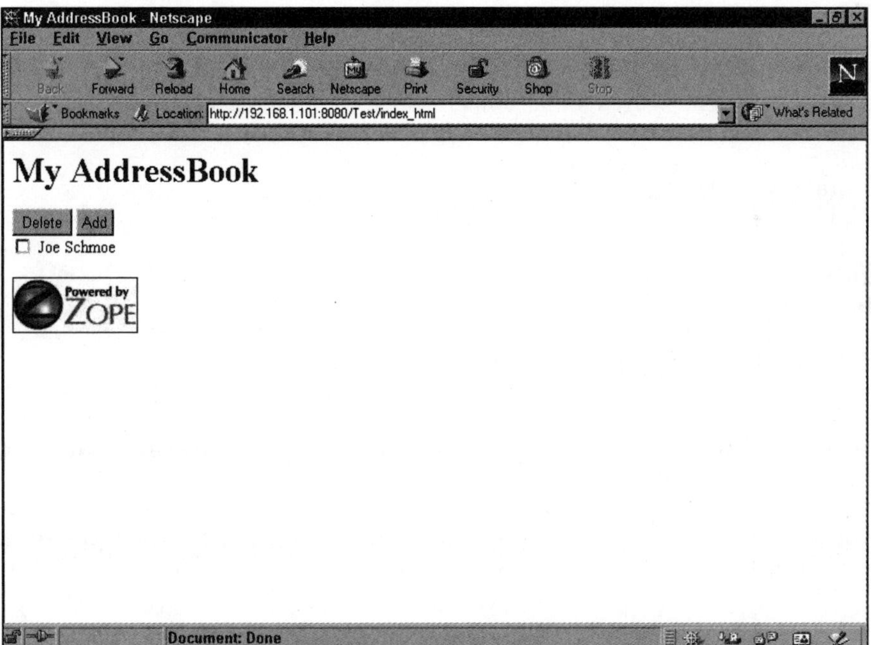

Figure 7-10: Revised AddressBook `index_html`

Clicking the Add button takes you to the `addEntryForm` method, whereas checking the boxes by any entry and clicking the Delete button will cause those entries to be removed.

The code for the product at this point can be found in the /chapter_07/Addressit_3 directory on the accompanying CD-ROM.

Traversing the AddressBook into the Entries

So far, you can instantiate an AddressBook, add entries to the AddressBook, list those entries, and even delete them if you don't like them. Pretty much the only thing you can't do right now is display an entry.

You can't get there from here

As the entries are stored in a dictionary within the AddressBook, it would seem that all you would have to do is traverse the Entries dictionary to the specific entry like this: /Test/Entries/1/index_html. But this does not work because Python's built in types are not traversable.

Fortunately, Zope's object publishing framework tries to find objects in several ways before giving up completely. One of the ways it attempts to find the right object is by trying to call the __getitem__ method with the unknown id as a key on the last known object (as if that object were a dictionary). So we can simply add our own __getitem__ method to the AddressBook class. Here is a simple version:

```
def __getitem__(self, id):
    return self.Entries[id]
```

This version would in fact intercept the object request, use the id as a key to retrieve the appropriate Entry object from within the Entries dictionary, and return the Entry object. Insofar as Entry objects have an index_html method, Zope will attempt to render it. That's where things break down again.

The object returned in this way is a *naked* or *bare* object. It doesn't have any sense of being contained within any other object, so any attempt to acquire anything from its environment (for example, standard_html_header) will fail.

The solution is to manually wrap the object in an acquisition context before returning it, like so:

```
def __getitem__(self, id):
    return self.Entries[id].__of__(self)
```

The __of__(self) portion of the previous code is subtle. As a result of adding this code, the Entry object will have a context when it is returned. Specifically, when Zope tries to walk up the containment tree from an entry and asks the entry to tell who its parent is, the entry will reply that it is an attribute __of__(self), self being in this case an AddressBook instance. Add the __getitem__ method to your AddressBook.py file, just before the addEntry method, and then refresh the product.

After restarting Zope, delete any existing AddressBooks, and add a new one with the same id (this is to avoid having a problem with the following test). Then go to its main view (for example, `192.168.100.101:8080/Test/index_html`) and add a new entry. Because a new AddressBook's `LastEntryID` property is initialized to 0, and this is the first entry that has been added to this new AddressBook, we can guess that the id of the new entry is 1. So try the following URL: `/Test/1/`. You should now see the entry's rendered `index_html` method.

Improving access to the entries

You should probably make it easier to get to the entries from the AddressBook, so let's change the AddressBook's `index_html` (`indexAddressBook.dtml`) method a little bit. Take a look at Listing 7-10.

Listing 7-10: IndexAddressBook.dtml

```
<dtml-var standard_html_header>
<h1><dtml-var title></h1>
<form action="." method="post">
<input type="submit" name="delEntries:method" value="Delete">
<input type="submit" name="addEntryForm:method"
value="Add"><br>
<dtml-in listEntries>
<input type="checkbox" name="EntryIDs:list" value="&dtml-id;">
<a href="./&dtml-id;"><dtml-var FirstName> <dtml-var
LastName></a><br>
</dtml-in>
<dtml-var standard_html_footer>
```

You can see that we've added a simple link around the rendered name in the entry listing. Now if you reload the AddressBook page, you should see links from any names listed. Clicking the links will take you to the Entry object in question.

Editing an Entry

Now that we can traverse to an entry and render it directly by going to a URL such as `/Test/1/index_html`, we can also traverse to the Entry object's `editEntryForm` method, which we added in an earlier section of the book. Try a URL such as `/Test/1/editEntryForm`, and you should at this point be able to see a form like that displayed in Figure 7-11.

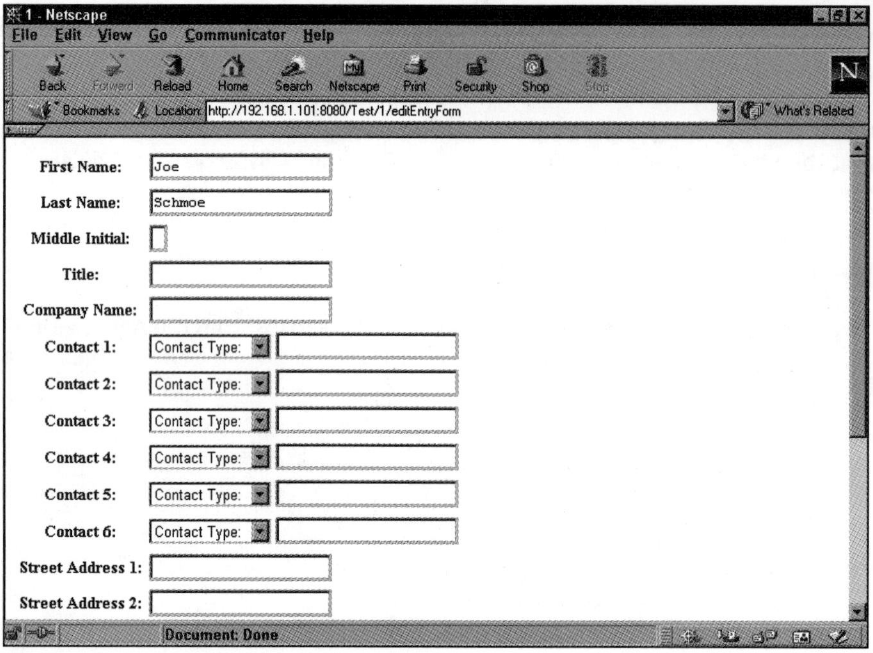

Figure 7-11: `editEntryForm.dtml` **form**

As you can see in Figure 7-11, the form does indeed render correctly. Some experimentation will also show that the `editEntry` method that the form submits to is also working correctly, and that you can now easily change the properties of an Entry object through the Web.

It's a little inconvenient to have to type in a direct URL to edit an Entry object, so let's make a small change to `entryDetails.dtml`, which is the file associated with Entry's `index_html` method. Take a look at Listing 7-11.

Listing 7-11: **entryDetails.dtml**

```
<dtml-var standard_html_header>
<form action="./editEntryForm" method="post">
<input type="submit" value="Edit Entry">
</form>
<h1><dtml-var FirstName> <dtml-var LastName></h1>
<table cellspacing="0" cellpadding="3" border="0">

<dtml-if Title>
 <tr>
  <th>Title:</th>
  <td><dtml-var Title>
 </tr>
</dtml-if>
```

```
<dtml-if Company>
 <tr>
  <th>Company Name:</th>
  <td><dtml-var Company>
 </tr>
</dtml-if>

<dtml-if "ContactType_1 or Contact_1">
 <tr>
  <th><dtml-var ContactType_1>:</th><td><dtml-var Contact_1>
 </tr>
</dtml-if>
<dtml-if "ContactType_2 or Contact_2">
 <tr>
  <th><dtml-var ContactType_2>:</th><td><dtml-var Contact_2>
 </tr>
</dtml-if>
<dtml-if "ContactType_3 or Contact_3">
 <tr>
  <th><dtml-var ContactType_3>:</th><td><dtml-var Contact_3>
 </tr>
</dtml-if>
<dtml-if "ContactType_4 or Contact_4">
 <tr>
  <th><dtml-var ContactType_4>:</th><td><dtml-var Contact_4>
 </tr>
</dtml-if>
<dtml-if "ContactType_5 or Contact_5">
 <tr>
  <th><dtml-var ContactType_5>:</th><td><dtml-var Contact_5>
 </tr>
</dtml-if>
<dtml-if "ContactType_6 or Contact_6">
 <tr>
  <th><dtml-var ContactType_6>:</th><td><dtml-var Contact_6>
 </tr>
</dtml-if>

<tr>
 <th valign="top">Address:</th>
 <td>
  <dtml-var Address1><br>
  <dtml-if Address2><dtml-var Address2><br></dtml-if>
  <dtml-if City><dtml-var City>, </dtml-if><dtml-var State> ⮐
<dtml-var ZipCode><br>
  <dtml-var Country><br>
 </td>

</table>

<dtml-var standard_html_footer>
```

Making the changes to `entryDetails.dtml` adds an Edit Entry button at the top of the page that makes it easier to access the `editEntryForm`.

After changing the file, reload the page for an entry (such as `/Test/1/`) and you'll see the button at the top of the page. Click it and you'll be taken to the `editEntryForm` method for that entry.

Congratulations! You've created a basic AddressBook application product. It is admittedly a little rough around the edges, but it has all of the basic functionality that such an application requires. In the next chapter, we show you how to add some polish and ease of use.

The code for the product at this point can be found in the `/chapter_07/Addressit_4` directory on the accompanying CD-ROM.

Summary

In this chapter we showed you step-by-step how to create a basic Web application as a Zope Python Product. We showed you:

✦ How to instantiate and edit AddressBooks

✦ How to add instances of the Entry class to the AddressBook

✦ How to list entries in the AddressBook

✦ How to delete entries from the AddressBook

✦ How to traverse the AddressBook into the entry instances

✦ How to edit the entry instances

In the next chapter, we show you how to increase the sophistication of the AddressBook's user interface.

✦ ✦ ✦

Enhancing the AddressBook

In This Chapter

In Chapter 7 we demonstrated the design and implementation of a fairly straightforward AddressBook application. In this chapter, we show you how to continue and improve the Address Book's functionality and user interface.

Adding a Standard Header

Until now, none of the DTML files that we've added to the AddressBook application have shared any code or layout besides the standard headers and footers Zope already uses. In order to make it easier to create standardized navigation for the application, a new header for the AddressBook is a good idea.

Add a `StandardAddressBookHeader.dtml` file to the `/Addressit/dtml/`directory with the following code:

```
<table width="100%" cellspacing="0"
cellpadding="2" border="0">
 <tr bgcolor="#CCCCFF">
  <td>
   <h2><dtml-var title_or_id></h2>
  </td>
 </tr>
</table>
```

And edit the `AddressBook.py` file to add the following line to the end of the Web presentation methods section:

```
standard_addressbook_header = DTMLFile ⮐
"dtml/StandardAddressBookHeader", globals())
```

Then edit indexAddressBook.dtml so that the beginning of the file reads:

```
<dtml-var standard_html_header>
<dtml-var standard_addressbook_header>

<form action="." method="post">
```

And edit the entryDetails.dtml file so that the beginning of the file reads:

```
<dtml-var standard_html_header>
<dtml-var standard_addressbook_header>
<form action="./editEntryForm" method="post">
<input type="submit" value="Edit Entry">
</form>

<table cellspacing="0" cellpadding="3" border="0">
```

Notice that both DTML files have had <dtml-var standard_addressbook_header> added to them, but both have also had some code removed. From the AddressBook's index_html method (indexAddressBook.dtml) we've removed the <dtml-var title>, and from the Entries index_html (entryDetails.dtml) we've removed the code that renders the first and last names of the Entry.

Now, the new standard_addressbook_header method will obviously replace the AddressBook's <dtml-var title> by rendering <dtml-var title_or_id>, but the Entry class currently has no title attribute or method, and you've just removed the code that renders the FirstName and LastName attributes. What you need to do now, is create a title method that returns an appropriately formatted name. Add the following method to the Entry class in Entry.py after the editEntry method and before the Web methods section:

```
def title(self):
    if self.MiddleInitial != "":
        return self.FirstName + " " + self.MiddleInitial + "." + " " +
self.LastName
    else:
        return self.FirstName + " " + self.LastName
```

This title method returns a string consisting of the FirstName, MiddleInitial, and LastName attributes (with appropriate punctuation and spacing) if the MiddleInitial attribute is *not* blank, but the title method returns a string consisting of the FirstName and LastName attributes only (separated by a space) if the MiddleInitial attribute *is* blank. The standard_addressbook_header will now render the Entry class' title method when it tries to render title_or_id.

Batching the Entries Display

The AddressBook application currently lists all of the contained Entries on a single page, regardless of how many entries there are. This is done by calling the `listEntries` method from the AddressBook's `index_html` DTMLFile.

The `listEntries` method is fairly simple. It just returns the dictionary's `values()` method, which returns a list that contains the objects in the dictionary:

```
def listEntries(self):
    "Method to list Entries"
    return self.Entries.values()
```

Note that if the `listEntries` method had instead returned `self.Entries`, the result would have been a list of key/value pairs, rather than a list of the values alone, which would have made accessing the attributes of the values (which are Entry instances) more difficult, though not impossible.

The code in `indexAddressBook.dtml` (which is mapped to `index_html` by the class) calls the `listEntries` method like this:

```
<dtml-in listEntries>
<input type="checkbox" name="EntryIDs:list" value="&dtml-id;">
<a href="./&dtml-id;"><dtml-var FirstName> <dtml-var
LastName></a><br>
</dtml-in>
```

which renders a checkbox and the first and last names for each returned object, linking the names to the actual Entry, which displays the Entry's `index_html`. However, now that the Entry class has a title method, you can simplify this by replacing the DTML that renders the first and last names like this:

```
<dtml-var standard_html_header>
<dtml-var standard_addressbook_header>

<form action="." method="post">
<input type="submit" name="delEntries:method" value="Delete">
<input type="submit" name="addEntryForm:method"
value="Add"><br>
<dtml-in listEntries>
<input type="checkbox" name="EntryIDs:list" value="&dtml-id;">
<a href="./&dtml-id;"><dtml-var title></a><br>
</dtml-in>
<dtml-var standard_html_footer>
```

which simplifies the DTML somewhat, and results in a nicer formatted name.

Scaling to many results

But what you should be concerned about here is that the page displays all of the Entries at once. When the AddressBook contains many Entries, this will result in two things:

- The page will be much longer, forcing users to scroll farther to find the entry they want.
- The page will take longer to download and render, forcing users to wait.

This clearly has a negative impact on the usability of the AddressBook. Fortunately, there is a fairly simple solution. Zope has optional attributes for the `<dtml-in>` tag that enable you to specify the beginning of the sequence you are iterating over, as well as how large the sequence is. Taking advantage of these optional attributes is fairly simple.

Rewrite the `indexAddressBook.dtml` file so that the `<dtml-in>` tag reads as follows:

```
<dtml-in listEntries size=20 start=start sort=LastName,FirstName,MiddleInitial>
```

You're doing three things here. First, you're telling the `<dtml-in>` tag to display 20 results at a time. Second, you're telling the tag to start at the sequence item whose number is contained in the "start" variable. Obviously the start variable needs to come from somewhere, so add the following to the top of the `indexAddressBook.dtml` file, just below the two header variables:

```
<dtml-unless start>
 <dtml-call "REQUEST.set('start', 1)">
</dtml-unless>
```

Here, you're checking if the start variable has already been set, or if the value was passed in from somewhere else, and if not, you set the variable to one. This means that the default starting point for a batch is the first item in the sequence, which is the expected behavior.

The third thing you're telling the `<dtml-in>` tag to do is to sort the result set by the LastName, FirstName, and MiddleInitial attributes. Using a compound sort means that the list is sorted first according to the LastName attribute, and in case of a tie, by the FirstName attribute. If the result is still tied, then the MiddleInitial attribute is the final tiebreaker. Sorting according to this format is standard office filing practice, and should be familiar to your users.

About orphans

If you go ahead and test the AddressBook application at this point and begin adding more Entries, you'll notice something curious as you get to the twenty-first entry, namely, that it's being listed on the page. (See Figure 8-1.) What's going on here and why isn't the batch being limited to 20 items like we asked?

It turns out that the <dtml-in> tag has an optional attribute called *orphan*. Orphans are "dangling" sequence items that you might want to aggregate with another batch (presumably they'd be lonely by themselves). The default value for the orphan attribute (meaning unless you set it explicitly yourself) is three, which means that if the next batch is smaller than three, its results are appended to the current batch so that they don't dangle.

If you want to disable the orphan functionality, all you need to do is set the orphan attribute to zero, like this: <dtml-in listEntries orphan=0>. However, you don't really need to do that for this AddressBook application.

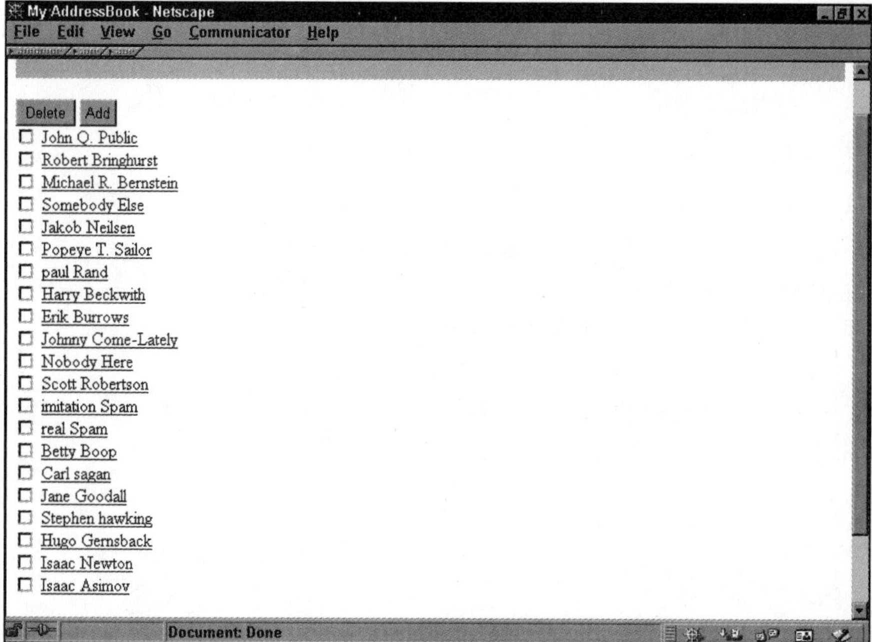

Figure 8-1: Orphans are added to the previous batch

Navigating among the batches

Okay, so how can the user get to the next batch? You could ask them to rewrite the URL to pass in a new start value, like so:

```
http://128.0.0.1/Test?start=21
```

This would work, as we can see in Figure 8-2, but it's unreasonable to expect users (even technically inclined users) to navigate by rewriting URLs in their browser's address field.

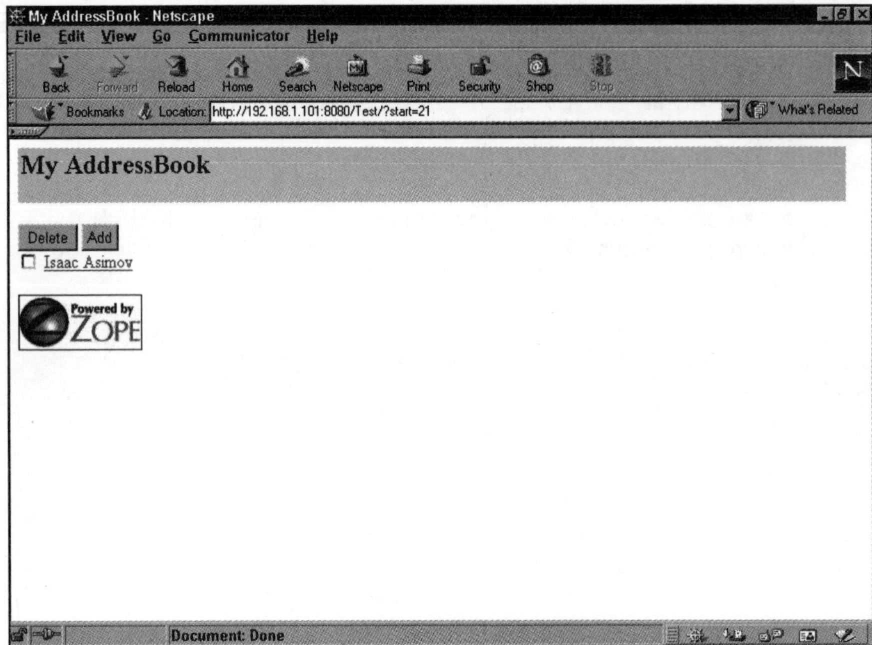

Figure 8-2: Manually displaying a different starting point

However, you can certainly automate this process by creating links on the page that pass in this value for the user in an easier to use way.

There's more than one way to create this sort of batch navigation, such as creating previous/next links that look like this:

```
< Previous  Next >
```

But we've found that generally speaking, a navigation interface should inform the user as to how much information is present and enable the user to skip to an arbitrary location within the set.

So, we'll show you how to build a general batch navigation interface that looks like this:

```
[1-20] [21-40] [41-53]
```

which will automatically expand to fit the number of results available.

First, edit `indexAddressBook.dtml` at the beginning of the file to match the following code:

```
<dtml-var standard_html_header>
<dtml-var standard_addressbook_header>
```

```
<dtml-unless start>
 <dtml-call "REQUEST.set('start', 1)">
</dtml-unless>

<dtml-in listEntries previous size=20 start=start>
<dtml-in previous-batches mapping>
[<a href="&dtml-absolute_url;?start= &dtml-batch-start- ⮐
number;"><dtml-var batch-start-number> - ⮐
<dtml-var batch-end-number></a>]
</dtml-in>
</dtml-in>

<dtml-in listEntries size=20 start=start>
<dtml-if sequence-start>
[<dtml-var expr="_['sequence-index']+1"> -
</dtml-if>
<dtml-if sequence-end>
<dtml-var expr="_['sequence-index']+1">]
</dtml-if>
</dtml-in>

<dtml-in listEntries next size=20 start=start>
<dtml-in next-batches mapping>
[<a href="&dtml-absolute_url;?start= &dtml-batch-start- ⮐
number;"><dtml-var batch-start-number> - ⮐
<dtml-var batch-end-number></a>]
</dtml-in>
</dtml-in>

<form action="." method="post">
.
.
.
```

You've just added three new sections of code to the AddressBook's `index_html` method between the `<dtml-unless>` block and the beginning of the form, each of which iterates over the same `listEntries` method that the main display does, further along the file.

The three new sections do the following:

✦ Render links to the batches before the current one

✦ Render an indicator of the current batch

✦ Render links to the batches after the current one

Let's take a closer look at each new section you've just added.

First, we've got the following code:

```
<dtml-in listEntries previous size=20 start=start>
<dtml-in previous-batches mapping>
[<a href="&dtml-absolute_url;?start= &dtml-batch-start- ⮐
number;"><dtml-var batch-start-number> - ⮐
<dtml-var batch-end-number></a>]
</dtml-in>
</dtml-in>
```

You can see that the code starts off by seemingly iterating over the current batch, as defined by the "start" attribute, except that we are also adding a "previous" attribute. The previous attribute causes the in tag to only iterate once if there are any previous batches, and sets various special batch variables to the previous sequence. The batch variable that you're interested in here is "previous-batches," which, when iterated over using the *mapping* keyword, creates a sequence of mapping objects that make "start-batch-number," "batch-end-number," and "batch-size" available as variables. You can see that the code here uses the "batch-start-" and "batch-end-" variables to construct a link that shows the range of the batch being pointed to, and passes the "batch-start-number" value in the URL as the value for "start."

The next section is a bit simpler:

```
<dtml-in listEntries size=20 start=start>
<dtml-if sequence-start>
[<dtml-var expr="_['sequence-index']+1"> -
</dtml-if>
<dtml-if sequence-end>
<dtml-var expr="_['sequence-index']+1">]
</dtml-if>
</dtml-in>
```

Here, the code is just iterating over the same current batch that further in the code will render the Entry list, but instead of rendering entries, it just tests to see if the code is executing on the first item in the batch, and if it is, it renders the following python expression: `"_['sequence-index']+1"`, which just adds one to the current sequence index. The sequence index starts with zero, not one, so you have to add one to it to get the number to match a user's expectations.

The second bit of code here does the same thing except that it tests whether the code is executing on the last item of the sequence and if so, renders the sequence index plus one.

And that's it for the current batch—it doesn't need to be linked to, it just must have a placeholder displayed.

Finally, the third bit of code is very similar to the first:

```
<dtml-in listEntries next size=20 start=start>
<dtml-in next-batches mapping>
[<a href="&dtml-absolute_url;?start= &dtml-batch-start- ⮐
number;"><dtml-var batch-start-number> - ⮐
<dtml-var batch-end-number></a>]
</dtml-in>
</dtml-in>
```

Similar, that is, except that we pass the "next" attribute instead of "previous," and iterate over "next-batches" using the mapping keyword instead of "previous-batches." Other than those changes, the code is identical, and produces a series of links to the batches following the current one.

With these three sections of code rendering navigation elements for the previous batches, current batch, and next batches, we have all that is necessary to display a functional batch-navigation device.

The result, after adding a few more Entries, looks like Figure 8-3 and Figure 8-4.

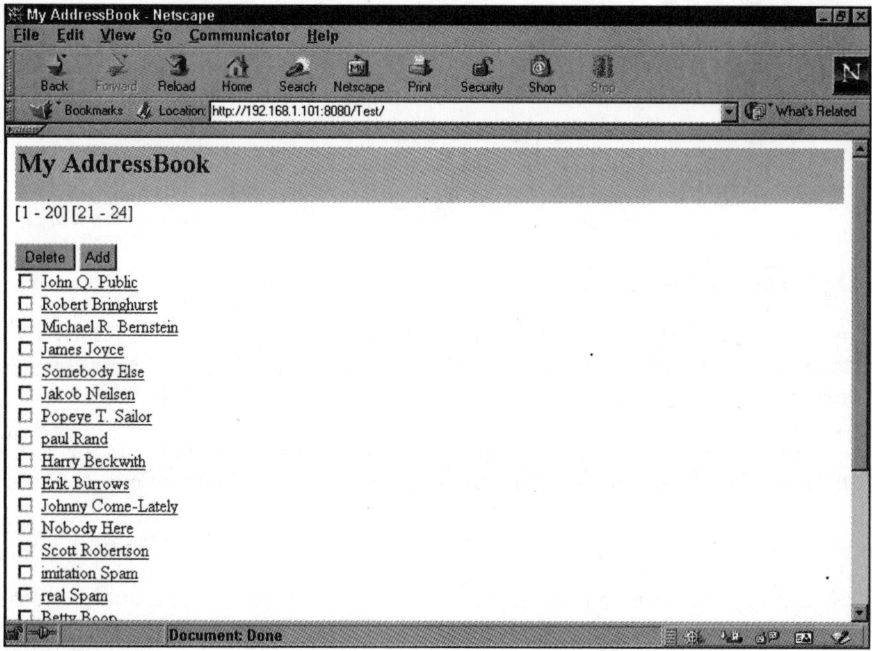

Figure 8-3: Batch Navigation 1

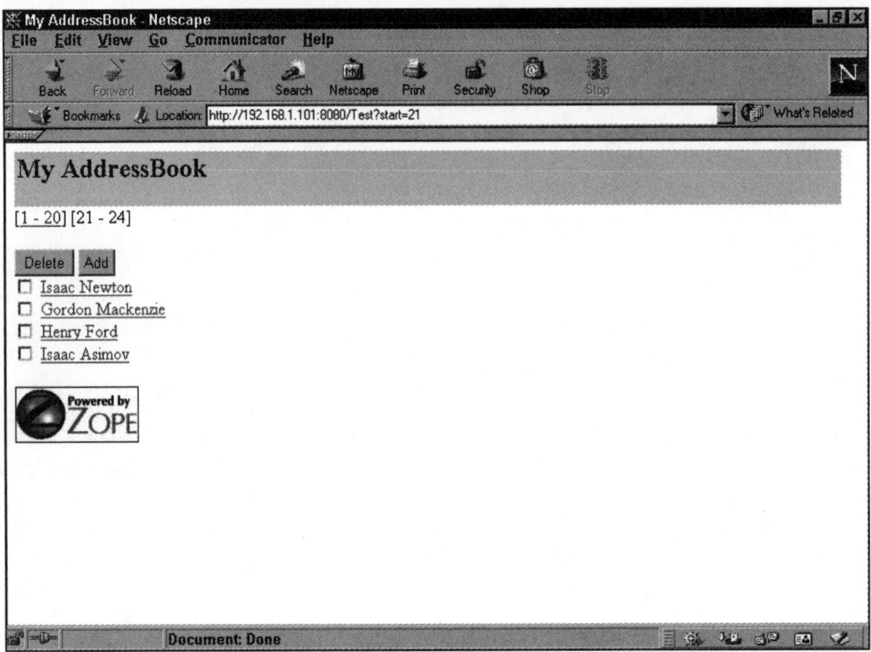

Figure 8-4: Batch Navigation 2

The code for the product at this point can be found in the `/chapter_08/Addressit_5` directory on the accompanying CD-ROM.

Grouping Entries

The changes you've made to the AddressBook in this chapter make it easier to manage and navigate Entries once you have more than 30 Entries. Now the AddressBook is capable of displaying any number of Entries by batching through them, so you can easily manage hundreds of Entries. However, suppose that you need to navigate among *thousands* of Entries, or that you need to categorize the entries in some way. If so, you should consider another enhancement: *grouping*.

There are two basic approaches for adding grouping to the AddressBook:

✦ Groups could be objects contained within the Addressbook, and containing Entries themselves.

✦ A Group could be a simple attribute of an Entry.

Both approaches have merit. In general, unless the Group has to have some attributes of its own beyond a simple label, the second approach is simpler. In this case, a group is simply a labeled category, so we'll go with the second approach.

Adding a GroupList attribute to the AddressBook class

Because the list of Groups that Entries can be categorized into is common to all Entries, a GroupList attribute should belong to the AddressBook class. This attribute can be a simple list of strings.

Change the AddressBook class' `__init__` method to read as follows:

```
def __init__(self, id, title):
    self.id              = id
    self.title           = title
    self.ContactTypeList = ['Email', 'Home', 'Mobile',
                            'Work', 'Pager', 'ICQ/IM',
                            'URL', 'Extension']
    self.Entries         = {}
    self.LastEntryID     = 0
    self.GroupList       = ['Unfiled', 'test1', 'test2']
```

The AddressBook class also needs a method similar to the `listContactTypes` method that will return the list of Groups, so add the following code to the AddressBook class (in `AddressBook.py`) just before the section labeled `#Methods to add, edit, delete and retrieve Entries`:

```
# Methods to manipulate groups

def listGroups(self):
    "Returns a list of Groups"
    return self.GroupList
```

More methods to manipulate the list of Groups will be created in a later section of this chapter.

Adding a Group attribute to the Entry class

In the Entry class, most of the attributes are initialized in the `editEntry` method, so you need to edit this method to take an additional optional parameter, Group, with its default value as "Unfiled." In addition, in the body of the method, the Group attribute must be set as well. Edit the `Entry.py` file so the `editEntry` method corresponds to the following code:

```
def editEntry (self, FirstName, MiddleInitial, LastName,
               Address1 = "",
               Address2 = "",
               City = "",
               State = "",
               ZipCode = "",
               Country = "",
               Company = "",
               Title = "",
```

```
                        Group = "Unfiled",
                        Contact_1 = "", ContactType_1 = "",
                        Contact_2 = "", ContactType_2 = "",
                        Contact_3 = "", ContactType_3 = "",
                        Contact_4 = "", ContactType_4 = "",
                        Contact_5 = "", ContactType_5 = "",
                        Contact_6 = "", ContactType_6 = "",
                        REQUEST = None
                        ):
        "Method for updating Entries"
        self.FirstName = FirstName
        self.LastName = LastName
        self.MiddleInitial = MiddleInitial
        self.Address1 = Address1
        self.Address2 = Address2
        self.City = City
        self.State = State
        self.ZipCode = ZipCode
        self.Country = Country
        self.Company = Company
        self.Title = Title
        self.Group = Group
        self.Contact_1 = Contact_1
        self.ContactType_1 = ContactType_1
        self.Contact_2 = Contact_2
        self.ContactType_2 = ContactType_2
        self.Contact_3 = Contact_3
        self.ContactType_3 = ContactType_3
        self.Contact_4 = Contact_4
        self.ContactType_4 = ContactType_4
        self.Contact_5 = Contact_5
        self.ContactType_5 = ContactType_5
        self.Contact_6 = Contact_6
        self.ContactType_6 = ContactType_6
        if REQUEST is not None:
            return self.editEntryForm(self, REQUEST)
```

After you've made this change to the `Entry.py` file, a corresponding change needs to be made to the `editEntryForm.dtml` file, so as to provide a way to set the Group for the Entry. Edit `editEntryForm.dtml` so as to add the following between the rows for the "Company" form element and the "Contact_1" form element.

```
  <tr>
    <th>Group:</th>
    <td>
      <select size=1 name="Group">
        <dtml-in listGroups>
        <option value="&dtml-sequence-item;" <dtml-if "_['sequence-⮐
item']==Group">selected</dtml-if>><dtml-var sequence-item>
```

```
</dtml-in>
      </select>
    </td>
</tr>
```

This little bit of code is similar to the form element you created earlier in this chapter for the contact type, namely, that the code iterates over the results of a method (in this case, `listGroups`), checks with each iteration if the sequence-item corresponds with the value of the Group attribute, and if so, causes that option to be selected in the form element.

At this point, you've made all the changes necessary to set a Group attribute on an Entry. Unfortunately, any AddressBooks that you have already created don't have a `GroupList` attribute, so refreshing the Product won't be very much help. You'll have to delete the existing AddressBook and create a new one after refreshing. After you've added an Entry, check its editing view and you should see something like the screen shown in Figure 8-5.

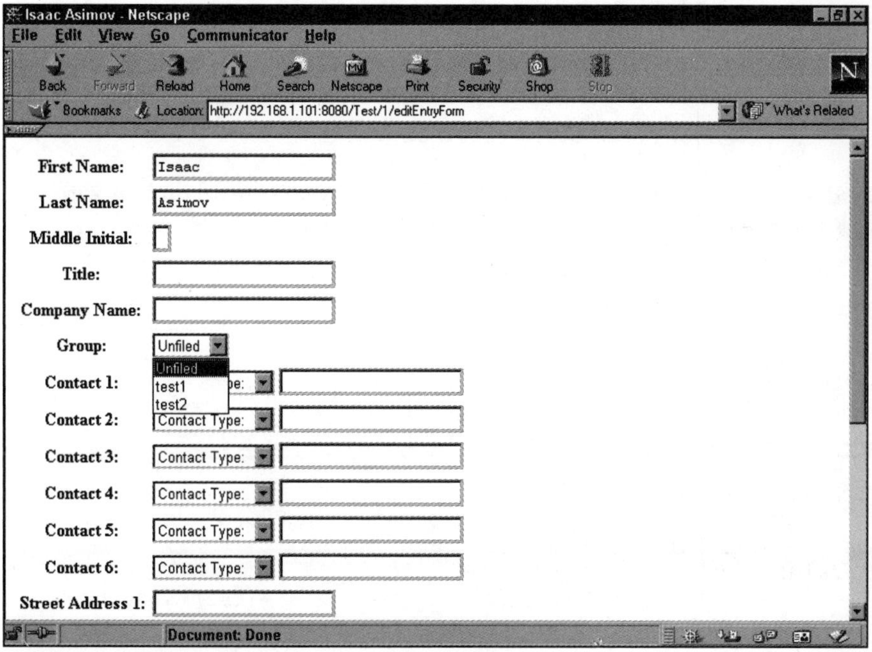

Figure 8-5: Editing an Entry with a Group attribute

Choosing another Group (such as test1) and submitting the change will demonstrate that the Group attribute is being persisted correctly in the ZODB (Zope Object Database).

Adding and Deleting Groups

In the previous section, you added the ability to set a Group attribute on an Entry object. This works in a substantially similar way to the various ContactType attributes, but with one important difference. You, as a developer, can't really anticipate how users are going to want to group the Entries in their AddressBooks the way you could anticipate the contact types. It's obvious then, that the AddressBook class needs some way of modifying the list of Groups besides editing the class' source code in `AddressBook.py`. In other words, the Group list must be configurable via its own management screens.

There is another design decision to be made here: whether the group management screens should be end-user screens or Zope management screens. The decision depends on who you see adding, deleting, and renaming groups — a site administrator or an end user. We are going to proceed under the assumption that the end user should be able to manage the groups.

There are three modifications that need to be made to the AddressBook:

- ✦ AddressBook needs a `manageGroupForm` DTML method.
- ✦ AddressBook needs a `addGroup` method.
- ✦ AddressBook needs a `delGroups` method.

First, add a `manageGroupForm.dtml` file to the `/Addressit/dtml/` folder with the following code:

```
<dtml-var standard_html_header>
<dtml-var standard_addressbook_header>

<h2><dtml-var title></h2>
<h3>Manage Groups</h3>
 <form action="." method="post">
 <table border=0 cellpadding=3 cellspacing=0>

 <dtml-in listGroups>
  <tr <dtml-if sequence-even>bgcolor="#CCCCCC"</dtml-if>>
   <td><input type=checkbox name="groups:list" ⮐
value="&dtml-sequence-item;"></td>
   <td><a href="&dtml-sequence-item;"><dtml-var sequence-
item></td>
  </tr>
 </dtml-in>
  <tr><td colspan=2>
   <input type=submit name="delGroups:method" value="Delete ⮐
selected Groups"><br>
   <input type=text name="group"><input type=submit ⮐
name="addGroup:method" value="Add a Group">
  </td></tr>
```

```
</table>
</form>

<dtml-var standard_html_footer>
```

The code here is fairly simple and reminiscent of an earlier version of the AddressBook's `index_html` method, except that here the code is iterating over `listGroups` instead of `listEntries`.

Another change is the code in the following line:

```
<tr <dtml-if sequence-even>bgcolor="#CCCCCC"</dtml-if>>
```

This checks to see whether the current sequence-item number is even, and if so, adds a gray background color to the table row. The upshot of this little bit of code is that every other row is gray, which is a technique known as *greenstriping* after the green and white striped printout paper that was used in dot-matrix printers. Whether in a printout or on-screen, greenstriping increases the legibility of information in tabular format, which is a common usability improvement in Web applications.

Next, you will need to make some changes to the `AddressBook.py` file. First, edit the end of the file (where the Web methods are defined) to add the `manageGroupForm` Web method:

```
# Web Presentation Methods

index_html = DTMLFile("dtml/indexAddressBook", globals())

addEntryForm = DTMLFile("dtml/addEntryForm", globals())

standard_addressbook_header = DTMLFile("dtml/StandardAddressBookHeader", ⮐
globals())

manageGroupForm = DTMLFile("dtml/manageGroupForm", globals())
```

Next, edit the "Methods to manipulate groups" section to incorporate the `addGroup` and `delGroups` methods outlined in Listing 8-1.

Listing 8-1: addGroup and delGroups

```
# Methods to manipulate groups

def addGroup(self, group, REQUEST = None):
    "Method to add Groups"

    if group not in self.GroupList:
        self.GroupList.append(group)
```

Continued

Listing 8-1 *(continued)*

```
            self.__changed__(1)

            if REQUEST is not None:
                return self.manageGroupForm(self, REQUEST)


    def delGroups(self, groups = [], REQUEST = None):
        "method to delete groups"
        if type(groups) != ListType:
            groups = [groups]

        for group in groups:
            if group == 'Unfiled': continue
            # You are not allowed to delete Unfiled

            try:
                index = self.GroupList.index(group)
                del self.GroupList[index]
            except ValueError:
                pass

        self.__changed__(1)

        if REQUEST is not None:
            return self.manageGroupForm(self, REQUEST)


    def listGroups(self):
        "Returns a list of Groups"
        return self.GroupList
```

The `addGroup` method is fairly self-explanatory. It takes a group parameter and an optional `REQUEST` parameter (with a default value of None). The method checks to see whether the Group name is already in the `GroupList`, and if not, adds it to the list. Then, the method checks that the `REQUEST` parameter's value is not equal to `None`, and if it isn't, (meaning that the `addGroups` method was invoked through the Web), the method returns the `manageGroupForms` method.

The `delGroups` method is a little more complex. It takes a list of group ids in the parameter "groups." The `manageGroupForm` page identifies each listed Group submitted via checkbox whose name is set to "groups:list." This is a technique whereby Zope will coerce the submitted values to a list, even if there is only one checkbox checked. Meanwhile, in a suspenders-and-belt fashion, the `delGroups` method also checks to see whether the group's parameter submitted to it is a list, and if not, changes it into one. This is done to ensure that the correct type is iterated over, even if the method is called from somewhere else other than the `manageGroupForm` page.

After `delGroups` has ensured that it is operating on a list, it iterates over that list to try and delete each group in turn, but first it checks to see whether the group it is trying to delete is the "Unfiled" group. As this is the group that Entries are set to by default upon their creation, deleting this group would probably be a bad thing, so the method will skip over an attempt to delete this Group.

Next, the `delGroups` method tries to find the index of the current Group in GroupList, and tries to delete the list item of that index. If the index lookup fails (and raises a `ValueError`), this would indicate that the list does not actually have a group of that name stored. This situation would pretty much only occur if someone else had already deleted the group in question sometime between when the `manageGroupForm` was rendered and when that particular group was iterated over in `delGroups`. So, `delGroups` will skip over the group if this exception is raised.

And that's it! If you refresh the Addressit product after saving the open files, you should be able to go to `/Test/manageGroupForm` in order to see the group management interface, as shown in Figure 8-6:

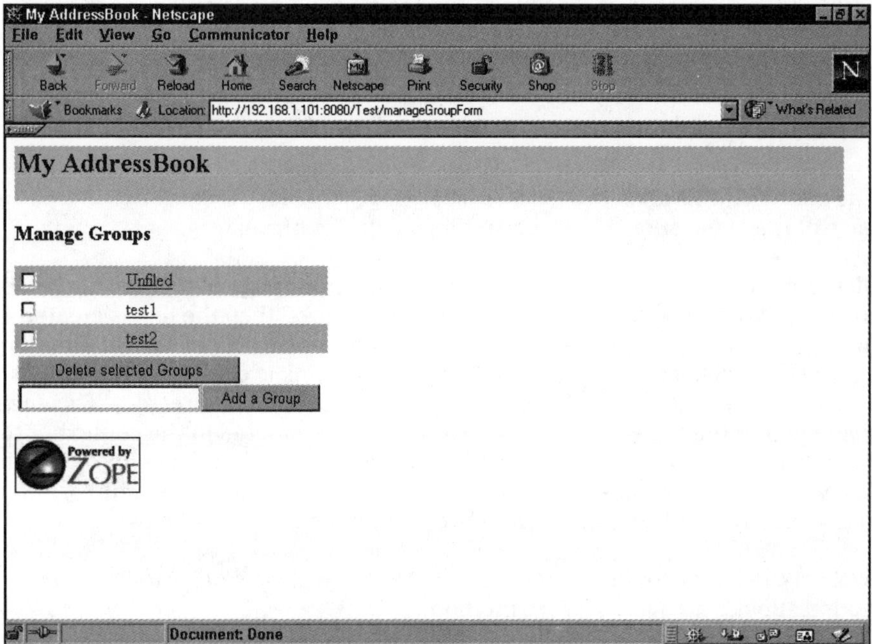

Figure 8-6: The manageGroupForm interface

Now that the user has an easy way to add and delete Groups, there is some clean up that needs to be done. The AddressBook should no longer be initialized with the test1 and test2 values in the GroupList attribute, only with Unfiled. So we need to make the following change to `__init__`:

```
def __init__(self, id, title):
    self.id             = id
    self.title          = title
    self.ContactTypeList = ['Email', 'Home', 'Mobile',
                            'Work', 'Pager', 'ICQ/IM',
                            'URL', 'Extension']
    self.Entries        = {}
    self.LastEntryID    = 0
    self.GroupList      = ['Unfiled']
```

You should also change `StandardAddressBookHeader.dtml` to link to the `manageGroupForm` method and generally improve the application-level navigation:

```
<table width="100%" cellspacing="0" cellpadding="2" border="0">
 <tr bgcolor="#CCCCFF">
  <td>
   <h2><dtml-var title_or_id></h2>
      <a href="<dtml-if "meta_type=='AddressBook'">.⮐
/<dtml-else>../</dtml-if>">Address Book</a>
     | <a href="<dtml-if "meta_type=='AddressBook'">.⮐
<dtml-else>..</dtml-if>/manageGroupForm">Manage Groups</a>
   <dtml-if "meta_type=='AddressBook Entry'"> | ⮐
<a href="./editEntryForm">Edit Entry</a></dtml-if>
  </td>
 </tr>
</table>
```

The code that this adds to `standard_addressbook_header` creates two links on every page of the application and one additional link on Entry pages.

The first link this code generates is a link to the front page of the AddressBook. If the meta-type of the current object is "AddressBook," then the link is created to point to `./`, or in other words, to the default view object of the *current* directory. Otherwise, if the meta-type is something else, the link is created to point towards `../`, or in other words, the default view object in the *parent* directory. This means that whether the `standard_addressbook_header` is rendered in the context of the AddressBook (or one of its methods) or in the context of an Entry (or one of the Entry's methods) the link will always point correctly towards the AddressBook's `index_html` method, and not toward the Entry's `index_html` method.

Similarly, the code for creating the second link will always point toward the AddressBook's `manageGroupForm` method.

The code creating the third link only renders if the current context's meta-type is "AddressBook Entry," and creates a link to the current Entry's `editEntry` method. Figure 8-7 and Figure 8-8 show the improved application navigation:

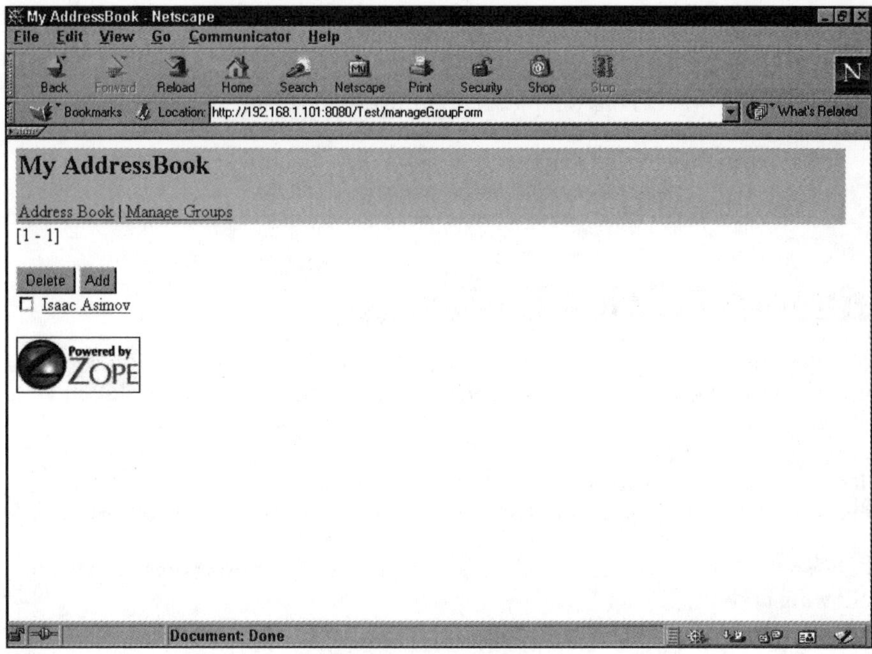

Figure 8-7: The Improved AddressBook Navigation 1

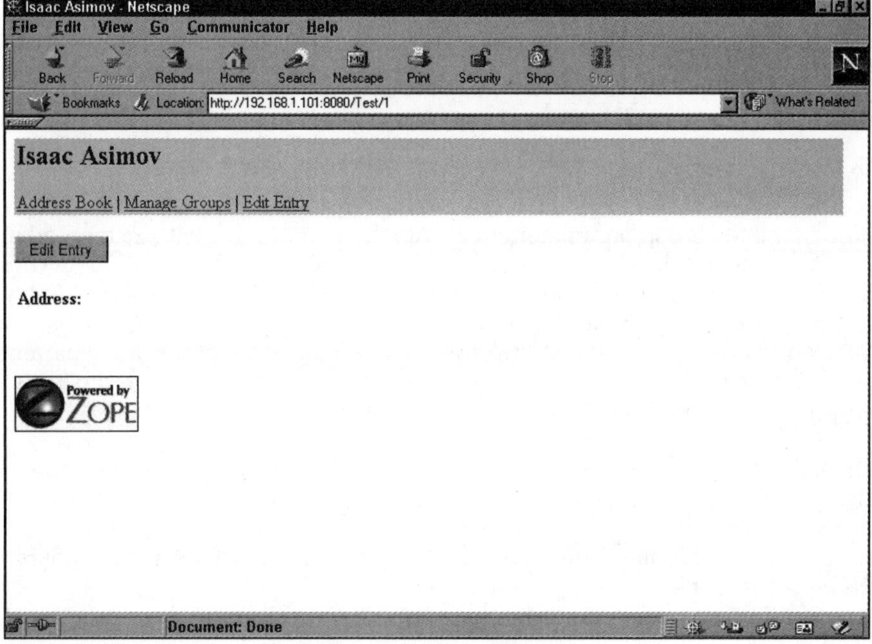

Figure 8-8: The Improved AddressBook Navigation 2

The simplicity of the code to create this navigation bar is one of the ways in which Zope demonstrates the power of its approach toward object publishing. Because object containment can be reflected directly in the URL, creating a link that leads to the containing object is as simple as pointing the link towards the parent directory.

The code for the product at this point can be found in the /chapter_08/Addressit_6 directory on the accompanying CD-ROM.

Retrieving Entries by Group

Now that you can categorize Entries by Group, we'll show you how to enhance the AddressBook class and the user interface to retrieve Entries according to which group the entries are in.

First, the listEntries method must be replaced with a listEntriesByGroup method. The new method will take a group parameter whose default will be "All":.

Remove the listEntries method from AddressBook.py, and replace it with the following code:

```
def listEntriesByGroup(self, group = "All"):
    ret = []
    if group == "All":
        for entry in self.Entries.values():
            ret.append(entry)
    else:
        for entry in self.Entries.values():
            if entry.Group == group:
                ret.append(entry)

    return ret
```

Note that if the group parameter equals All, the listEntriesByGroup method has identical functionality to the original listEntries method (returning all Entries). But if group equals some other value, the method iterates over the list of Entry objects, examines each Entry's Group attribute, and only appends it to a list object (labeled ret) if the Group attribute's value equals the value of the group parameter. After all entries that match this criteria are appended to the ret list, the list is returned by the method.

Changing the name of the method by which Entries are retrieved necessitates some changes to indexAddressBook.dtml as well.

First, add the following code to the beginning of the file, between the headers and the code that set's the default start value:

```
<dtml-unless SelectedGroup>
 <dtml-call "REQUEST.set('SelectedGroup', 'All')">
</dtml-unless>
```

This sets the default value of `SelectedGroup` to "All." Now change all occurrences of listEntries to `"listEntriesByGroup(_['SelectedGroup'])"`, including the quotes.

If you refresh the Addressit product, the AddressBook should at this point exhibit behavior that is identical to its previous behavior.

Let's demonstrate the new functionality of the `listEntriesByGroup` method. Create two new groups using the manageGroupForm screen: Good and Bad. Now create a couple of new Entries, and edit them so that there are at least one in each Group, and at least one that is still Unfiled.

Now, pass the SelectedGroup parameter in the URL like this: `/Test?SelectedGroup=Bad`, and you should now see the filtered list of Entries that correspond to the appropriate Group. (Remember that the Group attribute is case-sensitive.)

However, if you have more than one batch of Entries displayed and want to navigate among them, you'll notice that clicking on any of the batch navigation links reset the SelectedGroup parameter back to the default, and so causes the resulting page to display all of the Entries again. Clearly this is not what you want. In order to preserve the SelectedGroup parameter, you must cause the parameter to be passed along in the URL of the batch navigation links, just like the start parameter. Rewrite all of the links in indexAddressBook.dtml that look like this:

```
<a href="&dtml-absolute_url;?start=&dtml-batch-start-number">
```

to look like this, instead:

```
<a href="&dtml-absolute_url;?start=&dtml-batch-start-↩
 number;&SelectedGroup=&dtml-SelectedGroup;">
```

The batch navigation links should now have the expected behavior when navigating a particular Group.

However, as with navigating among batches, selecting the Group by rewriting the URL is clearly not very user-friendly, so you need to add a Group navigation device. Because the user is selecting from among a list of Groups, and this list is of unknown length (because the user is free to define as many Groups as he or she wishes), a drop-down selection box is the most appropriate solution. Add the following code to indexAddressBook.dtml after the form tag but before the two existing submit buttons ("Add" and "Delete"):

```
<input type="submit" name="index_html:method" value="View">
<select size=1 name="SelectedGroup">
  <option value="All">All Groups
```

```
<dtml-in listGroups>
  <option value="&dtml-sequence-item;"<dtml-if SelectedGroup>⮐
<dtml-if "_['sequence-item']==SelectedGroup">selected</dtml-if>⮐
</dtml-if>><dtml-var sequence-item>
</dtml-in>
 </select><br>
```

This code first creates an option in the select form element for "All Groups" that passes a value of "All," and then iterates over the `listGroups` method to create options for all the other Groups, including "Unfiled."

Your `indexAddressBook.dtml` file should now look like the code in Listing 8-2.

Listing 8-2: indexAddressBook.dtml

```
<dtml-var standard_html_header>
<dtml-var standard_addressbook_header>

<dtml-unless SelectedGroup>
 <dtml-call "REQUEST.set('SelectedGroup', 'All')">
</dtml-unless>

<dtml-unless start>
 <dtml-call "REQUEST.set('start', 1)">
</dtml-unless>


<dtml-in "listEntriesByGroup(_['SelectedGroup'])" previous ⮐
size=20 start=start>
<dtml-in previous-batches mapping>
[<a href="&dtml-absolute_url;?start=&dtml-batch-start-number;⮐
&SelectedGroup=&dtml-SelectedGroup;"><dtml-var ⮐
batch-start-number> - <dtml-var batch-end-number></a>]
</dtml-in>
</dtml-in>

<dtml-in "listEntriesByGroup(_['SelectedGroup'])" ⮐
size=20 start=start>
<dtml-if sequence-start>
[<dtml-var expr="_['sequence-index']+1"> -
</dtml-if>
<dtml-if sequence-end>
<dtml-var expr="_['sequence-index']+1">]
</dtml-if>
</dtml-in>

<dtml-in "listEntriesByGroup(_['SelectedGroup'])" next ⮐
size=20 start=start>
```

```
<dtml-in next-batches mapping>
[<a href="&dtml-absolute_url;?start=&dtml-batch-start-number;⮐
&SelectedGroup=&dtml-SelectedGroup;"><dtml-var ⮐
batch-start-number> - <dtml-var batch-end-number></a>]
</dtml-in>
</dtml-in>

<form action="." method="post">

 <input type="submit" name="index_html:method" value="View">
<select size=1 name="SelectedGroup">
  <option value="All">All Groups
<dtml-in listGroups>
  <option value="&dtml-sequence-item;"<dtml-if SelectedGroup>⮐
<dtml-if "_['sequence-item']==SelectedGroup">selected</dtml-if>⮐
</dtml-if>><dtml-var sequence-item>
</dtml-in>
 </select><br>

<input type="submit" name="delEntries:method" value="Delete">
<input type="submit" name="addEntryForm:method"
value="Add"><br>
<dtml-in "listEntriesByGroup(_['SelectedGroup'])" ⮐
size=20 start=start sort=LastName,FirstName,MiddleInitial>
<input type="checkbox" name="EntryIDs:list" value="&dtml-id;">
<a href="./&dtml-id;"><dtml-var title></a><br>
</dtml-in>

</form>
<dtml-var standard_html_footer>
```

As these changes were only to a `*.dtml` file, you can see the improvements by reloading the AddressBook's `index_html` view, which should look something like the screen shown in Figure 8-9.

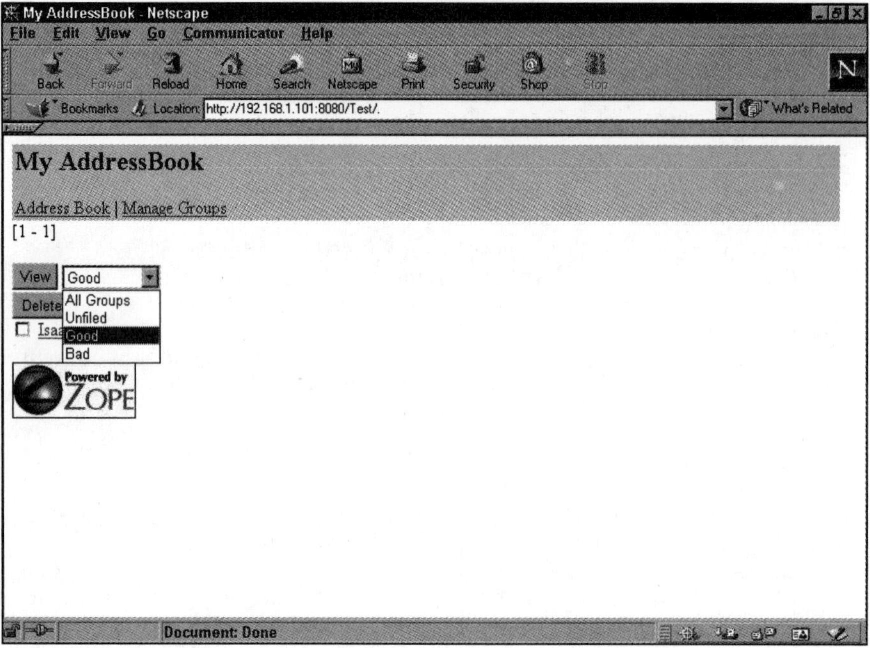

Figure 8-9: The Group selection box

Renaming Groups

So, now that the users of the AddressBook have the ability to define Groups and set a Group attribute on Entries (which is useful for filtering the Entry list displayed), it is much easier for those users to manage and navigate a large AddressBook (hundreds or even thousands of Entries). But another maintenance headache can now rear its ugly head.

What do users do if they want to rename one of the Groups? With the current version, a user would have to create a new Group, go through the list of the old Group, and edit the individual Entries to use the new Group name instead of the old one. Once the old Group was empty, it could be safely deleted.

This is an incredible pain in the *tuchis* (Yiddish for *butt*) if the group in question has more than a few Entries in it, so let's add a `renameGroups` method to the AddressBook class to take the drudgery out of this maintenance chore. Add the following code into the section of the AddressBook class that is labeled "# Methods to add, edit, delete and retrieve Entries" between the `delGroups` method and the `listEntriesByGroup` method:

```
    def renameGroup(self,
                    OldGroupNames,
                    NewGroupName,
                    REQUEST = None
                    ):
        "Method to rename one or more groups"

        if type(OldGroupNames) != ListType:
            OldGroupNames = [OldGroupNames]

        self.addGroup(NewGroupName)

        for OldGroupName in OldGroupNames:

            if OldGroupName != 'Unfiled':

                self.delGroups(OldGroupName)

                for entry in
self.listEntriesByGroup(OldGroupName):
                    entry.Group = NewGroupName

        if REQUEST is not None:
            return self.manageGroupForm(self, REQUEST)
```

The `renameGroups` method takes an `OldGroupNames` parameter (which should be a list) and a `NewGroupName` parameter, as well as the now familiar `REQUEST = None`. First, the method makes sure that the `OldGroupName` is in fact a list, and if it isn't a list, the method changes it into one. It then adds the `NewGroupName` to `GroupList`.

Then the `renameGroup` method iterates over the `OldGroupNames` list, and for each `OldGroupName` does the following:

- ✦ Deletes the `GroupName` if it's not "Unfiled"
- ✦ Uses `listEntriesByGroup` to retrieve all of the Entries that match `OldGroupName`
- ✦ Iterates over that list, setting each Entry's `Group` attribute to `NewGroupName`

After each inner loop in which the members of the `OldGroupName` are moved to the `NewGroupName`, the method increments the outer loop to move on to the next `OldGroupName`. After all of the `OldGroupName`'s are done, the method checks to see whether it was called through the Web, and if so, returns the `manageGroupForm` view.

This `renameGroups` method is a miniature study of code reuse in a way. The method is using two methods that we've previously defined: `delGroups` (used to delete the `OldGroupName`) and `listEntriesByGroup` (used to retrieve a subset of Entry objects that match `OldGroupName` for reassignment to `NewGroupName`). The `listEntriesByGroup` method was never intended to be called through the Web, but it is easy to see now why the delGroups method and all other methods that could be called that way need to check and see whether in fact they were. If the delGroups method had not been set up to check whether it had been called through the Web, it would have returned the manageGroupForm view early (to the renameGroups method), which would have caused an error.

There are two more changes you need to make to enable this feature. The first is to add an appropriate submit button that will lead to a renameGroupForm. To do so, rewrite the manageGroupForm.dtml file as follows:

```
<dtml-var standard_html_header>
<dtml-var standard_addressbook_header>

<h3>Manage Groups</h3>
 <form action="." method="post">
 <table border=0 cellpadding=3 cellspacing=0>

 <dtml-in listGroups>
  <tr <dtml-if sequence-even>bgcolor="#CCCCCC"</dtml-if>>
   <td><input type=checkbox name="groups:list" value="&dtml-sequence-item;"></td>
   <td><a href="&dtml-sequence-item;"><dtml-var sequence-item></td>
  </tr>
 </dtml-in>
  <tr><td colspan=2>
   <input type=submit name="delGroups:method" value="Delete selected Groups">
   <input type=submit name="renameGroupForm:method" value="Rename selected ⮐
Group"><br>
   <input type=text name="group"><input type=submit name="addGroup:method" ⮐
value="Add a Group">
  </td></tr>
 </table>
 </form>

<dtml-var standard_html_footer>
```

Next, you need to add a renameGroupForm.dtml file with the following code:

```
<dtml-var standard_html_header>
<dtml-var standard_addressbook_header>
<h3>Rename Group</h3>

<form action="renameGroup" method=post>
<dtml-in groups>
<input type="hidden" name="OldGroupNames:list" value="&dtml-sequence-item;">
</dtml-in>
Old Group Name: <dtml-var groups><br>
New Group Name: <input type="text" name="NewGroupName">
<input type="submit" value="Rename Group">
</form>

<dtml-var standard_html_footer>
```

The code here is not quite obvious. In order to take the selected Groups (that had their checkboxes checked) from the previous form and pass them along to the `renameGroups` method, the "groups" form value is iterated over here to create a hidden form field for each checked group. The hidden fields all have the name `OldGroupNames:list`, which again causes Zope to force the submitted values to a list, even when there is only one. This form also has a `NewGroupName` text field and a submit button.

Now you just need to add a declaration in the "# Web presentation methods" section of the AddressBook class to enable the new functionality. Add the following code to the end of the `AddressBook.py` file:

```
    renameGroupForm = DTMLFile("dtml/renameGroupForm", ↩
globals())
```

One of the interesting things about the way the `renameGroup` feature works, is that by checking more than one group name on the `manageGroupForm`, you not only rename several groups at once, but also their Entries are consolidated into the new Group as well. So, for example, if you have a "Competitors" group and a "Rivals" group, you can check them both, and click the Rename selected groups button. After you are presented with the `renameGroupsForm`, you can fill in the new group name as "Enemies," and click the submit button. Voila! You've combined both of the old Groups into a single new Group.

The code for the product at this point can be found in the `/chapter_08/Addressit_7` directory on the accompanying CD-ROM.

Sorting Entries by Column

You've made a lot of user interface and usability improvements in the AddressBook throughout this chapter, but the main view of the AddressBook could still use some work.

First, change the rendering code for the entry list so it displays the list in a more informative and usable way, as in Listing 8-3.

Listing 8-3: IndexAddressBook.dtml

```
<dtml-var standard_html_header>
<dtml-var standard_addressbook_header>

<dtml-unless SelectedGroup>
 <dtml-call "REQUEST.set('SelectedGroup', 'All')">
</dtml-unless>
```

Continued

Listing 8-3 *(continued)*

```
<dtml-unless start>
 <dtml-call "REQUEST.set('start', 1)">
</dtml-unless>

<dtml-unless sort_by>
 <dtml-call "REQUEST.set('sort_by',
'LastName,FirstName,MiddleInitial')">
</dtml-unless>

<form action="." method="post">
 <table border=0 cellpadding=2 cellspacing=0 width="100%">
  <tr>
   <td colspan=5>
    <table border="0" cellpadding="0" cellspacing="0"
width="100%">
     <tr>
      <td>
       <input type="submit" name="delEntries:method"
value="Delete">
       <input type="submit" name="addEntryForm:method" ⮐
value="Add"><br>
      </td>
      <td align="right">
       <input type="submit" name="index_html:method"
value="View">
       <select size=1 name="SelectedGroup">
        <option value="All">All Groups
<dtml-in listGroups>
         <option value="&dtml-sequence-item;"<dtml-if ⮐
SelectedGroup><dtml-if "_['sequence-⮐
item']==SelectedGroup">selected</dtml-if></dtml-if>><dtml-var ⮐
sequence-item>
</dtml-in>
        </select>
        <input type="submit" name="manageGroupForm:method"⮐
value="...">
      </td>
     </tr>
    </table>
   </td>
  </tr>
  <tr>
   <td colspan=5>
    <p align=center>
<dtml-in "listEntriesByGroup(_['SelectedGroup'])" previous ⮐
size=20 start=start>
<dtml-in previous-batches mapping>
[<a href="&dtml-absolute_url;?start=&dtml-batch-start-number;⮐
&SelectedGroup=&dtml-SelectedGroup;"><dtml-var ⮐
batch-start-number> - <dtml-var batch-end-number></a>]
</dtml-in>
```

```
</dtml-in>

<dtml-in "listEntriesByGroup(_['SelectedGroup'])" size=20
start=start>
<dtml-if sequence-start>
[<dtml-var expr="_['sequence-index']+1"> -
</dtml-if>
<dtml-if sequence-end>
<dtml-var expr="_['sequence-index']+1">]
</dtml-if>
</dtml-in>

<dtml-in "listEntriesByGroup(_['SelectedGroup'])" next ⮐
size=20 start=start>
<dtml-in next-batches mapping>
[<a href="&dtml-absolute_url;?start=&dtml-batch-start-number;⮐
&SelectedGroup=&dtml-SelectedGroup;">⮐
<dtml-var batch-start-number> - <dtml-var batch-end-
number></a>]
</dtml-in>
</dtml-in>
</p>

    </td>
  </tr>
  <tr>
   <td> </td>
   <th>Name</th>
   <th>Title</th>
   <th>Company</th>
   <td> </td>
  </tr>
<dtml-in "listEntriesByGroup(_['SelectedGroup'])" size=20 ⮐
start=start sort=FirstName,LastName,MiddleInitial>
  <tr <dtml-if sequence-even>bgcolor="#CCCCCC"</dtml-if>>
   <td><input type=checkbox name="EntryIDs:list" ⮐
value="&dtml-id;"></td>
   <td><a href="&dtml-id;"><dtml-var title></td>
   <td><dtml-var Title> </td>
   <td><dtml-var Company> </td>
   <td><a href="<dtml-var id>/editEntryForm">Edit</a></td>
  </tr>
</dtml-in>

</form>
</table>

<dtml-var standard_html_footer>
```

This improved version of the AddressBook's `index_html` method makes a number of changes as you can see in Figure 8-10.

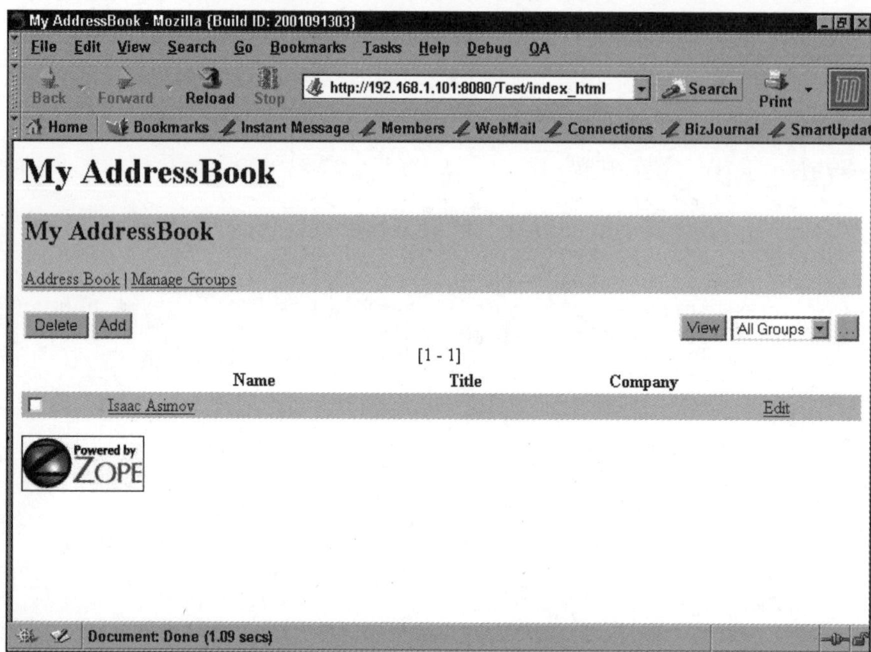

Figure 8-10: Improved `index_html` for the AddressBook

The improvements in this version are easily summed up. Starting from the top of the page and working down and left-to-right the improvements are:

✦ The form buttons, batch navigation, and Entry list are now in a single table.

✦ The group selection drop-down menu was moved to the right, and an ellipsis (...) button was added to point to manageGroupForm.

✦ The batch navigation was moved below the form buttons and centered.

✦ The checkboxes and name for each entry are now in separate columns of the table.

✦ Three more columns were added to the table, one each for the Entries' Title, Company, and another for an edit link pointing to the Entry's editEntry view.

✦ The Name, Title, and Company columns of the table have appropriate headers.

You can see that this has improved the usability of the AddressBook, even though we haven't added any new functionality yet.

Now that we're displaying three separate columns for each Entry (not counting the columns that contain the checkboxes and edit links), it would be nice to let users sort the Entries according to whichever column they find most convenient.

This is usually done by making the column titles into links. First though, you need to create and set a sort_by variable in the page so that the page can have a default. Add the following code just after the code that sets the start variable at the beginning of the indexAddressBook.dtml file:

```
<dtml-unless sort_by>
 <dtml-call "REQUEST.set('sort_by',
'LastName,FirstName,MiddleInitial')">
</dtml-unless>
```

Now change the batch navigation <dtml-in> tags to include a sort_expr="sort_by" attribute and replace the sort=FirstName,LastName,MiddleInitial from the main Entries loop with a sort_expr="sort_by" as well.

We're using a form of indirection here. The sort_expr attribute in the <dtml-in> tag indirectly gets the sorting string from sort_by. The expression in quotes for this attribute must be a valid Python expression, but the expression is not evaluated for each sequence-item to calculate the value that the items will be sorted by as you might think. Instead, the expression is evaluated once, and the result must be a valid sorting string, just as if you had passed it to the sort attribute. So, the default value of sort_by is FirstName,LastName,MiddleInitial (no spaces) and when the <dtml-in> tag evaluates sort_expr="sort_by", sort_by is evaluated to its contained value, and the <dtml-in> tag behaves just as it had been told to sort=FirstName,LastName,MiddleInitial.

If all this rigmarole to get the same sorting result seems unnecessary, remember that the code you added to the beginning of the file which sets the default sorting order can be easily overridden by setting the sort_by attribute before the code executes.

For example, you can pass in a sort_by parameter in the URL to change how the Entries are sorted. Rewrite the URL to /Test?sort_by=Company and you'll see that the Entries are now sorted differently.

So, now you need to expose this sorting functionality to the users, as you don't want them to have to rewrite URLs to sort the Entries.

Change the section of the file that creates the column headings to read as follows:

```
<tr>
 <td> </td>
 <th><a href="&dtml- _
absolute_url;?sort_by=LastName,FirstName,MiddleInitial&SelectedGroup⮐
=&dtml- SelectedGroup;">Name</a></th>
```

```
   <th><a href="&dtml-absolute_url;?sort_by=Title&SelectedGroup
=&dtml-SelectedGroup;">Title</a></th>
   <th><a href="&dtml-absolute_url;?sort_by=Company&SelectedGroup
=&dtml-SelectedGroup;">Company</a></th>
   <td> </td>
  </tr>
```

You can see that each column heading is now a link that passes on the current value of SelectedGroup and an appropriate value for `sort_by` depending on the Column in question. For example, the Name column passes on a value of `FirstName,LastName,MiddleInitial`, the Title column passes on a value of "Title," and the Company column passes on a value of "Company."

Similarly, the batch navigation links must be modified so as to pass on the current sorting information even while they pass on a modified start value:

```
<p align=center>
<dtml-in "listEntriesByGroup(_['SelectedGroup'])" previous 
size=20 start=start sort_expr="sort_by">
<dtml-in previous-batches mapping>
[<a href="&dtml-absolute_url;?start=&dtml-batch-start-number;
&sort_by=&dtml-sort_by;&SelectedGroup=&dtml-SelectedGroup;">
<dtml-var batch-start-number> - <dtml-var batch-end-
number></a>]
</dtml-in>
</dtml-in>

<dtml-in "listEntriesByGroup(_['SelectedGroup'])" 
size=20 start=start sort_expr="sort_by">
<dtml-if sequence-start>
[<dtml-var expr="_['sequence-index']+1"> -
</dtml-if>
<dtml-if sequence-end>
<dtml-var expr="_['sequence-index']+1">]
</dtml-if>
</dtml-in>

<dtml-in "listEntriesByGroup(_['SelectedGroup'])" next 
size=20 start=start sort_expr="sort_by">
<dtml-in next-batches mapping>
[<a href="&dtml-absolute_url;?start=&dtml-batch-start-number;
&sort_by=&dtml-sort_by;&SelectedGroup=&dtml-SelectedGroup;">
<dtml-var batch-start-number> - <dtml-var batch-end-
number></a>]
</dtml-in>
</dtml-in>
</p>
```

After you've made these two sets of changes to the file, reload the AddressBook's `index_html` page and you'll see that the column headers are now links, and that changing the sort order by clicking the links works. Navigating to a different batch will preserve the sort order now, as well as the selected Group.

Notice that while the batch navigation links pass in the selected Group and the sort order as well as the modified batch starting point, the column heading links only pass along the selected Group along with the modified sort order, while the current batch number is ignored. There is a very good reason for this. When a user resorts the Entries, the Entries they are looking at currently will likely be scattered throughout the re-sorted list, while the current batch number will be filled with different Entries altogether. Therefore, once the list has been resorted, it makes sense to present the beginning of the resorted list rather than some batch in the middle. By omitting the start parameter from the link, the resulting page has its start parameter reset to the default value, which is at the beginning of the list.

Dealing with case-sensitivity

You may have noticed that the sorting facility for `<dtml-in>` is case-sensitive. This means that words beginning with lower-case letters are sorted after upper-case letters. In other words, abrams will be listed *after* Zither.

The simplest and most elegant solution to this is to capitalize the various fields when they are edited. Make the following changes to `Entry.py`: Add "from string import capitalize" to the beginning of the `Entry.py` file, and edit the `editEntry` method to look like this:

```
    def editEntry (self, FirstName, MiddleInitial, LastName,
                   Address1 = "",
                   Address2 = "",
                   City = "",
                   State = "",
                   ZipCode = "",
                   Country = "",
                   Company = "",
                   Title = "",
                   Group = "Unfiled",
                   Contact_1 = "", ContactType_1 = "",
                   Contact_2 = "", ContactType_2 = "",
                   Contact_3 = "", ContactType_3 = "",
                   Contact_4 = "", ContactType_4 = "",
                   Contact_5 = "", ContactType_5 = "",
                   Contact_6 = "", ContactType_6 = "",
                   REQUEST = None
                   ):
        "Method for updating Entries"
        self.FirstName = capitalize(FirstName)
        self.LastName = capitalize(LastName)
        self.MiddleInitial = capitalize(MiddleInitial)
```

```
self.Address1 = Address1
self.Address2 = Address2
self.City = City
self.State = State
self.ZipCode = ZipCode
self.Country = Country
self.Company = capitalize(Company)
self.Title = capitalize(Title)
self.Group = Group
self.Contact_1 = Contact_1
self.ContactType_1 = ContactType_1
self.Contact_2 = Contact_2
self.ContactType_2 = ContactType_2
self.Contact_3 = Contact_3
self.ContactType_3 = ContactType_3
self.Contact_4 = Contact_4
self.ContactType_4 = ContactType_4
self.Contact_5 = Contact_5
self.ContactType_5 = ContactType_5
self.Contact_6 = Contact_6
self.ContactType_6 = ContactType_6
if REQUEST is not None:
    return self.editEntryForm(self, REQUEST)
```

Note that we are capitalizing the three name fields, as well as the Title and Company fields. This ensures that all of the fields used for sorting are capitalized whenever the Entry is edited. In order for this change to take effect, refresh the Addressit product, and then edit an entry that has some field in lower-case. The change should be immediate.

Since the `editEntry` method is called by the `addEntry` method when creating a new Entry object, no further changes need to be made to have new Entry object attributes capitalized upon their creation.

The code for the product at this point can be found in the `/chapter_08/Addressit_8` directory on the accompanying CD-ROM.

Summary

In this chapter you've enhanced what was a functional but very basic address book application to address scalability and usability issues in the interface. By creating a common application specific header, you made it easier to create a unified look-and-feel for the application, as well as common navigation bar.

The AddressBook created in Chapter 7 could have comfortably held a couple of dozen Entries that a user would have had no problem managing. But by allowing Entries to be batched, grouped, and filtered according to their group, and sorted according to selected columns, you've made it much easier to manage large numbers of Entries and navigate to the Entry you want.

There are further enhancements that could be made to this application, such as adding notes or pictures to Entries, creating links for e-mail and URL ContactTypes, and other enhancements that we won't explore in this book, but we encourage you to experiment with your own modifications.

The one thing that is really missing from the AddressBook at this point is important enough that we are dedicating an entire chapter to the subject: Security. In the next chapter, we will show you how to make your custom Zope Product secure by leveraging Zope's permissions and roles infrastructure.

✦ ✦ ✦

Zope Product Security

In This Chapter

Security and the Web

The Zope security framework

Determining your security requirements

Adding permissions

Associating permissions with roles

In chapters 6, 7, and 8 you developed a functional address book application with a reasonably sophisticated user interface. You may have noticed, however, that the entire functionality of the application is exposed to the Web, so that anyone who can access your server can view the AddressBook, add entries, or even delete entries. In almost every situation (except, perhaps, an intranet protected by a firewall where all users are trusted implicitly), this open access is not acceptable, and Web applications must implement some sort of security policy.

Security and the Web

Before we can show you how to add security to your application, however, some discussion is warranted as to what security actually *is*.

Security 101

What is security? A security professional would probably make a list similar to the following to define this term:

- **Confidentiality.** The data is only revealed to the appropriate entities.
- **Availability.** The system is accessible to the appropriate entities.
- **Integrity.** The data is in the state the last authorized entity left it in.

Leaving aside the issue of Availability for the moment, Confidentiality and Integrity basically imply a system of access-control. Access-control itself has two primary aspects:

✦ **Authentication.** The entities involved are who they say they are.

✦ **Authorization.** The entity is allowed to take the action in question.

Ensuring availability can mean two different things. It can mean that unauthorized entities cannot perform an action *in* the system that would deny the use of the system to legitimate entities (putting it firmly in the realm of access-control), or it can mean that unauthorized entities cannot isolate the system from the legitimate entities.

The Web is fundamentally insecure

The architecture of the Internet was not designed with any security considerations in mind, except in the sense that its decentralized packet-switched nature was designed to continue operating even if it was chopped into smaller pieces by a nuclear attack. As long as a path on any sort — no matter how indirect — existed between two nodes, they would still be able to communicate as full peers. So the Internet's primary design consideration (security-wise) was to ensure availability.

However, the early participants in the Internet were primarily researchers and academics, along with research assistants and students. The early social environment of the Internet can therefore be described as "collegial," inasmuch as people were assumed to be who they said they were, and no one worried about *deliberate* damage.

Because the Internet is now a venue for commercial activity, all sorts of motivations for formerly unthinkable actions exist that didn't before, and various security measures can be deployed on top of the underlying infrastructure to thwart those actions.

A full discussion about security is outside the scope of this book, but some further reading recommendations can be found at the end of the chapter.

The Zope Security Framework

Zope has had quite a few changes made to it to make it a better platform for building securable Web applications. Some of the security vulnerabilities identified and solved by Digital Creations and the Zope development community are general weaknesses of the Web development model that most environments that allow end users to create executable content still exhibit to this day.

Zope has two categories of code when it comes to security: Restricted Code and Unrestricted Code.

Any sort of executable code that can be edited TTW (through-the-Web) without access to the server's file system is considered restricted. This includes DTML Methods, Python Script Objects, and SQL Methods, among others. Restricted code is always subject to Zope's security machinery when executed, and can never access the file system of the machine it's running on.

On the other hand, code that must be edited through the file system, such as the application you've built in the preceding chapters of this book, is not subject to Zope's security machinery by default. The only default restriction file system-based code is subject to is that class methods that don't have a `docstring` aren't exposed to the object publication machinery at all. Once exposed to the publication machinery, however, no further restrictions are made on what the code may do, except for whatever limitations are imposed by the operating system. This, by the way, is why it is important to run your Zope site on a server that is run by a security-conscious system administrator. Potentially at least, a third-party Zope product could access any other resources that are available to the user that Zope is running as. But any operation that the code can perform within Zope is unrestricted as to who may perform it.

This isn't quite as bad as it sounds. There *are* situations where you simply don't need more security than this. For example, suppose you created a public discussion board in which the only public methods were a posting form and a viewing form. If you really don't need all sorts of management functions because you don't want to moderate or delete postings, this can work just fine. It's only when you need to limit some actions by some people (such as limiting who may post, or subjecting postings to a review process before they are publicly visible) that you need a more complex security policy.

Most Web applications in fact do have more complex needs than an exposed/hidden model. Those needs can be met with an ACL (Access-Control List).

ACLs are a security model in which actions in a system are protected by "permissions." If an entity has a particular permission with regard to an object, then the entity is capable of taking the associated action on that object. Formally, objects have access control lists associated with them that list all entities and the entities' associated permissions.

Zope expands and extends the authorization side of the access-control model in a few important ways:

✦ Roles

✦ Acquisition

✦ Ownership

✦ Local roles

Zope also has good solutions for the authentication portion of access control, we'll cover those later in this chapter.

Roles

In a system such as Zope, which has many different object types, and many possible actions on those objects, permission management can become unwieldy very quickly. Zope introduced the concept of a *Role* that could be associated with a user of the system. Roles are simply non-exclusive groups of permissions. Zope has four built-in roles by default: Anonymous, Manager, Owner, and Authenticated.

As you can see by examining the Security tab in the root folder (Figure 9-1), there are a lot of permissions. The Manager role has all permissions by default, Anonymous has a few permissions, and Owner has a few. Authenticated is a new role added in Zope 2.4, and doesn't have any permissions associated with it by default.

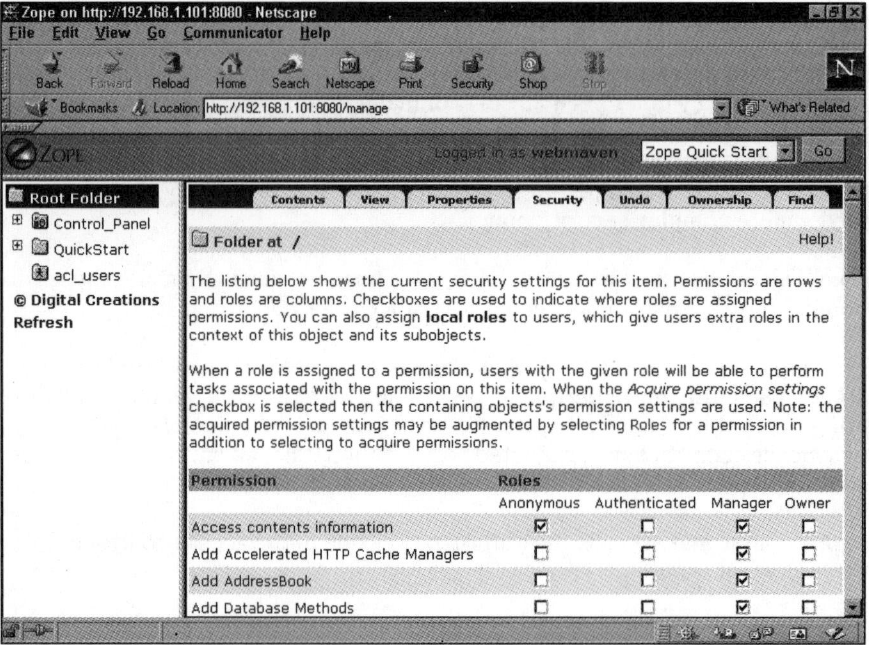

Figure 9-1: The Security tab

The purpose of the Manager role is fairly straightforward. A Manager can do pretty much anything inside of Zope. Anonymous is a role that is intended to represent a completely un-authenticated user. If there is some permission that you want everybody who accesses the site to have, give that permission to Anonymous. Owner is a relatively new role, and mostly is meant to be used to indicate which user owns a particular object. This has some interesting uses, security-wise, which we'll go into later in the chapter. Authenticated is an even newer role, and is basically a convenience role in that it is the exact inverse of Anonymous. If a user has been authenticated by any means, he or she gets this role, which enables developers to test for the Authenticated role instead of testing whether the user is not Anonymous.

Roles make it easier to manage permissions. By associating a permission with a role, and associating roles with users, you can avoid having to associate permissions with users directly, which makes security management much easier and less error prone. Technically, roles are aggregations of Permissions. You can also use roles as aggregations of Users, though they're not meant to be used that way. We expect that future versions of Zope will make it possible to assign roles to aggregations of users, which will probably be called Groups.

Acquisition

Like other attributes, assigned roles can be acquired or overridden at any point in the object hierarchy. This means that if an entity has been given the Manager role on the Root Folder of a Zope site, that role is acquired by all contained objects, so the entity has the Manager role over the entire site. This means that in Zope, roles (being groups of Permissions) do not have to be assigned explicitly to users with regard to each object. Zope assumes that an entity that has a role with regard to an object also has that role with regard to contained subobjects.

Note that the Permissions associated with a role can be changed in the Security tab. For example, the Permissions that the Anonymous role has can be changed in a subsection of the site to make it possible for un-authenticated users to add DTML Documents.

Ownership

As of version 2.2, Zope has had an Owner role to combat what is now known as the *Server-Side Trojan Attack*. This particular vulnerability, first identified and corrected in Zope, potentially affects all application servers that allow server-side executable content to be created by untrusted users. It works something like this:

1. An untrusted user creates executable content that will attempt to perform some operation for which the user does not have sufficient permissions (such as deleting the root object).

2. The untrusted user then gets another user (who has more privileges) to view (and therefore execute) the page in question by some method such as sending an e-mail message containing a URL pointing to the page, which when clicked, then runs the code that deletes the root object.

The Zope development community was the first to recognize this vulnerability and create a solution to it that was then incorporated into Zope version 2.2. The solution was to create the Owner role, which is given automatically to the user who creates an object. Zope now requires that restricted code run only if both the owner of the code *and* the user viewing (executing) it have sufficient privileges.

Local roles

In addition to being able to adjust the specific permissions associated with a role, Zope also enables you to give an entity a role on a particular object (and its subobjects). This is called a *Local Role* (as opposed to a "Global" one assigned in the user folder). The local roles screen is accessed by clicking on the local roles link in the Security tab, and looks like Figure 9-2.

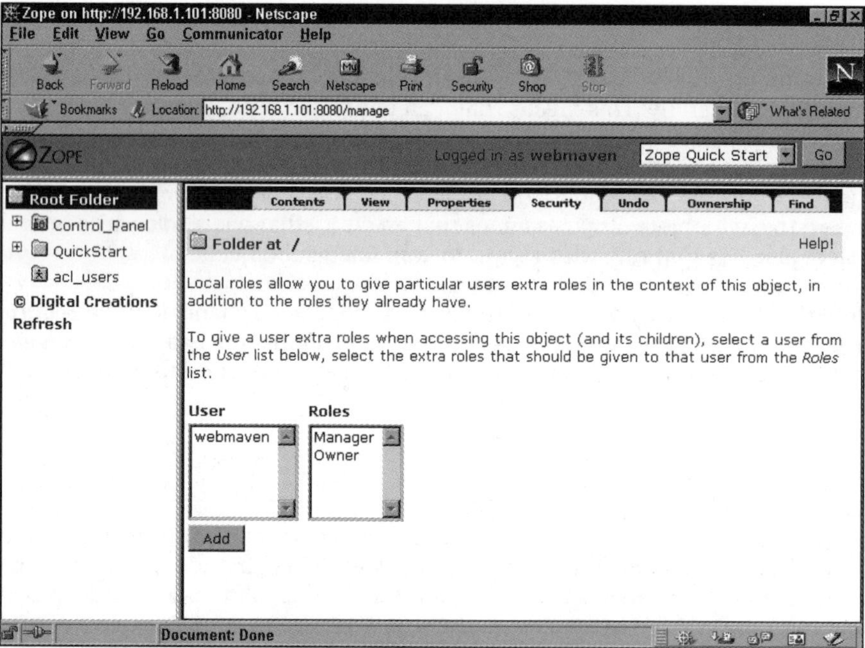

Figure 9-2: The Local roles screen

For example, you can delegate the management of a section of your site by giving someone the Local role of Manager on a subfolder. This will enable the user to take any actions whose permission's are associated with the Manager role, but only on the subfolder and its subobjects, not on any objects that are "above" it in the hierarchy, or "sibling" objects and their subobjects.

Note that roles are not exclusive. If you give the user another role lower in the site, that user will have *both* roles (and all associated permissions) from that point in the hierarchy down.

What Zope won't do for you

ZServer (Zope's built-in Web server) does not include support for SSL (Secure Sockets Layer). This means that Zope's built in authentication (which relies on standard browser authentication) sends both your username and password "in the clear," or unencrypted. Thus, the username/password pair is vulnerable to interception by some third party, who would then be able to access the system as the user whose username/password had been intercepted.

Insecure authentication may suffice for certain applications and situations, but you probably don't want to expose your manager level access in this way. Fortunately, you can use Zope in conjunction with Apache and SSL in order to secure the authentication protocol. Future versions of Zope may incorporate SSL directly into ZServer.

Zope also has available third-party add-on products in order to authenticate from other information sources such as a database, an LDAP (Lightweight Directory Access Protocol) server, or an NT domain controller, as a few examples. Add-on user folders exist for all of these options, as well as for a few others. Zope has a well-documented interface that user-folder implementations must follow, so you can pretty much drop in whichever option best suits your needs without having to change your site architecture at all.

What Zope will do for you

Once you've figured out how you want to handle authentication for your Web site (and whether the built-in authentication will suffice), Zope has a well-developed, flexible, and secure Authorization model. We've already covered the high points of the security system, and we'll cover it a bit more in the next section.

The important thing to remember is that because Zope has this security infrastructure built in, you don't have to re-implement any of it. Designing a security framework is pretty difficult, and for most Web applications out there, the programmers have devised their own from scratch because they didn't have an existing security framework to leverage.

In general, a product developer does not need to think about which users get what Permissions; that is up to the site administrator. The only thing a product developer needs to worry about is what permissions need to be created, and which roles get those Permissions by default.

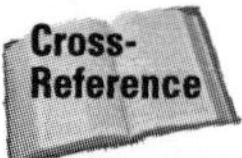

Chapter 13 covers security from the perspective of the site administrator.

Determining your Security Requirements

Okay. So you've created a cool Web application as a Zope product and now you need to add security. How do you go about it? It's actually pretty simple with Zope, as the Security framework does all of the heavy lifting. First though, you need to determine exactly what is going to be protected.

The Default policy

We want certain actions to be available to all users, and certain other actions to be more restricted. The policy we want to implement is roughly as follows:

1. We want anonymous users to be able to read the AddressBook and Entry detail pages.
2. We want to restrict adding, editing, and deleting Entries to certain people.
3. We want to restrict adding, renaming, and deleting Groups to certain people.
4. We don't want certain methods such as listEntriesByGroup externally available at all.

Listing the methods

First, you can see that we have two types of objects in the Addressit product: AddressBook objects and Entry objects. Table 9-1 shows the methods that exist for each.

Table 9-1
Methods in the Addressit Product

AddressBook.py	***Entry.py***
manage_addAddressBookForm	EditEntry
manage_addAddressBook	editEntryForm
listContactTypes	index_html
editAddressBook	

AddressBook.py	*Entry.py*
addGroup	
delGroups	
renameGroup	
listGroups	
addEntry	
delEntries	
listEntriesByGroup	
index_html	
addEntryForm	
standard_addressbook_header	
manageGroupForm	
renameGroupForm	

We can categorize these methods into a few types of actions:

- Viewing the AddressBook and Entries
- Managing the AddressBook, Entries, and Groups

You may notice that there is no mention of the `__init__` or `__getitem__` methods for either the AddressBook class or the Entry class. This is because Zope denies direct access to methods beginning with "_," even if you try to explicitly allow that access. Remember, methods beginning with an underscore are considered private methods of a class or module, and are not imported by default, so this part of the Zope Security policy is merely an extension of the existing Module/Package framework.

We can either create a Permission for each method, or we can create a Permission for each of these types of actions and associate the necessary methods with each Permission. Both approaches are valid. The approach you take depends on whether you're most concerned with giving the site builder as much control as possible, or whether you're more concerned with making the product easy to administer, and not populating the Security tab with unnecessary Permissions.

In the rest of this chapter, we'll take the second approach.

Reusing existing roles

Generally, the creation of new roles should be left to the site builder, and product developers should stick to the default roles Zope has. Adding roles is covered in Chapter 13. Table 9-2 lists the roles found in Zope and the type of actions we'll want to allow each role by default.

Table 9-2
User Actions in the Addressit Product

Anonymous	*Manager*	*Owner*	*Authenticated*
View the AddressBook	View management screens		
View an Entry	Edit AddressBook		
	Add Entries		
	Edit Entries		
	Delete Entries		
	Add Group		
	Remove Groups		
	Rename Group		

You can see that we aren't suggesting any actions be associated with the Owner or Authenticated roles. This is deliberate, as those roles will have special uses when we continue developing the AddressBook into a multi-user application in Chapter 10.

Meanwhile, we can simplify our task considerably if we collapse the Permissions down to "Viewing" and "Managing," as listed in Table 9-3.

Table 9-3
User Actions in the Addressit Product (Collapsed)

Anonymous	*Manager*
Viewing	Managing

Reusing existing Permissions

Zope has a number of built-in Permissions as well. Two that you should be especially aware of as a product developer are "View" and "Access Contents Information." "View" controls access to an object through the Web, and "Access Contents Information" controls access to attributes of the object. Both are granted to Anonymous by default, and are useful as default viewing Permissions on objects. With that in mind, let's map two Permissions (View, and Manage AddressBook) to all of the methods for the product:

Table 9-4
Methods Mapped to Permissions

Anonymous	*Manager*
View	**Manage AddressBook**
index_html (from AddressBook)	editAddressBook
index_html (from Entry)	addGroup
	delGroups
	renameGroup
	manageGroupForm
	renameGroupForm
	addEntry
	delEntries
	addEntryForm
	editEntry
	editEntryForm

It might seem as though we're loading too many Permissions onto the Manage AddressBook Permission, so it's a good idea to remember this rule of thumb: If permission for two or more actions are going to be given to the same people, then they should be covered by the same Permission. In this case, it doesn't make sense to cover group management and entry management by separate Permissions. All of these actions are actions that someone with a Manager role would be likely to have, so splitting them up, while certainly flexible, adds unnecessary Permissions to the Security tab.

Also, notice that we aren't associating the `standard_addressbook_header`, `listEntriesByGroup`, `listGroups`, or `listContactTypes` methods with any Permissions. This is because these methods do not need to be accessed from restricted code, such as through-the-Web DTML (Document Template Markup Language) methods, or directly traversed into by a browser. They are for internal use by the class, and only accessed from unrestricted code on the file system, so direct access to them will be turned off by default. This is one element of good security: Don't expose an interface at all unless you have to.

Adding Security

Okay, now that we've figured out which methods need protecting by which Permissions, let's show you how to actually go about it. (This is actually the easy part.) First, the `AddressBook.py` and `Entry.py` modules must import the security framework like this:

```
from Globals import HTMLFile, InitializeClass
from AccessControl import ClassSecurityInfo
```

Next, a `ClassSecurityInfo` object must be instantiated inside each class that is expected to interact with the security framework:

```
security = ClassSecurityInfo()
```

There that wasn't so hard, was it? Make the changes to both module files and add a ClassSecurityInfo instance to both the AddressBook class and the Entry class just after the `__init__` definition.

Next, add a line at the end of the `AddressBook.py` module file (outside the class definition) that reads as follows:

```
InitializeClass(AddressBook)
```

And add a similar one at the end of the `Entry.py` file:

```
InitializeClass(Entry)
```

`InitializeClass` is a special global method that will correctly apply any and all security declarations to the class that is passed to it, provided that class contains an instance of `ClassSecurityInfo`.

Refresh the product and try to access an instance of the AddressBook. In theory, Zope's default policy regarding access of methods that are not specifically associated with a Permission is to deny access, but as you can see, it doesn't quite work out that way for our Product.

The reason is a little obscure. The first culprit is the Item class that the Entry class and AddressBook class both inherit from (AddressBook inherits from `SimpleItem`, which inherits from Item). The `Item` class (found in the `lib/python/OFS/SimpleItem.py` file) specifically changes the default policy from "deny if not allowed" to "allow if not denied" for derivatives of that class (this is a holdover from older versions of Zope, and has been kept for backward compatibility). Fortunately, we can change this default back by adding the following code just after instantiating the `ClassSecurityInfo` object:

```
security.setDefaultAccess("deny")
```

This security declaration controls the ability of unrestricted code to call the unprotected methods of the Class. For example, before making this change, the following code would have worked from a DTML method outside of the class (assuming the existence of an AddressBook named Test):

```
<dtml-with Test>
 <dtml-var listContactTypes>
</dtml-with>
```

But after changing the default access policy back to "deny of not allowed," trying to render the above code results in an "Unauthorized" exception being raised, and a login dialog being displayed. Keep in mind that if your class does not have Item as an ancestor class, this step may not be necessary (but won't hurt either).

So far so good. We've restricted our code from being accessed by potentially malicious DTML and other restricted code within Zope. But we're not done quite yet.

As of Zope 2.5, the ZPublisher component of Zope does not use the security declarations directly when traversing and publishing objects, it only considers an object's `__roles__` attribute, and unfortunately, the `__roles__` attribute is not empty by default, but gets populated via a variety of magical processes. One of these processes is clearly visible in its effects in the management interface. After adding our security declarations so far, the View tab has disappeared from the management interface for the AddressBook instance. This is because the `manage_tabs` method checks to see whether the roles you have permit you to view the target URL defined in the tab. Because a Permission is not associated with the `index_html` method yet, the View tab is not displayed.

However, the Edit tab is displayed, even though the `manage_main` method doesn't have a Permission associated with it either. This is because methods beginning with `manage_` are considered "magic" and are automatically assigned to the Manager role by default. (Note that this circumvents the usual way of associating a method with a permission, which is then associated with a role.) So the `manage_tabs` method now detects this role and displays the tab.

ZPublisher only considers `__roles__` and doesn't check permissions directly. This causes traversal into methods to be allowed, even though default access should be denied. Which means, that even though you don't have a specific role or permission to access `index_html` (which causes it to not be displayed by the `manage_tabs` method), you can still traverse into it and access the object as `/Test/` or `/Test/index_html`. This goes for all the otherwise unprotected methods, requiring the product developer to either protect all methods explicitly, or otherwise "fix" the behavior of ZPublisher.

Fixing ZPublisher is fairly simple: just add the following line somewhere in your class, preferably near the `ClassSecurityInfo` instantiation:

```
__roles__ = ()
```

What this does is not very obvious. By default `__roles__` is equal to None, which causes ZPublisher to consider an object public, requiring no other security checks. Setting `__roles__` to an empty tuple instead solves this problem, and access to objects is (finally) denied by default, if it is not explicitly allowed.

All this seems unnecessary and insecure, but `Item`'s default policy, and ZPublisher's behavior regarding `__roles__` need to be maintained for backward compatibility with older Zope products. In a way, it's reassuring to know that the products you develop for Zope today are not likely to be broken with the next release.

As long as you add the default access declaration and set `__roles__` to an empty tuple, your product will be secure by default.

Adding Permissions

Let's re-expose the View tab by way of an example of how to add a Permission. If you add the following line just before the `index_html = HTMLFile ...` line (in the Web methods section), you will be associating the method with a Permission:

```
security.declareProtected('View', 'index_html')
```

This is one of three forms of declaration that you can make regarding methods in a class. The other two forms are `declarePublic('methodName')` and `declarePrivate('methodName')`, both of which only need to be passed the method name.

By adding the `declareProtected` statement, you are explicitly associating the method with the View permission. Because the View permission is associated by default with the Anonymous and Manager roles, you will now be able to see the View tab in the management interface and be able to access the `index_html` method of the address book as anonymous.

You should also add a similar declaration to `Entry.py` to associate the `index_html` method of the Entry class with the View permission.

`declarePublic('methodName')` re-allows unprotected access to a method, overriding the default policy if it is set to deny, and `declarePrivate('methodName')` disallows all access to a method, overriding the default policy if it is set to allow.

Next, you should add a security.`declareProtected('Manage AddressBooks', 'methodName')` line for each method in the AddressBook and Entry classes that is supposed to be exposed to the Manager role as listed in Table 9-4 (replacing `methodName` with the actual name of the method, of course).

Although the `manage_main` method is a "magic name" and is automatically associated with the Manager role (without bothering to associate it with a Permission) in the absence of any other declarations, it is appropriate to associate it with a Permission anyway. It is not, however, a good fit to associate it with the Manage AddressBooks Permission, as all of the other methods that are associated with it are meant to be accessed outside of the Zope management interface, and might be assigned to other roles than the Manager role (perhaps a custom role devised by a site administrator). Wouldn't it be nice if there were a Permission that specifically protected the Zope management interface? Well, there is. The Permission is called (appropriately enough) "View management screens," and is normally associated with the Manager role. Adding the following statement just before the `manage_main` method will associate the method with this permission:

```
security.declareProtected('View management screens',
'manage_main')
```

That's it! You've created and applied all necessary Permissions to the product. The pre-existing Permissions are already associated with the necessary roles, but you might be wondering about the new Permission you created, "Manage AddressBooks." How do you associate a Permission with a role?

Associating Permissions with roles

If you refresh the product and examine the Security tab, you'll see that the Manage AddressBooks Permission is already associated with the Manager role. This is because all permissions are assigned to Manager by default. After all, the Manager role is supposed to be able to perform any operation.

However, let's assume for the moment that you had a new Permission that you wanted to associate with one or more of the other roles, such as a special View AddressBooks Permission that you wanted to associate with the Anonymous and Manager roles. In that case, you would add a statement such as the following to your class:

```
Security.setPermissionDefault('View AddressBooks', ['Anonymous', 'Manager'])
```

`SetPermissionDefault` takes two parameters: the first is the permission name, and the second is a sequence (either a tuple or a list) of the roles that get the permission by default. For clarity's sake we suggest adding the following line to both classes (the Addressbook class in AddressBook.py and the Entry class in Entry.py) at the end of the class definition, rather than rely on the "magic" behavior:

```
security.setPermissionDefault('Manage AddressBooks',
['Manager'])
```

Note that you must declare all of the roles that have default access to a particular permission in a single statement (hence the requirement for a sequence of role names). Trying to associate each role with a Permission in its own statement will not work.

If you followed along in this chapter so far, your code should look something like Listing 9-1.

Listing 9-1: Address book code with security declarations

AddressBook.py

```
from OFS.SimpleItem import SimpleItem
from Globals import HTMLFile, InitializeClass
from Entry import Entry
from AccessControl import ClassSecurityInfo


# Module level declarations and methods

ListType = type([])

manage_addAddressBookForm = ⮐
HTMLFile("DTML/addAddressBookForm", globals())


def manage_addAddressBook(self, id, title, REQUEST):
    "Adds an AddressBook object to a folder"

    newAddressBook=AddressBook(id, title)
    self._setObject(id, newAddressBook)

    return self.manage_main(self, REQUEST)


# The Addressbook Class

class AddressBook(SimpleItem):
    "An AddressBook object"

    meta_type = "AddressBook"
```

```
    def __init__(self, id, title):
        self.id          = id
        self.title       = title
        self.ContactTypeList = ['Email', 'Home', 'Mobile',
                                'Work', 'Pager', 'ICQ/IM',
                                'URL', 'Extension']
        self.Entries     = {}
        self.LastEntryID  = 0
        self.GroupList = ['Unfiled']

    # create a ClassSecurityInfo object
    security = ClassSecurityInfo()
    security.setDefaultAccess("deny")
    __roles__ = ()


    def listContactTypes(self):
        "Returns a list of Contact Types"
        return self.ContactTypeList

    manage_options=(
    {'label':'Edit', 'action':'manage_main' },
    {'label':'View', 'action':'index_html'}
    )

    security.declareProtected('View management screens', ⮐
'manage_main')
    manage_main = HTMLFile("DTML/mainAddressBook", globals())

    security.declareProtected('Manage AddressBook', ⮐
'editAddressBook')
    def editAddressBook(self, title, REQUEST):
        "A method to edit Address Book Properties"

        self.title = title

        return self.manage_main(self, REQUEST)

    # Methods to manipulate groups

    security.declareProtected('Manage AddressBook', 'addGroup')
    def addGroup(self, group, REQUEST = None):
        "Method to add Groups"

        if group not in self.GroupList:
            self.GroupList.append(group)
            self.__changed__(1)

            if REQUEST is not None:
                return self.manageGroupForm(self, REQUEST)
```

Continued

Listing 9-1 *(continued)*

```
    security.declareProtected('Manage AddressBook', 'delGroups')
    def delGroups(self, groups = [], REQUEST = None):
        "method to delete groups"
        if type(groups) != ListType:
            groups = [groups]

        for group in groups:
            if group == 'Unfiled': continue
            # You are not allowed to delete Unfiled

            try:
                index = self.GroupList.index(group)
                del self.GroupList[index]
            except ValueError:
                pass

        self.__changed__(1)

        if REQUEST is not None:
            return self.manageGroupForm(self, REQUEST)


    security.declareProtected('Manage AddressBook', 'renameGroup')
    def renameGroup(self, OldGroupNames, NewGroupName, ⮐
REQUEST = None):
        "Method to rename one or more groups"

        if type(OldGroupNames) != ListType:
            OldGroupNames = [OldGroupNames]

        self.addGroup(NewGroupName)

        for OldGroupName in OldGroupNames:

            if OldGroupName != 'Unfiled':

                self.delGroups(OldGroupName)

                for entry in self.listEntriesByGroup ⮐
(OldGroupName):
                    entry.Group = NewGroupName

        if REQUEST is not None:
            return self.manageGroupForm(self, REQUEST)

    def listGroups(self):
        "Returns a list of Groups"
        return self.GroupList
```

```
# Methods to add, edit, delete and retrieve Entries


# This method intercepts requests for Entries, retrieves
# them from within the list, wraps them in the acquisition
# context of the AddressBook (so they appear to be
# subobjects), and returns them.
def __getitem__(self, id):
    return self.Entries[id].__of__(self)

security.declareProtected('Manage AddressBook', 'addEntry')
def addEntry(self, FirstName = "", MiddleInitial = "",
             LastName = "", REQUEST = None
             ):
    "Method to add an entry to an AddressBook"
    id = self.LastEntryID = self.LastEntryID + 1
    id = str(id)
    entry = Entry(id, FirstName, MiddleInitial, LastName)
    self.Entries[id] = entry
    self.__changed__(1)

    if REQUEST is not None:
        return self.index_html(self, REQUEST)

security.declareProtected('Manage AddressBook', 'delEntries')
def delEntries(self, EntryIDs = [], REQUEST = None):
    "Method to delete Entries"

    if type(EntryIDs) != ListType:
        EntryIDs = [EntryIDs]

    for id in EntryIDs:
        try:
            del self.Entries[id]
        except KeyError:
            pass

    self.__changed__(1)

    if REQUEST is not None:
        return self.index_html(self, REQUEST)

def listEntriesByGroup(self, group = "All"):
    ret = []
    if group == "All":
```

Continued

Listing 9-1 (continued)

```
            for entry in self.Entries.values():
                ret.append(entry)
        else:
            for entry in self.Entries.values():
                if entry.Group == group:
                    ret.append(entry)

        return ret


    # Web Presentation Methods

    security.declareProtected('View', 'index_html')
    index_html = HTMLFile("DTML/indexAddressBook", globals())

    security.declareProtected('View', 'addEntryForm')
    addEntryForm = HTMLFile("DTML/addEntryForm", globals())

    standard_addressbook_header = ⮐
HTMLFile("DTML/StandardAddressBookHeader", globals())

    security.declareProtected('Manage AddressBook', ⮐
'manageGroupForm')
    manageGroupForm = HTMLFile("DTML/manageGroupForm", globals())

    security.declareProtected('Manage AddressBook', ⮐
'renameGroupForm')
    renameGroupForm = HTMLFile("DTML/renameGroupForm", globals())

    #Declare permission defaults
    security.setPermissionDefault('Manage AddressBooks',
['Manager'])

# initialize the AddressBook Class
InitializeClass(AddressBook)
```

Entry.py

```
from Globals import Persistent, HTMLFile, InitializeClass
from Acquisition import Implicit
from OFS.SimpleItem import Item
from string import capitalize
from AccessControl import ClassSecurityInfo

class Entry(Item, Persistent, Implicit):
    "Address Book Entry"

    meta_type = "AddressBook Entry"
```

```
def __init__ (self, id, FirstName, MiddleInitial, LastName):
    self.id = id
    self.editEntry(FirstName, MiddleInitial, LastName)

# create a ClassSecurityInfo object
security = ClassSecurityInfo()
security.setDefaultAccess("deny")
__roles__ = ()

security.declareProtected('Manage AddressBook', 'editEntry')
def editEntry (self, FirstName, MiddleInitial, LastName,
               Address1 = "",
               Address2 = "",
               City = "",
               State = "",
               ZipCode = "",
               Country = "",
               Company = "",
               Title = "",
               Group = "Unfiled",
               Contact_1 = "", ContactType_1 = "",
               Contact_2 = "", ContactType_2 = "",
               Contact_3 = "", ContactType_3 = "",
               Contact_4 = "", ContactType_4 = "",
               Contact_5 = "", ContactType_5 = "",
               Contact_6 = "", ContactType_6 = "",
               REQUEST = None
               ):
    "Method for updating Entries"
    self.FirstName = capitalize(FirstName)
    self.LastName = capitalize(LastName)
    self.MiddleInitial = capitalize(MiddleInitial)
    self.Address1 = Address1
    self.Address2 = Address2
    self.City = City
    self.State = State
    self.ZipCode = ZipCode
    self.Country = Country
    self.Company = capitalize(Company)
    self.Title = capitalize(Title)
    self.Group = Group
    self.Contact_1 = Contact_1
    self.ContactType_1 = ContactType_1
    self.Contact_2 = Contact_2
    self.ContactType_2 = ContactType_2
    self.Contact_3 = Contact_3
```

Continued

Listing 9-1 *(continued)*

```
        self.ContactType_3 = ContactType_3
        self.Contact_4 = Contact_4
        self.ContactType_4 = ContactType_4
        self.Contact_5 = Contact_5
        self.ContactType_5 = ContactType_5
        self.Contact_6 = Contact_6
        self.ContactType_6 = ContactType_6
        if REQUEST is not None:
            return self.editEntryForm(self, REQUEST)

    def title(self):
        if self.MiddleInitial != "":
            return self.FirstName + " " + self.MiddleInitial ⮐
+ "." + " " + self.LastName
        else:
            return self.FirstName + " " + self.LastName

# Web Methods

    security.declareProtected('Manage AddressBook', ⮐
'editEntryForm')
    editEntryForm = HTMLFile("DTML/editEntryForm", globals())

    security.declareProtected('View', 'index_html')
    index_html = HTMLFile("DTML/entryDetails", globals())

    #Declare permission defaults
    security.setPermissionDefault('Manage AddressBooks', ⮐
['Manager'])


# initialize the Entry Class
InitializeClass(Entry)
```

That's it! You've added security to the Addressit product by leveraging Zope's security framework. After making the changes to the two modules, refresh the product to reinitialize it and apply the security assertions. You can now access the AddressBook anonymously (without logging in), but any attempt to add, edit, or delete entries will result in the application asking you to authenticate yourself.

The code for the product at this point can be found in the `/chapter_09/Addressit_9` **directory on this book's CD-ROM.**

Summary

In this chapter, you learned how security works on the Web, and what the Zope security framework will—and won't—do for you. You learned how to plan and apply security restrictions for Python products that will get applied by the Zope security framework, and how to associate those Permissions with default roles.

For further reading, check out *Secrets and Lies: Digital Security in a Networked World* by Bruce Schneier (John Wiley & Sons, 2000).

✦ ✦ ✦

CHAPTER 10

Creating a Multi-User AddressBook

✦ ✦ ✦ ✦

In This Chapter

Creating the Addressit class

Adding AddressBooks

Public and Private AddressBooks

Finishing touches

✦ ✦ ✦ ✦

In the first four chapters of this part of the book, we showed you how to build a Python Zope product, make it more sophisticated, and add security. However, the resulting object is really suitable for only a single person's use or, at most, for a small group of people who share their addresses.

If many people will use this application, they will want to manage their own addresses. You could give each person his or her own AddressBook, but that won't allow people to share their contacts. You could also create a shared `AddressBook` instance as well, but then everyone would have to check two places for their contacts.

The solution is to aggregate AddressBooks and allow people to see their contacts combined with the shared ones.

Creating the Addressit Class

The first thing that needs to be done is to create a specialized container to hold AddressBooks. Edit and save the __init__.py file to read as follows:

```
import Addressit,AddressBook

def initialize(context):

    context.registerClass(
        AddressBook.AddressBook,
        permission="Add AddressBook",
        constructors=(AddressBook.manage_addAddressBookForm,
                      AddressBook.manage_addAddressBook)
        )

    context.registerClass(
        Addressit.Addressit,
        permission="Add Addressit",
        constructors=(Addressit.manage_addAddressitForm,
                      Addressit.manage_addAddressit)
        )
```

You can see that we're registering a new object that we call an Addressit, with the attendant permissions and constructors.

Add an Addressit.py file with the code in Listing 10-1 to the Addressit product folder.

Listing 10-1: Addressit.py

```
from OFS.Folder import Folder
from Globals import DTMLFile, InitializeClass
from AccessControl import ClassSecurityInfo
from AddressBook import AddressBook

manage_addAddressitForm = DTMLFile("dtml/addAddressitForm", ⮐
globals())

def manage_addAddressit(self, id, title, REQUEST):
    "Adds an Addressit object to a folder"

    newAddressit=Addressit(id, title)
    self._setObject(id, newAddressit)

    return self.manage_main(self, REQUEST)

class Addressit(Folder):

    def __init__(self, id, title):
        self.id    = id
        self.title = title
```

```
    meta_type  ='Addressit'
    all_meta_types = (
    {'name':'AddressBook',
     'action':'manage_addProduct/Addressit/addAddressBookForm'},)



    # create a ClassSecurityInfo object
    security = ClassSecurityInfo()
    security.setDefaultAccess("deny")
    __roles__ = ()

    def listGroups(self):
        "Returns a list of Groups from all AddressBooks"
        AllGroups = ['Unfiled']
        for Object in self.objectValues():
            for Group in Object.listGroups():
                if Group == 'Unfiled':
                    continue
                AllGroups.append(Group)
        return AllGroups

    def listEntriesByGroup(self, group = "All"):
        "Returns Entries from all AddressBooks that match the ⮐
Group"
        AllEntries = []
        for Object in self.objectValues():
            for Entry in
Object.listEntriesByGroup(group=group):
                WrappedEntry = Entry.__of__(Object)
                AllEntries.append(WrappedEntry)
        return AllEntries


    # Web Presentation Methods

    security.declareProtected('View', 'index_html')
    index_html = DTMLFile("dtml/indexAddressit", globals())

    #Declare permission defaults
    security.setPermissionDefault('Manage Addressit', ⮐
['Manager'])

# initialize the AddressBook Class
InitializeClass(Addressit)
```

You may notice a few unfamiliar things about this Module. First, the `Addressit` class is derived from the `Folder` class, which is a basic container that has a management interface for displaying the objects it contains. This is, in fact, the same `Folder` class that you have already instantiated every time you've chosen `Folder` from the Add Object drop-down menu. We will specialize the `Addressit` class, but it will basically act like a folder.

The next new item appears right after the meta_type declaration. When deriving a class from Folder, you have the opportunity to specify what objects can be instantiated in it. You have two ways to do this, both of which involve specifying a tuple of dictionaries. Each dictionary in the tuple represents a single object type. Here, we've specified in the tuple the name of the object's meta type that we want to be able to instantiate (AddressBook) and the action to be taken when it is selected for addition to the Addressit container. Both of these are required parameters. An additional optional parameter of permission can be added to the dictionary, specifying the name of the permission that protects the object from being added, but because this has already been defined in the AddressBook class, you can dispense with this. The tuple of this dictionary is here assigned to all_meta_types, which is a complete list of addable types, and no other types of objects can be added to the Addressit container. If we had assigned the tuple to meta_types instead, the object would simply have been added to the list of objects already available for adding to a folder (this is what registering a class does, essentially). This can be useful, for example, if you want to make a class addable to a special container that can still contain other types of objects without making the class addable anywhere else (which would be the case if you registered the addable class). But, in this case, since Addressit instances should only contain AddressBook instances, and we still want to be able to add Addressbooks elsewhere, we assign the tuple to all_meta_types.

The Addressit class has a listGroups method that is different from the AddressBook class's method. It first retrieves a list of all contained objects from the Addressit instance (remember, only AddressBooks are addable to the Addressit) and then iterates through this list, calling the listGroups method on each object. It then iterates through this list, and if the name of the group doesn't match the string Unfiled, it appends it to a list. At the end of all this, the method returns the list of strings.

The other method that the Addressit class has is a listEntriesByGroup method, which likewise iterates through the objects in the Addressit instance, calling listEntriesByGroup on each object, passing in the group parameter. Because the entry objects are returned without their context wrapper by this method, we explicitly wrap the individual Entry objects in the AddressBook instance from which they came and then append it to a list. After the method is done appending the wrapped Entries, it returns the list. The rest of this class just defines constructor methods and a default view (index_html), so those need to be added next.

Add an addAddressitForm.dtml file to the DTML folder in the Addressit product folder, with the following code:

```
<dtml-var standard_html_header>

<form method=post action=manage_addAddressit>
<table border=0 cellspacing=0 cellpadding=5>
 <tr>
  <td>Addressit ID:</td>
  <td><input type=text name="id"></td>
 </tr>
 <tr>
  <td>Title:</td>
```

```
    <td><input type=text name="title"></td>
   </tr>
   <tr>
    <td colspan=2><input type=submit value="Add Addressit"></td>
   </tr>
  </table>
  </form>

  <dtml-var standard_html_footer>
```

This code is almost completely identical to the addAddressbookForm.dtml file, except for different labels on the form, and a different target (manage_addAddressit) for the form. Next add an indexAdressit.dtml file to the same folder, with the code from Listing 10-2.

Listing 10-2: IndexAddressit.dtml

```
<dtml-var standard_html_header>

<dtml-unless SelectedGroup>
 <dtml-call "REQUEST.set('SelectedGroup', 'All')">
</dtml-unless>

<dtml-unless start>
 <dtml-call "REQUEST.set('start', 1)">
</dtml-unless>

<dtml-unless sort_by>
 <dtml-call "REQUEST.set('sort_by',
'LastName,FirstName,MiddleInitial')">
</dtml-unless>

<form action="." method="post">
 <table border=0 cellpadding=2 cellspacing=0 width="100%">
  <tr>
   <td colspan=5>
    <table border="0" cellpadding="0" cellspacing="0"
width="100%">
     <tr>
      <td align="right">
       <input type="submit" name="index_html:method"
value="View">
       <select size=1 name="SelectedGroup">
        <option value="All">All Groups
<dtml-in listGroups>
         <option value="&dtml-sequence-item;"<dtml-if ⮐
SelectedGroup><dtml-if "_['sequence- ⮐
item']==SelectedGroup">selected</dtml-if></dtml-if>><dtml-var ⮐
sequence-item>
```

Continued

Listing 10-2 *(continued)*

```
</dtml-in>
        </select>
      </td>
     </tr>
    </table>
   </td>
  </tr>
  <tr>
   <td colspan=5>
    <p align=center>
<dtml-in "listEntriesByGroup(_['SelectedGroup'])" ⮐
previous size=20 start=start sort_expr="sort_by">
<dtml-in previous-batches mapping>
[<a href="&dtml-absolute_url;?start=&dtml-batch-start- ⮐
number;&sort_by=&dtml-sort_by;&SelectedGroup=&dtml- ⮐
SelectedGroup;"><dtml-var batch-start-number> - ⮐
<dtml-var batch-end-number></a>]
</dtml-in>
</dtml-in>

<dtml-in "listEntriesByGroup(_['SelectedGroup'])" ⮐
size=20 start=start sort_expr="sort_by">
<dtml-if sequence-start>
[<dtml-var expr="_['sequence-index']+1"> -
</dtml-if>
<dtml-if sequence-end>
<dtml-var expr="_['sequence-index']+1">]
</dtml-if>
</dtml-in>

<dtml-in "listEntriesByGroup(_['SelectedGroup'])" next size=20
start=start sort_expr="sort_by">
<dtml-in next-batches mapping>
[<a href="&dtml-absolute_url;?start=&dtml-batch-start- ⮐
number;&sort_by=&dtml-sort_by;&SelectedGroup=&dtml- ⮐
SelectedGroup;"><dtml-var batch-start-number> - ⮐
<dtml-var batch-end-number></a>]
</dtml-in>
</dtml-in>
</p>

   </td>
  </tr>
<tr>
 <th><a href="&dtml-absolute_url;?sort_by=LastName,FirstName, ⮐
MiddleInitial&SelectedGroup=&dtml-SelectedGroup;">Name</a></th>
 <th><a href="&dtml-absolute_url;?sort_by= ⮐
Title&SelectedGroup=&dtml-
SelectedGroup;">Title</a></th>
 <th><a href="&dtml-
absolute_url;?sort_by=Company&SelectedGroup=&dtml- ⮐
```

```
SelectedGroup;">Company</a></th>
 <td> </td>
</tr>
<dtml-in "listEntriesByGroup(_['SelectedGroup']) ⮐
" size=20 start=start sort_expr="sort_by">
  <tr <dtml-if sequence-even>bgcolor="#CCCCCC"</dtml-if>>
   <td><a href="&dtml-absolute_url;"><dtml-var title></td>
   <td><dtml-var Title> </td>
   <td><dtml-var Company> </td>
   <td><a href="&dtml-
absolute_url;/editEntryForm">Edit</a></td>
  </tr>
</dtml-in>

</form>
</table>

<dtml-var standard_html_footer>
```

This code is very similar (but not identical) to the equivalent method for an `AddressBook`. Basically, the differences are that this screen does not have the controls for adding or deleting `Entries` directly, and it uses a `<dtml-var absolute_url>` to correctly construct the links to the `Entries` (and their edit screens) inside their respective `AddressBooks`. (This is also why we took such care to wrap the entries with the AddressBooks from which they came in the Addressit class's `listEntriesByGroup` method; otherwise, `absolute_url` wouldn't work correctly.) And we've removed the `standard_addressbook_header`.

Now, you can refresh the Addressit product, and try instantiating some objects!

Adding AddressBooks

Adding an `Addressit` object is just like adding an `AddressBook`. Choose `Addressit` from the drop-down menu, and fill in the resulting form with the id of `test`. Click the Add Addressit button.

You are returned to the folder to which you added the `Addressit`, so click on the `test` object to see its management screen, which should look like the one shown in Figure 10-1.

As you can see, the interface looks like an ordinary folder, except that in place of a drop-down box to add objects, only an Add AddressBook button appears. This is because AddressBooks are the only type of object that can be added to the Addressit object, and the Zope management interface detects that only one kind of object is addable, so it displays a button instead of a drop-down.

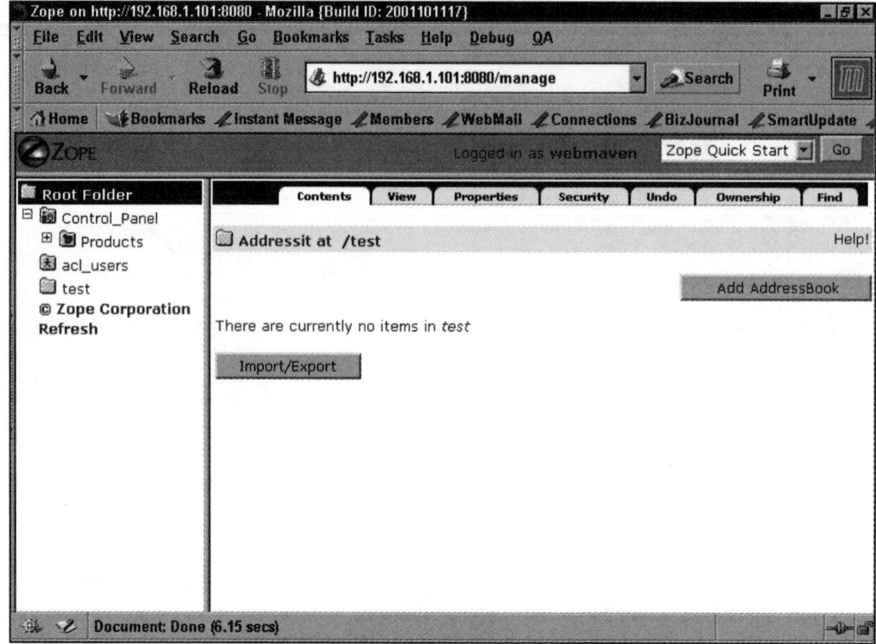

Figure 10-1: The Addressit Management Interface

Add a couple of `AddressBooks` to the `Addressit` (call them `01` and `02`), and you see them listed in the interface, just like an ordinary folder, as shown in Figure 10-2.

You can see that the Addressbooks are displayed here much as they would be in an ordinary folder. Clicking through to the individual AddressBooks reveals the usual management interface for the Addressbooks, and clicking through the View tab reveals the normal user interface for the AddressBook. (Hah! I could tell you thought I was going to pull out another screenshot!). Go ahead and add some entries and some groups to each AddressBook (give each AddressBook a *Musician* group), and assign some of the Entries to groups.

Now that you've populated the `AddressBooks` with users and groups, you can check out the Addressit's user interface. Click on the View tab in the Addressit object to see how the AddressBook contents are being aggregated. You should see something similar to the view shown in Figure 10-3.

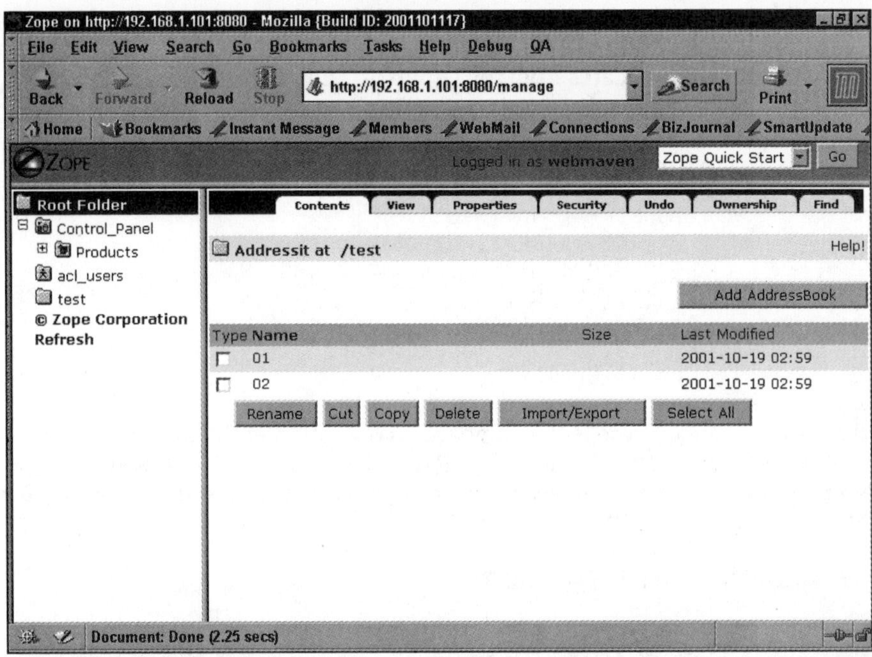

Figure 10-2: The Addressit Management Interface, with two `AddressBook` instances

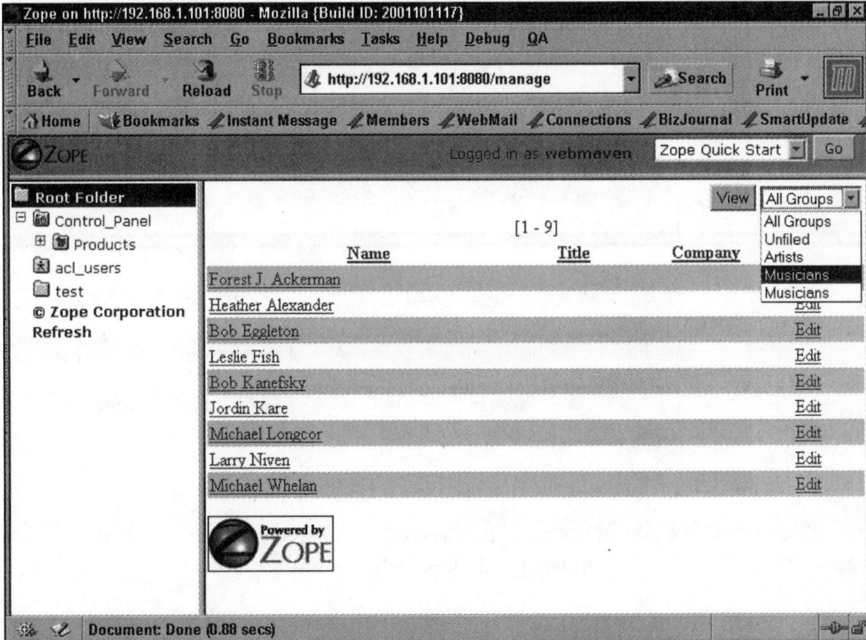

Figure 10-3: The Addressit index_html view

As you can see from the screenshot, the *Musicians* group name appears twice. This is because a *Musicians* group is defined in each `AddressBook`. Oops. The solution is simple: Eliminate duplicates from the Group list. Edit the `Addressit` class's `listGroups` method (not the `AddressBook` class's!) to read as follows:

```
def listGroups(self):
    "Returns a list of Groups from all AddressBooks"
    AllGroups = ['Unfiled']
    for Object in self.objectValues():
        for Group in Object.listGroups():
            if Group in AllGroups:
                continue
            AllGroups.append(Group)
    return AllGroups
```

What we've changed here is the comparison operation in the innermost loop. Whereas before it was checking to see if the Group in question was another `Unfiled` group, now it only checks to see if the group already exists in the `AllGroups` list, and if so, it skips appending it.

You can see the result in Figure 10-4.

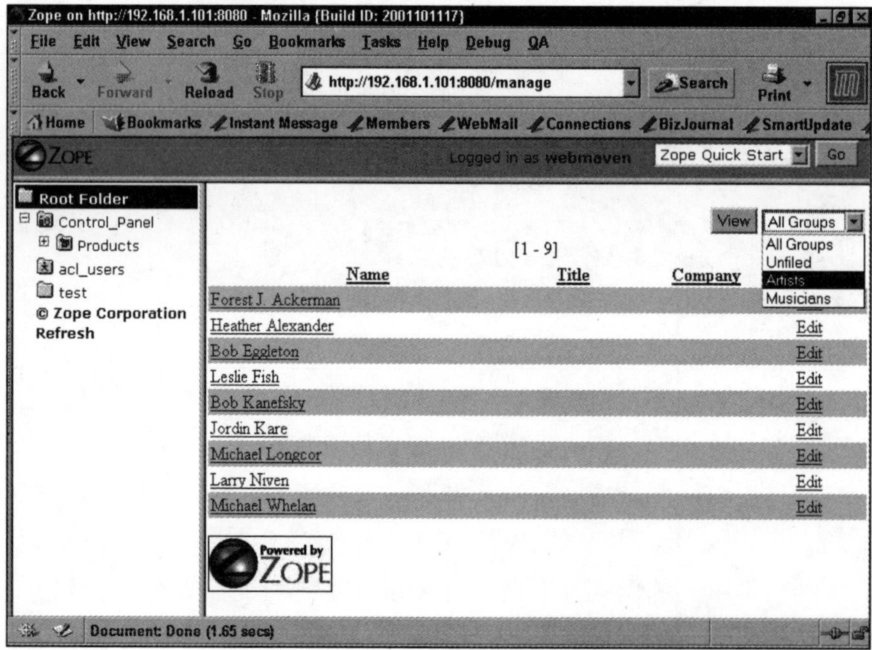

Figure 10-4: The Addressit index_html View, with redundant groups eliminated

Public and Private AddressBooks

At this point, the Addressit folder can aggregate any AddressBooks within it into a single navigable interface. However, it is doing so indiscriminately, which wasn't quite what we wanted. We wanted a user's private AddressBook to be seamlessly merged into a single view with any public AddressBooks.

Adding a Public attribute to the AddressBook class

The first step to getting this working is to add a `Public` attribute to the `AddressBook` class that defaults to `off`.

First, edit the `AddressBook.py` file as follows.

Add a Public variable to the `__init__`:

```
def __init__(self, id, title):
    self.id          = id
    self.title       = title
    self.ContactTypeList = ['Email', 'Home', 'Mobile',
                           'Work', 'Pager', 'ICQ/IM',
                           'URL', 'Extension']
    self.Entries     = {}
    self.LastEntryID  = 0
    self.GroupList = ['Unfiled']
    self.Public = 0
```

Next, change the `editAddressBook` method to change the value of the property depending on when the box is checked:

```
def editAddressBook(self, title, REQUEST, Public = None):
    "A method to edit Address Book Properties"

    self.title = title
    self.Public = Public
```

Edit the mainAddressBook.dtml as follows:

```
<dtml-var manage_page_header>
<dtml-var manage_tabs>

<form method=post action=editAddressBook>
<table border=0 cellspacing=0 cellpadding=5>
 <tr>
  <td>Title:</td>
  <td><input type=text name="title" value="&dtml-title;"></td>
 </tr>
  <tr>
  <td>Public:</td>
```

```
  <td><input type="checkbox" name="Public" <dtml-if ⮐
Public>checked="checked"</dtml-if>></td>
 </tr>
 <tr>
  <td colspan=2><input type=submit value="Edit
AddressBook"></td>
 </tr>
</table>
</form>
</body>
</html>

<dtml-var manage_page_footer>
```

Using the Public attribute

In order to use the `Public` attribute to control the visibility of the AddressBooks, you need to change the `Addressit` class's `listEntriesByGroup` and `listGroups` methods to skip non-public `AddressBook` instances, so edit those two `Addressit.py` methods as follows:

```
    def listGroups(self):
        """
        Returns a list of Groups
        from AddressBooks
        """
        AllGroups = ['Unfiled']
        for Object in self.objectValues():
            if not Object.Public:
                continue
            for Group in Object.listGroups():
                if Group in AllGroups:
                    continue
                AllGroups.append(Group)
        return AllGroups

    def listEntriesByGroup(self, group = "All"):
        """
        Returns Entries from AddressBooks
        that match the Group
        """
        AllEntries = []
        for Object in self.objectValues():
            if not Object.Public:
                continue
            for Entry in Object.listEntriesByGroup(group=group):
                WrappedEntry = Entry.__of__(Object)
                AllEntries.append(WrappedEntry)
        return AllEntries
```

Save the changes you've made to all three files, and refresh the product. Edit each AddressBook management interface at least once (whether you set the Public property on or off), in order to create and set the Public property; otherwise, you get an error when you view the Addressit because listEntriesbyGroup and listGroups both expect AddressBook instances to have a Public property.

You can now test your Addressit. Which AddressBooks are incorporated into the Addressit View depends on which have their Public property set.

Incorporating the user's private AddressBooks

Aggregating all public AddressBooks still isn't quite what we want. We also want the user's personal AddressBook to be merged into the public ones when they're viewing the Addressit object, even though it's not set to be public.

The trick is to figure out how to distinguish which AddressBooks *belong* to the particular user viewing the page. Fortunately, Zope has a fairly well developed security system that we can leverage. We can simply check for AddressBook objects that the user has a certain role for. We can choose one of two roles, Owner or Manager, to make the distinction. Either will work, but there are tradeoffs. The Manager role is currently the role that has the Manage AddressBook permission, which enables the user to add, edit, and delete Entries and groups. So it's easy to detect this role in determining whether to include a non-public AddressBook in the aggregation. On the other hand, the Owner role is a bit of a more natural fit, because we are looking for Addressbooks that are Owned by the current user.

The decision in this case becomes simpler when you realize that the user is unlikely to have an Owner role on an AddressBook unless he or she instantiated it himself or herself, whereas a Manager role is a prerequisite to being able to use the AddressBook at all. Therefore, we'll go with the Manager role.

So, we need to edit the listGroups and listEntriesByGroup methods in the Addressit class as follows:

```
    def listGroups(self):
        """
        Returns a list of Groups
        from all AddressBooks
        """
        AllGroups = ['Unfiled']
        for Object in self.objectValues():
            if not Object.Public:
                if not self.REQUEST.AUTHENTICATED_USER.has_role(['Manager'], ⮐
Object):
                    continue
            for Group in Object.listGroups():
                if Group in AllGroups:
                    continue
                AllGroups.append(Group)
        return AllGroups
```

```
  def listEntriesByGroup(self, group = "All"):
      """
      Returns Entries from all AddressBooks
      that match the Group
      """
      AllEntries = []
      for Object in self.objectValues():
          if not Object.Public:
              if not self.REQUEST.AUTHENTICATED_USER.has_role(['Manager'], ⮐
Object):
                  continue
          for Entry in Object.listEntriesByGroup(group=group):
              WrappedEntry = Entry.__of__(Object)
              AllEntries.append(WrappedEntry)
      return AllEntries
```

After making this change, a user will be presented with an aggregated view only of public `AddressBooks` and ones that the user has a `Manager` role on.

Unfortunately, we don't actually *have* a way of giving a user the manager role, because `AddressBooks` don't yet have a security tab. We can fix that too by changing the `manage_options` class property (which defines what tabs are displayed in the management view) of the `AddressBook` class (in `AddressBook.py`) from:

```
manage_options=(
{'label':'Edit', 'action':'manage_main' },
{'label':'View', 'action':'index_html'}
)
```

To the following:

```
manage_options=(
{'label':'Edit', 'action':'manage_main' },
{'label':'View', 'action':'index_html'}
)+SimpleItem.manage_options
```

This causes the `AddressBook` class to not simply override the `SimpleItem`'s class attribute with its own tabs, but to extend them instead. As the `SimpleItem` class adds the `RoleManager` class's Security tab to the `Item` class's History and Undo tabs, the `AddressBook` now has all of these, in addition to the Edit and View tabs defined in the `AddressBook` class itself.

In any case, after refreshing the product, you will find that the `AddressBook` management interface now has all the above-mentioned tabs, and that the security tab (which has a local-roles interface) enables you to assign a user a local role of `Manager` on an `AddressBook` to a user. Furthermore, the Addressit object now displays in a single aggregated view all public AddressBooks and whatever non-public AddressBooks the user has management privileges on. The user of course has to be authenticated (logged in) in order for this to work.

One final refinement: The edit links to the right of each listing are convenient but misleading, because there is one next to every single listing, and only those that are in AddressBooks that the user has management privileges on are actually editable. So the following code (near the bottom of `indexAddressit.dtml`) needs to be changed:

```
<td><a href="&dtml-absolute_url;/editEntryForm">Edit</a></td>
```

The change is simple; it just needs to be wrapped with the some conditional code to check the role of the current user on the `Entry` object (which is the current object in the sequence):

```
<td><dtml-if "AUTHENTICATED_USER.has_role(['Manager'],
_['sequence-item'])"><a href="&dtml-
absolute_url;/editEntryForm">Edit</a></dtml-if> </td>
```

After saving this change to `indexAddressit.dtml`, the `Addressit` user interface to a user that has his or her own `AddressBook` look like the one shown in Figure 10-5.

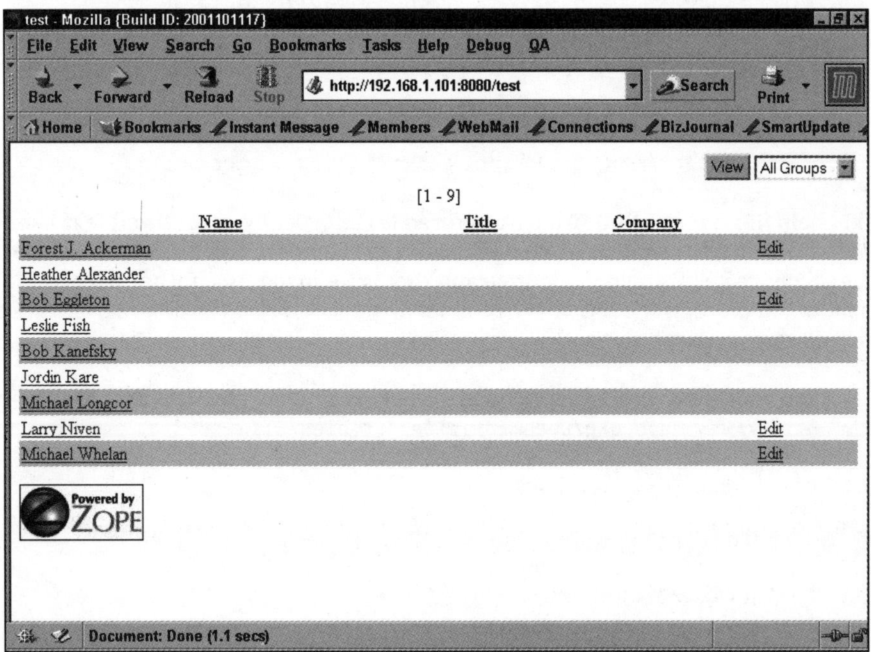

Figure 10-5: The `Addressit index_html` method

Finishing Touches

The Addressit application is now functionally complete, but it is lacking a few finishing touches before it is ready to be distributed as a product for other people to use.

Adding help

Documentation is something that everyone always wants more of, but no one wants to add. It is always helpful when a product has at least a rudimentary help file. Zope provides a straightforward mechanism for incorporating help directly into the management interface.

First, create a `/help` folder inside the products `/Addressit` folder. Then, add an Addressit.stx file to it with the following text in it:

```
Addressit

    The Addressit object is a specialized container for
    AddressBooks. Addressits aggregate the Addressbooks
    in them into a single view.

    Only AddressBooks that have their 'Public' property
    set to true and Addressbooks that the current user
    has management privileges on will be aggregated.
```

This help file is formatted using structured text. Basically, structured text uses indentation to determine structure in much the same way as Python does. The first line, because it's a single line paragraph that is followed by another paragraph that is indented more, will become a headline. The second and third paragraphs in the file will remain paragraphs.

You can find more information about structured text at this Web page: `http://www.zope.org/Documentation/Articles/STX`.

Next, edit `__init__.py` as follows:

```
import Addressit,AddressBook

def initialize(context):

    context.registerClass(
        AddressBook.AddressBook,
        permission="Add AddressBook",
        constructors=(AddressBook.manage_addAddressBookForm,
                      AddressBook.manage_addAddressBook)
        )

    context.registerClass(
        Addressit.Addressit,
```

```
        permission="Add Addressit",
        constructors=(Addressit.manage_addAddressitForm,
                      Addressit.manage_addAddressit)
        )

    context.registerHelp()
    context.registerHelpTitle('Addressit')
```

This registers the Addressit help topic automatically, incorporating it into Zope's help system. If you refresh the product at this point and click the help link on any management screen, you'll see that there is now an Addressit topic in the left pane of Zope's pop-up help.

But we're not quite done yet. Next, edit the `manage_options` definition in AddressBook.py as follows:

```
    manage_options=(
    {'label':'Edit', 'action':'manage_main',
     'help': ('Addressit', 'Addressit.stx')},
    {'label':'View', 'action':'index_html'}
    )+SimpleItem.manage_options
```

You can see that we've added another key/value pair to the first dictionary in the `manage_options` tuple. This first dictionary defines the Edit tab for the AddressBook object. The new member of the dictionary has a key of help and the associated value is a two-member tuple. The first of these members (`Addressit`) refers to the product directory that contains the appropriate help directory (you could point to a different product here, if you wanted). The second member of the tuple (`Addressit.stx`) refers to the appropriate filename in the help directory. If you now refresh the product, you'll find that any AddressBook instances now have a help link on their Edit tabs that pops up the Zope help with the Addressit help document.

You can in this way add separate help topics for each tab you define in any of your objects.

Adding an Icon

Zope icons are all 16×16 pixel GIFs. Adding one to a product is simple. First, add the icon to the product folder. In this case, the icon file names are `Addressit.gif` and `Addressbook.gif`.

Next, edit the `__init__.py` file as follows:

```
import Addressit,AddressBook

def initialize(context):

    context.registerClass(
        AddressBook.AddressBook,
        permission="Add AddressBook",
```

```
        constructors=(AddressBook.manage_addAddressBookForm,
                      AddressBook.manage_addAddressBook),
        icon = 'AddressBook.gif',
        )

    context.registerClass(
        Addressit.Addressit,
        permission="Add Addressit",
        constructors=(Addressit.manage_addAddressitForm,
                      Addressit.manage_addAddressit),
        icon = 'Addressit.gif',
        )

    context.registerHelp()
    context.registerHelpTitle('Addressit')
```

You can see that we added the `icon` declaration to the Addressit registration code immediately after the `constructors` declaration.

That's it. Refresh the product, and you should see an icon next to each `Addressit` instance, and one next to each `AddressBook` instance.

The code for the product at this point can be found in the `/chapter_09/Addressit` directory on the accompanying CD-ROM.

Summary

In this chapter, we walked you through a number of relatively simple adjustments and enhancements that transformed your single user `AddressBook` application into a multi-user `Addressit` application, which aggregates `Addressbooks` that are contained within it into a common view, depending on the status (Public or Private) of the `AddressBook` in question, and depending on what `Addressbooks` the user viewing the `Addressit` application has manager privileges on.

We also showed you how to add help to your product, as well as icons, in order to round out the product.

Further refinement is of course possible, though the wealth of usability improvements that can be made to the application is highly dependent on the audience that you are tailoring the application to. Moreover, for large numbers of `AddressBooks` and `Entries`, performance can begin to suffer, as the aggregation being used here is rather brute force. Subtler ways of building user interfaces exist, as you can see in Chapter 17.

✦ ✦ ✦

Zope Management

P A R T

✦ ✦ ✦ ✦

In This Part

✦ ✦ ✦ ✦

Content Management Strategies

✦ ✦ ✦ ✦

In This Chapter

Content management concepts

Using acquisition to enforce consistency

Using acquisition to share logic

Collaboration and versions

Applied security

✦ ✦ ✦ ✦

Unlike most of the rest of this book, which focuses on specific techniques and features of Zope, this chapter is intended to show how Zope can be used to support your efforts to build sites that are easily maintained and managed.

Most of the principles discussed in this chapter are well known and generally accepted, and yet most existing tools do little to support the application of these principles in the sites you build. Zope is designed around the concept of supporting a diverse Web-production team and provides features that make applying these principles easier than any other tool we're aware of. At the end of this chapter, we'll provide a list for further reading.

Content Management Concepts

Content management is probably one of the most difficult parts of the job of maintaining a Web site. Not only do you have to worry about getting all of the content up and into the correct place in a Web site, but you must also make sure the site is consistent in its appearance and presentation. Often, this must be done while dealing with several different departments. Throw in the hours of repetitive coding and you are likely going to go bald by your own hands.

In this chapter we first address the basics of the content manager's job by laying out what goals you should strive for in your site. We then break down some Web pages into manageable bites to illustrate what elements the content manager works with. Finally, we show you how Zope's powerful components are designed to solve the many problems content managers face, turning your job into a cakewalk.

Content management basics

The traditional view of the Web site has usually been that of a series of static pages laid out in a directory tree, with related pages nesting within folders and subfolders. Often a site starts out with only a handful of pages. The person in charge of the site (if there is one at all) has the relatively easy task of keeping these pages uniform in navigation and layout, as there are only a small number of pages to update.

As people in both the private and professional worlds began to rely on the Web more and more, some sites grew to monstrous proportions quicker than any single person could possibly keep up with. A corporate Web site that starts off as a model of clarity and consistency could eventually degenerate into confusing labyrinth as people start to add their own bits and pieces here and there without knowing (and at times not caring) what other people were doing. Even if some semblance of consistency could be found (likely through mind-numbing hours of cutting and pasting code on the part of the content manager), it would be a Sisyphean task to make sure all of the content and links remained current.

Even if this hypothetical Web site's growth is successfully managed and maintained, disaster will strike when someone in sales decides that some new high-level functionality needs to be implemented throughout the site, or worse yet, when the marketing department decides that the entire look of the site needs to be overhauled to better match the established corporate identity.

Assuming you don't just quit on the spot, what are you going to do? Most likely the solution would involve going through every single page of the Web site, isolating the content HTML (Hypertext Markup Language) from the HTML that determined navigation and presentation, and then a lot of deleting, cutting, and pasting. On a large enough site, even a simple change in navigation graphics could take a couple of weeks to complete if done by hand. A somewhat better solution would be to automate the cutting and pasting by using power tools such as grep (a UNIX command line tool for finding strings within a file) and Perl (a scripting language that excels at text processing), but this solution pre-supposes that the site was in a completely self-consistent state when you try to use these tools.

As challenges like these are identified, several core concepts, or *goals*, of content management are defined. There should, of course, be consistency, both for aesthetics and for ease of navigation. Content should be separated from presentation so that changing one has little impact on the other. Presentation should be separated from functionality. Also, forethought should be put into the design of the Web site to promote manageability while minimizing redundancy. (That may sound like a no-brainer, but as with many things, the gap between theory and implementation is often broad.) Finally, special cases and exceptions to the rule should be recognized, and implementing them made no more difficult than necessary, which means that it should be possible to easily override the consistency of the site.

Consistency

Even a site with good layout and design elements can be ruined if it is inconsistent. For this reason, consistency is an important goal for a content manager. When different portions of a Web site have a varying appearance, the impression visitors will receive is, at the very best, that the owner of the site is disorganized, and at worst visitors could be confused as to whether they actually left your site and are now looking at another site. This alone could be disastrous for a corporation trying to promote itself or sell its product online, as it makes it more difficult to establish the brand of the company or Web site.

Besides first impressions, consistency also helps visitors to a site find what they are looking for. When visitors first view a Web site, they rely heavily on visual clues to navigate their way around. If they get deeper into the site and suddenly find that the visual clues they came to rely on have changed, they could easily get lost.

The job of the content manager then is to enforce some set of rules on the Web site's appearance. Sometimes this can be as simple as merely setting up CSS (cascading style sheets) in the proper places and making sure that all of the authors contributing to the site link to them, or it can get as complex as writing an in-depth manual detailing all of the style rules of a Web site. Either way can put a considerable strain on both the content manager and the authors, as they all are forced to pay attention to not only the content they wish to provide, but also to the manner in which that content is presented. Although not a substitute for good communication among team members, a content management system that lets you set up templates, such as Zope, can help eliminate the need to cut and paste repetitive code.

Separation of content from presentation

If you are familiar with the use of cascading style sheets then you are probably aware of the benefit of separating your content from your presentation. Web pages that don't use CSS have HTML code that looks like this:

```
<table width=100 height=30>
<tr>
<td><font color="blue" face="arial,helvitica"><b>I once had
blue bolded text in a two celled table. And a picture to the
right of it.</b></font>
</td>
<td><img src="/somefolder/with/animage.gif" width=200
height=30></td>
</tr>
</table>
```

You could, however, link this document to a style sheet, which would significantly reduce the amount of code that you would have to create while developing your pages. Notice the difference in the amount of code that you need to write if you properly use a cascading style sheet:

```
<DIV class=Figure>
<img src="/animage.gif">
<p>
I once had blue bolded text in a two celled table. And a
picture to the right of it.
</p>
</DIV>
```

You can see that the HTML is much simpler and easier to understand, but this doesn't look like it will actually render anything like the original table code. The secret is in the style sheet. If you add the following code to the standard_html_header for your site, the rendering becomes much nicer:

```
<STYLE TYPE="text/css">
 .Figure { border:2px ridge #000;
           width: 200px; }

 .Figure P { font-weight: bold;
             color: blue;
             padding: 5px;
           }

 .Figure IMG {  border-left:2px ridge #000;
                border-bottom:2px ridge #000;
                padding: 5px;
                margin-left: 5px;
                margin-bottom: 5px;
         float: right;
         }
</STYLE>
```

What is happening here is that all of the code that is needed to tell your browser what type of font you want to use and what color it should be is contained in the style sheet, as well as additional control that you can't get using tables at all. Using a style sheet reduces the amount of code that you have to write, but there is also a bigger benefit if you use an external style sheet (rather than an inline style element as we're using here): multiple documents can link to the same style sheet, which means you can quickly change the look of all of those pages by only updating one document. This can be a real time saver especially if you have to update a lot of pages. Of course, putting the style sheet inline in the standard header is a time saver too, but if you have more than one standard header defined in your site, you could save even more time by linking to a common style sheet from each of them. Using a style sheet is also a good example of separating your content from your presentation, as all of the code that controls the style is in a separate document.

The problem with CSS, however, is that it is designed to control the appearance of HTML. Thus, the control that you get lets you change attributes such as the color, weight, and type of fonts that common elements of a document have, such as section heading, bullets, and paragraphs, as well as control to a fine degree other attributes such as margins, padding and borders. Unfortunately, style sheets don't offer any functionality for changing the *structure of the document*. Even if you used CSS to format the text in this document instead of inline `<font>` and `<b>` tags in a table, you would still have your work cut out for you if you needed to update the actual HTML structure (for example, moving the image after the text) for a hundred pages or more. Because the advantages of using CSS to control the appearance of your site are the same whether you use Zope or not, we won't be using style sheets in the rest of this book, but we strongly recommend that you take a look at using style sheets for your sites.

The problem in our example is that the content is intertwined with the code that controls the presentation. If you could somehow decouple the two pieces, when it's time to give the content a make over we would only have to change the code that controls the presentation, and presto! All 100 or so pages that we needed to update would be done.

Zope helps you to do this by allowing you to define and manage other types of content in addition to documents and images. You can create specialized content types such as press releases, address book entries, bug reports, or anything else you can imagine. Once you do this you can control how these documents are displayed in one place.

Extending Zope with new object types is covered in Chapter 16, which discusses ZClasses, and in chapters 6 through 10, which show you how to build Python Products.

Separation of Presentation from Logic

For a long time, the only way to add logic (behavior) to a Zope Web site was by using DTML or External Python Methods. DTML was certainly easier to use, as it could be created through the Web, but since DTML methods were also used to control presentation, it was difficult to avoid mixing Presentation and Logic into the same objects.

External Methods had the advantage of being entirely focused on Logic, but were difficult to create and use, since they require access to the server filesystem.

More recently, Python Script Objects offered through-the-Web functionality and a clean Logic orientation (Chapter 15). But many developers continue to use DTML for both purposes. So a new language was designed for the specific and sole purpose of being used for Presentation, and deliberately not powerful enough to be used to add Logic to your site, thus completing the separation. Chapter 18 discusses Zope Presentation Templates, and how they can be used to build user interfaces. Zope 2.5 is the first version to include Page Templates in the base distribution.

It is anticipated that in the future, most new development with Zope will use Page Templates for Presentation, and Python Script Objects for adding Logic, while Content will continue to come from object attributes or external sources such as relational databases. However, DTML still has its uses, and many existing Zope Products use it, so we've confined ourselves in this chapter to using DTML for our examples. However, we think that you will find that if you use Presentation Templates and Python Script Objects in preference to DTML, that your development will naturally separate Presentation from Logic.

Minimizing redundancy

It must be emphasized that no program or content management system can be a substitute for effective, two-way communication between you and other developers. As a content manager, the burden to create and foster such communication among all of the members of the project is on your shoulders. Zope cannot do this for you—no content management system can. What Zope can do is help to minimize the redundancies in your application that will naturally develop over time and are often made worse by poor communication among multiple developers working in tandem.

Redundancies in the architecture of your site or even in its code are not often apparent to a customer visiting your site or using your application. Why then, you might ask, should I concern myself with making an effort to minimize something the customer isn't likely to appreciate? Speaking from personal experience, a little bit of effort and planning at the beginning of a project will save a lot of time and frustration toward the end when small changes become big headaches.

Let's say, for example, that the content of your site is divided among several folders and the content in a few of these folders needs to access the same piece of information in a database. Creating an identical database method in each folder (as described in Chapter 12) would be redundant. If for some reason, you need to change this method, finding and updating every copy of it can become quite a chore. Your site should be constructed in a way that enables you to minimize the duplication of work and data. This idea may appear to be common sense, but surprisingly, even this simple mistake is made often. In this case, your job as a content manager is to ensure that only one copy of the database method exists, and that it is accessible from every folder in which in the data it returns is required.

An application that is weighed down by redundancy can achieve the same results as a lean, efficient one, but which would you rather have to maintain? Minimizing redundancy is really about making your job easier. There really isn't one right or wrong way to resolve this issue, but the solution should begin with an open and ongoing dialog by everyone involved in your project.

Using Acquisition to Enforce Consistency

Acquisition is probably the most useful tool Zope has for building Web sites. It's also arguably the most confusing. In fact, referring to it as a *tool* is misleading, as it is really more of a paradigm, and is deeply integrated into Zope's design.

So, what is acquisition?

Acquisition (more properly, environmental acquisition) is a flavor of object-orientation. If inheritance is based on "is-a" relationships, then acquisition is based on "in-a" relationships. In other words, acquisition is based on containment.

By now, you should be fairly familiar with Zope's containment hierarchy, as exposed in the Zope Management Interface by the file browser. However, Zope objects are not merely contained within their parent objects, they also acquire their attributes.

This is a little easier to show then to talk about, so we'll walk you through a short demonstration:

1. Make sure your Zope site has an `index_html` method in it.
2. Add a Folder named Demo, making sure that the "Create public interface" checkbox is not selected.
3. View `/Demo/index_html`.

As you can see, even though the Demo folder does not have its own `index_html` object in it, Zope fills in the blanks by searching up the containment hierarchy until it finds one. By itself this would be an extremely productive feature, but Zope doesn't stop there. If you examine the `index_html` object itself you'll find that it in turn calls `<dtml-var standard_html_header>` and `<dtml-var standard_html_footer>`, which are also located in the root folder. `standard_html_header` in turn calls `<dtml-var title_or_id>`, which is a method that is provided by Zope itself that returns the contents of a title property if one can be found or an id if not.

So, if we change the title property of the Demo folder via the Properties tab (say to "Test Title"), the rendering of the `/Demo/index_html` page will change appropriately, and the new rendering will have "Test Title" as the document's title.

You can see that once a method has been acquired, it operates within the context of the acquiring object, not within its original location in the containment hierarchy. This is extremely useful, as it becomes possible to acquire almost all of a page's characteristics and only override those portions that are unique to a particular section or page.

This particular demonstration of Acquisition will only work if `index_html` is a DTML Method, not a DTML Document. The reason for this is that Documents start searching for attributes in themselves first, and only then continuing on to their acquisition context and containment context. This is to allow attaching properties to the document itself. DTML Methods, however, do not look at themselves at all when searching for attributes, as they are considered attributes of their containers. Thus, The `index_html` method is acquired by the Demo Folder, and looks for the `standard_html_header` object starting from the Demo Folder as well, acquiring it from the Root Folder. The standard header then looks for the id property, again starting from the acquisition context, and finds it there. A standard header called from within a document would have looked in the document first, and found the `index_html` id, rather than finding it from the acquisition context.

Using acquisition to standardize layout

As we've already seen, `index_html` can be acquired from the root folder, and in turn acquires the standard header and footer methods. This gives site designers a convenient place to standardize the layout of the entire site, as they can insert the elements common to all (or even most) pages in the site, and be able to manage the look and feel from one location.

Take a look at the contents of the `standard_html_header` method:

```
<html><head><title><dtml-var title_or_id></title></head><body
bgcolor="#FFFFFF">
```

Not very easy to read, so reformat it into something a bit easier to scan:

```
<html>
<head>
 <title><dtml-var title_or_id></title>
</head>
<body bgcolor="#FFFFFF">
```

The HTML and DTML (Document Template Markup Language) in this method is prosaic, to say the least. Nevertheless, it provides a good starting point for a standard layout.

Let's start by adding a page to our site. Let's add an "About Us" page. Create a DTML document with an id of "about," a title of "About Us," and click the Add and Edit button. Edit the body of the document so it resembles the following:

```
<dtml-var standard_html_header>
It is our job to proactively leverage existing
 optimal information so that we may endeavor to
 distinctively conceptualize orthogonal
 results while striving for technical leadership.
<dtml-var standard_html_footer>
```

Viewing the page will show a screen similar to the screen shown in Figure 11-1.

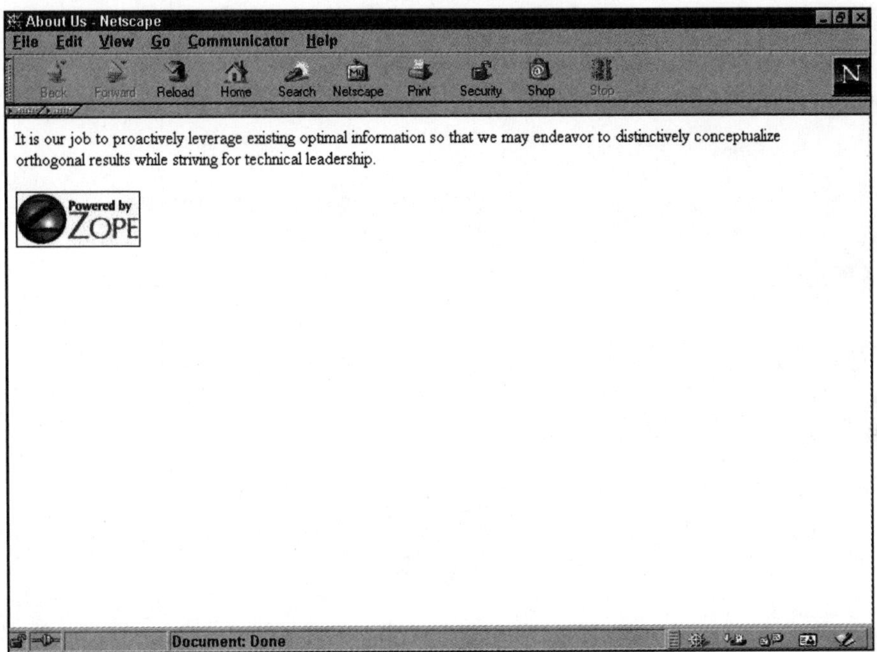

Figure 11-1: The About Us page

Let's say that we'd like to alter the layout in some way, for example, by adding a headline to the page. We could simply add the necessary code directly to the page in question like this:

```
<dtml-var standard_html_header>
<h1><dtml-var title_or_id></h1>
It is our job to proactively leverage existing
 optimal information so that we may endeavor to
 distinctively conceptualize orthogonal
 results while striving for technical leadership.
<dtml-var standard_html_footer>
```

But a better approach would be to add the code in question to the `standard_html_header` method instead, where it will be shared via acquisition by the entire site:

```
<html>
<head>
 <title><dtml-var title_or_id></title>
</head>
<body bgcolor="#FFFFFF">
<h1><dtml-var title_or_id></h1>
```

The resulting page looks like the page shown in Figure 11-2.

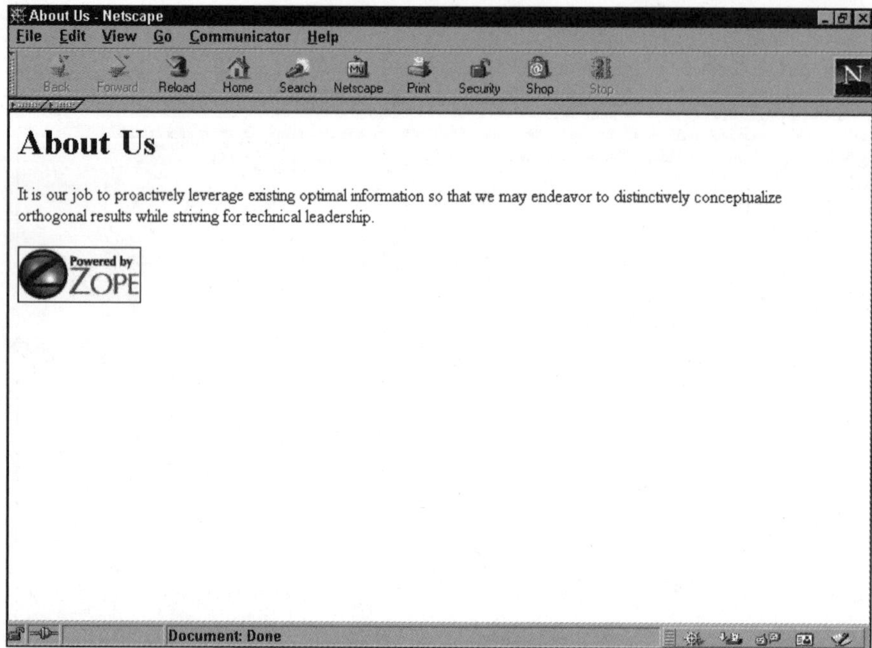

Figure 11-2: The About Us page with headline added

Taking page elements that are common to many pages in the site and moving them up the hierarchy is known as *factoring* your design, as it is conceptually similar to mathematically factoring a number into its component prime numbers.

Navigation

Navigation is one of those design elements that is amenable to being factored out and acquired by the site as a whole, as it is critical that navigation is consistent throughout a site. We don't get into a detailed discussion on designing navigation systems for Web sites in this book, but we offer an example implementation.

In your root folder, create a DTML method with an id of "navbar" and the following content:

```
<table width="120" align="left" cellpadding=5 celspacing=0
border=0>
 <tr>
  <td bgcolor="#CCCCCC" nowrap>
```

```
<ul>
 <li><a href="/">Home</a>
 <li><a href="/about">About Us</a>
 <li>Subsection 1
 <li>Subsection 2
 <li>Subsection 3
</ul>
</td>
</tr>
</table>
```

Then modify the standard header as follows:

```
<html>
<head>
 <title><dtml-var title_or_id></title>
</head>
<body bgcolor="#FFFFFF">
<dtml-var navbar>
<h1><dtml-var title_or_id></h1>
```

After which the About Us page should look like the page shown in Figure 11-3.

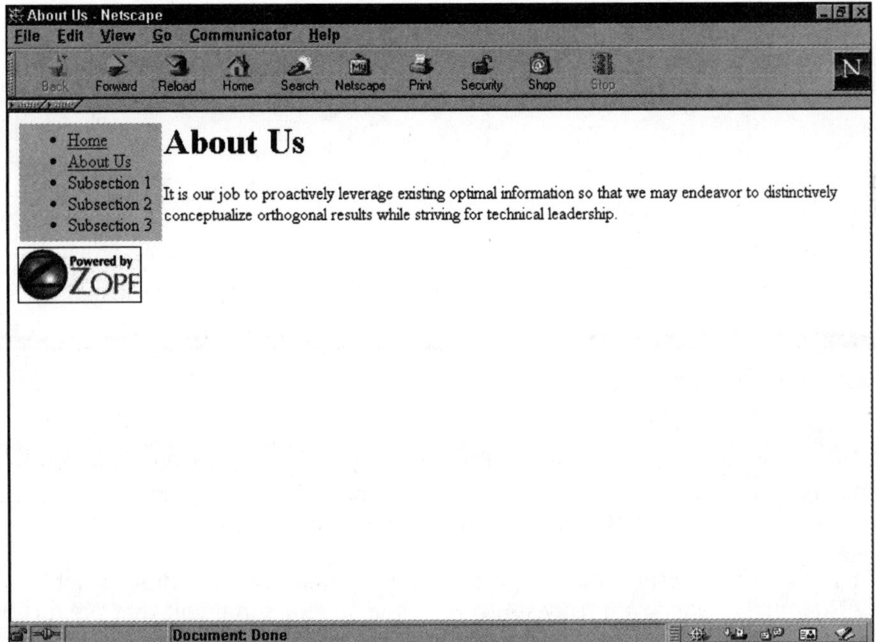

Figure 11-3: The About Us page with a standardized navigation bar

Now, if you create a new folder or page, it should acquire the page layout that you've defined at the root of the site. Create a folder with an id of products, and add an `index_html` DTML document to it with a title of "Products" and the following code:

```
<dtml-var standard_html_header>
Our products are second to none, because we're the leaders in
low-quality, low-margin, high-volume merchandise!
<dtml-var standard_html_footer>
```

The resulting page should look like the page shown in Figure 11-4.

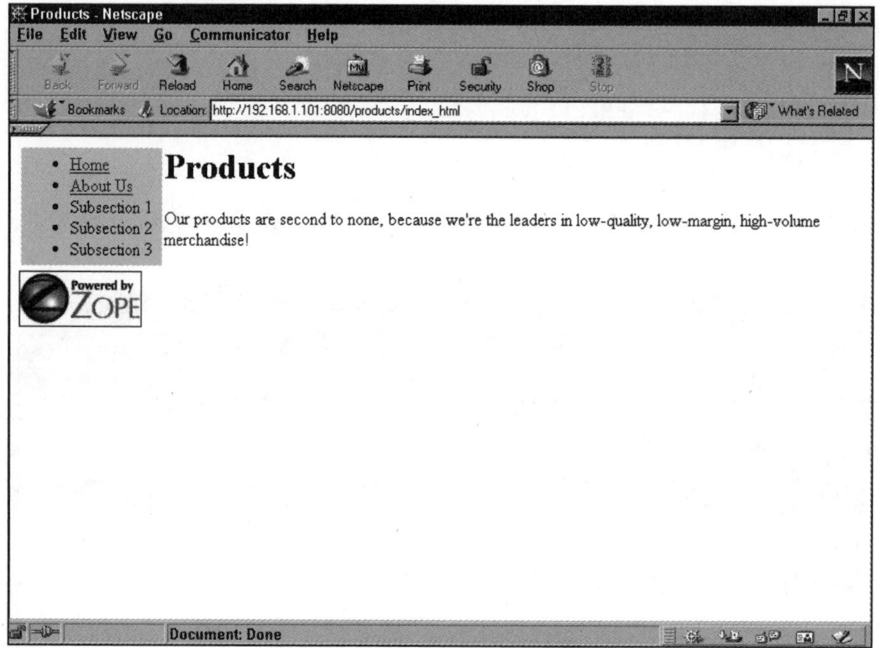

Figure 11-4: The Products page

As you can see, when you created this page, only those parts that were unique (the title and page content) actually needed to be created, as everything else is acquired from the folders above and incorporated seamlessly.

While this is wonderful from the point of view of creating Web sites, its implications for their maintenance are truly staggering. Imagine for a moment that the /products section of the Web site was brand new, and needed to be incorporated into the global navigation . . . on every page . . . *now*.

Well, if you're maintaining the site manually, as described earlier in this chapter, you might be sweating a bit, as it would take time to either cut-and-paste new HTML manually among all of the pages, or time to write a script that will automate the cutting-and-pasting process. And then still more time to review the resulting site before it can go live.

With Zope, the solution to all of this (if you've factored your code correctly) is to make the change in one place and simply let it be acquired throughout the entire site.

Using Acquisition to share Logic

Breaking your HTML into pieces that can be shared throughout the site is not the only use for Acquisition. Any logic that you want the whole site to share (or perhaps just a subsection) can be acquired as well.

Let's show you how to build a standardized e-mail comment form that your whole site can use, and have the comment routed automatically to the appropriate maintainer.

1. Add a Mail Host object to the root of your site by choosing it from the drop-down box in the Root Folder.
2. Leave the id as MailHost, and set the SMTP server to your mail server.

Generally if you are using an ISP the server will be `smtp.yourisp.com`, but yours might be different. If you're on an internal corporate network, ask your system Administrator what the appropriate settings are.

3. Click the Add button.
4. Next, add a DTML method to your root folder with an id of `standard_mail_form`, with the following code:

```
<dtml-var standard_html_header>
<H2>Comment on this page</H2>
<form action="standard_mail_action" method="post">
Your Name: <input type="text" name="name" size="30"><br>
<textarea name="comments" rows="8" cols="34">
Add your comment here.
</textarea><br>
<input type="submit" value="Send Comment">
</form>
<dtml-var standard_html_footer>
```

5. This will be the form that collects feedback and submits it to the form processing Method, `standard_mail_action`. Therefore, add another DTML method to the Root Folder with an id of `standard_mail_action` that contains the following code:

```
<dtml-var standard_html_header>
```

```
<dtml-sendmail mailhost="MailHost">
To: Feedback Recipient <&dtml-maintainer_email;>
From: Comment Form <webmaven@lvcm.com>
Subject: Website Comment

Feedback from : <dtml-var name>
About: <dtml-with "PARENTS[0]"><dtml-var absolute_url>⮐
</dtml-with>

Comments: <dtml-var comments>
</dtml-sendmail>
<h1>Thank you!</h1>
<p>Your comments have been sent.</p>

<dtml-var standard_html_footer>
```

You can see that the `standard_mail_action` Method attempts to send the e-mail to whatever e-mail address is in the `maintainer_email` attribute. In order for this to work, you need to create a string property on the Root Folder called `maintainer_email` and set its value to your e-mail address. Depending on your ISP's e-mail server policies, you might also need to change the From: address in the `standard_mail_action` Method to your own as well. You can also see a rather abstruse DTML string on the About: line. This DTML finds the parent of the current calling context and gets its absolute URL in order to inform the recipient which page specifically is being commented on.

Now, you can place a relative link in the standard footer of your site that points to `standard_mail_form`, like this:

```
<a href="standard_mail_form">Comment on this page.</a>
```

And the form and action will automatically append the appropriate URL to the e-mail, and send the e-mail to whomever is the site maintainer.

But there is another twist: Simply by overriding the `maintainer_email` property in a folder or subfolder, the e-mails for that whole section of the site will now go to someone else. In this way, the basic functionality (Logic) of the e-mail form and action are acquired throughout the site, and only the destination of the e-mail changes depending on where it gets called from.

As is, the form is fully functional, but since only users with the Manager Role have the appropriate permissions to send e-mail, the form is useless to anyone else. The remedy for this is also fairly simple. You need to give the `standard_email_action` method a *Proxy Role*. Click on the `standard_mail_action` object, and then click on its Proxy tab. The Proxy tab will present you with a list of available roles, including Manager. Select the Manager Role, and click the Save Changes button. The `standard_mail_action` method now has the Manager role, and can send e-mail on behalf of whatever user happens to request it, even Anonymous users.

That's it! You've added functionality throughout your entire site by using Acquisition.

More information on Proxy Roles and Security can be found in Chapter 13.

Collaboration and Versions

Versions are one of Zope's built in objects. They are used to compartmentalize changes to the Web site content or look and feel, so that conflicting sets of changes can't be made to the same object.

What is a version?

Chances are, more than one person will be working on your Web site at the same time. This can be a problem if people begin making changes to the same objects. In Zope, *versions* enable you to prevent users from overwriting each other's work. A version is an object that creates a separate development environment in which you can make changes that will not affect the work of others. You can stay in a version as long as you need to, and can even leave a version and come back to it later. The changes associated with a version can be saved to your site or discarded at any time.

Versions are also invaluable when updating large portions of your Web site. Often while making changes to one area, other parts of your site will be broken until you are finished updating. Versions enable you to complete this process without affecting the performance of your Web site by hiding your changes until you are ready for everyone to see them.

Imagine your boss has asked you to change the way the navigation on your company's Web site is displayed. The following sections in this chapter take you step-by-step through the process of updating a Web site with the use a version.

Creating a version

Creating a version is just like creating any other Zope object. Go to the Content screen of any folder in Zope. From the list of available objects, select Version. Zope will prompt you for the id and optional Title of the new version. When finished, click the Add button. Notice that the version you just added appears in the content list with a red diamond icon.

To create a version called "Updates," follow these steps:

1. While logged into Zope, select Version from the drop-down menu of addable objects.
2. Zope displays the add version page. Name your version "Updates" and set the title to "Navigation Updates." Click the Add button.

3. Zope returns you to the Root Folder's management screen and your new Version labeled "Updates" appears in the Root Folder's list of contents, as shown in Figure 11-5.

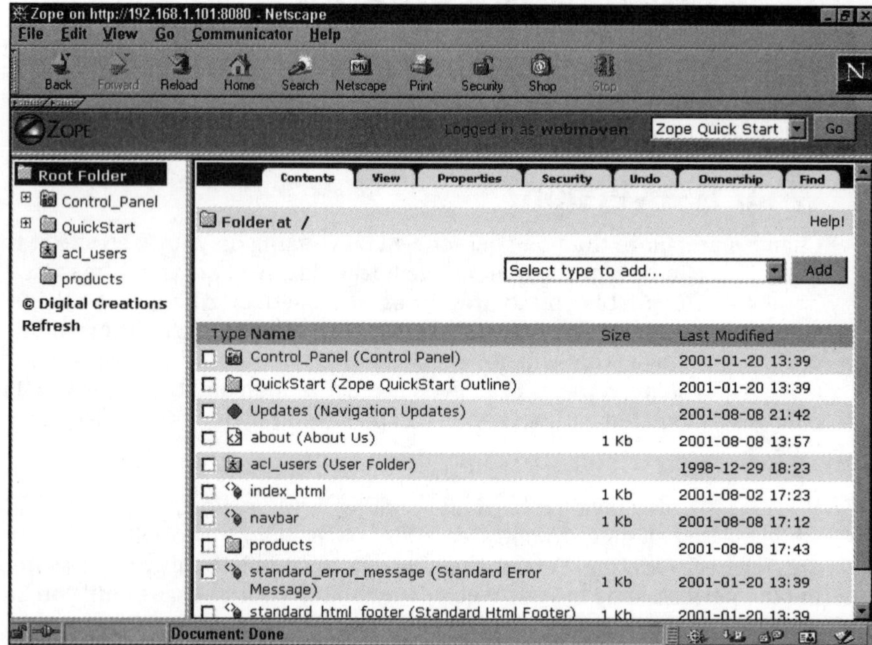

Figure 11-5: Adding a version

Joining and leaving a version

After creating the version you'll need to join it, as you won't be able to see any changes inside of version until you do. When you join a version, Zope sets a special cookie that your browser will pass back with every request. This cookie tells Zope that you are working in version that is different from the default version everyone else sees. The management screens will inform you that you are working a version by cleverly stating, "You are working in version */version name*." (See Figure 11-6.)

You can join or leave a version at any time. The project you are working on might take several days or even weeks to complete. In the meantime visitors to the Web site will continue to see the old site until you are ready to commit your changes. The cookie that is assigned to you is only good until the browser is shut down, so if you quit your browser or reboot your computer you will need to rejoin the version.

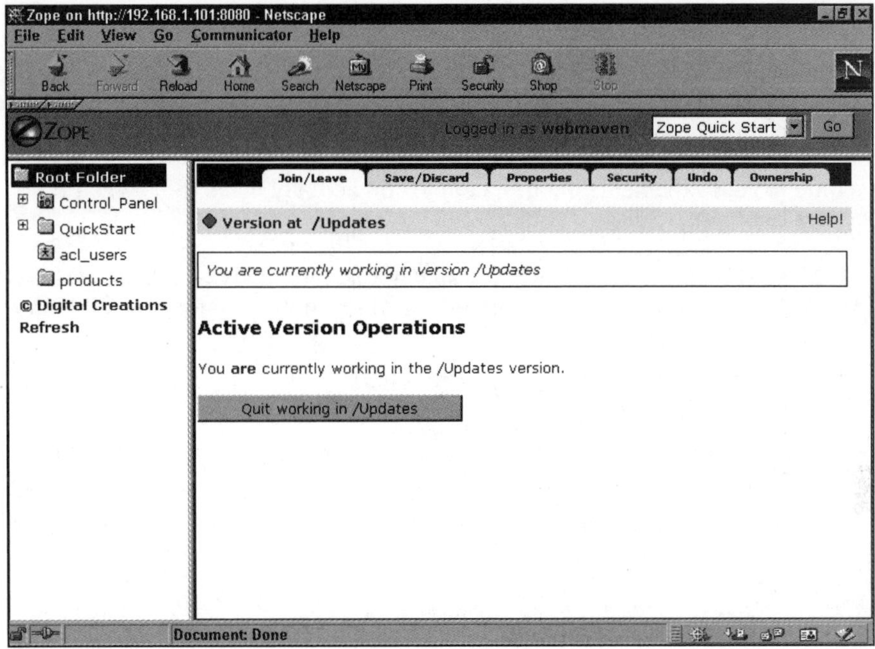

Figure 11-6: Joining a version

To join the version in our sample project, follow these steps:

1. From the Root Folder click the object with the red diamond labeled "Updates."
2. Zope displays the Join/Leave view for the Updates object.
3. Click the button labeled "Start Working in Navigation Updates." If you are already working in a version the button will be labeled "Quit Working in Navigation Updates."
4. Zope redisplays the Join/Leave page again and informs you that you are now working in a version. Notice that the button is now labeled "Quit Working in Navigation Updates."

Working in a version

Once in a version you can start making changes just as you would outside of it. If you make a change to an object in a version, a small red diamond appears to the right of the object's name in the management view, signifying that the object has been changed. Those that are not working in a version will be presented with an icon of a diamond and a lock. This signifies that this object has been edited in a version and is now locked. Locked objects can only be modified if you join the version. Deleting an object inside of version will lock the object outside of the version and also lock its containing Folder. Objects that are created inside of a version will not be visible until the version is committed, but their containing Folder will be locked.

It's time to get to the heart of our example and actually make the navigation updates to our demo site.

1. Make sure you are currently working in the version by clicking on the Update version object. If you aren't already working in the Version, click the Start Working in Navigation Updates button.
2. Take another look at the code in the `navbar DTML Method`. It should look something like this:

```
<table width="120" align="left" cellpadding=5 celspacing=0
border=0>
 <tr>
  <td bgcolor="#CCCCCC" nowrap>
   <ul>
    <li><a href="/">Home</a>
    <li><a href="/about">About Us</a>
    <li>Subsection 1
    <li>Subsection 2
    <li>Subsection 3
   </ul>
  </td>
 </tr>
</table>
```

3. Change the `Subsection 1` line to read:

```
<li><a href="/products/index_html">Products</a>
```

4. View the /products page and verify that your change is visible in the navbar.
5. Quit your version to get a feel for what others will see. Notice the lock symbol by the `navbar` method. Try editing it. If you view your site in your browser, you will see that your site has not yet been publicly changed.
6. Rejoin the version and view it again if you wish.

Now that you're happy with the change you made, it is time to commit it.

Saving or discarding your changes

Once you have made changes to your site in a version you can do one of two things: commit the changes so that the rest of the world can see how brilliant you are, or pretend that your changes never happened by discarding them. You don't need to be working in a version in order to commit or discard its changes.

Follow these steps to save or discard the Updates version:

1. From the Root Folder click on the version labeled "Updates."
2. Zope displays the Join/Leave page. Click the Save/Discard tab.
3. If there are any changes to be saved Zope will give you a text widget where you can make a comment about the changes you've made. If there are no changes to be made, Zope will inform you of this.
4. Enter in a note such as, "Added link to the product section," and click the Save button. Alternately, you can click the Discard button and Zope will revert all your changes back to how they were before you started working in the version. In either case, Zope will unlock all of your objects.

Things to consider when working with versions

If you add or delete objects while in a version, you are actually modifying the container, so the containing object will be locked from having other changes made outside of the version, including other objects being added or deleted.

Versions are mutually exclusive, and non-nesting. You can't create a version while in a version. In this respect, Zope Versions are less capable then CVS (Concurrent Versioning system) for versioning, and more resemble RCS (Revision Control System).

Committing a version causes all the transactions (changes) within it to be committed to the ZODB (Zope Object Database). This means that to undo the changes made by the version you can't roll back the version commit as a whole, you must roll back the individual transactions.

Applied Security

While security is dealt with more extensively in chapters 9 and 13 of this book, it's important to consider security from a content management perspective as well. Content management poses some interesting challenges for security, and the solutions that Zope has incorporated are elegant, allow Delegate responsibility, and perform Damage Control when necessary.

Delegation

Zope's model for delegation of authority is one of "customers who have customers." What this means is that management of any section of the object tree can be safely delegated to a user without that user being able to apply their privileges anywhere else.

Let's say that in our example you want to give Fred the sales manager control over the Products section of the Web site so that he can add and change products and their descriptions, but you don't want to give him the ability to alter the site's home page.

In Chapter 3, you learned about User Folders and users.

In order to safely delegate manger level access to Fred, you should add him to the User Folder at least one level above the folder he'll be managing. In this case, that would be the Root Folder, however don't give Fred's user any Roles just yet.

After you've added Fred's user to the Root Folder, go into the `/products` folder that you want to delegate to Fred and click the Security tab. You'll see a link in the description that reads "local roles." If you click this link you'll see a screen like the screen shown in Figure 11-7.

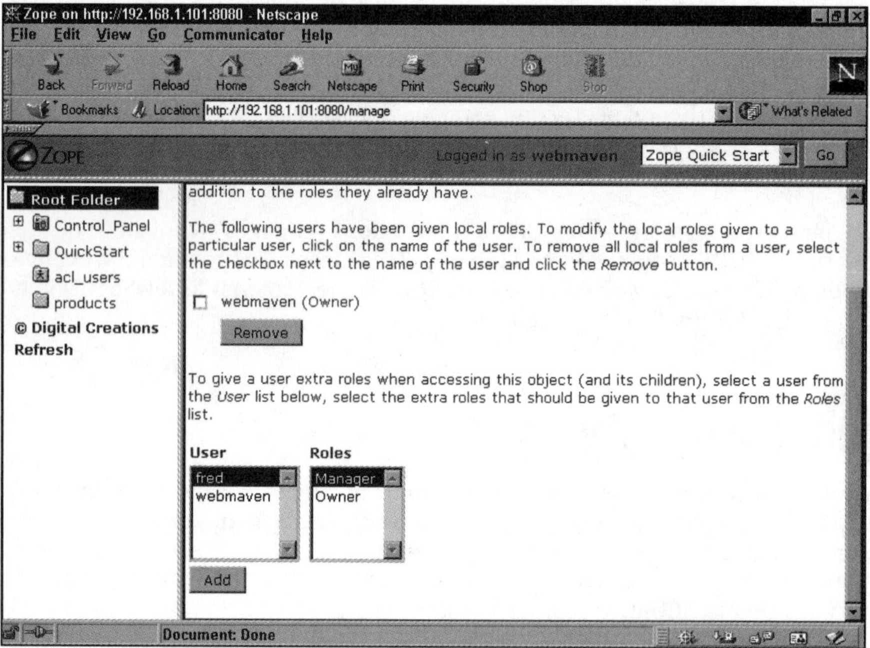

Figure 11-7: The local roles screen

Click both Fred's username and the Manager role from their respective list boxes, and then click the Add button. You have now given Fred a local role of "Manager." This means that Fred has a manager role in the `/products` folder and can do anything a manager could do. Of course, you could have simply added a user folder to the `/products` folder, and added Fred as a manager within that folder directly, but there are some subtle advantages to the use of local roles.

Now, let's assume that Fred has a subordinate, Sheila, that Fred wants to delegate the management of the Thingumbob product line. After creating a Thingumbob folder, Fred can create a user folder in the products folder by choosing the Add User Folder from the add list drop-down menu, shown in Figure 11-8.

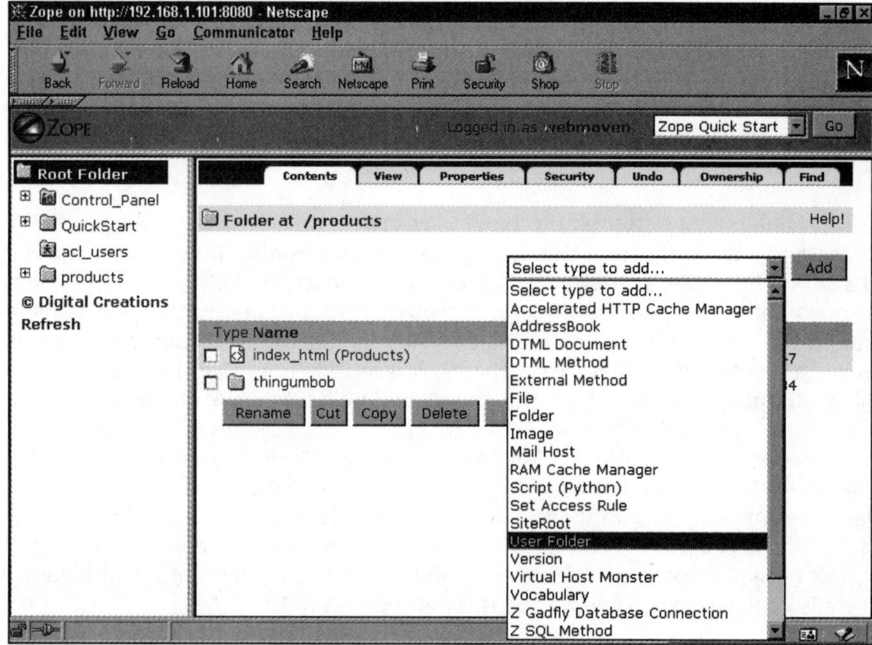

Figure 11-8: Adding a User Folder

After adding a user for Sheila, Fred can go ahead and give her a local role of manager within the Thingumbob folder.

Damage Control

All of this delegation is well and good, but doesn't really constitute damage control *per se*. Where damage control comes in is in the unfortunate situation where Fred doesn't meet the quarterly sales figures, and, because of some behind the scenes maneuvering by Sheila, Fred is fired.

In order to limit the amount of damage that Fred would be able to do to the company by expressing his unreasonable expectations of job security, you as the site administrator must revoke his access to the site immediately. This is fairly simple. You actually have two options in this case, you can:

✦ Delete the `fred` user.

✦ Remove Fred's local roles.

The former option is a quick fix, but will leave local roles scattered around the site. These are not harmful in-and-of themselves, but they do leave the possibility that someone in the future will create a new user with the same username, who would automatically get all of the privileges that had formerly been granted to Fred. So a more thorough procedure would be to remove all of the local roles Fred had been granted as well as the Fred user.

In either case, now someone needs to be assigned to manage the Products folder, and you don't want to do it. Fortunately, Sheila has been promoted to Fred's old job, and you can create a user for her in the root `acl_users` User Folder, and then give her a manager local role on the Products folder. (Don't forget to delete the Sheila user from the `/products/thingumbob` folder.)

Now it might seem redundant to have to re-create the sheila username in the root folder, and it is. Notice that this is only necessary because Sheila's user was created in a subfolder's User Folder. For this reason, if you expect this sort of shuffling of responsibility to occur often, you will probably want to centralize user management and create *all* users in the root folder, relying on local roles exclusively. This does mean that only the Root Folder manager will be able to add and delete users, so think carefully about which approach will end up being more efficient.

Centralizing the users also avoids the security problems caused by user name clashes. If Dave the VP has manager level access over the `/marketing folder`, and Dave the copyeditor is supposed to have read-only access to a `/marketing/news/releases/in-progress/` folder, Dave the copyeditor will actually have manager level access to that subfolder if their usernames are the same. If creating and managing users is centralized, problems like this can be avoided.

Even in the case of centrally managed users, Fred would still have been able to delegate management of the `/products/thingumbob` folder to Sheila by using the local-roles interface.

Anyway, now that Fred is out of the picture (and the system), he can't post any diatribes on the site that would embarrass the company, so your job is secure.

Summary

In this chapter you learned the basics of content management using Zope's acquisition features to increase maintainability, how to use versions to allow collaboration on the site and hide changes-in-progress until they're finalized, and how to use Zope's security infrastructure to safely delegate management of the Web site.

For further reading, check out the following titles:

Information Architecture for the World Wide Web by Louis Rosenfeld and Peter Morville (O'Reilly, 1998)

Cascading Style Sheets: Designing for the Web, 2/e, by Håkon Wium Lie and Bert Bos (Addison-Wesley, 1999)

The Art and Science of Web Design by Jeffrey Veen (New Riders, 2000)

✦ ✦ ✦

CHAPTER 12

Database Management

In This Chapter

This chapter introduces you to permanent data storage outside of the Zope-provided ZODB in the form of external database access. We will discuss types of databases, access methods from within Zope, and organize data within external databases.

About Relational Databases

We will be discussing one particular type of database — the *relational* database. To understand what a relational database is and how it differs from other database types, we will go through relational versus object databases, as well as some relational theory.

Database basics

Almost all of applications you will build or use in Zope will use some form of long-term data storage. This could be the user's preferences for quick-links on a Web portal, signatures for an online petition, or phone numbers in a company's internal phone list.

As discussed earlier in this book, Zope provides powerful data storage capabilities through its persistent object storage mechanism, the Zope Object Database, or ZODB. For many small and large applications, this is a more than sufficiently powerful tool for storing data. The ZODB has some shortcomings, however, so sometimes a more powerful, or simply a different kind of long-term data storage system is called for. The ZODB is an *object database*, which means it stores whole objects at a time, and stores related objects — such as properties of the object being stored — and any other objects that are referenced by the object being stored.

The ZODB provides a simple and effective system for storing data. Using the ZODB, it is easy to represent hierarchical relationships, such as one object containing another containing another. (This is typically a hard thing to do in a relational database.) The ZODB is also easy to administer, having virtually no setup or maintenance requirements.

The ZODB is great for small databases, and single-server Web sites. When it comes to more advanced setups, however, another kind of database is almost always required. This is because the ZODB has no facility for sharing, meaning that if you have 20 Web servers, there is no straightforward, efficient way to share a single ZODB among them.

This is changing, however, with the development of ZEO. ZEO allows sharing of a single ZODB instance.

The ZODB also has little capability of interfacing with other systems. In developing large systems using databases, you will find that often times the Web server needs to share data with the accounting system, the e-commerce engine, and any number of external systems. Using the ZODB alone, this becomes a daunting task, requiring adaptor code, and various other tricks. Using an external database, this often becomes a job of simply providing database mapping layers (views or stored procedures).

The most common type of external database is a relational database. This kind of database stores simple data only, such as numbers and strings, but also stores how that data is structured. Relational databases are structured as groups of tables. Tables can be thought of as lists of data structures, each containing zero or more rows of data. Each row in a table has one or more column, each column a single data element of a certain type. (For example; unsigned integer, variable-length string, binary digit, and so on.)

Relational database structure

To use a relational database in an application, the structure of the database must be designed. This structure is usually called a table schema, or just *schema*. For instance, to store a single-user address book application's data, we could use two tables: one to hold the address book's entries (the people in the address book), and another to hold the myriad ways to contact each person in the address book. The tables could look like Table 12-1 and Table 12-2.

Table 12-1
Addressbook_entries Table

First Name	*Last Name*	*Company Name*
Jane	Doe	ACME Inc.
John Q.	Doe	Ace Sprockets

First Name	*Last Name*	*Company Name*
Allesandro	Foo	Bit Monkey's LLC
Zaphod	Breeblebrox	Galactic Headquarters

Table 12-2
Addressbook_contacts Table

First Name	*Last Name*	*Phone Number*	*Phone Type*	*Address*	*City*	*State*	*Zip*	*Comment*
John Q.	Doe	555-1212	Cell	123 Boardwalk	Badwater	Alaska	99999	Spooky guy; try not to call.
Zaphod	Breeblebrox	123-4567	Home					Don't call during happy hour.

In the previous example, we begin to see how data is structured in a relational database. Each table contains records, or rows, comprised of columns. The columns define what each row of data contains, and the rows are the data. We can also see that these two tables are related. The Addressbook_entries table contains people. The Addressbook_contacts table contains contact information about those people. The relation between the two is the First_Name and Last_Name columns.

When designing a database schema, you must consider several elements of the data:

✦ What data is to be stored?

✦ How will the data be added to the database?

✦ How will the data be read from the database?

✦ How can the data be normalized?

The answers to these questions can help us design a table schema for recording purchases from an online storefront.

What data is to be stored?

Our virtual storefront has its own product catalog and inventory control system, so all we need to store in our database is what was purchased, when the purchase took place, and how the purchase was paid for. So, the data elements are going to be:

✦ The date of the purchase

✦ The order number

✦ The product number of each product purchased, and how much it cost

- The name, address, and phone number of the customer
- The credit card number, type, and expiration date

How will the data be added to the database?

Each time a purchase takes place in our storefront application, the application will have all of the data listed in the previous section. Because we will be using multiple tables to store our data, we will want to write the data in reverse order, writing the items of the order, then the order itself, so that anyone reading the database will not see the order until it is fully written to the database. The purchase in the store is complete, so we do not have to deal with partial orders or waiting for the user to hit a "confirm" button, so from the point the purchase is complete, we can write the whole order to the database at one time.

How will the data be read from the database?

This database is for historical tracking of orders from the storefront, so most likely the only way this data will be read will be from a reporting application that will simply list all of the transactions that occurred during the last month or week. It will start by looking up all of the orders within a certain date range, it will then look up the details of each order, and finally, format the information nicely in the report.

How can the data be normalized?

The term *normalized data* may be unfamiliar to you. Normalized data is a term used often in relational database circles and means data that has been simplified and broken down enough to be put into a table structure that closely models how the data itself is structured and used. Think of the example of the address book. A single table containing the name, company name, phone number, and address of each person in the book could have been used, but this table could not account for people with multiple phone numbers, nor people for whom you wish to store both a company and a home address. To account for this in a single table you could add more phone number and address columns, such as phone1, phone2, phone3, address1, city1, state1, address2, city2, state2, and so on, but this becomes problematic very quickly. First, you are adding a hard limit to how many addresses or phone numbers you are storing. Second, you are wasting space and resources on the database server by not using these extra columns for people with only one contact method. In programming parlance, adding extra columns like this would be considered "dirty."

A far better way to store address book data where multiple contact methods are allowed is to use one table to store the name and other non-replicated data about each person, and a second table to store the individual contact methods. This is a more normalized way to store the data. It makes more sense, and uses the table-oriented structure of the database to more closely model the data.

There is one last element of using multiple tables to normalize data. That is the use of keys. Think about the address book example. In this example we needed to relate the contact information entries to the individuals. Earlier in this chapter this was done by adding the "First Name" and "Last Name" columns to the Addressbook_contacts table. This allowed the relation of the contact information to the individuals by means of comparing the names. To make this work in most databases, the First Name and Last Name columns in both tables would be declared as unique keys. Moreover, possibly in the Addressbook_contacts table, the First-Name/Last-Name key could be declared as requiring a matching key in the Addressbook_entries table.

This table schema, to store orders from our storefront, will be using the concept of normalization to efficiently store order information. To do this, we need to think about the data being stored. Think about how an order invoice looks. Usually it has customer information on the top and then a list of items. The orders from the storefront are similar. They contain customer information and a list of products purchased. We could put all of this information into one table, with multiple columns for the products, adding a hard limit to the number of products able to be purchased, as in the following table structure:

Orders Table

Order Number

Order Date

Customer Name

Credit Card Number

Credit Card Expiration Date

Credit Card Type

Product #1 ID

Product #2 ID

Product #3 ID

Product #4 ID

Product #5 ID

This table structure would work just fine for our application, so long as nobody ever wants to buy more than five products at a time. For a small, private store, this might work, but a far better way to store the orders would be to use a second table to store the ordered items so that as many products as the customer likes can be purchased at one time.

The only problem with using a second table for ordered items is that it needs to relate some how to the order table. In most stores, each order is given a unique number — an order id — that will serve as the relation key in this example perfectly. All that needs to be done to the previous example is to remove the product columns and create a second table containing product ids and an order id for relation. The new table schema looks like this:

Orders Table

Order ID

Order Date

Customer Name

Credit Card Number

Credit Card Expiration

Credit Card Type

Order_Items Table

Order ID

Product ID

The new table schema stores our data well and even allows for growth later on. For instance, price and quantity columns could be easily added to the Order_Items table, whereas if all of the data were in one table, adding more columns for each product could prove to be quite an undertaking if 5, 10, or 100 product id columns were already present.

Most commercial relational database vendors have complete examples of the process of data normalization in their product documentation. For an additional resource, *Oracle8: The Complete Reference* (Osborne, 1997) contains a particularly good one.

Accessing relational databases: SQL

Nearly all modern relational databases are accessed by a computer language named SQL. SQL stands for Structured Query Language, and by some is pronounced *sequel*. Compared with Python or even DTML (Document Template Markup Language), it is a simple language, designed to be easy to learn, yet powerful to use.

The Query part of SQL is indicative of the client/server nature of relational databases. The client, be it a command-line tool or a Zope database adaptor, sends queries to the database server, be it MySQL, Oracle, or the Gadfly library within Zope.

There are several good books on the entire SQL specification, some devoted only to this topic, while some database books such as *Oracle8: The Complete Reference* (referenced in the previous note) contain a good SQL section.

SQL is submitted as sentences to the database server from the client. These sentences are composed of a SQL statement, followed by arguments and qualifiers to that statement. In some cases, statements can be nested, such as in subqueries allowed on Oracle, Postgres, and soon MySQL, but in most cases, there is only one query at a time.

The most commonly used SQL statements are SELECT, INSERT, UPDATE, and DELETE. In addition to describing these statements, we discuss the CREATE TABLE and DROP TABLE statements that enable you to actually add and delete tables to and from a database.

The SELECT statement

The SELECT statement is by far the most used statement in SQL. It is the only way to read data from a SQL-speaking database. All other statements are for manipulating data. Let's dive right in.

For the following examples we will use an example table with the structure shown in Table 12-3.

Table 12-3
Employees

Name	*SSID*	*Citizen*	*StartDate*
Alice	172-23-2821	Y	04/03/00
Asok	372-29-2892	N	11/02/98
Wally	212-39-2811	Y	01/10/01

Let's look at our first SQL query:

```
SELECT * FROM my_table
```

This is the most simple form of the SELECT statement. The previous sentence simply returns all columns of all rows of the employees table. The * in the previous sentence instructs SELECT to return all columns of the table. Because no logic was used to limit the number of rows returned from employees, all rows are returned.

To select only some columns, individual column names may be specified (separated by commas) instead of using the *, as in:

```
SELECT Name, StartDate FROM employees
```

This will return the name and start date of all the employees in the table.

To limit the number of rows returned, the SELECT statement uses a WHERE clause of the sentence. For instance, to select only non-citizen employees from the employee table, the following query will work:

```
SELECT * FROM employees WHERE Citizen = 'N'
```

This is about the simplest form of the WHERE clause. Depending on the database used, and the type of data being operated on, the logic that can be used in WHERE clauses can be quite complicated. In all SQL speaking databases, arbitrarily complex Boolean expressions can be used. For example:

```
SELECT Name FROM employees WHERE (Citizen = 'Y' AND StartDate > ⮐
DATE('01/01/2001')) OR SSID  ='372-29-2892'
```

The INSERT statement

New data is entered into a SQL speaking database using the INSERT statement. INSERT simply adds a single new row to the end of a table. For example, to add a new person to our employee table, we can use:

```
INSERT INTO employees VALUES ('Pointy Haired Boss', ⮐
 '214-28-1982', 'Y', '01/01/1968')
```

The UPDATE statement

The UPDATE statement changes the value of one or more columns of one or more rows of a table. For instance, if we wanted to change the start date of all employees in our table to January 1, 2001, we could use:

```
UPDATE employees SET StartDate = '01/01/2001'
```

Or, if Asok gained citizenship, we could use the following UPDATE statement:

```
UPDATE employees SET Citizen = 'Y' WHERE Name = 'Asok'
```

The DELETE statement

The DELETE statement deletes some or all of the rows from a table. To delete all of the rows of the employees table, the query is simple:

```
DELETE FROM employees
```

To just delete Wally, we can use a WHERE clause:

```
DELETE FROM employees WHERE Name = 'Wally'
```

The CREATE TABLE statement

To create a table, the CREATE TABLE statement is used. To create our employees table, we could use:

```
CREATE TABLE employees (Name VARCHAR(100), SSID CHAR(11), ⮐
Citizen CHAR(1),  StartDate DATE)
```

This is the basic syntax for CREATE TABLE. The datatypes allowed are database specific, but almost all support a simple set:

INTEGER

CHAR

VARCHAR

DATE

Most databases will also allow the specification of a default value, whether or not the column may allow null values, and whether or not the value in the column must be unique.

The DROP TABLE statement

The DROP TABLE statement simply removes an entire table from the database being used. Its syntax is very simple. To drop the employees table:

```
DROP TABLE employees
```

Be careful, however, as dropping tables are generally irreversible.

Real world: Specific RDBMS products

There are countless relational database options, and the number grows every day. For use with Zope, any database you choose must be supported by Python at least, and there must be a Zope adaptor for that database as well. Below are a few of the most popular database options for Zope.

MySQL

MySQL is one of the most popular databases in use today for small to medium Web sites. It is very fast, easy to manage, and has a huge, supportive user base. MySQL is an open-source product, but several companies offer commercial support.

MySQL has a few limitations. By default it is non-transactional, so enabling transactions and using them takes a little extra work. MySQL also does not support some of the more complicated SQL constructs, such as subqueries, triggers, and stored procedures. Most of these limitations are being overcome, however, as MySQL is improved on an almost weekly basis, and has been for years.

Oracle

Oracle is one of the biggest, oldest, most stable, feature rich, flexible, respected, and expensive relational databases in existence. Almost every other database product has only a sub-set of the features of Oracle. If money is no object, you can't go wrong with Oracle. Expense is Oracle's downfall, however. The software itself is often prohibitively expensive for small or medium size projects, and the hardware requirements of the database alone are also quite substantial.

Sybase

Sybase is a commercial database product comparable to Oracle. It is full-featured and stable, and has a loyal following. While Sybase may not be attracting many new customers in recent years, it is already deployed in many large systems around the world. For this reason, Zope could be used as a new front-end to existing systems.

PostgreSQL

PostgreSQL is another mature database. The core of PostgreSQL was developed over the last couple of decades at the University of California at Berkeley. The project eventually spun off as a separate and open-sourced product. PostgreSQL is incredibly feature-rich, and in comparison to Oracle or Sybase, consumes very little system resources. PostgreSQL is a reliable, cost-effective database, but does not come with the corporate support that Oracle does, or the blazing raw speed of MySQL.

ODBC

ODBC is a standardized database communication protocol, allowing any ODBC client to communicate with any ODBC server. This is in contrast to the database-specific protocols most database products use, which require their own Zope adaptor. Zope's ODBC database adaptor allows Zope to use any database product with ODBC support. In addition to the databases mentioned here, many more database products support ODBC, and so can be used with Zope.

Gadfly

Gadfly is a simple relational database product bundled with Zope. Every Zope installation out-of-the-box has the ability to create a new Gadfly database immediately. Gadfly supports only a subset of the full SQL language, and its performance and reliability are not quite on par with Oracle or MySQL, but it is a great learning tool. We will be using Gadfly as the relational database to use in the examples of the rest of this chapter.

Connecting Zope to a Relational Database

To be able to use an external relational database from within Zope, you must create a Zope database connection object, which allows SQL queries to be sent to the database and responses to be read. In order to create a connection object, a number of steps must be followed. We discuss each of these steps in the following sections.

Getting an adaptor

Zope accesses databases using a Zope Database Adaptor. This is a Zope product that implements the right application programming interface (API) to allow SQL

Methods to make use of the adaptor to communicate via SQL to a database in a common way. Essentially, the adaptor is the Zope abstraction of the specifics of using a database. One of the most interesting things an adaptor does is to check for and make use of the transactional ability of some databases. (This topic is discussed in more detail in the "Advanced Techniques" section of this chapter.)

The only database adaptor that comes bundled with Zope is the Gadfly adaptor, which is fully self-contained so that all Zope instances can make use of a relational database out-of-the-box. To use any other database, you must download the adaptor from the Internet. A good place to look is at `http://www.zope.org/Products/external_access`.

In addition to needing a Zope adaptor to obtain access to an external database, you will almost certainly need to get the Python module that allows Python, which Zope is written in, to communicate with the database. To make things even more involved, the Python module will almost certainly need to have libraries installed from the database itself to work. If Zope and the database are running on the same machine, this is taken care of for you, but if they are not on the same machine, you will need to install the database client libraries on the machine Zope is running on.

Each Python module and Zope Database Adaptor is different, and will have slightly different installation methods, but they will all be somewhat similar. For example, we will go through the steps of getting Zope access to a local (meaning installed on the same machine) MySQL database. We will assume MySQL and Zope are already installed.

The first step is to install the MySQL Python module. (Because MySQL is so common, this may actually be already done for you.) Both MySQL and Python come with the Python-MySQL module, and will install it for you if you choose to do so when you install either product. If you did not choose to do this, you will need to download the MySQL-Python module from `www.python.org`. Go to the download section of the Web site, and from there click the link to The Vaults of Paranassus. From the main page, enter **MySQLdb** into the search box. Download the MySQLdb package, and follow the installation instructions that follow.

Next, you will download the MySQL Zope adaptor from `www.zope.org`. Enter **zmysqlda** into the search box on the main page. Several items will come back; click one with the simple title of "ZmySQLDA." There may be several; download the one with the latest date. Follow the installation instructions in this package, and you are done! From within a Zope folder you may use the product drop-down list to create a new connection to your MySQL database.

Connecting and disconnecting

To create a connection to a database from within Zope, you will need to go to a folder within Zope, one either at or below the level from which the connection will be used, and create a database connection object. The root (/) folder is a good choice for database connection objects, but could get cluttered if too many exist.

To create a new connection object, go to the folder in which you want to put the new object, and from the product drop-down list, select to add the adaptor instance of your choice. If you are using MySQL, this will be called "Z MySQL Database Connection." See the database connection add screen in Figure 12-1.

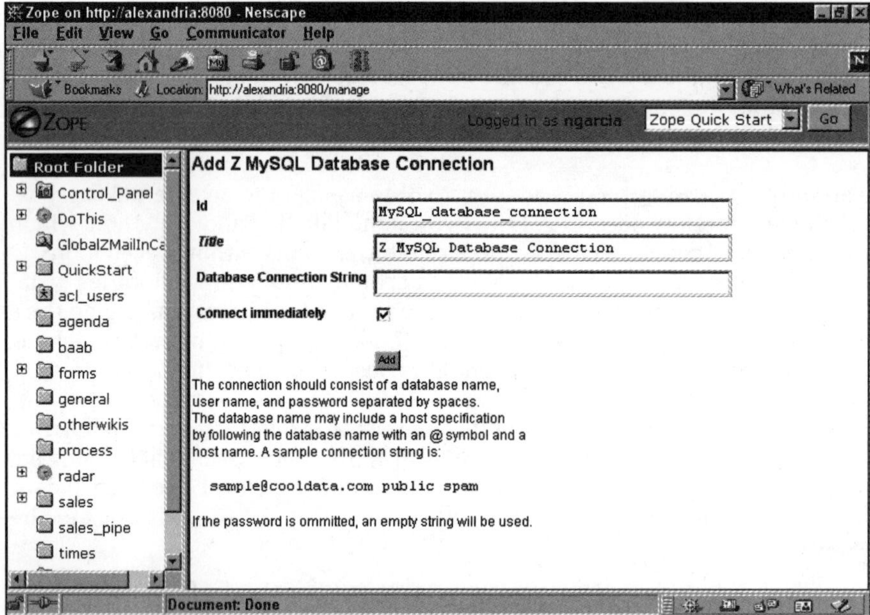

Figure 12-1: MySQL Database Connection Add screen

From the add screen, give your new connection object an id and a connection string.

The connection string is a somewhat tricky thing. Often it is hard to get right, and when you get it wrong, the error messages are not very helpful. The most verbose form of the connection string syntax is:

```
DB_Name@Server_Name User_Name Password
```

The `@Server` portion can be left off if the database server is on the same machine as the Zope process, and the Password can be left off if the database user account has no password.

Testing SQL statements

All Zope database adaptors enable you to run SQL queries from within the Test tab of their management screens, which you can get to by simply clicking the connection object.

Using the test screen, you can run simple queries to look around in your database or to do one-time tasks, such as renaming a table or altering a column.

Browsing tables

Some database adaptors have a Browse Tables tab in their management screens. This function enables you to visually browse the existing table schema. Tables and their columns can be seen. Often, this is useful for visualizing the database structure.

SQL Methods: The Basics

Zope may use database adaptors to communicate with databases, but everything else within Zope, be it Python-written products, DTML, or scripts (Python or Perl) uses SQL Method objects. The SQL Method is a Zope product written in Python, but it forms the glue between the adaptor API and DTML or anything else.

Any time a database is to be accessed, you should create an instance of the SQL Method product (simply called a SQL Method) to do the work. A SQL Method acts just like a method of any programming language. It has a name, it takes arguments, it has a body, and it returns a result.

- The name of a SQL Method is its Zope ID.
- The arguments of a SQL Method are defined as named variables.
- The body of a SQL Method is one or more SQL queries.
- SQL Methods return Result Objects.

SQL Methods are created and used in different ways, depending on the environment. To be called from DTML, they are created through the Zope management screens, just like any other product. From Python in External Methods, or in Python-written products, they are imported and instantiated just like any other class. What they do have in common, however, is the body. No matter how SQL Methods are used, the rules on their SQL written bodies are the same, and the same Zope added functionality exists.

Static SQL methods

Any SQL Method may have a simple, unchanging SQL body. A query such as:

```
SELECT * FROM employees
```

will always work. These can get frustrating to use in a hurry, however, as they do not allow you to vary the statement in any way. This is necessary in WHERE clauses of statements, and especially when specifying new data for the INSERT statement.

Dynamic SQL methods

Dynamic SQL simply means the ability to add a simple subset of DTML to your SQL Method bodies. These tags are then evaluated at run time, so that dynamic data can be inserted into the SQL queries.

The dtml-sqlvar tag

The `dtml-sqlvar` tag is the equivalent of DTML's `dtml-var` tag. At run time, the tag is simply replaced with the value it references. The `dtml-sqlvar` tag, in contrast to the `dtml-var` tag, properly escapes and quotes the value according to the rules of the specific database. The `dtml-sqlvar` tag does not have as many options as the `dtml-var` tag, however.

See the DTML reference section in Chapter 4 for all tag options.

`dtml-sqlvar` is probably most often used for INSERT and UPDATE statements. For example, to add a new employee to our employees table:

```
INSERT INTO employees VALUES (<dtml-sqlvar name type=string>,
<dtml-sqlvar ssid type=string>, <dtml-sqlvar citizen
type=string>, <dtml-sqlvar startDate type=date>)
```

As you can see, the most often used option to `dtml-sqlvar` is the type option. The most often argument of it, is string. See the DTML reference for more options.

The dtml-sqltest tag

You can use the `dtml-sqlvar` tag to represent the variable components of WHERE clauses in SQL, such as in:

```
SELECT * FROM employees WHERE Name = <dtml-sqlvar Name
type=string>
```

However, this can become cumbersome with more complex data types, such as dates. Zope provides a mechanism to construct WHERE clause elements that do proper quoting and type conversion. This mechanism is the `dtml-sqltest` tag. This tag allows the previous statement to be represented as:

```
SELECT * FROM employees WHERE <dtml-sqltest Name type=string>
```

This statement evaluates to exactly the same SQL as the first example, but is a little bit easier to understand. It simply compares the named variable to a column of the same name. The operator, in this case equality can be changed, as can the datatype. Check the reference section of this book for a complete list of options.

The dtml-sqlgroup tag

The `dtml-sqlgroup` tag is one of a family of tags including:

- `dtml-sqlgroup`
- `dtml-and`
- `dtml-or`

This family of tags enables you to represent complex Boolean logic in an easy to understand way. Essentially, `<dtml-sqlgroup>`, and its end-tag, `</dtml-sqlgroup>`, evaluate to left and right parenthesis, respectively. `dtml-and` evaluates to the AND SQL operator, and `dtml-or` evaluates to the SQL OR operator. These tags are usually used in conjunction with the `dtml-sqltest` tag. For example:

```
SELECT * FROM employees
   <dtml-sqlgroup where>
         <dtml-sqltest Name type=string>
   <dtml-and>
          <dtml-sqlgroup>
                <dtml-sqltest SSID type=string>
          <dtml-or>
                <dtml-sqltest StartDate type=string>
          </dtml-sqlgroup>
   </dtml-sqlgroup>
```

This is a pretty simple example of the use of `dtml-sqlgroup`. The interesting thing going on here behind the scenes is that `dtml-sqlgroup` is smart enough to know that if the `Name` argument is not passed in to the SQL Method when it is called, that part of the WHERE clause will be left out. Optionally, the word *required* can be added as an option to `dtml-sqltest` tags, requiring that clause to be used. This kind of adaptive logic can be useful in applications such as searches where some or all of the fields of the search are optional. It can also lead to some confusing bugs, so be careful.

Using SQL Methods from DTML

The easiest way to use SQL Methods is from DTML methods of documents. The SQL Method object can be created from the product drop-down list within a Zope folder, using easy-to-use graphical interfaces. You can easily see what arguments are being used, and edit the SQL body of the method online. You can see the SQL Method add/edit screen in Figure 12-2.

Be careful to note that the arguments to SQL Methods must be single words on individual lines of the arguments text area.

To illustrate the use of SQL Methods for the rest of this section, we will use two SQL Methods, which are shown in Figures 12-3 and 12-4.

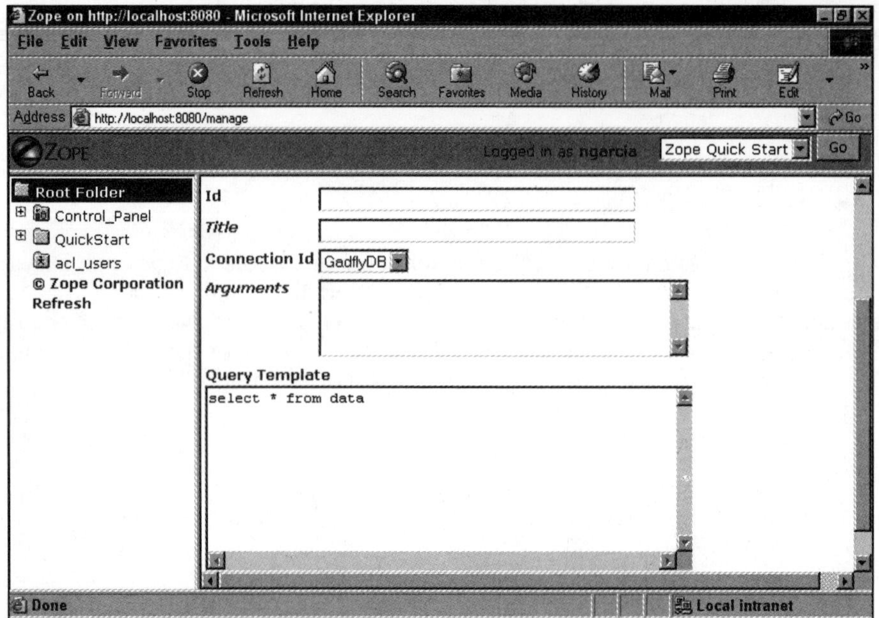

Figure 12-2: SQL Method add screen

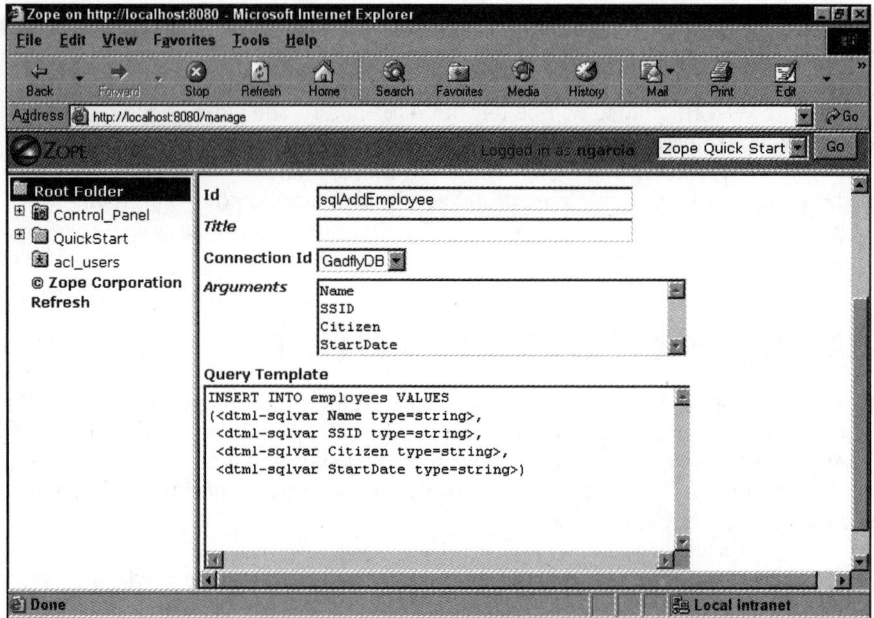

Figure 12-3: sqlAddEmployee SQL Method edit screen

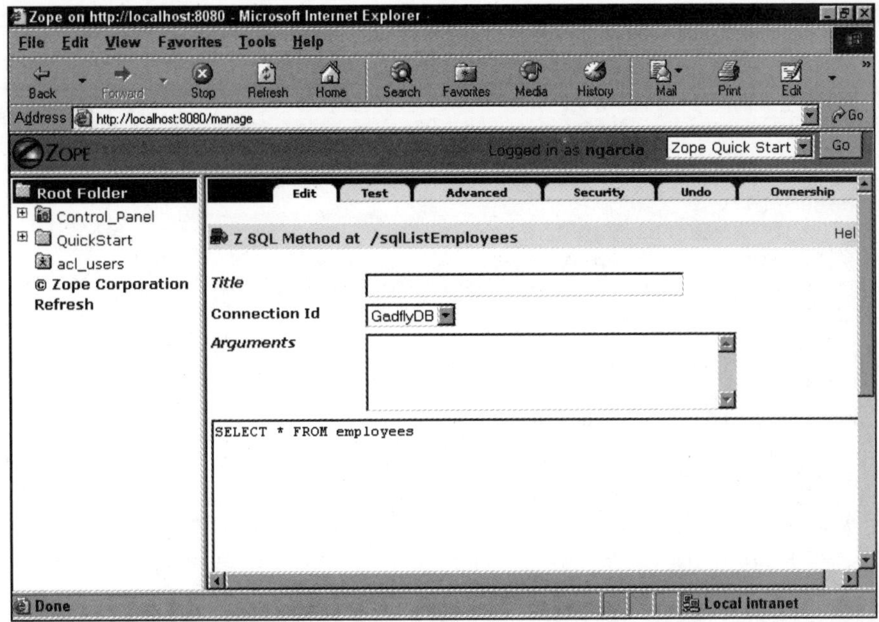

Figure 12-4: sqlListEmployees SQL Method edit screen

As with all things in DTML, SQL Methods are accessed via tags: `dtml-var`, `dtml-call`, and `dtml-in`.

Using the dtml-call tag

The `dtml-call` tag is the simplest way to call SQL Methods, but it is also the least powerful. `dtml-call` enables you to call SQL Methods and pass them arguments, but it does not enable you access to any return value. This is best used for calling SQL Methods that perform INSERTs, UPDATEs, or DELETEs, not SELECTs. We can call our example insert SQL Method in this way:

```
<dtml-call "sqlAddEmployee(Name='Phil', SSID='55-666-777',
Citizen='N', StartDate='01/01/0001'">
```

Adding this line to any DTML method with access to the `sqlAddEmployee` method will cause an insert of Phil's data into the Employees table.

Using the dtml-in tag

To retrieve data from a database we use the `dtml-in` and `dtml-var` tags. The most powerful way to do this is with the `dtml-in` tag. As we learned previously, this tag is for iterating through lists or tuples of objects. SQL Methods return a tuple of Result objects, so this is perfect. If we want to iterate over all the people in our employee table, the following DTML would work perfectly:

```
<dtml-var standard_HTML_header>
<table>
<!-- A table header -->
<tr><td>Name</td><td>SSID</td><td>Citizen?</td><td>Start ⮐
Date</td></tr>
<!-- Iterate through the employees -->
<dtml-in sqlListEmployees>
   <!-- For each employee, print out the column data -->
   <tr>
   <td><dtml-var Name></td>
   <td><dtml-var SSID></td>
   <td><dtml-var Citizen></td>
   <td><dtml-var StartDate></td>
</tr>
</dtml-in>
</dtml-var standard_html_header>
```

Using SQL Methods from External Methods

External methods are methods written in Python that reside in files inside of the Extensions directory of Zope. These methods can access the Zope folder hierarchy, and through this, SQL Methods. (To fully understand this section, you will need to skip ahead to Chapter 15 to find out about External Methods, then turn back to find out how to use SQL Methods from them.) All external methods are passed a self object reference. This object is a reference to the folder that contains the external method proxy object. This object reference then can be used to get references to other objects from within the Zope folder hierarchy using the `hasattr` and `getattr` methods. Here is an example of a Python External Method that calls the `sqlListEmployees` SQL Method from the previous section, and returns a list of maps of the rows.

```
Def employeeMapList(self):
    # Call the sqlListEmployees method, which is a property
    # on our folder, which is self.
    results = self.getattr('sqlListEmployees')()

    # Turn the result object into a list of maps
    mapList = []
    for result in results:
        resultMap = {}
        for column in results._names
            resultMap[column] = result[column]

        mapList.append(resultMap)
    return mapList
```

Using SQL Methods from Python Products

Python-written Zope products, as with External Methods, are beyond the scope of this chapter, so read chapters 6 through 10 to learn about Python Products and then turn back to learn how to use SQL Methods from them.

The basic steps to using SQL Methods from Python Products are:

1. Import the SQL class.
2. Create a new SQL Method object.
3. Set the new SQL Method as a property on the product.
4. Call the SQL Method.

It's important to note that what database connection is to be used with any SQL Method is determined at SQL Method instantiating time, not run time. Further, this connection is specified by id, not by reference. This is why the SQL Method must be a property on the Product to work, as the SQL Method, when called, makes calls on the connection object through traversal, and for it to be able to access the Product's traversal tree, it must be a property of the Product.

Importing the SQL method class

As always with Python, any external classes must be imported into the current namespace by means of the import statement. The simplest way to import the SQL Method class is with:

```
from Products.ZSQLMethods.SQL import SQL
```

Instantiating new SQL method objects

Now that the SQL class is imported, a new SQL Method object may be instantiated by using the class name SQL. The constructor of SQL is:

```
SQL(id, title, connectionID, arguments, sqlBody)
```

Because SQL Methods may be added to Zope folders, the SQL class extends `OFS.SimpleItem`, and so must have an id and Title. The id should be something meaningful, whether you will be adding the SQL Method to a folder or not. The title is optional.

`ConnectionID` is the id of the database connection to be used. As stated earlier, this name is resolved to an object reference at run time through acquisition.

Arguments is a list of string names for arguments that can then be used in dtml-sql* tags within the SQL body.

The `sqlBody` option is just that: the SQL queries to be executed.

Calling SQL methods

The most common way to use SQL Methods from Python Products as stated earlier in this chapter, is when the SQL Method is a property of the Product. In this way the SQL Method may be called as a method of the product. This is demonstrated as:

```
# Declare the ID to use for the SQL Method
methodId = 'sqlListEmployees'

# Instantiate the new SQL method object, and make it a
# property on this product.
setattr(self, methodId, SQL(methodId, '', 'employeesDB',
   'SELECT * FROM employees'))

# Call the SQL Method just like any other method
result = self.sqlListEmployees()
```

This is by far the most common way to use SQL Methods from Python Products. However, SQL Methods that are already in existence and in a Zope folder may be called from Python Products, just as External Methods do, through the self object.

If you write a new product in Python that uses SQL Methods from Zope folders, all that must be done is to place the SQL Method objects at or above the Folder where your product is to be instantiated. Once that is done, the SQL Method can be called, just as in the last line of the pervious example.

SQL Methods used from within products need not be set as a property of the product more than once. If the product inherits from Persistent, the SQL Method needs only be instantiated and set as a property on the product once. The best time to do this is from within the Product constructor.

Advanced Techniques

Now that you know the basics of using external databases with Zope, we can investigate some of the advanced techniques available to you.

Acquiring parameters

Up to this point, all parameters to SQL Methods in our examples have been explicitly passed to the method when it is called. This is often the most desirable way to pass data to SQL Methods, and certainly offers the greatest degree of control, but this is not the only way. If no arguments are passed to a SQL Method that specifies needed arguments, the SQL Method will collect its arguments from the environment. This is especially useful in calling SQL Methods from DTML. In this case, the SQL Method will get its arguments from the REQUEST object, which is often where the arguments come from anyway. This saves you some typing at least, and at most it saves you from some possible typos.

Traversing to SQL method results

Because of the near magical ability of Zope to access all objects via their URLs, it is possible to get the result of a SQL Method simply by going to its URL and passing arguments on the query string.

For example, if you had a SQL Method named employee_lookup in your Zope Root Folder that took an argument named SSID, and had a body of:

```
SELECT * FROM employees where <dtml-sqltest SSID type=string>
```

then you could access the result of this query by going to the URL:

```
/employee_lookup?SSID=212-39-2811
```

If the SQL Method was connected to our example Gadfly database, you would get Wally's employee record. This would be very undramatic to look at in your browser, however.

To add some display logic to the result, you could append the id of a DTML method to the URL. If you had a DTML method named `employee_display` with the following body in the same folder as your previous SQL Method:

```
<dtml-var standard_html_header>
<table>
<tr><td>Name</td><td>SSID</td><td>Citizen?</td><td>Start
Date</td></tr>
<tr>
<td><dtml-var Name></td>
<td><dtml-var SSID></td>
<td><dtml-var Citizen></td>
<td><dtml-var StartDate></td>
</tr>
</table>
<dtml-var standard_html_footer>
```

this DTML Method could add display logic to our SQL Method simply by going to the following URL:

```
/employee_lookup?SSID=212-39-2811/employee_display
```

The result of this URL would be a nice HTML page displaying Wally's employee data in a clean table.

Pluggable Brains

Often working with SQL Methods you will find yourself frustrated with the Result Objects they return. These objects work, but are really only good for iterating through linearly, and are not very helpful beyond that.

To address this problem, Zope added the concept and mechanism of *Pluggable Brains*. This mechanism essentially enables you to add methods to result objects by mixing result objects with an externally defined class. This is done in the advanced tab of SQL Method management screens. There you will find two text fields, one labeled Class Name, and one labeled Class File. If, in the Extensions directory of your Zope installation, you put a file containing a Python class with some methods for using SQL Result objects, you can specify this file and class name in these fields. This done, all result objects returned from this SQL Method will also have the methods defined in the class you specified. This must be done for each SQL Method you wish to use in this way, and you must access the directory structure of your Zope installation, but this is an effective way of making result objects more useful.

Caching

Just as Zope can use caches to speed up DTML pages, Zope has caches for SQL Methods. Caching of SQL Method results can dramatically speed up your application, but can also lead to over consumption of memory and misrepresentation of data if you are not careful.

SQL Method caching is applicable only in cases where the result of the query does not change often or at all. If, for instance, you build an inventory control application, and set up caching on the SQL Method that checks for the availability of products, you could over-sell products, because when the first time the SQL Method was run, you had 100 products, and so it stored that value in the cache. Later, you could sell 1,000 units of the product, and the product availability method would still be handing out 100 as the number of available. SQL Method result caching is powerful, but must be used with care.

Often, SQL Method result caching can be helpful. For instance, if you built an application that takes signatures for an online petition, you could supply a very large cache to the SQL Method that looks up signatures for display on your main page. Because it's not important that viewers see the absolute most up-to-date number of signatures, and because it could slow down the application quite a bit to pull all of that information from the database every time, caching is very applicable. In this case, page load times could be reduced from ten seconds to sub-second easily.

All caching control for SQL Methods is accessible from within the SQL Method objects in Zope under the Advanced tab (see Figure 12-5) of their management screens. There are only three controls:

✦ Maximum rows to retrieve

✦ Maximum results to cache

✦ Maximum time to cache

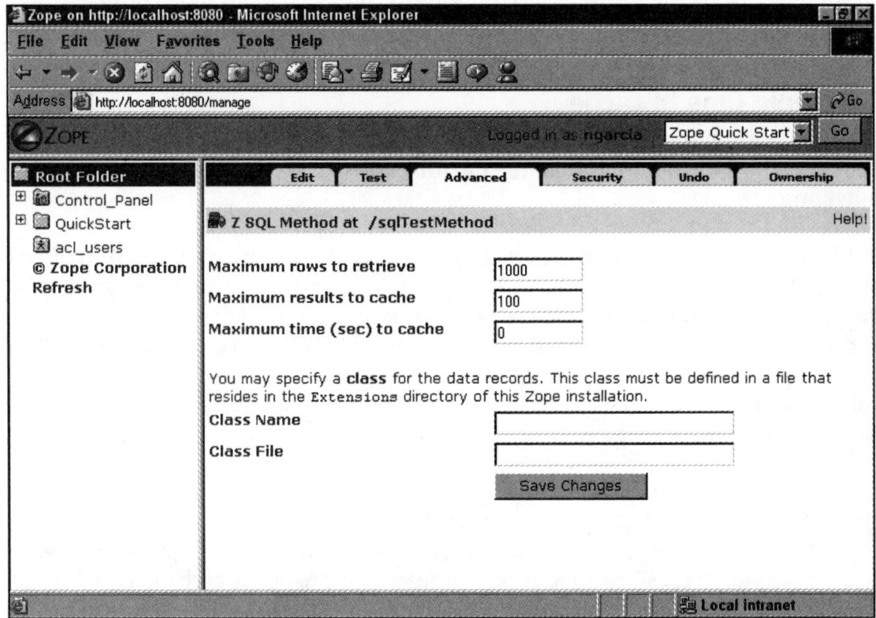

Figure 12-5: The advanced tab

These three controls allow a surprisingly large amount of control over the performance of SQL Methods. We will go over each individually here.

Maximum rows to retrieve

Some people find the existence of this field to be curious. There are some applications in which limiting the number of results from a SQL Method may be desirable, and this can be done here; however, a better way to do it is within the SQL statement itself using a LIMIT clause in your SELECT statements, as this reduces load on the database server.

You may choose to make use of this limiting function, but if you do not wish to limit the result size of your queries, this value may be set to zero (0) and the result size will be unlimited by Zope.

Maximum results to cache

This is the first real caching control. Combined with the third field, Maximum Time to Cache, it controls whether caching takes place at all, and how much. If Maximum Time to Cache is set greater than zero, then this field determines how much of the result of this query to keep in memory, and return in subsequent calls. This value should always be higher than the number of rows expected to be returned, otherwise if caching is used, data could be lost.

Maximum time to cache

While Maximum Results to Cache controls how much memory is used during caching, Maximum Time to Cache controls whether to cache or not, and if so, for how long.

If this field is set to Zero (0), no caching takes place for this SQL Method. If it is greater than zero (for example, if it is set to 60), Zope will cache results of this query for one minute. That means that if Maximum Results to Cache is set to 1,000 and the query returns 800 rows, the first time this SQL Query is cached, 800 rows of data will be stored in memory, and those same 800 rows will be returned to all subsequent calls for the next 60 seconds. After 60 seconds, the cache is flushed, or emptied, and the process repeats itself.

All Zope caching works on a per-thread basis. Zope uses a thread pool to handle requests, so that multiple requests can be handled at one time. If your Zope thread pool contains 10 threads, then Zope can handle 10 requests at one time. However, because caching is on a thread basis, to see a caching speedup, all 10 threads must take their initial cache miss to initialize. The larger the thread pool, the more simultaneous requests Zope can handle, but the longer it takes caching to work.

Transactions

Transactions, along with the stability of most mature database products, are what make relational databases so popular in large, high budget applications. They are the saviors of data integrity. Transactions make certain that the data in a relational database's tables are correct, with no references to rows that don't exist, and no otherwise partially completed operations.

Transactions work all of this magic by simply grouping SQL queries together and making sure that if any query of the group fails, that any changes made to the database are undone. Also, in most cases, no changes to a database from a transaction are visible to other users of the database until the entire transaction is completed.

This action of protecting data is utilized on most relational databases that support it via the BEGIN, COMMIT, and ROLLBACK statements. The BEGIN statement begins a transaction. The COMMIT statement completes a transaction. The ROLLBACK statement tells the database to undo any changes made since the beginning of this transaction.

To use transactions manually, as done from a command-line tool, the general sequence of events is:

1. Begin a transaction using the BEGIN statement.
2. Enter a series of queries: SELECTs, INSERTs, UPDATEs, DELETEs, and so on.
3. If anything goes wrong, send the ROLLBACK statement to undo the damage.
4. If everything went well, send a COMMIT to make the changes permanent and visible.

Zope uses transactions internally in servicing all queries, as discussed in Chapter 14. If you write an application in Zope that uses a database and that database supports transactions, Zope automatically extends the scope of the Zope transaction to include the database use.

What this essentially means is that a Zope application using a transaction-capable database generates an error in the form of an exception, and that exception is not caught within the application, Zope will catch it, display it to the user, and rollback any changes made to persistent Zope objects, as well as send a ROLLBACK command to the database. This provides a very simple-to-use mechanism for making use of transactions within Zope. Basically, you don't have to think about it.

Building a SQL Application

Now that you are familiar with the integration of Zope and relational databases, let's use these powerful tools to build a SQL-based application to solve one of life's most troubling problems. Where should we go for lunch?

You know the problem. You're at the office, you're hungry, and you don't want to eat alone so you invite a few people to eat with you, and then no one can agree where to go! Enter the "Wheel of Food"—an application designed to not only settle disputes in the office but also to keep track of what places there are to eat.

The application lets you and your co-workers keep track of all the restaurants in your area. Each co-worker can cast or retract a vote for up to three restaurants where he or she wishes to eat. After the voting is done, the tables can be reset for the next day so that the whole process can start over.

This example uses the Gadfly database. (If you are feeling adventurous you can create an application using a different database, but you may need to translate the SQL methods.)

Setup a workspace

Rather than having to build a full re-instantiable Zope product, we will simply build the whole Wheel of Food application in a folder under the Zope Root Folder. This folder will be called "WOF," and so the URL to the new application will be `<your zope instance URL>/WOF`.

The first step in building the Wheel Of Food application is to create the `/WOF` folder. Open a Web browser, go to Zope's management screen, and in the Root Folder, create a new folder with the id of WOF.

Create a new Gadfly connection

The next step in building the Wheel Of Food application is to create a connection to the database that will be used. As stated earlier in this section, the application will use the Gadfly database, which comes bundled with Zope.

From within the `/WOF` folder, select to create a new "Z Gadfly Database Connection" from the product drop-down list. This will bring up the Gadfly database connection add form, as shown in Figure 12-6.

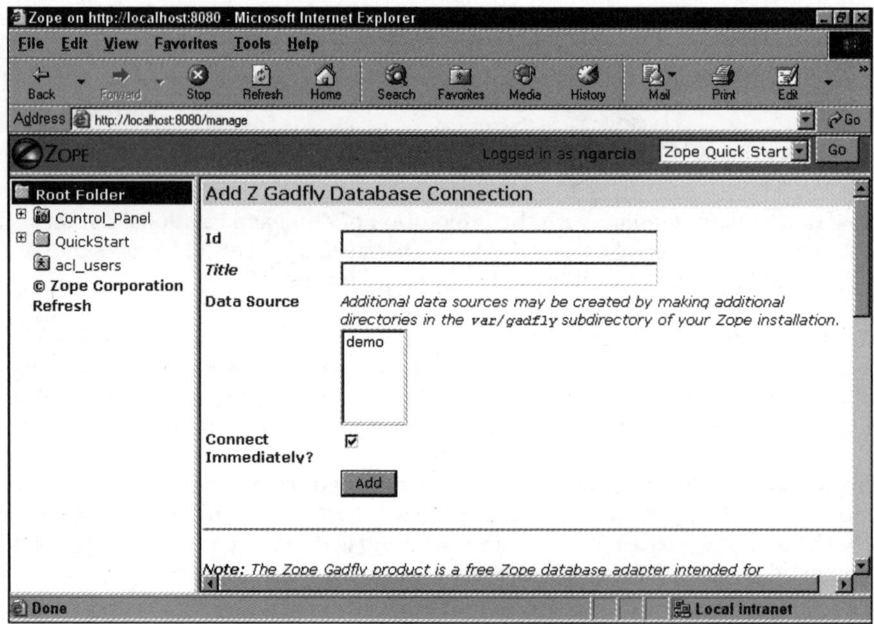

Figure 12-6: Gadfly database connection Add screen

In the id field, enter **wof_db**. This is the id of the connection object we will use for the application.

Select the "demo" data source. This is where the data in our database will be stored on the server filesystem. If you wish, you can create other data sources as directed in the Add screen, or you can just use "demo." (This is really only a problem if other people are using this Zope instance, in which case there could be tables already created that could conflict with your program.)

Last, click the Add button. This will create the `wof_db` Gadfly database connection object in our `/WOF` folder so that you can begin using our database.

Create the table schema

The Wheel Of Food will be tracking two types of information. These are:

- ✦ Restaurants
- ✦ Votes for restaurants from users

Restaurants will be simply added and deleted from a list. That can be stored in a simple table, containing only the names of the restaurants.

Votes for restaurants need to contain a reference to what restaurant is being voted for and who voted for it. This can be stored in a separate table with two columns: restaurant name and user name.

To create the table schema the WOF will access, we will create a SQL Method with the CREATE TABLE statements and run it.

From inside the `/WOF` folder, create a new SQL method with an id of "sqlCreateTables," and a body of:

```
CREATE TABLE restaurants (name VARCHAR)
CREATE TABLE votes (restaurant_name VARCHAR, user_name VARCHAR)
```

Make sure the `connection_id` field is set to `wof_db` and click the Add and Test button. This will create the `create_tables` SQL Method and run it, to create the tables that the Wheel of Food will use. You can click the Browse tab from within the database connection object to look at the tables you just created.

The column type VARCHAR was used to hold the string values in the restaurants and votes tables so that simple strings of any length can be used without the need to add or remove padding characters or worry about the maximum length of restaurant names.

Create the SQL methods to access the database

The next step in creating the Wheel of Food application is to create all the SQL Methods that the application will use to access the database. Let's think about all of the various ways the application will read from or write to the database:

- ✦ Adding a restaurant
- ✦ Deleting a restaurant
- ✦ Adding a vote for a restaurant
- ✦ Listing restaurants
- ✦ Listing all voters
- ✦ Listing all the people who voted for a restaurant
- ✦ Resetting the votes

Each of these types of database access will get its own SQL method to perform exactly that function. Let's create them now.

Adding a restaurant

This SQL method will need to take one argument, the restaurant name. Create a new SQL method inside the `/WOF` folder with an id of "sqlAddRestaurant."

In the arguments box, enter "name" on one line.

For a body, enter the SQL:

```
INSERT INTO restaurants VALUES (<dtml-sqlvar name type=string>)
```

Make sure the connection_id field is set to `wof_db`, and click the Add button.

Deleting a restaurant

Create another SQL Method object, this time with an id of "sqlRemoveRestaurant," that takes an argument of `name`, and has a body of:

```
DELETE FROM restaurants WHERE <dtml-sqltest name type=string>;
DELETE FROM votes WHERE restaurant_name = <dtml-sqlvar name
type=string>
```

Adding a vote for a restaurant

Create a SQL Method with an id of "sqlAddVote" that has two arguments on separate lines, one of `restaurant_name`, another of `user_name`. The body should contain:

```
INSERT INTO votes VALUES (<dtml-sqlvar restaurant_name
type=string>, <dtml-sqlvar user_name type=string>)
```

Listing restaurants

This is the first SQL Method of this application that returns anything useful. This method will be called form the application to iterate through the list of restaurants in the database. It will do this in order to display the votes for each restaurant.

Create a new SQL Method with an id of "sqlListRestaurants," and a body of:

```
SELECT name FROM restaurants
```

Listing all voters

So that the application can build a nice looking grid of votes with restaurants on one side and voter names on the other, we need a method to get the names of all the voters. To do this, create a SQL Method with an id of "sqlListVoters," and a body of:

```
SELECT DISTINCT user_name FROM votes
```

Listing votes for a restaurant

This SQL Method will return a list of user names who voted for an individual restaurant.

Create a new SQL Method with an id of "sqlListRestaurantVotes," that takes a `restaurant_name` argument, and has a body of:

```
SELECT user_name FROM votes WHERE <dtml-sqltest ⮐
restaurant_name type=string>
```

Resetting the votes

This last SQL Method will delete all of the votes in the votes table so that the application can be re-used. Create a SQL Method with an id of "sqlResetVotes" that has a body of:

```
DELETE FROM votes
```

Write the DTML for the user interface

The interface of the Wheel of Food is one screen. At the top will be a listing of all of the restaurants and who voted for each. At the bottom will be a small interface for adding and deleting restaurants, and a button for erasing all the existing votes. Users will vote by clicking the name of the restaurant in the list.

The main page

So that the application can be accessed by simply going to the `/WOF` directory of the Zope server, the main page of the application will be a DTML Method in the `/WOF` folder with an id of "index_html." Create this DTML Method with a body of:

```
<dtml-var standard_html_header>
<dtml-var vote_table><br>
<a href=reset_votes>Reset the Vote Table</a>
    
<a href=index_html>Refresh the Table</a>
<br>
<form name=add_restaurant method=post action=add_restaurant>
Add a restaurant: <input type=text name=restaurant_name>⮐
<input type=submit><br>
</form>
<form name=remove_restraunt method=post
action=delete_restaurant>
<select name=restaurant_name>
  <option value="">Select a Restaurant to Delete</option>
<dtml-in sqlListRestaurants>
  <option><dtml-var name></option>
</dtml-in>
</select>
<input type=submit value='Delete Restaurant'><br>
</form>
<dtml-var standard_html_footer>
```

Adding restaurants

When a user enters a new restaurant from the main page, the name of the new restaurant is submitted to `add_restaurant`. Create a new DTML document with an id of "add_restaurant" in `/WOF` with a body of:

```
<dtml-call
"sqlAddRestaurant(name=REQUEST.get('restaurant_name'))">
<dtml-var index_html>
```

This DTML document simply calls the `sqlAddRestaurant` SQL Method and then includes the `index_html` document, so that the user can keep going.

Removing restaurants

The `remove_restaurant` document will work just like `add_restaurant`. Create a new DTML Document with an id of "remove_restaurant" with a body of:

```
<dtml-if restaurant_name>
  <dtml-call
"sqlRemoveRestaurant(name=REQUEST.get('restaurant_name'))">
</dtml-if>
<dtml-var index_html>
```

Listing restaurants and restaurant votes

The `index_html` document includes a document named vote_table. This document will create a table showing the whole list of restaurants, and which users voted for which restaurant. Create a new DTML document with an id of "vote_table" and with the following body:

```
<table border=1>
<tr>
<td>Restaurant Name</td>
<dtml-in sqlListVoters>
    <td><b><dtml-var user_name></b></td>
</dtml-in>


<dtml-in sqlListRestaurants>
    <tr>
    <td><a href="vote?restaurant_name=<dtml-var name
html_quote>"><dtml-var name></a></td>
    <dtml-call "REQUEST.set('users', [])">
    <dtml-in "sqlListRestaurantVotes(restaurant_name=name)">
        <dtml-call "users.append(user_name)">
    </dtml-in>
            <dtml-in sqlListVoters>
              <dtml-if "user_name in users">
            <td>X</td>
        <dtml-else>
            <td> </td>
        </dtml-if>
    </dtml-in>
    </tr>
</dtml-in>
</table>
```

Voting

To record votes, users click the name of the restaurant on the main screen. This is simply a link to "vote" with the name of the restaurant in the URL. Create another DTML method with an id of "vote" and a body of:

```
<dtml-call "sqlAddVote(restaurant_name=restaurant_name,
user_name=AUTHENTICATED_USER.getUserName())">
<dtml-var index_html>
```

Resetting votes

Create one last DTML document with an id of "reset_votes" with the body of:

```
<dtml-call sqlResetVotes>
<dtml-var index_html>
```

Summary

In this chapter, we introduced the basics of relational databases and demonstrated how Zope provides a robust architecture for storing, manipulating, and accessing information in relational databases. We demonstrated creating SQL methods, accessing them from DTML, External Methods, and Python Products. We demonstrated advanced techniques such as acquiring the query parameters, and we built an application based on a relational database.

✦ ✦ ✦

CHAPTER 13

User Management and Security

✦ ✦ ✦ ✦

In This Chapter

The Zope security framework

Creating and managing users

Understanding roles

Setting permissions

Gaining access when accidentally locked out

Proxy roles

Local roles

Authentication adaptors

✦ ✦ ✦ ✦

One of the most difficult things about deploying a Web site, Web application, or intranet, is making sure that what you've deployed is secure. In Chapter 9, we introduced the basic concepts underlying network security in general and Web application security in particular. We also covered adding application-specific permissions to your Zope products and associating permissions with default roles.

In this chapter, we cover security from the point of view of the site administrator, a topic that was briefly touched on in Chapter 11 by way of damage control and delegation.

The Zope Security Framework

Zope provides several tools for securely giving people the appropriate access to your server:

- ✦ User Folders
- ✦ Permissions
- ✦ Roles and Local Roles

User Folders enable you to create and manage users within Zope, or to use external user information within Zope. *Permissions* govern whether a particular entity can take a specific action. *Roles* group permissions together in a way that makes them easy to assign to users.

Together, User Folders, Permissions, and Roles form Zope's security framework. This framework is one that all Zope products use and extend, making it easy for site administrators to specify which permissions need to be granted to which users, and in what context, even though those permissions control access to applications and products written and provided by many developers. Zope creates a highest common denominator for Web application security that all product developers can leverage, simplifying the task for the site administrator.

Creating and Managing Users

A secure site that no one can use is something that is fairly easy to accomplish. Just don't connect the server to a network, and never grant anyone permission to even see the server.

A Web site that no one can access isn't very useful, however, so some way of giving access to some people, but not to others, is a good thing. A way of giving different users different levels of access in different locations is even better. In Zope, users are represented by User objects that are stored in special User Folders. User Folders are always named `acl_users`.

Adding a user

Adding a user to a User Folder is pretty simple. Follow these steps:

1. Click an existing User Folder. All user folders are named `acl_users`. We suggest clicking on the acl_users folder in your root folder.
2. Click the Add button.
3. Fill in the form for the new user (see Figure 13-1) with the username and password for that user. For this example, use `bob` and `uncle` as the username and password, respectively. The password must be typed once each in the Password and Confirm fields.
4. For the moment, don't click any roles for the user and leave the Domains blank.
5. Click the Add button.

Congratulations! You've added a user!

Editing a User

Users can have user passwords and allowed domains reset by clicking the user and editing the user's password field, as shown in Figure 13-2.

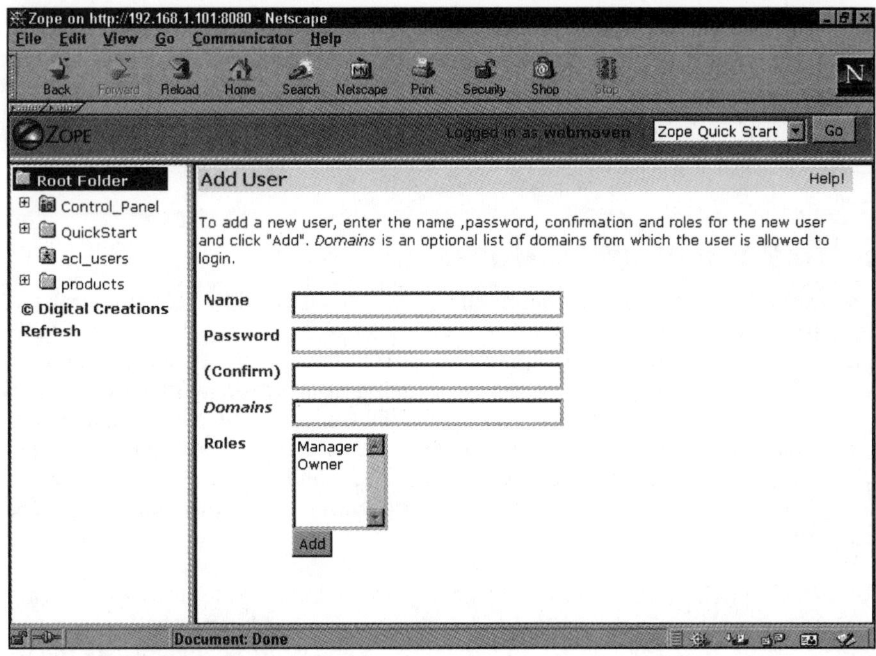

Figure 13-1: Adding a user

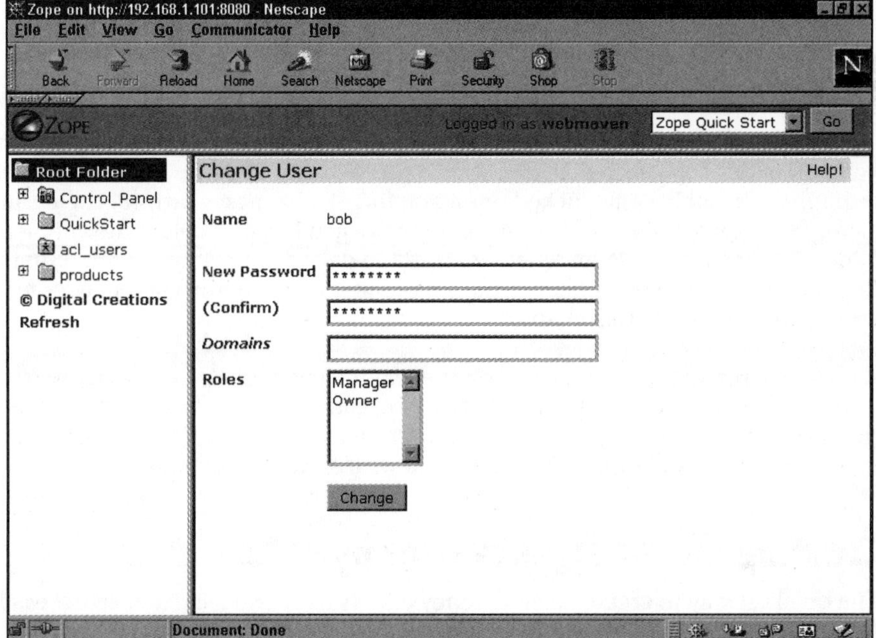

Figure 13-2: Editing a user

After you've edited the password in the Password and Confirm fields, click the Change button and the user's password will be changed.

You can also edit the users to give them roles. Let's give Bob a manager role. Click on the Bob user again, and select Manager from the Roles list, then click the Change button. Bob now has a Manager role.

Setting the allowed domains

The user object also has a Domains property. This is used to limit the Internet locations from which the user can authenticate themselves. If the field is left blank (as it usually is), all locations are equally valid. You can specify a location such as "corporation.com" in order to only allow logins from within an internal network, or you can specify an IP address such as "192.168.0.1" and only allow logins from that particular internal IP address. You can also add asterisks as wildcards to the IP address in order to specify a range such as "192.168.0.*," and finally, you can specify multiple allowed Internet locations by separating them with spaces: 192.168.*.* joe.homenetwork.com.

You can also define a user without a password that has a role (for example, a custom role of "Employee") provided that a domain has been specified. Anyone who accesses Zope from within the specified domain automatically gets the role, even without logging in. This is not generally recommended, because it can weaken security, but the flexibility is available.

The Emergency User

The emergency user has two uses. The first is a way to login if you accidentally lock yourself out of Zope. Don't laugh because this actually happens all the time. For example, you can become locked out if you forget your password, set the permissions wrong on a object, delete the user you logged in as, or delete the acl_users folder. The second use is for when you need to delete the acl_users folder in the Root Folder on purpose because you want to install one of the custom user folders we discuss later on in this chapter.

A couple of restrictions are placed on the emergency user. You can't create or own objects. The exception to this rule is that you can create acl_user folders. The only thing you can do is edit existing objects and users. This is useful for restoring the system back to a state where you can login with a normal account.

Creating the emergency user by hand

The quickest way to create an emergency user is to create a file named access in the top-level directory of your Zope installation with your favorite text editor. Assuming you installed Zope in the default location as described in Chapter 2, the location of this file would be C:\Progam Files\WebSite in Windows and

/usr/local/Zope-2.x.x in Linux. The file only needs to contain two items: the name of the emergency user and the password. These two values must be separated by a colon on a single line. For example, to create an emergency user named superman whose password is lois, you would put this line in your access file:

```
superman:lois
```

After you've created this file you must restart Zope. Then go to the Zope management screen and you should be able to login as superman.

The previous example shows how easy it would be for someone to get into your Zope site if he or she has write access to the directory where Zope is installed. Make sure that this directory is properly protected!

You should remove the access file as soon as you're done with the emergency account.

Creating the emergency user with zpasswd.py

In the previous example, the emergency users password is left clear as day for anybody to see if he or she has the ability to read the access file. This is very insecure. Alternatively, the password can be stored as a one-way hash using either the SHA or CRYPT algorithm. One-way hashes are secure because they can't be unencrypted. In other words, you can't take a hash and turn it back to the original password. Of the two methods, the SHA algorithm is the most modern and is the preferred algorithm to use because it supports longer passwords. CRYPT is the historical format used by most UNIX systems and passwords must be limited to eight characters in length.

Because you can't create a hash by hand (maybe you could if you're a mathematical genius, but we can't), a utility script is provided in the top-level directory of your Zope installation. You run this script like you would any other Python script. (See Chapter 5 for more details.) The script expects one argument, which is the name of the file where the user name and password should be stored. The script prompts you for everything else.

Here's an example of running the script on a Windows machine:

```
C:\> cd "\Program Files\WebSite"
C:\PROGRA~1\WebSite> bin\python zpasswd.py access
Username: superman
Password:
Verify password:

Please choose a format from:

SHA - SHA-1 hashed password
CRYPT - UNIX-style crypt password
CLEARTEXT - no protection.
```

```
Encoding: SHA
Domain restrictions:

C:\PROGRA~1\WebSite>
```

After you run the script the contents of the access file will look something like this:

```
superman:{SHA}5ICcNROns7lfa7Z8xMGoXILdP1M=
```

Understanding Roles

Zope generally assumes that a connection to it is anonymous, that is, the connection is not associated with a particular user unless the browser sends authentication information that Zope can verify. The authentication consists of the username and password.

After Zope has associated the user (or, more precisely, the browser with which the user is accessing Zope) with a User object, Zope checks to see if that user is permitted to perform the action that was requested. Zope does this by checking to see if the user has access to the appropriate Permission that is protecting the action in question. Because Zope has dozens of Permissions in a default installation, and more can be added by installed Products, assigning Permissions directly to User objects would be needlessly tedious and time-consuming. For this reason, Zope has implemented the concept of *roles*.

Roles are basically aggregations of permissions that come in an easily labeled chunk. Zope has several default roles as described in the following sections.

The Anonymous role

The Anonymous role is associated with all users. Associating permissions with this role enables both authenticated and un-authenticated users to perform actions protected by those permissions. As a result, Anonymous has Permissions associated with it that are strictly associated with viewing information, at least by default.

The Authenticated role

Authenticated is a role that can be considered the inverse of Anonymous, all users who are logged in have the Authenticated role. The Authenticated role does not have any Permissions associated with it by default.

The Manager role

The Manager role pretty much has all Permissions granted to it, which will give any user who has the Manager role granted to him or her the ability to fully configure and use the server (at least within Zope).

The Owner role

Owner is a very special role. When a user accesses an object that attempts to perform some action within Zope, Zope will only permit the action if both the accessing user and the object's owner (typically the user who created it) have the requisite Permissions.

This protects against the "server-side Trojan" attack, which is possible when you allow untrusted users to create executable content on a server. Basically the scenario goes like this:

1. An untrusted user creates some server-side code that would attempt to do some operation for which he or she does not have sufficient Permissions (such as delete a folder in the root of the Zope server).
2. The untrusted user then tricks someone who does have sufficient Permissions (such as the owner of the site) to view the page with the malicious code.
3. If the code is only restricted by the Permissions of the viewing (executing) user, then this code would run, deleting the folder in question.

For this reason, the Owner role is used to associate an object with the user that created it. Specifically, the creating user gets a local role of Owner on the object. Zope's security infrastructure only allows executable code to perform operations that both the owner and the viewing user have sufficient Permissions for. In the previous example, if the untrusted user does not have sufficient Permissions to delete the folder, the malicious code will not execute and will raise an error.

Creating roles

Creating a new role within Zope is fairly straightforward. It is done from the Security tab and is outlined here:

1. Click the Security tab.
2. Scroll to the bottom of the screen where you will find a text box with the heading "User Defined Roles," and an Add role button.
3. Type **Employee** into the text box.
4. Click the Add Role button.

You should now see a screen that looks like the screen shown in Figure 13-3, with a new Employee column.

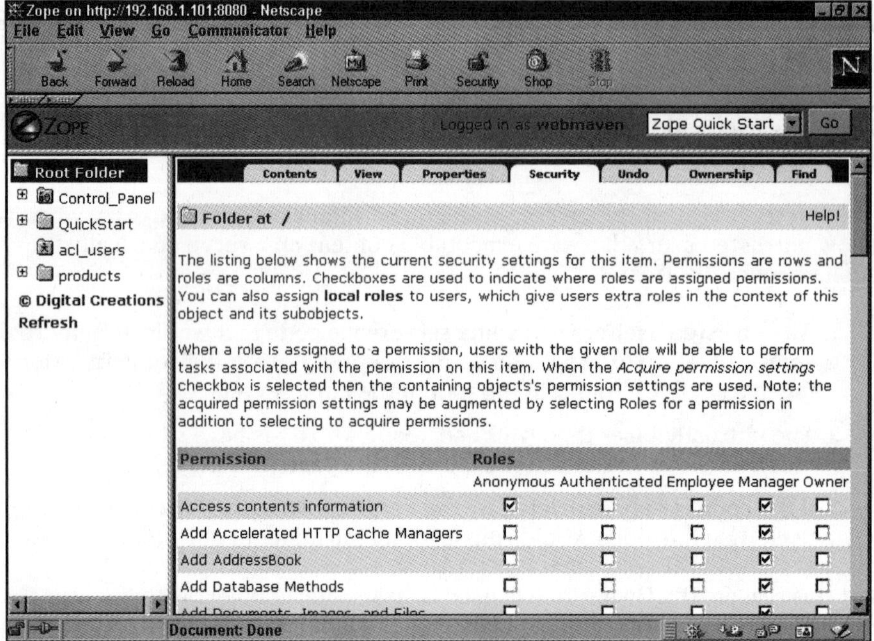

Figure 13-3: Adding a custom role

Custom roles that are added by you are not automatically available throughout your entire Zope site, unless you define them in the Root Folder's Security tab. If you define a role in a subfolder's Security tab, only that subfolder and its contained objects will have the role available.

Setting Permissions for Roles

Once you've created a custom role, you need to associate Permissions with it for the role to be able to grant those Permissions to users that have it. This can be done from the Security tab as well. Each role has its own column in the Security tab's main table, with one Permission in each row. Checking the checkboxes where the roles and Permissions intersect grants the Permission to the role.

Check the Access contents information Permission's for the Employee role, and then scroll down to the end of the table and click the Save Changes button. You can see that the checkbox is still checked after the page refreshes.

There are two other ways of associating Permissions with roles: The first is to click the Role name, which brings up a form that lists all of the Permissions that a particular role has, as can be seen in Figure 13-4.

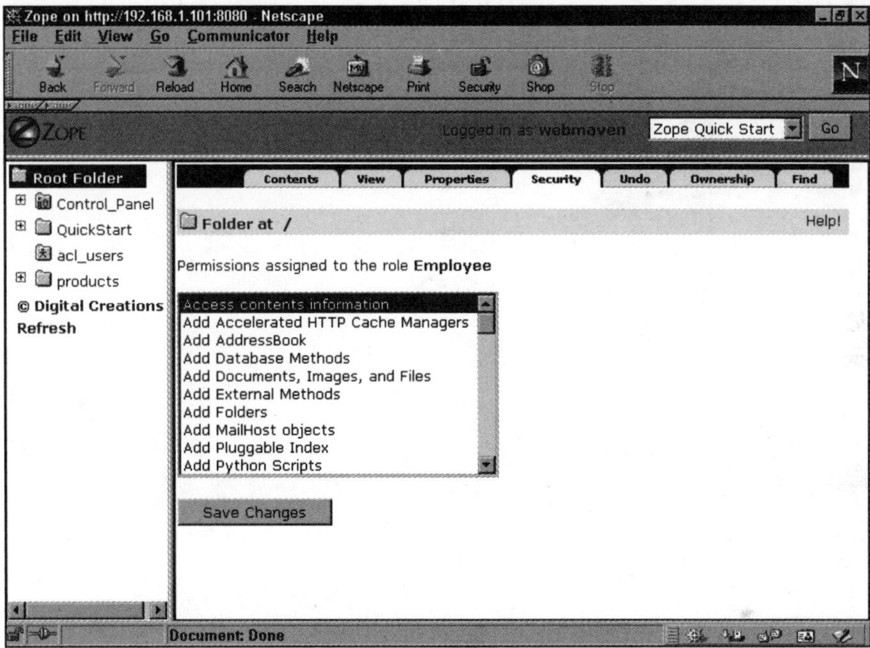

Figure 13-4: The Employee role Permission form

Holding down the control key and clicking another Permission selects it, and clicking the Save Changes button applies the changes.

The second way to associate Permissions with roles is to click the Permission name, which gives you a form that lists all of the roles that have that Permission associated with them, as shown in Figure 13-5.

As before, you can Ctrl-click the roles in order to select or deselect them, and clicking the Save Changes button applies the changes.

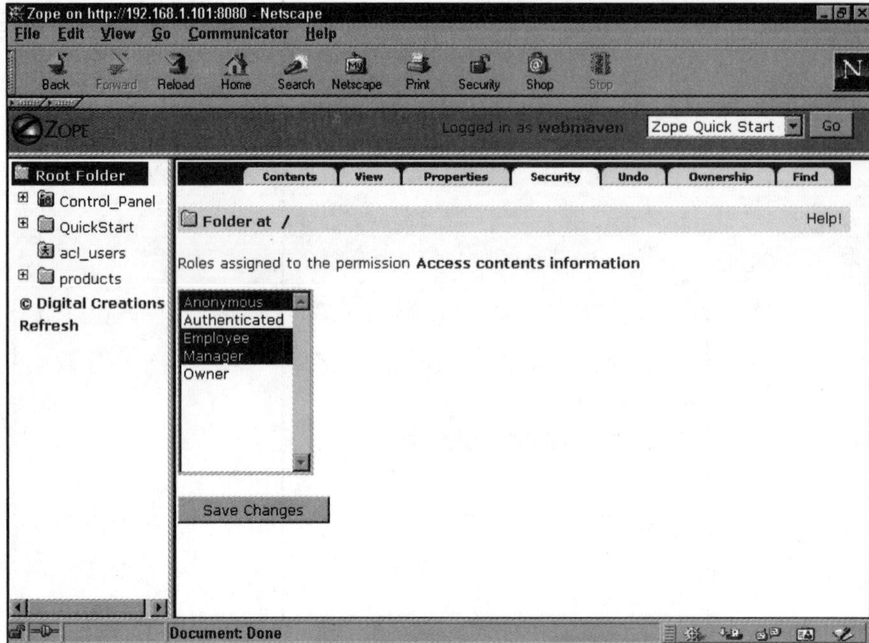

Figure 13-5: The Access Contents Information Permission roles form

Proxy Roles

Suppose you have a special method you want to make available to anonymous users, but for security purposes you want to make sure that they can't call it directly, and possibly pass on their own parameters to it. Zope makes this easy by enabling you to assign a proxy role to another method to allow it to call your special method.

Giving a proxy role to a method

Following is an example. Create a DTML (Document Template Markup Language) method in your root folder called Special, and edit it so that it has the following code:

```
<h3>This will only render securely</h3>
```

After you have saved the changes to the code, click the Security tab. You can see that the security settings on the DTML method are a bit different than the settings you've seen before. Firstly, many Zope objects will have different permissions associated with them. Secondly, many of them don't have any security settings set explicitly, but instead expect to acquire their security settings from their containers. That's what the "Acquire permission settings?" column is for.

Uncheck the Acquire permission settings? column for the “Access contents information” and “View” Permissions, and check the Manager role’s column for both as well. Then click Save Changes.

Because you unchecked the Acquire permission settings? column for these two Permissions, the method no longer acquires the permission’s assignment to Anonymous, and only the Manager role can view and/or access the method.

Now, create another DTML method named `proxytest` and edit it as follows:

```
<dtml-var standard_html_header>
<dtml-var Special>
<a href="./Special">link to Special</a>
<dtml-var standard_html_footer>
```

Click the methods Proxy tab. You’ll see a screen that looks like the screen shown in Figure 13-6. Click the Manager role in the form to select it, and click the Save Changes button. You have now given the `proxytest` DTML method the Manager proxy role.

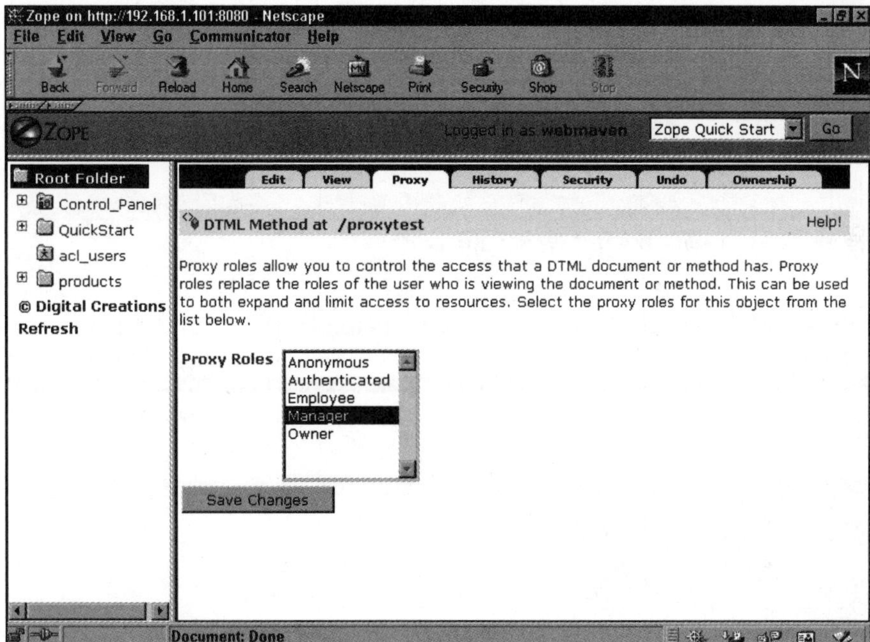

Figure 13-6: The Proxy tab

Testing the proxy role

To test the proxy role, log out of Zope and try to access `proxytest`. You should see a screen like the screen shown in Figure 13-7.

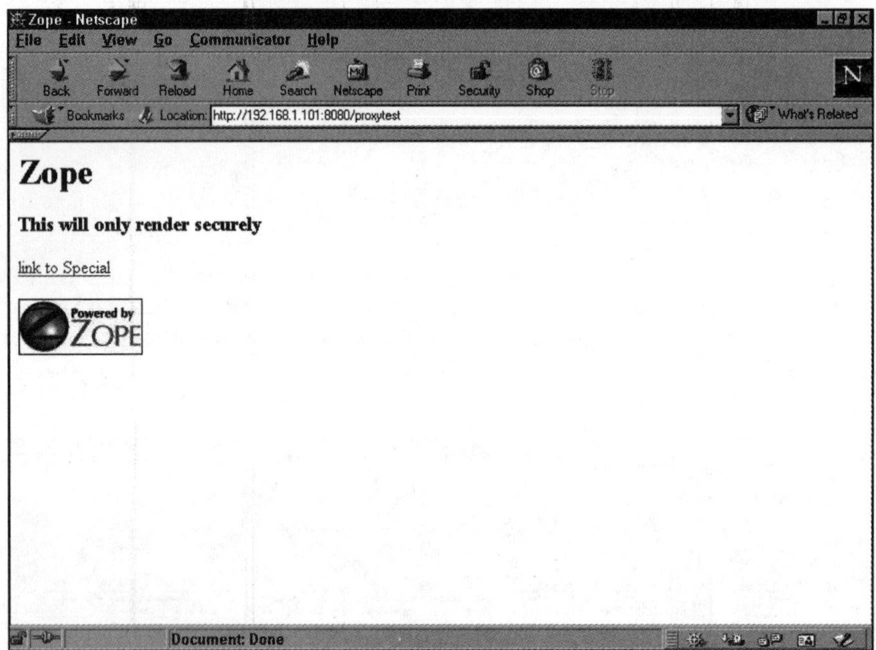

Figure 13-7: Viewing the `proxytest` method

After verifying that the `proxytest` method can render the `Special` method, try clicking the "link to Special" link in order to access `/Special` directly. Zope should detect that Anonymous does not have sufficient permissions in order to view the method directly, so you should be prompted for a username and password, as shown in Figure 13-8.

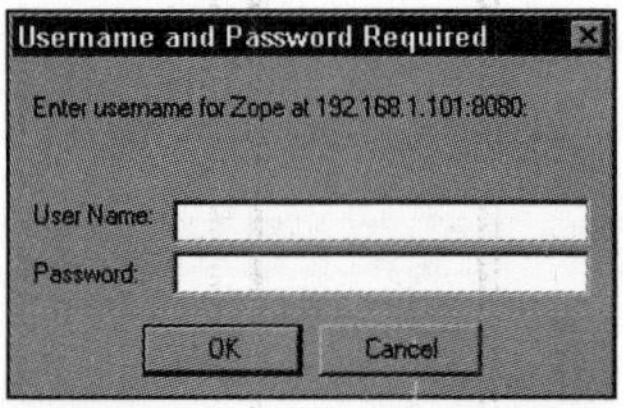

Figure 13-8: Zope prompt for a username and password

As you can see, Proxy roles enable you to give methods or other Zope objects roles in order to access other objects or perform operations on behalf of users to whom you don't want to give those roles. In this way, you can expose Zope's functionality to your users in an indirect but safe way, without having to grant them undue privileges.

Local Roles

In Chapter 11, we showed you how to create a user and give that user a local role that would only apply to a subsection of your site. Local roles are used in a number of ways by Zope. One of those ways is to assign users a local role of "Owner" for the objects that they create, as mentioned earlier in this chapter in the section, "The Owner role."

As we mentioned earlier in this chapter, roles are collections of Permissions that you can assign to a user. In the previous section we had you grant the Manager role to the Bob user. This gave Bob the ability to do just about anything anywhere in the site. Although this was a convenient way to give Bob the ability to make changes to the site, there might be a time when you would like to be a little bit more restrictive or selective with which areas of the site Bob could or should edit. So, go back to the root folder's user folder, and remove Bob's manager role.

Now, you could create an `acl_user` folder in each subfolder you want Bob to access and give him the appropriate role. This would become quite tedious to maintain. You would have to maintain redundant sets of information. Every time Bob needed to change his password you would be forced to go to each `acl_user` folder in your entire site and make those changes.

Zope's solution to this problem is Local roles. A Local role is a way of saying, "Give this user this role while the user is accessing this object or its subobjects." With this ability you can grant Bob manager access to the Sales folder on your site but only give him limited or no access to the Accounting folder.

We're going to take you through an example so that you can get a feel for how this is done. First, make sure that you have a user named "Bob" that does not have any roles. Then, create two folders at the root level of your site. Name one folder "sales" and the other "accounting." (Refer to Chapter 3 if you are not sure how this is done.)

Now you need to set the Permissions of the folders. For our imaginary site let's pretend that the `/Sales` folder is going to contain some literature about your company's products. The information in this folder is something that you want everybody to read but only a few people to edit. Assuming that you haven't changed Zope's default Permission settings, you shouldn't need to change for the sales folder. By default, Zope grants the Anonymous user the View permission for documents and folders.

The /accounting folder on the other hand, might contain more sensitive information. So we want to make sure that only people who we have explicitly granted access to can view its contents. This can be easily accomplished by selecting the Security tab in the /accounting folder. Click the "Acquire permission settings?" heading (see Figure 13-9) and then any highlighted items in the multiple selection box, so that they are no longer highlighted. Depending on your operating system and/or browser, you might need to hold the Control key down while doing this. Once this is done, click the Save Changes" button. You will be returned back to the screen with the permission/role matrix. Verify that all of the Permissions under "Acquire permission settings?" have been removed by scrolling down the page and verifying that all of the checkboxes are unchecked in the "Acquire permission settings?" column.

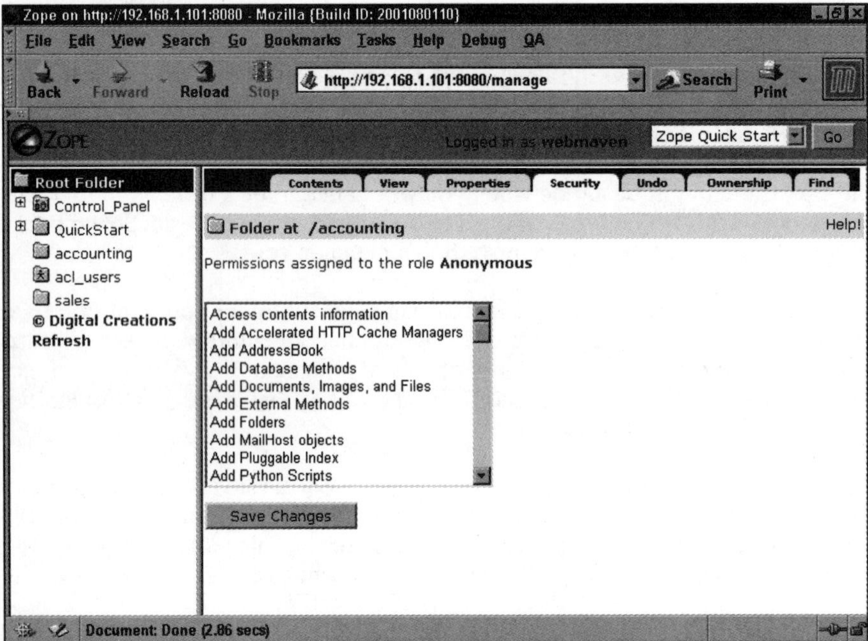

Figure 13-9: The Permissions granted to the Anonymous role

Since we've turned off acquisition for all permissions, we would now need to explicitly grant those permissions back to the Manager role for the /accounting folder, except that Zope automatically takes care of that for us (otherwise we would be locked out of managing the /accounting folder right now too).

The last thing we need to do is to grant Bob the Manager role for the Sales folder. Go back to the Root Folder and click the Sales folder or select it from the navigation view in the left hand side of the management interface. Click the Sales folder's Security tab. This screen is almost identical to the Security tab in the Accounting folder.

The local roles interface is sometimes overlooked because the link to the management screen is buried in the first paragraph of text at the top of the security page. Go ahead and click the link labeled "Local Roles" and you will be taken to a page like the one shown in Figure 13-10.

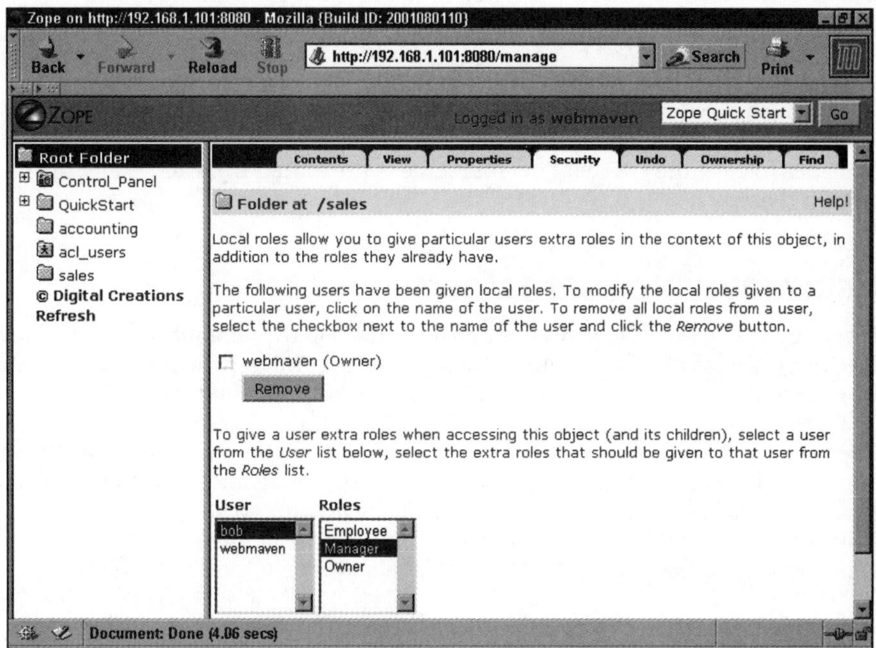

Figure 13-10: The Local Roles screen

On this page there are two multi-select boxes. The first box contains a list of every user that has been defined in all `acl_users` folders in the tree to this point. This means that if you had created a user in the root's `acl_users` folder and also had a user in an `acl_user` folder in a subfolder, both users would be available from this list. The second list contains all the roles that have been created and can be given to a user. You might notice that you can't assign the Anonymous or Authenticated roles through this interface.

Click `bob` in the user list and in the second list click the Manager role. Finally, click the Add button. The page will update and you will notice two immediate changes. The first is that the message, "Your changes have been saved" will be displayed at the top of the page. In addition, Bob should appear in the list preceded by a check box. To the right of the user in parentheses are the roles that the user has been granted locally. If Bob's name now appears in the list with the word "Manager" in parentheses, you have done everything right.

You can now test that this local role worked by first logging out or closing all of your browser windows. Then go directly to `http://localhost:8080/sales/manage` and login as Bob. The management screen for the sales folder will be displayed. Now test that Bob can't manage the `/accounting` folder by going to `http://localhost:8080/accounting/manage`. You should be prompted to log in again because Bob doesn't have permission to manage the Accounting folder.

Finally, try to simply *view* the `/accounting` folder by going to `http://localhost:8080/accounting/` and you will be prompted to login. Since only users with the Manager role have permission to view the `/accounting` folder (we turned off acquisition of the Anonymous viewing permissions), and Bob doesn't have a local Manager role for the `/accounting` folder, he is prevented from accessing the information there.

Using multiple user folders

Given that redefining the same user again and again throughout the Zope object hierarchy is a waste of time and a maintenance nightmare, you might legitimately wonder why Zope even lets you create multiple `acl_user` folders at all.

The reason is that Zope is built to accommodate a "customers who have customers" approach. In other words, if Bob has subordinates (or clients) to whom he wishes to give special access within a folder that he manages, but nowhere else in the site, it makes sense to allow him to create an `acl_user` folder in the folder he manages, which lets him create users that don't exist elsewhere in the site hierarchy.

Care must be taken not to overuse this approach, however, as the situation can arise (as described in Chapter 11) where a user must be "promoted" to a role in a higher folder, or where the same person has multiple user objects scattered throughout the site.

In general, a user object should be defined at the highest point to which the user could conceivably need special access, and local roles should be used in subfolders down from that point. Making this determination is a little easier when the user in question is actually a customer (as customers rarely need to be promoted) rather than an employee.

Removing a Local role

Later on you decide that Bob should no longer have the ability to manage the sales folder. To remove Bob from this folder, follow these steps:

1. Return to the Sales folder's Local roles page.
2. Click the check box next to Bob's name.
3. Click the Remove button.

Bob's name and roles should be removed from the list of Local roles.

Local roles gotchas

If you've assigned a user a Local role and later delete that user, the Local role will remain. This might cause a problem later on if you create a user with the same name. This user will automatically get these local roles which might not be what you intended.

Authentication Adapters

While Zope's built-in User Folders are very flexible, some Web sites (particularly intranets) must obtain user information and passwords from other sources. Fortunately, Specialized User folders are available from various developers, and can be found on the Zope Web site. One word of caution: because these adapters are not part of the official Zope release they may not work with the latest version of Zope. If you find an adapter that you really want to use and it doesn't work (make sure you test on a copy of your site), try e-mailing the author or the Zope mailing list.

A description of selected User Folder products rounds out the rest of this chapter.

Installing a custom acl_user folder in the Root Folder

If you want to install a custom `acl_users` folder (see on the next sections in this chapter for more details about some available adapters). You'll need to be logged in as the emergency user. This is because the first step you'll need to do is to delete the existing `acl_users` folder as no more than one user folder may exist at a location at any time. Deleting the `acl_users` folder will temporarily lock everybody but the emergency user out of the site.

MySQL User Folder

URL: `http://www.zope.org/Members/vladap/mysqlUserFolder`

Provides the ability to authenticate users from a MySQL database, track sessions, associate custom information with a user (such as e-mail address, first name, last name, and so on) and provides sample registration methods so that an anonymous user can register on your site and get an account.

SSL Certificate Authenticator

URL: `http://www.zope.org/Members/zhivago/SSLCertAuth`

Uses SSL v3 client certificates to authenticate users.

Cookie User Folder

URL: `http://www.dataflake.org/software/cookieuserfolder`

Extends Zope to use cookies instead of basic HTTP (Hypertext Transfer Protocol) authentication. An additional benefit from this product is that you can setup custom login/logout pages is html instead of relying on the browser's standard login window.

NT User Folder

URL: `http://www.zope.org/Members/htrd/NTUserFolder`

Authenticates a user against an NT Domain. Only works with the Windows version of Zope.

SMB User Folder

URL: `http://www.zope.org/Members/mcdonc/smbUserFolder`

This User Folder also authenticates users from an NT Domain. Unlike the NT User Folder this one runs on other platforms in addition to Windows.

etc User Folder

URL: `http://www.zope.org/Products/etcUserFolder`

Authenticates users from a UNIX standard password file. The file it uses is configurable and it doesn't have to be the one used by the system. The User Folder only looks for the first two colon-delimited fields. The first field should be the user name and the second should be the encrypted password.

Generic User Folder

URL: `http://www.zope.org/Members/Zen/GenericUserFolder`

This User Folder lets site administers roll their own authentication using Zope through the Web management system. You can edit seven DTML methods that let you control just about every aspect of the authentication process. This includes what the login page looks like, what page the user sees after logging in, the logout page, how the user is authenticated, what domains the user can login from, what users are in the system, and which roles the user has.

The default install demonstrates how to set up the system for two users. This isn't very practical but it should be fairly straightforward for someone who's read this book to extend his or her system to use SQL or External methods from a database or other such system.

Login Manager

URL: `http://www.zope.org/Members/tsarna/LoginManager`

This is a User Folder that can authenticate users from more than one source. For instance, when a user logs in you can configure the Login Manager to first check the ZODB and then a SQL server. This can be done for the credential search. In other words, you can configure the Login Manager to first look for a cookie, and if that fails, try basic HTTP authentication.

UserDB

URL: `http://www.zope.org/Members/otto/userdb`

This simplistic User Folder authenticates users from almost any SQL database for which Zope has an adapter. The default install makes you pick a preexisting Database connection (see Chapter 12). This connection should have a table named "users" in it that contains fields for username, password, domains, and roles.

If you want to modify the queries that are used by UserDB, click the Properties tab. UserDB doesn't care if a table named users exists or not. All it cares about is that when it runs the queries on the page these queries return a Result set that contains the appropriate fields.

LDAPLoginAdapter

URL: `http://www.zope.org/Members/jens/LDAPLoginAdapter`

The LDAPLoginAdapter is a replacement User Folder that authenticates against an LDAP server. The nature of the LDAPLoginAdapter is "read-only," meaning at present it does not allow you to create, edit, or delete users in LDAP. You will need to populate the LDAP directory by other means.

LDAPUserManager

URL: `http://www.zope.org/Members/jens/LDAPUserManager`

The LDAPUserManager allows you to add, edit, or delete users and roles on the LDAP server. It's designed to be run in conjunction with the LDAPLoginAdapter. The LDAPLoginAdapter is a replacement for a Zope User Folder. It does not store its own user objects but builds them on the fly after authenticating a user against the LDAP database.

Summary

Zope's sophisticated security and user management schema eases the burden on a Web application developer. Adapting Zope to match your organization's security environment is especially convenient with the variety of third-party authentication adapters available.

In this chapter you:

- ✦ Managed users and roles.
- ✦ Created the emergency user.
- ✦ Learned about products could extend Zope's security framework.

✦ ✦ ✦

Advanced Zope Concepts

P A R T

IV

✦ ✦ ✦ ✦

In This Part

✦ ✦ ✦ ✦

CHAPTER 14

Core Zope Components

✦ ✦ ✦ ✦

In This Chapter

Using Acquisition

Persistence and the ZODB

ZPublisher

Using DocumentTemplates

✦ ✦ ✦ ✦

This chapter is for the hard-core Python developer who either wants to take his or her custom product beyond what's here today, or who wants to use some of the core components of Zope in other applications.

Acquisition

Acquisition is a concept similar to Inheritance. The difference is, instead of receiving a predetermined set of additional data and functionality based on what classes an object inherits from, objects pick up additional attributes depending on where they're contained.

> **Note**
>
> The Acquisition package isn't distributed without Zope. If you want to use it in an application outside of Zope you will need to do some detective work based on what operating system you use. On Windows you'll need to grab two files from the lib/python directory named `Acquisition.pyd` and `ExtensionClass.pyd` and put them either in your application's directory or in your Python's path. On Linux you'll need to grab `Acquisition.so` and `ExtensionClass.so`.
>
> Chances are, you're reading this section in order to have a better understanding of Zope. If this is the case the only thing that you need to do in order to run the Acquisition examples in the following sections is to make sure that you're in the lib/python library.

In the following example, which assumes that the Acquisition module is in your Python path, you will create a user object whose e-mail address will change, depending on whether the user is at work or at home.

```
from Acquisition import Implicit
class Location(Implicit):

    def __init__(self, domain):
        self.domain = domain


class User(Implicit):

    def __init__(self, user):
        self.user = user

    def getEmail(self):
        return self.user + '@' + self.domain

bob = User('bob')
office = Location("boringjob.com")
office.user = bob
home = Location("yahoo.com")
home.user = bob
```

If you call `office.user.getEmail()`, the method would return "bob@boringjob.com," whereas calling `home.user.getEmail()` would return "bob@hotmail.com." If you look at the `getEmail()` method, which is defined in the User class, you may notice that it uses `self.domain` to build the e-mail address, yet the User class doesn't assign the value anywhere. The user object obtains the domain attribute from its parent, which is either the office or home location.

Understanding wrappers

This magic is accomplished with a special object called an Acquisition *wrapper*. You don't see it happen, but when you access the attribute of an object that inherits from `Acquisition.Implicit`, the attribute isn't returned: a wrapper is. This wrapper has a reference to both the attribute and the attribute's parent.

Wrappers appear to your program to be exactly like the objects they wrap. For example, if you access `color`, you'd be accessing the wrapped object's color attribute. Wrappers accomplish this using the special Python method `__getattr__ ()`. If an object has this method, Python will call it every time an attribute is accessed. The return value of the method will be used as the value of the attribute. In the case of wrappers, if the object doesn't have the attribute color, the wrapper will check to see if the object's parent does. If the parent is a wrapped object, then the same checks will be preformed. This happens until either an attribute of the appropriate name is found or the top of the hierarchy is hit.

One consequence of this wrapping of attributes is that comparison with the `is` operator will fail. For example, note the difference between an ordinary object and one that inherits from acquisition:

```
>>> from Acquisition import Implicit
>>> class Ordinary: pass
...
>>> o = Ordinary()
>>> class ACQClass(Implicit): pass
...
>>> parent = ACQClass()
>>> a = ACQClass()
>>> parent.o = o
>>> parent.o is o
1
>>> parent.a = a
>>> parent.a is a
0
```

The reason why the `is` check returns false is because `parent.a` is a wrapper object where as `a` is an ACQClass object.

Manipulating wrappers

Acquisition wrappers provide several convenient attributes for manipulating the underlying object and its parent. Table 14-1 lists each of these attributes. They are only available if the object is wrapped.

Table 14-1
Acquisition Wrapper Attributes

Attribute	*Description*
`aq_self`	The unwrapped object. Note that an object can be wrapped several times. Like peeling an onion, you can use `aq_self` to get at each subsequent layer.
`aq_base`	Returns the underlying object completely striped of all wrappers.
`aq_parent`	Returns the wrapped object's parent.
`aq_inner`	Returns the object wrapped only by containment.
`aq_chain`	Returns the acquisition chain, which is a list of each of the object's ancestors.
`__of__(parent)`	Method used to arbitrarily create wrappers.

Unwrapping a wrapped object

The attribute, `aq_self`, is the object that is being wrapped by the wrapper. The underlying object, however, could be wrapped multiple times (you'll see how this is possible when we introduce you to the `__of__` method later in this chapter). On the other hand, `aq_base` is the fully unwrapped object.

```
>>> from Acquisition import Implicit
>>> class ACQClass(Implicit): pass
...
>>> a = ACQClass()
>>> a.b = ACQClass()
>>> id(a.b)
8202360
>>> id(a.b.aq_base)
8200488
>>>
```

Notice in the previous example, that the `id` method produces different results, which proves that `a.b` is a wrapped object. There are several reasons why you would want to unwrap an object. The most obvious is when you want to test whether two objects are the same. Another reason is if you want to make sure you do not acquire something accidentally.

Testing whether an object is wrapped

The `aq` attributes only exist for wrapped objects. You may often see code like the following that tests to see whether an object is wrapped:

```
if hasattr(object, 'aq_base'):
  object = object.aq_base
```

Accessing an object's parents

You can get a reference to an object's parent using the `aq_parent` attribute. This leads to all sorts of interesting possibilities, but probably the most convenient aspect is that using acquisition wrappers to get an object's parent avoids Python's problem with circular references (see the sidebar titled "The Problem with Circular References" for more information).

Where `aq_parent` gives your object's immediate parent, the `aq_chain` attribute returns a list of each of the ancestors of the wrapped object.

```
>>> from Acquisition import Implicit
>>> class ACQClass(Implicit):
...   def __init__(self, id):
...     self.id = id
...
>>> a = ACQClass("a")
>>> a.b = ACQClass("b")
>>> a.b.c = ACQClass("c")
>>> a.b.c.d = ACQClass("d")
>>> for object in a.b.c.d.aq_chain:
...   print object.id
...
d
c
b
a
```

Wrapping objects manually with __of__

There may be times when you want to make an object participate in acquisition even though you are not accessing the object as an attribute of another object that inherits from acquisition. This is where the `__of__` method comes in. Unlike the attributes that start with `aq`, the `__of__` method is available to all objects that inherit from acquisition. The `__of__` method takes one argument: the object's parent, and returns a wrapped object.

One use for this is when you have an object that stores a series of sub-objects in a list or a dictionary. If you manually wrap each sub-object as you access them, you will be able to acquire the parent's sub-objects.

```
from Acquisition import Implicit

class Category(Implicit):

  def __init__(self):
    self._categories = {}
    self.id = id

  def addCategory(self, id):
     self._categories[id] = Category(id)

  def getCategory(self, id):
    return self._categories[id].__of__(self)
```

You might be thinking that it would be easier to just store the wrapped object in the dictionary instead of wrapping the object every time it is retrieved. This would work if you were using acquisition by itself. However, you should not do this if you use acquisition in conjunction with the ZODB (Zope Object Database). For technical reasons the ZODB unwraps every object when it is stored.

The Problem with Circular References

Something that sometimes trips up new users of Python is circular references. A circular reference is when you have two objects that have references to each other as in this case:

```
parent.mychild = child
child.myparent = parent
```

The problem is that Python uses a technique called *reference counting* to manage objects in memory. Basically Python keeps count of how many references to an object there are. When you create an object with code like:

```
object = SomeClass()
```

Continued

Continued

Python sets the reference count for this newly created object to one. If later in your code you create another reference to this same object, Python increases the count to two.

```
anotherRef = object
```

Likewise when you delete a reference with the del statement, Python decrease the reference count by one. As in:

```
del anotherRef
```

Periodically, Python checks to see if there are any objects that have a reference count of zero and if so removes them from memory. The problem with circular references is that when you have two objects that point to each other, you need to be careful when deleting your objects. If you are not careful, they will continue to live and occupy memory long after you think that they've been deleted.

To understand how this works we can use a function called getrefcount() which (surprise, surprise) returns the count of how many references there are to a given object. The use of getrefcount() might be slightly misleading the first time you use it because the method returns a count that is usually one higher than you would expect. For example, if you have only one reference to an object, the method will return two. This is because the method itself has a reference to your object while it's getting you the count. Now having said that, we're going to use the method to show you what happens if you're not careful when deleting objects that have a circular reference to each other.

Start by importing the getrefcount() method from the sys package and then define a class named klass as follows:

```
>>> from sys import getrefcount
>>> class klass: pass
...
```

Next use getrefcount() to determine how many references there are to this class.

```
>>> getrefcount(klass)
2
>>>
```

Notice there are two. There's one reference in your current namespaces that you created when you created the class. The second reference is held temporarily by the getrefcount() function. If you were to create an instance of klass and used getrefcount() again on klass, the results would be three.

```
>>> parent = klass()
>>> getrefcount(klass)
3
```

This is because each object instance has a reference to its class (which by the way can be accessed as parent.__class__). Now create a couple of instances of klass and store a reference to each other. If you like you can use getrefcount() to determine how many references there are to each of the instances.

```
>>> child = klass()
>>> getrefcount(klass)
4
>>> getrefcount(parent)
2
>>> getrefcount(child)
2
>>> parent.mychild = child
>>> child.myparent = parent
>>> getrefcount(klass)
4
>>> getrefcount(parent)
3
>>> getrefcount(child)
3
>>> dir()
['__builtins__', '__doc__', '__name__', 'child', 'getrefcount',
'klass', 'parent']
>>> del parent
>>> del child
>>> getrefcount(klass)
4
>>> dir()
['__builtins__', '__doc__', '__name__', 'getrefcount', 'klass']
```

Notice how even after you deleted child and parent, the reference count of `klass` is still four. How can this be? The output of `dir()` (which lists the names in the current namespace) shows that `child` and `parent` have been deleted. Why then is the reference count of `klass` still 4? The reason is because of that pesky circular reference you created. When you tried to delete `parent`, Python noticed that the reference count for the object was still greater than 0 (because child's `myparent` attribute contains a reference to `parent`) and so it didn't delete the object from memory. Likewise when you tried to delete `child`, neither did its reference count did not drop below 1 because the now phantom `parent` object still has a reference to the `child` object.

The only thing that the `del` statement accomplished was to remove the names from the current namespace and make it impossible for you to work with those objects. You have what programmers call "a memory leak" because there are objects taking up memory and there's no way to recover them.

The only way to avoid this problem is to break the circular reference before deleting your objects. Assuming that we hadn't yet deleted the `parent` and `child` instances, the proper way to delete the objects with a circular reference would be something like this:

```
>>> del child.myparent
>>> del child
>>> del parent
>>> getrefcount(klass)
2
```

Context versus containment

Two words that are tossed around a lot while talking about acquisition are *context* and *containment*. Containment is the concept that one object is contained by another.

```
>>> from Acquisition import Implicit
>>> class ACQClass(Implicit):
...   def __init__(self, id):
...     self.id = id
...
>>> a = ACQClass("a")
>>> a.b = ACQClass("b")
```

In the previous example it can be said that a contains b. Now consider this example:

```
>>> from Acquisition import Implicit
>>> class ACQClass(Implicit):
...   def __init__(self, id):
...     self.id = id
...
>>> a = ACQClass("a")
>>> a.b = ACQClass("b")
>>> a.x = ACQClass("x")
>>> print a.b.x.id
x
>>>
```

In the previous example, x is accessed through b. The b attribute acquires the x attribute through acquisition from the a object. In this case it can be said that the x object is in the context of b. This is because b does not contain the x object. Note that b could have an effect on x's behavior, as shown in the following example:

```
>>> from Acquisition import Implicit
>>> class ACQClass(Implicit):
...   def __init__(self, id):
...     self.id = id
...
>>> a = ACQClass("a")
>>> a.b = ACQClass("b")
>>> a.x = ACQClass("x")
>>> print a.x.aq_parent.id
a
>>> print a.b.x.aq_parent.id
b
```

This is where the use of the aq_inner attribute comes into play. It will return an object only wrapped in its container versus its context. Continuing from the same example used previously, you can see how aq_inner returns x wrapped only in its container, which is a, even though it was acquired through b.

```
>>> print a.b.x.aq_inner.aq_parent.id
a
```

ZODB and Persistence

If you've done a bit of programming in Python or another object-oriented language and you're like us, you're probably addicted to creating object hierarchies to model your problems.

This is natural—humans think in outlines. We categorize information this way. For instance, think of how scientists categorize living creatures into kingdom, phylum, class, order, suborder, family, genus, and species. The top-level categories (known as kingdoms) include Animalia, Plantae, Fungi, Protista, and Prokaryotae. Within a given kingdom you have subcategories (called phylum or divisions). For example, some of the living creatures in the Animalia kingdom can be further categorized depending on whether they have spines.

Objects are great for modeling this kind of information. But if you've programmed with objects for a while, you are probably familiar with the pains that are associated with trying to make this kind of information permanent. You have a couple of choices. You could create your own file format and write all of this information out to disk, or you could try mapping this information to a SQL (Structured Query Language) database. Both options could quickly become the brunt of your programming chore while writing and marinating your application.

Luckily, Python provides a simple module called *Pickle* that takes care of converting objects to a format that can easily be stored on disk or moved around on a network and then converted back to objects again. This process is known as *marshaling*. The creators of Zope couldn't leave well enough alone and combined the Pickle module into a package called ZODB (Zope Object Database), which provides a rich set of features such as Transactions, Undo support, and caching. If you've read through Part II and created the application we outlined, you're already familiar with how little effort is needed on your part to use the ZODB. Most of the work is completely transparent to the developer, which is good because it frees you to worry more about the problem you are trying to solve instead of worrying about manipulating bits on a hard disk.

The ZODB can't be compared directly to a SQL database because it's missing one important piece of functionality. It does not include any searching capabilities. The ZODB was designed specifically to store and retrieve objects and to make this process as transparent as possible for the developer. Searching the ZODB, however, is left entirely up to your application.

One method that can be used to accomplish this is to start at the top of the hierarchy and search each object and its attributes. Besides being tedious, this process can be time and resource intensive when searching a large database. Luckily there's an alternative called ZCatalog that provides indexing and searching capabilities. To find out more about the ZCatalog see Chapter 17.

In the next couple of sections in this chapter we give you some in depth examples showing you the intricacies of the ZODB and how you can use it in applications that you create outside of Zope.

You are going to need a copy of the ZODB. We assume that you have Zope already installed on your computer and that it will be the version you are working with.

Alternatively, you can download and install a copy of the ZODB by itself without Zope from A.M. Kuchling's Web site at `http://amk.ca/zodb`. The installation instructions for installing ZODB won't be described here because they involve compiling (which Linux users might be familiar with but will probably be a bit cumbersome to Window's users). Regardless, if you're interested in using the ZODB in your own application without Zope, `http://amk.ca/zodb` is the best place to start.

Unlike traditional relational databases, the ZODB imposes no structure on the data that's stored in it. This is left to the programmer to decide.

Using the ZODB in other applications

For a quick introduction to the ZODB, drop to the command line, change to the `lib/python` directory under your Zope directory, and fire up the Python interpreter. Now you are ready to run the following commands:

```
>>> from ZODB import FileStorage, DB
>>> storage = FileStorage.FileStorage("c:\\temp\\test.fs")
>>> db = DB(storage)
>>> connection = db.open()
>>> root = connection.root()
```

The use of two backslashes "\\" is necessary in the previous example. Python uses the backslash to identify an escape sequence. See the section entitled "Escape Sequences" in Chapter 5 for more information.

The root object that you've just obtained behaves like a dictionary, with one notable difference. Any object you put in this dictionary that conforms to the rules of persistence (which is explained in the next section of this chapter) will be saved to the filename, `test.fs`, whenever you commit a transaction. To see how this is done add a tuple to the root object and commit the batch.

```
>>> mytuple = ("Lions", "Tigers", "Bears", "Oh My!")
>>> root['mytuple'] = mytuple
>>> print root['mytuple']
('Lions', 'Tigers', 'Bears', 'Oh My!')
```

If you were to quit now the changes you made would not be stored in the database. This is because the ZODB is transactional. In a transactional system many changes can be made at once but aren't saved until they are committed. This is a powerful feature that lets your program discard changes and rollback to a known good state for any reason. To make the changes to the database permanent, you need you need to commit the current transaction. This is done by calling the `get_transaction()` method, which the ZODB installs into the `__built-ins__` namespace the first time it is imported. (This makes this method global and available anywhere in your program without needing to import it every time.) Once you get the current transaction, call its `commit()` method, which saves all of your changes out to your storage. This can be done in one step as shown here:

```
>>> get_transaction().commit()
```

Finally, it's a good idea to close your storage before exiting your program so that the file is written out to the disk properly. Although this isn't technically necessary since the ZODB (or the FileStorage at least) was designed to guarantee that the data will be saved to the disk when you call `commit()`.

```
>>> storage.close()
```

That's it! You can quit your application at any time and when you come back your data will still be there. In fact, for demonstration purposes, why don't you quit out of the interpreter now and restart it. Then rerun the following code to see that your object is permanently stored in the database:

```
>>> from ZODB import FileStorage, DB
>>> storage = FileStorage.FileStorage("c:\\temp\\test.fs")
>>> db = DB(storage)
>>> connection = db.open()
>>> root = connection.root()
>>> print root['mytuple']
('Lions', 'Tigers', 'Bears', 'Oh My!')
```

Storing objects and subobjects

In the previous example we stored a simple list of strings into the root object of the ZODB. You can store objects of your own design but they need to inherit from a mix-in class named *Persistent*.

Consider this set of classes used for tracking bookmarks:

```
fromZODB import Persistentclass BookMark(Persistent):
   def __init__(self, title, url):
       self.editBookMark(self, url)

   def editBookMark(self, title, url):
       self.title = title
       self.url = url
```

Now you can store instances of this class in the ZODB like this:

```
mybookmark = BookMark('Codeit','http://www.codeit.com')
root['mybookmark'] = mybookmark
get_transaction().commit()
```

If you make changes to the object later on (perhaps by using the object's `editBookMark()` method) the only thing you need to do to make your changes permanent is to commit the transaction.

```
mybookmark.editBookMark('Codeit (Spanish Version)', ⮐
'http://www.codeit.com/sp/')get_transaction().commit()
```

The Persistent mix-in class provides the special `__getattr__` and `__setattr__` methods that are aware of the transaction. They detect whenever the attributes of your object are accessed or changed. This lets the ZODB know when it should save your object and its children automatically. For this reason you should never define `__getattr__` or `__setattr__` methods in classes that inherit from Persistent.

You don't have to store every object directly in the root object. Any of the object's attributes that inherit from Persistent will be saved as well. The same is also true for any of the sub-object's objects. In fact, Zope only stores one object in the root object, called application. You can retrieve the sub-objects via traversal or with methods that return the objects references directly.

Notifying the ZODB when an object has changed

As you can see you don't have to do much to save objects that have changed. There are a few notable exceptions. Persistent overrides `__setattr__` to detect changes, which works whenever you make changes directly to an object's attributes. But if you modify a mutable object such as a dictionary or list, the ZODB has no way of knowing that a change has occurred. If this happens you must notify the ZODB that your object has changed by setting your object's `_p_changed` attribute equal to 1. For example, let's create a class that lets you organize multiple bookmarks into sub-folders:

Attributes that start with _p_ are for the ZODB's own devious purposes. You should never create any attributes that start like this.

```
class BookMarkFolder(Persistent):
    def __init__(self):
        self._bookmarks = {}
        self._sub_folders = {}

    def addBookMark(self, bookmark):
        self._bookmarks[bookmark.title] = bookmark
        self._p_changed = 1

    def delBookMark(self, title):
        if self._bookmarks.has_key(title):
            del self._bookmarks[title]
            self._p_changed = 1
```

```
    def addSubFolder(self, name):
        self._sub_folders[name] = BookMarkFolder()
        self._p_changed = 1


    def delSubFolder(self, name):
        if self._sub_folders.has_key(name):
            del self._sub_folders[name]
            self._p_changed = 1

    def getSubFolder(self, name):
        return self._sub_folders[name]
```

Here's an example of this program in action:

```
# Code to open ZODB & import BookMark class goes here
bookmarks = root['bookmarks'] = BookMarkFolder()
get_transaction().commit()

bookmarks.addSubFolder('Favorites')
Favorites = bookmarks.getSubFolder('Favorites')
Favorites.addBookMark(BookMark('Geek News',
                               'http://slashdot.org'))
Favorites.addBookMark(BookMark('Python Reference',
                               'http://python.org'))

get_transaction().commit()
```

Meet the rules of persistence

For the ZODB to do its magic, you must follow a few rules:

1. Only "Pickable" items (see the documentation for the Pickle module that comes with the standard Python installation or read it online at `http://www.python.org/doc/current/lib/module-pickle.html`) can be stored in the database. ("Pickable" items include all of the standard types such as strings, numbers, lists, tuples, dictionaries, and object instances.) Certain things like files, sockets, classes, and Python code objects cannot be stored in the database.
2. Objects that inherit from Persistent will be saved automatically whenever their immutable attributes change or when you specify that an object has changed by setting `_p_changed = 1`.
3. Objects should not create attributes that start with `_p_`. These attributes are reserved for the ZODB.
4. Attributes that start with `_v_` are volatile and will not be saved to the database when the transaction is committed. Objects that our retrieved from the ZODB will not have these attributes. You can use `__setstate__` (which is called whenever an object is retrieved from the database) to restore these variables.

Creating attributes that won't be saved in the ZODB

Attributes that start with _v_ are considered volatile. They won't be saved when a transaction is committed. You use this when you have attributes, such as file objects, that shouldn't or can't be saved in the database. You can define a method called __setstate__ that the ZODB will call whenever it loads the object from the database. The ZODB will pass your object the state of your object, which is a dictionary of your object's attributes. You can add your volatile attributes back at this time.

For instance, imagine you have code that keeps a file handle open for logging purposes. Because file objects aren't pickable, the easiest way to do this is to store the name of the file that you want to open in a regular attribute. When ZODB brings the object out of the database it calls the __setstate__ method where the object reopens the file.

```
from ZODB import Persistent
from time import ctime
class Logger(Persistent):
   def __init__(self, logname):
     self.logname = logname
     self._v_file = open(logname, 'a')

   def __setstate__(self, state):
     Persistent.__setstate__(self, state)
     self._v_file = open(self.logname, 'a')

   def log(self, msg):
     self._v_file.write(ctime() + msg + "\n")
```

Another useful aspect of volatile variables is that if you modify one, your object is not automatically saved in the database. You'll see this feature in action later in this chapter in the section titled "Using subtransactions and other tricks to save memory."

Aborting transactions

Using the transactions abort() method, changes you make can be reverted back to the state they were in at the time of the last commit.

```
>>> from ZODB import FileStorage, DB, Persistent
>>> class Counter(Persistent):
...    def __init__(self):
...      self.count = 0
...    def __repr__(self):
...      return str(self.count)
...    def increase(self):
...      self.count += 1
```

```
>>> storage = FileStorage.FileStorage("c:\\temp\\test.fs")
>>> db = DB(storage)
>>> connection = db.open()
>>> root = connection.root()
>>> counter = Counter()
>>> root['counter'] = counter
>>> get_transaction().commit()
>>> print counter
0
>>> counter.increase()
>>> print counter
1
>>> get_transaction().abort()
>>> print counter
0
```

This is similar to what Zope does when it catches an error that wasn't handled by your Product.

Caching and memory management

The ZODB is capable of storing hundreds of thousands of objects. You can actually store more objects in the database than you can fit into memory. As objects are pulled from the database, the ZODB tracks how often they are used and automatically reclaims the space of objects that haven't been accessed for a certain period of time.

For the most part this is completely transparent and there isn't much that you need to worry about. But if you feel the urge to tinker, the database object (the one you get when you execute `db = DB(storage)` in Python) exposes a couple of functions that can be used to control how many objects are in the cache, how long an inactive object can sit in the cache before being used, and a couple of methods to manually flush the cache.

Changing the number of objects kept in the cache

You can control the number of objects that are allowed to be in the cache before ZODB attempts to reclaim their space using the `db.setCacheDeactivateAfter()` method. You use this method by calling it with an integer argument. For example, to set the cache to hold a 1,000 objects, you would use:

```
db.setCacheSize(1000)
```

To get the current cache size you can use getCacheSize on the database object like this:

```
size = db.getCacheSize()
```

Here's a quick way to get a reference of the database object, in case it's not currently in scope. Every persistent object that has been saved in the ZODB has an attribute named `_p_jar`, which is a reference back to the current connection object. Connection objects have a method named `db()` that will return the database instance.

```
db=self._p_jar.db()
```

Changing amount of time an inactive objects remained in the cache

It's also possible to change how long an object can sit around unused in the cache before it is removed with a call to `setCacheDeactivateAfter()`. It takes one argument, which is the number of seconds that the object can be unused before it becomes a candidate for removal. You can set it so that objects are removed from the cache after two minutes of inactivity like this:

```
db.getCacheDeactivateAfter(120)
```

Just like setting the cache size, you can use the `getCacheDactivateAfter()` method to determine what the existing time out value is.

```
time_out = db.getCacheDeactivateAfter()
```

Emptying the cache manually

You can clean the cache manually (remove objects that aren't being used) by sweeping it—no pun intended. Normally you do not need to worry about this task since the ZODB handles it for you as part of its normal operations. However, if and when you perform a sweep, the ZODB will go through each of the caches (usually there's one cache per thread) and remove objects that haven't been accessed in a certain amount of time. The database object provides two methods for sweeping the caches. Both methods take a single argument, which is the number of seconds that an object has been unused in the cache.

The first method, called a full sweep, performs a single pass through each of the caches and removes all the dereference objects and inactive objects. Here's how to remove all objects that haven't been used in sixty seconds:

```
db.cacheFullSweep(60)
```

The second method, known as a minimize sweep, is more aggressive and would make multiple sweeps through the cache to empty. Here's how to perform a minimize sweep:

```
db.cacheMinimize(60)
```

Using subtransactions and other tricks to save memory

Unused objects are normally removed from memory based on the target cache size. This is true unless the object has been modified. Zope won't remove an object from the cache until its contents have been saved. One problem this presents is that you can quickly run out of memory if your application has made changes to a large amount of objects or your objects are rather large.

Luckily ZODB enables you to commit changes in the middle of a transaction to get these changed objects out of memory. This process is called subtransactions. To commit a subtransaction you call `commit()` with a value of true. When this happens the ZODB will immediately dump the objects out of memory to the disk. It's up to you to decide when this is necessary and how often. The more subtransactions you commit, the less memory that's used, but the trade-off is that processes go slower. If the transaction is aborted, the subtransactions will be rolled back as well.

Suppose we want to load large files into the ZODB—files that might be several hundreds of megabytes large. We could just create an object that stores all of the binary data into a Python string. A class that would do this would look something like this:

```
class PersistentFile(Persistent):

  def __init__(self, name, file):
    self.Name = Name
    self.loadFile(file)
    self.CurrentPos = 0

  def loadFile(self, file):
    # Note: This method assumes that the argument named file is
    # an opened file handle
    self.Data = file.read()
    self.Size = len(self.Data)
    self.CurrentPos = 0

  def read(self, size=None):
    if self.CurrentPos >= self.Size:
      # We've reached the end of the file so...
      return None


    if size == None:
      # No size was entered so return everything.
      read_to_pos = self.Size - self.CurrentPos
    else:
      read_to_pos = self.CurrentPos + size

    data = self.Data[self.CurrentPos:read_to_pos]
    self.CurrentPos = read_to_pos

    return data

  # Implement the other file operations like seek,
  # readline, etc... here
```

This would work fine for small files as long as you didn't load a lot of them in a single transaction. Imagine what would happen if you tried to load a 100-MB file into the ZODB. Even if you tried to commit a subtransaction it wouldn't do you much good because the whole object would be over 100 MB in memory. On top of that, each thread in your application has its own copy of this object in its cache. It's not hard to imagine how quickly you could run out of memory with this approach.

The solution to this problem is to break your file up into several smaller chunks and spread it over multiple persistent objects that are linked together. This rather large example shows you how to put most of the existing features of the ZODB to use. You should pay close attention to a couple of things. First notice that we use a volatile attribute named `_v_CurrentPos`. Two reasons for this one are that modifying a volatile variable doesn't cause the ZODB to think to need to save the object, which would be annoying for a large file if it needed to be rewritten to the ZODB every time we read it. And, secondly it allows each thread that uses the ZODB to read independently of the other threads because each time an object is pulled from the disk into the cache `_v_CurrentPos` is reset to zero thanks to the use of the `__setstate__` call `import sys`.

This technique is used with Zope's file objects that enable users to store large file objects into the ZODB. These should not be confused with Python's file object that enables you to manipulate files on the file system. Zope's file object can be larger than the available memory of the machine. When uploading the file if there wasn't away to get the object out of memory quickly your server might crash. This is accomplished by breaking the file up into a linked list of smaller persistent objects. Each object contains about a 65k bites of data with a pointer to the next object. As each object is created a subtransaction is committed. The beauty of this system is when the object is being loaded into memory pervious chunks will be removed as the number of objects hit the Target Cache size.

```
sys.path.append("c:\\program files\\website\\lib\\python")
from ZODB import FileStorage, DB, Persistent

CHUNKSIZE=1024
class Chunk(Persistent):

    def __init__(self, data):
        self.Data = data
        self.NextChunk = None

    def setNextChunk(self, chunk):
        self.NextChunk = chunk

class PersistentFile(Persistent):

    def __init__(self, Name, file):
        self.Name = Name
        self.FirstChunk = None
        self._v_CurrentPos = 0
        self.NumberOfChunks = 0
        self.Size = 0
```

```
        self.loadFile(file)

    def __setstate__(self, state):
        Persistent.__setstate__(self, state)

        self._v_CurrentPos = 0


    def getChunk(self, chunk_number):
        if (chunk_number > (self.NumberOfChunks-1)) or ⮐
(chunk_number < 0):
            raise IndexError

        current_chunk = self.FirstChunk

        while(chunk_number > 0):
            chunk_number -= 1
            current_chunk = current_chunk.NextChunk

        return current_chunk

    def loadFile(self, file):
        # Note: This method assumes that the argument named
        # file is an opened file handle

        previous_chunk = None
        while(1):
            data = file.read(CHUNKSIZE)

            # Check to see if we've hit the end of the file
            if data == '': break

            self.Size += len(data)
            self.NumberOfChunks += 1
            chunk = Chunk(data)

            if previous_chunk is None:
                self.FirstChunk = chunk
            else:
                previous_chunk.setNextChunk(chunk)

            previous_chunk = chunk

            # Free up some memory by commiting a subtransaction
            get_transaction().commit(1)

            self._v_CurrentPos = 0


    def read(self, bytes_to_read=0):
        if self._v_CurrentPos >= self.Size:
            # We've reached the end of the file so...
            return ''
```

```
        read_to_offset = self._v_CurrentPos + bytes_to_read
        if (bytes_to_read == 0) or (read_to_offset > ⮐
self.Size):
            # No size was entered so return everything.
            bytes_to_read = self.Size - self._v_CurrentPos

        data = ''
        chunk_number, chunk_offset = ⮐
divmod(self._v_CurrentPos, CHUNKSIZE)
        self._v_CurrentPos += bytes_to_read

        current_chunk = self.getChunk(chunk_number)
        while(bytes_to_read > 0):
            bytes_to_read -= (CHUNKSIZE-chunk_offset)
            data += current_chunk.Data[chunk_offset:CHUNKSIZE]
            current_chunk = current_chunk.NextChunk
            chunk_offset = 0

        return data

    # Implement the other file operations like seek,
    # readline, etc... here

storage = FileStorage.FileStorage("c:\\temp\\test.fs")
db = DB(storage)
connection = db.open()
root = connection.root()

f = open("setup.bmp","rb")
pfile = PersistentFile(f.name, f)
root[pfile.Name] = pfile
get_transaction().commit()
```

Thread safety

If you're writing a multi-threaded application, you might be wondering about issues such as concurrency. As long as each thread opens its own connection to the ZODB your application will be mostly thread safe with a few exceptions. This is because each thread keeps its own cache of objects and only one connection can commit its changes to the database at a time. If two or more different connections try to commit changes made to the same object(s), one connection will succeed and the others will raise a ConflictErorr. It's up to you to work the process out. For example, Zope treats every request as a transaction if a ConflictError is detected. Zope automatically tries to reprocess the request three times before giving up and displaying an error to the user.

The best way to avoid ConflictErrors in your application is to spread the load of writes around your object hierarchy.

Alternatively your object can handle the conflict. If your object defines a method named `_p_resolveConflict()`, it will be called and passed three values:

✦ The original state

✦ The state of the object that was saved before your save

✦ The state as of the object as it is in the current thread

Using these values you can determine how your object was changed by the previous commit, update your current object and have it written back to the database.

A good example of a system where it would be difficult to spread changes to other objects would be an inventory control system that keeps track of the quantity of a particular product that you have on hand. Two things can happen to this quantity: it can be increased or decreased. If two threads do either of these things at the same time it is possible that you're numbers will get out of sync.

Imagine that you started off with a copy of your product object that had a quantity on hand set at 10. In one thread there's an attempt to increase the quantity on hand by 5 because a new shipment was received in the warehouse. In another thread at the exact same time, somebody ordered one of the products, so this thread will attempt to decrease the quantity on hand by 1. One transaction will be saved first, and the other thread will receive a ConflictError. If this protection wasn't in place and the thread that was trying to increase the inventory by 5 is saved first, then the value would be temporarily set to 15. Right after that the thread that was decreasing the value would save and set the quantity on hand to 9. What should have happened—regardless of what order it happened in—is that the quantity on hand should have be equal to 14.

To resolve the conflict so that an error isn't raised, define a method named `_p_resolveConflict` in your object. This hook will be called with three arguments that will let you examine all the different states and then update your object accordingly. For example, if you compared the value of quantity on hand that was in the thread that just committed versus the original value, you can determine that the value was increased by 5. Taking that into account, you can then subtract 1 from the current value to get 14. Here's the code you would use:

```
class Product(Persistent)

  def __init__(self)
    self.OnHand = 0

  def increaseInventory(self, count):
    self.OnHand = self.OnHand + count

  def decreaseInventory(self, count):
    self.OnHand
```

```
def _p_resolveConflict(self, oldState, savedState, newState):
  # Figure out how each state is different:
  savedDiff = savedState['OnHand'] - oldState['OnHand']
  newDiff= newState['OnHand'] - oldState['OnHand']

  # Apply both sets of changes to old state:
  oldState['OnHand'] = oldState['OnHand'] + savedDiff + newDiff

  return oldState
```

Undoing transaction

After a transaction has been committed it's possible to undo it. In order to do this you'll need a storage that supports it. The default File Storage that we've been using in the examples throughout this chapter is one such storage.

Tip: To determine whether your database supports undo capabilities, you can call the `supportsUndo()` method on your db object, which returns true if the database has undo support.

To undo a transaction, you need to get its id using the `undoLog()` method. This method returns a list of dictionaries that contains information about each transaction. Once you have the id you can pass it as an argument to the undo function. Note that you won't notice any changes until you commit the transaction and open a new connection to the database.

```
>>> root['blah'] = 1
>>> get_transaction().commit()
>>> del root['blah']
>>> get_transaction().commit()
>>> db.undoInfo()
[{'time': 1010037367.1700001, 'id': 'AOHHpB6XjUwAAAAAAMsrg',
'user_name': '', '
description': ''}]
>>> db.undo('AOHHpB6XjUwAAAAAAMsrg')
>>> get_transaction().commit()
>>> root = db.open().root()
>>> root.keys()
['blah', 'setup.bmp']
>>>
```

Removing old transactions to save space

You can pack the ZODB to remove the unwanted undo information. This will reclaim some disk space. Simply call the `pack()` method on the database. All the undo transactions will be removed by default if you call the pack method with no arguments. Optionally, you can call the pack option with an integer, which will remove all the transactions that are that many days older than the number. For instance, to remove all the undo transactions older than a day you would call the pack function like this:

```
db.pack(1)
```

Working with, saving, and aborting versions

Versions are a group of transactions that can be committed and undone together. Changes made to a version are not visible outside of the version, except that objects edited in a version are locked. No other connections will be able to edit those objects unless they themselves are working in the same version.

To work in a connection you specify an arbitrary string to be the name of the version as part of the open argument, as follows:

```
connection = db.open('New Changes')
# Then get the root object as normal
root = connection.root()
```

All calls to `get_transaction().commit()` will only affect connections that are using the same version.

The changes that are committed in a version are saved to the disk, which means that you can quit your program any time and when you open a connection to the same version they'll still be there. If you want to make the changes visible to the all connections, you can commit the version like this:

```
db.commitVersino('New Changes')
```

Discard all the changes made in a version call like this:

```
db.abortVersion('New Changes')
```

ZPublisher

The component responsible for object publishing is called ZPublisher. It's a lightweight ORB (Object Request Broker), which is another name for object publishing. *Object publishing* is the process of taking an HTTP request (or similar protocol), finding the object that the request refers to, and returning the results after handing the objects the details of the request.

Traversing objects

The process of finding the object that is referred to by a network request is called *traversal*. The ZPublisher takes a URL, breaks it up into names, and then attempts to move from one object to the next until it finds the last object in the URL. For instance, a URL such as `http://codeit.com/object1/object2/object3` could be expressed in Python as `root.object1.object2.object3`.

The ZPublisher doesn't simply convert all of the slashes in a URL to periods. For each step in the URL the ZPublisher looks at the previously found object (or the root object if it's the start of the traversal process) to see whether it has an attribute with the name of the next step. If this doesn't work, the ZPublisher checks to see whether the previously found object is a dictionary and if the next object is in it.

In other words, ZPublisher tries to get the next object by doing the equivalent of a `object.nextobject` or `object["nextobject"]` in Python. This is assuming that the URL was `http://yoursite.com/object/nextobject`.

Controlling the traversal process with __bobo_traverse__

For the ultimate in control, you can define a method named `__bobo_traverse__()`. If this method is defined, ZPublisher won't even attempt to find the next object as an attribute or as a dictionary item.

Bobo was ZPublisher's old name before Zope was open sourced. The name `__bobo_traverse__` is a left-over legacy from before this time.

`__bobo_traverse__()` takes two arguments (besides `self`): `request` and `name`. The `request` argument, as the name implies, is a reference to the request object. The `name` argument is a string containing the name of the next object. Using these two pieces of information you can determine what the next object should be. The method can return a single object, a sequence of objects (in case you want to add more parents to the chain), or None if the object isn't found.

Practical uses for this hook include building objects dynamically during the traversal function or inserting additional objects into the parents' chain (to change the behavior of acquisition).

For example, you could write a method that builds an object by querying a SQL database. This example assumes that you have created the `sqlGetEmployee` SQL method somewhere in the hierarchy where it can be acquired.

```
def __bobo_traverse__(self, request, name):
    res = self.sqlGetEmployee(name=name)
    if len(res) > 0:
       return Employee(res[0])
    else:
       return None
```

Security and traversing

As you can imagine, you don't want people from the outside world to call every method that exists in your application. This is why ZPublisher imposes the following security rules:

1. All object's classes and methods that are to be public must define a doc string.
2. The name of a sub-object that you wish to access through the Web cannot start with an underscore.
3. If the object has an attribute named `__roles__` and it's a list of strings, a user must have one of the corresponding roles. If `__roles__` is `None`, the object is considered public and can be accessed by anyone. If `__roles__` is an empty list, the object is private and cannot be accessed through the Web.
4. Methods of an object can be protected in a similar fashion, by defining a list named `method__roles__`.

Publishing the object

Once the object is found via traversal, ZPublisher attempts to "publish" the object by either calling it if possible, calling the `index_html()` method if it exists, or returning a string representation of the object.

It would be pretty uneventful if all that the publishing process did was find an object and return the static content. Zope would be no different than a vanilla http server serving up static content. What Zope does is let you create your own functions that cannot only create dynamic content but also manipulate the various objects in the application.

So, one thing that methods need then are arguments that it can get out of the request. Traditional CGI scripts were forced to write routines to get the information out of the request themselves. With ZPublisher, there's no need to do this. Instead, you can define the methods and arguments that your objects have and ZPublisher will try to figure out the names of these methods for you. This process is called *marshaling arguments*.

Marshaling arguments

By default an HTTP request is searched for arguments that are passed in either via an HTTP GET or an HTTP POST operation. After traversing the object, ZPublisher determines how to call the object and will automatically map the corresponding values in the request to the arguments of the method. For instance, imagine that you have an object that defines the following method:

```
def himom(self, momsname):
    "Takes the name of your mother and says hi to her."
    return "Hi, %s!" % momsname
```

If this method was accessed via the URL `http://site/myobject/himom?momsname=Sylvia`, the value of `momsname` would be "Sylvia." Similarly, you could use a form that posted its information to this method:

```
<html>
<body>
<form action="http://site/myobject/himom" method="post">
Enter your mom's name here: <input type="text" name="momsname">
</form>
</body>
</html>
```

and you'd get the same result.

The beauty of this is that you had to write hardly any code at all to accomplish this! With a CGI script you might have had to look at the QUERY_STRING environment variable and "unescape" it yourself. ZPublisher automatically converts all of the escape sequences to the character equivalents for you.

If you define a method that takes an argument and it's not in the request, ZPublisher will raise an exception. You can get around this by assigning your argument a default argument like this:

```
def himom(self, momsname="Mom"):
    "Takes the name of your mother and says hi to her."
    return "Hi, %s!" % momsname
```

This way if no argument exists, the default greeting will be "Hi, Mom!"

Your methods can also define two special arguments REQUEST and RESPONSE. If either of these arguments is defined, ZPublisher will hand your argument the object corresponding to its name.

A typical idiom used while publishing objects via the Web is to default the REQUEST object to `None` in the method definition. Then you test the REQUEST before returning a value from your method to determine whether you were called via the Web or internally.

```
def editMomsName(self, momsname, REQUEST=None):
    self.momsname = momsname
    if REQUEST is not None:
        # We were called via the web return an html document
        return """<html>
                  <body>
                  <blink>Hi, %s!</blink>
                  </body>
                  </html>""" % self.momsname
```

Type casting arguments

By default all arguments are marshaled as strings. Some Python methods that you write will need the arguments to be a specific type. You can have the ZPublisher attempt to convert an argument to a specific type by naming the argument with a special suffix. For example, if you name an argument `status:int`, ZPublisher will attempt to convert the status argument to an integer. ZPublisher will raise an exception if it can't convert the argument to the type you specified. Table 14-2 contains all the formatting codes.

Table 14-2
Type Conversion Codes

Code	*Description*
`boolean`	Converts the argument to true or false.
`int`	Converts the argument to a Python integer.
`long`	Converts the argument to a Python long.
`float`	Converts the argument to a Python float.
`string`	Converts the argument to a Python string.
`required`	Causes ZPublisher to raise an exception if the argument is blank.
`ignore_empty`	Removes the variable from the request if it evaluates to an empty string.
`date`	Converts the argument to a DateTime object.
`list`	Converts the argument to a list, even if there is only one value.
`lines`	Creates a list of values from a string containing line breaks.
`tokens`	Creates a list of values from a string by splitting words that are separated by spaces.
`tuple`	Creates a Python tuple from one or more values.
`text`	Converts the line breaks regardless of the browsers OS to be that of the OS the server is running.
`record`	Combines multiple variables into one variable.
`records`	Combines multiple variables into a list of records.

Converting an argument to a number

Imagine you have a method that calculates how much to tip a waiter in a restaurant. You'll need to make sure that the price you paid is converted to a float before performing the calculation.

```
class TipCalculator(SimpleItem):
  "This class defines methods useful for eating out."

  tip_percentage = .15

  def calculateTip(self, price):
      "This method expects a float."

      return "You should tip %s." % price * self.tip_percentage
```

If you attempted to call this method via the Web by going to a URL such as `http://yoursite.com/calc/calculateTip?price=28.00`, you would receive a type error because price is converted to a string and Python doesn't know how to multiply strings. What you want to do is make sure that price is converted to a float first. The proper URL should be `http://yoursite.com/calc/calculateTip?price=28.00:float`.

Alternatively, and probably more realistically, you would have the user fill out a form such as the following, where the user would enter in the price of dinner first:

```
<html>
<body>
<form action="calculateTip">
Enter in the price of your dinner:
<input type="text" name="price:float" size="6">
<input type="submit">
</form>
</body>
</html>
```

Another interesting aspect of this approach is that if the user enters something into the text box that can't be converted to a float, such as the phrase, "I'm a dummy," ZPublisher will raise a TypeError, which let's you know that your user entered in the wrong kind of value.

It's not possible to catch this type of error in one of your methods with the normal `try:...except:...` clause because the ZPublisher will try to convert the variable to the appropriate Python type before your method is ever called.

Converting arguments to a list

If more than one argument with the same name is in a request (`somemethod?arg=1&arg=2`, for example) ZPublisher will automatically convert the argument into a list. You would use the `:list` or `:tuple` conversion code to make sure that the argument is always converted to a list even if there is only one item.

Here's an HTML example of a typical form for which you can pick more than one option. By naming the select box `ids:list` we make sure that ZPublisher converts the `ids` argument to a list even if there is only one item selected.

```
<html>
<body>
<form action="removeIDs">
Select the IDs that you want deleted.

<select name="ids:list">
  <option value="item1">Item 1</option>
  <option value="item2">Item 2</option>
  <option value="item3">Item 3</option>
</select>

<input type="submit">
</form>
</body>
</html>
```

Here's the Python method that would handle that request:

```
def removeIDs(self, ids):
   """Removes one or more ids from the dictionary and returns
   count of items deleted."""

   count = 0
   for id in ids:
     del self.dictionary[id]
     count += 1

   return "%s items were removed from the dictionary!"
```

Requiring arguments

You can have the ZPublisher check to make sure that an argument was entered by a user with the `:required` conversion code. (All right, we know what you are thinking. This really isn't a conversion, but don't blame us (we didn't name them.)

```
<html>
<body>
<form>
You'd better enter something or I'm going to cry!
<input type="text" name="something:required">
<input type="submit">
</form>
</body>
</html>
```

If your user clicks the submit button without filling anything into the text box, the ZPublisher will raise an exception complaining that the required field was blank.

Combining conversion codes

ZPublisher lets you combine multiple codes together. For example, you can specify that an argument should be converted to a list of integers or that its a required float. To achieve this effect, simply add additional conversion codes separated by colons as shown in the following examples:

```
<select name="ids:int:list:required">
<option value="1">First Option</option>
<option value="2">Second Option</option>
<option value="3">Third Option</option>
</select>
```

Combining variables with the record conversion code

The record conversion code can take multiple form variables and combine them into a single object. Try this out. Create a two DTML Method, one named `personForm` and the other named `showPerson`. Add the following DTML/HTML to the personForm:

```
<dtml-var standard_html_header>

<form action="showPerson">
Enter your
First Name:<input type="text"
name="person.first_name:record"><br>
Last Name:<input type="text"
name="person.last_name:record"><br>
E-mail:<input type="text" name="person.email:record"><br>
<input type="submit">
</form>

<dtml-var standard_html_footer>
```

When the user fills out this form and presses submit, all the html variables whose names start with `person.` and end with `:record` will be added to the person object and then posted to your `showPerson` method. Change the `showPerson` method to have the following DTML and HTML:

```
<dtml-var standard_html_header>
Name: <dtml-var "person.first_name"> ⮐
<dtml-var "person.last_name"> <br>
E-mail: <dtml-var "person.email">
<dtml-var standard_html_footer>
```

Now go back and view the `personForm` method, enter data in the form, press submit, and see what happens.

Creating a list of records

The `records` conversion code can be used to create a list of records. It uses the same format that the `record` code does except that it can be used multiple times. For example, you could use it thus:

```
<dtml-var standard_html_header>

<form action="showPerson">
<input type="text" name="employees.first_name:records"><br>
<input type="text" name="employees.last_name:records"><br>
<input type="text" name="employees.email:records"><br>

<input type="text" name="employees.first_name:records"><br>
<input type="text" name="employees.last_name:records"><br>
<input type="text" name="employees.email:records"><br>

<input type="submit">
</form>

<dtml-var standard_html_footer>
```

This will create a list named "employees" where each element in the list is a record object that has `first_name`, `last_name` and `email properties`. You could then modify the `showPerson` method to use this list as follows:

```
<dtml-var standard_html_header>

<dtml-in emlpoyees>
Name: <dtml-var "person.first_name"> <dtml-var ⮐
"person.last_name">
E-mail: <dtml-var "person.email"><br>
</dtml-in>

<dtml-var standard_html_footer>
```

Using the REQUEST object

The REQUEST object is a huge data dictionary that contains every piece of information regarding the current request. It contains everything from the current user, the server's public environment variables, what cookies the site has set on the user's browser, to what form variables were posted in the request. In addition, the REQUEST contains several convenient functions for manipulating URLs.

The information and functionality can be broken down into five groups:

- **Environment.** These are all of the environment variables that are required or are a standard part of the CGI specification. Table 14-3 lists the variables you'd most likely need to read while working with the ZPublisher.
- **Special.** Variables (listed in Table 14-4) and methods (listed in Table 14-5) provided for your convenience.
- **Cookies.** Methods and variables used for manipulating cookies in the user's browser.
- **Forms.** A list of all form values and the methods to manipulate them. See Table 14-4.
- **Other.** Variables that you have set (using `REQUEST.set()`) in your application.

Table 14-3
CGI Environment Variables

Variables	*Description*
SERVER_SOFTWARE	The name and version of the software answering the request.
SERVER_NAME	The server's hostname or IP address.
GATEWAY_INTERFACE	The CGI version.
SERVER_PROTOCOL	The name and version of the protocol of the request.
SERVER_PORT	The port from which the server took the request.
REQUEST_METHOD	The method the request was made. Either "GET," "HEAD," "POST," and so on.
PATH_INFO	Extra path information after the script.
QUERY_STRING	The raw (undecoded) information that followed the "?" in a URL.
REMOTE_HOST	The name of the host, if known, making the request.
REMOTE_ADDR	The IP address of the host making the request.
CONTENT_TYPE	The content type of the request. This variable is only present if the method was a POST or PUT.
CONTENT_LENGTH	The length of the data that was sent to the server during a POST method.
HTTP_USER_AGENT	The name of the browser and version that made the request.
HTTP_ACCEPT_LANGUAGE	The user's default or preferred language.

You can access the variables from Table 14-3 or Table 14-4 in a couple of ways. First, you can get a reference to the REQUEST object by defining it as an argument to your method. Once you have a reference to the REQUEST object, you can access the REQUEST variables as either attributes of the REQUEST object or as if the variable was an item in the REQUEST dictionary.

```
def showBrowserAndIP(self, REQUEST):
   browser = REQUEST['HTTP_USER_AGENT']
   ip = REQUEST.REMOTE_ADDR
   return "Browser: %s <br>IP: %s" % (browser, ip)
```

Second, you can define the variable as an argument in your function and ZPublisher will pass it to your function like it would pass any other HTTP argument:

```
def showBrowserAndIP(self, HTTP_USER_AGENT, REMOTE_ADDR):
return "Browser: %s <br>IP: %s" % (HTTP_USER_AGENT,REMOTE_ADDR)
```

The REQUEST object is usually passed to DTML methods as well. This means you can access any of these variables directly with the `<dtml-var ...>` tag. For instance, inside a DTML method you can print the IP address of the person accessing your pages like this:

```
<dtml-var REMOTE_ADDR>
```

Table 14-4
Convenience Variables

Variable	*Description*
PARENTS	A list of objects traversed in order to get to the object that was published. For example, in Zope, `PARENTS[0]` would be the root object.
RESPONSE	The response object. Useful for setting headers and cookies.
PUBLISHED	Reference to the object that was published.
URL	The URL of the request without the query string.
URL0, URL1, ..., URL*n*	URL0 is the URL string that was used to make the request. URL1 is the URL with the last item removed. URL2 is the last two items removed, and so on.
URLPATH0, URLPATH1, ..., URLPATH*n*	Identical to URL*n* variables without the host and port in the URL.
BASE0, BASE1, ..., BASE*n*	Similar to the URL0 and kin but instead starts with the full URL and removes the last item with each step. BASE0 starts with first item in the URL (the server and port) and then adds an item. BASE1 is the server portion of the URL plus the next directory. URL2 is the server portion of the URL plus the next two items. Note, when using ZServer by itself, BASE0 and BASE1 are identical.
BASEPATH0, BASEPATH1, ..., BASEPATH*n*	Identical to BASE*n* variables without the host and port in the URL.
AUTHENTICATED_USER	Reference to the user currently logged in. If no user is logged in, this variable references the Anonymous User.

The variables from Table 14-4 are not part of the CGI standard but are provided by the ZPublisher for your convenience.

Using the PARENTS variable to build navigation elements

The PARENTS variable can be thought of as the path used to access your objects. Using this list you can achieve all sorts of interesting effects in your applications. Consider the "breadcrumbs" idiom often used in Web sites. The breadcrumbs are the list of links that appear at the top of a Web page that show where you are in a Web site's hierarchy. The list of links that appear just under the tabs in the Zope management screen is an example of breadcrumbs.

Breadcrumbs derives its name from the story of Hansel and Gretel, two children who went exploring in the woods. To make sure they didn't get lost, they left a trail of breadcrumbs that they could follow to get back home. The only flaw in their plan was that birds ate their trail. This probably won't happen to your Web site, but if it does, we'd like to hear about it!

You can build your own breadcrumbs with a simple bit of code similar to the following code block that loops through PARENTS list and builds a string of HTML that contains the names and links of the published objects parents:

```
def buildBreadCrumbs(self, PARENTS)
  link = '<a href="%s">%s</a>'
  breadcrumbs = link % (PARENTS[0].absolute_url(), _
PARENTS[0].title_or_id())

  for parent in PARENTS:
    breadcrumbs += " : "
    breadcrumbs += link % (parent.absolute_url(), _
parent.title_or_id()

  return breadcrumbs
```

Using URLn and BASEn

The URL*n* and the BASE*n* are handy variables but their purposes and differences are hard to understand without a few examples. Imagine that you went to a method whose URL is `http://localhost:8080/offices/ny/department/accounting/index.html`. The variable URL0 in this case would be `http://localhost:8080/offices/ny/department/accounting/index.html` where as BASE0 would be `http://localhost:8080/`. URL1 would be `http://localhost:8080/offices/ny/department/accounting` and BASE1 would be `http://localhost:8080/offices`. URL2 would be `http://localhost:8080/offices/ny/department/` and BASE2 would be `http://localhost:8080/offices/ny`. (See Table 14-5.)

The previous example is not entirely true. If you are running ZPublisher with ZServer BASE1 and BASE0 would both be `http://localhost:8080/`. This is a throwback from before ZServer was used. Usually ZPublisher expects BASE0 to be the host portion of the site and BASE1 to be the script name used to access Zope.

Table 14-5
Convenience Methods

Method	*Description*
`get_header(name, default=None)`	Returns a specific HTTP header or None if the header does not exist. Optionally, you can specify a different value to be returned if the header is not found instead of None.
`items()`	Returns a list of all keys and values in the REQUEST object.
`keys()`	Returns a list of all keys in the REQUEST object.
`setVirtualRoot(path, hard=0)`	Alters the path in URL, URL*n*, URLPATH*n*, BASE*n*, BASEPATH*n*, and `absolute_url()` so that the current object has path. If hard is true, PARENTS is emptied.
`values()`	Returns a list of values in the REQUEST object.
`set(name, value)`	Adds a new variable to the REQUEST object.
`has_key(key)`	Returns true if the REQUEST has the key.
`setServerURL(protocol=None, hostname=None, port=None)`	Modifies the protocol, hostname, and port. Using this method will change the values returned by SERVER_URL, URL, URL*n*, BASE*n*, and `absolute_url()`.

Using the RESPONSE object

The RESPONSE object enables you to manipulate, well... the response to the user. Using the RESPONSE object you can set cookies in the user's browser, redirect the user to a different page, manipulate various HTTP headers, and stream data back to the user's browser in smaller chunks instead of all at once (as is the default for returning pages). Table 14-6 summarizes the various methods and properties of the RESPONSE object.

Table 14-6
RESPONSE Object Methods and Properties

Method	*Description*
`setHeader(name, value, literal)`	Sets an HTTP return header "name" with value ("value"), clearing the previous value set for the header, if one exists. If the literal flag is true, the case of the header name is preserved; otherwise, word capitalization will be performed on the header name on output.
`setCookie(name, value, **kw)`	Sets an HTTP cookie on the browser. The response will include an HTTP header that sets a cookie on cookie-enabled browsers with a key "name" and value ("value"). This overwrites any previously set value for the cookie in the Response object.
`addHeader(name, value)`	Sets a new HTTP return header with the given value, while retaining any previously set headers with the same name.
`appendHeader(name, value, delimiter=",")`	Appends a value to a cookie. Sets an HTTP return header "name" with value ("value"), appending it following a comma if there was a previous value set for the header.
`write(data)`	Returns data as a stream. HTML data may be returned using a stream-oriented interface. This allows the browser to display partial results while computing a response to proceed. The published object should first set any output headers or cookies on the response object. Note that published objects must not generate any errors after beginning stream-oriented output.
`setStatus(status, reason=None)`	Sets the HTTP status code of the response. The argument may either be an integer or one of the following strings: OK, Created, Accepted, NoContent, MovedPermanently, MovedTemporarily, NotModified, BadRequest, Unauthorized, Forbidden, NotFound, InternalError, NotImplemented, BadGateway, ServiceUnavailable, which will be converted to the correct integer value.

Method	Description
`setBase(base)`	Sets the base URL for the returned document.
`expireCookie(name, **kw)`	Causes an HTTP cookie to be removed from the browser. The response will include an HTTP header that will remove the cookie corresponding to "name" on the client if one exists. This is accomplished by sending a new cookie with an expiration date that has already passed. Note that some clients require a path to be specified. This path must exactly match the path given when creating the cookie. The path can be specified as a keyword argument.
`appendCookie(name, value)`	Returns an HTTP header that sets a cookie on cookie-enabled browsers with a key "name" and value ("value"). If a value for the cookie has previously been set in the response object, the new value is appended to the old one, separated by a colon.
`redirect(location, lock=0)`	Causes a redirection without raising an error. If the "lock" keyword argument is passed with a true value, the HTTP redirect response code will not be changed even if an error occurs later in request processing (after `redirect()` has been called).

Create Dynamic Text with DocumentTemplates

In Chapter 4 we showed you how to create dynamic Web pages using DTML methods and documents. In this section we will show you how to use and extend the underlying class library that generates dynamic text documents based on templates. The examples in this section will be used to generate HTML. Although DTML isn't limited to the use of HTML, it's just such a natural fit that it's almost difficult to imagine better examples. So we're going to take the path of least resistance for this section. We'll leave it up to you, if desired, to find other uses for DTML.

The name of the library is DocumentTemplate. It can be found under `lib/python/DocumentTemplate` of your Zope installation. With this library you can create callable template objects.

A callable object is a Python object that implements the `__call__` hook. Objects that implement this hook can be treated as functions within Python code.

Let's jump right in and create one of these template objects and we'll show you how to use it.

```
from DocumentTemplate import HTML

template_source = """
<html>
  <head>
    <title><dtml-var title></title>
  </head>

  <body>
  <dtml-var content>
  </body>
</html>
"""

template_method = HTML(template_source)
```

Once you have created an a template instance you can now call it.

```
results = template_method(title="This Document!",
                          content="Oh lookey, I've been " + \
                                  "dynamically generated by" +\
                                  " this template!")
```

And it produces the following results:

```
<html>
  <head>
    <title>This Document</title>
  </head>

  <body>
  Oh lookey, I've been dynamically generated by this template!
  </body>
</html>
```

A template takes a string as an argument when it is initialized. This string is the template source and it consists of text and tags. The tags are replaced with dynamic content when the template is rendered (called). The dynamic content is produced from the namespace that is constructed with the values that you passed in while calling the template.

See Chapter 4 for a reference of all the tags and what they can do.

Initializing templates with default arguments

You have already seen how a basic template is instantiated and used from the previous example. Optionally a template can be instantiated with a mapping object, named arguments, or both to create a default namespace that is searched if a value can't be found from the arguments that are passed in when the template is called. Using the same example as previously (one you should be quite familiar with by now!) we can change it to use some default values via named arguments.

```
template_method = HTML(template_source, ⮐
{title:"Missing Title"}, content="Missing Content")
```

Now you can call the template without any arguments.

```
results = template_method()
```

And it produces the following results:

```
<html>
  <head>
    <title>Missing Title</title>
  </head>

  <body>
   Missing Content
  </body>
</html>
```

Calling templates

Templates can be called with multiple object instances, mapping objects, and named arguments. These objects are searched based on the order they are passed to the template when it's called. This is true except for named arguments that, if present, will be used first. Continuing from our previous example, imagine you had an object with a `title` property of "The latest and greatest news story!" If you passed it to the `template_method` as the first argument, the results would look like this:

```
>>> class k: pass
...
>>> o = k()
>>> o.title = "The latest and greatest news story!"
>>> print template_method(o)

<html>
  <head>
    <title>The latest and greatest news story!</title>
  </head>

  <body>
   Missing Content
  </body>
</html>
```

Working with templates stored in files

Instead of cluttering your source code with long format strings you can put your templates into individual files. In fact, this is such a convenient way of working with templates that the DocumentTemplate library provides a class that can be instantiated with a filename instead of the source of the template.

If you put the template code from the beginning of this section into a file named `template.dtml` and save it to the same place as where your code is then you can use the script like this:

```
import sys
sys.path.append("c:\\program files\\website\\lib\\python")

from DocumentTemplate import HTMLFile

template_method = HTMLFile("template.dtml",
                           title="No Title",
                           content="No Content"
                           )
```

Document template security

DocumentTemplates have basic security checks that prevent attributes that start with the underscore from being used in templates. If desired you can extend your templates to perform other security checks while rendering.

In the following script we subclass the HTML object and provide the `guarded_getattr()` hook. The hook takes two arguments (besides "self") the object, and the name of the attribute that is being accessed in the DTML. So back to the script. In it we've implemented the hook and check to see whether "bob" is the one attempting to render the attribute. If it is "bob," we return the value of the attribute, if it's anybody else, we raise a RunTime exception.

```
import sys
sys.path.append("c:\\program files\\website\\lib\\python")

from DocumentTemplate import HTML

class SHTML(HTML):
    # This HTML object only let's bob access object attributes
    def guarded_getattr(self, object, attribute):

        if user == "bob":
            return getattr(object, attribute)
        else:
            err_msg = "You are not authorized to use "+\
                      "%s's '%s' attribute in DTML!"
            raise RuntimeError,  err_msg % (object, attribute)
```

```
class k:
    #Dummy class used
    def __init__(self, title):
        self.title = title


template_source = """
<dtml-var title>
"""

template_method = SHTML(template_source)
o = k("This is a test")

user = raw_input("Enter your user name: ")
print template_method(o)
```

There's one other hook that you can define named `gaurded_getitem()` that will be called when using mapping objects within DTML expressions. Using a modified version of the preceding script we've defined the hook and changed the DTML used in the template to show you how it works.

```
import sys
sys.path.append("c:\\program files\\website\\lib\\python")

from DocumentTemplate import HTML

class SHTML(HTML):
    # This HTML object only let's bob access object attributes
    def guarded_getitem(self, mapping, item):
        if user == "bob":
            return mapping[item]
        else:
            err_msg = "You are not authorized to use "+\
                      "%s's '%s' entry in DTML!"
            raise RuntimeError,  err_msg % (object, attribute)


template_source = """
<dtml-var expr="dict['title']">
"""

dict = {'title':'Title inside a key'}
user = raw_input("Enter your user name: ")
print template_method(dict=dict)
```

The key thing that we should point out in the previous example is that you had to explicitly pass your mapping object in as a named argument. This is because DTML does not search mapping objects if you pass them in like an object. So to get around this, we call the function as follows, `template_method(dict=dict)`.

Creating your own tags

To finish this section on DTML, we'll show you how to create your own tags. Creating tags can lead to some exciting possibilities. For instance there's the Calendar tag (originally created by Ty Sarna, now maintained by the Zope community, and available at `http://www.zope.org/Members/jdavid/Calendar`) that renders an HTML representation of a calendar. This is great way to generate a dynamic calendar with little HTML coding effort.

We're not going to create anything so complex in this chapter, but we will show you the basics of creating tags so that, if you like, you can impress the world with the next innovative tag.

There are two types of tags that can be created: block and singleton tags. *Block* tags are two-part tags that consist of an opening and a closing tag. Examples of these tags are the `in` and `if` tags. The other type of tag is the *singleton* tag, such as the `var` and the `call` tags that don't have a closing counterpart.

Creating a tag is a simple matter of implementing all of the required interfaces and registering it as an available command. We'll start with the singleton tag.

Creating a simple singleton tag

We'll start with the equivalent of a hello world example, and then show how to make more complicated aspects of tags like using arguments and expressions, and working with values from a templates namespace.

Here's the most basic of tags that simply inserts the phrase "Hi Mom!" when rendered. It can be used in a template by inserting `<dtml-himom>` into a templates source. Singleton tags need to implement three things in their class:

- ✦ A `name` attribute, which is used to match your class to the tag when it is used in a template. For instance in the example that follows, we set name equal to "himom".
- ✦ A constructor (`__init__`) method that takes one attribute called "args." For now we'll pass on this method since we don't need it for our first example.
- ✦ A `render()` method, which is hook that is called by the template when the tag is rendered. This hook needs to take one argument, usually called "md," which is a TemplateDictionary (your guess is as good as ours as to why it's called md). The Method Dictionary is the namespace passed to the template. We'll ignore the TemplateDictionary for now since we're only going to insert the "Hi Mom!" phrase.

Without further ado here's a Python script that creates our "himom" tag, registers it, and then builds a sample template to test it:

```
import sys
sys.path.append("c:\\program files\\website\\lib\\python")
from DocumentTemplate.DT_String import String
```

```
# Create a class for our tag
class HiMomTag:

    name = 'himom'

    def __init__(self, args):
        pass

    def render(self, md):
        return "Hi Mom!"

    __call__ = render

# Register our new tag so we can use it in a template
String.commands['himom'] = HiMomTag

# Test it out by creating a template.
from DocumentTemplate import HTML
template_src = "<dtml-himom>"
template_method = HTML(template_src)
print template_method()
```

If you save all this code into file and run it with Python, it will produce the following results:

```
Hi Mom!
```

Using arguments in tags

Let's put the "Dynamic" in DTML by using arguments in your tag so that you can insert a message to your mother.

It's now time to talk about a tag's constructor. It's important to note that your tag's `__init__` method is only called when the template is instantiated. In other words when you run the following code:

```
template_method =HTML(template_source)
```

When this happens the tag class is passed its `args` as a string. You need to parse the string and set the appropriate attributes on your tag instance so that you can use the values when the tag is rendered later. The value of `args` is everything between the beginning and end of the tag (`<dtml-`*`name`* and >). For example if your template's source contained:

```
<dtml-himom msg="the dogs dead." btw="Oh, and I won't be home for dinner!">
```

then the value of `args` will be equal to `msg="the dogs dead." btw="Oh, and I won't be home for dinner!"`.

You could attempt to parse this string yourself (if you're a masochist) or you could use a handy method provided as part of the DocumentTemplate library called `parsed_params()`. This method takes a string as its first argument, and then a series of named arguments that specify what values should be present in the `args` string and what they should default to if not present. Knowing this, we can update are tag to parse the `args` when the object is instantiated and modify our tag's render method to use the attributes if they're present.

```
import sys
sys.path.append("c:\\program files\\website\\lib\\python")
from DocumentTemplate.DT_String import String
from DocumentTemplate.DT_Util import parse_params

# Create a class for our tag
class HiMomTag:

    name = 'himom'

    def __init__(self, args):
      args = parse_params(args,msg="",
                              btw="")
      self.msg = args['msg']
      self.btw = args['btw']

    def render(self, md):
      if self.msg == "":
        return "Hi Mom!"
      else:
        return "Hi Mom, %s %s" % (self.msg, self.btw)

    __call__ = render

# Register our new tag so we can use it in a template
String.commands['himom'] = HiMomTag

# Test it out by creating a template
from DocumentTemplate import HTML
template_src = """<dtml-himom msg="the dog's dead." btw="Oh, ⮐
and I won't be home for dinner!">"""
template_method = HTML(template_src)
print template_method()
```

Running this script we get:

```
Hi Mom, the dog's dead. Oh, and I won't be home for dinner!
```

Getting values and rendering Python expressions

All right you got us. The last example wasn't very dynamic because it was based on the values directly inserted into the templates source. To make it truly dynamic we want to interact with those values that you pass to the template when you render it (or use the defaults).

This is done using the md parameter of your tag's render method. This dictionary is an aggregated representation of all the namespaces passed to the template when it is rendered. Imagine calling a Template Method and passing it an object that expects to insert the value for "title" into a document it's creating. To get this value from within the render method of your tag you would simply write:

```
title = md["title"]
```

and the md will return the value, regardless of whether you called the template method like:

```
# This assumes that o has a title attribute
results = template_method(o)
```

or

```
results = template_method(title="The title")
```

One other thing that you'd likely want to do is evaluate a Python expression (the same way the var tag does) using values that are part of the template_method. You can accomplish this with the help of the Eval class, which provides a method for safely evaluating Python expressions while working with the md. The Eval class will follow all the security precautions that DTML follows, even the custom ones you provide.

To use the Eval class import it from the DT_Util module that's inside the DocumentTemplate library. Then instantiate an Eval instance with your python expression. This instance has a method named "eval" that returns the results of your Python expression using a TemplateDictionary.

We've taken the himom example as far as we can so to demonstrate using values and expressions in a template. Let's build a tag that can print out a pretty version of Python's types.

```
import sys
sys.path.append("c:\\program files\\website\\lib\\python")
from DocumentTemplate.DT_String import String
from DocumentTemplate.DT_Util import parse_params, Eval,
html_quote

#from pprint import PrettyPrent

import pprint

# Create a class for our tag
class PPrintTag:

    name = 'pprint'
```

```
    def __init__(self, args):
        get = parse_params(args,name=None,
                           expr=None).get
        self.name = get('name')
        self.expr = get('expr')
        if self.expr is not None:
            self.expr = Eval(self.expr).eval

    def render(self, md):print template_method(o)

        if self.name is not None:
            ret = md[self.name]
        else:
            ret = self.expr(md)

        ret = pprint.pformat(ret)
        return html_quote(ret)

    __call__ = render

# Register our new tag so we can use it in a template
String.commands[PPrintTag.name] = PPrintTag

# An example that inserts a title attribut into
# a document
from DocumentTemplate import HTML
template_src="""<dtml-pprint name="title">"""

template_method = HTML(template_src)
class k: pass
o = k()
o.title = "I'm a title"
print template_method(o)


# Here's an exampl using an expresion
template_src = """<dtml-pprint expr="x+ 20">"""
o.x = 10
template_method = HTML(template_src)
print template_method(o)
```

Block tags

Block tags have an opening and closing tag that usually surround data and other tags. In the previous example we showed you how to create a tag whose attributes use Python expressions. What expressions can't do is evaluate tags, whereas block tags can.

To create a block tag, define an attribute at the class level named "blockContinuations" and set it to an empty tuple. This tells the DocumentTemplate library that this is a block tag. This attribute is also used to let the DocumentTemplate library know what other special tags there are that can exist only within the opening and closing of this block tag. We'll explain more about this in a moment.

So for now, here's an example of a note tag that produces the HTML equivalent of a yellow sticky note.

```
import sys
sys.path.append("c:\\program files\\website\\lib\\python")
from DocumentTemplate.DT_String import String

note_format = """
<table border=1 bgcolor="#FFFE7B" width="250" height="250">
<tr height=10><td valign="top">Note:</td></tr>
<tr><td valign="top">%s</td></tr>
</table>"""

class NoteTag:

    name = 'note'
    blockContinuations = ()

    def __init__(self, blocks):
        self.note = blocks[0][2]

    def render(self, md):
        note = self.note(md)

        return note_format % note

    __call__ = render

# Register the tag
String.commands[NoteTag.name] = NoteTag

from DocumentTemplate import HTML
template_src="""<dtml-note>My first note!</dtml-note>"""
template_method = HTML(template_src)
print template_method()
```

Running this script produces the following HTML:

```
<table border=1 bgcolor="#FFFE7B" width="250" height="250">
<tr height=10><td valign="top">Note:</td></tr>
<tr><td valign="top">My first note!</td></tr>
</table>
```

The biggest difference between a block tag and a singleton tag is in the constructor. Instead of taking a single string argument, it takes a two-dimensional list, named "blocks." Each item in the list represents a block in the tag. Each block has three elements:

✦ The first element is the name of the tag.

✦ The second element is the argument string for the block. It's in the same format as the argument string that is passed to the singleton constructor.

✦ The third element is a template method, the same type that you create when you make a method with the HTML class. This method was built using the source of all the text that was in between the `<dtml-note>` and `</dtml-note>` tags.

Block tags can have speacil tags that are only allowed inside of the block tag. A good example of this is the `<dtml-else>` tag that is only allowed between a `<dtml-if>` and `</dtml-if>` tag. To tell the DocumentTemplate library that your block tag has one of these special tags you add its name to the `blockContinuation` tuple of your tag's class.

The following code has been modified so that your note tag can have a subject and a body block. The subject will be all the text between the `<dtml-note>` and `<dtml-body>` tag. The body will be everything between the `<dtml-body>` and `</dtml-note>` tags. If the `<dtml-body>` tag doesn't exist then there will be no subject.

```
import sys
sys.path.append("c:\\program files\\website\\lib\\python")
from DocumentTemplate.DT_String import String


# Create a class for our tag

note_format = """
<table border=1 bgcolor="#FFFE7B" width="250" height="250">
<tr height=10><td valign="top">Note: %s</td></tr>
<tr><td valign="top">%s</td></tr>
</table>"""


class NoteTag:

    name = 'note'
    blockContinuations = ("body",)

    def __init__(self, blocks):
        #get = parse_params(args,name=None,
        #                       expr=None).get
        if len(blocks) > 2:
            raise RuntimeError, "Note tags can only have one ⮐
inner body tag!"
        elif len(blocks) == 2:
```

```
            self.header = blocks[0][2]
            del blocks[0]
        else:
            self.header = None

        self.note = blocks[0][2]

    def render(self, md):
        if self.header is not None:
            header = self.header(md)
        else:
            header = ""

        note = self.note(md)

        return note_format % (header, note)

    __call__ = render

# Register the tag
String.commands[NoteTag.name] = NoteTag

from DocumentTemplate import HTML
template_src="""<dtml-note>Read This<dtml-body>I have written a
second note!</dtml-note>"""
template_method = HTML(template_src)
print template_method()
```

Summary

After reading this chapter you should have a picture of how the core components combine to form Zope and how to use them in applications outside of Zope. Specifically, you learned how to make objects acquire properties from their parents, keep objects persistent, how to use the lightweight object request broker (ZPublisher) to make your objects available over a network, and to create your own DTML tags.

✦ ✦ ✦

CHAPTER 15

Scripting Zope

✦ ✦ ✦ ✦

In This Chapter

Overview of scripting

Jumping in with Python scripts

Under the hood of a Python script

Calling Python-based scripts

External methods

Perl-based scripts

✦ ✦ ✦ ✦

In previous chapters, you learned about DTML, a simple but powerful method of creating dynamic content, and Products, a more complex and thorough way of writing applications in Zope to handle business logic. Sometimes, however, a problem is too large to be handled elegantly in a DTML document, yet not quite large enough to warrant building an entire application around it. Sometimes, all you really want is the ability to write a small chunk of code to do something that would otherwise be cumbersome in DTML. This is where *scripts* come in.

Consider the following problem. Suppose you have an area of your Web site that needs to display the directory hierarchy up until the point of the page you are on, with each level being a link to that level. This would give you an effect similar to the object listing at the top of the management interfaces editing screens, a sort of "breadcrumbs" trail leading you from the top of your structure to where you currently are. You start by getting the folder that the document being viewed is in; then you get each parent of that object until you reach the Zope application or some arbitrary stopping point. After you have all of the objects, you take each one in turn and build a URL for it and join them all together for displaying. If you attempted to do this in DTML, you'd have a host of unwieldy pieces of code. What you really want is to be able to hand this task off to a small program written in Python. Simply pass it an object and it returns a series of URLs. To do that, you use a script.

Zope comes bundled with two powerful scripting solutions: Python Scripts and External Methods. A third option, Perl Scripts, is available as an add-on product.

Jumping in with Python Scripts

The following sections assume at least a rudimentary knowledge of the Python language. Please see Chapter 5 for a primer.

Creating a Python-based script

To create a Python-based script, select Script (Python) from the Add menu in the management interface. Enter an id and click Add and Edit. You're presented with an editing screen like the one shown in Figure 15-1.

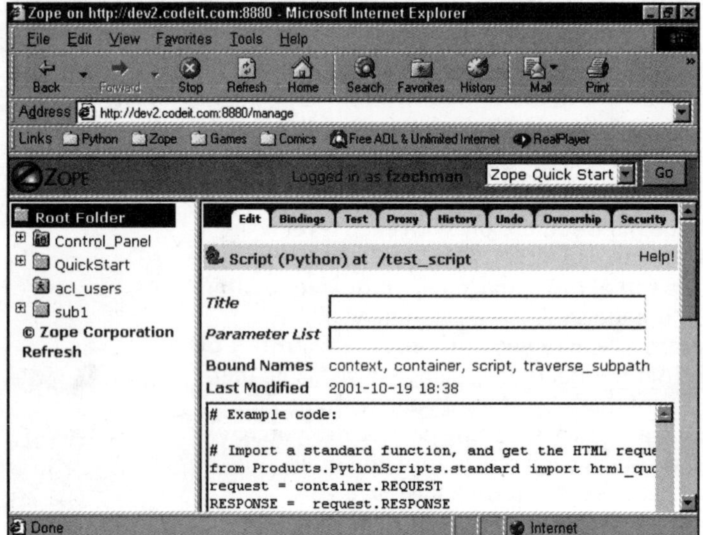

Figure 15-1: Editing a Python script

The Parameter List is just like the parameter list in a normal Python method. It is a comma-separated list of variables to be passed into the function. Default values are specified with the syntax <parameter>=<value>. Ways of passing arguments to these scripts will be described in more detail later.

The large text area is the body of the script and is where the actual Python code is placed. Almost anything you can do in a normal Python method can be done here. A few restrictions are explained later in this chapter.

When you first create a Python Script, it contains some example code that demonstrates several useful functions. Let's take a moment to examine these before you move on to one of your own.

```
# Example code:

# Import a standard function, and get the HTML request and response objects.
from Products.PythonScripts.standard import html_quote
request = container.REQUEST
RESPONSE =  request.RESPONSE

# Return a string identifying this script.
print "This is the", script.meta_type, '"%s"' % script.getId(),
if script.title:
    print "(%s)" % html_quote(script.title),
print "in", container.absolute_url()
return printed
```

The first thing the script does is to import a function from a module in Products.PythonScripts.standard. This module provides access to several useful functions for use in Python Scripts and can be examined in closer detail by opening up the standard.py file located in your Products/PythonScripts directory. This particular function, html_quote, converts characters that have special meaning in HTML to special syntax that can be displayed without being interpreted. The next thing we do is get the REQUEST object from the scripts container. This is a useful shortcut that can be used in place of passing the REQUEST to the script as an argument.

See "Calling scripts" later in this chapter for more information on passing parameters to scripts.

Notice that the script is actually printing values. Unlike a Python module run from the command line, or code run through Python's interactive shell, the values printed here don't go to the terminal where you started Zope. Instead, they are put into a special variable called `printed` that this script eventually returns. This can be a useful tool for returning complicated, formatted output to a calling object, or even to print out an entire HTML page, although we don't recommend doing that.

As a final note, you'll see that the code uses a variable called `script` and accesses several properties. This is a special bound variable and is explained in greater detail later on in this chapter under the section "Binding variables."

Now let's create a small script, the classic "Hello world!" Create a Script (Python) object with an id of `hello` and edit it. If the script has code in it already, go ahead and erase it. Fill out the fields as shown in Figure 15-2 and save.

To test your script, simply click the Test tab at the top of the form. You should get a screen with the text `"Hello World!"` on it. Easy as that!

But the script doesn't do much good if you can't pass it a parameter. Edit the script again to be like the one shown in Figure 15-3. Notice that we added a parameter to the script and supplied a default value of `World`. This means you can pass in the name that you would like the script to greet, but you may optionally leave it out and the default value of `World` will be used. Click the Test tab again. This time, you notice that it brings up a screen with an input box for the name parameter we specified. Go ahead and enter your name and click the Run Script button. It should say hello to you now! Try it again without the parameter and verify that the default works.

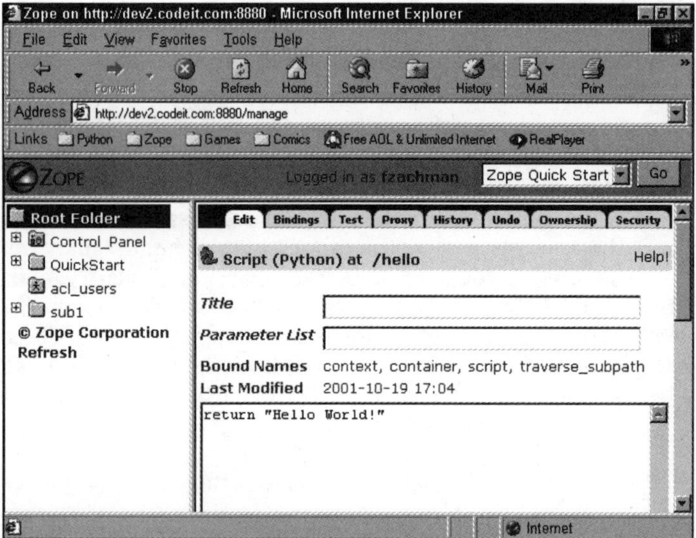

Figure 15-2: A simple script

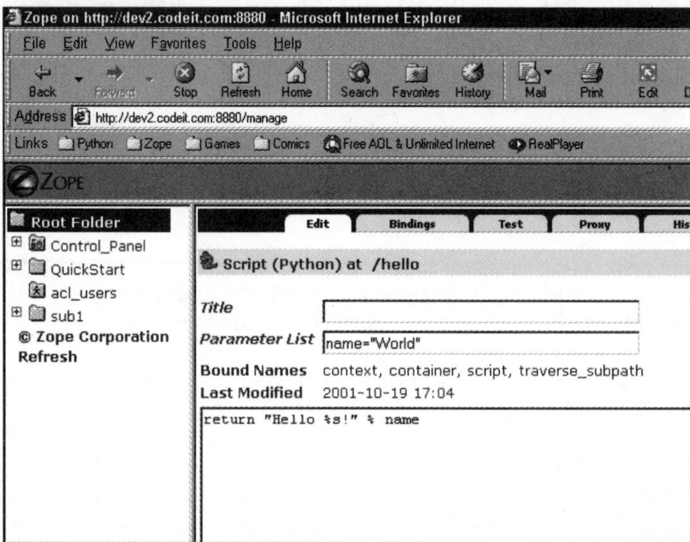

Figure 15-3: Passing parameters

Script security

Like most objects in Zope, certain security methods are enforced on scripts to limit their ability to damage both the Zope instance and the machine that is hosting it. Because Python scripts could potentially be extremely harmful, several restrictions are placed on them, altering how you might expect them to run.

Python normally supplies a set of functions available to all programs. These built-ins enable you to perform many useful, and potentially harmful, operations. Because of the danger posed by these functions, Python-based scripts give you access to only a limited subset. The following is a complete list of the standard built-ins available to Python-based scripts:

`ArithmeticError`	`TypeError`	`isinstance`
`AssertionError`	`ValueError`	`issubclass`
`AttributeError`	`ZeroDivisionError`	`len`
`EOFError`	`abs`	`list`
`EnvironmentError`	`apply`	`long`
`FloatingPointError`	`callable`	`map`
`IOError`	`chr`	`max`
`ImportError`	`cmp`	`min`
`IndexError`	`complex`	`oct`
`KeyError`	`delattr`	`ord`
`LookupError`	`divmod`	`pow`
`NameError`	`filter`	`range`
`None`	`float`	`repr`
`OSError`	`getattr`	`round`
`OverflowError`	`hasattr`	`setattr`
`RuntimeError`	`hash`	`str`
`StandardError`	`hex`	`tuple`
`SyntaxError`	`int`	

Most of these functions behave as you would expect them to in normal Python. However, `range` and `pow` are limited from producing overly large numbers and sequences. Of the missing functions, most deal with the filesystem (`open`, for example) or have the capability to affect the Zope process (such as `exit`).

In addition to the standard built-ins, Zope also provides a few bonus built-ins. `DateTime`, `test`, `namespace` and `render` are DTML utility functions. And to make up for removing the `type` function from the built-ins, Zope provides an alternative, `same_type`, which enables you to compare the type of two objects in much the same way as `type`.

Besides restrictions to standard built-ins, Zope also restricts what you may import into your scripts. Python-based scripts have access to only the following modules: `Products.PythonScripts.standard`, `AccessControl`, `string`, `random`, and `math`. Zope also monitors scripts for excessive looping and raises an error if it detects a potential infinite loop. This is to prevent a Python-based script from monopolizing CPU time and possibly reducing performance of the rest of the server or even locking it up.

And, finally, like all objects in Zope, Python-based scripts adhere to the standard security policies. The scripts themselves cannot access objects that the user calling the script does not have access to unless a Proxy Role has been placed on the script. Also, as in DTML, Python-based scripts cannot access variables whose names begin with an underscore. Zope considers these private and raises an error if you attempt it.

Binding variables

You notice an area between the Parameter List and the body of the script labeled Bound Names with a list of variables. These are hooks back into Zope's framework, giving you access to traversal and other useful information. Click the Bindings tab of the management interface. You should get a screen like the one shown in Figure 15-4.

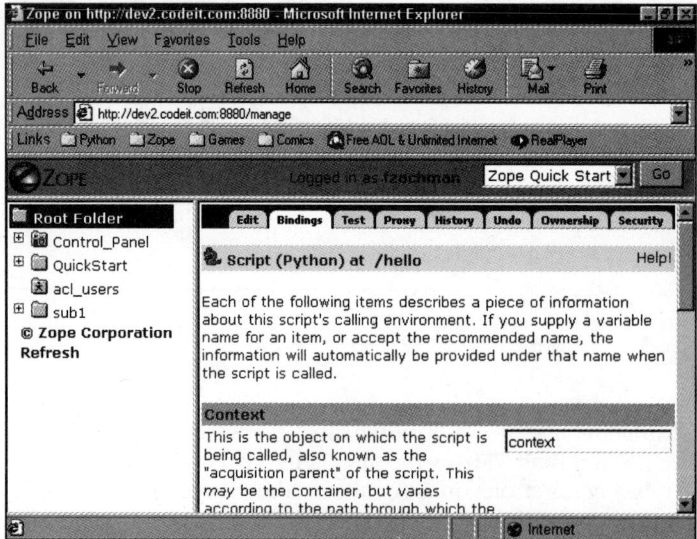

Figure 15-4: The Bindings screen

When you create a Python-based script, Zope automatically creates default values for four of the five available bound variables. Here is a list of the variables and what they are used for:

✦ **Context.** This is the object on which the script is called. Usually, this is the same as the Container, but as we learned in the section about Acquisition in Chapter 14, through the trickeries of Traversal, we can essentially make any script, anywhere, be called on any other object in the Zope Hierarchy. The default value for this variable is `context`.

✦ **Container.** This is the actual container (usually a Zope folder) where the script resides. This is useful for calling other methods stored in the same folder. The default value is `container`.

✦ **Script.** This refers to the script object itself and defaults to `script`.

✦ **Namespace.** By default, this variable is left blank, but its recommended value is an underscore character. If this script is called from DTML, this variable is set to be the namespace of the caller. Normally, a script searches for its parameters in the `REQUEST` object if no parameters are passed in (see "Calling scripts from DTML," later in this chapter.) If this variable is set, it instead searches through the namespace (eventually getting to the request object).

✦ **Subpath.** If this script was traversed to in a URL, Subpath contains all the elements of the URL that occur after the script. If a script named `some-script` was called in the URL `/foo/some-script/bar/spam`, Subpath would be a list containing the strings `bar` and `spam`. This variable defaults to `traverse_subpath`.

A simple script probably won't use any of these variables, but they can come in very handy for more complex problems. They're also quite helpful for debugging your scripts.

Under the Hood of a Python Script

A Zope Python script is, in essence, a Python method defined through Zope. Zope takes the parameters and body you supply and converts it into a callable python method, which runs just like you would expect it to. A lot of trickery is involved behind the scenes in order to get your function to be called on the right object and obey Zope's security restrictions, but if you think of it as a normal python method with limited access, you'll do fine.

Calling Python-Based Scripts

You can call a Python-based script just like you would any other object in Zope. The two primary methods are, of course, calling it from inside of another Zope object (including other scripts and DTML methods), and calling it directly via a URL. For most Zope Web applications, the former will probably be the most used way.

However, for advanced functions, usually where another client that understands HTTP wants to talk to your server, calling a script from the URL can be a powerful tool. We'll look at both of these methods in the following sections.

Calling scripts from DTML

Calling your scripts from inside DTML is done in much the same way as you would call a DTML method. If you just need to run the code but aren't interested in displaying any returned results, simply use the `dtml-call` syntax. To display the returned results, use the `dtml-var` syntax. It becomes interesting when you must decide how to pass parameters to your scripts.

Parameters can be passed two ways, explicitly or implicitly. Explicitly passing one or more parameters to a script requires you to treat it exactly as you would a normal python function call. Suppose you had a Python-based script called `retrieveCustomerInfo` that took the parameter `customerId`, processed some information, did some formatting, and returned some information about that customer. Now suppose you had a DTML document that looped through a list of `customerId` and displayed their information. It would probably look something like this:

```
<dtml-in customerIds>
  <dtml-var expr="retrieveCustomerInfo(customerId=_['sequence-
item'])"><BR>
</dtml-in>
```

Simple enough, right? But there are shortcuts — ways to get your parameters to be passed without explicitly specifying them. If you don't pass any parameters to a script that requires one or more, Zope examines the `REQUEST` object to see if it can find the required parameters there. This behavior also works if you have a form that submits directly to a Python-based script. Any form variables that match parameters of the script will be matched up. Any form variables that don't have a counterpart in the Parameter List will be ignored and unavailable in the script.

As mentioned earlier, if the `Namespace` variable is bound, the script also attempts to find the needed variables in calling objects `Namespace`. These are usually other objects, such as a folder.

See Chapter 4 for details about Zope's `Namespace` and what might be found there.

Let's test this out using our Hello World script created earlier in the chapter. Create a DTML Document called helloDoc in the same folder as your script with the following bit of code in its body:

```
<dtml-var expr="hello(name='John')">
```

Now view the page. You should see the value returned by the script displayed. You notice that the name `'John'` was passed explicitly to the script. Now let's alter it a little bit. Change your page to look like the following:

```
<dtml-call "REQUEST.set('name', 'John')">
<dtml-var hello>
```

View the page again. You now see that even though we didn't explicitly pass the parameter `name` in, Zope searched the request and matched the value up anyway.

Now, let's do one final example to make it all a bit more interactive. Here we create a form that enables a user to input the name to be passed to the script. We also use a common programming technique of having the form post back to itself and deal with the displaying of the results. Edit helloDoc to contain the following code:

```
<form action="./" method="POST">
  Name: <input type="text" name="name" value="">
  <input type="submit" value="Submit">
</form>
<p>
<dtml-if "REQUEST.get('REQUEST_METHOD')=='POST'">
  <dtml-var hello>
</dtml-if>
```

Try the page and enter your own name. When you submit, it says hello to you! And again, we've taken advantage of implicit argument passing. Since form variables are placed on the REQUEST, the script will automatically retrieve them.

Note that we could have changed the action of the form to submit directly to the hello script, but the results would not have been formatted with your header and footer. There are times when this may not be such a bad thing—for example, if you call a RESPONSE.redirect() at the end of the script. But in general, you'll still be calling it from another object.

Calling scripts from a URL

Navigating to a script via URL is fairly simple. The interesting thing is that you can change the Context that a script is called in, and thus the object that it is called on, via the intricacies of Zope's acquisition framework. Suppose you have a directory structure similar to the one in the following list:

- ✦ (Folder) plants
  - (Object) ficus
  - (Object) figs
- ✦ (Folder) animals
  - (Object) dogs
- ✦ (Folder) tasks
  - (Script) feed
  - (Script) water

To call the `Water` script on the `ficus` object, you would call `/plants/tasks/ficus/water`. Because of the way Zope does Acquisition, it is able to properly find all the objects in the URL, and because of the way we've called our script, the context that `water` operates in is the `ficus` object. To call `feed` on the `dogs` would be handled the same way by calling `/animals/tasks/feed/dogs`.

For more information on acquisition, see Chapter 14.

A practical example

Let's take our breadcrumbs example from the beginning of the chapter and actually implement it. Create a Python script called `breadcrumbs` with the following code in the body:

```
# Take the object that this script is called on (the context)
# and traverse up to the root, getting the ID of each object.

object = context
path = []  # A list of id's, one for each object.

while 1:
# The root application doesn't have an ID attribute, instead it
# has a method that returns the id. So we check to see if the
# objects id is a method or a string. If it is a method we've
# reached the top of our trail.

  if same_type(object.id, ''):
    path.append(object.id)
    object = object.aq_parent  # Get the parent of this object
and loop
  else:
    break

# Because we started at the bottom and went up, we'll
# want to reverse the order of the trail so that the
# first item is at the top most object.

path.reverse()

# Since we didn't include the root object in our list of
# breadcrumbs we'll want to prepopulate it.
breadcrumbs = "<a href='/'>/</a>"

for i in range(0, len(path)):
  id = path[i]
  url = "/%s" % (string.join(path[:i+1], '/')) # URL is all ⮐
id's up to this one
  href = "<a href='%s'>%s</a>" % (url, id)
  breadcrumbs = "%s%s/" % (breadcrumbs, href)

return breadcrumbs
```

Now, edit your `standard_html_header` to include the following code somewhere below the body:

```
<dtml-var breadcrumbs><BR>
```

Create a directory structure a few layers deep with an `index_html` that includes the `standard_html_header` in each one. View the page at the bottom of the tree. You should see a page similar to the one shown in Figure 15-5. Each link at the top should take you back to the particular directory as named.

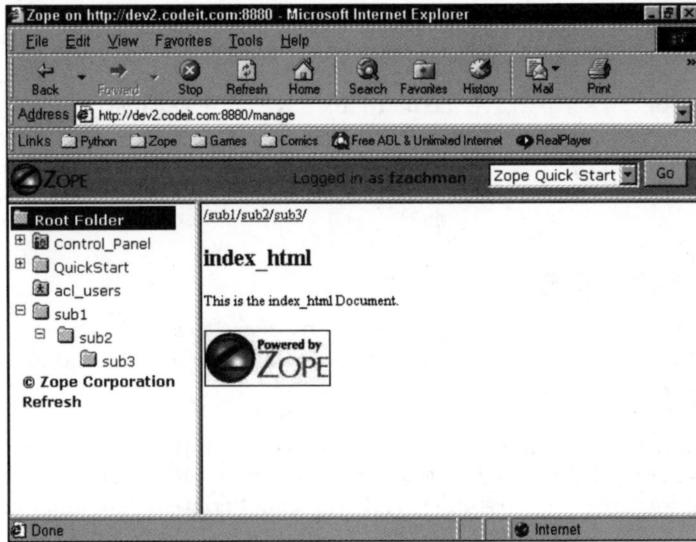

Figure 15-5: Breadcrumbs

External Methods

Zope provides another method of scripting with Python, that of External Methods. They're called External Methods because the code that you write lies outside of the ZODB and instead resides in the filesystem. An external method is simply a method, written in Python, whose module is in the `/Extensions` folder of the Zope installation. To create one, you need access to the filesystem directly, or at least enough to FTP/SCP your file to the appropriate location.

Open up an editor and create a file called `Hello.py` with the following contents:

```
def helloMethod(name="World"):
    return "Hello %s!" % name
```

Save the file to the `/Extensions` directory under your Zope installation. If you don't have access to the filesystem where your Zope installation is running, you need to talk to your system administrator.

After the module is on the filesystem, you need to create a Zope External Method object. From the Zope Add menu, select External Method. Enter **externalHello** for the Id, **Hello** for the Module Name, and **helloMethod** for the Function Name. Click add. You should now have a Zope object called `externalHello`. You can call this from DTML or traverse it from the Web just like you would a normal Python-based script. It behaves in much the same way.

Why external methods?

So, the big question is, why would you want to go through all the trouble of an External Method when you could just create a Python-based script? As we saw in the previous section, Python-based scripts are powerful, but they are also limited. If you have a particular module you want to import, chances are it won't be available in a simple Python-based script. External methods have far fewer restrictions. With them, you can access arbitrary packages, the filesystem, or the network. This lessening of security in the script itself is offset by the fact that you must have access to the filesystem.

A practical example

In order to perform the following example, you need access to an FTP server. If you don't have access to one, you can use Zope's built-in FTP server to upload the file to the root of your Zope instance.

Suppose that each day you need to upload some data via FTP to a remote server. The file is a simple comma-delimited text file created from some data pulled from a SQL database and formatted in a python script. The exact contents are unimportant, as long as it's a simple text file.

Open up a text editor and create a file called `dailyUpload.py` that looks like the following, replacing the values for HOST, PORT, USER, and PASSWORD with your FTP information:

```
from ftplib import FTP
from StringIO import StringIO
from string import join
from DateTime import DateTime

# Replace the contents of the following
# variables with your own FTP values.

HOST = '##Your FTP Server##'
PORT = '##The Port it connects to. Blank for default##'
USER = '##User name##'
PASSWORD = '##Password##'
```

```
def ftpData(self, data):
    # Create the file object from the string data supplied
    file = StringIO(data)

    # Next, login to the FTP server.
    ftp = FTP()
    ftp.connect(HOST, PORT)
    ftp.login(USER, PASSWORD)

    # DateStamp the data then upload it.
    date = DateTime()
    dateStamp = join([str(date.year()),
                      str(date.month()),
                      str(date.day())], '-')
    filename = 'file_%s' % dateStamp
    command = "STOR %s" % filename
    ftp.storlines(command, file)

    # Logout
    ftp.close()
```

Place the file in the `/Extensions` directory of your Zope installation. Now create an External Method object with an id of `dailyUpload`, a module name of `dailyUpload`, and a Function name of `ftpData`. Create a simple text file in your editor and upload it to a File object called `data` in the same directory as your External Method. The contents don't matter. Now create a Python script like the one shown in Figure 15-6.

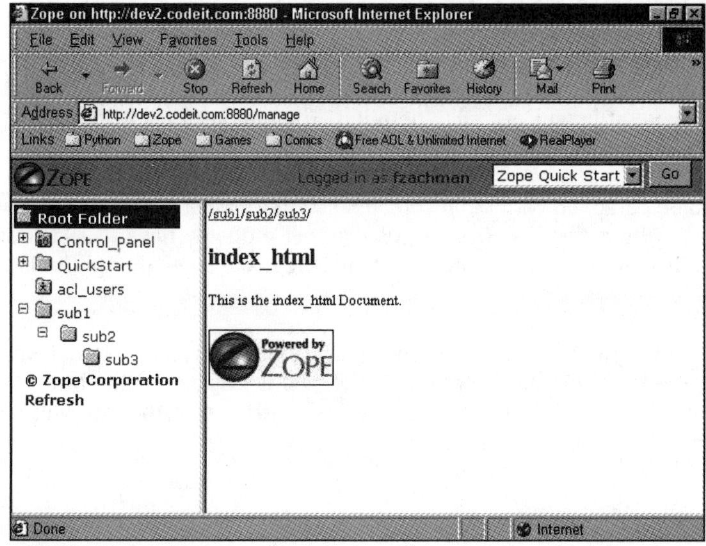

Figure 15-6: uploadData script

Test the script and then log in to your FTP server to verify that the data was successfully transferred.

Changes to External Methods are not immediately available to Zope. If you edit the code of an External Method, you need to edit Zopes External Method object. Restarting the server will also refresh the code.

Perl-Based Scripts

Because Zope is itself written in Python, it's relatively easy to provide Python-based Scripts and External Methods. But for all its power, Python just doesn't do some things as well as other languages. Perl is a powerful language, similar to Python, that many Web developers are already familiar with. As such, there are Perl versions of both the Zope embedded scripts and External methods.

This section assumes you are installing in a Linux environment.

Unlike Python scripts, Perl scripts don't yet have the restrictions that limit the amount of Memory or CPU time taken up by them. As such, it's possible for someone to write a Perl script that will monopolize server time and could bring your Zope installation to a halt.

Before installing Script (Perl)

Before you can install Perl-based scripts, you need to make sure that Perl is installed. Installing Perl is beyond the scope of this book, but the rest of the setup requires that you have at least Perl 5.6.0 installed. You can get Perl from the Comprehensive Perl Archive Network at `www.cpan.org`.

Perl needs to be compiled with Multi Threading support. Most binary distributions are compiled without threads. This means you will probably have to install and compile it from source. For the CPAN source version, make sure you run Configure with the `-Dusethreads` flag.

After Perl is installed, you need to install the `pyperl` module. In a nutshell, this enables you to embed Perl inside of Python. None of it is Zope specific, but it is needed by the Zoperl product later on. Pyperl and Zoperl can both be downloaded from `http://downloads.activestate.com//Zope-Perl/`.

Installing Zoperl

Now that we have both Perl and Pyperl installed, we need to install Zoperl. This can be downloaded from the same location as Pyperl at `www.activestate.com`. Extract the archive to a directory and open the README file. You should follow the instructions available for the version of Zoperl that you're installing. The easiest way to install it is to simply run the `install.pl` script. It prompts you for a list of products to install. You want to install the PerlExternalMethod and PerlMethod products. It may also prompt you to install Hack::Names. This is normal and is required by some versions of Zoperl. After the installer has run, restart your Zope instance and you should be ready to go.

The README of Zoperl goes into detailed instructions for installing the entire process on Windows. If you are running Zope on a Windows machine and would like to get Zoperl working, please refer to the instructions therein.

Using Perl-based scripts

Perl-based scripts in general work exactly like their Python counterparts as far as passing parameters to them and returning results is concerned. They also have the same access to Zope objects.

Here's an example that returns the id of the object in the current context:

```
my $context = shift;

$data = "Hello. You are viewing: $context->title_or_id";

return $data
```

Summary

In this chapter, you discovered how to program Zope via several scripting methods, including External Scripts, Python Script Objects, and Perl Script Objects. Scripts are useful for automating a series of operations and/or adding business logic to a Web site.

✦ ✦ ✦

CHAPTER 16

ZClasses

✦ ✦ ✦ ✦

In This Chapter

What are ZClasses?

Creating a simple ZClass

ZClasses and property sheets

Automatically generating ZClass views

Creating simple applications using ZClasses

ZClasses and security

Creating CatalogAware ZClasses

Subclassing ZClasses from Python base classes

Distributing ZClass products

✦ ✦ ✦ ✦

While Zope comes with a rich variety of built-in object types such as Images, Files, Documents, Folders, and Methods, occasionally you may need to define a new object type that will work within Zope.

New object types are defined within Products. There are two ways to define new object types within Zope:

- ✦ File system–based Python Products
- ✦ Through-the-Web Products using ZClasses

Python product development is covered extensively in Part II of this book. In this chapter, we explain when and how to use ZClasses to define new object types.

What are ZClasses? OOP and Classes

In standard OOP (object-oriented programming) parlance, a *class* is a blueprint or prototype that defines the variables and the methods common to all objects of a certain kind, which are also known as *instances* of the class.

So, all Folder objects within Zope are really instances of the Folder class. Everything about how Folders behave is defined within that class. For example, the functionality that enables Folders to contain other objects and list the objects within them.

However, not all folders are identical. Folders can contain different objects and they can have different properties. These attributes are not defined in the class, which is only concerned with those things that instances have in common.

Through-the-Web ZClasses

You may be wondering, if all of Zope's standard objects are defined in Python Products, then why not use those instead of ZClasses?

Well, creating Python Products requires knowledge of the Python programming language. Beginning Zope users may not have the required programming skill to create a Python Product for Zope. Therefore, Zope has a way for users to define new object types through the Web by creating what are called *ZClasses*.

ZClasses enable you to create Products and new object types (classes) entirely through the Web, without resorting to creating files on the file system.

ZClass-based products can be redistributed to other Zope users, and can generally be modified after they've been installed if the user has management privileges on the Root Folder, unless the developer has chosen to disallow such modification.

ZClass disadvantages

So if ZClasses are so great, why not use them for everything? Why are the standard object types developed as Python Products, instead of ZClasses?

ZClasses do have some disadvantages. Many programmers like using powerful filesystem-based development tools such as editors, versioning systems, debuggers, and so on. Because ZClasses are stored entirely within the ZODB (Zope Object Database), they aren't accessible to filesystem-based tools. This imposes a practical upper limit to the complexity of ZClass-based products, and the browser textarea editing that Zope provides isn't very productive compared to a powerful text editor.

It's expected that in future versions of Zope, the distinction between file system-based products and through-the-Web products will diminish, or even disappear, but for the moment, ZClasses and Python Products are still distinct.

Creating a Simple ZClass

In this section, we show you step-by-step how to create a simple ZClass. All of the interesting parts will happen inside the special Products folder, which is in the Control_Panel, as you can see in Figure 16-1.

As you can see, the Products folder contains a number of listings. If you haven't added or created any through-the-Web products to your Zope installation yet, then all of the products are indicated by "closed box" icons. As we shall soon see, through-the-Web products have "open box" icons.

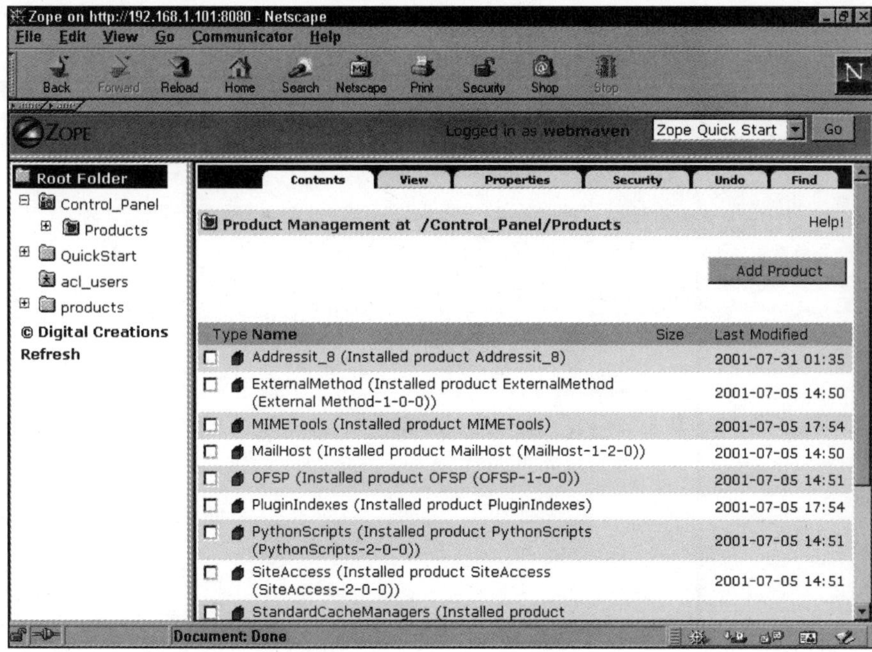

Figure 16-1: The Products folder

Creating the product

In the `/Control-Panel/Products` folder, click the Add Product button. You'll be presented with a form similar to the form shown in Figure 16-2.

Type **SimpleProduct** for the id for the Product, and click the Generate button. You'll be returned to the `/Control_Panel/Products/` folder, and you should see "SimpleProduct" in the list, as shown in Figure 16-3.

Click SimpleProduct and take a look at the screen that appears, which should look like the screen shown in Figure 16-4.

You can see a few new things in your product that distinguish it from other container-type objects:

✦ A Folder object with a question mark in its icon called "Help (SimpleProduct)." The Help folder can be used to contain product-specific help topics.

✦ Two new tabs, Define Permissions and Distribution.

Another difference that is only apparent if you examine the Add list drop-down menu is that there are several new objects available to add in your Product, including ZClass, Zope Permission, and Zope Factory.

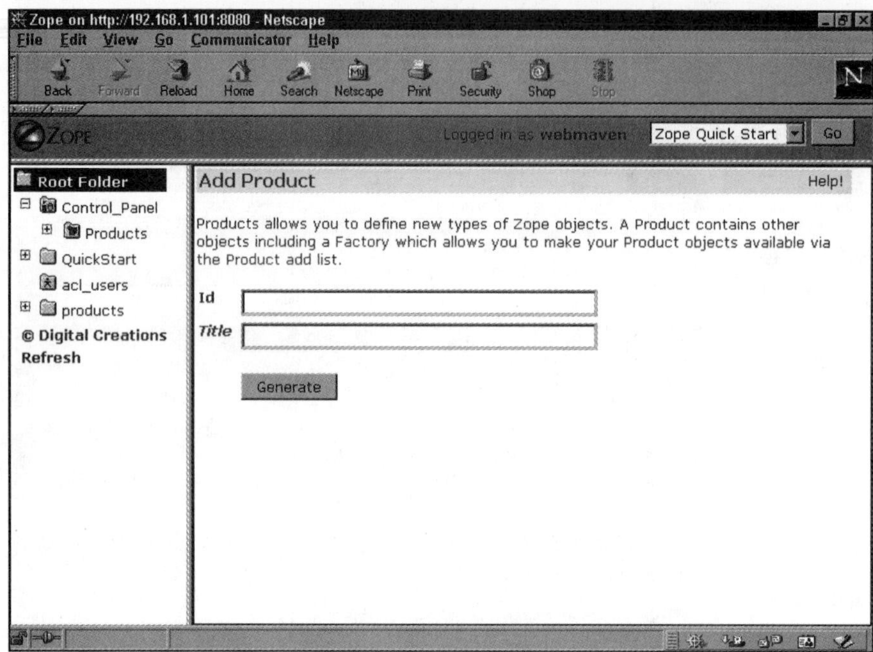

Figure 16-2: The Add Product form

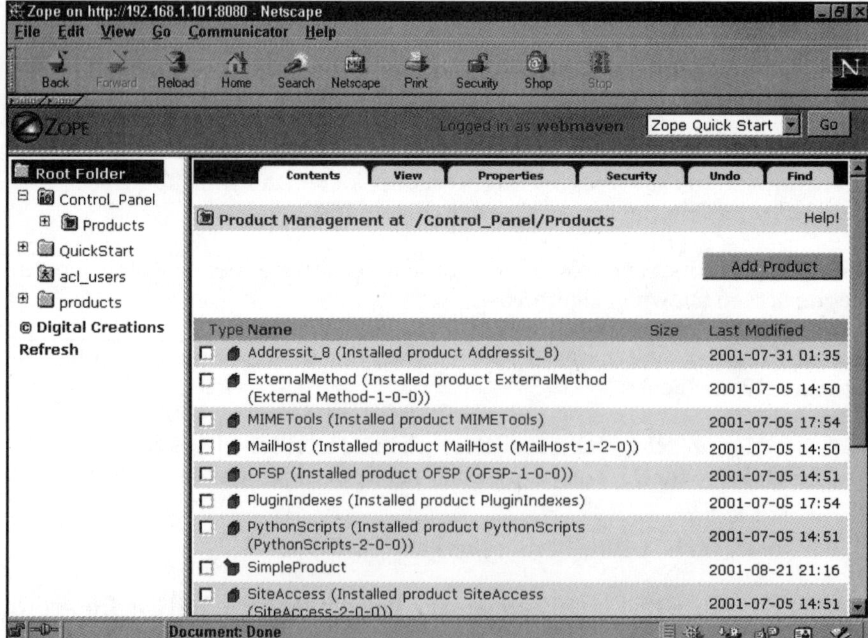

Figure 16-3: The SimpleProduct in the Products folder

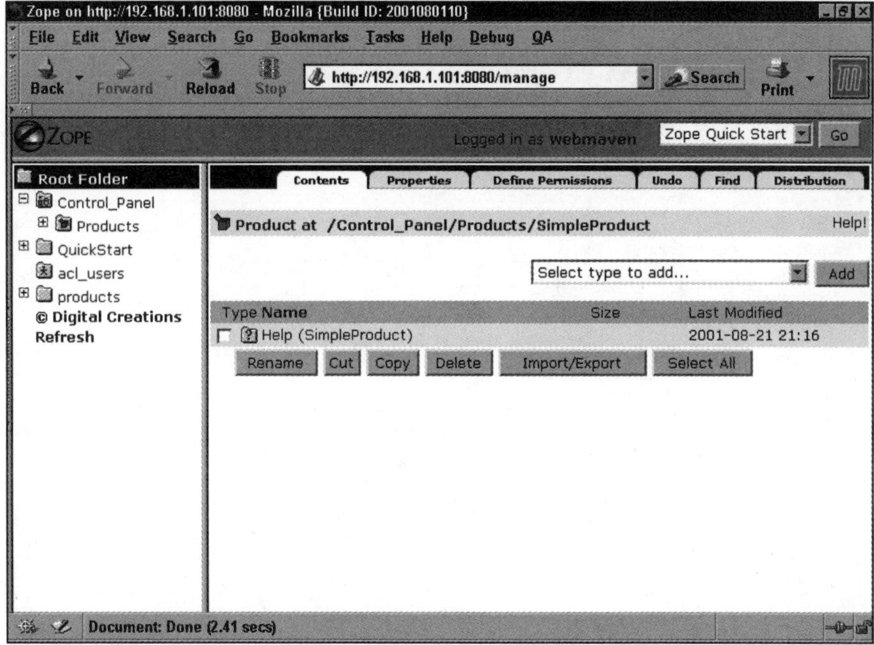

Figure 16-4: The Empty SimpleProduct

Creating the ZClass

So let's create a new object type. We won't have you create anything particularly complex to begin with, just an object that displays a single property.

Using the Add list drop-down menu in the SimpleProduct Contents tab, choose ZClass, which will display the Add ZClass form, as shown in Figure 16-5.

This form has several elements, but we're not concerned with most of them just yet. For now, set the id of the ZClass to **SimpleZClass** and the meta-type to Simple. Leave the two checkboxes ("Create constructor objects?" and "Include standard Zope persistent object base classes?") checked, and click the Add button. You should be returned to the SimpleProduct Contents view, where you should see several new objects as shown in Figure 16-6.

The second object listed, with the white box icon, is the actual SimpleZClass ZClass.

There are also two DTML methods: `SimpleZClass_add`, which is the method that actually creates an instance of your ZClass where it gets called, and sets its id and title, and `SimpleZClass_addForm`, which is the form that is displayed when you choose to add a Simple object from the Add list drop-down menu. This form let's you choose the id of the instance, and pass it along with the other given variables on to the `SimpleZClass_add` method for the actual construction.

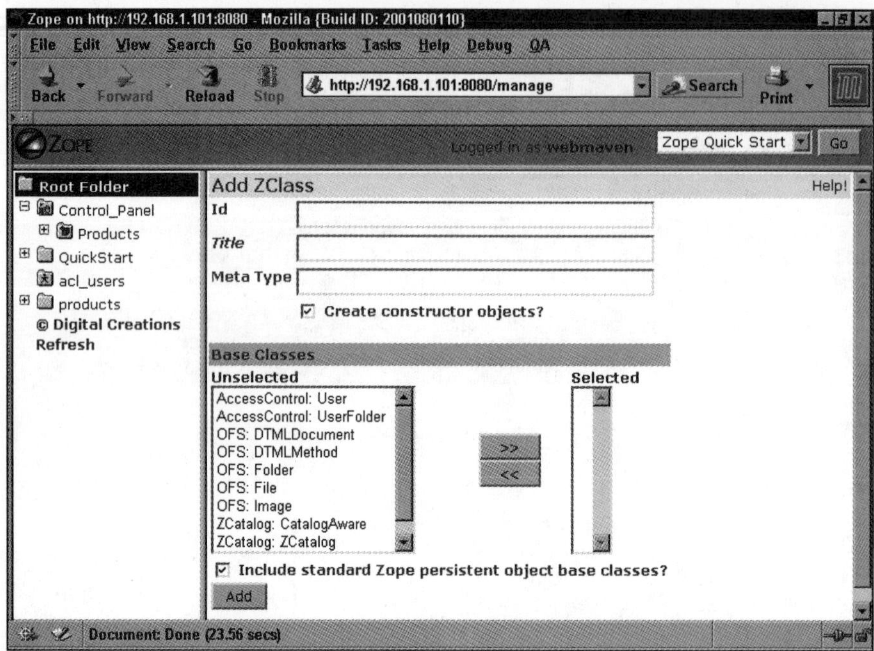

Figure 16-5: The Add ZClass form

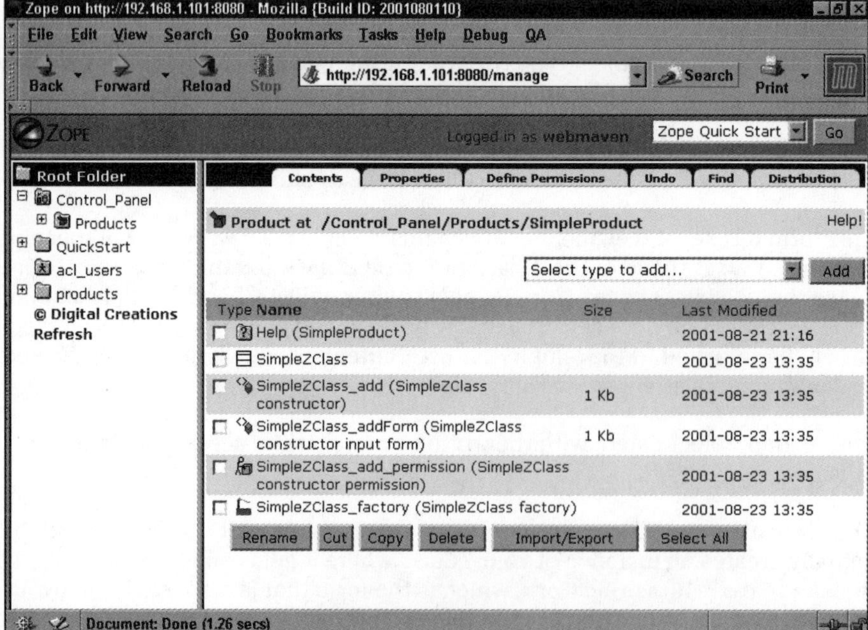

Figure 16-6: The SimpleProduct with SimpleZClass

`SimpleZClass_add_permission` is represented by a stick figure carrying a box, and defines a permission that you can associate with the ability to create "Simple" objects. You can use this to control who can and cannot create objects within your site, just as with any other object. You can also control the name of the permission using this object.

`SimpleZClass_factory` is a special object that tells Zope about the name of the object in the Add list, as well as what method must be called when it is selected in the list (in this case it is `SimpleZClass_addForm`), and what permission a user needs to have to be able to add this object (in this case `SimpleZClass_add_permission`).

At this point, you can go ahead and actually add "Simple" objects to normal folders. So, navigate to your root folder and choose "Simple" from the "Add" list drop-down menu. You'll be presented with a form to set the id of the object. Use and id "simpletest" and click "Add". This will actually create the object in the folder.

Unfortunately, the Simple object, which is an instance of the SimpleZClass ZClass, doesn't actually do anything yet, so let's show you how to enhance it a bit.

Adding a default view

When Zope publishes an object, the first thing it looks for is an `index_html` method. If it can't find one for the object, it tries to acquire one. In this case, your `SimpleZCLass` object does not have an `index_html` method, so it acquires one from containing Root Folder.

Go back to the `/Control_Panel/Products/` folder, and click the SimpleProduct item. Then click the SimpleZClass item. You should be on the Methods tab by default, so choose "DTML Method" from the Add list drop-down menu, and name the method **index_html**. Click the Add and Edit button to change the default code for a method to the following:

```
<dtml-var standard_html_header>
<h3>This is a Simple object.</h3>
Not much to see here yet.
<dtml-var standard_html_footer>
```

After you click Save Changes, you can click the text. SimpleZClass, in the path at the top of the frame to return to the Methods tab of the ZClass. Next, click the Views tab of the ZClass, which should look like Figure 16-7.

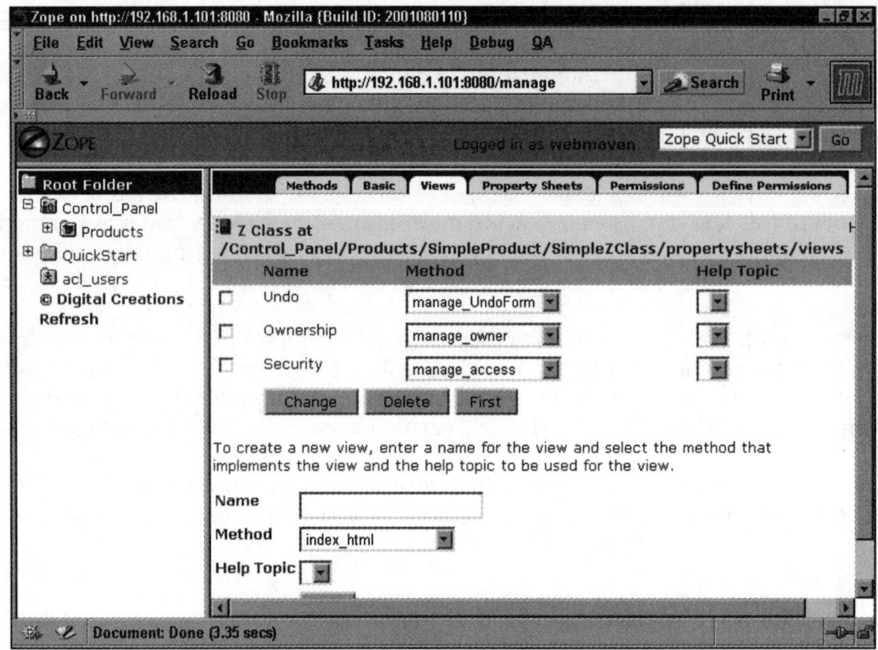

Figure 16-7: The SimpleZCLass Views tab

You can see here that three views are currently defined for the ZClass: Undo, Ownership, and Security, which not coincidentally are the three tabs available when you click on the simpletest Simple object we added to the root folder earlier.

What you're going to do next is add a View tab to the ZClass. Type in the name **View** into the Name field of the form at the bottom of the Views tab. Make sure that the method selected in the Method drop-down menu is `index_html`, and click the Add button. (See Figure 16-8.)

Now that you've added a "View" view to the ZClass, take a look at the instance that you already added to the Root Folder at `/simpletest` by clicking on it in the Root Folder. You should see that the ZClass now has a new tab named "View." Click it to see the ZClass `index_html` method, as shown in Figure 16-9.

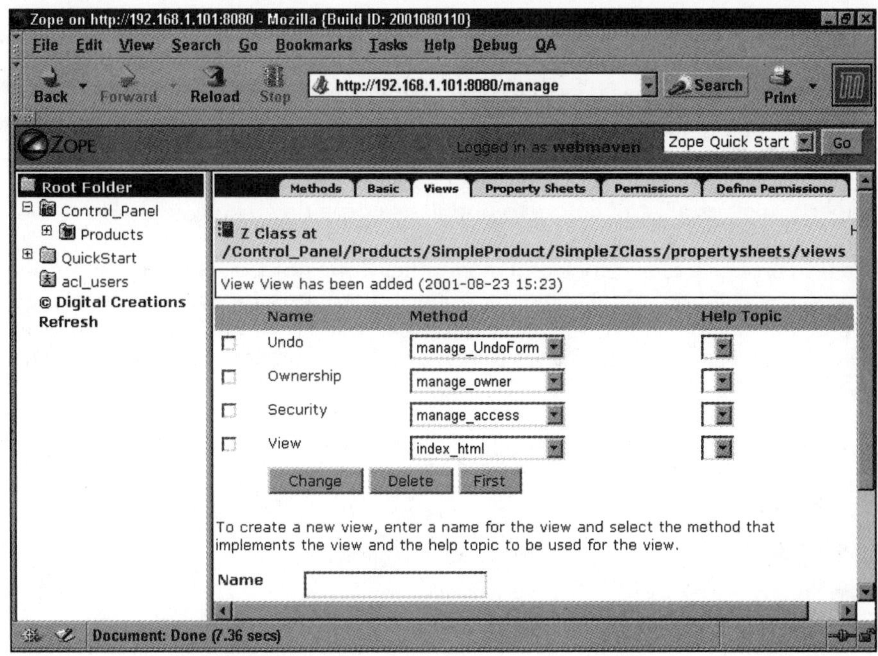

Figure 16-8: After adding the "View" view

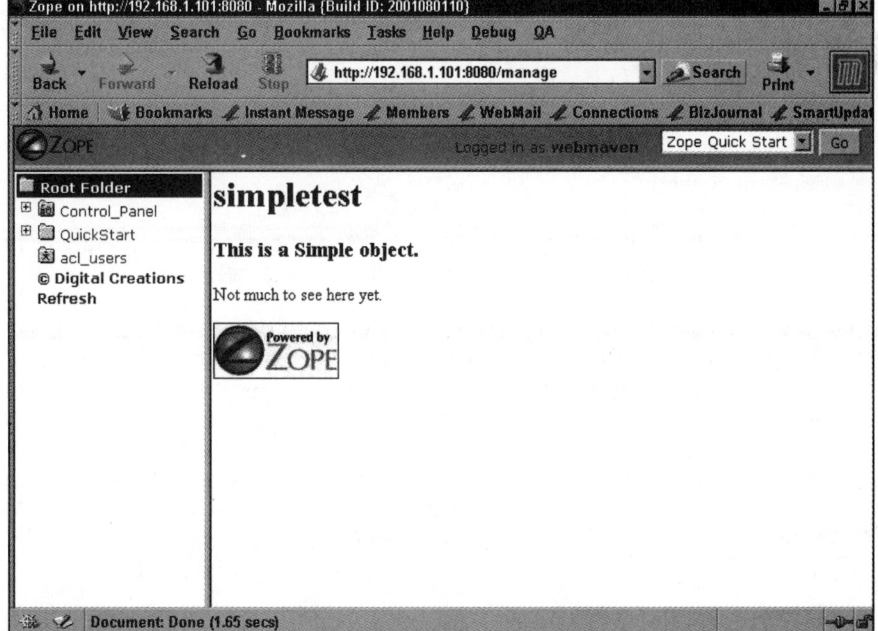

Figure 16-9: The ZClass rendered `index_html` method

ZClasses and PropertySheets

Adding new object types is all very well, but if those objects can't have custom attributes, then they won't be much use. Zope objects have attributes called Properties that can be generically created and assigned values through the Properties tab. In this way, you can edit a Folder object's title, or add a custom property such as a list of colors to populate a drop-down box.

The title property of a Folder, and most other Zope objects, is a built-in property. However, specialized objects need specialized property types, and occasionally default values. To support this, you can define and add your own custom properties to your ZClasses, build interfaces to manage them, and access those properties from DTML.

Zope has several property types you can use:

- Boolean
- Date
- Float
- Int
- Lines
- Long
- String
- Text
- Token
- Selection
- Multiple Selection

Most of these represent ordinary attribute types, and correspond directly to their namesakes from Python. A few deserve a bit more explanation.

Lines properties are basically a list of strings. The typical representation of a lines property is a form text element containing rows separated by carriage returns. This property can be iterated over from within DTML to access its individual strings. Like the list type in Python, the order of the elements is preserved.

Text properties are essentially string properties, except that Zope takes care of converting the line ending character supplied by the browser to a standard internal representation. It's meant to store values from a text form element.

Tokens, like lines properties, are sequences of strings. Unlike lines, which separate their elements with carriage returns (enabling multiple words in each string), Tokens separate the strings with spaces, so that what is stored is a sequence of single word strings, rather than arbitrary strings.

Selection and *Multiple Selection* properties are used to store the values of selection and multiple selection form elements.

Using simple property types

In order to use properties, they must first be added into the ZClass. ZClasses have special objects for containing property definitions called *property sheets*.

You can add a Property Sheet by navigating to the Simple product by clicking the Control Panel in the Root Folder, and then clicking on Products, and finally clicking on SimpleProduct. Next, click the SimpleZClass.

ZClasses have a tab for managing property sheets, called, of course, "Property Sheets." Click the Property Sheets tab as shown in Figure 16-10.

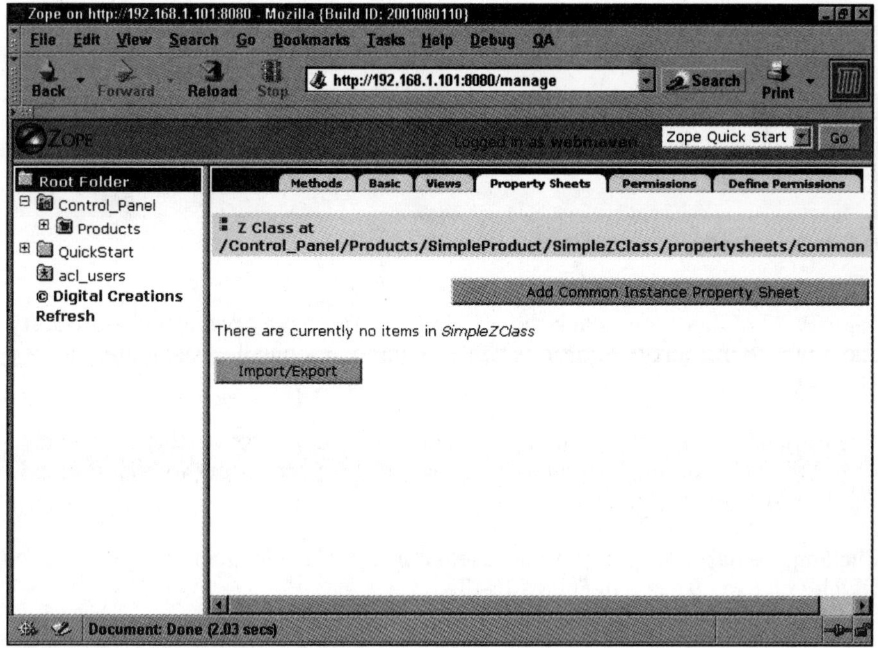

Figure 16-10: The Property Sheets tab

As you can see in Figure 16-10, the SimpleZClass doesn't have any property sheets defined, so you don't have anywhere to place your property definitions yet. You can remedy this quite easily by clicking the Add Common Instance Property Sheet button, which brings up a simple form requesting an id and a title, as shown in Figure 16-11.

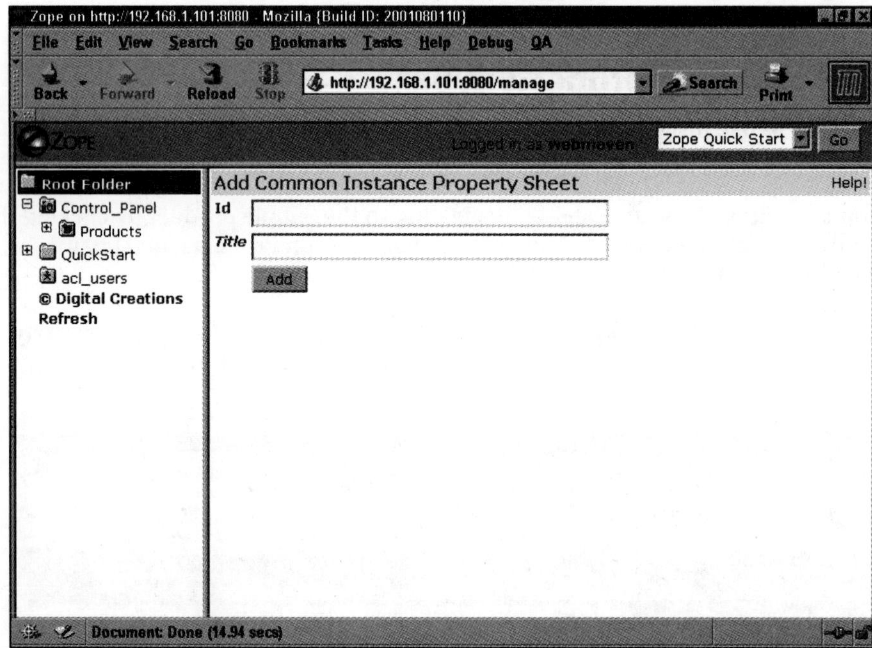

Figure 16-11: The Property Sheet Add form

Fill in an id of **Basic**, and click the Add button. You have now added a property sheet whose property definitions will be shared among all of the instances of your ZClass (hence, a "common instance" property sheet).

The Property Sheets tab (which you were returned to after adding a property sheet) now shows the existence of the "Basic" property sheet we just created, as Figure 16-12 demonstrates.

Clicking the Basic property sheet reveals the interface for managing properties, which you can also see in Figure 16-13.

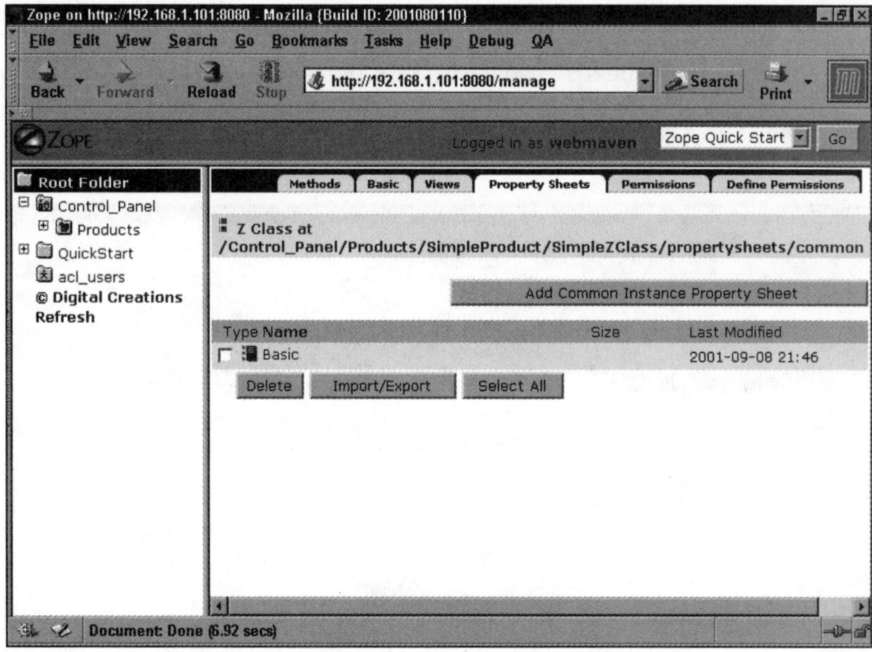

Figure 16-12: The Property Sheets tab, with the Basic property sheet

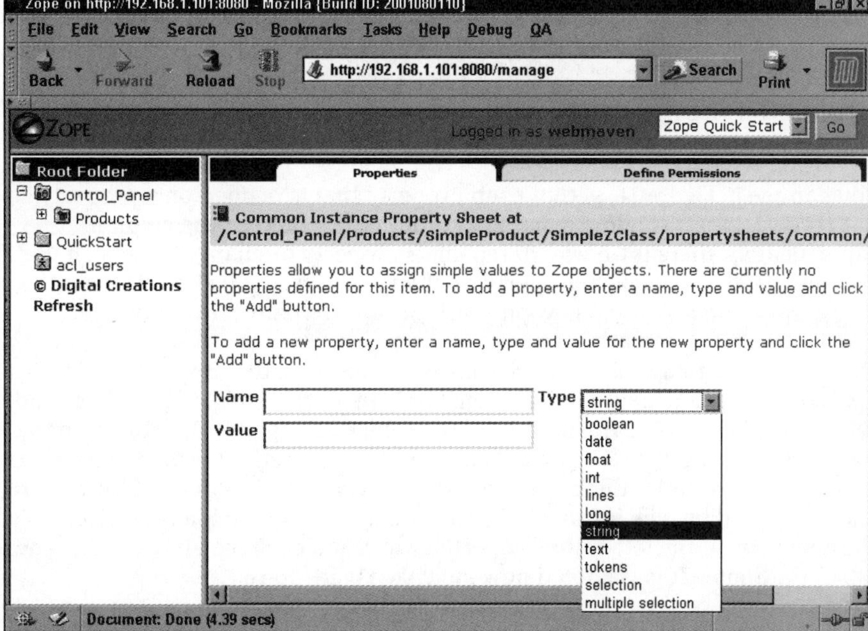

Figure 16-13: The "Basic" property sheet

Figure 16-13 also illustrates the types of properties that can be added, as described earlier in this chapter. For now, add a string property to the property sheet with a name of "title." Fill in the name field with **title** and make sure that the drop-down is set to "string." Leave the Value field blank. Click the Add button, and your property sheet should now look like Figure 16-14.

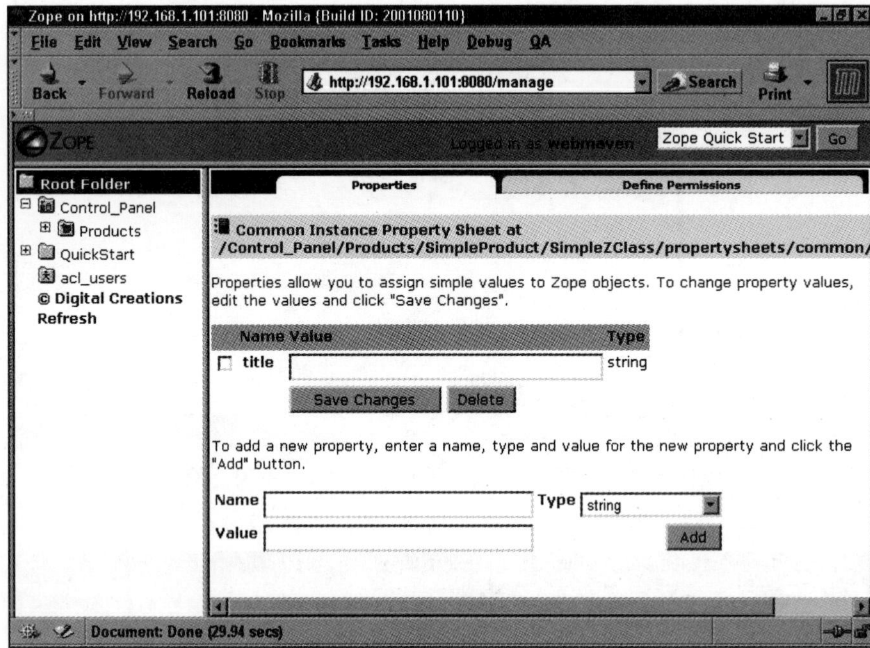

Figure 16-14: Adding the "title" string property

You can see in Figure 16-14 that each property that is defined on a property sheet has three columns: a name column, a value column, and a type column. Unfortunately, there is no way to rename a property or change its type. If you find that you need to rename a property or change its type, you should delete the property in question and add a new one with the appropriate name and type.

One of the nice things about ZClass property sheets is that Zope can automatically construct a management tab for them. Navigate back to the SimpleZClass and click the Views tab. Scroll to the bottom of the screen and type **Properties** into the Name field. Select propertysheets/Basic/manage from the method drop-down menu, as shown in Figure 16-15. Click Add, and you'll see a new View defined for the property sheet. It would be nice for this to be the default view of the Simple object, so check the checkbox to the left of the Properties view, and click the First button. The View tab of the SimpleZClass should now look like Figure 16-16.

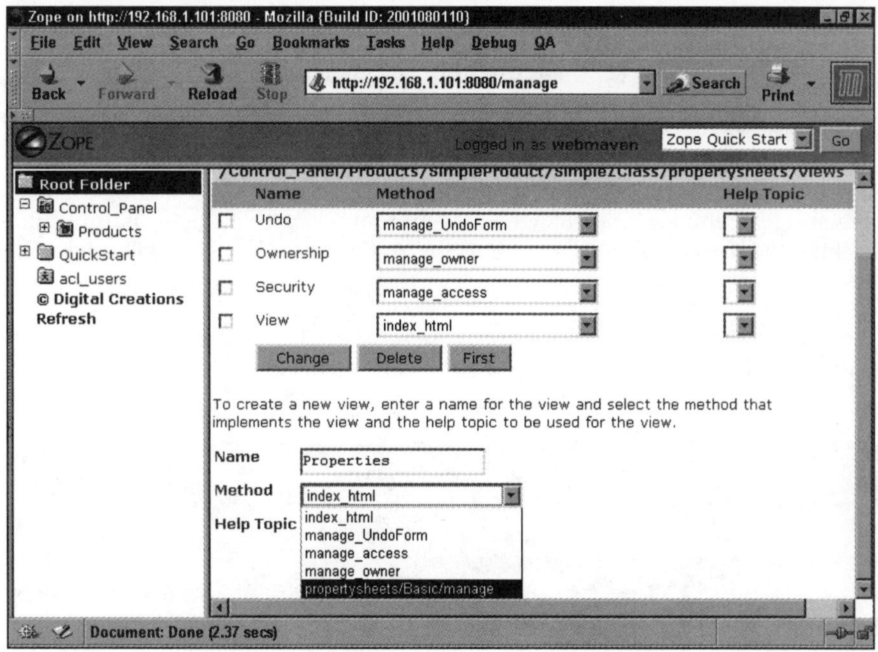

Figure 16-15: Adding the "Properties" view

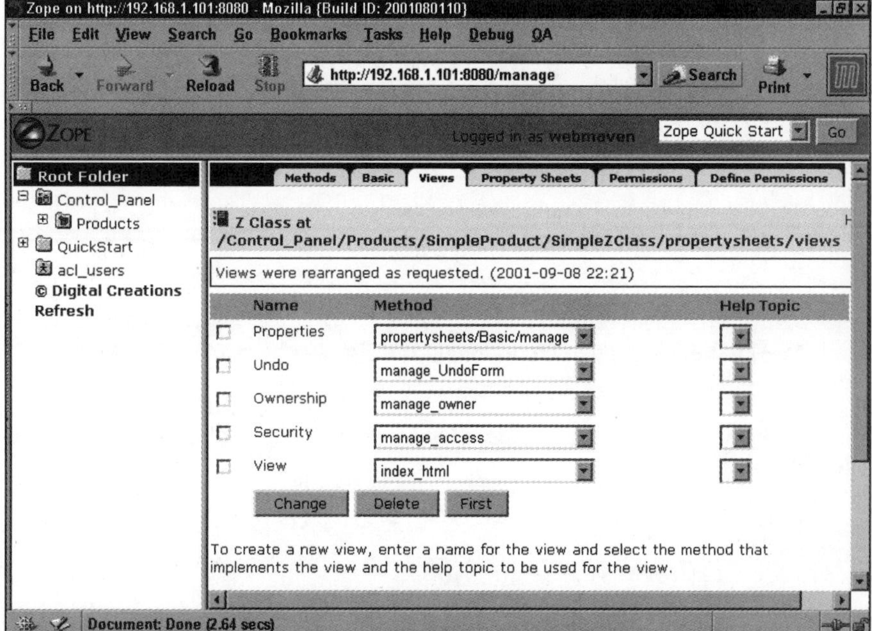

Figure 16-16: The Views tab, after adding the "Properties" view

If you now click on the simpletest instance of your ZClass, you'll see that the Properties view is now displayed by default, and that Zope constructs a form to manage the properties for the Basic property sheet automatically.

Using this form is the same as using the Properties tab for any other Zope object: make the changes you want and click the Save Changes button. As an example, type **A Title for simpletest** into the title field, and click Save Changes. Zope presents a screen telling you that the changes have been made with a single OK button. Clicking the button will returns you to the Properties tab, which will reflect the change that you made.

Clicking the View tab reveals that the title property is being acquired and rendered in the objects `index_html` method, as you can see in Figure 16-17.

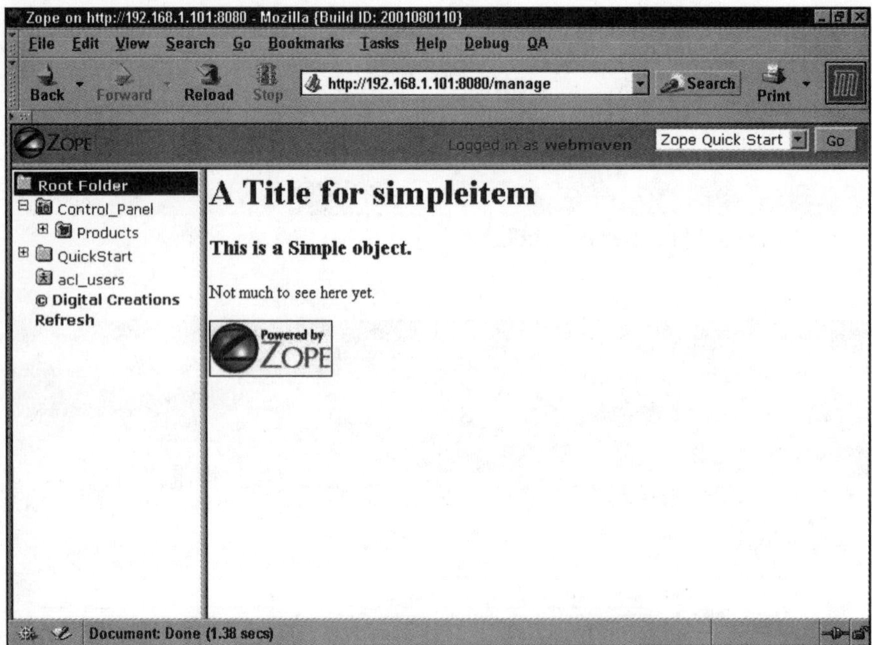

Figure 16-17: The title property rendered in the Simple object's `index_html`

Recall that the `index_html` method calls `standard_html_header`, which contains the following code:

```
<html>
<head>
 <title><dtml-var title_or_id></title>
</head>
<body bgcolor="#FFFFFF">

<h1><dtml-var title_or_id></h1>
```

The `title_or_id` method tries to render an object's title if it can find one, or the object's id if it cannot. Until now, the simpletest instance has only had an id, but because we added a title property, the simpletest instance is rendered as the object's title, and as a header in the page.

It's important to realize that while property sheets define the properties of all instance of a ZClass, the values of the properties in those instances are independent of one another, so setting a second Simple instance's title does not influence the value of the other instances' title property.

Using select and multiple-select properties

Sometimes, instead of letting the owner of an object set a property to any value, you may want them to choose from among a limited number of choices. This is what the *select* and *multiple-select* properties are for.

However, for these property types to work, they must get the allowed values from somewhere. Typically, these properties get the allowed values from another property, either in another property sheet, or acquired from above the object instance.

For example, add a Values property sheet to the SimpleZClass and add a `color_list` lines property to it. Fill out the lines property so that it matches Figure 16-18, and save the changes.

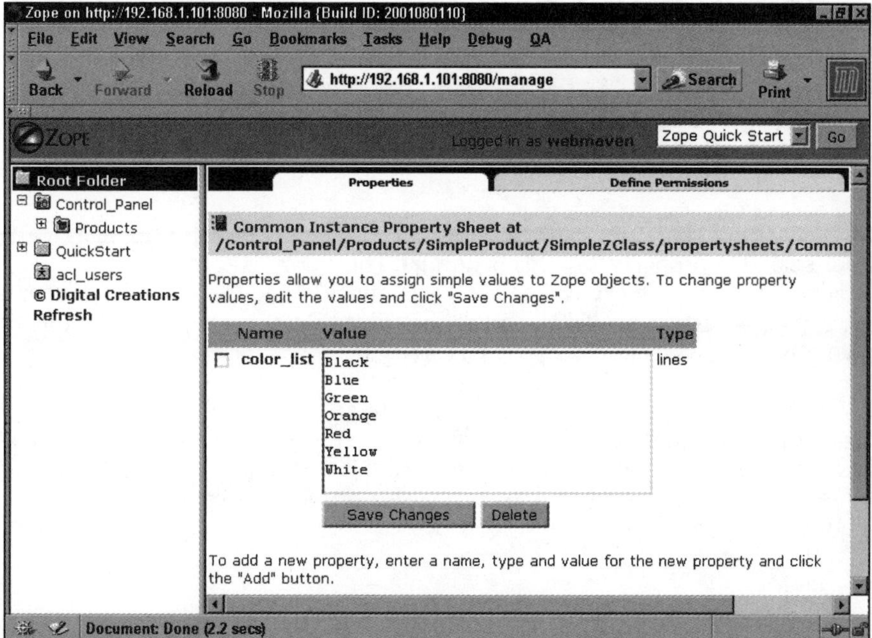

Figure 16-18: The Values property sheet

After you've created the property holding the list of values, go to the "Basic" property sheet and add a select property by entering the name color, choosing selection from the Type drop-down menu, and setting its value to color_list. This is how you inform Zope of the source of the allowed values.

After creating the "color" property, the property sheet should look like Figure 16-19.

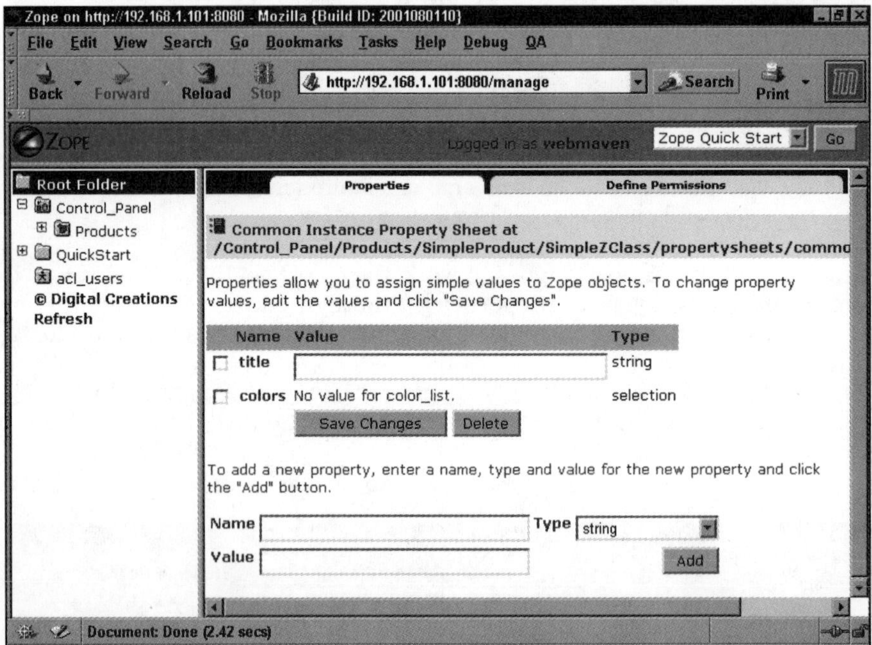

Figure 16-19: The Basic property sheet with the Color select property

You may notice that Zope can't find the `color_list` attribute for populating the color selection property, but this is normal. The color_list property definition is not an actual property, and so isn't subject to acquisition. In the ZClass instance, the color_list property is available, and so the color selection property is populated correctly.

There are a couple of ways to correct this, but none of them ideal. You could put the color_list property in a location where both the ZClass instances and the ZClass itself can acquire it, such as in the Root Folder, but that moves the list of permitted values outside of the product and can cause a problem when you distribute the product.

If you create a color_list property on the Simple product's Properties tab instead, the ZClass will acquire it just fine, but the instances won't. You could duplicate the color_list property definition in the Values property sheet as well as an actual property on the product, but that will probably be confusing if and when the two get out of synch.

All in all, we recommend you leave the color_list property definition in a property sheet dedicated for this purpose (in this case, the Values property sheet), and simply ignore that the color selection property in the Basic property sheet reports an error.

Automatically Generating ZClass Views

In this chapter, you've already seen how to create a management tab dynamically from a property sheet, but they are hardly what you want to present to the end users of your site.

Fortunately, Zope has a facility for generating end-user interfaces fairly easily.

This facility for creating end-user interfaces has a few drawbacks. Unlike the method used to create management tabs, these automatically generated methods are not self-updating, so if you change the ZClass, you will either have to re-generate the methods in question, or you'll have to hand edit them.

Hand edit? Yes, the methods generated in this way are actual DTML (Document Template Markup Language) method objects, and can be customized to your heart's content. Keep in mind that any changes you make will be lost if the methods are re-generated again.

Generating a View interface

In the SimpleZClass, delete the `index_html` method that is currently used to view the ZClass instances. Then, use the Add drop-down menu to select Property Sheet Interface. The form, which looks like Figure 16-20, has an id field in which you should type **index_html**, a title field that you may leave blank, a select field for choosing the property sheet in which you should choose "Basic," and another select field for determining the type of interface to generate ("view" or "edit") in which you should choose "view."

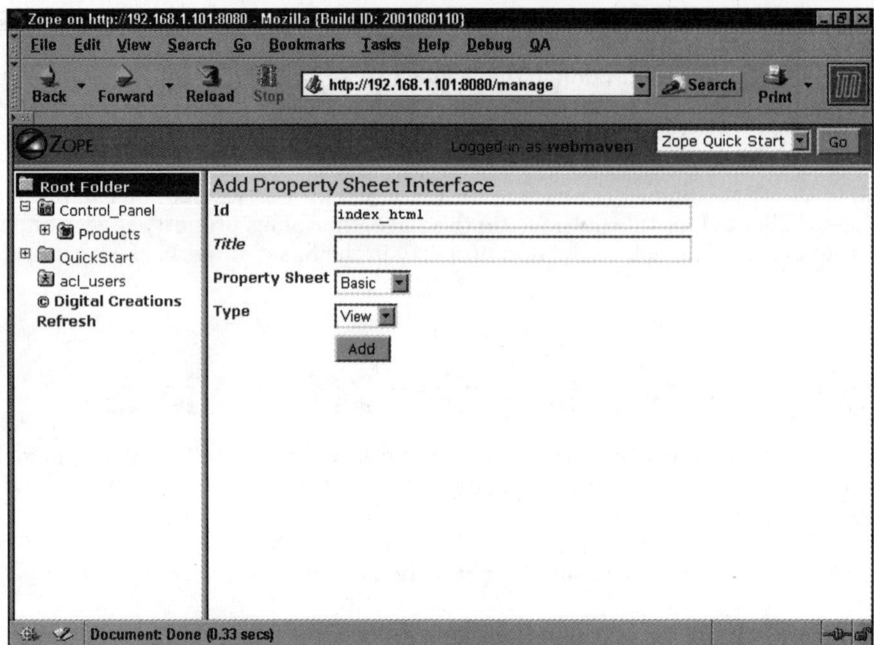

Figure 16-20: The Add Property Sheet Interface form

After filling out the form, click the Add button. This generates the interface method and returns you to the ZClass Methods tab. Because this facility creates a "normal" DTML method, you can click it in order to examine the code that was generated. The code of the new `index_html` method should look like this:

```
<dtml-var standard_html_header>
<table>
  <tr><th align=left valign=top>Title</th>
      <td align=left valign=top><dtml-var title></td>
  </tr>
  <tr><th align=left valign=top>Colors</th>
      <td align=left valign=top><dtml-var colors></td>
  </tr>
</table>
<dtml-var standard_html_footer>
```

If we take a look at the View tab of the simpletest instance in the Root Folder, we'll see this code rendered, as is shown in Figure 16-21.

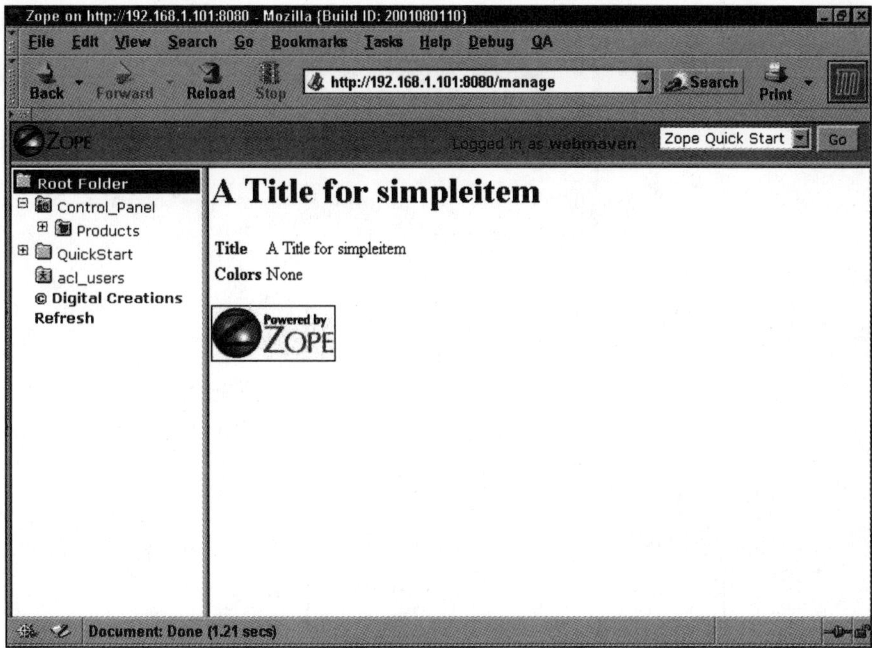

Figure 16-21: The rendered View interface

Generating an Edit interface

Creating an "Edit" interface for your ZClass is substantially similar to creating a View interface, but the end result is a little different.

In the SimpleZClass Methods tab, choose Property Sheet Interface from the Add drop-down menu, and fill out the form as follows: set the id to "edit_form," leave the title field blank, set the Property Sheet drop-down menu to "Basic" and set the Type drop-down menu to "Edit." Once you've set the form fields appropriately, click Add.

Examining the contents of your new edit_form method reveals the following code:

```
<html><head><title><dtml-var title_or_id></title></head>
<body bgcolor="#FFFFFF" link="#000099" vlink="#555555">
<dtml-var manage_tabs>
<form
action="propertysheets/Basic/manage_editProperties"><table>
  <tr><th align=left valign=top>title</th>
      <td align=left valign=top>
             <input name="title:string" size="35"
                    value="<dtml-var title html_quote>"></td>
```

```
    </tr>
    <tr><th align=left valign=top>colors</th>
        <td align=left valign=top>
              <dtml-if "_.has_key('colors')">
              <select name="colors">
                <dtml-in "_.string.split('color_list')">
                  <option
                    <dtml-if "_['sequence-item']=='colors'">
                    SELECTED</dtml-if>
                    ><dtml-var sequence-item></option>
                </dtml-in>
              </select>
              <dtml-else>
                No value for colors
              </dtml-if></td>
    </tr>
    <tr><td colspan=2>
      <input type=submit value=" Change ">
      <input type=reset value=" Reset ">
    </td></tr>
  </table></form>
  </body></html>
```

You can see that more code is generated here than for the View method, most of it to iterate over the color_list property and create the select form element.

In order to see how this method renders, you'll have to type in the URL directly (in this case, `http://yourserver/simpletest/edit`). You should see something similar to what is shown in Figure 16-22.

You may notice that the color drop-down menu is not functioning properly and is not displaying the list of colors we've defined in color_list. Unlike the automatically generated view of the property sheet that we defined for the Properties tab, the generated DTML method assumes that the options for colors, namely color_list, is a tokens property, instead of a lines property. The assumption is buried in the following DTML line:

```
<dtml-in "_.string.split('color_list')">
```

`split` is a method of the string module, and generally expects two parameters: a string and a separator. In the absence of an explicit separator, split uses the default separator, which is a space. You may recall that tokens properties are sequences of strings separated by spaces.

Resolving this problem is fairly simple. Just replace the previous line with the one that follows :

```
<dtml-in color_list>
```

And that's it! The edit method will now work as advertised.

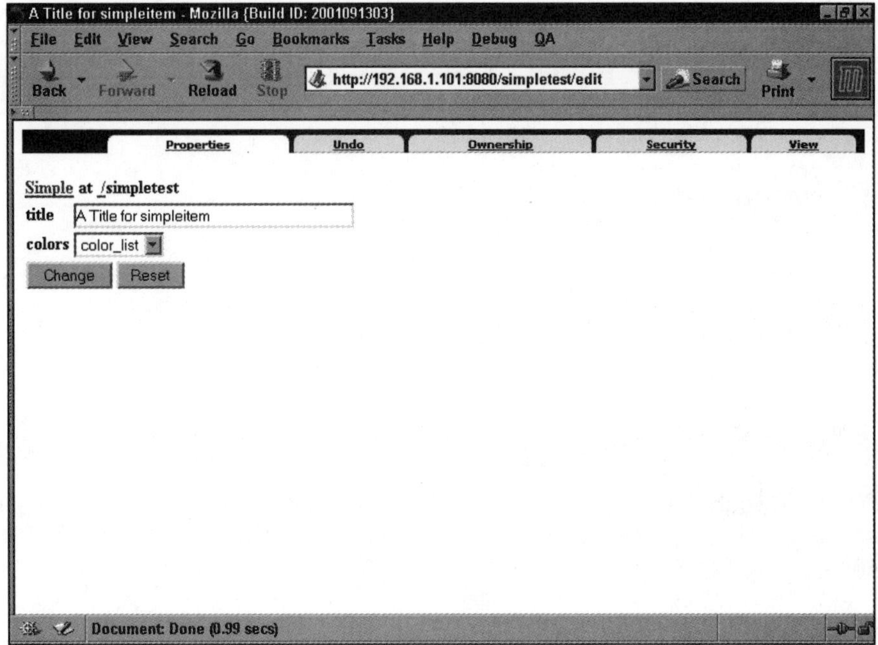

Figure 16-22: The SimpleZClass edit_form method

There are a few other minor tweaks to get this to work well as an end user-accessible edit screen. First, the code must be modified to use the standard headers and footers, and the management tabs must be removed. In addition, a reference to the edit screen should be added to the `index_html` method.

After making the changes to the edit_form method, your code should look like the following listing:

```
<dtml-var standard_html_header>
<form
action="propertysheets/Basic/manage_editProperties"><table>
  <tr><th align=left valign=top>title</th>
      <td align=left valign=top>
            <input name="title:string" size="35"
                   value="<dtml-var title html_quote>"></td>
  </tr>
  <tr><th align=left valign=top>colors</th>
      <td align=left valign=top>
            <dtml-if "_.has_key('colors')">
            <select name="colors">
              <dtml-in color_list>
                <option
                  <dtml-if "_['sequence-item']=='colors'">
                  SELECTED</dtml-if>
```

```
                ><dtml-var sequence-item></option>
              </dtml-in>
            </select>
            <dtml-else>
              No value for colors
            </dtml-if></td>
  </tr>
  <tr><td colspan=2>
    <input type=submit value=" Change ">
    <input type=reset value=" Reset ">
  </td></tr>
</table></form>
<dtml-var standard_html_footer>
```

Creating Simple Applications Using ZClasses

Until now, you've built a fairly useless ZClass as a demonstration. In order to illustrate some of the more complex aspects of building custom object types in this way, a more concrete example is helpful.

In this section, we show you how to build an application for creating and managing frequently asked questions. The application will consist of a folder-like FAQ manager object, and Q & A objects that can be placed in it.

First, of course, you'll need to create a product for the various object-types to "live" in. Add a ZFAQ product to the Products folder.

FAQManager ZClass

The first object that you'll need to create is the container. We'll call this class the *FAQManager*. Add a ZClass to the ZFAQ product. Set both the id and the meta-type to FAQManager and leave the Include standard Zope persistent object base classes? and Create constructor objects? boxes checked. Select ZClasses: ObjectManager from the list of unselected base classes, and click the button with the two greater than symbols (>>). You will see that the ZClasses: ObjectManager class now appears in the "selected" list instead of the unselected list. Next, repeat the procedure with the OFS: Folder class. The form should now look like the form shown in Figure 16-23.

When you have the Add form set as in Figure 16-23, click the Add button.

The ObjectManager and Folder classes overlap significantly. The main reason for Subclassing both is that an ObjectManger enables you to restrict the object-types that may be added to it, whereas Folders have a management interface that supports copy-and-paste, renaming, and other niceties. By subclassing both, we get both sets of functionality. The order in which the ZClass inherits from these two classes is important.

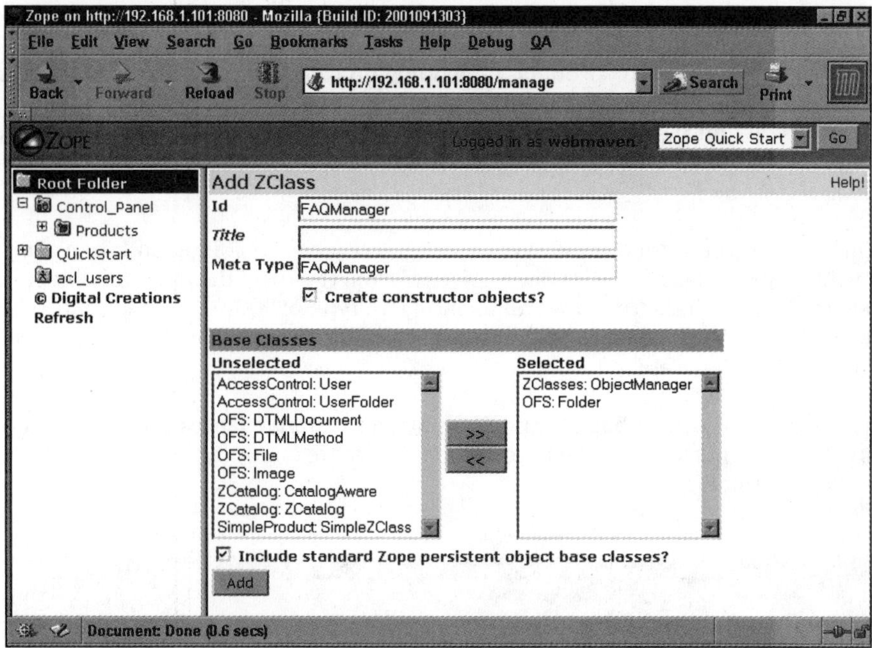

Figure 16-23: The Add form for the FAQManager ZClass

Click the FAQManager ZClass. You'll see that it has a tab that the SimpleZClass didn't: a Subobjects tab. This is used to control what objects may be contained within the FAQManager. Right now, we don't yet have an object type to place within the FAQManager, so we'll leave it alone.

Let's add a FAQManager and see what it looks like so far. In your Root Folder, choose FAQManager from the drop-down list of addable objects. In the Add FAQManager form that appears, give the FAQManager an id of **faqtest**, and click the Add button.

Clicking faqtest shows a single Contents tab that informs you that there are no items in faqtest. It also does not have any provision for adding any objects. If you try accessing faqtest through a browser (`http://yourserver/faqtest`), you'll see that it simply acquires the `index_html` method of the Root Folder, and obviously doesn't have one of its own. All in all, not very useful . . . yet.

QandA ZClass

So our FAQManager doesn't have any objects to add. Fortunately this is easily remedied. The QandA ZClass is actually very simple, consisting of two text properties ("question" and "answer") and a Boolean property ("display"). The trickiest part of creating the QandA ZClass is its *location*, which must be inside the FAQManager ZClass. By placing it there, QandA ZClass instances will only be addable within the

FAQManager, and nowhere else. If you wanted to be able to add QandA instances elsewhere, you could either create its own product, or you could place them directly within the ZFAQ product, depending on whether you later wanted to distribute the FAQManager and QandA separately or as a single product. In this case, though, you don't want the QandA distributed separately or the instances to be addable anywhere else, so the ZClass should be created inside the FAQManager ZClass.

Click the ZFAQ product in the `/Control_Panel/Products/` folder, and then click the FAQManager ZClass. Here, choose "ZClass" from the drop-down list of objects, and fill in the Add ZClass form with an id and meta-type of "QandA." The QandA ZClass doesn't need any base classes, but make sure that the two checkboxes are selected. Finally, click Generate.

At this point, if you go back to the FAQManager instance faqtest, and take a look at it in the management interface, you'll see that there is now an Add QandA button as you can see in Figure 16-24.

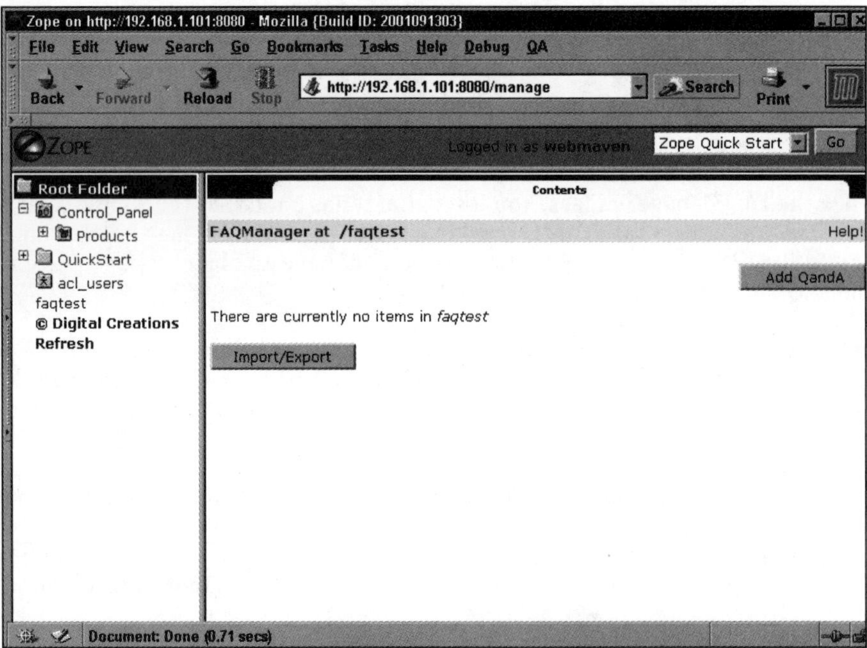

Figure 16-24: The FAQManager Contents tab after the QandA ZClass has been added to the FAQManager ZClass

Clicking the Add QandA button presents a simple Add QandA form consisting only of an id text field and an Add button. Add an id of "001," and click the button. After Zope adds the `001` QandA instance to the FAQManager, you'll see that the interface now has the usual folder interface, including Cut, Copy, Paste, and Rename buttons.

Our QandA instances need properties, so let's add them. To make the QandA objects easier to manage, it would be useful to have the folder interface list the question as well as the id. However, the only property that folder-like objects list in the interface in this way is the title property. While it is possible to get the title property to return the value of another property (or a computed property) through some sleight-of-hand, it's actually completely unnecessary. All you have to do is use the title property to store the question in the first place and relabel the field on the form.

In the QandA ZClass, click the Property Sheets tab and then click the Add Common Instance Property Sheet button. Give the property sheet an id of "basic," and click Add. In the Property Sheets tab, click the Basic property sheet, which should now be visible. Add a Boolean property named "display," and two text properties named "title" and "answer."

Now that you've added the necessary property definitions to the QandA Basic property sheet, you need to create a form to edit the values and add it as a view.

Navigate back to the main Methods tab of the QandA ZClass and select Property Sheet Interface from the Add drop-down menu. In the Add Property Sheet Interface form, fill in the id field as "edit_form," leave the property sheet drop-down field on "basic," and change the type drop-down menu to "Edit." Click the Add button.

Next, you need to add an Edit tab. Go to the QandA ZClass's Views tab and add a view named "Edit" using the `edit_form` method. Because we want this to be the default tab for the QandA object, select the checkbox to the left of the Edit view and click the First button.

At this point you should go back to the faqtest FAQManager instance in your Root Folder and take a look at the changes there. The `001` instance of the QandA ZClass that you already added should still be there, but if you hadn't already added one, or you removed it, add it now.

Click the `001` instance and you should now see the Edit tab we just created, as can be seen in Figure 16-25. Type **Why?** in the title field, and **Because.** in the answer field, and click the Change button.

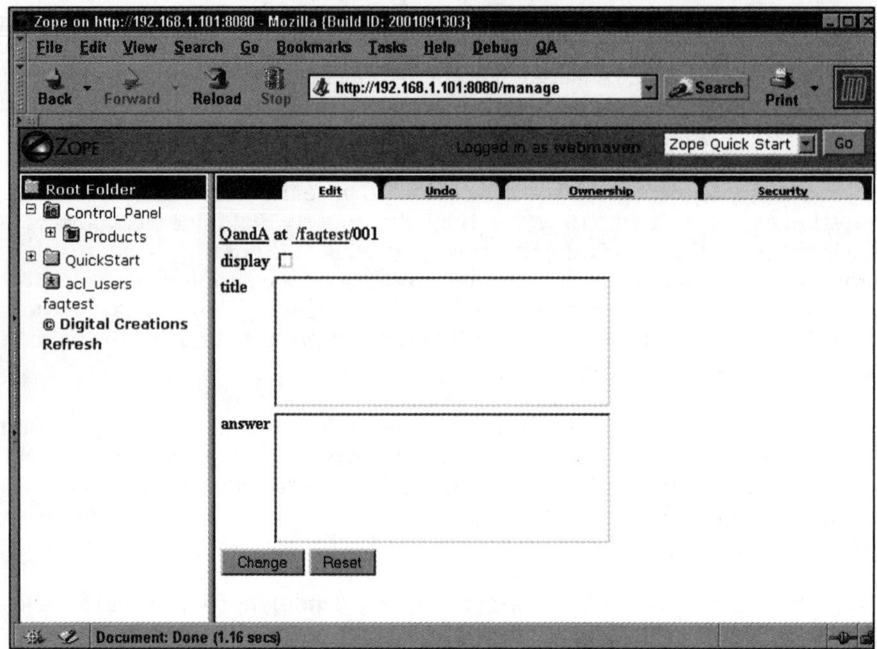

Figure 16-25: The QandA Edit tab, as generated

If you now take another look at the FAQManager management interface, you can now see that the value of the title property is in fact being displayed by the id, just as we intended.

However, you didn't really want to have the name of the field be "title;" you wanted it to be "question," so we need to go in and alter the edit method. Navigate to the QandA ZClass, and click the `edit_form` method. Find the line that contains the following code:

```
<tr><th align=left valign=top>title</th>
```

and change it to match the following:

```
<tr><th align=left valign=top>question</th>
```

Then click the Save Changes button. If you now go back to the QandA instance in faqtest, you'll see that the Edit tab now labels the first text field as "question." So far, so good.

Next, you may have noticed that after editing the QandA instance and pressing the Change button, the confirmation screen you are presented to then returns you to the QandA's property sheet screen, rather than to the FAQManager interface, as would be more convenient. This can be fixed by creating a method that intermediates between the `edit_form` method and the `manage_editProperties` method that the `edit_form` targets as its action currently.

Create an `edit` DTML method in the ZClass Methods tab alongside the `edit_form` method. Place the following code into it:

```
<dtml-call
"propertysheets.basic.manage_changeProperties(REQUEST)">
<dtml-call "RESPONSE.redirect(URL2+'/manage_workspace')">
```

and click Save Changes. Next, change the target of the `edit_form` method form action to the `edit` method. Find the line in `edit_form` that reads:

```
<form
action="propertysheets/basic/manage_editProperties"><table>
```

and change it to read:

```
<form action="edit"><table>
```

and click Save Changes. If you now go back to the faqtest instance and edit the 001 QandA object, you'll find that after clicking the Change button you are immediately redirected to the FAQManager Contents tab.

Finishing the FAQManager interface

You're almost done creating a functional FAQ tool. The only thing missing now is a display interface for the FAQManager object.

This method (`index_html`) must do two things:

- ✦ Iterate through the contained QandA objects to render a list of questions that are linked to question-and-answer pairs lower in the document.
- ✦ Iterate through the same objects again to render the question-and-answer pairs.

Create an `index_html` DTML method in the FAQManager ZClass with the following code:

```
<dtml-var standard_html_header>

<dtml-in "objectValues('QandA')" sort=id>
<a href="#&dtml-id;">&dtml-title;</a><br>
</dtml-in>
```

```
<dtml-in "objectValues('QandA')" sort=id>
<a name="&dtml-id;"><hr>
<b>Q: <dtml-var title></b><br>
<b>A:</b> <dtml-var answer><br>
<a href="#">Return to top</a>
</dtml-in>

<dtml-var standard_html_footer>
```

You can see that this code is a very simple display method, but it has the disadvantage of displaying all QandAs even if they don't have an answer yet. This is why we added the display property, in order to control the display. Change the `index_html` method to the following:

```
<dtml-var standard_html_header>

<dtml-in "objectValues('QandA')" sort=id>
 <dtml-if "display">
<a href="#&dtml-id;">&dtml-title;</a><br>
 </dtml-if>
</dtml-in>

<dtml-in "objectValues('QandA')" sort=id>
 <dtml-if "display">
<a name="&dtml-id;"><hr>
<b>Q: <dtml-var title></b><br>
<b>A:</b> <dtml-var answer><br>
<a href="#">Return to top</a>
 </dtml-if>
</dtml-in>

<dtml-var standard_html_footer>
```

Now, only those QandA objects that have the display property checked will be listed in the FAQManager's `index_html` method.

You've now created a ZClass based extension of Zope. You (and other users with the Manager role) can add instances of the FAQManager in various places in your site and create and manage the contained QandA objects in order to easily maintain an FAQ list.

Creating CatalogAware ZClasses

Here we describe the necessary alterations to a ZClass-based product to make the instances automatically cataloged and indexed.

See Chapter 17 for more information about ZCatalog and searching.

Making a ZClass catalog aware

Catalog awareness in class instances means that the following conditions are met:

- ✦ Objects are indexed in the catalog automatically when they are added to the site.
- ✦ Objects are unindexed when they are removed from the site.
- ✦ Objects are re-indexed when they are changed.

All of this is accomplished by subclassing the ZClass from CatalogAware, and making a few changes to its add and edit methods.

First, a point that perhaps does not get stressed enough: when creating a CatalogAware ZClass, it's important that the ZClasses: CatalogAware class is added first to the list of classes that the ZClass subclasses.

Create a CatalogThing product in your `Control_Panel/Products` folder and add a ThingClass ZClass to it. Type **ThingClass** in the id field in the ZClass add form and set the meta type to Thing. Leave the two checkboxes on the form checked, then select ZCatalog: CatalogAware in the base class list and click the >> button.

After you have set up the ZClass add form correctly, click the Add button.

Now that you've successfully generated a CatalogAware ZClass, you just need to edit the methods to correctly call the special CatalogAwareness methods of your class.

Editing the constructor

In the CatalogThing product, click the `ThingClass_add` method. The method should contain the following code:

```
<HTML>
<HEAD><TITLE>Add ThingClass</TITLE></HEAD>
<BODY BGCOLOR="#FFFFFF" LINK="#000099" VLINK="#555555">

<dtml-comment> We add the new object by calling the class in
               a with tag.  Not only does this get the thing
               added, it adds the new thing's attributes to
               the DTML name space, so we can call methods
               to initialize the object.
</dtml-comment>

<dtml-with "ThingClass.createInObjectManager(REQUEST['id'], ⮐
REQUEST)">

  <dtml-comment>
```

```
          You can add code that modifies the new instance here.

          For example, if you have a property sheet that you want ⮐
     to update from form values, you can call it here:

            <dtml-call "propertysheets.Basic.manage_editProperties(
                       REQUEST)">

       </dtml-comment>

     </dtml-with>

     <dtml-comment> Now we need to return something.  We do this via
                     a redirect so that the URL is correct.

                     Unfortunately, the way we do this depends on
                     whether we live in a product or in a class.
                     If we live in a product, we need to use
                     DestinationURL
                     to decide where to go. If we live in a class,
                     DestinationURL won't be available, so we use
                     URL2.
     </dtml-comment>
     <dtml-if DestinationURL>

      <dtml-call "RESPONSE.redirect(
            DestinationURL+'/manage_workspace')">

     <dtml-else>

         <dtml-call "RESPONSE.redirect(
               URL2+'/manage_workspace')">
     </dtml-if>
     </body></html>
```

Following the line that reads:

```
<dtml-call "propertysheets.Basic.manage_editProperties(REQUEST)">
```

add the following line:

```
<dtml-call index_object>
```

Remove the `<dtml-comment>` and `</dtml-comment>` tags that surround that section, then click Save Changes.

Cataloging changes to the object

As with the Simple ZClass you created at the beginning of this chapter, you can create property sheets to store attributes of your ZClass instances. However, because you want to be able to search for these properties in the catalog, they must be reindexed whenever the object changes as well.

Add a Basic property sheet to the ThingClass ZClass, and create a title string property in it. Next, generate an edit property sheet interface with an id of "edit_form." Change the target of the form in `edit_form` from `propertysheets/Basic/manage_editProperties` to `edit`, and add an `edit` DTML method object with the following code:

```
<dtml-call "propertysheets.Basic.manage_changeProperties ⮐
(REQUEST)">
<dtml-call reindex_object>
<dtml-call "RESPONSE.redirect(URL2+'/manage_workspace')">
```

After these changes have been made, the Zclass instances will be reindexed whenever their properties are edited, as well.

Finally, add a view for the `edit_form` method and make it the first view by default.

After all of these changes have been made, you can test whether the ZClass instances are indexed correctly. Add a ZCatalog named "Catalog" to the Root Folder by selecting ZCatalog from the drop-down menu and filling in the Add ZCatalog form with an id of Catalog. Then add an instance of your ThingClass to the Root Folder as well by selecting "Thing" from the drop-down menu. The Add Thing form will only have a single id field, which you can fill out with an id of stuff. Click Add.

At this point, you should go back to the ZCatalog in your Root Folder, and click the Catalog tab. You should see the /stuff object listed as being cataloged.

Furthermore, if you edit the /stuff object's title property (for example, by setting it to "A Lot of Stuff" and saving the changes), you can examine the ZCatalog's Vocabulary object to see that the three words, "lot," "of," and "stuff" were indexed when the Thing object's properties were changed.

More information on the use of ZCatalog for indexing and searching objects can be found in Chapter 17.

Subclassing ZClasses from Python Base Classes

Until now, we've showed you how to create ZClasses and subclass from Zope's built-in Python classes. In Part II of this book, we discussed creating your own Python products. You can also subclass your own Python classes in your ZClasses.

Why Subclass Python classes?

As ZClass-based products are in many ways less capable than full Python products, it would seem as though combining them in this way would be a step backwards, but it does offer some distinct advantages:

- ✦ Presentation and logic can be more clearly separated.
- ✦ Multiple ZClass-based products can subclass the same Python product.
- ✦ The Python product can be upgraded without losing the ZClass product customizations.

Creating the Python base class

In your Zope installation's `/lib/python/Products` directory on your computer's file system, create a directory called "SimpleBase." In the `/lib/python/Products/SimpleBase` directory, create a file called "Simple.py" with the following contents:

```
class Simple:
    """
    A Simple Base Class
    """

    Name = ""

    def hello(self):
        """
        Say Hello
        """
        return "Hello, " + self.Name

    def edit(self, NewName):
        self.Name = NewName
```

Then, create an `__init__.py` file that contains the following:

```
from Simple import Simple

def initialize(context):
    context.registerBaseClass(Simple)
```

and an empty `refresh.txt` file.

Restart Zope, and verify that the product has been properly registered by going to the `Control_Panel/Products` folder and checking for the SimpleBase product, which should have a closed box icon.

Subclassing the ZClass from the base class

Now, create a new ZClass (you can create this in the SimpleBase product, or create a separate product if you like) called "SimpleTTW," and subclass "SimpleBase: Simple," which should appear in the list of available base classes.

After you've created the SimpleTTW ZClass, add an `index_html` DTML method to it with the following code:

```
<dtml-var standard_html_header>
<dtml-var hello>
<dtml-var standard_html_footer>
```

Then, add an `edit_form` DTML method with the following code:

```
<html><head><title><dtml-var title_or_id></title></head>
<body bgcolor="#FFFFFF" link="#000099" vlink="#555555">
<dtml-var manage_tabs>
<dtml-if save>
<dtml-call "edit(REQUEST.Name)">
</dtml-if>
<H2>Edit SimpleTTW</H2>
<form action="edit_form"><table>
<tr><th>Name</th>
    <td><input type=text name=Name></td>
</tr>
<tr><td></td><td><input type=submit value="Save Changes"
name="save"></td></tr>
</table></form>
</body></html>
```

At this point, you should add Views to the ZClass, one for `edit_form` named "Edit," and one for `index_html` named "View." Make the Edit view first.

Create an instance of SimpleTTW in the Root Folder, and click on it. You'll be presented with the Edit view, where you can change the value of the Name property. Filling in the form and clicking the Save Changes button will submit the form to itself, but the conditional code at the beginning of the `edit_form` method will detect that this was a form submission and will call the `edit` method on the object. This method, which the SimpleTTW ZClass inherits from the Simple Python class, applies the change to the `Name` attribute.

After making the change, click the View tab to see that the greeting returned by the "hello" method called from the `index_html` method is incorporating the changed value.

You can see that the methods defined by you in the SimpleBase product are in fact made available to the DTML methods that you defined for the SimpleTTW ZClass.

Distributing ZClass Products

Now that you have created your own ZClass-based Products, you may want to install them on other Zope servers, or even share them with other site administrators. To do this, you need to create a *distribution* of your product.

To distribute your Product, select the Distribution tab from within the product. For example, click the Distribution tab within the ZFAQ product.

The form on the Distribution tab gives you fine control over the distribution you create. The Version field specifies the version that will be visible in the products list for whoever installs the product. Every time you make a distribution, the number will be incremented, but you can change it to whatever number you want. We suggest leaving it at 1.0 unless you have some reason to do otherwise.

Next on the form, there are two radio-buttons that let you select the kind of Distribution you want to create. If you want others to be able to customize and/or redistribute your Product, select the "Allow Redistribution" option. If you want to disallow redistribution, select the "Disallow redistribution and allow the user to configure only the selected objects:" option, and you can choose which objects your users can customize in your Product. The list defaults to having no objects selected, which won't allow any changes to the distributed product. If you want them to be able to change the FAQManager ZClass, select that ZClass. If you want the whole product to be customizable but still disallow redistribution, select all of the objects in the list. Notice that the QandA Zclass, which is contained within the FAQManager Zclass, is not listed within this object list. This means that there is no way to allow or disallow customization of the QandA ZClass independently from the FAQManager ZClass. Whether the QandA Zclass is customizable is dependent on the whether the FAQManager ZClass is customizable. To get around this limitation, the QandA object would have to have been created in a separate product.

After you made your decisions regarding the redistribution and customization of the ZFAQ product distribution, click the Create a distribution archive button. Zope will now create a file called `ZFAQ-1.0.tar.gz`, and attempt to download it to your computer. Save the file on your desktop or in a "Downloads" directory on your computer.

The `ZFAQ-1.0.tar.gz` file can be installed in a Zope installation just like any other downloaded product. If you think that your product would be useful to other Zope users, we suggest that you add your product to your zope.org member folder to make it generally available.

Summary

In this chapter, you learned about creating through-the-Web products using ZClasses, defining property sheets and views, and building a simple Web application using them. You also learned to add permissions to ZClasses, make your ZClasses CatalogAware, subclass Python classes in your ZClass products, and distribute your through-the-Web products.

✦ ✦ ✦

CHAPTER 17

Searching Content

In This Chapter

Adding and populating ZCatalogs

Configuring and querying the ZCatalog

Accessing ZCatalogs from Python

More about ZCatalog

Most of this book describes using Zope to accomplish fairly ordinary Web site building and maintenance tasks. Even Part II of the book, which shows you how to build custom object types using Zope's object oriented framework, isn't that different from building a similar application using JavaBeans, for example.

In this chapter, we are going to introduce one of Zope's features that sets Zope apart from other Web development environments — its integrated framework for indexing and searching objects and their attributes.

Adding and Populating ZCatalogs

Zope has built-in searching and indexing capabilities that enable you to easily find objects in your site that conform to various criteria (such as containing some text) via ad-hoc queries.

What is a ZCatalog?

ZCatalogs are Zope's general-purpose search engines and indexers. A ZCatalog examines objects, indexes whatever properties you've marked as significant, and enables you to query the ZCatalog for objects whose properties match your criteria. Additionally, ZCatalogs don't return the actual objects in their results, but instead return a special lightweight object with whatever metadata you've told the ZCatalog to retain for the object and a pointer to the actual object if you need it.

Adding a ZCatalog to your site

In your root folder, click on the drop-down to select ZCatalog from the list of addable products. Fill the Add ZCatalog form that comes up with an id of `Catalog`, leave the title field blank, and leave the vocabulary drop-down set on the default of `Create one for me` (we'll go into more detail about Vocabularies in the "About Vocabularies" sidebar in the "More about ZCatalog" section). Click the Add button.

You should now have a ZCatalog instance named `Catalog` in your root folder. The icon for a ZCatalog is a folder with a magnifying glass, and the ZCatalog user interface does resemble that of a folder somewhat. But there are a few differences, as shown in Figure 17-1.

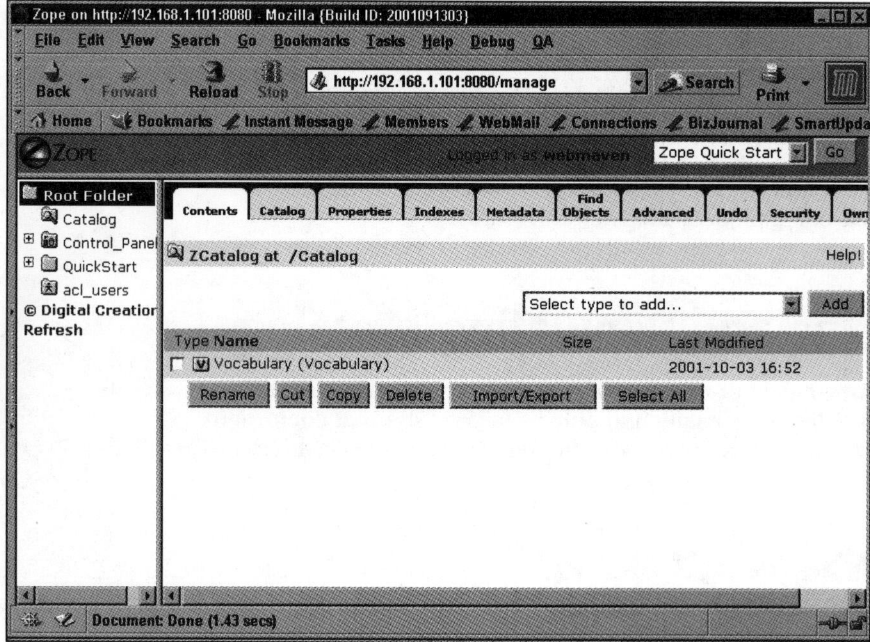

Figure 17-1: The ZCatalog Contents tab

ZCatalogs have several tabs that folders do not have, including the following:

Catalog

Indexes

Metadata

Advanced

The Find tab that folders have is replaced with a Find Objects tab in a ZCatalog.

Populating a ZCatalog

ZCatalogs can be populated in two ways: manually and automatically. Populating a ZCatalog manually is fairly simple; just go to the Find Objects tab in a ZCatalog (shown in Figure 17-2), and select the criteria for the objects that you want to catalog and index.

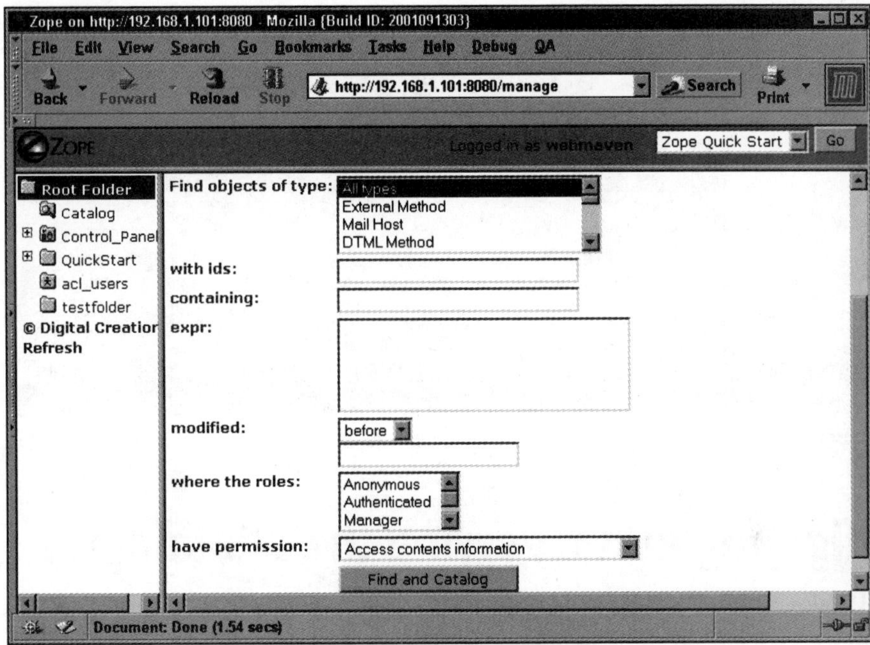

Figure 17-2: The ZCatalog Find Objects tab

For the time being, leave the default settings in the form, and click the Find and Catalog button at the bottom of the form. The operation may take a few moments, so be patient while Zope works.

After Zope is done finding and cataloging the objects that meet the criteria you specified (in this case, all objects stored in the ZODB), the browser is redirected to the Catalog tab of the ZCatalog, and it shows you how long it took to complete the operation, as shown in Figure 17-3.

As you can see, the find objects operation found all objects in the ZODB, all of which are now recorded in the ZCatalog.

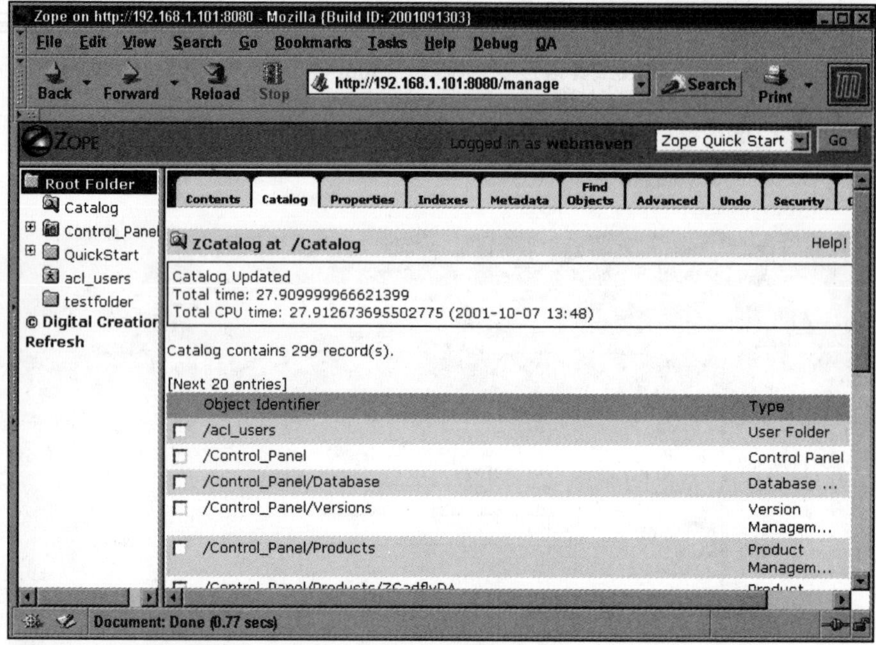

Figure 17-3: The Catalog tab, after finding objects

Configuring and Querying the ZCatalog

ZCatalogs store two types of information about the objects that they catalog: indexes and metadata. Indexes are the lookup tables that the ZCatalog consults in order to determine which objects match a particular query, and metadata is the information about an object that a ZCatalog stores in order to make its result sets more meaningful.

ZCatalog indexes

The ZCatalog uses indexes to determine which objects that it knows about match a particular query. In order for you to query a ZCatalog about a particular object attribute, that attribute must be indexed by the ZCatalog in an Index. As you can see in Figure 17-4, the ZCatalog's index tab has several indexes by default.

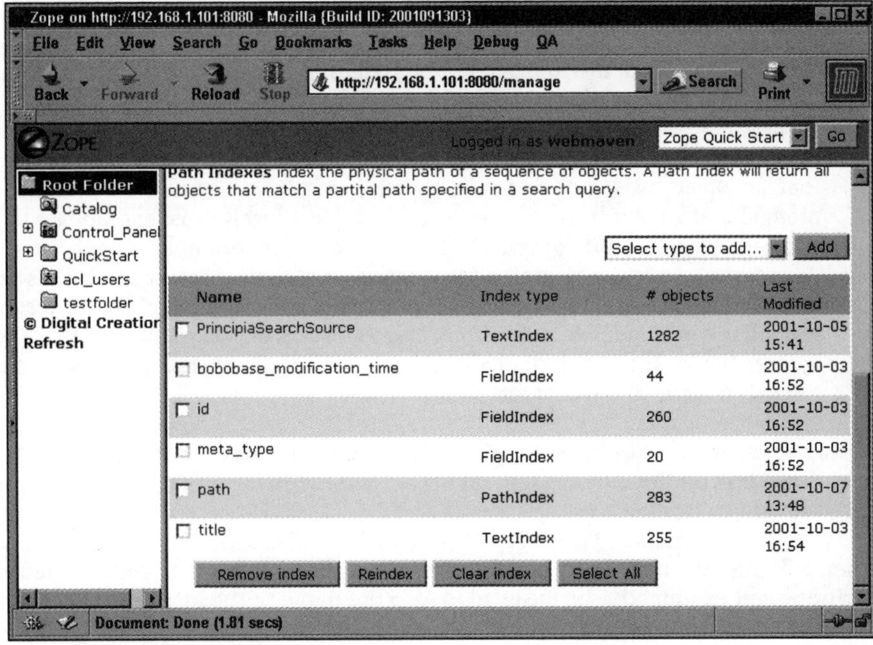

Figure 17-4: The ZCatalog Indexes tab

The following are the four built-in types of indexes:

- ✦ **Text indexes.** These indexes break up text contained in an attribute into individual words. The more times a particular word appears in an attribute indexed by a text index, the higher its score. Results are sorted by score, highest to lowest from the most relevant to the lest relevant. Text indexes are often referred to as full-text indexes. `PrincipiaSearchSource` and `title` are text indexes included in a ZCatalog by default.
- ✦ **Field indexes.** These indexes treat the object's attribute as a single unit, and they are used to keep track of object attributes that conform to a particular value. Field indexes included in a ZCatalog by default are `bobobase_modification_time`, `id`, and `meta_type`.
- ✦ **Keyword indexes.** These indexes take a sequence of objects and break them up into keywords, which are then indexed individually. A Keyword index returns any objects that have one or more indexed keywords that match any keywords from the query. They are particularly useful for building categories.
- ✦ **Path indexes.** These indexes break up the physical path to an indexed object into all its subpaths. A Path index returns all objects that match a partial path specified in a search query. By default, a ZCatalog includes a path index named `path`.

You may be wondering what the heck `bobobase_modification_time` and `PrincipiaSearchSource` are. These attribute names date back to the dim prehistory of Zope, before the source had been released, and even before it was named Zope. In those days, the ZODB had been called Bobo, apparently chosen as "a name so stupid, it would have to be replaced," and the ZPublisher was called Principia. `bobobase_modification_time` is an attribute that stores the last time that an object was modified, and `PrincipiaSearchSource` is an attribute or method that an object can use to expose whatever text is most appropriate to be indexed with a Text index. A book object for example might have a `PrincipiaSearchSource` method that returns a concatenation of the book's title, author name, description, and keyword attributes. This would ensure that a single text index would index all of the book objects' textual attributes, making them easily searchable. There is further detail in the "More about text indexes" section towards the end of the chapter.

Adding a new index is easy, just choose the type of index you want to add from the drop-down box on the Indexes tab, fill in the Add Index form that comes up, and click the Add button.

When a ZCatalog indexes an object, it uses the defined indexes to determine what attributes get examined. The index id is also the name of the attribute that it will examine for each cataloged object. It's easy to see, then, that the `title` index will operate on the title attribute of cataloged objects. As you know, not all objects within Zope have a title attribute. In those cases, the index ignores the object.

Removing an index is similarly easy. Just select the checkbox next to the indexes you wish to delete, and click the Remove Index button.

Clearing an index does just what it sounds like. It wipes an index clean of the values that it has stored, and of the associations from those values to the objects they came from. You can clear an index by selecting the checkbox to the left of the index, and clicking the Clear Index button.

Reindexing examines the objects the Catalog knows about, and updates the values stored by the indexes that you've selected. You can use this to repopulate an index after it has been cleared, but this will not find any new objects that are not in the ZCatalog already. You can reindex the ZCatalog's indexes by selecting the checkbox next to an index, and clicking the Reindex button.

ZCatalog indexes don't have to target attributes, they can also be directed to index object methods. This means that you can index on the result of some calculation. Suppose that your object has a method for returning a list of `related_items`, and that the method calculated which objects were related according to some criteria you selected. By indexing this method, you can search the ZCatalog for all objects that consider themselves related to the currently displayed object (not just the objects that the current object's `related_items` method returns).

ZCatalog Metadata

Metadata, or "data about data," are the attributes that the ZCatalog stores for each object, not for the purposes of querying, but for the purpose of returning results. In Figure 17-5, you can see the metadata that a ZCatalog is set to store by default:

✦ `bobobase_modification_time`

✦ `id`

✦ `meta_type`

✦ `title`

✦ `summary`

Notice that this list of stored attributes does not necessarily match the list of indexed attributes, but can overlap with them. Generally speaking, only those attributes that you want to see returned in a result list should be stored as metadata. You might be asking yourself why the indexed attributes aren't returned with the result objects as well, and why the information in them must be stored again as metadata in order for it to be returned with the results. The answer is that storing the indexed attributes and the metadata separately is a tradeoff between storage space and speed. The indexes are all optimized for lookup speed, in order to return the result objects as quickly as possible. Passing the indexed information to the result objects would slow this functionality down. Also, the result objects themselves are optimized to be as lightweight as possible (because a great many of them might be returned at once, and therefore have to be loaded in memory), and contain no more information (metadata) than is required, along with a reference to the actual cataloged object. Forcing the result objects to contain all indexed attributes would make them much larger, and cause the ZCatalog's performance to decrease.

Adding a new metadata field is simple. Just type the name of the attribute that you want to track into the Add Metadata field at the bottom of the Metadata tab, and click the Add button. Deleting a metadata field is as simple as selecting the checkbox next to the field name and clicking Delete.

It's worth noting that as with Indexes, metadata fields can reference methods, not just attributes. So, for example, if your object has a method that returns the result of a calculation (say, popularity), you can store that as metadata as well, and return this in your query results list.

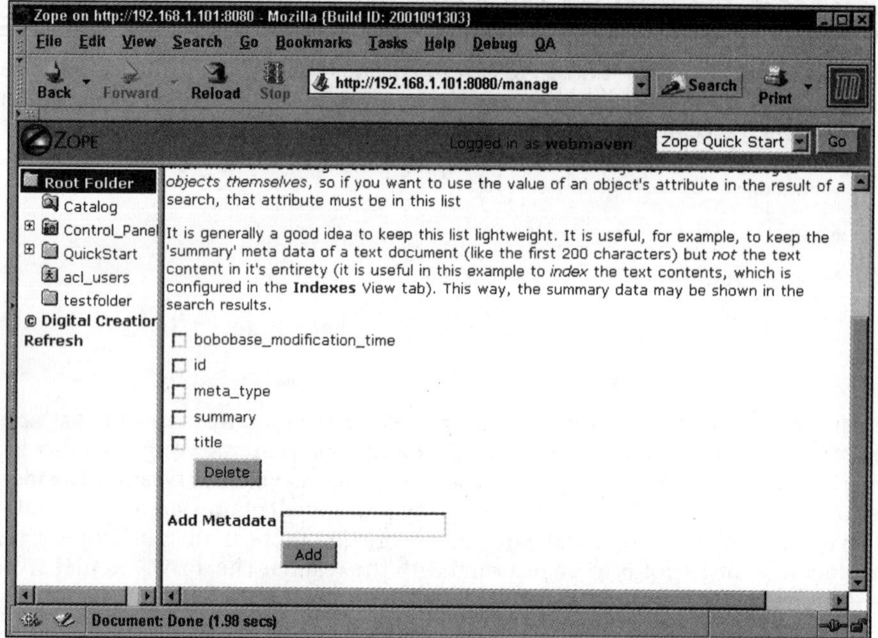

Figure 17-5: The ZCatalog's Metadata tab

Building search interfaces

Zope includes the capability to automatically generate search interfaces for ZCatalogs based on the indexes and metadata stored in the ZCatalog.

In the root folder, choose Z Search Interface from the drop-down box. An Add Search Interface form comes up (see Figure 17-6), with several fields. The first is a list of the searchable objects (ZCatalogs) that you can set the search interface to target. Select Catalog. Next is the report id, which is the id of the DTML Method that will display the results list. Type **search_results**. You may leave the report title and search input title blank, but type **search_form** into the search input id field. All that remains is to choose the form of the report that will be generated.

You can choose a tabular format or a records format for the report. They both contain and present the same information; the only difference is in the HTML code that is generated. In the tabular format, each result in the result list gets a row in a table, with each metadata field in its own cell and the metadata columns labeled at the top of the table. In the records format, each result in the result list is in its own paragraph, with the metadata fields separated by commas. I generally use the tabular format.

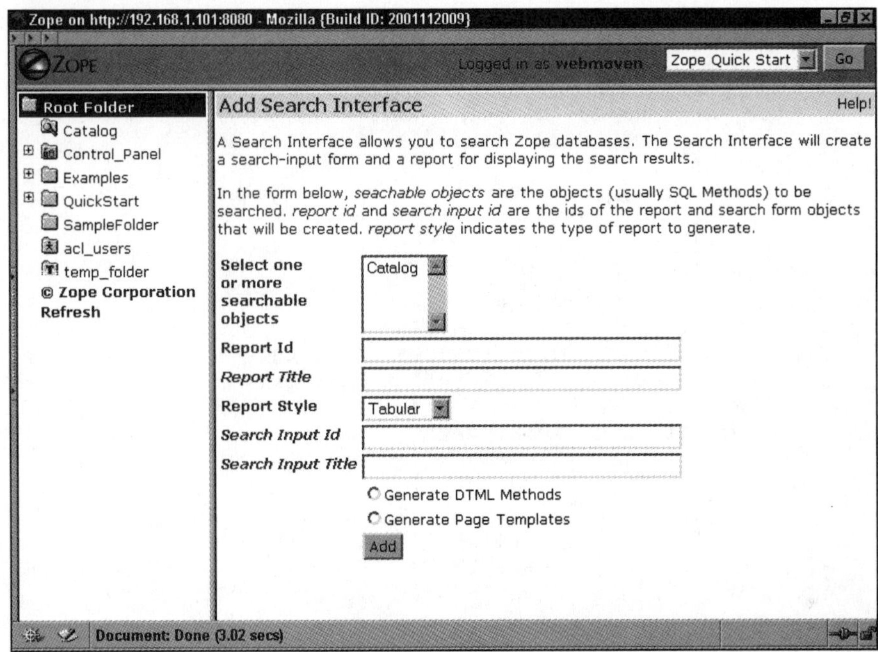

Figure 17-6: The Add Search Interface form

At the bottom of the form, you also have the option of selecting whether DTML Methods or Page Templates will be generated. Page Templates are a relatively new addition to Zope, so while we encourage you to explore their use (and read Chapter 18), the rest of this chapter will only discuss using DTML Methods. So select the DTML Methods radio button.

After you've filled in the form, click the Add button, and after a brief pause, you are returned to the Contents view of the root folder. Two new DTML methods are there: `search_form` and `search_results`.

Listing 17-1: The search_form method

```
<dtml-var standard_html_header>

<form action="search_results" method="get">
<h2><dtml-var document_title></h2>
Enter query parameters:<br><table>

<tr><th>Id</th>
    <td><input name="id"
             width=30 value=""></td></tr>
<tr><th>Path</th>
    <td><input name="path"
             width=30 value=""></td></tr>
<tr><th>Title</th>
    <td><input name="title"
             width=30 value=""></td></tr>
<tr><th>PrincipiaSearchSource</th>
    <td><input name="PrincipiaSearchSource"
             width=30 value=""></td></tr>
<tr><th>Meta type</th>
    <td><input name="meta_type"
             width=30 value=""></td></tr>
<tr><th>Bobobase modification time</th>
    <td><input name="bobobase_modification_time"
             width=30 value=""></td></tr>
<tr><td colspan=2 align=center>
<input type="SUBMIT" name="SUBMIT" value="Submit Query">
</td></tr>
</table>
</form>
<dtml-var standard_html_footer>
```

You can see in Listing 17-1 that the input names match the various indexes that they search.

It's easy to compare the code from Listings 17-2 and 17-3 to see the differences and similarities between the tabular and records formats for results lists. The most significant thing about both of these code listings is the line `<dtml-in Catalog size=50 start=query_start>`, which seems to indicate that no parameters are being passed into the ZCatalog. In fact, the ZCatalog is picking up the form fields and their values from the HTTP request (accessible in Zope through the `REQUEST` object), so no values need to be passed in explicitly. This is why the attribute, the index, and the form field all share the same id — to make this transparency possible.

Listing 17-2: The search_results method (tabular)

```
<dtml-var standard_html_header>
<dtml-in Catalog size=50 start=query_start>
   <dtml-if sequence-start>

      <dtml-if previous-sequence>

        <a href="<dtml-var URL><dtml-var sequence-query
                >query_start=<dtml-var
                previous-sequence-start-number>">
        (Previous <dtml-var previous-sequence-size> results)
        </a>

      </dtml-if previous-sequence>

      <table border>
        <tr>
          <th>Title</th>
          <th>Meta type</th>
          <th>Id</th>
          <th>Summary</th>
          <th>Bobobase modification time</th>
          <th>Data record id </th>
        </tr>

   </dtml-if sequence-start>

        <tr>
          <td><dtml-var title></td>
          <td><dtml-var meta_type></td>
          <td><dtml-var id></td>
          <td><dtml-var summary></td>
          <td><dtml-var bobobase_modification_time></td>
          <td><dtml-var data_record_id_></td>
        </tr>

   <dtml-if sequence-end>

      </table>
      <dtml-if next-sequence>

         <a href="<dtml-var URL><dtml-var sequence-query
            >query_start=<dtml-var
            next-sequence-start-number>">
         (Next <dtml-var next-sequence-size> results)
         </a>
```

Continued

Listing 17-2 *(continued)*

```
      </dtml-if next-sequence>
   </dtml-if sequence-end>

<dtml-else>

  There was no data matching this <dtml-var title_or_id> query.

</dtml-in>

<dtml-var standard_html_footer>
```

Listing 17-3: The search_results method (records)

```
<dtml-var standard_html_header>
<dtml-in Catalog size=20 start=query_start>
   <dtml-if sequence-start>

      <dtml-if previous-sequence>

        <a href="<dtml-var URL><dtml-var sequence-query
                 >query_start=<dtml-var
                 previous-sequence-start-number>">
        (Previous <dtml-var previous-sequence-size> results)
        </a>

      </dtml-if previous-sequence>


   </dtml-if sequence-start>

        <p>
          <dtml-var title>,
          <dtml-var meta_type>,
          <dtml-var id>,
          <dtml-var summary>,
          <dtml-var bobobase_modification_time>,
          <dtml-var data_record_id_>
        </p>

   <dtml-if sequence-end>


      <dtml-if next-sequence>
```

```
          <a href="<dtml-var URL><dtml-var sequence-query
             >query_start=<dtml-var
             next-sequence-start-number>">
          (Next <dtml-var next-sequence-size> results)
          </a>

       </dtml-if next-sequence>
    </dtml-if sequence-end>

 <dtml-else>

   There was no data matching this <dtml-var title_or_id> query.

 </dtml-in>

 <dtml-var standard_html_footer>
```

You can see the rendered `search_form` in Figure 17-7, and you should see something similar if you view the `search_form` DTML method.

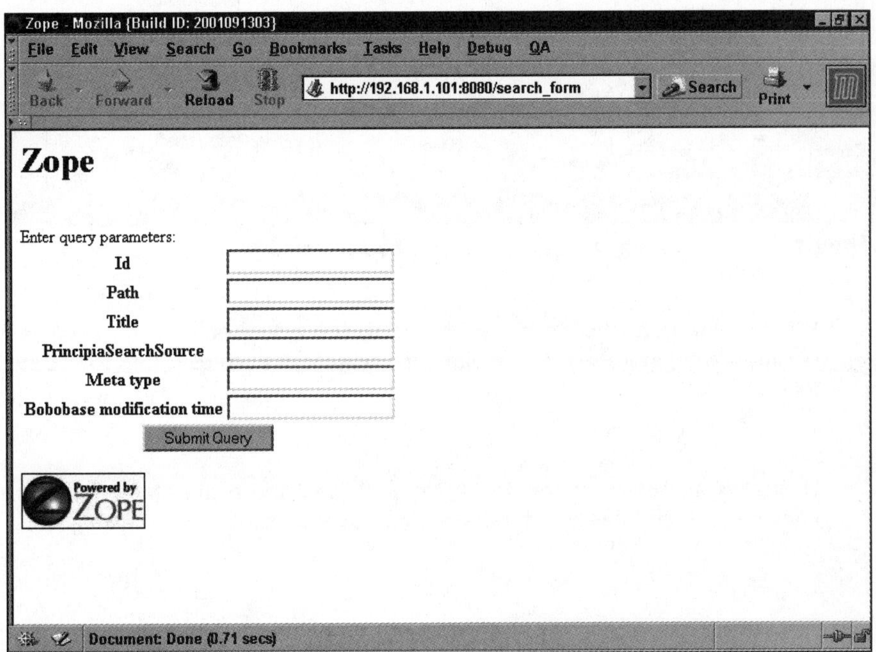

Figure 17-7: The `search_form` generated interface

You can see that the search form has a field for each index. When you click on the Submit Query button without entering any search parameters, the Catalog returns all objects that it has cataloged. Depending on whether you selected a tabular format or a records format when you generated the search interface, you see a results page like the one shown in either Figure 17-8 or Figure 17-9.

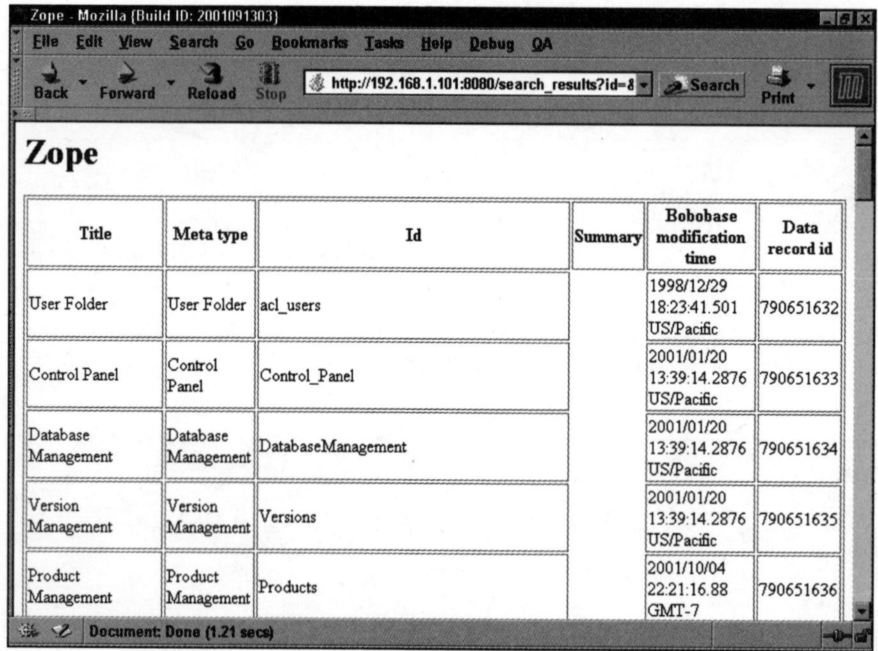

Figure 17-8: The `search_results` method (tabular format)

You can link from the search results list to the actual objects by changing the occurrence of <dtml-var id> in either the Tabular or Records results format to the following code:

```
<a href="&dtml-getURL;"><dtml-var id></a>
```

This takes advantage of the getURL attribute that the result object (colloquially known as a brain) has, which refers to the actual object that was cataloged.

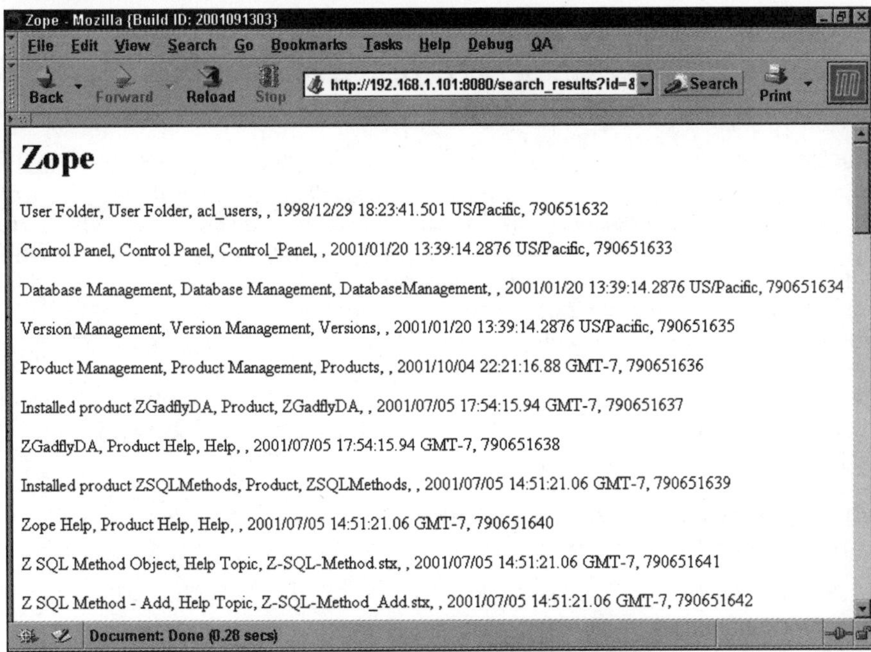

Figure 17-9: The `search_results` method (records format)

Accessing ZCatalogs from Python

You can access ZCatalogs from Python script objects and from within Python-based product code, not just using DTML search interfaces. This lets you use your sites logic and behavior to query the ZCatalog programmatically.

Accessing ZCatalogs from Python script objects

Consider the following Python script object, named `about_objects`:

```
x = context.Catalog({'PrincipiaSearchSource': 'about'})
z = []
for y in x:
    z.append(y.getObject())
return z
```

You can call the script from a DTML method, like this:

```
<dtml-var standard_html_header>
<dtml-in about_objects>
<a href="&dtml-absolute_url;"><dtml-var id></a><br>
</dtml-in>
<dtml-var standard_html_footer>
```

Calling from a DTML method, as in the preceding code, produces a list of links to all cataloged documents containing the word `about`. The catalog is being passed a dictionary, where the key is the index id, and the value is the indexed value that we're looking for.

Notice that the Python Script takes the result object list `x`, and by calling the result objects' `getObject` method, builds a list of the actual cataloged objects (`z`), which it returns instead of the list of result objects. This allows the DTML to call the individual objects' `absolute_url` method, instead of the result objects' `getURL` method. Both approaches are valid, but there is a tradeoff. The `absolute_url` method is common to all objects, making it easier to pass almost any object list to this DTML, which can make code reuse a little easier. However, result objects are typically much lighter weight that the actual objects they represent, which makes them (and their associated `getURL` method) a better choice if the list is either very long, or the objects very large, either of which will increase the amount of memory Zope requires to retrieve the object list.

A hybrid approach can sometimes work, by having the Python Script simply return the result object list like this:

```
x = context.Catalog({'PrincipiaSearchSource': 'about'})
return x
```

In order for this to work and allow the DTML to just call `absolute_url`, the Catalog must store `absolute_url` as metadata for the cataloged objects. This approach gives you the advantages of both DTML portability, and reducing the system load, at the cost of increasing the amount of metadata that the ZCatalog stores.

The catalog query can easily be made dynamic by using a variable name instead of a literal (not surrounded by single quotes), in order to pass in a dynamic value, as in the following example:

```
x = context.Catalog({'PrincipiaSearchSource': searchtext})
z = []
for y in x:
    z.append(y.getObject())
return z
```

Make sure that the Python script object has a `searchtext` parameter defined, and call the Python script object from DTML, like this:

```
<dtml-in expr="about_objects(searchtext='here')">
<a href="&dtml-absolute_url;"><dtml-var id></a><br>
</dtml-in>
```

You can find more information about creating and using Python Script Objects in Chapter 15.

Accessing ZCatalogs from Python products

Accessing a ZCatalog from within a Python product is just as easy as from within a script object, assuming that the class in question inherits from `Acquisition.Implicit`:

```
def catalog_results(self, REQUEST):
    """
    Returns results from the catalog
    """
    x = self.Catalog({'PrincipiaSearchSource': 'about'})
    z = []
    for y in x:
        z.append(y.getObject())
    return z
```

As you can see, the only real difference between a Python product and a Python script object is how the ZCatalog is accessed initially. After you access the Catalog, the Python syntax is identical.

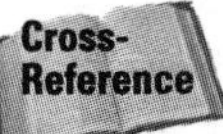

More information on writing Zope Python products is in chapters 6 through 10.

Complex queries from Python

It's possible to do more complex queries from Python than the examples we've given you so far.

One interesting thing you can do is pass more than one key/value pair to the ZCatalog:

```
x = context.Catalog({'PrincipiaSearchSource': 'an', 'id':
'dtContent'})
```

When you pass two query parameters in this way, the Catalog only returns the items that satisfy both conditions. This is equivalent to a Boolean AND operation.

In order to get a Boolean OR you need to add together the results of two separate queries, like this:

```
x = context.Catalog({'PrincipiaSearchSource': 'an'})
y = context.Catalog({'id': 'dtContent'})
z = x + y
return z
```

Unfortunately, this does not produce a true Boolean OR, as the result is merely a concatenation of the two lists, and the results that meet both requirements appear twice. We can rewrite the code to eliminate duplicates as follows:

```
x = context.Catalog({'PrincipiaSearchSource': 'an'})
y = context.Catalog({'id': 'dtContent'})
z = []
for w in x:
    for q in y:
        if q.getObject() == w.getObject():
            break
    else:
        z.append(w)

for q in y:
    z.append(q)

return z
```

This is a bit cumbersome, but it gets the job done. This code loops through each result in the first sequence `x`, checking it against each item in the second sequence `y` (in a second loop). The code here has to check the actual cataloged objects (not the results themselves) by retrieving them using `getObject()`. Only if there is no match does the result from the first sequence get appended to the returned sequence `z`. Then the second sequence `y` is appended to the returned sequence `z` in it's entirety (since it contains no duplicates with the list), which is then returned. Now the script returns a true Boolean OR of the two sets.

Making Zope Product Classes auto catalogable (CatalogAwareness)

Making a Python Zope Product that automatically catalogs itself when it's created, and reindexes itself whenever it's changed is fairly easy and straightforward. The class needs to subclass from `CatalogAware`, and it needs to call `self.reindex_object()` whenever the object is changed. Here is the Hello Product from Chapter 6 after it has been made CatalogAware:

```
from OFS.SimpleItem import Item
from Globals import Persistent, HTMLFile
from Acquisition import Implicit
from Products.ZCatalog.CatalogPathAwareness import CatalogAware

manage_addHelloForm = HTMLFile('DTML/manage_addHelloForm', ⮐
globals())

def manage_addHello(self, id, REQUEST):
    "Method for adding a Hello object"
    newHello = helloClass(id)
    self._setObject(id, newHello)
```

```
    return self.manage_main(self, REQUEST)

class helloClass(Item, Persistent, Implicit, CatalogAware):
    def __init__(self, id, Name = 'World'):
        self.id = id
        self.Name = Name

    meta_type = "Hello Object"

    manage_options = ({'label':'Edit', ⮐
'action':'manage_editHelloForm'},)

    def hello(self):
        return "Hello, " + self.Name

    def edit(self, Name, REQUEST):
        "method to edit Hello instances"
        self.Name = Name
        self.reindex_object()
        return self.index_html(self, REQUEST)

    # Web Methods

    index_html = HTMLFile('DTML/index_html', globals())

    manage_editHelloForm = ⮐
HTMLFile('DTML/manage_editHelloForm', globals())
```

As you can see, only one line needed to be added, and one other line changed, in order to make this Class automatically Catalog itself (CatalogAware). The Class will now automatically catalog itself with the ZCatalog (named Catalog) whenever an instance is added (or copy-and-pasted), and automatically remove itself from the ZCatalog whenever it is deleted. The only thing the class needs to do itself is reindex itself when it is changed. It's worth noting that CatalogAwareness does not hook into the persistence machinery, so reindexing will not happen by itself even if the attribute that changed was immutable. You always have to trigger `reindex_object()` on the class instance yourself.

Note In the preceding example, the Module is importing the CatalogAware class from Products.ZCatalog.CatalogPathAwareness, rather than from Products.ZCatalog. CatalogAwareness. This is to take advantage of improvements made to that version of CatalogAware that use the objects' physical path within the ZODB to uniquely identify an object, rather than use the Objects' URL, as the previous version of CatalogAware did. This avoids several problems related to virtual hosting several domain names on the same Zope server, and also avoids problems associated with accessing the same server using different IP addresses or network names. You should always use Products.ZCatalog.CatalogPathAwareness. CatalogAware to make your Zope Products CatalogAware.

More about ZCatalog

There is more to the ZCatalog than automatically generating search interfaces. Here is some more in-depth information.

More about text indexes

As described earlier in the chapter, a text index is used to index human-readable text. You can search the index for objects that contain certain words. Text indexes also enable you to make more advanced searches than just looking for a word. ZCatalog's Text Index can do the following:

- Use Boolean query expressions such as `word1 AND word2`. This returns all objects that contain both words. Supported Boolean expressions include `AND`, `OR`, and `AND NOT`.
- Control search order by grouping queries using parentheses: `(word1 AND word2) AND NOT word3)`. This returns objects that contain both of the first two words, but does not return any that contain the third word.
- If your catalog contains a Globbing Vocabulary object (the default Vocabulary has Globbing enabled), you may also use wildcards in your search queries, such as searching for `Zo*` to return objects that contain `Zoroaster`, `Zope`, and `ZODB`.

More about field indexes

Unlike text indexes, which break up attributes into words that are indexed separately, a field index treats the value of an attribute as an indivisible whole, and it indexes the entire value of the attribute. This makes field indexes very useful for indexing attributes whose value must be one of a limited set of choices (for example, selection properties) and for attributes whose value must be treated as a whole, such as Ids, even if they do have spaces in them.

About Vocabularies

A simplistic approach to searching for a word in various objects would be to use a regular expression to determine whether the word existed as a substring of the relevant attributes, but this would be a very resource-intensive operation and would not scale particularly well. All ZCatalog indexes are intended to minimize search times by creating lookup tables to make the determination faster. Because human-readable text passages conform to certain rules of grammar, a text index can use rules to determine in advance what substrings are likely to be relevant, and store only those in the lookup table. However, because these rules are different for every language (and sometimes for each subject), ZCatalogs break out this functionality to a separate object called a Vocabulary. When you create a Text index, you must choose which Vocabulary it uses.

Here are some of the rules that Vocabulary objects use to determine what substrings are worth indexing:

- **Breaking up the text into words.** In western languages, words are delimited by whitespace or punctuation on either end of the substring. In many Asian languages, single characters are considered words, or else the determination is made from context.
- **Choosing which words to ignore.** In English, there is no point in indexing words such as "a," "of," "and," "it," and so on. In other languages, the list of ignorable words (called stop-words') will be different.
- **Indicating synonyms.** In English, the words "present" and "gift" can be considered synonyms, and you would want a search for "gift" to also bring up objects that contain the word "present," but this does not make sense in any other language. However, note that in some situations, this does not necessarily make sense in English either, and "present/now" or "present/display" may make a more suitable pair for your context.
- **Indexing the stem words only.** Someone searching for the word "park" would also be interested in occurrences of the words "parking" and "parks." A Vocabulary uses rules to trim suffixes from words in order to make sure that the stem words only get indexed, and also trimming these suffixes from the query strings. This makes sure that variants based on different tenses show up in a search. However, these rules are different from one language to another, with some languages having prefixes, or even compound words that need to be split up further and indexed separately.

When you create a Vocabulary object, you must choose which splitter to use, and whether to make the Vocabulary object Globbing. Three splitters are available: the standard ZopeSplitter, an ISO-8859-1 Splitter, and a Unicode aware Splitter. Globbing vocabularies are more complex vocabularies that allow wild card searches on English text to be performed because they also index word fragments. However, they use a lot more memory and space in the ZODB than non-globbing vocabularies.

The different splitters are intended to be used depending on the character set of the content being indexed. The standard ZopeSplitter is basically for use on objects containing ASCII encoded English text, and is primarily useful for that purpose. The ISO-8859-1 splitter is able to recognize and index characters that lie outside the ASCII character-set, and takes its name from the standard that defines the characters in the Latin-1 character-set used by many Western European languages such as German, French, Danish, and so forth. The Unicode splitter is intended to be used with texts encoded using the Unicode standard, which encompasses practically all known human languages.

Creating a Vocabulary object is fairly simple. Within a ZCatalog instance, delete the existing Vocabulary object by selecting the checkbox next to it, and clicking the Delete button. Next, choose Vocabulary from the drop-down list. In the form that comes up, you can set the id of the Vocabulary object (you should type in **Vocabulary**), the Title (which you can omit), the type of Splitter (choose ZopeSplitter), and whether the Vocabulary object is Globbing (non-Globbing is the default, select the checkbox to make the Vocabulary Globbing).

Once you've made your selections, click Add, and a Vocabulary with the settings you've selected will be added to the ZCatalog.

By default, ZCatalogs are instantiated with three field indexes: bobobase_ modification_time, id, and meta_type. The search_form DTML method that you generated earlier uses a text field to query the meta_type of the objects that were cataloged, but this isn't very useful. An object's meta_type can only be equal to one of a limited number of choices, so it doesn't make sense to potentially give a wrong result because of a mistyped query. So, we are going to show you how to modify the search interface to take advantage of the field index.

Find the section in the search_form DTML method that reads as follows:

```
<tr><th>Meta type</th>
    <td><input name="meta_type"
               width=30 value=""></td></tr>
```

And replace it with the following code:

```
<tr><th>Meta type</th>
    <td>
     <select name="meta_type">
      <option value="">
      <dtml-in expr="Catalog.uniqueValuesFor('meta_type')">
      <option value="&dtml-sequence-item;"><dtml-var sequence-
item>
      </dtml-in>
     </select>
    </td>
</tr>
```

Click Save Changes, and take a look at the search_form. You see a drop-down box that contains a listing of every meta_type that the ZCatalog has indexed. If you leave the drop-down with no field selected or the first blank option selected, the meta_type is not considered in the query, but if you select a meta_type, only objects that have that meta_type will be returned.

More about keyword indexes

Keyword indexes take a sequence of strings and break them up into their individual strings and index them individually. In this way, they are a little like text indexes (in that they break up an attribute into its components) and like Field indexes (in that the individual strings are then treated as indivisible). As their name suggests, they are very useful for indexing attributes that serve as sequences of keywords, which can then be used to place objects into categories.

Typically, a keyword index would index either a line or multiple select property (in a ZClass) or a list of strings (in a Python class). As an example, let's say that you are trying to categorize a collection of books in a departmental library that are listed on your company Intranet. You create a ZClass with `author`, `title`, and `description` properties, and a multiple-selection property called `categories` that is populated from another property, `category_list`.

In the catalog that the books will be indexed in, you create a `categories` keyword index. Now let's suppose that you have the following categories to choose from for your books (partial list):

- Programming
- Marketing
- Java
- HTML
- Sales
- Python
- Branding
- Microsoft
- Design
- Typography
- Zope

You can see that a book about designing Web sites would probably be categorized under both Design and HTML, while this book (the *Zope Bible*) would be categorized under Programming, Python, and Zope.

In your search interface, you would provide a multiple selection form element, like the following:

```
<select name="categories:list" multiple>
 <dtml-in expr="Catalog.uniqueValuesFor('categories')">
 <option value="&dtml-sequence-item;"><dtml-var sequence-item>
 </dtml-in>
</select>
```

This lets users select as many categories as they are interested in, and the ZCatalog returns any objects that match one or more of the categories, with those that match to most listed first.

Notice how the form uses the unique`ValuesFor()` method rather than the `category_list` property. This ensures that only those categories that actually have books associated with them are listed as valid choices.

More about path indexes

Path indexes take a path attribute and break it up into a sequence of successive shorter paths by removing the object on the end of the path. Thus, a DTML document located at `/marketing/branding/style_guide/logos.html` is indexed under the following subpaths:

- ✦ `/marketing/branding/style_guide`
- ✦ `/marketing/branding`
- ✦ `/marketing`

Searching for any of these subpaths returns the document and any other objects stored under the subpath. The following code lists all documents stored in or under the `/marketing` folder and links to them:

```
<ul>
<dtml-in expr="Catalog(meta_type='DTML Document', path='/marketing')">
 <li><a href="&dtml-getURL;"><dtml-var title_or_id></a>
</dtml-in>
</ul>
```

Path indexes are particularly useful if you are using your site's containment hierarchy to categorize and structure the content of your site.

The Advanced tab

The Advanced tab in a ZCatalog lets you perform some maintenance operations, and controls some finer details that determine how the ZCatalog operates.

The Advanced tab has two sections, Catalog Maintenance and Subtransactions. The Catalog Maintenance section of the tab has two buttons on it, Update Catalog and Clear Catalog. The Update Catalog button is similar in its operation to selecting all the indexes on the Indexes tab and clicking the Reindex button. This clears all the indexes, and recatalogs all cataloged objects, repopulating the indexes and updating the object's metadata.

Clicking the Clear Catalog button does just as its name suggests, clearing the catalog of all cataloged objects and metadata. For all intents and purposes, the Zcatalog forgets about all the objects it has cataloged and their stored metadata. It doesn't remove the indexes you've set up in the ZCatalog, though it does wipe them clean.

The Subtransactions section is a bit more involved. It controls whether Zope commits cataloging transactions a little at a time, or tries to do so all at once.

Using subtransactions reduces the amount of memory ZCatalog needs when cataloging large numbers of objects, but also slows the cataloging operations down. So you're trading memory for speed. Subtransactions are enabled by default. When subtransactions are enabled, you can disable disable them by clicking the Disable button. When subtransactions are disabled, you can enable them by clicking the Enable button.

ZCatalog subtransactions are not compatible with ZSQL methods. If you are cataloging objects and using ZSQL methods in the same transaction, you must disable subtransactions in the ZCatalog.

When Subtransactions are enabled, you can also determine the threshold above which a subtransaction will be committed. The default is 10,000 objects. Lowering the number causes subtransactions to be committed more frequently, lowering the number of objects that need to be kept in memory at any one time during a cataloging (or recataloging) operation, and further slows the cataloging operation down, and increasing the number effects the reverse tradeoff, keeping more objects in memory to speed the cataloging operation. How much memory is saved or used, and how much the cataloging operations are sped up or slowed down, depends very much on the specifics of the objects that you're cataloging. If your objects are large, and you find that cataloging operations are causing your server to run out of memory, you can try lowering the subtransaction threshold.

Summary

In this chapter, you learned how to catalog content in your Zope site in order to search and retrieve it quickly, based on the indexed attributes of the objects. You also learned about storing metadata about the objects in the ZCatalog, in order to make the search results more informative.

All of the different index types were discussed, including text indexes, keyword indexes, field indexes, and path indexes, along with their uses in various contexts.

We also introduced using ZCatalog queries from DTML and from within Python Script Objects and Python Products.

The ZCatalog is a very powerful tool for developing Web sites, especially when combined with `CatalogAware` ZClasses and Python products to automatically catalog and index a site's content as it is added to and changed.

✦ ✦ ✦

CHAPTER 18

Zope Page Templates

✦ ✦ ✦ ✦

In This Chapter

The problem with DTML

Template Attribute Language

TAL Expression Syntax

Macro Expansion TAL

✦ ✦ ✦ ✦

In this chapter, we'll discuss the drawbacks of DTML and you'll meet Zope Page Templates, a new presentation scripting technology introduced in Zope 2.5. As always, we provide some references for further reading at the end of the chapter.

The Problem with DTML

Throughout the rest of this book, we used DTML (Document Template Markup Language) for all code that is specific to the presentation layer of our examples, and in some cases we've shown you how to code logic in DTML as well. However, DTML has some serious shortcomings:

- ✦ DTML tags are not friendly to HTML editors.
- ✦ DTML source is not renderable by a WYSIWYG (What You See Is What You Get) editor.
- ✦ DTML encourages mixing of presentation and logic.

To be sure, the present form of the DTML syntax was a great improvement over the original syntax. Witness the following equivalent pieces of code:

```
<!--#in objectValues('DTML Document')-->
<!--#var title-->
<!--#/in-->

<dtml-in objectValues ('DTML Document')>
<dtml-var title>
</dtml-in>
```

The former code was the old original DTML syntax, which was eventually improved to be cleaner and easier to both read and type. Both syntaxes are still supported within Zope, but you won't find too much code written in the old style anymore. Nevertheless, despite these improvements, DTML still has problems.

DTML tags are not friendly to HTML editors

No generally available HTML (Hypertext Markup Language) editor understands DTML tags or knows what to do with them. A few, such as Macromedia's Dreamweaver, can be set to ignore tags that they are unfamiliar with, but this does not necessarily let you edit the page.

Suppose your code is doing something simple, such as determining which of several background colors to use for a table cell, as in this code fragment:

```
<td <dtml-if sequence-even>bgcolor="#CCCCCC"<dtml-else>
bgcolor="#FFFFCC"</dtml-if> >
```

Leave aside for the moment the fact that most editors will simply choke at what they see as a completely malformed `<td>` tag — an HTML editor that lets you set attributes on a tag will likely balk at what it sees as a duplicated `bgcolor` attribute. Some editors might even attempt to fix the code and remove the redundant `bgcolor` attribute.

You could instead duplicate the HTML completely, like this:

```
<dtml-if sequence-even><td bgcolor="#CCCCCC">
<dtml-else><td bgcolor="#FFFFCC">
</dtml-if>
```

But now the editor will complain about opening a new table cell without closing the previous one. So you go ahead and completely duplicate the entire tag, including whatever DTML code was supposed to populate the cell with content. Duplicating code is of course a recipe for a site that is difficult to maintain, and weren't we using Zope to avoid that in the first place?

Now you break apart your HTML into reusable pieces, and put them into their own methods. Hmm. Weren't we already doing that with `standard_html_header` and `standard_html_footer`? Which brings us to the next point. . . .

DTML Methods and Documents are not renderable by WYSIWYG editors

This is an issue only partly related to the previous one. Because DTML Documents and Methods are not *complete* HTML documents, a WYSIWYG editor can't render them in order to give an HTML designer any idea as to what it will look like. Consider the following DTML Document:

```
<dtml-var standard_html_header>
<h2><dtml-var title_or_id></h2>
<p>
This is the <dtml-var id> Document.
</p>
<dtml-var standard_html_footer>
```

There is just no way that an HTML editor can interpret this as a valid HTML document, even if it ignores the DTML tags. The capability to inline and render modular code sections is a powerful capability for application servers such as Zope, but its implementation in DTML (and similar server-side scripting technologies) leads to pages whose HTML is scattered among various DTML Documents and Methods, with no way to edit the page as a whole.

As a result, HTML designers are limited to creating HTML templates in their favorite tools, and then handing them off to developers who proceed to chop them up into headers, footers, navigation bars, and so on, and inserting the necessary DTML code to pull in data from the ZODB (Zope Object Database) to both reassemble the pieces into pages and populate the page with content.

Sadly, this process is entirely one way, and the designer cannot edit the DTML-ified version with his or her favorite tools, as the template is no longer in any one place. Furthermore, if the designer wants to tweak his or her design, he or she has to create a new template and hand it off to the developers again for the whole process to be repeated. This creates a lot more work for the developers that they could have been spending creating new functionality for the site.

DTML encourages the mixing of presentation and logic

DTML enables you to do some powerful things. Unfortunately, not all of these things are directly related to rendering the presentation layer. These include such capabilities as instantiating objects, deleting objects, setting cookies, redirecting the browser, and so on.

To be fair, at the time that the DTML syntax was originally created, Python code for Zope was limited to filesystem-based external methods, and Python Script objects didn't yet exist. For any logic you wanted to add to your site through the Web, you pretty much had to use DTML. Once ZODB-based Python Script objects were added to Zope, there was less need for these capabilities within DTML, but they remain in Zope for backward compatibility. Unfortunately, it can be difficult to discipline yourself and enforce the separation between presentation and logic when to a large extent you're using the same syntax for both.

When presentation and logic are mixed together in this way, the code is much more difficult to understand, debug, and modify. Maintainability of both presentation and logic suffer. Separating the logic out into Python products, and restricting the use of DTML to presentation only is a good practice, but product code, being on the filesystem is more difficult to work with than through-the-Web code. Python Script objects (added to Zope in version 2.3) finally enabled developers to cleanly separate presentation and logic from each other and still write code through the Web, but the temptation to cross the line from presentation logic to application logic when working in DTML is always there.

Clearly, an alternative to DTML that did not have these problems was called for. Enter TAL (Template Attribute Language).

While DTML has its drawbacks as a templating language for HTML pages, it is still quite useful when you need to dynamically create other file formats such as comma-delimited text files. For this reason, and for reasons of backward compatibility, Zope will continue to support DTML in the foreseeable future.

TAL (Template Attribute Language)

In Zope 2.5, Zope is integrating a new syntax and paradigm for developing Page Templates that avoids the problems of DTML, and introduces some interesting new capabilities. The new syntax is based on XHTML (Extensible Hypertext Markup Language) attributes, which can be attached to ordinary HTML tags. Following is an example of a dynamic greeting:

```
<b>Hello, <span tal:replace="user/getUserName">User
Name</span>!</b>
```

In this sample, an ordinary `<span>` tag has been augmented with an additional attribute. This is an XML namespace attribute, as indicated by the colon (:) in the attribute name. The `tal:replace` attribute indicates that the result of the path expression that it is assigned as a value should replace the entire tag that the attribute is on, giving the following rendering:

```
<b>Hello, Bill!</b>
```

Assuming, of course, that the user viewing the rendered page has a username of "Bill." We'll get back to path expressions later in the chapter, as these are one of the expression types defined by the TALES (TAL Expression Syntax).

What's interesting here is that unlike with DTML, or practically any other templating solution, both the rendered and unrendered code are valid HTML (or XHTML), so the editor you use to create the template won't have any more problems with the unrendered page than the browser does with the rendered one. All the editor needs to be able to do is ignore any unfamiliar attributes and most good editors do this very well.

Page template basics

In your Root Folder, choose Page Template from the drop-down list of objects, and you'll see an Add Page Template form like the form shown in Figure 18-1.

Type Test for the id and click Add and Edit. You should now see a form like the form shown in Figure 18-2.

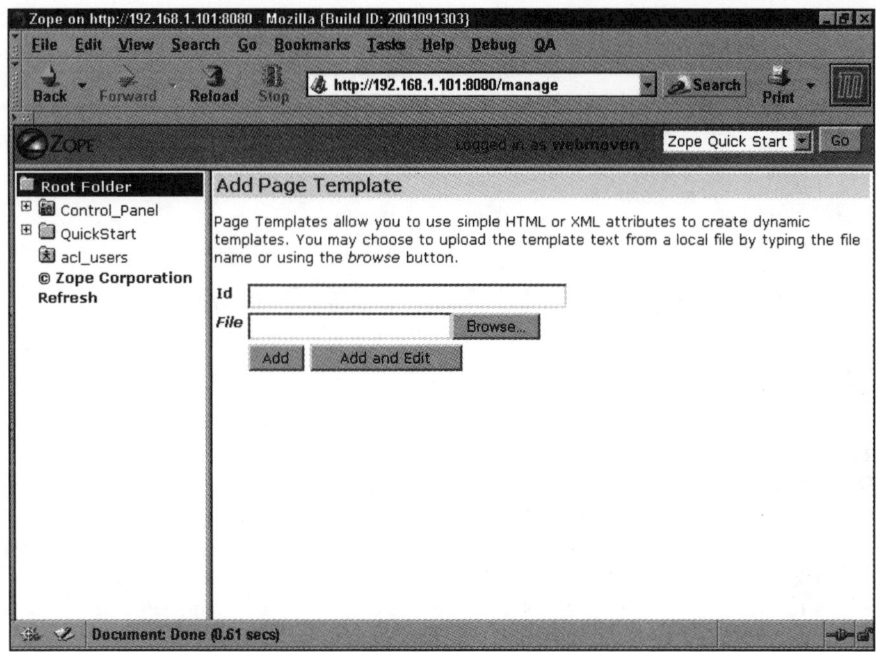

Figure 18-1: The Add Page Template form

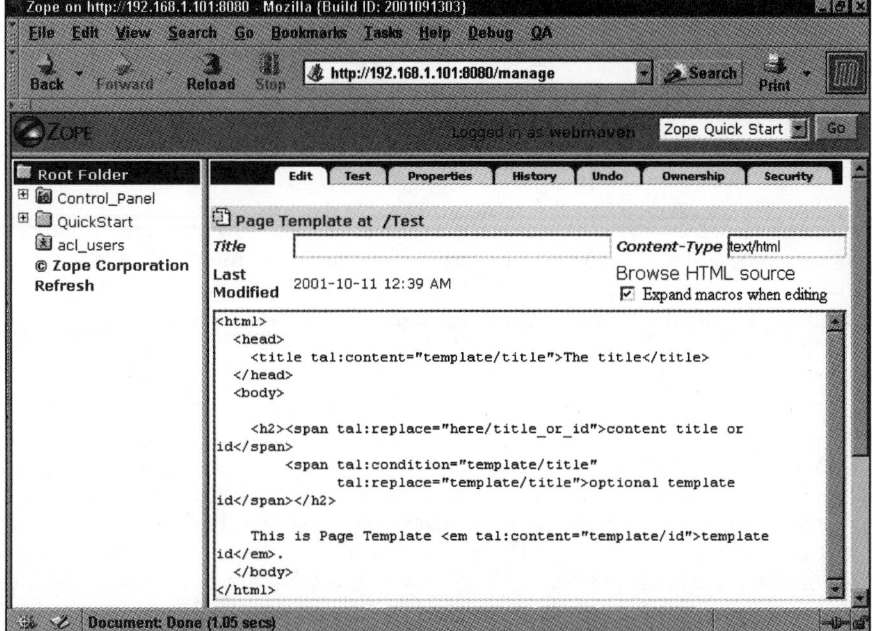

Figure 18-2: The Edit Page Template form

Rather a lot is going on in the default template content, so before you go any further, change the title property to The Test Document, and edit the content of the template as follows:

```
<html>
  <head>
    <title tal:content="template/title">The title</title>
  </head>
  <body>

    <b><span tal:replace="template/title">The Title</span></b>

  </body>
</html>
```

Then click Save Changes.

Although TAL uses XHTML attributes to add processing instructions to templates, the examples in this chapter are not actually valid XHTML, for clarity's sake. Doctypes are not declared for any of the examples in this chapter, nor do we include an XML declaration at the beginning of the code. This means that while the examples will be processed correctly by Zope, and the rendered template will display correctly in a browser, the examples will not validate correctly by the W3C XHTML validator at `http://validator.w3.org/`. We would like to encourage you to explore the transition to XHTML, and ensuring that your pages validate. More resources about XHTML are listed at the end of this chapter.

At this point, you can check out the rendered version of the template by clicking the Test tab, which displays a page like the page shown in Figure 18-3.

It's easy to see what has happened here. The `<span>` tag, with the `tal:replace="template/title"` attribute set on it, has been replaced with the text, "The Test Document," by the template rendering process.

Because the TAL syntax is designed to be valid XHTML, browsers, as well as editors, can parse the unrendered templates. You can view the unrendered source in a browser by clicking the Browse HTML Source link at the top of the Page Template editing form, which displays something like Figure 18-4.

You can see that in this case, the words, "The Title," which are enclosed in the `<span>` tag are plainly visible, as the unrendered template has not replaced the tag.

However, the `<title>` tag in the template's head section is plainly not being replaced, or it wouldn't show up in the browser window's title bar. The reason the behavior is different is in the two TAL attributes. The `TAL` attribute on the `<title>` tag is `tal:content="template/title"`, whereas the attribute on the `<span>` tag in the body of the page is `tal:replace="template/title"`. Plainly, `tal:replace` is intended to replace the entire tag with the result of the expression, and `tal:content` is intended to replace the content of the tag only, leaving the tag itself intact.

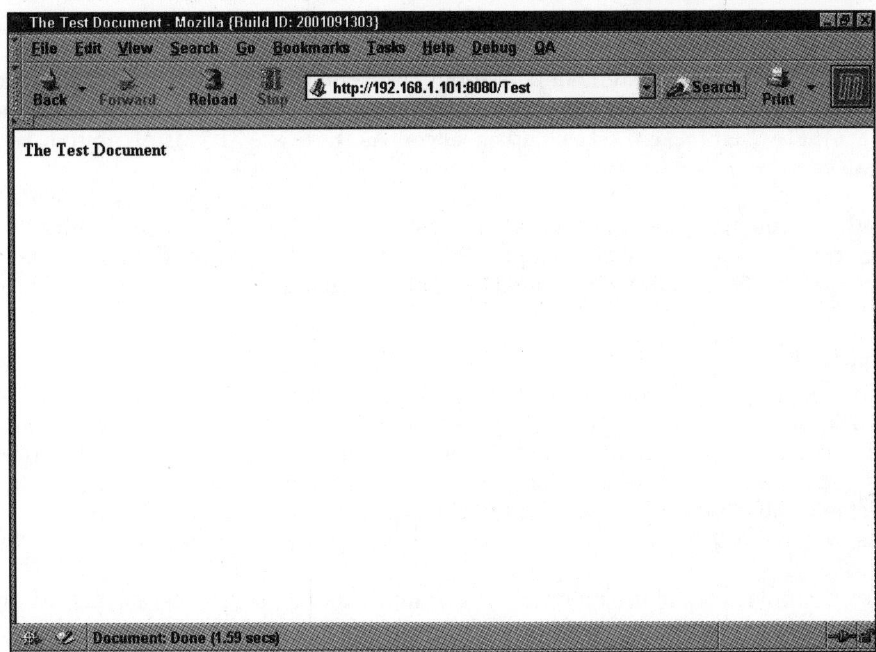

Figure 18-3: The rendered Test Page Template

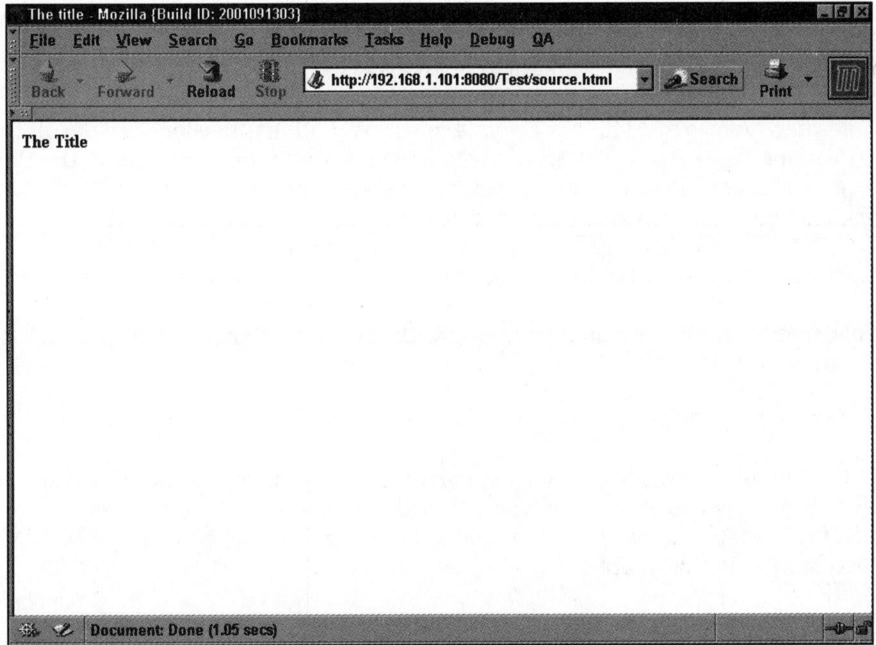

Figure 18-4: Browsing the unrendered template source

TAL statements

TAL defines several statements for adding presentation logic (as opposed to application logic) to Page Templates. They are: `replace`, `content`, `repeat`, `condition`, `attributes`, `define`, `omit-tag`, and `on-error`. As these are XHTML attributes, they must be lowercase only.

TAL statements follow the general form `tal:statement="expression"`, with the expression being one of several possible types, and optionally containing one or more flags. These will be explained later in the chapter.

replace

The `replace` statement, which we have already encountered, is one of the workhorses of Page Templates. It replaces the XHTML element that it is set on with the result of its expression, which is set as the value of the attribute. The expression can be prefixed with one of two flags: `text` or `structure`. `text`, which is the default behavior, causes the result of the expression to be escaped to HTML entities, such that `&` becomes `&`, `>` becomes `>`, and `<` becomes `<`.

For example, both of the following TAL statements replace the `<span>` tag with the templates escaped title attribute:

```
<span tal:replace="template/title">The Title</span>
<span tal:replace="text template/title">The Title</span>
```

This replaces the `<span>` tag with the unescaped `title` attribute:

```
<span tal:replace="structure template/title">The Title</span>
```

Note that `"template/title"` is a *path expression*. Path expressions are one of the expression types that a TAL statement can use. More information about the types of expressions that TAL statements can use is found later in this chapter in the TALES (TAL Expression Syntax) section. For now, you just need to know that `"template/title"` evaluates similarly to `<dtml-var title>`, except that it uses the `title` attribute of the template, instead of an acquired `title` attribute.

This element is simply removed (along with the content enclosed by the tag) from the rendered HTML:

```
<span tal:replace="nothing">A TAL Comment</span>
```

This example also demonstrates the use of one of the names built-in to TAL. `nothing` is a special expression name that is equivalent to Python's `None`, or an SQL `NULL`. More details about the built in names in TAL can be found in the TALES section later in this chapter.

content

The `content` statement is almost identical to the `replace` statement, except that it only causes Zope to replace the contents of the tag, not the whole tag. Like `replace`, the content statement also has the optional flags `text` and `structure`, and the default behavior is also `text`.

For example, these statements populate an `<h1>` tag with the escaped `title` attribute of the template:

```
<h1 tal:content="template/title">The Title</h1>
<h1 tal:content="text template/title">The Title</h1>
```

This statement replaces the contents of the `<h1>` tag with the unescaped `title` attribute:

```
<h1 tal:content="structure template/title">The Title</h1>
```

This statement leaves the `<h1>` tag empty:

```
<h1 tal:content="nothing">An Empty H1 tag</h1>
```

repeat

DTML has the `<dtml-in>` tag for repeating a block of code once for every item in a sequence, and TAL has the `repeat` statement that is used for the same purpose. The `repeat` statement takes a variable name and an expression. The expression should evaluate to a sequence. An empty sequence causes the entire repeat statement to be removed from the rendered template.

The variable name is used to access both the individual item in the sequence, as well as information about the current iteration via an iteration object, which is only accessible through the use of a built-in attribute named `repeat`.

For example, this statement iterates over the list of objects returned by `objectValues` from the current context, and renders the id of each object as a list item in an unordered list:

```
<ul>
 <li tal:repeat="list here/objectValues" tal:content="list/id">An ID</li>
</ul>
```

In the previous code we are combining two TAL statements in the same `<li>` tag, one to iterate over the sequence, and one to render the content of the tag. Also, `here/objectValues` is another path expression. `here` refers to the current rendering context, so this `repeat` statement is roughly equivalent to `<dtml-in objectValues> <li><dtml-var id></dtml-in>`. Also, notice how the `content` statement's path expression starts with the variable name (`list`) defined in the `repeat` statement.

This demonstrates one of TALs strengths relative to DTML, namely that you must explicitly specify the namespace that a variable lookup should occur in. DTML by contrast only has a single namespace stack, which can make it difficult and confusing to get at the value you actually want, if it isn't at the top of the stack

The following code iterates over the same list of objects, but renders them as numbered rows in a table, using the index (starting from zero) to number the rows:

```
<table>
 <tr tal:repeat="list here/objectValues">
  <td tal:content="repeat/list/index">0</td>
  <td tal:content="list/id">An ID</td>
 </tr>
</table>
```

Notice how in this case, the repeat statement is on the `<tr>` tag, while the content statement is on the `<td>` tags. Also demonstrated is the special iteration object accessed through the `repeat` name in the first `content` statement's path expression.

`repeat` has several special variable names associated with it, as listed in Table 18-1.

Table 18-1
repeat Variables

Variable name	*Description*
`index`	The iteration number, starting from 0
`number`	The iteration number, starting from 1
`even`	This variable is true (1) when the iteration index is an even number, otherwise it's false (0)
`odd`	This variable is true (1) when the iteration index is an odd number, otherwise it's false (0)
`end`	This variable is true (1) if the iteration is the last in the sequence
`length`	The total number of iterations in the `repeat` sequence
`letter`	Designates the iterations with lowercase letters, "a" through "z", then "aa" - "az", then "ba" - "bz", eventually progressing to "za" through "zz" and then "aaa" through "aaz", and so on
`Letter`	Same as letter, using uppercase

condition

The `condition` statement takes an expression as an argument. If the expression evaluates as true, then evaluation of other statements on the element will proceed, and if it evaluates to false, the element is removed from the rendered page.

For instance, this example only renders if a Boolean `showme` attribute (which can be acquired) in the current context is true, though you should note that non-existence of a `showme` attribute raises an error, rather than evaluating to false:

```
<span tal:condition="here/showme">showme is true</span>
```

The error for a non-existent attribute can be avoided by modifying the code as follows:

```
<span tal:condition="here/showme | nothing">showme exists ⮐
and is true</span>
```

As a path expression that can't be resolved to an object or attribute raises an error rather than evaluating as false, the *pipe* (|) character provides a way of specifying alternatives. Specifying alternative paths can be used in other TAL statements that take path expressions as well. Here, the alternative path consists of the built in variable `nothing`, which always evaluates to false.

The following example creates a list of objects from the current context's `objectValues` method whose `visible` property evaluates to true:

```
<table>
 <tr tal:repeat="object here/objectValues">
  <td tal:content="object/id">An object id</td>
 </tr>
 <tr tal:condition="not:here/objectValues">
  <td>There are no objects here</td>
 </tr>
</table>
```

Here we are using the `not:` prefix, which inverts the truth of the evaluated expression. If there are no objects in `here/objectvalues` (that is, the expression is false), then the first table row will not render, but `not:` causes the condition statement on the second row to evaluate as true, and the second row is rendered. (See Table 18-2.) The practical upshot is that either we get a series of rows that list contained object ids, or we get a single row that informs us that there are no objects to list. More information about the not: flag can be found at the end of the Path Expressions section later in this chapter.

Table 18-2
True and False Values in TAL

True	*False*
Numbers besides zero	The `nothing` variable name
Non-blank strings (including those containing a single space)	The number zero (0)
Anything else that isn't false	A blank string
	An empty list
	An empty tuple
	An empty dictionary
	Python `None`

attributes

Besides being able to replace an entire element with the result of an expression, and being able to replace just the contents of an element, TAL also enables you to set other element attributes by using the `attributes` statement. `attributes` takes pairs of attribute names and expressions. Because there can only be a single `attributes` statement on an element, multiple attribute/expression pairs are separated with semicolons (;).

For instance, this example takes a list of objects from `objectValues`, and renders them in a table, making alternate rows different background colors:

```
<table>
 <span tal:repeat="list here/objectValues">

 <tr tal:condition="repeat/list/even"
     tal:attributes="bgcolor string:#FFFFCC">
  <td tal:content="list/id">An ID</td>
 </tr>

 <tr tal:condition="repeat/list/odd"
    tal:attributes="bgcolor string:#CCFFFF">
  <td tal:content="list/id">An ID</td>
 </tr>

 </span>
</table>
```

Notice how we're using the `condition` statement to determine which version of the table row will be rendered based on whether the row is odd or even, and then using the `attributes` statement to set the appropriate `bgcolor` attribute on the row.

define

The define statement enables you to assign the value of an expression to a label, which is available to other TAL statements in the template.

There are two kinds of variables in TAL: local variables and global variables. *Local* variables are only valid within the scope of the element in which they are defined and its child elements. If a child element redefines the variable, the change is only in effect for the child element and its children.

Global variables are available to any element after the element on which they are defined, even those not contained within that element. Redefining the variable only affects those elements that follow the element on which the variable was redefined.

For example, the following code defines a local variable (local variables are the default), redefines it in a child element, renders it in the child element's scope, exits the child element, and renders the variable again, this time within the parent scope. This renders the string, "The number is two, the number is one."

```
<span tal:define="number string:one">
 <span tal:define="number string:two">
  The number is <span tal:replace="number">A number</span>,
 </span>
 the number is <span tal:replace="number">A number</span>
</span>
```

In the next example, the variables are global. As a result, the variable redefinition on the child element does not revert when the child element's scope is exited, and in fact, the variable is available outside the defining element as well. So, this renders the string, "The number is two, the number is two. The number is still two."

```
<span tal:define="global number string:one">
 <span tal:define="global number string:two">
  The number is <span tal:replace="number">A number</span>,
 </span>
 the number is <span tal:replace="number">A number</span>.
</span>
The number is still <span tal:replace="number">A number</span>.
```

omit-tag

Unlike the `contents` statement, which replaces the contents (and any child elements) of the element on which it is defined, the `omit-tag` statement does the reverse: it removes the element on which it is defined while leaving the contents and child elements intact.

`omit-tag` takes an expression as an optional argument. If the expression evaluates to true, the element is stripped away, leaving the contents of the element and its children intact. If the expression evaluates to false the element is left in place.

For example, this code strips the element if visible evaluates to true:

```
<span tal:omit-tag="here/visible">
 The tag will be omitted
</span>
```

This code replaces the content of the tag and then removes the surrounding tag, which is functionally equivalent to the replace statement:

```
<span tal:omit-tag=""
      tal:content="string:Hello, World.">
 A Greeting
</span>
```

This code doesn't do anything:

```
<span tal:omit-tag="nothing">Still spanned.</span>
```

`omit-tag` is always the last statement to execute on a tag, because it removes all other statements along with the tag itself. Also notice that in the second example the content statement is taking a string expression (rather than the path expressions we've seen so far). More information on the order in which TAL statements execute as well as string expressions can be found later in this chapter.

on-error

Besides manipulating the rendering of the Page Template in various ways, it's also important to respond appropriately to errors in that manipulation. The `on-error` statement provides that facility.

The `on-error` statement takes an expression and an optional prefix of either `text` or `structure`. When the processing of the Page Template raises an error, an `on-error` statement is searched for starting with the current element being processed. Failing to find an `on-error` statement on the current element causes the search to expand to the parent element (the element surrounding the current element), continuing up the template's element hierarchy.

When the first `on-error` statement is found, it is evaluated as a `content` statement and the result is evaluated and replaces the contents and child elements of the element that the `on-error` statement is on.

For example, the following code triggers the `on-error` statement if there is no "visible" attribute or property defined where the template can acquire it, and a suitable error message is substituted:

```
<table>
 <tr tal:repeat="object here/objectValues">
  <span tal:condition="object/visible"
        tal:on-error="string:no property named visible!">
  <td tal:content="repeat/object/index">0</td>
```

```
    <td tal:content="object/id">An ID</td>
    </span>
  </tr>
</table>
```

Order of TAL statement execution

As we've seen in several of the examples given for the different statements, TAL statements can be combined within a single element. When statements are combined in this way, you cannot rely on the parent/child relationships between elements to control execution order, so a hierarchy of execution priorities is defined. TAL statements on a single element are executed in the following order:

1. `define`
2. `condition`
3. `repeat`
4. `content or replace`
5. `attributes`
6. `omit-tag`

The content and replace statements are mutually exclusive, and you can't have them both defined on the same element. Similarly, the replace and omit-tag statement combination, while not actually forbidden, is nonsensical, and doesn't have any more effect then a plain replace statement.

If you find that you need to override this execution order, simply place the statement you want to execute first on an enclosing `<span>` tag, along with a `tal:omit-tag=""` statement.

TALES (TAL Expression Syntax)

TAL is meant to be a general-purpose solution to the problem of creating dynamic templates that are nevertheless viewable in a browser and editable in their unprocessed state. While Zope currently has the only implementation of TAL, care has been taken not to incorporate any Zope-specific functionality into TAL, per se. Nevertheless, there is a need for implementation-specific functionality in order to integrate with Zope and leverage Zope's strengths.

The expressions TAL statements take as arguments and which, when evaluated, supply the TAL statements with data to operate on and to incorporate into the rendered Page Template, are where implementation specific functionality can be exposed. Appropriately then, TALES (TAL Expression Syntax) allows comprehensive access to Zope's objects and methods through several different types of expressions. TALES, however, is specific to Zope, and would probably be replaced with some other expression syntax in a different TAL implementation (for example one that depended on a more traditional three-tier application server or middleware). TALES has three different types of expressions: path expressions, Python expressions, and string expressions, and one expression modifier, "not."

Path expressions

Path expressions are the default type of expression in TAL, and are indicated by the use of an optional `path:` flag.

Path expressions are interpreted as the path to some object in the ZODB. The object is returned as the result of the expression, unless it is callable, in which case the result of calling the object is returned.

Every path must begin with a variable name, and TAL requires certain built-in names to be available as starting points for traversal in order to expose TAL functionality. The built-in names are:

- **nothing.** This is a special value intended signify a non-value. It is equivalent to Python None, or SQL Null. In the Java language this would be called `void`.
- **default.** This is another special value, indicating that the existing text should be left alone as it is in the Page Template, and not replaced. This is most useful as the last path expression in a sequence of alternatives separated by the pipe (vertical bar) character.
- **options.** This is a dictionary of the keyword arguments (name/value pairs) passed directly to the template. In Zope, these keyword arguments are passed from Python code.
- **repeat.** This is the various repeat variables, explained in the section on the TAL repeat statement.
- **attrs.** A dictionary that contains the initial values (unaltered by the attributes statement) of the attributes of the element to which the current statement is attached.
- **CONTEXTS.** This is a list of built-in variable names. If you overload a built-in name with a local or global variable definition, the actual built-in name can still be accessed as a subobject of CONTEXTS.

Besides accessing the built-in variables that a TAL implementation requires, you also need to be able to traverse to objects in the ZODB. To make the task of traversing to the correct object easier, seven different starting points are defined in the ZOPE implementation of TALES:

- **root.** This is the ZODB root object, also known as the Zope application object. Using this is equivalent to using PARENTS[-1] from DTML.
- **here.** This is the current rendering context, or the object on which the template is being called.

- **container.** This is the object that contains the Page Template object. It is similar to a Python Script object's container.
- **template.** This is the Page Template object being rendered.
- **request.** This is the ZPublisher request object. It contains information regarding the HTTP request, as well as object publication-specific information. URL parameters are accessed directly through `request` (`request/variablename`), and form values are accessed through a special `form` variable (`request/form/fieldname`).
- **user.** This is the object that corresponds to the user viewing the object being rendered.
- **modules.** This is an object that grants access to all available Python modules and packages, many of which will not be available to restricted code such as Page Templates.

Using path expressions

Constructing the appropriate path for your path expression is fairly straightforward if you know what you are trying to do. For example, if you want to include the title of the object on which you are rendering the template in the template's rendered output, start with the variable name `here` and add the `title` attribute object, which will result in the path expression, `here/title`. What might be more useful would be to call the method `title_or_id` instead, like this: `here/title_or_id`. Or, if you wanted to get all of the sibling objects from the current context, you would use `here/objectValues`.

However, if you don't want to use the title of the object in the current rendering context, but instead want to use the Page Template object's title property, you would use a path expression of `template/title`.

Similarly, if you want to get the username of the current user, you would use the path expression `user/getUserName`, or if you wanted to get the referrer from the current HTTP request, you would use a path expression of `request/referer`.

Any or all of the path expressions can be used in various TAL statements, for example:

```
<span tal:replace="template/title">The Title</span>
```

Specifying alternate paths in an expression

Path expressions can take more than one path. Multiple paths must be separated using the vertical bar character (`|`), and are tried from left to right. The evaluation of the path expression stops as soon as a path has been successfully evaluated.

In this way, you can specify more than one path to try for a particular expression, as well as the order in which they will be tried. For example, here we are trying to test for the trueness of an attribute in a condition statement:

```
<span tal:condition="request/showme | here/showme">
 showme is true
</span>
```

It's important to note that as the Page Template tries to resolve each path, starting from the variable, the first object it fails to traverse in the path expression will cause it to switch to evaluating the next path, but if no more paths are available, an error is raised. To avoid an error, the last path could either be `nothing` (a false value), or `default`.

Getting an object without rendering it

Sometimes, you want to call and render several of an object's attributes:

```
<div>
  <span tal:content="root/book1/title>Book Title</span>,
 written by <span tal:content="root/book1/author>Author
Name</span>,
 rated <span tal:content="root/book1/rating>Rating</span>.
</div>
```

This actually causes Zope to access the `book1` object several times, slowing the rendering of the page. However, assigning the `book1` object directly to a variable using a `define` statement will render the object, and make it impossible to access its attributes. The solution is to use a nocall: flag on the assignment, as is demonstrated in the following code:

```
<div tal:define="book nocall:root/book1">
  <span tal:content="book/title>Book Title</span>,
 written by <span tal:content="book/author>Author Name</span>,
 rated <span tal:content="book/rating>Rating</span>.
</div>
```

Depending on how expensive accessing the object is, this can result in a significant speedup. Using `nocall:` in this way is roughly equivalent to using `<dtml-with>`.

Python expressions

Python expressions are prefixed with the mandatory flag `python:` and must be a valid Python expression. They are useful for passing arguments to methods and objects that would otherwise be awkward or impossible to pass using path expressions, but you should not use them to try and embed application logic in your templates. Instead, use Python Script objects for your application logic.

Here is an example that retrieves a list of folder objects only from the current rendering context:

```
<ul>
 <li tal:repeat="list python: here.objectValues('Folder')"
     tal:content="list/id">An ID</li>
</ul>
```

A space is not required between the `python:` flag and the expression itself, but is recommended for clarity and legibility.

You can also use Python expressions to do comparison tests. The following example iterates over the root folder's objectValues, and tests whether the object is a Folder, and if so, calls objectValues on it again, rendering all object's id attributes:

```
<ul>
 <li tal:repeat="object root/objectValues">

  <span tal:condition="python: object.meta_type == 'Folder'"
        tal:omit-tag="">
   <b tal:content="object/getId">The folder id</b>
   <ul>
    <li tal:repeat="object root/objectValues">
     <i tal:content="object/getId">The object id</i>
    </li>
   </ul>
  </span>

  <span tal:condition="python: object.meta_type != 'Folder'"
        tal:omit-tag="">
   <i tal:content="object/getId">The object id</i>
  </span>

 </li>
</ul>
```

String expressions

String expressions are useful for simple substitutions as well as for composing path expressions together as an alternative to using multiple `<span>` elements within a text block.

String expressions require a prefix of `string:` and may contain multiple substitutions in the form of `$name` or `${name}`, where `name` takes the form of a path expression. The evaluated path expressions are always escaped (text), so this is inappropriate for inserting structure path expressions.

Here is an example of using string expressions:

```
<p tal:content="string: Hello, ${user/getUserName}. You ⮐
are viewing the '${here/title_or_id}' page.">Generic
greeting</p>
```

A literal dollar sign ($) must be escaped by doubling the symbol ($$) to prevent it from being interpreted as the variable prefix, like so:

```
<p tal:content="string: You have paid $$15.00">Price</p>
```

The not: expression flag

The `not:` expression flag is a flag that can be prefixed to any of the other expression types (including their flags) in order to interpret the evaluated expression as a Boolean, and to return the inverse Boolean value. If the expression cannot be evaluated as a Boolean directly, the `not: flag` will cause it to be coerced to a Boolean according to the following rules:

- ✦ Integer 0 is false.
- ✦ Positive integers are true.
- ✦ Empty strings, lists, or other sequences are false.
- ✦ Non-values (such as NULL, None, the TAL variable nothing, and so forth) are all evaluated as false.

Here's a small example which when the user is Anonymous, simply removes the entire element, but otherwise renders the username:

```
<p tal:condition="not: python: user.getUserName()⮐
== 'Anonymous'" tal:content="user/getUserName">The user
name</p>
```

Of course, in this case it might have been easier to replace the `==` operator with a `!=` operator and forego the `not:` flag, but in many other circumstances (such as evaluating path expressions), you do not have that option.

METAL (Macro Expansion TAL)

One of DTML's most useful features is the ability to include DTML methods inside other DTML Documents and Methods. As noted at the beginning of this chapter, this leads to presentation code being scattered over several methods with no way to view or edit the page as a whole. METAL is a language for macro pre-proccessing that provides the benefit of this feature of DTML without the accompanying drawbacks.

Macros enable you to define a section of presentation code in one template and include it in other templates, so that any changes you make to the macro are visible in all the templates that share it.

Unless you specifically disable the feature (by unchecking the "Expand macros while editing" checkbox), macros are always fully expanded in the source of the templates that include them, making it easy to view all of the code that will be interpreted to render the page, and to view this code in a browser in its uninterpreted form.

Simple code reuse

So, how do you create the equivalent of `<dtml-var navbar>` using METAL?

Start by creating a Page Template in the root of your site with an id of "navigation," and edit the template body as follows:

```
<html>
  <head>
    <title tal:content="template/title">The title</title>
  </head>
  <body>
 <table metal:define-macro="navbar" border="1" align="left">
 <tr>
  <td>
   <ul>
    <li tal:repeat="object python: root.objectValues('Folder')">
     <a tal:attributes="href object/absolute_url"
        tal:content="object/title_or_id">The object title</a>
    </li>
   </ul>
  </td>
 </tr>
</table>
   <h2><span tal:replace="here/title_or_id">content title or id</span>
        <span tal:condition="template/title"
              tal:replace="template/title">optional template id</span></h2>

    This is Page Template <em tal:content="template/id">template id</em>.
  </body>
</html>
```

So far, so good. You've defined your first macro Notice that the macro definition is only part of the Page Template. It's important that the Page template as a whole is an actual HTML file, which makes it easily editable in a WYSIWYG editor. Next you need to call the macro from within another Page Template. In the Test Page Template (or another if you wish), place the following code within the body of the HTML page, right after the beginning `<body>` tag:

```
<table metal:use-macro="here/navigation/macros/navbar">
</table>
```

Notice that macros are accessed from the macros variable on the Page Templates that contain them. Click the Save Changes button. You'll notice immediately that the code that you added to the second template was immediately upon saving replaced with the code that you defined as the macro in the navigation Page Template, resulting in code that looks something like this:

```
<html>
  <head>
    <title tal:content="template/title">The title</title>
  </head>
<body>
<table metal:use-macro="here/navigation/macros/navbar"
       border="1" align="left">
 <tr>
  <td>
   <ul>
    <li tal:repeat="object python:
root.objectValues('Folder')">
     <a tal:attributes="href object/absolute_url"
        tal:content="object/title_or_id">The object title</a>
    </li>
   </ul>
  </td>
 </tr>
</table>
</body>
</html>
```

Note that editing any content or child elements on the template contained in the element with the `metal:use-macro` statement will not have any effect on the template or the original macro. Macros can only be edited within their original Page Templates.

When the "Test" Page Template is rendered, the macro is expanded in place, and then rendered. If the macro body contains any macros in turn they are expanded first, before the macro is included in the template.

Macro slots

Macros are clearly useful in the context of editable Page Templates, but they require their definition to be on a whole XHTML element. This prevents the use of ordinary macros for creating a standardized look and feel because of the way you would need to break the start and end tags of the page body between two macros.

METAL provides an answer, in the form of an inside-out macro. Create a standard_page Page Template in your Root Folder with the following content:

```
<html metal:define-macro="standard_look">
 <head>
  <title tal:content="here/title">The title</title>
```

```
  </head>
  <body bgcolor="#FFFFFF">
   <table metal:use-macro="here/navigation/macros/navbar">
   </table>
   <span metal:define-slot="content">
    Insert content here.
   </span>
  </body>
</html>
```

Clicking Save Changes expands the navbar macro. We can preview the look and feel by clicking the Test tab.

Applying this standardized look and feel to our test page is rather simple. Just edit the Test Page Template as follows:

```
<html metal:use-
macro="root/standard_page/macros/standard_look">
  <head>
    <title >The title</title>
  </head>
<body>
<span metal:fill-slot="content">
This is the content from the test page template
</span>
</body>
</html>
```

Click the Save Changes button. After saving the changes, you can see that the expanded macro did not simply replace the entire contents of the Page Template, but took the element with the `metal:fill-slot` attribute and matched it to the appropriate metal:define-slot element in the macro, and did a reverse substitution so that the expanded template retained the fill-slot element:

```
<html metal:use-
macro="here/standard_page/macros/standard_look">
 <head>
  <title tal:content="here/title">The title</title>
 </head>
 <body bgcolor="#FFFFFF">
  <table border="1" align="left">
 <tr>
  <td>
   <ul>
    <li tal:repeat="object python:
root.objectValues('Folder')">
     <a tal:attributes="href object/absolute_url"
        tal:content="object/title_or_id">The object title</a>
    </li>
   </ul>
  </td>
 </tr>
```

```
</table>
  <span metal:fill-slot="content">
This is the content from the test page template
</span>
 </body>
</html>
```

In this way, a standardized look and feel can be created and maintained, with the expanded macros making every page on the site viewable and editable. In our example here, no edits to the Test Page Template will be retained unless they are within the span element that has the `fill-slot` attribute. Several designers can easily edit the standard_page, the Test page, and the navigation page with its navbar macro without overwriting each others changes, as long as they do not disturb the METAL attributes. Furthermore, the Page Templates can easily access business logic encapsulated in PythonScripts, external methods, SQL Methods, and even DTML without putting that logic into the page, and confusing the designers and their editing tools with the mixed-in code.

Some examples of combining Page templates with Python Script objects are included in Zope 2.5. They are located in the `/Examples/` folder object.

Summary

In this chapter, you learned about an exciting new technology incorporated into Zope version 2.5: Zope Page Templates.

You learned the problems with DTML that Page Templates were designed to avoid, and the basics of creating and editing a Page Template through the ZMI (Zope Management Interface). You also learned the TAL, TALES, and METAL languages, along with how to use these syntaxes to create dynamic data-driven templates that are viewable in a browser, editable in WYSIWYG editors, and can incorporate macros to create standardized page components and overall look and feel.

For further reading, check out the following books:

XHTML by Chelsea Valentine and Chris Minnick (New Riders, 2001)

HTML and XHTML: The Definitive Guide by Chuck Musciano and Bill Kennedy (O'Reilly, 2000)

XHTML For Dummies by Ed Tittel, Chelsea Valentine, and Natanya Pitts (Hungry Minds, 2000)

✦ ✦ ✦

CHAPTER 19

Debugging

✦ ✦ ✦ ✦

In This Chapter

Understanding Zope's error messages

Using Zope's debug mode

The Python debugger

Logging

✦ ✦ ✦ ✦

Let's face it, nobody's perfect, not even you. Occasionally products you've written will crash, hang, produce inconsistent or flat-out wrong results. When this happens — and it will happen — you want to make sure that you have at your disposal a variety of ways with which to track down and eliminate bugs. Zope provides many different options when it comes to debugging, some of which should be familiar to long-time Python users.

This chapter discusses each of the available debugging options. The following is sample code that we will refer back to for the different examples we present in this chapter. The code is for an instantiable product, such as the ones we learned how to make in Chapter 6, with some very basic functionality. If you notice any errors in the code, those are intentional. We *are* learning how to debug, after all.

__init__.py:

```
import TestModule

def initialize(context):
  context.registerClass(
        TestModule.TestProduct,
        permission="Add Test Object",
        constructors=(TestModule.manage_addTestForm,
                      TestModule.manage_addTest)
  )
```

TestModule.py:

```
from OFS import SimpleItem

def manage_addTestForm(self, REQUEST):
  "This is the form that allows you to add a Test object"
  return """<html>
 <body>
 <form method="post" action="addTest">
 ID: <input type="text">
 <input type="submit" value="Add Test">
 </form>
 </body>
</html>"""

def manage_addTest(self, id):
  "Add a Test object."
  newTest = TestProduct(id)
  self._setObject(id, newTest)

  return self.manage_main(self, REQUEST)

class TestProduct(SimpleItem.Item):

  meta_type = 'Test Product'

  def __init__(self, id):
    self.id = id
    self.status = 'Initialized'

  def setStatus(self, new_status):
    "Set a new status"
    if self.status == new_status:
      return "I already had it that way!"
    else:
      self.status = new_status
      return "Status changed to %s" % new_status

  def Status(self):
    "Return the object's current status"
    return self.state
```

For the examples we use in this chapter we created an instance of TestProduct in the root of our Zope instance, called "Test."

Error Messages

The first step in understanding how to debug a problem in your Zope application is to understand Zope's error messages. A typical error message will look something like Figure 19-1. You can reproduce this error yourself by going to `http://localhost:8080/Test/Status`. As you can see, there isn't much helpful information there. If you were running Zope in debug mode, you would see a much more informative, albeit confusing, error message, as shown in Figure 19-2.

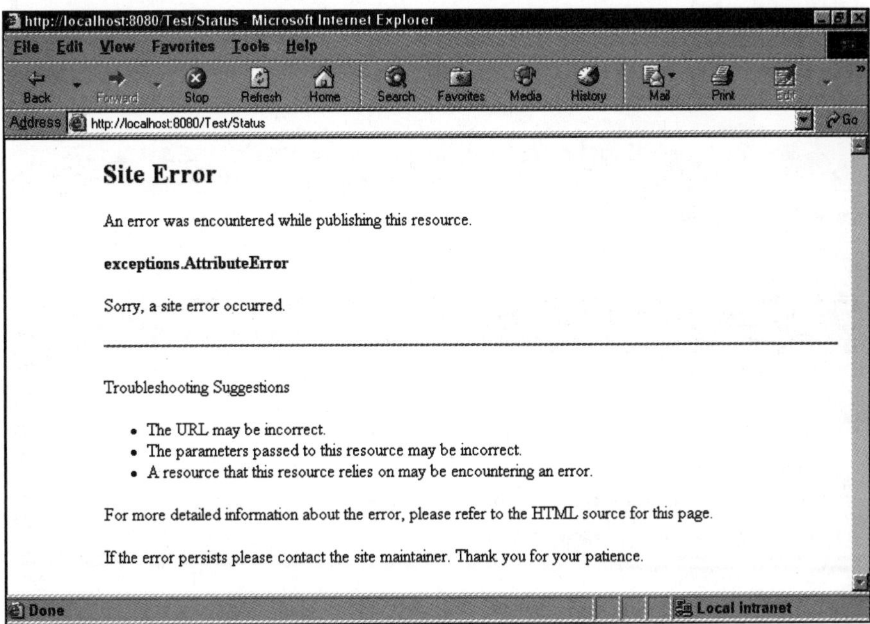

Figure 19-1: A typical Zope error message

That extra information that you see is called a *traceback*. A traceback tells you what function calls Zope used to get to this point. Now, how do we find that information if we're not running in debug mode? As you can see in Figure 19-3, when Zope is not running in debug mode, the traceback information can be found as a comment in the HTML (Hypertext Markup Language) source code of the error message page.

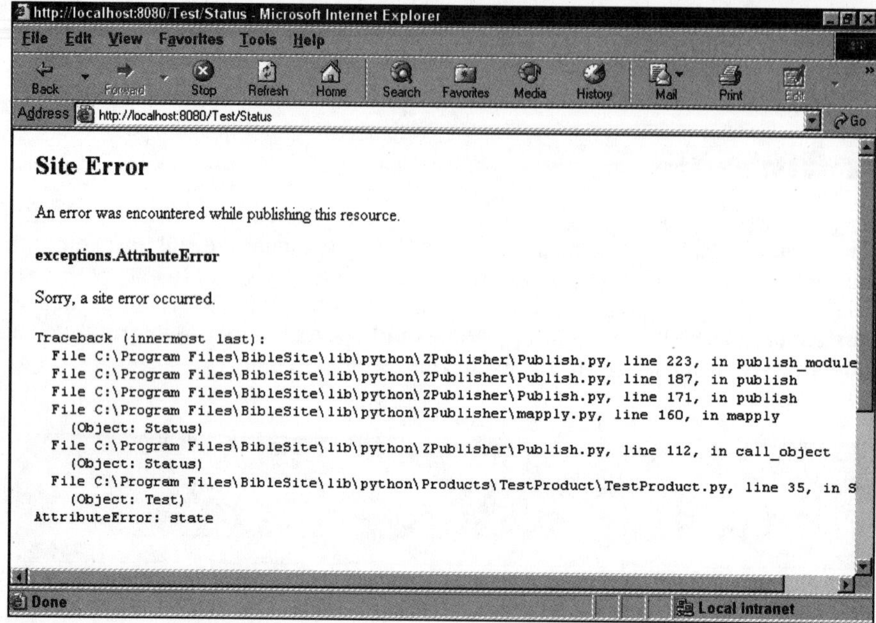

Figure 19-2: A Zope error message, when running in debug mode

```
Status[1] - Notepad
File  Edit  Search  Help
<TABLE BORDER="0" WIDTH="100%">
<TR VALIGN="TOP">

<TD WIDTH="10%" ALIGN="CENTER">
 
</TD>

<TD WIDTH="90%">
  <H2>Site Error</H2>
  <P>An error was encountered while publishing this resource.
  </P>
  <P><STRONG>exceptions.AttributeError</STRONG></P>

  Sorry, a site error occurred.<p>
<!--
Traceback (innermost last):
  File C:\Program Files\BibleSite\lib\python\ZPublisher\Publish.py, line 223, in publish_module
  File C:\Program Files\BibleSite\lib\python\ZPublisher\Publish.py, line 187, in publish
  File C:\Program Files\BibleSite\lib\python\ZPublisher\Publish.py, line 171, in publish
  File C:\Program Files\BibleSite\lib\python\ZPublisher\mapply.py, line 160, in mapply
    (Object: Status)
  File C:\Program Files\BibleSite\lib\python\ZPublisher\Publish.py, line 112, in call_object
    (Object: Status)
  File C:\Program Files\BibleSite\lib\python\Products\TestProduct\TestProduct.py, line 35, in Sta
    (Object: Test)
AttributeError: state

-->
  <HR NOSHADE>

  <P>Troubleshooting Suggestions</P>
```

Figure 19-3: Traceback information in the HTML source of the error page

Let's examine what kind of information is provided for us in the traceback. The first thing you'll notice is that the traceback gives you some function names, some module file names, and some line numbers. The data, from top to bottom, delineates the path of function calls that were made to get to the point of the error. Each line gives you the name of the file that the function call is in and the line number of the function call. The first few lines are of the publishing process. Using the filenames you can easily find the point at which we begin to enter our product.

After all of the lines detailing the function calls, it tells you what error was raised, which in this case is an `AttributeError`. If we go and take a look at our code, we will see what the error is. The attribute that we are trying to return, `self.state`, doesn't exist. The correct attribute would be `self.status`.

Debug Mode

Zope's debug mode is helpful for tracking down bugs. When in debug mode, tracebacks will be displayed on the error page rather than in a comment in the source code. External methods, if modified, are reloaded every time they are accessed, so you don't have to manually reload them. All of this comes at the cost of performance, so you don't want to leave your production servers running in debug mode.

There are two ways to make Zope start up in debug mode. The first way is to pass the `-D` switch to the start script. In Windows, from your Zope directory, type **start –D**. In Linux you need to use **./start –D**.

Alternately, you can set the environment variable `Z_DEBUG_MODE=1`. In Windows you can type **set Z_DEBUG_MODE=1**. In Linux, if you're using bash, you can type **export Z_DEBUG_MODE=1**. For other shells, refer to the documentation for your particular shell.

Calling Zope from Python

One of Zope's most useful features is the ability to simulate HTTP (Hypertext Transfer Protocol) requests from within Python, including the interactive shell. Let's examine how we would make such a request.

First, make sure that Zope is not running. Only one application can have the ZODB (Zope Object Database) open at one time, so if your Zope instance is running, you will not be able to load it in Python. Once you've shut down Zope we need to import the appropriate modules, Zope and ZPublisher. Once we have the module imported, we can use the provided functions to imitate an HTTP GET. If we hit an error, we'll get a standard Python error. Let's look at an example.

First, we call up the Python interpreter from within the `lib\python` directory of our Zope installation. If you are using a binary installation of Zope you can start the interpreter with the command `..\..\bin\python`, otherwise you can probably just type `python`. Remember that this command will only work from the `lib\python` directory. Under Linux the command is exactly the same, except that instead of a backslash, you would use a forward slash: `../../bin/python`.

You'll be greeted with the interpreter's startup message:

```
Python 2.1 (#15, Apr 16 2001, 18:25:49) [MSC 32 bit (Intel)] on
win32
Type "copyright", "credits" or "license" for more information.
>>>
```

The >>> is the interpreter's prompt and lets you know that it is ready for input. Now we need to import the Zope and Zpublisher modules:

```
>>> import Zope, ZPublisher
>>>
```

These modules could take a few minutes to load. When it's done loading you should be returned to the interpreter's command prompt. If Zope is still running you'll get the following message before being returned to the command prompt:

```
ZODB.POSException.StorageSystemError: Could not lock the
database file. There must be
another process that has opened the file.
<p>
>>>
```

What this means is that you still have Zope running. You need to exit the interpreter, shut down Zope, and then try again. To exit the interpreter in Windows, press Ctrl+Z. To exit the interpreter in Linux, press Ctrl+D.

Assuming that we have successfully imported Zope, we should now be able to simulate an HTTP request using the ZPublisher module:

```
>>> ZPublisher.Zope('/')
Status: 200 OK
X-Powered-By: Zope (www.zope.org), Python (www.python.org)
Content-Type: text/html
Content-Length: 308

<html><head>
<base href="http://127.0.0.1/Zope/" />
<title>Zope</title></head><body bgcolor="#FFFFFF">

...Page Content...

<p><a href="http://www.zope.org/Credits" target="_top"><img
src="http://127.0.0.
```

```
1/Zope/p_/ZopeButton" width="115" height="50" border="0"
alt="Powered by Zope" /
></a></p></body></html>


>>>
```

ZPublisher will return exactly what it would return to a browser, including the HTTP headers.

If you need to access a protected function, you can pass a username and password using the `u` parameter:

```
>>> ZPublisher.Zope('/', u="joe:123")
>>>
```

The Python debugger (pdb)

Some of you may already be familiar with the Python debugger (pdb); some of you may even be familiar with the GNU debugger (gdb) whose interface was the basis for the Python debugger. This section explains some of the basics uses for the debugger, as well as how to debug our Zope programs with it.

In the previous section we learned how to make calls to Zope from within Python. Now we are going to learn how to call Zope and be automatically entered into the debugger so we can step through the various function calls that Zope goes through to publish an object. All we need to do is pass in a new argument to our function call that we learned earlier in this chapter.

Let's try calling the `setStatus` function of our Test object, having Zope run it in the debugger so we can step through it:

```
>>> ZPublisher.Zope('Test/setStatus?new_status=Ready', d=1)
* Type "s<cr>c<cr>" to jump to beginning of real publishing
process.
* Then type c<cr> to jump to the beginning of the URL traversal
  algorithm.
* Then type c<cr> to jump to published object call.
> C:\Program Files\WebSite\lib\python\<string>(0)?()
pdb>
```

You may notice a couple of different things here. First, we're passing a variable to `setStatus`. Because we're simulating an HTTP request, you can pass variables the same way you would in a URL (uniform resource locator). Second, we're passing a second argument to the call. This argument is the one that tells Zope to run this request in the debugger.

You may also notice that Zope has returned three statements, and then a different prompt. This new prompt is the Python debugger's prompt. It tells us that we've entered the debugger and it is now waiting for input.

The three statements that Zope returns detail three different breakpoints that have been pre-selected. The first breakpoint is set at the beginning of the publishing process. The second breakpoint is set where Zope begins the traversal function to find the object you're requesting. The third breakpoint is set at the point where Zope begins the actual process of publishing your object. The three statements also give you instructions on how to use the debugger's commands to get to these points. Let's examine those. The two different commands are `s` and `c`. The `s` is the "step" command. It enables you to step into a function. The `c` is the "continue" command. It tells the debugger to continue executing statements until it encounters the next breakpoint, or there are no more commands to execute. A few more commands that will come in handy when in the debugger are: `p`, the "print" command, which can be used to display variables, and `n`, the "next" command, which executes the current line of code and moves the pointer to the next one.

While the `s` command and the `n` command may seem similar at first glance, there's a big difference between the two. If the line of code that you are about to execute is a function, the `s` command will take you to the first line of code in that function. The `n` command on the other hand will execute the function in its entirety and take you to the next line of code after the function has been executed.

Sometimes the pre-defined breakpoints aren't really convenient, and you'll want to set a breakpoint yourself in a specific function. Fortunately the debugger provides for just that situation. In order to set a breakpoint we need to import our product from the pdb prompt (after entering the debugger the way we outlined earlier in this chapter):

```
pdb> from Products.TestProduct.TestModule import TestProduct
pdb>
```

In addition to using these commands you can also execute other standard Python commands. Other commands specific to the debugger are beyond the scope of this chapter but can be found online at `http://www.python.org/doc/current/lib/module-pdb.html`.

Once our product is imported, we can set a breakpoint using the `b` command:

```
pdb> b TestProduct.setStatus
Breakpoint 3 at C:\Program Files\ZopeSite\lib\python\Products\↵
TestProduct\TestModule.py:25
pdb>
```

This command tells the debugger to set a breakpoint in the `setStatus` function of the TestProduct object. We can now, using the commands we learned previously, step through the debugger to our breakpoint. As instructed, we use `s` and then `c` to step to the first breakpoint:

```
pdb> s
> C:\Program Files\BibleSite\lib\python\<string>(1)?()
pdb> c
```

```
> C:\Program
Files\BibleSite\lib\python\ZPublisher\Publish.py(122)publish()
-> def publish(request, module_name, after_list, debug=0,
pdb>
```

This is the beginning of the publishing process. As you can see, we've stepped to the very beginning of the publish function in the Publish module of the ZPublisher package.

Now, we hit `c` again to continue on to the second breakpoint:

```
pdb> c
> C:\Program Files\BibleSite\lib\python\ZPublisher\Publish.py
(111)call_object()
-> def call_object(object, args, request):
pdb>
```

Here we begin to traverse through to the object that we're calling. In this case the variable "object" is our function, setStatus.

A third `c` will take us to the breakpoint we just set:

```
pdb> c
> C:\Program Files\BibleSite\lib\python\Products\TestProduct\
TestModule.py(26)setStatus()
-> import pdb; pdb.set_trace()
pdb>
```

You can use the `l` (list) command to display a short snippet of the source code surrounding our breakpoint:

```
pdb> l
 21          self.id = id
 22          self.status = 'Initialized'
 23
 24        def setStatus(self, new_status):
 25          "Set a new status"
 26 B->      if self.status == new_status:
 27           return "I already had it that way!"
 28          else:
 29            self.status = new_status
 30            return "Status changed to %s" % new_status
 31
pdb>
```

You can see that the debugger is showing us where our breakpoint is set with the `B->` identifier. From here, you can use the other commands we've learned to continue examining the function to solve any problems. Once you're done with your debugging, keep hitting `c` until you're returned to the Python interpreter's prompt.

Post-mortem debugging

The debugging method we outlined in the previous section is really more useful for tracking down complicated problems that aren't immediately identifiable. When you have a problem that is raising an error, "post-mortem" debugging becomes more useful than the above method.

Our TestProduct has a function that contains a mistake. If we try to call this method, Zope will raise an `AttributeError`. The Zope function that we've been using in the previous sections to make HTTP requests from within Python has another parameter that it can take that will, when it encounters an error, allow us to enter into the debugger at the point where the error occurs.

```
>>> ZPublisher.Zope('Test/Status', pm=1)
>>>
```

Our `Status` function is trying to return the state attribute, which does not exist, and will raise an `AttributeError`. Passing `pm=1` to the Zope call raises the `AttributeError` instead of the default behavior of returning the HTML code of the error page. Once the error has been raised, we can import the Python debugger and use its `pm` function to step straight to the line that raised the error:

```
>>> import pdb
>>> pdb.pm()
> C:\Program Files\WebSite\lib\python\Products\TestProduct\⮐
TestProduct.py(35)Status()
-> return self.state
pdb>
```

Once again, from here we can use the debugger's commands and Python code to figure out what our problem is.

Triggering the Python Debugger via the Web

Sometimes it may not be fast or easy enough, or even possible, for you to debug your problem simulating HTTP requests through the interactive shell. In these cases you need to have a way to call up the debugger from your code.

First (and this is very important), make sure your Zope instance is running in debug mode. If you're not running in debug mode and you trigger the debugger, your Zope instance will be paused waiting for input from the debugger — input you won't be able to give it because the process has detached itself from the terminal. The other thing you'll have to watch out for is that the debugger only pauses one thread this way, while your site continues to work. If someone else were to try and load the page that has the debug trigger in it, you will be switched out of whatever debugging you were doing into the thread that they just triggered. This can make it difficult to do effective debugging, so you will want to make sure that you have a controlled environment, or that Zope is not running multi-threaded while you're debugging.

In order to trigger the debugger, you must add one simple line to your code. At the appropriate section of your source code, preferable before the error occurs, insert the following line:

```
import pdb; pdb.set_trace()
```

For the purposes of our example, we're inserting the code into TestModule.py as follows:

```
def setStatus(self, new_status):
  "Set a new status"
  import pdb; pdb.set_trace()
  if self.status == new_status:
    return "I already had it that way!"
  else:
    self.status = new_status
    return "Status changed to %s" % new_status
```

When Zope hits this line of code, it will trigger the debugger in the controlling terminal. In your Web browser it will appear as though the server is not replying. This is because it is waiting for your input:

```
--Return--
> C:\Program Files\WebSite\bin\lib\pdb.py(895)set_trace()->None
-> Pdb().set_trace()
(Pdb)
```

From here, hitting "n" will step you from the `set_trace()` function, into the function where we set out breakpoint:

```
(Pdb) n
> C:\Program Files\WebSite\lib\python\Products\TestProduct
\TestModule.py(27)setStatus()
-> if self.status == new_status:
(Pdb)
```

In this case, I set the breakpoint directly after the doc string in the `setStatus()` function. You can use the `l` command to display the surrounding source code:

```
(Pdb) l
 22          self.status = 'Initialized'
 23
 24        def setStatus(self, new_status):
 25          "Set a new status"
 26          import pdb; pdb.set_trace()
```

```
 27  ->      if self.status == new_status:
 28            return "I already had it that way!"
 29          else:
 30            self.status = new_status
 31            return "Status changed to %s" % new_status
 32
(Pdb)
```

Notice that the debugger tells you what line it is set to execute with a `->`.

From here, you can use any of the previously discussed debugger commands to locate the problem.

This kind of debugging can be used from External Methods as well as from Products.

Logging

Another way to determine whether your product is working correctly or not is to use the provided mechanisms for logging information. You can use Zope's logging functions to insert short informative statements about what your product is doing. The way we do this is by using the zLOG module.

zLOG module

The zLOG module provides an interface to Zope's logging engine. Let's take a look at how we can use it in our product. The function that we are most interested in is the LOG function, so we will begin by importing that:

```
from zLOG import LOG
```

Now that we have the LOG function available to us, we can use it to write messages to Zope's log file. LOG takes a few arguments that enable you to organize your messages. The first three arguments are required: "subsystem" is simply a string describing the product or module that generated the error; "severity" is a number, floating point, or integer, that quantifies the degree of seriousness of your error; "summary" is a string that you use as your informative statement. There are three arguments that are optional: "detail," a string that you can use as a longer description; "error," which is a standard three-element tuple consisting of an error type, value, and traceback; "reraise," which will cause the error provided in the "error" argument to be re-raised. If you provide the "error" argument, a summary of this information will be added to the error detail.

The zLOG module provides some standard severity variables that you can import and use for your logging calls. In order of severity, from lowest to highest, the severity variables are: TRACE, DEBUG, BLATHER, INFO, PROBLEM, WARNING (has the same severity as PROBLEM), ERROR, PANIC. You should import the ones you plan to use for your messages when you import the LOG function, like this:

```
from zLOG import LOG, INFO
```

You can then make the call to write to the log file like so:

```
LOG('TestProduct', INFO, 'Well, you got this far at least!')
```

When running in debug mode, the following message will appear on the console:

```
2001-10-18T22:55:10 INFO(0) TestProduct Well, you made it this
far at least!
```

Note that when using TRACE, DEBUG, and BLATHER, most logging engines will ignore them because their integer value is less than 0.

Remember, at this point we're running our tests in Zope, so any changes that we make to our product will have to be refreshed. You can refresh the Product by using its Refresh tab, if the product has a refresh.txt file. Otherwise, the only way to refresh a product is to stop and restart Zope.

Profile logging

When your product is hanging the server, or spinning out of control in an infinite loop, sometimes it can be useful to turn on logging of profile information. Turning on profile logging incurs a significant performance hit on the server so it should be used pretty sparingly, after you've determined that you can't debug your problem any other way. A profiler reports the performance of a running program and returns statistics that could be useful in finding bottlenecks.

Turning on profile logging is done with the `-M <filename>` switch. The specified filename is the name of the file that will contain the profile information. Alternately, you can set an environment variable, `PROFILE_PUBLISHER`, the contents of which should contain the path to the file you want to contain the profile information. You should find a program called `requestprofiler.py` in the utilities directory of your Zope installation, which will read and interpret the profile log file.

Control panel

The Control Panel also holds a couple of utilities that are useful for debugging. There is a link in the Control Panel to Debug Information. Here you will find two tabs, one for Debugging Info, and one for Profiling. The Profiling tab will normally have information on how to enable profiling, unless you have the environment variable discussed above set. Note that the Profiling tab will not be active if you use the `-M` switch. It will only be active if you set the environment variable.

Debug information

The Debug Info screen is by far one of the most useful tools in Zope's debugging arsenal. Refer to Figure 19-4 for an example of the contents of the Debugging Info tab. More often than not, this is the first place I will go to see if any threads are hung, and if they are, what they were trying to execute and what parameters were passed to it. All this info is available from this one screen, making it invaluable to the beginning stages of debugging certain problems. Of course, if all four of your threads are hung, you're not going to be able to get to this screen, so it's not always a foolproof solution.

The first information you will find in this page is exactly the same information that is present on the main Control Panel page:

- Version of currently running Zope instance
- Version of Python running Zope
- Platform Zope is running on
- Process id Zope is running under
- Current running time

Now starts the interesting and useful information. The first piece of useful information is a multi-select list labeled "Top Refcounts." It lists some classes, and a number next to that class. The number is the number of times the object has been referenced by the objects loaded in memory. Objects with a higher refcount are being used more than the objects with a lower refcount. The importance of these numbers lays in the fact that the more refcounts there are, the more memory your Zope instance is using. If you notice an extremely high refcount for an object and your Zope instance is using a lot of memory, you may be able to perform some optimizations and save some memory.

Next comes a table that we can use to give us an idea of how memory is being utilized. It reports the same types of objects that we see in the "Top Refcounts," and it also has a column for the refcounts at a particular time, and the refcounts at a time a few minutes later. The final column gives you the difference in the refcounts from one time to the next. This is helpful because it gives us an idea of whether memory usage is increasing, and how fast. If the difference between refcounts (the delta) is significant, and continues to increase, then you may have a memory leak, some kind of circular reference, or a recursion problem that just continues to load new references to objects in memory. Problems like these can crash a server pretty quickly, so this table is crucial in determining if you have a problem like this or not.

The final table on this page (Figure 19-4) has a list of the currently active threads. There will never be more rows than the number of threads that you specified, although there may sometimes be less, as threads aren't all initialized at startup. If a thread has been initialized, but isn't processing any requests, it will say "None" in the "opened" column. If a thread is in the middle of processing, you will see the date and time that the processing began, and the time in the seconds that it has been processing the page. The next column, “info,” contains all of the variables in the REQUEST object for that page. There is a lot of useful information in there, such as what page is being requested (PATH_INFO), what page they came from (HTTP_REFERER), any form variables that may have been posted to the page, the username of the requester, and so on. This information is useful for duplicating a request to a page that may be hung or processing too slowly.

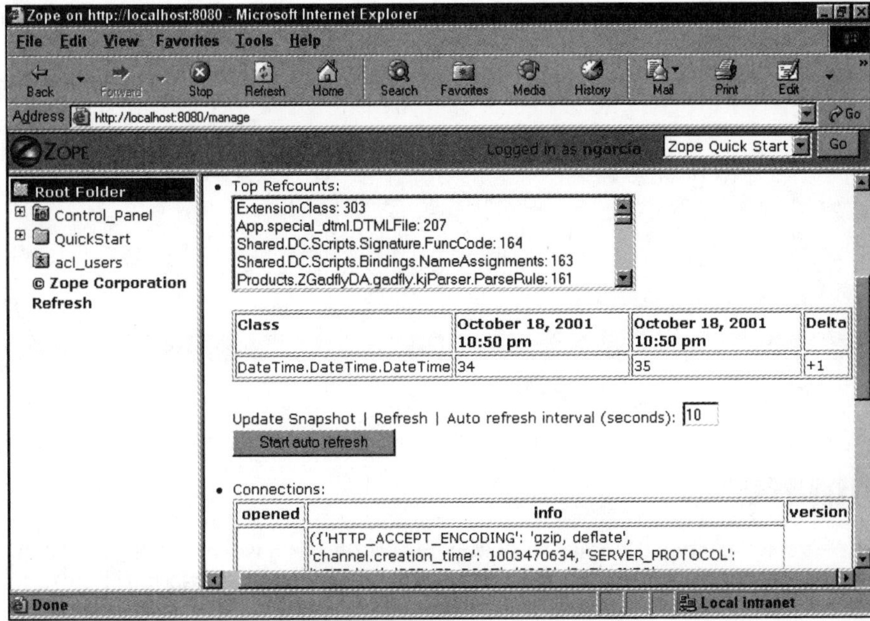

Figure 19-4: The Zope Debugging Info screen

Profiling

The Profiling tab in the Control Panel provides some information gathered using the Python profiler. As you can see in Figure 19-5, it details a list of different functions, plus some statistical data on the calling of each function. There are five different columns that provide statistical information. “ncalls” is the number of calls to that particular function. “tottime” is the total time spent executing that function, not including time spent calling other functions. “percall” is “tottime” divided by “ncalls.” “cumtime” is the total time spent executing that function, including time spent calling other functions. “percall” is “cumtime” divided by “ncalls.”

What is this data useful for? Primarily, this data is intended to be used to single out the functions in your product that are running slowly and are affecting performance. Any bottlenecks in your system will show high “tottime” and “percall” and should be revised.

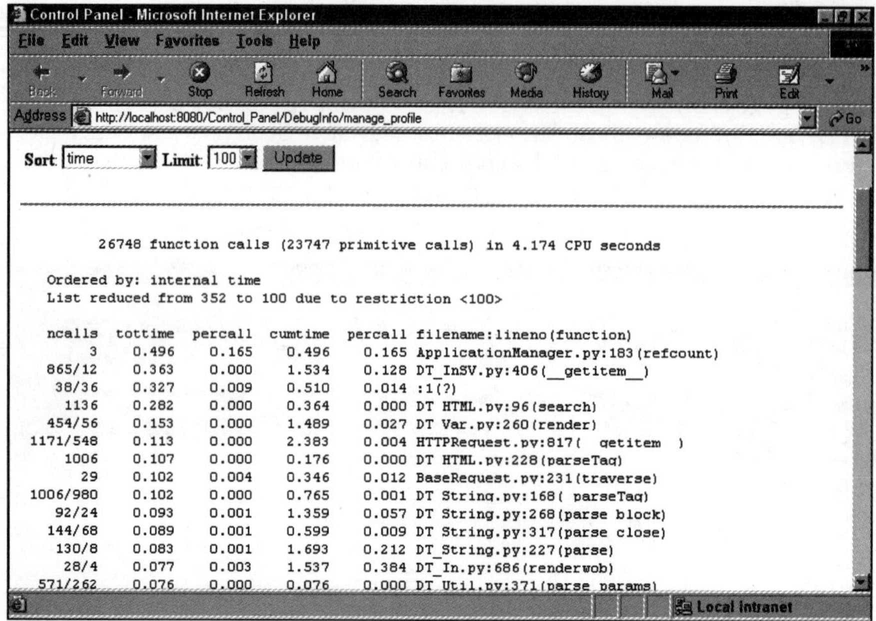

Figure 19-5: The Zope Profiling screen

Summary

As we've seen, when it comes to debugging, Zope has a wealth of options available to us. Whether our problems are simple, such as typos or syntax errors, or more complicated, such as locked threads or memory leaks, there is always an option for figuring out where things are going wrong. Simple problems can be debugged using the logging facilities; more complicated problems require the use of the debugger. Because Zope is written in Python many of its debugging options are rooted in Python's debugging utilities. Python's maturity gives us well-developed tools that fit nicely within the Zope framework and enable us to examine our work quickly and efficiently.

✦ ✦ ✦

CHAPTER 20

Alternative Methods of Running Zope

✦ ✦ ✦ ✦

In This Chapter

Interfacing Zope with other Web servers

Zope and scalability

✦ ✦ ✦ ✦

Although Zope is quite self-contained and includes everything that you need to create and deploy Web applications within a single application, there are times when you want Zope to run a little differently to accommodate your needs. For example, you might want Zope to run behind another Web server, or you may want to deploy Zope as a cluster of servers, rather than a single process. In this chapter, we'll discuss and demonstrate some of those alternatives.

Interfacing Zope with Other Web Servers

Several of the reasons that you would want to run Zope in conjunction with other Web servers are as follows:

- ✦ You are already running a Web server and don't want to put all of your existing pages into Zope just to take advantage of its capabilities.
- ✦ Many of the files you deliver are large (for example high-resolution graphics or streaming media files), and it doesn't make sense to serve them up dynamically from Zope when a static file server will work more efficiently.
- ✦ You have a virtual hosting environment and only want some of the sites served by Zope.
- ✦ Your boss insists that you use a "standard" Web server.

Luckily for you, Zope can easily integrate with other Web servers.

Zope and Apache

Zope and Apache fit together so well and so easily that it's hard to believe. We'll assume that you want Apache to run on port 80 (the standard Web server port), that the Web site you're serving up is `www.smallco.com`, and that you have Zope running on an IP address of 127.0.0.1, and the default port of 8080.

In your Zope Web site's root folder, add a Virtual Host Monster object by selecting Virtual Host Monster from the Add object drop-down. The form that appears at the bottom of the subsequent page has only an id field. Type in **Apache** and click the Add button.

In Apache's `httpd.conf` file, add the following code to the end of the file:

```
<VirtualHost *>
 RewriteEngine On
 RewriteRule ^/(.*) _
http://127.0.0.1:8080/VirtualHostBase/http/www.smallco.com:80/$
1 [P]
</VirtualHost>
```

Locate the mod_proxy configuration section of the same `httpd.conf` file, and make sure that the ProxyRequests and ProxyVia options are enabled, as in the following code:

```
<IfModule mod_proxy.c>
 ProxyRequests On
 ProxyVia On
</IfModule>
```

If you now restart Apache, you should be serving all of your content out of Zope's root folder. Of course, perhaps this wasn't what you need. If you want to serve different sites out of different Zope folders, you'll need to change the rewrite rule.

For example, if you want to serve the `smallco.com` site out of the `/hosted_sites/smallco` folder, change the rewrite rule as follows:

```
RewriteRule ^/(.*)
http://127.0.0.1:8080/VirtualHostBase/http/www.smallco.com:80/
hosted_sites/smallco/$1 [P]
```

These are two simple examples. Apache rewrite rules are extremely flexible, and can handle practically any requirement that you have, but a full description of their use would take up an entire chapter of this book.

Searching for apache or rewriterule on Zope.org will present you with many examples and configurations.

Zope and Microsoft IIS

Microsoft IIS (Microsoft Internet Information Server) is a popular Web server for Microsoft NT and is included with the Windows NT 4.0 Option Pack 3. If you happen to be running IIS, there will be a couple of hoops to jump through regarding IIS's authentication process and coupling IIS and ZServer via PCGI (Persistent Common Gateway Interface).

As such, we first discuss how to get PCGI configured properly, and then talk about a couple of different options you have when configuring the authentication situation. We assume you have NT 4.0 and IIS running with their default settings and have Zope's root directory as `C:\Program Files\Zope\`.

Introducing ZServer to IIS through PCGI

In Zope's root directory, you should find a file called `Zope.cgi`. Copy this file into IIS's cgi-bin directory at `C:\Inetpub\wwwroot\cgi-bin\` and rename it to Zope.pcgi. Persistent CGI is a good solution for Web applications like Zope that have a relatively high start-up costs and are meant to be long-running in process. Unlike regular CGI scripts that are run when the Web server is asked for the appropriate URL, return their results, and then shut down. Persistent CGI programs remain running between HTTP requests in order to avoid the startup and shutdown costs. Since Zope is relatively large as Web applications go, it is a good idea to run Zope in this way.

We now want to add a new extension mapping to IIS for PCGI. What we must do is tell IIS to run Zope's `pcgi-wrapper.exe` whenever it sees the .pcgi extension. (The `pcgi-wrapper.exe` application is what passes requests and results back and forth between IIS and Zope.) Go to Start ➪ Windows NT 4.0 Option Pack ➪ Microsoft Internet Information Server ➪ Internet Service Manager. This opens the Microsoft Management Console.

Locate your Web site beneath Internet Information Server and right-click it to open its properties. Click the Home Directory tab and then the Configuration button. Click Add under the App Mappings tab. For Executable, insert **"C:\Program Files\Zope\pcgi\Win32\pcgi-wrapper.exe" %s**. For Extension, insert **.pcgi**.

Finally, we must make Zope look for that `Zope.pcgi` when it starts up. To do this, add the path to the file in Zope's startup script using the -p switch by either editing the `start.bat` file in the Zope root directory or by editing the registry key if you have Zope installed as a Windows NT Service. (The syntax will look similar to `-p C:\Inetpub\wwwroot\cgi-bin\Zope.pcgi`.)

To edit the registry key, run regedit. The path is `HKEY_LOCAL_MACHINE\SYSTEM\CurrentControlSet\Services\Zope\Parameters\Start`. Add **-p C:\Inetpub\wwwroot\cgi-bin\Zope.pcgi** and click OK.

Editing Windows' registry makes it really easy to truly mess up your system. Be sure to edit only the key we instruct you to.

Start both IIS and Zope. Try accessing your Web site by pointing your browser at `http://localhost/cgi-bin/zope.pcgi`. If it yields the same page as `http://localhost:8080/`, you know that you have everything set up correctly. Now to make sure authentication is passed properly.

The public Web site: having Zope verify authentication

If you try to access Zope's management interface through `http://localhost/cgi-bin/zope.pcgi/manage`, you will receive the typical request for a username and password. Unless you enter the username and password you set up while installing Zope, you will get an authentication error. What is happening here is that Zope sends out a request for authentication, but when IIS receives the response, it looks at it and figures that it doesn't match anything in its system, so tosses it out without passing it along back to Zope.

The solution for this is to make IIS pass along all of the information without getting itself involved by giving anonymous access to the `Zope.pcgi` file. So, go back into the Microsoft Management Console and right-click the `Zope.pcgi` file in the cgi-bin folder and then click the File Security tab. Click the Edit button under Anonymous Access and Authentication Control. Three options appear: Allow Anonymous Access, Basic Authentication, and Windows NT Challenge/Response. Make sure Anonymous Access is the only box checked. This will pass all authentication information directly to `Zope.pcgi`, and therefore, to Zope.

Click OK and try to access `http://localhost/cgi-bin/zope.pcgi/manage` again. When you enter the username and password you should gain access to Zope's management interface. Congratulations! You set up Zope to run behind IIS.

Zope and Scalability

A persistent question posed by people considering Zope is "Does Zope scale?"

What is scalability?

Scalability, in computer systems as well as in business models, is the quality a system possesses when its percentage of overhead stays the same or even decreases as the number of transactions grows.

Ideally, your Web server's performance (in terms of how quickly it was serving requests for documents) bears a direct linear relationship to how many requests were being served, and the ability of the server to serve those requests bears a direct linear relationship to the cost of its hardware. In practice, neither of those is true for any system, but it's much less true for dynamic publishing environments than it is for Web servers serving static files.

Here's how the non-linear relationship works: Suppose you're serving up static files on a Web server. As your site becomes more popular, more people hit your site. As the load on your site increases, you notice performance starts to degrade and the server's response time starts to increase. Then you notice that as even more people hit your site, the rate at which the server slows down actually increases. Each additional visitor to your site is imposing a proportionately greater performance penalty — a 10 percent increase in hits causes a 15 percent increase in response time, and another 10 percent increase in hits causes another 20 percent increase in response time. Eventually, your site crawls to a halt.

Now, you decide to buy a new server to replace your old one. You decide to spend twice as much on the hardware this time, figuring that that should give you a comfortable margin for error. However, after the new server is in place, you notice that although it certainly performs better than the old server, it also starts to slow down with an increase in hits, and it didn't take a 100% increase to do it either!

You call various vendors and find out that as you spend more money on hardware, the price/performance ratio actually decreases. In effect, you pay more and more for ever-diminishing returns. You discover that there is a "sweet-spot" where you can get the most bang for your buck, but unfortunately, that machine isn't powerful enough to handle your current load, much less future increases. If only there were a way to divide the work between several computers.

Clustering and load balancing

Not surprisingly, there *is* a solution for divvying up the work between several computers. In fact, there are several solutions, with variations.

If, like with our hypothetical Web site owner's site, your server is serving up static content, you can use *round-robin DNS* to distribute the load among several servers. This basically directs each request for `www.yoursite.com` to one of several IP addresses on your internal network. As each request comes in, the next IP address on the list is chosen to fulfill it. As long as all of the servers have identical content, the user will never notice with which machine his or her browser is actually communicating.

This approach, which has the advantage of simplicity, has one drawback: not all HTTP (Hypertext Transfer Protocol) requests are created equal. Larger files place more of a load on the server that is fulfilling the request. Because requests are simply passed to each server in turn, it is a statistical certainty that some servers will be hit harder than others, increasing the load on them. In addition, there are other factors that will conspire to distribute the load unevenly across your servers, such as the fact that the DNS server that the user's browser consults to resolve the domain name into an IP address caches (remembers) the IP address, sometimes for a couple of days. If that DNS server is used by many users, then those users will all be hitting the same server until the cache expires and a new IP address is retrieved. Now, over time, on average, the load will tend to be even across the servers, but in the short term, some servers will be hit harder than others due to these and other factors.

Because servers that are being hit harder decrease in their response time, and your goal is to maximize the efficiency of your cluster of servers (as that's what we're describing), you need to find a way to distribute the load more evenly in the short term, not just in the long term. Otherwise, some servers will be overworked and decrease in efficiency, and others will be under-utilized. This is where *dynamic load balancing* comes in.

Dynamic load balancing is done by a device often referred to as a *Layer 4 switch*. Layer 4 switches hand requests off to a cluster of computers. To the rest of the Internet, `www.yourdomain.com` resolves to a single IP address, which actually belongs to the switch. Meanwhile, behind the scenes, the switch transparently hands off the request to servers in the cluster. The servers, meanwhile, are able to inform the switch as to how hard they're working, so the switch can always choose the server with the lightest load for the current request.

Explaining these and other load balancing techniques further is really beyond the scope of this book, but it's important to understand what, in general, is going on here.

So far, we've only been discussing static Web sites. The situation changes in several particulars when the Web site in question is producing all or part of its page views dynamically.

A setup that is producing pages dynamically is generally called an *application server*. An application server typically has three parts: a Web server, a database, and some form of middleware tying the two together. Note that in some usages, "application server" can refer to the middleware part alone.

All three parts of the application server can reside on the same server, and for some simple setups (Apache, Perl, and MySQL, for example), this is perfectly adequate if the system is not expected to serve a lot of requests. However, under higher load situations, the differing requirements of each component suggest separating them so that a hardware configuration tuned to its needs can be provided.

At the very least, you should separate the database sever from the other two components. This is because replicating a database is far more work than replicating static files on a Web server. In a dynamic Web site, you want to present the same data to many users. If the Web site also collects information that is added to the database (such as book or music recommendations), that information must be reflected in the site no matter which server is replying to the request.

The easiest way to do this is to cluster the Web servers and have each one use the same database server as its information store.

By now, you may be wondering what all this has to do with Zope. Zope is an integrated solution, with the Web server (ZServer), middleware (ZPublisher), and data storage (ZODB) components in a single package. Load balancing or clustering Zope servers seems rather more difficult than with a traditional setup.

Zope Enterprise Objects

In order to cluster and load-balance Zope servers, Zope needs to emulate the separation of data storage from Web serving that a more traditional application server setup does. Fortunately, such a system exists called ZEO (Zope Enterprise Objects).

What is ZEO?

ZEO enables Zope to run on multiple computers and ensures that all of the Zope servers share their databases both for incorporating data into the pages served up by the server, as well as incorporating and storing information supplied by the browser. ZEO uses a client/server architecture. The Zope installations on multiple servers are the ZEO *clients*. All of the clients connect to a single *storage server*.

ZEO clients and servers communicate using Internet protocols so they can be in the same rack or across the city. You can use ZEO to distribute a Zope site all over the world, if you want.

ZEO isn't for everyone

Zope is generally capable of serving millions of hits per day on fairly prosaic commodity hardware. If you find that your performance is suffering, and deploying on multiple servers is going to make sense from a price and performance perspective, then you should use ZEO. But keep in mind the additional complexity of deploying any clustering solution, and balance that against the simplicity and elegance of running Zope as a single application.

Throughout the rest of this chapter we assume you are installing ZEO to coordinate multiple physical servers, but it is also possible to use ZEO to increase performance on multi-processor systems. This is because Zope runs in a single process, even though it is a multi-threaded application. By running a ZEO client and a ZEO Storage Server as separate processes, Zope can better take advantage of multiple CPUs in a multi-processor system.

Installing ZEO

It's important to make sure that all of the Zope installations you'll be tying together into a single cluster use the same version of Zope, and that the ZEO client installations all have the same add-on products installed.

Any additional systems or resources that one of the ZEO clients needs to access to should be available to all of them. This can include HTTP access to other sites or servers that you wish to access via XML-RPC; mail servers that you need to access via SMTP or POP3; any relational databases that are accessed from the site; and other external resources on which your server may depend.

It's also important that the network connection between the ZEO clients and the server is reliable, whether it is a local network, across the Internet, or around the world. Unreliable or poor connections will slow down the interaction between the ZEO storage server and the ZEO clients.

Because ZEO is not distributed as part of Zope, you'll need to download it from the Zope.org site at `http://www.zope.org/Products/ZEO`. As of this writing, the most recent version of ZEO is 1.0 beta 5. Choose a more recent version if one exists and if it is more appropriate for your situation.

Running ZEO

We are first going to show you how to configure and run both the ZEO client and the ZEO storage server on the same machine.

Download and unpack the ZEO package (ZEO-1.0b5.tgz) in your Zope installation directory. This will create a `ZEO-1.0b5` directory in your Zope installation directory. Next, copy the ZEO directory and all of its contents out of the ZEO-1.0b5 directory into the `/lib/python/` subdirectory of your installation.

Finally, you need a `custom_zodb.py` file in your Zope install directory with the following contents:

```
import ZEO.ClientStorage
Storage=ZEO.ClientStorage.ClientStorage(('localhost',8800))
```

The `custom_zodb.py` file is used to tell Zope to run as a ZEO client. This code passes a tuple that must have two elements: a string that contains the address to the server, and the port number on which the server is listening. On Linux and other UNIX systems, `'localhost'` refers to the machine on which the code is running. Another alternative is `'128.0.0.1'`, which has the same effect. If you are testing this on one of Microsoft's consumer operating systems (Windows 95, 98, ME), you may find that neither of these work, in which case you should provide your system's actual IP address.

Your next step is to start up the ZEO server by launching the `start.py` located in the `lib/python/ZEO` directory:

```
python lib/python/ZEO/start.py -p 8800
```

If you're running Windows, place the previous code into a start_server.bat file, and save it into the Zope installation directory where the start.bat file is located. Run the start_server.bat file.

This starts the ZEO server. Instruct it to listen on port 8800. Notice that the port on which you start the server should match the port that you pass to the ClientStorage in `custom_zodb.py`. Next, in another terminal window, start up Zope as you usually would, using `z2.py`:

```
$ python z2.py -D
```

On Windows, just run the start.bat file as you normally would.

```
------
2001-10-23T08:40:18 INFO(0) client Trying to connect to server:
('localhost', 8800)
------
2001-10-23T08:40:18 INFO(0) ClientStorage Connected to storage
------
2001-10-23T08:40:20 INFO(0) ZServer HTTP server started at Tue
Oct 23 01:40:20 2001
        Hostname: WEBMAVEN
        Port: 8080
------
2001-10-23T08:40:20 INFO(0) ZServer FTP server started at Tue
Oct 23 01:40:20 2001
        Hostname: webmaven
        Port: 8021
------
2001-10-23T08:40:20 INFO(0) ZServer PCGI Server started at Tue
Oct 23 01:40:20 2001
        Inet socket port: 8090
```

Notice how you're informed that the "client Trying to connect to server" and then that the "ClientStorage Connected to storage." This shows that the ZEO client has managed to connect to the ZEO server.

Direct a browser to `http://yoursite.com:8080/manage` (or whatever URL on which your ZEO client is listening) and log into Zope.

If you go to your server's Control Panel, you'll see that the database section now reports both the size and the location of the ZODB (Zope Object Database) that the ZEO Client has mounted, as shown in Figure 20-1.

Running ZEO on one computer in this way does not, unfortunately, improve the speed of your site, and in fact, may slow it down by increasing the load a little. (The exception to this is when you have a multiprocessor system, but those aren't very common yet.) To take full advantage of the scalability ZEO provides, you need to run the ZEO client on several servers, connecting to a single storage server.

Running ZEO Clusters

Setting up a ZEO cluster is pretty much the same as running ZEO on a single machine. First, start the ZEO storage server, and then start one or more ZEO clients.

The point of this is that as with the more traditional application server technologies, the ZEO clients can be "round-robined," load-balanced, and otherwise clustered to provide scalability. By using ZEO, there is no practical upper limit to the performance of your site, or the number of machines that it runs on.

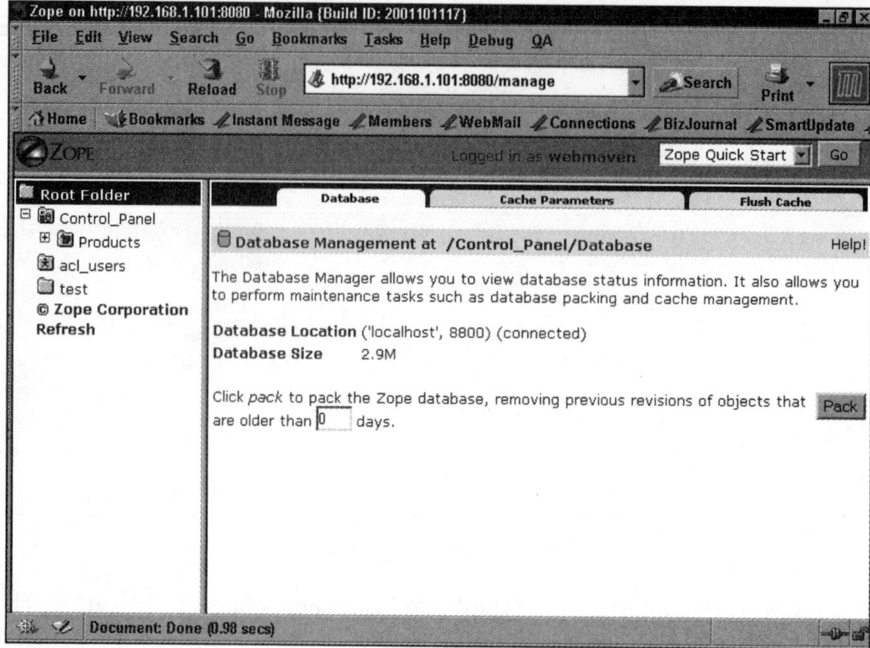

Figure 20-1: The Database screen of a ZEO client

Summary

In this chapter, you learned about interfacing Zope with other Web servers, and learned how to configure Zope to run in a clustered configuration.

For further reading, check out the following books:

Apache: The Definitive Guide by Ben Laurie, Peter Laurie, and Robert Denn (O'Reilly, 1999)

Apache Server 2 Bible by Mohammed J. Kabir (Hungry Minds, 2001)

Capacity Planning for Web Services: Metrics Models and Methods by Daniel A. Menascé and Virgilio A.F. Almeida (Prentice Hall PTR, 2001)

Web Performance Tuning: Speeding Up the Web by Patrick Killelea and Linda Mui (O'Reilly, 1998)

✦ ✦ ✦

What's on the CD-ROM

This appendix provides you with information on the contents of the CD-ROM that accompanies this book. For the latest information, please refer to the ReadMe file located at the root of the CD-ROM.

There are several programs included on this CD-ROM:

- Zope 2.5
- Codeit Addressit
- Macromedia Dreamweaver
- Adobe GoLive 5.0
- Adobe Acrobat Reader

Also included are source code examples from the book and an electronic, searchable version of the book that can be viewed with Adobe Acrobat Reader.

System Requirements

Make sure that your computer meets the minimum system requirements listed in this section. If your computer doesn't match up to most of these requirements, you may have a problem using the contents of the CD-ROM.

For Windows 9*x*, Windows 2000, Windows NT4 (with SP 4 or later), Windows ME, or Windows XP:

- PC with a Pentium processor running at 120 MHz or faster
- At least 64 MB of RAM
- Ethernet network interface card (NIC) or modem with a speed of at least 28,800 bps
- A CD-ROM drive — double-speed (2x) or faster

For Linux:

- ✦ PC with a Pentium processor running at 90 MHz or faster
- ✦ At least 64 MB of RAM
- ✦ Ethernet network interface card (NIC) or modem with a speed of at least 28,800 bps
- ✦ A CD-ROM drive — double-speed (2x) or faster

You will need at least 200 MB of hard drive space to install all the software from this CD-ROM.

Using the CD-ROM with Microsoft Windows

To install the items from the CD-ROM to your hard drive, follow these steps:

1. Insert the CD-ROM into your computer's CD-ROM drive.
2. Double-click My Computer.
3. Double-click on "Zope Bible" CD-ROM icon.
4. Browse the directory structure.

Using the CD with Linux

To install the items from the CD to your hard drive, follow these steps:

1. Log in as root.
2. Insert the CD-ROM into your computer's CD-ROM drive.
3. Mount the CD-ROM.
4. Launch a graphical file manager.

What's on the CD

The CD-ROM contains source code examples, applications, and an electronic version of the book. Following is a summary of the contents of the CD-ROM arranged by category.

Source code

The Addressit application that is developed in chapters 6 through 10 is available in all the intermediate versions in the folders `/chapter_06/`, `/chapter_07/`, `/chapter_08/`, `/chapter_09/`, and `/chapter_10/`.

Applications

The applications described in the following sections are on the CD-ROM.

Zope

Zope is the leading open source application server. Ready to install versions of Zope 2.5 for Windows, Linux, and Solaris, as well as the Zope 2.5 source code are all included on the CD-ROM. Zope is Open Sourced under the Zope Public License 2.0.

Codeit Addressit

The Addressit Application that was developed in chapters 6 through 10 is available as a finished product as well. Licensed under the GPL.

WYSIWYG HTML Editors

A WYSIWYG (What You See Is What You Get) HTML editor lets you design and build Web pages visually. The two that we've included also allow control and direct editing of the HTML code itself, which is important if you are designing dynamic Web site templates.

- **Macromedia Dreamweaver:** an HTML editor for Windows and Macintosh computers. 30-day trial. For more information: `www.macromedia.com`
- **Adobe GoLive:** an HTML editor for Windows and Macintosh computers. 30-day trial. For more information: `www.adobe.com`

Electronic version of *Zope Bible*

The complete (and searchable) text of this book is on the CD-ROM in Adobe's Portable Document Format (PDF), readable with the Adobe Acrobat Reader (also included). For more information on Adobe Acrobat Reader, go to `www.adobe.com`.

Electronic version of *Python 2.1 Bible*

The complete (and searchable) text of *Python 2.1 Bible* by Dave Brueck and Stephen Tanner (Hungry Minds, 2001) is on the CD-ROM in Adobe's Portable Document Format (PDF), readable with the Adobe Acrobat Reader (also included). For more information on Adobe Acrobat Reader, go to `www.adobe.com`.

Troubleshooting

If you have difficulty installing or using the CD-ROM programs, try the following solutions:

- **Turn off any anti-virus software that you may have running.** Installers sometimes mimic virus activity and can make your computer incorrectly believe that it is being infected by a virus. (Be sure to turn the anti-virus software back on later.)
- **Close all running programs.** The more programs you're running, the less memory is available to other programs. Installers also typically update files and programs; if you keep other programs running, installation may not work properly.

If you still have trouble with the CD-ROM, please call the Hungry Minds Customer Care phone number: (800) 762-2974. Outside the United States, call 1 (317) 572-3994. You can also contact Hungry Minds Customer Service by e-mail at `techsupdum@hungryminds.com`. Hungry Minds will provide technical support only for installation and other general quality control items; for technical support on the applications themselves, consult the program's vendor or author.

✦ ✦ ✦

Installing Zope from the Red Hat RPMs or Source Code

This appendix provides instructions for installing Zope from both RPM files and source code.

Installing on Linux from RPM

RPM is a package format for Linux-based operating systems. RPM stands for *Red Hat Package Management,* but it is used in many other Linux distributions in addition to Red Hat Linux.

Downloading the RPMs

First, the RPM files must be downloaded to your computer. RPM files for Zope are maintained by Jeffrey Rush, and can be found at `http://starship.python.net/crew/jrush/Zope/`.

Follow the link for the most recent version of Zope and select the Group A package, which contains the entire Zope environment in a single package. Then select one of the two options from Group C; either the ZServer (Python-based HTTP sever) or the Persistent CGI (PCGI) option. Choose PCGI only if you wish to set up Zope to work "behind" Apache. In this chapter, we assume you chose the ZServer option.

Save both files to your user's home directory.

Option 1: Installing with GnoRPM

You can use the GnoRPM GUI utility to install both packages. From a command-line interface as the root user, type **gnorpm**. This should launch the GnoRPM utility on your Linux desktop, as shown in Figure B-1.

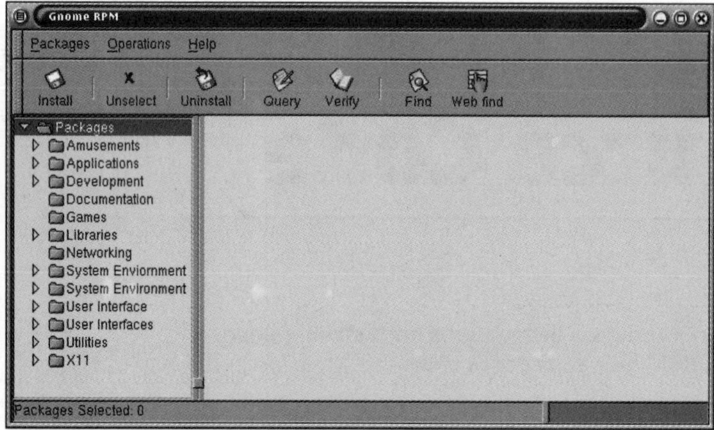

Figure B-1: GnoRPM initial screen

Click the Install button, which pops up an Install dialog box, as shown in Figure B-2. Then click the Add button in the install dialog box. This pops up an Add packages file browser, as shown in Figure B-3.

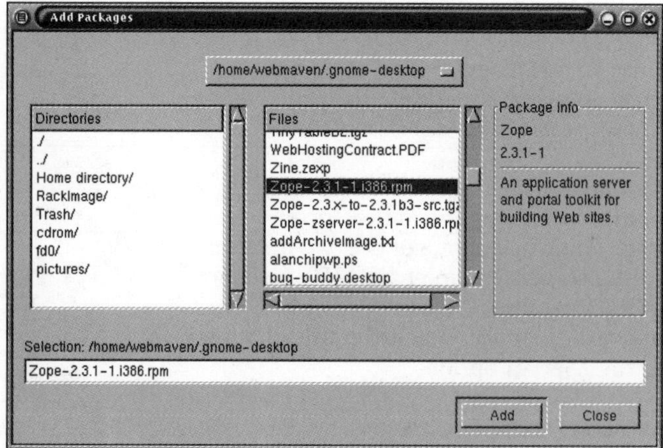

Figure B-2: GnoRPM Install dialog box

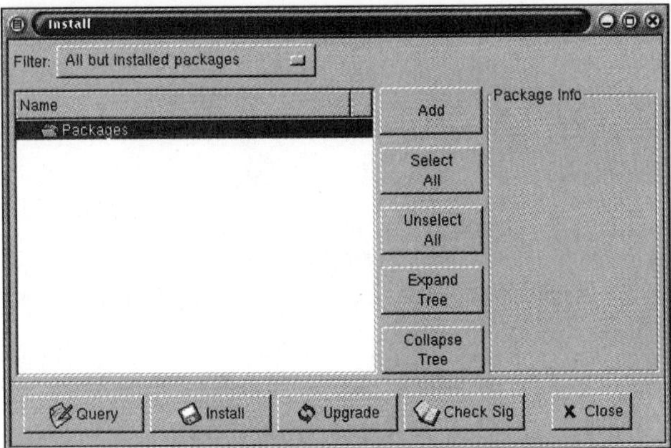

Figure B-3: GnoRPM Add Packages browser

Change the directory to your home directory (where you saved the downloaded files), and click the first of the two RPM files you downloaded. Then click the Add button. This adds the package to the previous dialog box. Repeat the last two steps with the second package and click Close.

You will see, as in Figure B-4, that the install dialog box now has two packages listed under `Packages/Development/Web Applications`, and that each package has a checked box next to its name. Click the Install button at the bottom of the install dialog box, and GnoRPM will proceed to install the Zope packages for you.

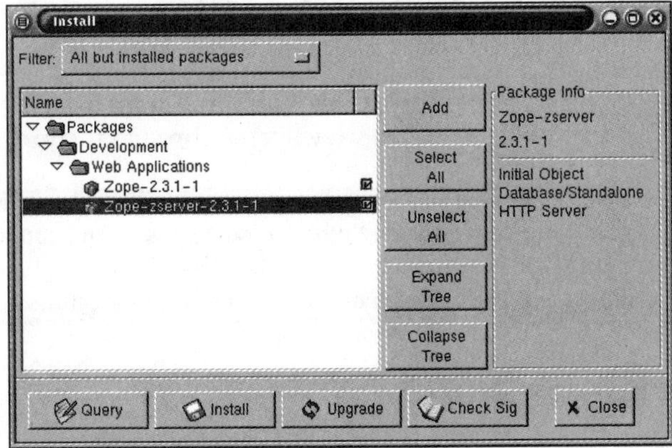

Figure B-4: GnoRPM Add Packages browser with Zope packages

After installing the two packages, click the Close button in the install dialog box and exit GnoRPM by using the Quit menu option under the Packages menu.

Option 2: Installing with the command line RPM utility

As an alternative to using GnoRPM, you can use the command line RPM utility from the directory in which you saved the two RPM files:

```
# rpm \install Z*.rpm
```

This assumes, of course, that the only RPM files in that directory that begin with "Z" are the two Zope RPM files.

Starting and stopping Zope when installed from RPMs

Once you have successfully installed Zope using RPM, your system is now configured to start Zope when the system is booted up. If you wish to start Zope without rebooting, enter the following from a command line while you have root privileges:

```
# /etc/rc.d/init.d/zope start
```

Similarly, the following will shut Zope down without having to shut your system down:

```
# /etc/rc.d/init.d/zope stop
```

Installing from Source Code on Linux

Installing Zope from source code is not particularly difficult, but is a little more involved than installing the binary distribution. In this section we first examine the reasons for installing from source code, and then we will step through the process.

If you are examining an existing Zope installation and you would like to know if it was a binary or source install, a quick way to find out is to check the `/lib` subdirectory of the Zope installation. If it contains a `python2.1` directory, then it's a binary install. Otherwise, it should contain only `python` and `Components` subdirectories.

Why install from source code?

First, you may be asking yourself, "Why would I even want to install Zope from source code?" There are a few basic reasons why you would want to do so:

- For security
- If you are using your own Python
- For installing the latest development code from CVS (Concurrent Versioning System)

Security

Whenever you install a binary, there is a possibility that it was compiled with additional or modified code that may be malicious. This would be called a *trojan* (think wooden horse, not safe sex). Even getting the binary from a known source may not guarantee its integrity, as the Internet is an insecure network, and someone could conceivably "spoof" your machine into thinking that the download it was receiving was coming from somewhere it wasn't. Then again, it's possible that the site from where you downloaded the binary was itself compromised, and the legitimate download was replaced with a modified one. The binary you receive could be digitally signed to ensure its integrity, but even then you are relying on the skill and truthfulness of the packager.

While giving credence to these possibilities may seem paranoid to some, others take them very seriously. A thorough discussion of the security risks inherent in relying on binary software distributions is outside the scope of this book, but many professionals in the field consider the availability of source code to the software you install a major security advantage.

The extent of the measures that you go to in verifying the provenance and functionality of the software you install is, of course, up to you. For most users, installing all software only from source code is likely to be overkill.

Using your own Python

The binary distribution of Zope does not assume that Python is installed on your system. Consequently, a binary version of Python is included in the binary Zope distribution. This can present problems if the version of Python installed on your system has modules or Packages installed that you would like to access from within Zope. Under these circumstances, you would want to compile Zope from source code to have it use your existing Python installation.

Installing the latest development code from CVS

If you wish to participate in the ongoing development of Zope, you will probably want to get the very latest (possibly unstable) code for Zope from CVS (Concurrent Versioning System), in order to examine recent modifications, make your own modifications, and test the modified code. In order to use the source code retrieved from CVS, it must still be compiled in exactly the same fashion as any other source code installation. While we will not cover downloading the latest code from CVS in this book, you can find instructions at `http://www.zope.org/Resources/CVS_info`.

Getting the source code

In order to compile the source code for Zope, it is necessary to first download it. This can be done in exactly the same fashion as downloading any other distribution of Zope. Go to the Zope Web site and click Download. You should see a link labeled "Current stable release" (as of this writing, this was 2.5.0). Follow the link, and click the link `Zope-2.5.0-src.tgz` (or the equivalent if there is a more recent version) and download the file to your system.

Installing from source code

Okay, so you've got the source code. Now what? You need to do the following five tasks:

- ✦ Move the tarball into `/usr/local`.
- ✦ Check the existing Python installation for version and threads.
- ✦ Unpack the Zope source-code tarball and rename the resulting directory.
- ✦ Change to permissions on the directory.
- ✦ Complete and test the install.

Move the tarball to the /usr/local directory

First, as the root user, move the gzipped tarball to the `/usr/local/` directory with **mv Zope-2.5.0-src.tgz /usr/local/**.

Checking the existing Python

Version 2.5 of Zope requires Python 2.1 or higher. This version of Zope is compatible with Python 2.2, but only 2.1 is officially supported at this time. Accordingly, you should determine which version of Python is installed on your system:

```
# python

>>>Python 1.5.2 (#1 Aug 25 2000, 09:33:37) [GCC 2.96 20000731
(experimental)] on Linux-i386
```

Hmm. Looks like you'll have to upgrade Python on your system. Go to `www.python.org/2.1.1/rpms.html` and download the python RPMs for your system. Installing the Python RPMs is substantially similar to installing the Zope RPMs described earlier in this chapter.

Next, check to see whether the Python on your system was compiled with the thread module:

```
>>>import thread
>>>
```

If the `import thread` command does not return an error, you are good to go. If `import thread` does return an error, you may need to recompile Python on your system. This isn't very likely though, as Python 2.1.x has threading compiled in by default.

One last note about Python: You must have the development libraries installed for a source installation of Zope to succeed. The Python development libraries can be obtained in RPM format from the Python Web site along with the base RPM file.

Unzipping the archive

Now you need to unpack the gzipped tarball into the /zope directory with the following command:

```
# tar -xzvf Zope-2.5.0-src.tgz .
```

Now, rename the resulting directory to something a little easier to type with **mv Zope-2.5.0-src Zope**.

Change permissions

When Zope is started as root, it switches to the "nobody" user by default, to make sure that the Zope process is not running with excess privileges.

It's necessary, therefore, to make certain that the "nobody" user has the appropriate permissions to run and access the subdirectories. This can be done with the following commands:

```
# chown -R nobody Zope
# chmod 770 Zope
```

Completing the installation

Now change directories into the newly created Zope directory:

```
# cd Zope
```

Then run the wo_pcgi.py script:

```
# python wo_pcgi
```

This installs Zope with only ZServer as the HTTP server. If PCGI support is required, then run the w_pcgi.py script instead.

This begins a rather lengthy installation process, which first compiles various C extensions, and eventually concludes just like a normal binary installation. As with a binary installation, you should make note of the emergency user user name and password at the end of this process.

After the installation is complete, and you've made note of the emergency user name and password, test your Zope install by starting it from the command line with **./start** and using a browser to access Zope by typing in the following into the location bar: **http://localhost:8080**.

A quick review

Here is a quick review of the commands you will be entering:

1. Move the tarball into the `/usr/local/` directory with **mv Zope-2.5.0-src.tgz /usr/local/.**
2. Unzip and untar the compressed file with with **gunzip Zope-2.5.0-src.tgz** and then **tar -xvf Zope-2.5.0-src.tar.**
3. Rename the resulting directory to something a little easier to type with **mv Zope-2.5.0-src Zope.**
4. Make sure the files have the proper permissions with **chown -R nobody Zope** and then **chmod 770 Zope.**
5. Change into the directory with **cd Zope.**
6. Install Zope with **python wo_pcgi.**
7. Run the start script with **./start** and then point your Web browser at `http://localhost:8080/`.

For further details on setting up and administering your Zope installation, see Chapter 2.

Summary

In this appendix you learned how to

✦ Install Zope from RPM files

✦ Install Zope from source code

RPM files can be a convenient way of installing Zope binaries when you want a simple standard installation and little to no customization.

Installing Zope from source code may be a little more involved than installing the binary version, but it is no more difficult. It also has certain advantages regarding security, using your installed version of Python, or compiling the current development code obtained from CVS.

✦ ✦ ✦

Index

C

H

I

M

O

P

Q

R

V

W

Hungry Minds, Inc. End-User License Agreement

READ THIS. You should carefully read these terms and conditions before opening the software packet(s) included with this book ("Book"). This is a license agreement ("Agreement") between you and Hungry Minds, Inc. ("HMI"). By opening the accompanying software packet(s), you acknowledge that you have read and accept the following terms and conditions. If you do not agree and do not want to be bound by such terms and conditions, promptly return the Book and the unopened software packet(s) to the place you obtained them for a full refund.

1. **License Grant.** HMI grants to you (either an individual or entity) a nonexclusive license to use one copy of the enclosed software program(s) (collectively, the "Software") solely for your own personal or business purposes on a single computer (whether a standard computer or a workstation component of a multi-user network). The Software is in use on a computer when it is loaded into temporary memory (RAM) or installed into permanent memory (hard disk, CD-ROM, or other storage device). HMI reserves all rights not expressly granted herein.
2. **Ownership.** HMI is the owner of all right, title, and interest, including copyright, in and to the compilation of the Software recorded on the disk(s) or CD-ROM ("Software Media"). Copyright to the individual programs recorded on the Software Media is owned by the author or other authorized copyright owner of each program. Ownership of the Software and all proprietary rights relating thereto remain with HMI and its licensers.
3. **Restrictions On Use and Transfer.**
   - **(a)** You may only (i) make one copy of the Software for backup or archival purposes, or (ii) transfer the Software to a single hard disk, provided that you keep the original for backup or archival purposes. You may not (i) rent or lease the Software, (ii) copy or reproduce the Software through a LAN or other network system or through any computer subscriber system or bulletin-board system, or (iii) modify, adapt, or create derivative works based on the Software.
   - **(b)** You may not reverse engineer, decompile, or disassemble the Software. You may transfer the Software and user documentation on a permanent basis, provided that the transferee agrees to accept the terms and conditions of this Agreement and you retain no copies. If the Software is an update or has been updated, any transfer must include the most recent update and all prior versions.
4. **Restrictions on Use of Individual Programs.** You must follow the individual requirements and restrictions detailed for each individual program in Appendix A of this Book. These limitations are also contained in the individual license agreements recorded on the Software Media. These limitations may include a requirement that after using the program for a specified period of time, the user must pay a registration fee or discontinue use. By opening the Software packet(s), you will be agreeing to abide by the licenses and restrictions for these individual programs that are detailed in Appendix A and on the Software Media. None of the material on this Software Media or listed in this Book may ever be redistributed, in original or modified form, for commercial purposes.

5. Limited Warranty.

(a) HMI warrants that the Software and Software Media are free from defects in materials and workmanship under normal use for a period of sixty (60) days from the date of purchase of this Book. If HMI receives notification within the warranty period of defects in materials or workmanship, HMI will replace the defective Software Media.

(b) **HMI AND THE AUTHOR OF THE BOOK DISCLAIM ALL OTHER WARRANTIES, EXPRESS OR IMPLIED, INCLUDING WITHOUT LIMITATION IMPLIED WARRANTIES OF MERCHANTABILITY AND FITNESS FOR A PARTICULAR PURPOSE, WITH RESPECT TO THE SOFTWARE, THE PROGRAMS, THE SOURCE CODE CONTAINED THEREIN, AND/OR THE TECHNIQUES DESCRIBED IN THIS BOOK. HMI DOES NOT WARRANT THAT THE FUNCTIONS CONTAINED IN THE SOFTWARE WILL MEET YOUR REQUIREMENTS OR THAT THE OPERATION OF THE SOFTWARE WILL BE ERROR FREE.**

(c) This limited warranty gives you specific legal rights, and you may have other rights that vary from jurisdiction to jurisdiction.

6. Remedies.

(a) HMI's entire liability and your exclusive remedy for defects in materials and workmanship shall be limited to replacement of the Software Media, which may be returned to HMI with a copy of your receipt at the following address: Software Media Fulfillment Department, Attn.: *Zope Bible*, Hungry Minds, Inc., 10475 Crosspoint Blvd., Indianapolis, IN 46256, or call 1-800-762-2974. Please allow four to six weeks for delivery. This Limited Warranty is void if failure of the Software Media has resulted from accident, abuse, or misapplication. Any replacement Software Media will be warranted for the remainder of the original warranty period or thirty (30) days, whichever is longer.

(b) In no event shall HMI or the author be liable for any damages whatsoever (including without limitation damages for loss of business profits, business interruption, loss of business information, or any other pecuniary loss) arising from the use of or inability to use the Book or the Software, even if HMI has been advised of the possibility of such damages.

(c) Because some jurisdictions do not allow the exclusion or limitation of liability for consequential or incidental damages, the above limitation or exclusion may not apply to you.

7. U.S. Government Restricted Rights. Use, duplication, or disclosure of the Software for or on behalf of the United States of America, its agencies and/or instrumentalities (the "U.S. Government") is subject to restrictions as stated in paragraph (c)(1)(ii) of the Rights in Technical Data and Computer Software clause of DFARS 252.227-7013, or subparagraphs (c) (1) and (2) of the Commercial Computer Software - Restricted Rights clause at FAR 52.227-19, and in similar clauses in the NASA FAR supplement, as applicable.

8. General. This Agreement constitutes the entire understanding of the parties and revokes and supersedes all prior agreements, oral or written, between them and may not be modified or amended except in a writing signed by both parties hereto that specifically refers to this Agreement. This Agreement shall take precedence over any other documents that may be in conflict herewith. If any one or more provisions contained in this Agreement are held by any court or tribunal to be invalid, illegal, or otherwise unenforceable, each and every other provision shall remain in full force and effect.

Zope Public License (ZPL) Version 2.0

This license has been certified as open source. It has also been designated as GPL compatible by the Free Software Foundation (FSF).

Redistribution and use in source and binary forms, with or without modification, are permitted provided that the following conditions are met:

1. Redistributions in source code must retain the above copyright notice, this list of conditions, and the following disclaimer.
2. Redistributions in binary form must reproduce the above copyright notice, this list of conditions, and the following disclaimer in the documentation and/or other materials provided with the distribution.
3. The name Zope Corporation™ must not be used to endorse or promote products derived from this software without prior written permission from Zope Corporation.
4. The right to distribute this software or to use it for any purpose does not give you the right to use Servicemarks (sm) or Trademarks™ of Zope Corporation. Use of them is covered in a separate agreement (see `http://www.zope.com/Marks`).
5. If any files are modified, you must cause the modified files to carry prominent notices stating that you changed the files and the date of any change.

Disclaimer

THIS SOFTWARE IS PROVIDED BY ZOPE CORPORATION "AS IS" AND ANY EXPRESSED OR IMPLIED WARRANTIES, INCLUDING, BUT NOT LIMITED TO, THE IMPLIED WARRANTIES OF MERCHANTABILITY AND FITNESS FOR A PARTICULAR PURPOSE ARE DISCLAIMED. IN NO EVENT SHALL ZOPE CORPORATION OR ITS CONTRIBUTORS BE LIABLE FOR ANY DIRECT, INDIRECT, INCIDENTAL, SPECIAL, EXEMPLARY, OR CONSEQUENTIAL DAMAGES (INCLUDING, BUT NOT LIMITED TO, PROCUREMENT OF SUBSTITUTE GOODS OR SERVICES; LOSS OF USE, DATA, OR PROFITS; OR BUSINESS INTERRUPTION) HOWEVER CAUSED AND ON ANY THEORY OF LIABILITY, WHETHER IN CONTRACT, STRICT LIABILITY, OR TORT (INCLUDING NEGLIGENCE OR OTHERWISE) ARISING IN ANY WAY OUT OF THE USE OF THIS SOFTWARE, EVEN IF ADVISED OF THE POSSIBILITY OF SUCH DAMAGE.

This software consists of contributions made by Zope Corporation and many individuals on behalf of Zope Corporation. Specific attributions are listed in the accompanying credits file.